~BWITI~

AN ETHNOGRAPHY OF
THE RELIGIOUS IMAGINATION
IN AFRICA

1/2/83

To Rena and Mike —
Happy new year and
365 days of good
reading. There is
even some history
here.

Jim

BWITI

An Ethnography of
the Religious Imagination
in Africa

JAMES W. FERNANDEZ

DRAWINGS BY
RENATE LELLEP FERNANDEZ

Princeton University Press
Princeton, New Jersey

*Me ve bôn be Fang nten vi akal nzông be nga
lere me mimbu mibé. Me ve fe Kabiyen nten vi
akal mbamba nlem a lere me mimbu mite ye
mimbu mise ening edzea. Me nga yen nye
mbeng.*

Contents

List of Figures

List of Photographs

All photographs are by James W. and Renate L. Fernandez.

FANG CULTURE (*following page 230*)

1. The Chief of the village of Assok Ening, Essono Mba, posing before the collapsing Council House (aba) of Mvok Mba M'Oye. Assok Ening, Oyem District.
2. A newborn child, still with the whiteness of the land of the ancestors from whence it has come, is placed on the back of the next oldest sibling, as a sign of the continuity of the genealogical line. Assok Ening, Oyem District.
3. The close relationship encouraged between the infant and its next oldest sibling. Assok Ening, Oyem District.
4. Young village boys and girls play together until, approaching puberty, their interests diverge. Assok Ening, Oyem District.
5. The boys' earliest interest in courtship is expressed in the dancing male and female bamboo figures going a-courting on a string. Assok Ening, Oyem District.
6. Boys practicing spear throwing. Assok Ening, Oyem District.
7. Striking small stones as accompaniment, girls gather to sing the rhythm songs particular to their sex. Assok Ening, Oyem District.
8. Young men (nduman), escaping the ennui of their decentered villages, leave on a courting expedition. Azok, Mitzik District.
9. Young men playing mbek in the Council House. Assok Ening, Oyem District.
10. Young girl on the margins of puberty (mon mininga).
11. Young boy (mon fam).
12. Young married woman (ngwan nga).
13. Young husband (ndum fam).
14. Man at the height of his powers (nyamoro).
15. Another nyamoro.
16. The tiredness of the old (nom mininga).
17. Old man (nom fam).
18. Ndebot: a house of people. Evinayong, Spanish Guinea.
19. Mvogabot: people who look across the courtyard at each other. Kougouleu, Kango District.
20. Preparing the leaf package of pounded food (zom).

Initiation Sequences

Preface and Acknowledgments

THIS BOOK is about efforts at "world reconstruction" that have been going on in small and often isolated villages in the Equatorial Forest of West Africa.* The word "reconstruction" brings to mind great wars and great depressions and attempts by mankind to repair and overcome the grievous damage to peoples brought about by these events—the results of false hopes and sullen and resentful feelings working away in inadequate human institutions. Perhaps the Western reader, whose interest is provoked by the possibility that we will be addressing ourselves to these great afflictions and their repair, will be disappointed that all this is going on in what are, to him, the obscure backwaters of the globe—as, geopolitically, they no doubt are. On the Gabon Republic, the locale of this study, my colleague Brian Weinstein has written an estimable book about nation-building that relates more to the larger world.[1] But here I shall be sticking to the anthropologist's task and we shall be dwelling in these equatorial villages from first to last. This is an account of a thoughtful group of people who have turned away from a larger world order which in the usual course of events they might have been expected to join.

And yet an anthropologist must argue that there is no study of mankind from which mankind cannot learn. False hopes and sullen, resentful feelings are present here as elsewhere—counteracted, to be sure, by the pleasures and mounting euphoria of ritual activity. There is the same desire for more comprehensive and stable structures, for a more enduring and satisfying worldview. We may even claim the presence of an ultimate wisdom in the events and in the attempts at reconstruction we shall describe—the wisdom of knowing that the realities in which men and women dwell are in large measure the realities they have made for themselves. We have been beguiled since time immemorial—and anthropologists most of all perhaps—with the thought that the objective key to reality lies beyond the frontier where other realities dwell. Now that terrestrial frontiers have practically all been surveyed and traversed we continue to beguile ourselves with cosmic frontiers. There may well be other living realities with which to communicate. Yet finally the universe curves back upon itself and the world we live in is the world we have constructed or reconstructed by our methods—methods fundamentally similar to the microcosmogony going on in the Equatorial Forest, which in the end comes down to an argument of images. This may be the only way that a

---

* This book has two sets of notes. Those marked with an asterisk are printed at the foot of the page. Other notes are given in a separate section at the back of the book.

cosmos can be made to emerge. As Hannah Arendt has argued, man in his search for objective reality always ends up "confronting himself alone."[2] In such reflective cosmologies as we have before us, confrontations of a final and steadier state are constant.

This book may be about the capacity of an emergent religious culture to create its own realities. But any student will be quick to recognize how little of his own understanding he has created for himself. As I have discussed in the introduction the genealogy that frames the "personae" of the book, I might here recite a genealogy of influences and obligations. To me the best work in anthropology has been done, to speak only of a generation or age grade now passed on, by Malinowski, Ruth Benedict, E. E. Evans Pritchard, Marcel Griaule, and Clyde Kluckhohn. It is not so much the theoretical perspectives of these works—I claim one of my own—but rather their embeddedness in local idiom, their skillful presentation of local points of view that impresses. Whatever their theoretical contribution, and their works are all major "points de repère" in anthropology, they did not allow that essential academic interest to override local realities as, alas, has often enough been the case in anthropological studies. They have all been ethnographers first and ethnologists second. I hope to have maintained that priority here.

My particular mentor was Melville Herskovits who, like Franz Boas, his own teacher, ranged widely in anthropology from physical anthropology to folklore. I could not expect, perhaps none of my generation could expect, to contribute so eclectically as he. But it was he who focused my African interests on religion and it was he, out of his more pronounced relativism, who initiated my interest in the "creation of cultural realities." Two other mentors may be mentioned. Francis L. K. Hsu, who has uniquely occupied middle ground in anthropology between East and West and between the British and the American tradition, constantly stimulated my interest in the role of affect in human affairs. And William Bascom, who came out of physics to anthropology, continually asked, "What are the operations, the techniques by which the unseen is made visible?" I have tried to make clear some of those operations here.

This work was largely undertaken in Gabon and I owe many debts to French scholars, administrators, and missionaries. I would first thank Pierre Alexandre whose own Bulu work, both linguistic and ethnographic, has informed my own. At every turn he has sought to facilitate this study. I am indebted to Governor Hubert Deschamps for discussions of his work on oral history, to Georges Balandier for kind discussions of his Fang data and the colonial situation, to the District Administrator of Oyem, Serge Pasquier, and of Medouneu, Mebunge Simon, who were most helpful in my task, as was Laurent Biffot, then Research Director of ORSTOM in Libreville. Also in Libreville our friend from Bitam days, Eko Jean Marc, then Minister of Education, was a constant source of insight as was the Oyem Député Ndong

Philippe, the master of the mvet troubadour legends. To various missionaries I owe a debt for hospitality and comprehension of my task: to Pastor Bruneton of Oyem, to Pastor Mangome of Bitam, to Père Sillard of Libreville, and particularly to M. l'Abbé Raponda-Walker, that formidable Africanist, in 1960 still active in his eighties in Libreville. As fortunate for me was the extraordinary opportunity in 1962 to exchange correspondence with Gunter Tessmann, the first ethnographer of the Fang, 1904-1909, still active, though on other matters, in his ninth decade in Brazil. May all students of Fang be as enduringly vigorous.

This study might have begun in Spanish Guinea (Rio Muni)—it ended there—were it not for visa difficulties. My Spanish colleagues Augusto Panyella and Jordi Sabater were unfailingly helpful in advising and preparing me for Fang studies from their own extensive knowledge. The Spanish Administrator of the District of Ebebiyin, the late Captain Basilio Olanchea, displayed great understanding and showed me every kindness under trying circumstances, as did Captain Juan Alonso, Administrator at Akurnam.

Within my own age grade I particularly thank for various forms of solidarity and counsel Warren d'Azevedo, Keith Basso, T. O. Beidelman, Judith Gleason, Philip Leis, Igor Kopytoff, Wyatt MacGaffey, David Sapir, James Spencer, Robert Thompson, Edward Tiryakian, and Brian Weinstein.

This book carries a dedication to Fang themselves and to my wife, Renate Lellep. It is as much if not more their book than mine. I am particularly indebted to Renate Lellep for the drawings and for many of the photographs. I have received invaluable assistance from young Fang with whom I have worked: Mve Essono Etienne, Ze Sima Martin, Oyono Edu Secundino, Eco Essono Federico. Mbolo abui!

I am grateful to Judith May of Princeton University Press for such careful and perspicacious editing of the demanding manuscript. Susan Gall and Donna Norvell showed great patience in carefully typing it—and typing it again—and again. Isis Carvallo and Nancy Schwartz were indispensable in bibliographic and indexing matters. And thanks to Gail Filion, editor at Princeton University Press, for being undaunted by such a daunting project.

I also thank Charles Cullen, Hannah Kaufman, and the Princeton University Computer Center for advice on constructing the comprehensive index. Pauline Caulk and Darcy Evans patiently entered the index data. Laury Egan designed the book with an admirable sense of its content.

The research was supported by a grant from the Foreign Area Program of the Ford Foundation. I am indebted to the Foundation and to the late Dorothy Soderlund, chief administrator of the program. Dartmouth College and Princeton University have provided supplementary funds for data analysis and write-up. Princeton University has provided a generous subvention in aid of publication.

Linguistic Note

FANG is a northwestern Bantu language with a characteristic Bantu form class system, proliferating verbal roots, classified substantives, and systematic concordances. Its utterances are much shorter, however, than most Bantu languages and there is a more pronounced dependence on tone. The orthographic system involved in rendering Fang in the present work has posed several problems. At the time of the study and in the area where it was carried out there were seven competing orthographic systems in use: Gabon Catholic and Gabon Protestant, Cameroon Catholic and Cameroon Protestant, Spanish Guinea Catholic, IFAN, and the Cameroon and Gabon administrative orthography. (The American Peace Corps introduced an entirely new orthography in the mid-1960's). There was also the problem that research was carried out predominantly in three different dialect areas: in the Ntumu-Fang dialect area of the Oyem District, in the Ntsi or Betsi dialect area of Medouneu (influenced by the Okak dialect), and in the Meke dialect area of Kango District. Further complexities were introduced when Samuel Galley's valuable *Dictionnaire Fang-Français et Français-Fang* was published posthumously in 1964. It has seemed to me that any orthography employed here should not impede consultation of that rich resource even though it was mainly compiled by Galley in the Ndjole and Lambarene regions among speakers of the Nzaman or central Fang dialect felt by him to be the "most pure."[3] Galley himself had wished his Dictionary to be available to as wide a Fang population as possible. Rather than seeking a highly scientific orthography he tried to stay close to existing conventions. His system is thus in some respects more cumbersome than desirable. For example he makes much more use of the semi-vowels y, w, and v than I could hear or find useful. In order to avoid new letters he preserves the cumbersome ny and n̠y gutterals which we will write as the ŋ of certain contexts.

I also heard in my areas more tendency to the diphthong than Galley, who argues—it may be true for southern Fang dialects—that Fang syllables can contain only one vowel. Even when two seem to be heard, he says, one is always dominant, transforming the other into a semi-vowel. Thus for *bia* (song) he writes *bya*. Another shift from north to south is the difficult dorso-velar *kp* and *gb* occurring with the initial nasal *n*. This combination is common among Ntumu: *nkpwek*, "favorite but flighty young wife." But further south the labial component is surpressed by the initial nasal, *nkwek*.

We will, like Galley, write words as if they were valent for all Fang dialects. Many can be written that way without asking too much of the speakers of individual dialects. But where there are inescapable differences we will indicate the dialect involved within parentheses: (N) Ntumu, (B) Betsi, (M) Meke, (Z) Nzaman, (O) Okak. Thus, *nkpwek*(N) and *nkwek*(Z). There will also be variations in the spelling of some Fang words due to the varied orthographic sources consulted.

The system for rendering Fang in this work follows, with some attention to Galley, that employed by Pierre Alexandre in his monograph, *Le Groupe dit "Pahouin"* in the International African Institute Ethnographic Monograph series.[4] This system conforms to the conditions of typewritten presentation and corresponds closely to the system employed by the Bulu people in their extensive written literature which penetrates widely into Northern Gabon and is readily understood by Fang. Alexandre's modification of the Bulu Protestant orthography obviates any further need to choose among the many available systems which have grown up, as they all have, in the battleground of sectarian evangelization and colonial policy.

The following phonetic shifts distinguishing Fang from Bulu may be noted: the Bulu glottal stop between vowels, *sa''ale*, becomes a Fang velar explosive *g, sagele*; dental explosive *t* in Bulu, *kalata*, becomes an alveolar rolled *r* in Fang, *kalara*; the palatal explosive *ty* in Bulu is replaced by *ki* in Fang. The post-alveolar *j* in Bulu is given greater fricative emphasis, *dz*, by Fang. the Bulu palatal semi-vowel becomes an alveolar affricative *dj* in Fang. Fang tend to nasalize initial consonants and suppress final explosives. The accentuation of their syllables is nowhere as pronounced as among the Bulu. The Bulu say of Fang that they swallow their words, and this is a just commentary on the difficulties of Fang as opposed to Bulu.

The values of the letters of the orthography used here are the following:

Vowels:

a - like the Italian *a*, as in English "father."
e - according to its environment:
     1. before final *n* as in English "ten."
     2. before final *k* as in English "sung."
     3. otherwise an intermediate sound as between English "moss"
  and "must."
é - as *ey* in English "they."
i - as in English "if."
í - as *i* in English "machine."
o - like the French *o*, as in English "nor."
ô - as in English "note."
u - like the German *u*, as *oo* in English "noon."

Long vowels, which occur infrequently, are doubled. Consonants have the ordinary English sounds with the following exceptions:

j - is the voiced affricate, as in English "John."

ng - is the nasalized *ng* of English "singing." Modern usage often employs the tilde which we will omit except as indictive before *k* or *g*: *ñkol, ñgoe*. In certain contexts in more southern Fang *ng* is followed by a slight semi-vowel, *y*, not noted here.

r - slightly rolled in Fang, approximating the Spanish double *rr*.

g - is the voiceless velar fricative in intervocalic position, and otherwise is hard and gutteral.

An occasional emphatic aspirated *k* is transcribed *kh*.

z is everywhere pronounced *dz*, and is so written in many orthographies.

Though Fang is a tonal language—whether a two- or three-tone system with a rising and falling tone is debated—we only note here the falling tone which indicates the negative: *ma yem*, "I know": *ma yem*, "I don't know." In etymological discussion prompted by the Fang and Bwiti penchant for "word play" and the "breaking of words," *abukh bifia*, and where we are attempting to distinguish the verbal or radical sources for a particular substantive, we will indicate tone in the following manner: (h) for high tone; (m) for mid tone; (l) for low tone. Thus *sok*(h), "to drink like an animal," and sok(l) "to search out hidden truth."

Many of the transcriptions, particularly in Part III, are in Popi Fang, the Bwiti "Latin" or religious "language" adopted from the Metsogo people of southern Gabon. This is a simulated "language" not fully understood by the members of Bwiti although there are many recognizable Tsogo words and phrases. I did not hear any sounds in this church "language" that differed from those heard in Fang itself, although there may well be some. In any event we will write Popi according to the above orthography.

~BWITI~

AN ETHNOGRAPHY OF
THE RELIGIOUS IMAGINATION
IN AFRICA

Entering into
an Equatorial Microcosm

THE ROAD TO XANADU:
CULTURE AS REPRESENTATION

MANY LONG NIGHTS, over two years, of participation in Bwiti chapel life on the Equatorial line led to this book. Anthropological observation turned into participation in chapels in the deep forest, close by sacred rivers, and along the estuaries or beaches on the edge of the sunless sea. It is now more than a decade since those nights but I remember them vividly. This is not only because in preparing fieldnotes for publication and looking again at slides and photos one is reanimated by former experiences. It is because the members of Bwiti have created a potent religious universe. As awkward as I am of foot and tongue, I can still perform some of the striking dances and sing some of the memorable songs of midnight and first light. The reader should know that the object of investigation exerts strong attraction on those who have participated in it.*[1] This is not to be taken lightly, although one main purpose of Bwiti is to ease the oppressive burden of everyday human experience, to infiltrate with a spiritual buoyancy vacancies in the laden tissues of mankind's afflicted corporeality.

This book has to do with the anthropology of the religious imagination. It is a work of cultural anthropology, treating culture as representations. The titles and other references from Lowes' work[1] are chosen with a purpose. Lowes took a powerful but mysterious work of the poetic fancy, Coleridge's *Kubla Khan*, and showed in detail the experiences out of which it rose—the specific passages of Coleridge's voluminous reading which established lingering images in the poet's mind. He then showed how these images, even the most incongruous, coalesced in the deep well of that mind to rise again in phantasmagoric, but magical, potent expression. Lowes pursued his search for the sources of Kubla Khan very thoroughly. Nothing which might contribute to an understanding of the working of the mind in its imaginative acts, whether in daylight or in dream, was too trivial. I agree with him. The reader

---

*[1] I have not tried to discuss these songs and dances in musical terms in this book. But the reader may wish to consult a selection of Bwiti music published by Folkways Records, New York: *Music From an Equatorial Microcosm: Fang Bwiti Music (with MBiri Selections)*, Recorded and Annotated by James W. Fernandez, Ethnic Folkways Records FE 4214. A very extensive tape collection of Bwiti songs and sermons has been deposited in the Archives of Folk Music, University of Indiana, and is available for consultation.

will thus find us pursuing the antecedents of the Bwiti cult in Fang experience in considerable detail. Like Lowes we will follow the "profoundly significant part played in imaginative creation by the association of ideas."[2] And like Lowes we will accept that it is only in the detail of our investigation that we can do justice to the richness of the associative process which is at the core of the imaginative act.

Kubla Khan comes to mind in connection with Bwiti for a number of reasons. There is the fact that the poem has in good part an "Abyssinian locale" despite its Asian references. The damsel with the dulcimer reminds one of the Bwiti cult harp. The harp represents the voice of the female object of devotion in Bwiti, Nyingwan Mebege, the sister of God who is syncretized with the Virgin. There is something about the "flashing eyes" and "floating hair" of the ominous protagonist of the poem—Beware, Beware!—that reminds one of the Bwiti initiate deeply influenced by the narcotic *Tabernanthe iboga* and on the point of seeing the ancestors. There is the fact that Coleridge composed the poem upon waking from a long dream and perhaps under the influence of laudanum, to which he was certainly addicted. The members of Bwiti, the *Banzie*, often claim that all the imaginative elaborations of liturgy and belief that they introduce come to them in dream communications with the ancestors or under the influence of *eboga*, to which they are deeply attached. They are one of the few African religious movements to argue their potency from the constant use of a psychoreactive drug.

But these are all accessory associations. Basically, Bwiti links to Kubla Khan because it is an imaginative constellation of images which gives pleasure to its Fang participants. It is an equatorial pleasure dome. And, like Lowes in Xanadu, we want to pursue the sources of that dome in Fang culture and account for its pleasures in the enduring etymological sense of that term: reconciliation. Bwiti, it can be shown, is a religious microcosm which "placates" and "reconciles" those who are troubled and separated in their relationships to one another, both gods and men. It satisfies by providing a whole experience for those to whom life does not provide enough of anything they feel they need, who feel they are not taking part or who, at best, feel they are allotted an insignificant part of the whole.

The Plan of the Work

Anthropologists as a rule must travel a long road to come to their particular Xanadu. The reader will find, however, that the road here taken to Bwiti differs from the customary anthropological presentation, which generally begins, because of the importance of environment to societies living close to the margin of survival, by placing its subjects in their ecological situation. This study begins rather by placing Fang in imagined time. For although it is often assumed that time is of little concern to ahistorical peoples without written records, in fact, Fang preserve good historical knowledge five to seven generations deep in the genealogy. They also have a good memory of and have been significantly affected by major events of the colonial period. Bwiti is an expression of that fact.

We begin with historical documents that shed light on early European contact and the early colonial situation with which Fang had to contend. Of particular interest are the images Europeans held of Fang and the attitudes that accompanied these images.[3] We then shift to examine Fang views of their own past based on real or imagined events which are hung upon the genealogical structure. Thus, the study begins by treating that "double-history" that has been so influential in the beliefs and attitudes of Fang. It then moves on to consider Fang as they represent themselves in social space, as they represent real space, as they represent sex relationships, political relationships, and economic relationships, the relationships of the generations, and the relationship of the individual to his own achievements and to his mortal destiny. Throughout these chapters of Part I, an attempt is made to account for a malaise in Fang life which manifests itself not only in a "double history" but also in the decentering of the village, money-mindedness, high divorce rates, failures of intergenerational good will, and the "apotheosis of evil." The intention of this chapter development is to provide in Part I a road through Fang culture of the past and present that will lead the reader in Part III to that Xanadu of the Fang imagination, the Bwiti religion.

In Part II we pause along the road to reflect upon the problems of interpreting the meaning of Fang religion. For the meanings of Fang life and Bwiti experience are not just lying about self-evident to be picked up and displayed. Meaning is treated here as an emergent rather than a residual property of experience. It is clear that the meanings assigned by the first Fang ethnographer, Gunter Tessmann, emerged out of his particular interaction and dialogue with Fang. The meanings he assigned were significantly different from those assigned by Father Trilles and by other missionaries or by the members of Bwiti themselves. So our own meanings emerge out of our own particular interaction. Every interpreter seeks to "step between" those whom he studies and those for whom he writes.[4] But he does not achieve an Archimedean point. He is still in part the creature of circumstances. The concepts and images he selects and fashions are significantly influenced by a particular interaction. They emerge from a particular dialogue. There *is* one sea anchor in such an ocean of interpretive uncertainty. And that is to stay, as we seek to do, as close as possible to local idioms and local actions. In Part II, in any case, we shall examine some of those emergent concepts and images, at the same time seeking to see through them to how the traditional religious situations they represent might have incorporated the dilemmas and malaise discussed in Part I.

While we do not ignore the important impact upon Fang of missionary

Christianity, our interpretation of Bwiti, it should be remarked, has its center of gravity in Fang culture itself. The continuity of that culture and its reinterpretation in Bwiti is the main emphasis here. This is not surprising insofar as we lived with Fang and not with missionaries and in that experience were made aware of such cultural continuities. It is also not surprising that those who study these movements from a missionary or evangelical perspective tend to emphasize the profoundly transforming impact of Christianity. In keeping with our orientation we will employ Fang terms, out of a lexicon continuous with their old religious views, for divinities that might otherwise be labeled Jesus and God. For the Bwiti Savior figure we will use the term most often employed by Banzie, Eyen Zame (He Who Sees Zame) and for the Deity itself we will use the Fang name, Zame. The name is used as often as the French "Dieu." And it preserves some of the qualities of the this-worldly efficient diety, Zame ye Mebege, of the old Fang divine genealogy. Those qualities are present in the Bwiti deity.

In Part III, we seek to show how the malaise and increasing isolation of parts of Fang culture achieve some assuagement and reconciliation in Bwiti and, at the same time, how this imaginative coalescence makes use of the diversity of experiences still resonant and relevant in a declining culture. As with Coleridge's *Kubla Khan* we cannot understand this imaginative religion without understanding some of these resonant experiences which it compiles in narcotic dream or conscious design.

While Bwiti draws on the Fang past it is also very much in dialogue with colonial culture and particularly with the missionary presence. We show some of that dialogue in Part II, and point up its consequences in Part III. There is some urgency in that dialogue and this is seen in the fact that the Banzie, the members of Bwiti, are loquacious about their religion, ever ready to explain themselves and virtually with a missionary animus. This dialogue of acculturation provided my field notebooks with much voluntary exegesis and even more extensive explanation under inquiry. Recently in anthropology there has been an emphasis on the unconscious and unexplainable elements in meaning and knowledge.[5] Questions are raised about the truth-value of local exegesis. No doubt much that is meaningful surpasses conscious association. At the same time not all explanations in traditional societies are forced and thus pseudo-conceptions. And this is certainly not the case in such transitional societies as Fang. No forcing in Bwiti is required. The problem is one of separating out the pseudo-conceptions from an insightful reasoning-out of what Banzie feel to be truly meaningful. There is plenty of this "reasoning-out" in Bwiti. In fact it was often forced upon an ethnographer already surfeited with a full day's notetaking. This "intellectually self-conscious" quality, incidentally, is often encountered in African religious movements[6] although the tendency is for observers to maintain or impose a Western "ethnologic," as we see below, in the understanding of these intellectual operations—this reasoning-out process. One of the central concerns of Part III of this study is explication of the various "edifying" ways in which the "knowledgeable ones" of Bwiti "reason out" their religion to the membership.

There are several other elements of the plan. Recent work[7] has shown the value of presenting social dramas in cultural life. When incompatibilities in beliefs, values, and attitudes come into palpable tension or open conflict one may gain insight. Each chapter begins with a revealing event that is epiphanic in Fang or Fang Bwiti culture as we lived it. The remainder of each chapter seeks, in part, to provide an ethnographic background and ethnologic explanation for the event. The events alone offer insight, one hopes, into a range of Fang and Fang Bwiti life. For the key events of the chapters of Part III, episodes have been chosen that in some respects resonate with key events of the corresponding chapters in Part I. But the correspondence is not perfect. Our experience in Bwiti was not perfectly correspondent with our experience in Fang culture.

What we have in Parts I and II, then, is an "ethnography of acculturation"—of Fang in transition. It assumes the existence of several basic ethnographies of Fang or closely related people.[8] Parts of these ethnographies need correction and such will be provided. It is probably true to say that most anthropological work in recent decades has been done in transitional circumstances and thus is acculturation study. In Part III, however, we are faced with a religious culture which seeks to return to that kind of whole, well-bounded, well-integrated, and isolated community that anthropologists used to study or assumed in their studies. In a way our subject moves us against the current of anthropological method. Many of the same individuals appear in these events and that includes the ethnographer.[9] But nothing is more natural than for an anthropologist living within the situation he studies to practice the extended case method.[10] He lives with and comes to know well the same set of individuals who tend to be those involved, though in different ways, in the succeeding events that come to attention. As their roles change in those events one gets a fuller notion of personality and also a better idea of the possibilities for development and change in social relations and frame of reference. The same status and the same frame of reference are not brought to bear on every event in people's lives. Even within the most closed and isolated communities people operate with various frames of reference. This is much more the case in a situation of acculturation.

The extended case method is also advantageous as "extension." It enables the reader to extend, as do members of the culture themselves, his experiences with a small group of individuals to an understanding of broader aspects of the society. For Fang, like all men, extend the lessons of their experience with a limited number of people—experience anchored in the nuclear family primarily—to other experiences within their culture of greater scale and depth.

We gain a power of understanding, or better, we are, like Fang themselves, enabled to find things to stand for or represent the more inchoate experiences of social life from our primary experiences with self and a limited number of others.

THE KINDS OF EXPLANATION TO BE OFFERED

Religion in this secular and pragmatic age needs explaining. It may be argued that religion, par excellence, should be the object of explanation if "all explanations are attempts to explain away impediments of some kind. They are efforts to deprive puzzles, mysteries and blockages of their force."[11] This is even more the case with religions that have the appearance of the exotic— that is, whose dependence on ritual, upon cosmology, and upon therapy differs sharply from the more redemptive and theologically speculative religions to which the West is accustomed. My explanation is basically genetic and semantic. I hold, first, that there has been a set of historical circumstances and experiences that bring a people to expectations propitious for religious revitalization. Second, the meaning of that revitalization is composed from the residue of these experiences. Thus, a people's religion cannot be understood or explained without taking historical circumstances into account.[12] For religion, at least Bwiti, has the particular power to reconcile past and present, the corporeal and the social, the I and the Other. It is, through the sign-images that it employs, *internuncial* between the past and the present of the society which institutionalizes it and the past and present of the corporeal individual who participates in it.

The cosmological and liturgical structure of Bwiti, no doubt, has a relevance to universal mental operations which are at work in the composition of all religions. The work of Claude Lévi-Strauss will come to the reader's mind. I came upon *Tristes Tropiques* when I was in the field in Gabon and I owe a debt to that book, for it caused me to see Fang in a new way. But I was earlier influenced by Lowes and the search for associations and I am more interested in the content of Fang thought than in the structure of the "savage mind." Nevertheless, I am concerned with what Lévi-Strauss calls *bricolage* or fabulation, that tendency in the nonscientific mind to meet the challenges of its situation by making use of what lies at hand, namely, the "remains and debris of events . . . the fossilized evidence of the history of an individual or a society."[13] Along the road to Xanadu we will examine live events and we will note also the remains of Fang culture many of which we will later find taken up again by the Bwiti masters of religious thought. The road we travel should enable us the better to understand the way they structure new and convincing events for their membership by tying together the remains of the past.

To say that I desire to explain, as did Lowes, how this imaginative creation takes place through the association of ideas is to take up again an old, old concern in psychology and elsewhere in the culture sciences. I do not intend simply to rework old atomistic points of view or limit myself to distinctions such as preoccupied Lowes: the Coleridgian notions of fancy ("unchecked sublimal flow of images in association") as in *Kubla Khan* and imagination ("the determining will constructively at work consciously manipulating and adjusting and refashioning the associated images of memory into conformity with a design) as in the *Ancient Mariner*.[14] I am mainly concerned with those devices of representation, sign-images, which I consider to be the basic building units of the religious imagination in its acts of cosmos building. These are images which for a variety of cultural or physiological reasons have powerfully significant associations and which can be used and ordered in various ways to rebuild the cosmic edifice—to return to the whole.*[2] The various schema of this edification will be an object of our inquiry. How do the Banzie construct their pleasure dome, that quality space in which they dwell as they undergo an assuaging series of transformations?

We have before us a religion that seeks to recapture the totality of the old way of life. But this cannot simply be done by nativism. It must be by syncretism. Fang have been too much influenced by the colonial world, by the missionary message, and particularly by the linear and sequential processes of their newly acquired literacy.[15] Not many of the members of Bwiti may be literate, but most of their leaders, the "knowledgeable ones," are. This not only prompts them to exegesis, it commits them to a greater sense of progressive development. One of the interesting things about Bwiti is the syncretic tension between the search for "saving circularities" of an older world view and a more modern commitment to the sequential transformation of religious experience which is not only assuaging to troubled states but redemptive—converting. The interplay between sequence and circularity is a basic dynamic, and it is not simply dialectical. We cannot be guided exclusively by dialectical thought in either the epistemological or the political sense.

Politically one must know that there has been an important element of deprivation in Fang experience which energizes Bwiti, though it is doubtful

---

*[2] The sign-image or significant image is that image whose associations make it particularly apt for use by Fang or Fang in Bwiti in their expressive activities. By "apt for use" we mean that these significant images are especially suitable for predication upon inchoate subjects of attention giving them both concreteness as well as possibilities of performance. The sign image, whose meanings are mostly tacit or implicit, is to be distinguished from the explicitly defined symbol, on the one hand, and the signal on the other—the more or less associationless orienter of activity. Because of the implicitness of the sign-image, it is necessary to search for its associations by anthropological participation in culture. For the distinction between signals, signs, and symbols see J. W. Fernandez, "Symbolic Consensus in a Fang Reformative Cult," and for an explanation of the systematics of the predication of sign-images on inchoate subjects see J. W. Fernandez, "The Mission of Metaphor in Expressive Culture."

that Bwiti can simply be labeled a religion of the oppressed.[16] In Part I we will make clear the deprivations that exist in Fang life both in fact and feeling. They are many and motivating. But the determined search for dialectical oppositions or contradictions either political or mental can vitiate our understanding although, granted, it may enhance the action orientation of the observer. Religions like Bwiti seek "interpenetration without contradiction." While the dialectical point of view desires sharp and useful contradictions to emerge from inquiry, religions like Bwiti are at a stage of argument and action that desires the emergence of the opposite—a general and assuaging sense of unity.

Though the influence of literacy in religion tends, by making it possible to write things down for recurrent reference, to lead to dogmatic and canonical attitudes, there is very little of that in Bwiti. Perhaps this is because the literacy is latent and not practiced widely. Bwiti, like the antecedent Fang religion, is not a complete and closed system of thought always consistent in its presentation. There is no priesthood powerful enough to define orthodoxy and heresy clearly. The notions of many participants often owe as much to their own experiences—which in the spirit of Fang egalitarianism they do not hesitate to introduce—as to what the leaders say. Banzie emphasize speaking with one voice but consensus is still hard to establish. To reify or codify either Fang or Bwiti belief, therefore, is to misplace the concreteness of their experience. Particularly in this transitional period, Fang move in ambiguity. It is a discouraging time of failed or vestigial concepts. Bwiti seeks to clarify some of these ambiguities, but the reality of the religion is a dynamic and ambiguous organization of diversity.[17] This diversity challenges the Bwiti leaders, the "knowledgable ones," in the overarching order they seek to achieve.

If we must be cautious about overreading the intellectual nature of consensus in Bwiti, or overinterpreting the dogmatic application of central ideas and images, we must also be cautious in judging the ethnologic by which the Bwiti cosmos is put together. While there is some tendency to proceed by rules from given premises to necessary conclusions, the syllogisms which appear most in Bwiti are what may be called "syllogisms of association." They operate by elipsis, by enthymeme, by dropping common or middle terms, rather than by compliant implication. And rather than being self-contained, they force contextualization upon the listener, requiring him or her to bring empirical experience to bear from beyond the statements being made in the rituals or the sermons.[18] This forced contextualization and transcendence of religious statements has itself, as we shall show, cosmogonic function.

This may be the same thing as to say that the logic of Bwiti cosmogony is more synthetic than analytic—a logic of analogy, concord, and inclusion rather than one of syllogism, equation, or mutual exclusion. Bwiti religious intelligence, which comes in visions and dreams, in intuitions and intimations, often in psychoreactive states, works primarily with images and by the analogic association of these. Fang recognize this in their way. When in my extended discussions I asked them "to examine certain subjects or problems very carefully" (*fak adzo*) we often ended up circling back on the original subject seeking to rephrase it in other terms. This is perfectly natural in a people given more to action than to formal thought—however reflective they may be in certain ways and, perhaps, have always been.[19] Given their penchant for analogic thinking and their action orientation, I quickly came to appreciate two of their proverbs: *ba dzô mam menkot, ba yem mam menkot* (things said with twists must be understood with twists) and *mbôfak* (*nkôbot* or *entemege*) *emwan nsôsôm* (the thinker is the son of the hunter). In pursuing Fang ideas the reader should not be surprised to find some twists. We are pursuing willful game which is not going to run down the path straight ahead of us. It may even double back. Our very presence affects it.

Important syntheses take place in relation to the key words that recur thematically in the discourse of a people. As the Bohannans have shown for the Tiv (a people very similar to the Fang), in respect to religion, complexities of beliefs and actions tend to cluster around keywords—as "nebulae of associated ideas."[20] In the case of Fang, while there is rarely a systematization of these clusters of associated ideas—no theology or highly systematic philosophy—yet they arise in many different situations as "points de repère" in social interaction. The usefulness of an empirical search for an overall organization of these keywords is dubious. Fang are too pragmatic and empirically oriented for that. But a careful examination of the associations of these words—they cluster around the most crucial abstractions of their lives, "preparation" (*akômnge*), "witchcraft capacity" (*evus*), "protective benevolence" (*mvam*), "respect" (*engang*), "good luck" (*maa*), "pleasurable activity" (*elulua*)—and the main situations in which they appear can bring us, together with the study of other devices of representation, close to the actualities of Fang belief. We will be particularly attentive to terms for emergent qualities of Fang and Bwiti life such as *mvwaa* (even-handed tranquillity) and will distinguish between these emergent qualities achieved by various special ritual forms of kinesthesia and synesthesia and the residual everyday qualities of life.

GENERALITY OF OBSERVATIONS

Every ethnographer is faced with the problem of the generality of his observations. How widespread are the practices he has observed, the beliefs he has noted? Even in the most dogmatic, closed, and small-scale society individual differences are present and important in processes of change. The description of cultural practices and beliefs is thus a matter of accounting for distributions about a mean, a mode, a median. The establishment of these points is a statistical matter best accomplished by sample survey—the method of extensity.[21] We practiced extensive research only in demographic matters. Our method was primarily that of intensity—repeated and in-depth discussions with a limited number of knowledgeable informants, and, where possible, repeated observation of practices and collection of public statements and other texts.

We worked intensely thus with some eighteen informants and lived for many months in three different villages in Fang country: Assok Ening (Oyem) among the southern Ntumu, Etsam (Medouneu) among the Okak, and Kougouleu (Kango) among the Méké. But an addition we stayed for more than a week's time in at least ten other villages ranging from the Ntem River facing the Cameroons to the shores of the Ogoowe, the southern extension of the Fang in central Gabon. This included a month in Rio Muni. Altogether we worked with over two hundred Fang in two years. Work began in the bush, moved to a peri-urban milieu around Libreville, then returned to the bush to avoid either a rural or an urban bias. Registered here are the findings we came to regard as the mode in Fang and Bwiti belief and practice.

But a warning is still in order. Fang have an egalitarian and open society. There is so much "palaver" and dispute in Fang life that I was soon forced to reflect on the problems of consensus in cultural beliefs and social practices.[22] One must listen to Fang wisdom on this matter, as found in proverbs repeatedly put forth to us. They say *ayong ese da kik ngui anena* (each clan cuts up the wild pig in its own fashion). They say *nda foré, binong bibe* (one house, two beds). They say *fofon ye ngem gem* (*adzidzit ye ongengem*) (each animal [bat] has his particular way of feeling shame). Perhaps it would be wise to coin my own proverb in the spirit of Fang wisdom, *nyugele ase a tsile akikh nten* (*dzile aba die amien*) (every teacher writes his unique book).

The upshot is that we shall avoid speaking of *the* Fang doing, saying, or believing such and such. Rather, when the custom is fairly widespread among them we shall say Fang say, Fang do. And we will try to present individual Fang or Banzie voices. As Fang say, "he who listens to the rain (many voices) understands nothing" (*a wok mvung, ka yili dzum*).

Sir Thomas Browne said in *Religio Medici*, "We carry with us the wonders we seek without us: there is all Africa and her prodigies in us." Indeed the Dark Continent has been for Europeans a screen upon which to project some obscure—prodigious—preoccupations. But method in anthropology must guard against discovering imposed wonders. In the universal sense, it is true, all men witness common "wonders" as their minds and bodies come into being, mature, and decline. We shall see some of these "wonders" constructed into Bwiti. But the interpretations given to these "wonders" of the human condition are to be sought in the culture itself. No doubt satisfactory ethnography must be written with imagination. But in every case, that imagination should be tied down to local images, local actions.

Argumenti Personae

We will list below (pp. 18-23) the names and brief biographies of Fang and Fang-Bwiti men and women who appear in these pages. The Fang are mainly from the village of Assok Ening and the family of Mba M'Oye, Clan Bukwe, Oyem District, Northern Gabon. The Banzie appearing here have a wider provenience for we consider two other chapels beside the Bwiti chapel in Assok Ening: the mother chapel at Kougouleu, the Libreville region, close to the coast, and the Ayol Chapel midway between the coast and northern Gabon.

In part we seek here what Max Weber called "subjective interpretation"— insight into the subjective meaning of Fang and Bwiti cultural realities. In good measure this will be insight into ongoing arguments. For we find our subjects involved in characteristic arguments both of their own and of their culture. These make use of a Fang repertory of images. Uncertainties of self and of other are faced in characteristic ways. Characteristic arguments are put forth to further characteristic intentions.

But can these subjects, these "characters" be placed into a drama? Nowhere are the parts of any of the characters written out. Throughout our experience there was a spontaneity and an emergent quality. Some Fang saw more of a plot than others but none an entire play. One cannot ignore, particularly in this transitional period, the ambiguities and ambivalences, the sense of the inchoate, which Fang confront and for which they must find images of concretization and performance. We will not speak, therefore, of dramatic performance or "dramatis personae" in Fang life itself. The round of life, if not uncertain, is simply undramatic in its day-in and day-out preoccupations with getting a forest living.

The dramatist or those who use dramatic metaphors are, as Plato pointed out in the *Republic* (Book X), likely to be several degrees removed from the reality of human affairs.[23] We will speak rather of the arguments that each person is making for himself, for his family and kin-group and on behalf of his culture. Fang are an argumentative people and it is no surprise that one of the most active institutions among them was the men's council house (*aba*), an arena of argument aptly called the "palaver house" by Spanish administrators. It is true that these arguments are often residual and must be interpolated. But occasionally they emerge in an unexpected moment of epiphany or denouement and become evident as a selfishness or altruism, self-indulgence or restraint, clairvoyance or opacity, wisdom or folly. Then, indeed, there is a tendency for protagonists and antagonists to take shape in village life. Men and women, aware that they are arguing at cross-purposes, bring into play for redefinition or rededication the rules and images of right action that they live by. But though these events are emotionally dramatic and suggest dramas they are not really dramas themselves. To say that they are is simply to overinterpret the coherence and intentionality of Fang interaction.

In the Bwiti religion, however, these "dramatic suggestions" are taken up and made into ritual dramas. Narratives are provided and scenarios are created and the parts of participants become fairly well known. Arguments are enacted with foregone conclusions. Banzie become dramatic persons and thus defeat the inchoateness of everyday life. They find images to predicate upon their inchoate selves. They are given dramatic new names and become something through performance.

In Bwiti we find, often quite explicitly formulated, the dramatic perform- ance of metaphors, the recurrent enactment of narratives, and the repeated exploration of themes. But then Bwiti is, as Fang daily life is so manifestly not, a religious drama of the triumphant passage through life and the over- coming of death. Just the same, plenty of arguments take place, disturbing the flow of that dramatic passage.

THE SETTING OF THE ACTION AND ITS REPRESENTATIVENESS

The action takes place (1958-1960) in villages in the Equatorial Rain Forest of northern and central Gabon. Two statistics are telling: rainfall and popu- lation density. The lushness of this forest may be comprehended in the average rainfall of 150 inches per year. Gabon lies in that limited region of West Africa where there are two rainy seasons—warm late spring rains (*sugu esep*) and the cooler and heavier autumn rains (*sugu ôyôn*). It is a region of very low population density, five people or less per square kilometer, and the forest—the predominant reality—stretches hundreds of kilometers to the east of these villages with virtually no habitation at all.

Most of the Fang action takes place in Assok Ening (Figure 1.1), a village in the Woleu-Ntem region of northern Gabon. It lies on the frontier between the southern Ntumu and northern Fang-Fang dialect groups of Fang. It is a regroupment village which means that "village families" (*mvogabot*) for- merly living apart have been persuaded by the government, interested in ease of administration, to live together. Assok Ening is a regroupment of four former villages of two different clans. That two different clans share the same village is a modern development. Assok Ening in that sense is very much a transitional village. With its 379 inhabitants it is also larger than the average Fang village—105 persons is average village size in the Woleu Ntem, while 85 persons per village is average for all Fang regions.

Most of the action in Assok Ening takes place in the family of Mba M'Oye. It has 65 members, the largest family in the village. There are 8 *nyamoro* (mature, usually middle-aged, men with wives and children), 22 women

The Genealogical Line (22 Names)

Village of *Assok Ening*
Mvogabots: 1. Mba M'Oye
2. Ekong Oye
3. Angwia Ndekwu

▲ MALE
● FEMALE

1.1 Family Relationships of Those Appearing in this Account married in as wives, and 35 youth, which is to say newly married men, unmarried boys and girls, and children. The family has two council houses, which is below the Fang average of three council houses per mvogabot. Moreover, the family directs most of its action to the council house of Ngema, Mintze, and Asseko Mve. Besides these council houses, the family possesses 40 dwellings of which 27 are the traditional bark, raffia, and thatch sleeping or cooking huts and 13 are the new "cold houses" with cement floors, wattle and daub walls and, eventually, zinc roofs. There were no zinc roofs in Assok Ening during the time of the action.

Most of the action in the mvogabot of Mba M'Oye takes place in the *ndébot* (house of people) of Ngema Mve and his brothers of the same father. Every Fang mvogabot is made up of a number of ndebot associated with a nyamoro. An ndebot is thus the household of an old or middle-aged man frequently living with his uterine brothers but always with his wives and his sons and their wives and children. There are seven ndebot in the family of Mba M'Oye. In these ndebot with their strong primary family ties lie the seeds of the fission of the mvogabot. In many Fang mvogabot one of the three council houses will be acting as a center of resistance to mvogabot unity, expressing the desire of the several ndebot associated with it to break away on their own. In Mba M'Oye some of this fissionary impulse was found in the second council house. But generally Mba M'Oye was remarkably well integrated.

Our focal setting, the village of Assok Ening and the village family of Mba M'Oye, are thus larger entities than the Fang norm. The family enjoys unusual integration. Fang villages of the period of fieldwork comprised, on the average, two mvogabot of between 40 and 50 members each. But while this village and this family have an exceptional character, their actions are not much removed from the mode. In my view life in Assok Ening is simply more agitated and more subject to modernizing pressures. The result is that the underlying problems of Fang life in transition—the conflicting arguments of their lives—are more likely to surface. That the family has unusual integrity is due primarily to the wealth, wisdom, and persuasiveness of one man, Ngema Mve. But men such as he are found on occasion among Fang of any village. Still there is always a danger in letting one village and one family represent *the* Fang. We shall be calling, therefore, on observations from other villages of the western equatorial forest.

In our discussion of Bwiti we shall also refer to the more established chapels of the New Life Branch of the religion: first, the mother chapel, the direct successor of the founding chapel at Kougouleu (Kango District) close to Libreville and the Estuary—the heartland of Bwiti—and second, one of the most active chapels in the southern Woleu-Ntem region at Ayol village. Both of these chapels are located in the same equatorial milieu but both are much closer to the coast and to the European and missionary influences which are an important dynamic in Bwiti. The religious microcosm in both these chapels is much more coherent than in the new Asumege Ening (New Life) chapel in Assok Ening.

A final question arises in respect to representativeness. Because we are concentrating on the Bwiti microcosm we only incidentally consider the relationship of Bwiti to other religious activities and movements in its region and in Africa generally. I have published a number of articles comparing Bwiti to other African religious movements I have studied,[24] and this is the second of four projected monographs on religious movements studied in the 1960's.[25] But the more important question, perhaps, is the relation of Bwiti to other movements in its region. We have recently been well reminded how widely diffused religious elements and influences in Africa can be.[26] We will try to give adequate treatment here to southern Gabonese influences on Fang Bwiti. Going further afield in the region and particularly to the lower Congo, the pioneer survey by E. Andersson and the work of John Janzen and Wyatt MacGaffey,[27] when compared to the Bwiti material, shed light on its place.

THE TIME AND TENSE OF THE INQUIRY

It has been a frequent convention in anthropological writing to employ the present tense in cultural description even though the research may have taken place at some period in the past and involves customs at various stages of change or lag. The use of the "historical present" may "fix" culture for greater clarity of presentation, but its consequence is to overemphasize the stability of tradition. This method of presentation, however, will be employed in Part III in our description of the Bwiti religion, with the justification that the object of Bwiti *is* the achievement of a fixed and stable microcosm as enduringly present and as free from the "ravages of time" as possible. In Part I we will employ the past tense understood as referring predominantly to the situation of Fang culture in the mid-twentieth century, and especially in the decade of the 1950's to which the Bwiti religion which we knew was responding.

If we had written this ethnography in Fang instead of in English we would have had, perhaps, a more adequate tense structure with which to work. For Fang has not only a recent past and a remote past, in addition to a perfect past tense, but it also has, by the use of auxiliaries, a conditional or narrative (aoristic) past and a potential or continuous present. Their use might have achieved a better sense than was possible in English of the way, among Fang, that an unspecified past persists in orienting the present and the way the present is potential with the past. Such retrospective potentiating of the possibilities of the present is very much an objective of the Bwiti religion.

The tense problem which I treat here as mainly a problem of available grammatical categories—customary verbal extensions of the Bantu radical—raises the question of a Fang sense of time. What would the phrase, "ravages of time," since we have used it, mean to them? Since Fang who were involved in this inquiry did not employ the concept of time, the question is, as has been recognized in African studies, an academic one.[28] "Time" was not discussed as a general problem-concept nor compulsively calibrated among Fang in the villages or in Bwiti except in respect to exact timing of rituals. Time, as such, was very much bound up with events and activities and thus had a situational character of considerable diversity. Agricultural time was different from human body time, from genealogical time, and from forest or game time. I believe the phrase "ravages of time" would mean to Fang of this study a falling apart of the resonances and associations between events of the past and events of the present by reason of acculturation and all it brought with it of new discrepant realities and broader horizons.

Bwiti, it seems to me, is seeking to respond to such ravages by "time binding,"[29] by trying to bring past and present into "coexistence."[30] This "time binding" or return to "coexistence," this placation or communion of tenses, seems to me to be very much what religious renewal is and always has been about in Fang experience. There was little concern for future time. Beyond the natural course of present events, such as a human life or an agricultural cycle, I could not discern much interest in time to come, and surely not in the endless and finally imageless future of the linear time of the Western macrocosm. There was very little attempt to imagine or prophesy time in that dimension. Indeed, the distant, eventual future was, grammatically, in the use of the auxiliary "nga," homophonically the same as the distant past tending to collapse into it.[31] In Fang Bwiti the feeling seems to have been that if past and present could be brought into coexistence and communion the future would fulfill itself. Though there was an occasional politically oriented Bwiti leader or one with ideas of a future postcolonial society, and though millenarian hopes were sometimes expressed in some chapels, for the great majority of Banzie their microcosm could be brought into being NOW.[32]

Argumenti Personae: Brief Biographies (Parts I and II)

The Family (ndébôt) of Mba M'Oye

Ngema Mve

> The central figure of Part I, if there is one. A practical-minded man and the most influential in the village. Age 52. Work purifies, he argues, and work conquers all. Ngema has many wives and few children. He has worked many years with the European and is convinced of the

advantages of their way of life. "When are my fellow villagers going to learn the ways of the world?" he asks impatiently.

Nana Michelle

Ngema's first wife. Clan Essabalun.

Zang

Ngema's second wife and mother of Marie. Clan Effak.

Minkpwe

Ngema's sixth wife and recently his favorite.

Ada

Ngema's newest wife, his ninth. Clan Essangi.

Ekomo Ngema Marie

Ngema's only daughter. A strong-minded woman whom Ngema has kept in the village in order that she should have children to strengthen his family lines. Age 25. She argues for the preeminence of her mother, Ngema's second wife, against the claim of the other wives.

Asseko Mve

Ngema's younger brother with few wives and many children. Age 48. Since his descendants may take over the family, he argues for a greater share in decision-making than is allowed him by Ngema.

Mintza Mve

Ngema's older half-brother—same father but different mother. Retired from an active part in village life to dedicate himself to his grandchildren and to the Catholic religion. Age 68. "When are the villagers going to stop this fetish foolishness?"

Essono Mba

The Chief of the village. His writ does not run very far with his fellow villagers. A great believer in the old religion and the old forces of the supernatural. "How is my vitality and potency," he asks, "being affected by the ancestors and the witches?"

Efop

Essono's second wife. Age 35. Clan Nkojeng.

Mve Essono

Son of the Chief and Efop. Age 18. He is his father's favorite son, *abeng musô* (remover of sand/flea eggs from the toes). "What will my fortune bring me in the future?" he asks.

Ondo Mba

Essono's resentful younger brother. Age 58.

Ndutumu Zogo

A family member whose linkage to the lineage is not clear. Age 45. He argues for a version of clan genealogy that makes him of direct descent.

Muzwi Mebiame

A man with one wife and no children who has made himself an authority on genealogical matters. Age 50. Having no future in the genealogy, he argues for a symbolic presence.

Alogo Engonga

A man whose mind and body have been badly damaged by tertiary neurosyphilis. Age 56. He makes no arguments.

Muye Alogo Michel

His son and a man of many projects. Age 30. One of the leading members of the local Bwiti cult. Caught between coming to terms with the powers of this world and the powers of the next. He argues that villagers should cooperate to make money.

Ngema Obama Antoine

A young tailor recently returned to the village in psychological distress. Age 21. "Why has my fortune turned out so disastrously?" He argues that the ancestors intended to make him wealthy.

Bibong Asumu Leon

A strong-minded and strong-bodied man who is the local representative of the opposition political party. Age 42. "How can I best take a lead in Assok Ening and best represent my party's interest here?"

Fernando Ndong

The ethnographer, age 28. He and his wife share Ngema Mve's house. He asks too many questions and is always doing paper work. "What does he want, really?" He argues that the outside world would be very interested in the Fang way of life and that is why he is here.

Kabiyen

His number one wife, age 25. She cooks in the kitchens with the other women, goes to the plantations and fishes and bathes down at the river. She is better loved than her nosy husband. "Was it true that her father had given money to her husband when he married her?"

The Family (ndébôt) of Ekong Oye

Muzwi Ekwaga

The father of Mba Muzwi. Age 65.

Mbe Muzwi

A young man of the village trying to increase his fortune by magical means. Age 23.

Obunu Alogo

The local trickster and a man with a lively and often outrageous imagination. He breaks taboos and abuses his fellows with impunity. Age 48.

The Family (ndébôt) of Angwia Ndekwu

Sima Ndong

A young man suffering from elephantiasis. One of the most eloquent of villagers. Age 33.

Ze Ndong
>His younger brother to whom Sima has been ceaselessly protective and benevolent. A valuable assistant to the ethnographer.

Metogo Zogo
>A local dance leader (*nganga*) of Bwiti. He is clairvoyant and often acts mysteriously. Age 32. He argues for Bwiti as the only salvation.

Observers upon or Accessories to the Action

Ayang Ndong
>An old man of clan Essisis, Medouneu District. A great authority on his people. Age 76. He argues that all things Fang are degenerating.

Bikuh Oyono
>A suspected adulterer. Clan Bukwe.

Edu Ada
>A blind troubadour singer of the mvet cycle of Hero Tales. Appreciated for his ribald sense of humor.

Eye Zolo
>A dead blacksmith. Clan Bukwe.

The Chief of Medouneu
>A man of clan Bukwe, Chief of the next village to Assok Ening. His authority is very uncertain and he is constantly testing it. He argues for the reality of the power invested in him by colonial authorities.

Mendame Simon
>A local man who showed his bare backside at a funeral gathering.

Ndende
>A man and his disciples from Bakota country who removed sorcery by witchcraft.

Père Dominick
>A local White Father with long experience among Fang and well liked. He has been frequently frustrated by their demonic beliefs. He argues for the intelligence of Fang but decries their lack of heartfelt conviction on religious matters.

Ze Azi
>A nonagenarian of the village of Koomessi, Oyem District, Clan Nkojeng. He makes no arguments.

DRAMATIS PERSONAE: BRIEF BIOGRAPHIES (PART III)
MEMBERS OF THE "NEW LIFE" FAMILY OF BWITI

The Mother Chapel of Asumege Ening (Begin the Life)
Bwiti at Kougouleu Village, Kango District, Estuary Region

Ekang Engono ("Aki Kos Zambi Avanga"/"The Parrot's Egg, God the Mediator")

The protagonist of Part III and the leader, nima na kombo, of the mother chapel of Asumege Ening. He is the direct successor to the founder, Ndong Obam Eya. A man who has "died many times," he embodies the "even-handed tranquillity" of one who "knows death." In his visions he has seen and been able to create significant new rituals, dances, and songs in Bwiti. When not involved in leading the rituals or dramatically pronouncing the "évangiles," he is scarcely to be seen in the village. He is off hunting in the forest.

Michel Bie Ngounya ("The Knowledgeable One")

The Yemba, "knowledgeable one," of the mother chapel. He explains to visitors and to inquiring members the meanings of Bwiti. He often gives the leader's sermons or gives sermons of his own. An able energetic man with a flare for dramatic statement, it is suspected that he may be seeking to establish his own chapel. He may be losing his allegiance to his role in the ritual drama of the leader and subtly arguing for a different dispensation.

The New Chapel of Asumege Ening Bwiti at Assok Ening, Oyem District,
Woleu-Ntem Region

Zogo Ebu ("Zambi Avanga"/"God the Mediator")

The father of the Nganga Metogo Zogo and the founder of Disumba Bwiti in Assok Ening. Conservative about his rituals, he finally failed to involve dramatically a substantial part of his membership. After long argument three-quarters left him to build a new chapel.

Metogo Zogo ("Onwan Misengue"/"Bird of the Two Earths") and Muye Michel ("Ngadi"/"The Bolt of Lightning")

Already identified as members of an Assok Ening family (mvogabot), they set up the new chapel of Asumege Ening after separating from Zogo Ebu. They are mildly arguing among themselves as to who should assume the leadership. Metogo Zogo is much the more dramatic personage and Muye the more matter-of-fact.

Oyana Ndutumu ("Mvon"/"the Initiate")

A daughter of Zogo Ebu's brother who returned to the village after divorce. She was initiated into Bwiti and dramatically experienced all that was expected of her. Her initiation provoked an argument that led to the splitting apart of the Disumba chapel.

Ona Pastor ("Koko Nangunda"/"The Rocky Sepulcher")

A Bwiti expatriate from Spanish Guinea who has joined the Kwakum Oyem chapel but often dances in Assok Ening. He is typical of the wanderers (*ntobot*) who attach themselves as clients in many Bwiti chapels. One of the most knowledgeable of Banzie, he can explain at length any aspect of the religion, although his explanations mostly learned in

Disumba Bwiti differ in important ways from local Asumege Ening explanations.

Mvomo Asumu André ("Nanga Misengue"/"The Portals of the Two Earths") The "knowledgeable one" of the Kwakum chapel (Oyem) and soon to be the leader. Expanding on Asumege Ening Bwiti from the Estuary, he is creating a coherent and dramatically compelling style of Bwiti, influential in the Assok Ening chapel. He helped organize the Assok Ening chapel.

The Established Asumege Ening Chapel at Ayol in Medouneu District

Eko Obama ("Mosingi"/"The Civet Cat") A long-time lumber camp worker in the peninsular forests across from Libreville. He first danced Bwiti in the lumber camps, and returned in his mid-forties to organize Bwiti in his natal village. He was much influenced by Ndong Obama Eya, the founder of Asumege Ening, and has journeyed to the Kwakum chapel as a representative of this branch of Bwiti.

PART I
THE ROAD

❖ 1 ❖

Narratives of
Fang-European Contacts,
1840-1910

Môt a wí a môt ka etôm.
(The man who kills a man without a dispute.)

THE STRANGER

WHEN I ARRIVED in northern Gabon I was a week's time hitchhiking and
hiking up and down the roads and back into the forest in the region of Bitam,
Oyem, and Minvoul before I was able to locate a suitable village. It was an
uncomfortable and hot week. First contacts are difficult. They carry many
misunderstandings. One is tryng to make enduring relationships with people
one hardly knows but hopes to come to know very well indeed. There is a
tendency to be painfully sensitive to all sorts of clues, relevant and irrelevant,
and to overinterpret or fall back on stereotypes.

Assok Ening was a village that immediately attracted me. Not far from the
main road, it was a regroupment of several clans, with a marketplace, an
infirmary, and a school provided by the administration. It promised much
material on culture contact. Hiking up off the main road amidst the astonishment of women and children, I went directly to what appeared to me the
main men's council house. Two elderly men were inside making rattan baskets. They spoke no French and called a schoolboy to speak with me. When
it was understood that I was looking for a place to live in the village, there
was some exchange of looks, but the older man stepped outside to the large
talking drum and began to beat upon it for several minutes. With the customary
tattoo he announced the presence of a European and then called by name
those family members who were in the nearby fields and forests. They gathered
quickly, along with most of the village. My request was repeated and greeted
with immediate debate. There was an argument as to which houses I might
be shown and to whose family I was properly "the stranger." Finally I was
shown the house of Ngema Mve, which had a concrete floor, two large main
rooms, and four sleeping rooms. Since this was more than adequate I expressed
immediate interest, but nothing could be done immediately, for the whole

family had to be gathered on the issue. Two days later in Bitam I received the following letter:

Cher Monsieur:

The family has raised the question of your lodging with us and is agreeable that this should be so. We consider you to be our stranger and shall look after your well being. Please come this evening or the next to discuss details.

Mve Essono for the Family of
Mba M'Oye

That evening's discussion was once again a very public one. All the windows of Ngema's house were open and villagers leaned in at every portal. The room was full. Everyone was anxious to know why a European (*ntangen*) wished to live among them. The speculation was particularly intense because it was said I had come to establish a commerce. Some had heard that I was a *mwan amerika* (a child of America), and since this phrase was often used for Protestant missionaries, some thought I might be intending to set up a mission station. When, as it turned out, I wanted only to live among them to learn their way of life, there was evident disappointment, and some drifted away.

There had been a debate in the family the day before as to the terms on which I would be accepted. Though this had been resolved, some parts of it were repeated so that I should not take my place for granted nor underestimate the price of my lodging. Leon Bibong felt it necessary, as a local representative of the opposition political party then anxious for independence from France, to wonder why, when the Gabonese were trying to free themselves from European domination, a European should be accepted into village life. "Why has he come?" he asked with a dark edge to his voice. Sima Ndong, though he was not of the family of Mba M'Oye, then spoke. Because of his eloquence, he was often allowed to speak in the affairs of other families. He asked, "When have we not been disappointed in the European? We have always had the highest hopes in him but he has not taught us to make the simplest thing he knows—a match! He always comes among us full of promises but in the end he turns away from us and deceives us!" Then Ngema Mve spoke. He said, "All these things are true but when has a European come and wanted to live in our village? Did not the fathers say that we must show men who came with good hearts every hospitality, until they should have shown their 'bad heart' (*nlem abé*). Now it is our place to offer him hospitality." These remarks were received with sounds of approval.

The room was then cleared and the family and I began negotiating for the rent of the house. It was finally decided that two of the bedrooms of the house should be kept for two of Ngema's wives and the rest of the house should be mine for a price one-half of that which was originally demanded by the family. I would have bargained more vigorously since the price was still large, but I was too mindful of the deceptions practiced by Europeans just alluded to, and wished to begin generously. Sima Ndong later confided that I agreed to pay too much for the rent of that house, but that was later when he was in a dispute with Ngema.

My reception by the family of Mba M'Oye already at that early moment brought into play their ambivalent notions about themselves and about the European—notions that were to reappear thematically during several years among them. While hospitality was almost always extended to us in the different villages, there was at the same time an uncertainty and even a suspicion about the future of our relations. The history of Fang-European contacts shows good reasons for this. That history reveals Europeans imposing paradoxical images such as that of the noble savage and acting upon inconsistent premises such as the "civilizing mission." In a sense Fang, questing themselves, as we see in Chapter 2, were accessories to varieties of European quest which they came to regard as deceitful.

THE INTERIOR CALLING

The Fang first appear in a report by T. Edward Bowditch on his mission to Cape Coast Castle and Ashantee in 1819. He referred to them as Paamway, the name current among the coastal peoples and later adopted for them by the Spanish. They were reported to live about a month and a half's journey[1] northeastward from the Gabon Estuary in the vicinity of the large east-flowing river, Wola or Wole, "the largest river in the world from which come all the great rivers in this country." The Woleu, which becomes the Benito in Rio Muni, actually flows west and is a relatively minor watercourse among its larger geographical neighbors, the Ntem-Campo, the Sanaga, and the Ogooué. It seems more likely that Fang at this time, in their migration southwestward, were found at the headwaters of the Ntem, between that river and the Sanaga, and not so far south as the Woleu.

In this early account, based on secondhand native testimony, inaccuracies in the reports of custom accompany geographical misrepresentations. Of the Paamway, Bowditch tells us "all the nations on this route were said to be cannibals, the Paamways not so voraciously so as the others because they cultivate a breed of large dogs for their eating." Bowditch's preoccupation with the cannibalism of all the peoples of Gabon introduces a leitmotif of European interest and understanding in the region.

Like Bowditch, almost all Europeans in the first half of the nineteenth century were confined to the coastal regions of West and Equatorial Africa, often because of the stratagems of coastal inhabitants. The coastal peoples benefited as middlemen in trade with the interior, and resisted attempts by Europeans to make direct contact. They employed threats as well as insidious commentary on the barbarity of the interior tribes. These reports were a source of the reputation for savagery and cannibalism acquired by Fang.

At the same time, coastal accounts intrigued as much as they repelled, for the missionaries felt a call to the conversion of these pristine interior tribes untouched by the corruption of the coast—its immoral European elements, its fleshpots, its monuments to mammon, its sycophantic and untrustworthy natives. Their "manifest destiny" was the penetration to and illumination of the heart of darkness.[2]

The first direct contacts with Fang were made by two American missionaries, Wilson and Griswold, representing the American Board of Foreign Missions. They arrived on the Gabon on the 22nd of June, 1842.[3] A month later, in a letter to the home board, the Rev. Griswold, in explaining the wisdom of the site selected, was already extolling the opportunities for access to the interior tribes. He drew an entrancing picture of the "millions of southern central Africa which had never yet been visited by the Christian Missionary."[4] Nor was it long before the Pangwe people came to personify this beckoning interior. In August the Rev. Wilson made a reconnaissance to the upper waters of the estuary, the confluence of the Kama, where he met with a group of Pangwe on a trading expedition. He found them noble savages indeed. "Those of whom we saw were vastly superior in their personal appearance to the maritime tribes . . . I have no hesitation in pronouncing them the finest Africans I have ever met with. They wear no clothing (and) jeer the bushman of this region because they wear cloth to conceal their personal defects and external diseases."[5]

He credited their virtues to a mountainous and healthful habitat "where the cutaneous and other diseases common to the maritime regions are unknown." The Prudential Committee of the Home Board did not miss this reference and, in commenting upon Wilson's report, suggested hopefully that it was the interior which might be best suited to missionary operations.

> The country will be pleasant and healthful and the people, untainted by the vices of civilization, will first know the whiteman not as an avaricious trader, not as the fomentor of strife and bloodshed but as the minister of peace and the herald of mercy.[6]

Pursuant to these beliefs, the Rev. Griswold in May and June of 1844 pushed back to the borders of Fang country and was thus the first European of record to visit Fang in their villages. But the exertion of this trip was too great. Not long after his return he succumbed to a fever, dying July 14 of that year,[7] the first in a succession of losses that depleted the Gabon Mission station.

In September 1848, the Rev. William Walker left the Baraka station at the mouth of the Gabon and, journeying some twenty miles back in from the head of the estuary on the Kama, visited three Pangwe towns. Their nobility was manifest: "More perfect specimens of masculine vigor I have never seen. The competitors at the Olympic games might have envied such bones and muscles so perfectly developed."[8] While he found them in a state of "wild independence" with no trace of demeaning customs such as slavery, yet there was a commercial animus in them which augured ill. For "they have learned that not a tenth part of the goods obtained for ivory on the coast ever reaches them."[9]

Walker mentioned Fang cannibalism in passing. It is this which the coastal peoples flee: "if they are killed they do not care much for that. But they express a great horror of being cut up and eaten like so many pigs." He concluded that they must bend every effort to move in among the waves of "this equatorial tide in its unceasing progress out of the interior before it crashes, flounders and breaks up upon the beach!"[10]

In fact the Americans were stalemated in the estuary region until their ejection by the French in the late 1880's, but their efforts were continued with greater penetration northward, in the Muni Estuary, Spanish Guinea, and much later on the Ogooué and in the Cameroons. From the Corisco Presbyterian Mission at the mouth of the Muni Estuary the Rev. James Mackey in September 1853 made an expedition back into the Cristal Mountains. He repeated it in 1857.[11] From an ethnographic viewpoint his report is useful. It solves, for example, the problem as to the source of Fang brass work which, it is supposed, was traded down from the Cameroons. He pointed out that brass kettles and other trade articles were simply melted down and reworked. He also observed the importance of the "men's council and guard house" (aba), the place where justice is administered. In three days in one village he never saw it without its complement of men in discussion. His report is fundamentally a confirmation of the pristine conditions he probably expected to find: vitality ("The Panwis are the noisiest tribe I have yet met with in Africa . . . they seem to delight in all manner of sounds"); and fertility ("The proportion of children in the Panwi towns is much greater than towns nearer the sea").

There are several interesting features in these early American contacts. The Americans were impressed with the virtue of Fang. They even found them to have talent in theological matters. Reverend Bushnell recites with approbation the way an intelligent Pangwe held a Bakele in warm discussion respecting the salvation of their respective tribes. "The Bakele assured him that the Pangwes, being cannibals, were sinners above all others, and consequently could not go to heaven."[12] The missionaries were most concerned with the European-inspired abominations these children of nature might be exposed to on the coast. And, in fact as the missionaries on the Gabon Estuary began to give up any hope of reaching Fang in their plateau home, more and more commentary was given over to the fear that Fang, who were now reaching the coast, were sinking into immorality and would succumb to degenerate coastal ways.

THE FRENCH SEARCH FOR A PEOPLE
WITH WHOM TO BUILD A COLONY

The French felt a similar attraction to the interior. They established themselves at Libreville in 1842 in the belief that the Gabon Estuary was the mouth of a very large and deeply penetrating river. The lure of the estuary,[13] however, soon faded, as exploration at the head of this arm of the sea and up its adjacent rivers, proved them all unnavigable. It was on one of these voyages up the Como that the first French contacts with Fang villages were made by Lieutenant Pigeard at about 25 leagues from where the Como empties into the estuary. This was in September of 1846.[14] In November of the same year his colleague, Lieutenant Mequet, made a further reconnaissance up the Como, giving us the first extended description we have of Fang in French. He called them ''M'Pawins.''[15]

The ''pièce de résistance'' of Mequet's exploration up the Bekoué was the opportunity to meet on two different occasions with these M'Pawins—these ''eaters of men, the terror of MPongues.'' In contrast to the coastal peoples (MPongue, Bekali, Bulu, Tshekiani) who were neither trustworthy nor attractive, he found the Fang well formed, athletic, very European of countenance, and with more the air of Neapolitan fishermen than of negroes. Their hands and feet were of an aristocratic mold.[16] He observed them gracefully involved in a rather staid dance between men and women, probable *bele-bele*, still a favorite. After much cajolery, he succeeded in inviting the two chiefs aboard his ship in order to impress them with the industry and power of the whites. Profoundly impressed as the chiefs were, their dignity was not disturbed. At last Mequet asked them directly if they were anthropophages. It was a question that preoccupied the French more than the Americans. The chief responded, ''No,'' smiling in a sincere manner. Mequet was disposed to accept this answer. ''I consider them much too advanced on the ladder of civilization to eat their fellow beings though they may have done so formerly.''[17]

While Mequet's report set the tone for later contacts, the denial of cannibalism was generally ignored. This disposition can be seen in his companion-in-arms, Braouezec, who a decade later explored beyond Mequet's route on the Bekoué[18] and up the Como to the foothills of the Cristal Mountains. He gave a good account of the Pahouins, ''Faon (*sic*) et Makei,''[19] whom he accompanied on an elephant hunt. It is strikingly similar to Mequet's in every aspect except anthropophagy. He found the Fang intrepid, resourceful, and brave compared to the coastal MPongwe. The Fang fought in broad daylight, the terror of their neighbors, confronting the guns of their enemies with spears and elephant-hide shields, both adeptly employed. Their villages were clean and their houses well made, and they wore their hair pulled back in the manner of the eighteenth-century queue. Their egalitarianism was extreme, verging on communism. Their religion was less impressive, "a mixture of fetishism and superstition"; and unlike their neighbors, the MPongwe and Akelis, they are anthropophagous, buying captives with elephant tusks to "approvisionner leurs festins."

While these observations contained some truth they reiterated the gathering stereotype. In part, Braouezec was taken in by Fang themselves. They described to him their "terrible enemies" in the mountains, a race of short, broad men, the Bakoui, who kept them constantly on their guard. They were referring here to the pygmies with whom Fang had long had a tie of clientship in which Fang were dominant. Thus a Fang sense of playful exaggeration and sardonic self-deprecation contributed to the accumulating notions about them.

Mequet concluded his visit, as did so many who followed him, by arguing that in view of the industry and bravery of the Fang, every effort should be made to establish direct contact with them. "Through them, free of intermediaries and foreign competition, we can attract to us all the ivory of the country."[20]

NOBLE CANNIBALS IN NARRATION

While men of administration and commerce were beginning to strengthen their contacts with this dynamic people of untapped potential, explorers with a more professional purpose made efforts to meet the Fang. One of these was the gorilla hunter, Paul DuChaillu, an American of French Creole birth. In him the Fang sense of exaggeration met with a popular nature-romanticism. DuChaillu's accounts of his two explorations in Gabon in the late 1850's and mid-1860's were widely published in Europe and America.[21] He was one of the nineteenth century writers who made Africa come alive in Western minds. The German geographical journal *Globus* quickly picked up his stories in the early 1860's, but they were soon obliged to defend him against attack. He is not a liar like the Frenchman, Douville, we are told. His accounts are simply a little decorated in spots.[22]

DuChaillu visited the Fang in the Cristal Mountains behind the Muni Estuary in late August and early September of 1856, encountering suspicion among intervening tribes that he would establish direct trading relationships with interior peoples.[23] Though he was energetically forewarned that he would be "murdered by the cannibals and eaten," his encounter with Fang was carried off calmly from his side. For the first two Fang he met, on the other hand, it was a moment of "perfect silence and terror." They took him for a "spirit who had just come down out of the sky."[24] They soon became accustomed to him, however, and he was able to remark their intelligent look, though he was troubled by a tendency toward sagittal peaks in their head form which, despite their obvious ingenuity, seemed to indicate a low scale of intelligence. The abundance of children, he concluded, rested on premarital chastity.

In fact, much of what DuChaillu says could be an elaboration of what was said in the 1840's by the other Americans. Like them he is impressed with the craftsmanship displayed in Fang weapons. "They turn out a very superior article of iron and steel much better than that brought to them from Europe."[25] But DuChaillu's best narrative powers are aroused by cannibalism. He had heard about it but disbelieved it until he saw a woman lugging along the thigh of a human body as any housewife returning from the butcher with a steak. He compiles gluttonous event upon event—the consuming even of those dead of disease, the tales of necrophagy told on the coast, the piles of human bones behind the houses. Still, he does not allow us to generalize from these "horrid customs." Though the Fang seem and are "regular ghouls, they are yet the finest, bravest-looking set of negroes I have seen in the interior."[26] DuChaillu's ambivalent account established the Fang as "the noble cannibals of the equator," a view contained in the previous reports but never as dramatically stated. Despite the skepticism provoked by his adventures, DuChaillu's "genie" can be traced through succeeding accounts, just as he picked up and accentuated earlier reports.

In view of this lingering influence, Tessmann, the first anthropologist with long experience with the Fang, felt obliged to assess DuChaillu's contribution from a scientific point of view. He criticized the theatrical descriptions of hunting scenes, the tendency to report as Fang customs some that in actuality were a mixture from many different equatorial tribes.[27] One might question whether DuChaillu actually reached the Fang in the Cristal Mountains. He reports the plateau to be 5,000 feet,[28] about twice as high as it is. He confuses and reverses the directions of the various rivers confluent to the Muni,[29] mistakes marriage customs and the emphasis upon chastity, and greatly exaggerates the ritual observances and size of cult objects of the ancestral cult.[30] DuChaillu's trip closely approximates that of the Reverend Mackey.[31] Indeed he left for the interior from Corisco Island, the Presbyterian mission base. There he would have had an opportunity to consult with Mackey or with other missionaries familiar with the Fang frontier. But he does not mention them.

What Tessmann most emphatically condemns is DuChaillu's report on Fang cannibal customs. Here he calls upon the scientific testimony of one of the greatest of nineteenth century explorers, the ubiquitous Richard Burton.[32] Burton, serving at the time as British Consul to Fernando Poo, took advantage of a trip to Libreville to journey up the Gabon Estuary expressly to spend a day among the Fang, "a people who during the last two seasons have excited so much curiosity among the Anthropologists." This day, the 13th of April 1862, was spent on the upper Bekoué in roughly the same area described by Braouezec.

Burton warns that these are first impressions but not in themselves to be despised, since "the longer we remain in a place the more our sensations are blunted (becoming) like a manuscript, from which by careful correction everything salient or interesting is eliminated."[33] Nevertheless, he comes far closer to a balanced account of Fang cannibalism than DuChaillu. "The cannibalism of the Fang is by no means remarkable limited as it is to the consumption of slain enemies." In contrast to DuChaillu's experience, no trace of the practice was seen in the village where he stayed.[34] The corpse is secretly eaten by the men only. The people shouted with laughter when a certain question was asked—the sick are not devoured, the dead are decently interred.[35]

While these observations accord with anthropological knowledge, Burton could not resist the gratuitous remark which countered his observations and highlighted the phenomenon. "The Rev. W. M. Walker[36] and other excellent authorities agree that it is a rare incident even in the wildest parts but it is rendered unusual only by want of opportunity." After his return to the coast and to the exaggerated atmosphere in respect to the interior created by both trader and tribesmen, he feels compelled to add a footnote to his report:

> P.S. You will bear in mind that the Fang whom I visited were a comparatively civilized race, who have probably learned to conceal the customs which they have found distasteful to the whiteman. In the remoter districts, they may still be determined cannibals.[37]

Burton was not the man to scotch the notion of the noble cannibal.[38] It was a mythology that intrigued him, too, though he could not be as enthusiastic in its service as DuChaillu.

By the time of Burton's brief visit, attitudes and beliefs about the Fang were well crystallized. Few visitors and explorers were able to escape them entirely, though each new visitor gave, according to his patience and capacity for observation, his particular emphasis. Thus Roullet in 1866 exploring the Como, the northern confluent that flows into the Gabon Estuary, noted the Fang "as a people mild and peaceful, fearful only when injured in their rights."[39] They possessed "le sentiment de la justice" and one could travel among them without fear. Roullet declared himself frankly surprised by DuChaillu's accounts of cannibal gluttony. "If they are given to anthropophagy it is only in such rare circumstances that many Pahouin have never eaten human flesh." Yet, like Burton, while Roullet's experience obliged him to dispel the mystery of the Fang he yet gave credence to other tales of the interior. His Fang informants mention two phenomena in particular, the Samapalas and the Bocquis. The second are a race of men with ancient European ancestry and the first, men of cloven hooves. The editors of the journal mildly reprove Roullet for the credulity of his report here[40] and remind him of the similar belief among American Indians upon seeing Spaniards on horseback. The explorer's fancies, if dispeled by the eye, were still supported by the imagination *and* by Fang willingness to feed the fantasies of their visitors.

From the 1870's on, the avenue of exploration shifted north and south—north to the German penetration of the Cameroons and south to the French exploration up the Ogooué.[41] Larger forces began to work in Equatorial Africa. Exotic preoccupations gave way to practical considerations.

The Fang as Objects of Exploitation

A decade of French exploration of the Ogooué culminated with de Brazza's thrust through to Stanley Pool in 1876-1878. But de Brazza was preceded in the lower portions of the river by Griffon du Bellay[42] whom de Brazza later took as his companion in exploration.

The immediate predecessor to de Brazza was the Marquis de Compiegne, who explored the Ogooué in the period 1872-1874, but not very thoroughly beyond Ndjole and the confluence of the Okano. He encountered both the Pahouin and their congeners, the Osyeba, but his impressions seem largely taken over from DuChaillu and du Bellay.[43] In Compiegne we find, quite noticeably, that sour note concerning the detrimental effects of Pahouin contact with the civilization of the coast. The Marquis photographed a Pahouin chief wearing a towering Kolbach, the hivelike parade helmet of the French Imperial Army. "But how preferable," he remarked, "to this ridiculous accoutrement is the simple war gear of the primitive Pahouin."[44] Compiegne quotes the hopes held by previous explorers of Pahouin energy and honesty: "Alas, one has to recognize today the Pahouins are far from having responded to this expectation—from civilization they have taken all the vices but none of the virtues. The closer they approach the coast, the more lazy, thieving and dishonest they become."[45]

From this point on one detects a sense of deception and distrust between European and Pahouin. One is reminded of the cautious hopes of du Bellay a decade before:

> Such is the Pahouin Race, the most interesting of all those who inhabit Gabon, and soon the most important for us, because they advance with long steps towards our factories. One sees them come with pleasure because if it is possible to make something of this country it will be with these people so well adapted. But one cannot ignore that they will be very captious subjects and difficult to manage. If they are habitually amenable and hospitable enough, they also have a stormy and versatile character served by an industry and energy that few blacks possess.[46]

In contrast to this optimistic estimate, the Marquis de Compiegne, disenchanted, even fearful of the future prospects of Fang hegemony, sought to strengthen the colonizing mission with the express purpose of preventing this numerous but degenerating race from taking over the French Congo.[47]

Savorgnan de Brazza is still remembered in Equatorial Africa for the honesty of his dealings with the Africans he encountered. In the 1950's there were many old men, Fang and Miene alike, who claimed to have been a cook or porter on his expeditions. In him seem to have reposed those desirable traits of honesty and power dispensed with wisdom and restraint which Africans thought they recognized and could admire in Europeans. In the late 1890's, after political forces in Republican France had removed de Brazza from any position of influence in colonial affairs, Africans still petitioned for his presence in disputes and negotiations. Missionaries deplored the passing of his wisdom and justice from the scene. In 1905 he came back, on government request to investigate abuses against the natives of the French Congo, but died in Dakar on his return.

De Brazza's encounter with the Pahouin (Mfan-Osyeba is the name he gives to the Ogooué Fang)[48] is an example of his finesse in personal relations. They intercepted him and his expedition above the mouth of the Okano on the Ogooué. But while they treated him hospitably, they did not wish to allow his further advance. Finally, after spending some time with them, amusing and awing them with magic tricks and legerdemain, de Brazza stood before the elders one evening with his two hands extended, a bullet in one and trade goods in the other. They were to make their choice. The trade goods were chosen and he was allowed to proceed. The respect he gained enabled him later to settle a dispute between the Okande and the Osyeba. He became known on the middle Ogooué as a "pacificateur."

De Brazza saw the Fang as a people potentially useful in schemes of French colonialization. Unfortunately, he remarks, they have generally been treated with rough methods and Draconian reprisals. Thus, "this intelligent active people who should help us develop Gabon act towards us with mistrust," and an effective rapprochement becomes more and more difficult with the passing years.[49] For Compiegne, the Fang were already corrupted by coastal influences. Their own lack of character led to demoralization. De Brazza looked for the cause in overbearing and uncomprehending oppression by administrators who, like the Marquis de Compiegne, had strong political misgivings about the advancing Fang. In either case, the older image had begun to decline in the face of economic and commercial considerations. the romantic paradox of nobility and cannibalism was difficult to sustain against the utilitarian interests of colonial development.

Cannibal Idealism Reasserted

In the last quarter of the nineteenth century, however increasingly they were mistrusted, Fang were still fortunate, insofar as their European and American reputation was concerned, to have struck responsive chords in the personalities of two of the liveliest commentators on things African that the end of the century produced—Trader Horn and Mary Kingsley.

Horn's occasional use of the native languages and his mention of the Presbyterian missions at Kangwe and Samkita establish his presence on the Ogooué in the 1870's. But just what the actual dimensions of his experiences were is difficult to determine. "The correctful thing in all literary books," he tells us, "is to remember that even the truth may need suppressing if it appears out of tangent with the common man's notion of reality."[50]

What can be deduced from a romantic narrative focused around a beautiful, white cult priestess (whom he doubtless adopted from Rider Haggard) are the facts that Horn was a trading agent for Hatton and Cookson on the Ogooué, that he probably established their farthest upriver trading post on the island, Isangue, across from present-day Ndjole, and that he was constantly involved in negotiation and battles with the Ogooué River Fang between Lambaréné and Ndjole for free passage and trading rights.[51] He appears to have provisioned de Brazza on his first passage through to Stanley Pool and to have gathered gorilla skeletons for European museums and for General Grant on his West African sojourn. The Fang appear throughout the narrative as cannibals. But they are also "the most moral race on earth . . . the women chaste and the men faithful . . . The cannibals know that clean morals make a strong fighting race."[52] Horn had great admiration for the Mpangwes and describes with appreciation their lusty style of palaver and battle. The cannibalism seems not to have bothered him at all. His code hinged on the survival of the fittest and he was not altogether sure whether Christianity—by that light—was, as he said, a better form of fetishism or not.

For all that it is the work of an elderly raconteur trying to suit a public taste, Horn's account has its uses. It helps size up the difficulties of the early traders who attempted to bypass the middlemen tribes. Though its coloration is patent, its presentation of the noble cannibal takes the most archetypic form, and reveals a set of attitudes.

Likewise, through Mary Kingsley, in whose cherished memory the Royal African Society was founded, a great deal that had been implicit in the previous encounters with the Fang was directly stated. Her lively accounts of intrepid explorations along the Ogooué in the 1890's in the service of ichthyology are full of observations on Fang.[53] And the observations are keen,[54] though they may be difficult to accept in the "opera bouffe" style in which she presents herself—laced up in Victorian dress while falling out of canoes and stumbling into pitfalls, descending on amazed villagers in drenched disarray and all the while steadily spiriting away another unknown variety of fish.

Mary Kingsley was powerfully intrigued by African character and what she regarded as its most significant manifestation, fetishism. She summed up her notions in something she called "The African Idea" whose study was, she tells us in the enthusiasm of describing it, her "chief motive for going to West Africa." "Stalking the wild West African idea is one of the most charming pursuits in the world."[55] In her two principal works[56] she devoted more attention to the discussion of fetishism and African spirituality than to any other subject, including politics and economics in which she was also strongly interested.[57] She took her research seriously enough to consult directly with the great English anthropologist, Sir Edward Tylor, about her facts and theories.[58] From him she obtained the culture concept, though she disputed his dream theory of religion.[59]

For the Fang she developed a special affection. Her farewell is particularly touching. "I parted company with the terrible Mpangwe whom I hope to meet with again for with all their many faults and failings they are real men."[60] Her positive impression is the more intriguing because before she meets them and even when she is among them she frequently comments on their villainous looks, their excitability, their treacherous reputation. Kingsley invites us to attend with anxiety the outcome of her sojourn with these "wild wicked looking savages." She refers to their cannibalism. She starts out by spoofing some of the reports she has heard of it,[61] but ends up taking it seriously as a necessary element of Fang character. She is unable to confirm any of the things she has heard about this practice—in fact does not try, refusing to make, in contrast to most of her reports of Fang custom, a sober ethnographical evaluation of the evidence.

> [The Fang] has no slaves, no prisoners of war, no cemeteries so you must draw your own conclusions. No, my friend, I will not tell you any cannibal stories. I have heard how good M. du Chaillu fared after telling you some beauties and now you must come away from the Fang village and down the Rambwé River.[62]

To some extent, of course, Mary Kingsley was, like Horn, "correctfully" suppressing the truth for the sake of her narrative. She wants to keep us in suspense about the Fang. Are they, as she was told, terrible and treacherous and depraved or, as she began to find out, are they "a fine sporting tribe . . . distinctive, powerful and intelligent, an indefatigable race and plucky" who can "teach the coastal tribes activity and courtesy."[63] "A certain sort of friendship arose between the Fang and me," she says.[64] But what was its basis?

What Mary Kingsley liked in Africans and what she found in the Fang was the personification of "The African Idea." We have to be careful lest we take her wit and hyperbole too seriously. But she took the African idea seriously enough. This was partly for purely historical reasons. "It was always highly interesting to observe the germ of any of our own institutions existing in the culture of a lower race."[65] Though she talked frequently of African inferiority, it is also clear that she found "The African Idea" strongly relevant and not outmoded and antiquarian. "Although a Darwinian to the core, I doubt if evolution in a neat and tidy perpendicular line with fetish at the bottom and Christianity at the top represents the true state of things."[66] The fascination exerted by fetishism had its dangers. "I must warn you that your own mind requires protection when you send it stalking the savage idea through the tangled forests, the dark caves, the swamps and the fogs of the Ethiopian intellect . . . the fascination of the African point of view is as sure to linger in your mind as the malaria in your body. Never then will you be able to attain to the gay happy cock-sureness regarding the Deity and the Universe of the suburban agnostics."[67]

What she discovered about fetishism is that though it was everywhere defined by Europeans as the worship of a material object, "it is not, on the contrary, Africans who worship material objects but ourselves. The African's mind works along the line that things happen because of the action of spirit upon spirit: it is an effort for him to think in terms of matter. We think along the line that things happen from the action of matter upon matter."[68] In returning to England her materialism is excited by a steam locomotive as a "magnificent bit of machinery," but her study of fetishism has revealed to her other realms of meaning—other forms of excitement where reality is spiritual, and in that lies the danger she mentions. For the European it is "this steady sticking to the material side of things" that has given him his domination over matter and over others. "The African Idea" is a threat to all that. Cannibalism, she implies, is the acid test of the materialist; it tests our perception of reality, and, approached unflinchingly, can give us a new vision. Cannibalism on the spiritual level is an entirely different thing from cannibalism approached from a materialist perspective.

All along Mary Kingsley had sought to explain the value in various customs that were seen by Europeans as degraded and childlike: polygamy, the bride-price, the palaver. But in understanding cannibalism we have the noble qualities that emanate from the African idea fully perceived. These qualities cluster around a sense of life and justice unclouded by the hypocrisy of material commitment—where men can treat with men, spiritually, free of the pressures of vested interests.

Flint has pointed out that Mary Kingsley was articulating notions out of which could spring both the colonial doctrine of "indirect rule" and assertions of negritude and African personality.[69] There can be no doubt that she was one of the early ones to put these ideas into words, casting them up in the face of what she called the "superior culture instincts" of her compatriots. She was also working out the implication of the old image of the "noble cannibal."

There is a lot in Mary Kingsley's work which is outmoded. Her feeling that African languages "are not elaborate enough to enable a native to state his exact thought,"[70] is an example. She is not quite sure what to make of African mental processes. At one point she speaks of the "African mind muddle"[71] and of African dependence upon gesture rather than speech, but elsewhere she announces that "the African's mind does not run on identical lines with the European. Negroes follow their ideas much more carefully than white men . . . who seem to the African to make great jumps in their thought course.''[72] It cannot be said, despite her wealth of commentary, that she ever satisfactorily resolved the problem of the ''noble cannibal.'' But she explored deeper into the tension we feel in that image.

THE FANG FALL BETWEEN MERCHANT MATERIALISM AND THE CIVILIZING MISSION

For those not directly involved with the colonial enterprise and the materialism which nourished it, the Fang continued as noble cannibals even into the twentieth century. Their contradictory qualities embraced mysterious elements of origin and character. Perhaps the high point of this lingering preoccupation is a book dating from 1905,[73] in which, because of their common qualities of nobility and barbarity, the Fang are linked in kinship with Teutonic folk. The hints at their Caucasian antecedents which we have seen in earlier accounts are finally laid to their proper source. They are discovered as a lost German tribe.

But for the French carrying forth the ''civilizing mission'' along the equator the Fang had long since ceased to be exotic subjects of contemplation. The notes of warning concerning them sounded by Compiegne in the early 1870's were accompanied by the beginning of a policy of reprisals against their depredations, a policy which de Brazza deplored. Merchants complained ever more frequently of Fang pillaging of trade goods in transit.[74] By no means did the administrators, however, simply reflect the merchants' view of equatorial problems. They recognized the degree to which instability, on the upper Ogooué, for example, had been provoked by the merchants themselves, first by fanning the appetite for goods and second by attempting to bypass established trading treaties. The concern for native interests reached such a point that the Undersecretary of State in the Ministry for Marine and Colonial Affairs had, in fact, to remind the Lieutenant Governor of Gabon and his administrators of their primary responsibilities to the merchants.[75] An outbreak between the Okande and the Pahouin in the summer of 1894 seemed well on the road to solution until a trader representing the house of Daumas among the Okande took their side and killed two Pahouins, an act which embroiled the administration for more than a year and led inevitably to the burning of villages and other official reprisals.[76]

A classic example of the struggle between the commercial interests and administrative concern for social and political stability arose around the grounding of the trading steamer, *Eclaireur*, on an Ogooué sand bank above Lambaréné in the dry season of 1897. The captain, to lighten the load, placed his entire cargo of rubber on the sand spit, from where it was swept away by a sudden rise in the water level. Attempts to reclaim these balls of rubber in Pahouin villages downstream bore little fruit, and the commercial company involved, Chargeurs Reunis, turned to the administration claiming pillage and theft. With some reluctance an administrative detachment with forty militia accompanied by several merchants set out to enforce the ordinances of 1669 and 1681 concerning flotsam and jetsam. The most defiant village, 450 meters in length, was entirely burned down, throwing some six hundred inhabitants into the inhospitable forest. In the engagement and exchange of fire one merchant and one administrator were wounded. Rifles, powder, and other goods were recovered, but very little rubber.[77] Since the loss approached the sum of 30,000 francs the director of Chargeurs Reunis in Paris, in a subsequent letter to the Minister of Foreign Affairs, reminded him of the imperious necessity "of preventing such acts of pillage and of effectively chastising the native populations thus assuring the security of navigation and trade along the only commercial highway of the colony."[78]

To this pressure for further reprisals the administration in Libreville responded that the original loss was due entirely to the imprudence of the captain of the *Eclaireur* who then embroiled the administration in his incompetence. Finally, A. Dolisie, Commissaire General of the Government in Libreville, responded with some acerbity to the Agent General's request for arms and further reprisals:

> Even a European trader of long experience on the Ogoowé refused to give up his rubber except against remuneration. I have very little difficulty in imagining that the Pahouins ignore the ordinances of 1681 in respect to floated cargoes and I conceive that rifle fire constitutes a rather inept means of explaining it to them . . . now we have men dead and villages burnt and much greater difficulty in obtaining the restitution of the rubber.[79]

The merchants would be much better served, Dolisie argued, to proceed with greater subtlety and to go unarmed. "For myself," he concluded, "I await a more exact explanation to appreciate the reasons which led us immediately to the use of arms."

To this occasional administrative resistance to the "main forte" in the service of commerce was added a much more persistent missionary protest. In 1899-1900 the Fang clans above Ndjole, whose own trade routes had been opened by administrative decree, closed them again and called for a palaver to settle the trade right involved. Several traders sought to force these routes. Their goods were stolen, themselves threatened, and several porters wounded. The Ndjole authorities were new and apparently filled with coastal tales of the terrible Pango. Declaring a state of insurrection, they sent in Senegalese militia and burnt out the recalcitrant villages. A veteran missionary, Ellenberger of the Paris Mission Society, deplored these reprisals, for they de-

stroyed his attempts to reach an accommodation between the dissident clans
and the administration.

> Why has the attitude of peace been renounced. If there is a country where
> patience accomplishes infinitely more than violence, it is assuredly this
> one. The Pahouin is an orator and the true victory to be gained is to be
> more eloquent than he. One "palavers" one or two weeks or more but
> once understanding is reached everything returns peacefully to order.
> But spilled blood is never pardoned. They will exile themselves, the
> unfortunates, deep in the bush, but the desire for vengeance will persist.[80]

Despite a series of these complaints dating back to the 1880's, the mercantile
argument seems to have been the persuasive one, and severe reprisals continued in the hope that the Fang would sensibly conceive of their colonial
responsibilities and the limits of their power. In 1899 the Pahouin of Fernan
Vez refused to come into the post and discuss trading relations with the
merchants and administration. Because of this insolence and to set an example,
five of their villages were destroyed.[81] This "punition gratuite" was frequent
enough to make entirely understandable the widespread call by which the
arrival of a European was announced on the talking drum of Fang villages—
Môt a wí môt ka etôm (man who kills man without a dispute).

A FINAL ACCOMMODATION

Fang were not, however, forest innocents under colonial onslaught. They
were quick enough to appropriate or pillage goods if the situation seemed
favorable. A favorite riddle of theirs runs: "Who is the elephant from which
everyone has the right to take his cut of meat . . . the white man."[82] They
were not disposed to reach an accommodation with the French, whom they
saw as invaders. They perceived that other powers had interests in Africa,
and those Fang who reached the coast early enough tried to achieve some
sovereignty by playing off one power, in most cases the American missionaries, against the French. In 1884 Chief Eyano of the village of Bilogwe north
of Libreville condescends to address a letter in English to the French commandant:

> Do not come or send anyone here to talk about giving our land to your
> government as long as the world stands our land is from Bote Point to
> Malandi . . . one of our number is not a heathen to give away his land,
> etc. for rum. That is Rev. Mr. Hill. Goodbye.[83]

This intransigence, the more offensive for being expressed in English, animated the French against American missionaries, who became "points de
repère" in Pahouin resistance to French hegemony. The Americans were soon

forced out of the Gabon. The method—cultural, not political—was to require mission instruction in French.[84] The Fang continued, however, to try to manipulate the colonizing powers, setting Germans against French, Spanish against French, and vice versa.[85]

For those who did not live on frontiers which they could cross at will, however, resistance was at best sporadic. The political life of Fang was unstructured and decentralized. There was little base upon which to organize concerted resistance to colonial encroachment. Their conquests of other African peoples were the consequence of a tumultuous process of village displacement, a kind of tumbling of one village over another which forced out those in its path not by organization, but by sheer weight of numbers and persistent small-scale attacks and harassment. Fang resistance to the colonial presence, therefore, was customarily exhausted in ephemeral revolts accompanied by the killing of a militiaman or two, perhaps a trader or an administrator. Interclan rivalries were so intense that anti-European enmity could not organize itself to any enduring purpose.

The one important exception to this was a lengthy campaign waged above Ndjole against administrative and mercantile appropriation of Fang trade routes. The leader of this campaign, a village chief named Emane Tole, had great influence with other villages and other clans and was able to organize an effective intermittent blockade for a number of years from 1895 onward. Largeau, author of the *Encyclopédie Pahouin* and one of the early authorities on the Fang, described Emane Tole as a savage of "extreme violence," very difficult to surprise and "impossible really to punish with the resources we have at our disposition."[86]

At the turn of the century, to judge by administrative documents, Pahouin discontent with the colonial condition reached its apex. Revolts flared north of Libreville at Lambaréné, around Sindara, on the Ngounie, on the upper Como, and above Ndjole. But the most significant event amidst this agitation, as noted by the Commissaire General Albert Grodet, was the fact that Emane Tole, betrayed by his own people, was delivered up to the administration in 1902. Grodet took this to mean that even the most resistant Fang were finally deciding, in the face of a determined French administration, to live in "bonne intelligence" with their "commandants."[87] He was right. Fang appear to have come to terms with their colonizers. Only three revolts of any importance occurred after 1905, the effective date of Fang pacification. The noble cannibal had become a colonial subject.

If this accommodation with the colonial world on the part of the Fang was reflected in the betrayal of Emane Tole, then on the French side an increasingly sour and dyspeptic view of the once romanticized Pahouin is evidenced in the reports of administrators who were now journeying extensively among them. J. B. Roche, participating in a Franco-Spanish expedition delimiting the Rio Muni frontier in 1901, found little to attract him among these impoverished, bellicose and thieving people. Their language was hard and aggressive, their superstitions of the most degrading and barbarous character, their villages and houses dirty, their women unattractive. He repeated the old folklore of their daily cannibal diet, and complimented their sense of justice which, however, he found helpless to manifest itself effectively.[88]

Roche did not, however, underestimate the intelligence and initiative of his hosts. ''I am persuaded,'' he warned the authorities, ''that given the bellicose and thieving instincts of the Fang, and their poverty, on the day when one of the intelligent ones raises the standard of revolt against us, he will be followed by thousands of volunteers who, above all, if they are pushed on by the fanaticism of a new religion, will create for us the greatest difficulty.''[89] The assessment of Fang potentialities for belligerence made by Grodet after the surrender of Emane Tole was, however, more perceptive. Roche was writing at the height of the last sporadic struggle for autonomy by various scattered villages. Nothing more concerted was ever to develop, no major military leader and organizer was to come forward. But the ensuing accommodation with colonial control after the turn of the century did not extend to the religious realm. Here indeed a new religion, as forecast by Roche, was born. For it is from about this time that there is evidence of Bwiti among the southern Fang.[90] It was in large part a response to their increasing sense of degradation—a degradation reflected, perhaps, in the historical accounts we have examined by that shift from a noble cannibalism to a degenerate and unredeemed anthropophagy. And, in a way, Bwiti was to be a reaffirmation of ''The African Idea.''

CONCLUSION: THE SPECTACLE OF CREATIVE FORCE

In examining the history of these contacts one sees that the image of the ''noble savage'' was more than the literary convention it is often made out to be.[91] It appeared in the perceptions of the most objective of explorers. It was always a paradoxical image, strongly infused with the doubts of the romantic movement as to the value of civilization. At the same time this image provided support for equally prevalent European feelings of superiority, not to mention the libidinal satisfactions to be found in contemplating exotic practices prohibited at home.

But the perceptions examined here were also shaped by the political and economic environment in which they were expressed. We see a transition in the nineteenth century from what Curtin has called, in respect to the British, an ''era of Humanitarianism'' ending in 1850, to an ''era of Imperialism'' commencing in 1880.[92] The thirty years from 1850 to 1880 constitute a transitional period. It would be too much to call the early European views of the Fang strictly humanitarian, for they all had the abivalence characteristic of the noble savage stereotype. What can be said is that Fang in the early period were at least scrutinized for their customs with a curiosity largely free from political and material considerations, though not from some enduring ethnocentric images.

The years 1860-1865 in Gabon provide a better terminating date for these attitudes than 1850: Schnapper has pointed out that up to this period the idea of "protection" was dominant in French colonial thinking, largely preoccupied, as it was, by rivalry with the English and by the suppression of slavery.[93] Politically it was hoped that the natives, if left to themselves, would—under French protection—cause commerce to flourish around fortified trading posts such as that established at the Gabon Estuary in Libreville. In fact the French looked forward expressly to the coming of such supposedly energetic people as the Fang whose activity and intelligence would greatly expand the production of colonial crops on the coast[94] . . . a production faltering in the hands of the lassitudinous coastal peoples. But as slavery was abolished and the English quarrel repaired, this agenda was brought to face the economic problem: under protection alone there was no profit in commerce. It became clear that the Africans vegetated under such conditions or imposed such heavy tariffs on trade with the interior as to create impossible burdens on merchant and interior tribesmen alike. In response to a commercial malaise a policy of forcible intervention and control of African affairs developed, leading eventually to full-scale imperialism and direct colonial occupation and rule. It became increasingly difficult to contemplate any African culture with benevolent disinterest.

The shift from the lofty paternalism of protection to outright occupation and direct rule is reflected in the relations with the Fang. And in fact one finds "hardheaded" views of the Fang beginning to appear in the mid-1860's. Of course, the noble cannibal notion had powers of resistance. Dating back in France at least to Montaigne, it had undergone previous transformations. It was reinvigorated in the mid-eighteenth century by the atmosphere of imperial splendor—the calculated appeal to vainglorious sentiment perpetrated by the Third Empire.[95] Even in the period of concentrated commercial imperialism from 1880 on, such idiosyncratic explorers as Mary Kingsley revived these notions as a necessary intellectual framework for their experiences. But the Third Republic was the vehicle of more practical overseas ambitions and nationalist emotions that made the noble cannibal an increasingly less relevant mythology.

For commercial reasons alone the simple and uncivilized lot of the savage could no longer be praised. In such a state he was hardly a good producer or consumer. It was his abject poverty and unenlightened condition that, as in the reports of Roche, had to be emphasized. The new doctrine and ethical imperatives of the "civilizing mission"—*la mission civilisatrice*—replaced the noble savage by economic necessity.

The discrepancy between the theory of the civilizing mission and the facts of the colonial enterprise, with the inevitable hypocrisies which resulted, has been well documented not only by colonial historians but by practically all persons of sensibility who went out to Africa in any way compelled by its ethic.[96] That this discrepancy between doctrine and deed acted among the Africans to erode European moral authority has been shown clearly by Albert Schweitzer in respect to the Fang and related peoples.[97] A reverse image of this hypocrisy, moreover, is commonly seen in many African religious movements (Bwiti among Fang) in which an almost biblical Puritanism appears and sets rigid requirements for cult followers while implicitly criticizing the whites by their own standards.[98]

The civilizing mission was proclaimed in many modes and with varying intensity throughout the later colonial period. Insofar as the doctrine relates to our work in central and northern Gabon the following direct statement of its claims is relevant. It appears in a document concerning native relations and local authority promulgated in 1909 and circulated to the commandants among the Fang in 1912.

> It is important in every respect that the natives have before them the spectacle of our creative force and our organizational genius. Our occupation of the country aims to procure the advantages of stability, security, industry and economy for the population . . . to free them from internecine struggles and the avid and cruel tyranny of their chiefs and fetishists guaranteeing justice and order. . . . this native policy, honest, prudent, and paternal, does not preclude a measure of discipline. The native will not be docile and confident unless he is taken well in hand from the beginning. Having the sentiment of his weakness he will abandon himself without reserve to our tutelage.[99]

Despite the development of the doctrine of the "mission civilisatrice," however, the paradoxical idea of nobility joined with cannibalism seems to have been too much a part of the West's own ambivalence about its material accomplishments to have disappeared entirely. Though it flourished most unambiguously in the early period, it reappears from time to time until the mid-twentieth century. In Gabon, French anticlericalism often expressed itself in this idiom. The Fang, it continued to be said, was in his pristine condition a man of admirable moral quality who, however, was brought low by the conversion forced upon him by the missionaries—conversion to principles that were neither fully understood nor manifestly superior to those he had always practiced. The missionaries for their part decried the low morals of the merchants and traders who, as vehicles of the worst in western materialism, corrupted a native population of traditional integrity and spontaneous spirituality. It was not unusual for administrators to prefer the savage to both merchants and missionaries.

Thus the "noble savage" periodically reappears in Gabon and in relation

to Fang—usually at times of disgruntlement among the various echelons of
the colonial enterprise. But its great influence upon the perceptions of Europeans had fully passed by the beginning of the twentieth century. By that
same period, correspondingly, Fang had relinquished their claims of equatorial
dominance. They began in various ways and with periodic relapses to adjust
themselves to the inexorable conditions of colonial life—to a paternal tutelage
laden with paradoxical notions and moral ambiguities often accompanied by
arbitrary and unpredictable actions. The shifting images held of Fang for more
than a century, in short, were bound to be reflected in Fang themselves and
to be, inevitably, a part of any negotiation with them—be it simply a matter,
as it was for me, of finding a house. But these incidents of the entree into
Fang culture are of only passing interest. For, once lodged, I was to discover
among Fang themselves a "spectacle of creative force," the Bwiti religion—
an "African Idea," a set of images of surpassing interest and power, a
sequence of enacted narratives as compelling to Fang participants as anything
DuChaillu, or Burton, or Trader Horn, or Mary Kingsley had crafted for a
European audience avid for exploration of the unknown.

⁓2⁓

Compositions of the Past

Nzé e mana minlang mi ligé
(Hunger ends, legends remain.)

ZE AZI RECALLS AZAPMBOGA

IN MY FIRST MONTHS in Assok Ening, I mapped the village and noted down many genealogies and the historical accounts which accompanied them. Some inhabitants felt unable to give a satisfactory answer to my questions and suggested that I should go to Koomassi and talk with Ze Azi, a nonagenarian and the oldest man in the district. Several of his daughters, all now dead, had married into Assok Ening years previously and Ze Azi was well known. He was the mother's brother to some already old men. He was also in the unusual position of having outlived any claims they could make against him upon the death of these women. As one "beyond" the brideprice, he was also beyond most of the internecine strife and covetousness of Fang life. And since he had also lived to such a great age, it was clear that he was a good man with a benign witchcraft capacity. If he had been a sorcerer, he would have died long before. Sorcerers might obtain great wealth and power, but they did not live long. Their witchcraft being was quickly wasted by the injuries it received in its assaults on others.

So I went to see Ze Azi at Koomassi, the village at the bottom of one of those domelike monadnocks that occasionally thrust up 500 to 1,000 feet above the northern equatorial forests. Ze was an old man indeed. His body seemed past appetite, past hunger. He seemed ancient as he sat propped up in one dark corner of the council house, his polished walking stick in one hand, his fly whisk in the other. He wore only the loin cloth of former days. Between the folds of his upper body, now collapsing upon its frame, could yet be seen the purple geometric patterns of the tattoo work so often found in older Fang. His eyes, one of which was glazed over with a cataract, were both deeply buried in his head. With great effort he arranged himself so we could speak into his good ear.

I wanted to talk genealogical history but Ze's mind for many years now had been ranging beyond family matters, and in our conversation it kept drifting away to the legendary past. The history he would tell us in his very high and dry voice was of the *ôban* (the raid against Fang and the southern

Ntumu that took place in the last decade of the nineteenth century). This he had seen with his own eyes. "Some of us fled and others of us took refuge in a cave in the mountain here. They were a strong and cruel people who came down from the north and ravaged our villages. Those who tried to fight them were slaughtered. They came from beyond *azapmboga* where our fathers many generations ago passed through with the help of Pygmies. The Pygmies helped us to live in the forest but this forest life has weakened us and we could not fight against those who came down from beyond azapmboga." The old man then bestirred himself from these disgruntled observations on Fang impotence to speculate about life on the savanna and early life in the forest before brotherly strife had driven Fang apart.

Ze Azi also wanted me to talk about the country from which I came. He had never been to the ocean although he had long wished to see it. In the early days it had been thought, he said, that the European came out of it and smelled of it. He said that with a twinkle in his one eye. When I said that I had come down by air and not by sea he remarked, "Yes, the Europeans have powers that only our ancestors possessed." This set him off again to reciting some of the miraculous accomplishments of the famous heroes of the troubadour legends . . . the men of Engong. They had once used the top of this very rocky hill as an arena for their battles, leaping up and over it in several bounds.

This interview with Ze Azi stands out in my mind—he died not so long after—because in this old man, whose mind drifted back and forth between fact and fiction, we see the state of the old Fang culture, collapsing about its framework yet still possessing many fictions by which it was able to sustain itself in the face of the facts of the colonial world. In this chapter, after beginning with some facts of tribal identity, we want to examine some of these fictions: first, the notion, largely lost in the twentieth century as it was for Ze Azi, that Fang were conquerors and, lying behind this notion, some of the images of their rather disjointed myths and legends of origin and migration. We then examine two more organized bodies of animating lore: the troubadour legends of the great race of Engong and a literary version of Fang origins and migrations, *The Journey of the Children of Afri Kara*. This latter was a melding, like Ze Azi's mind, of fact and fiction. Finally, since we began in the first chapter by examining European views of Fang, we end by examining Fang views of their relations with the European. These were expressed in the Whiteman-Blackman legends. This quite diverse lore could be put to quite diverse uses. And Fang had quite diverse uses for it. In part, like the narrators of the colonial adventure, Fang folk narrators responded, in their narrative re-compositions of perduring Fang themes, motifs, and sign images, to time and circumstance. The Fang troubadour epic was of a certain time and place as was *The Journey of the Children of Afri Kara*.

"Conquérants en Disponibilité"

Fang, as they have called themselves, were the southern and eastern subgroup of the Pahouin, a category which came to include the Bulu, the Ewondo, the Eton, and the Beti of the Cameroons. In the early days the term Pahouin referred only to Fang themselves.[1] In reality, their rapid migration, which raised the preoccupations discussed in Chapter 1 was only part of a very large movement of populations toward the ocean. This movement followed a northeast to southwest axis on as much as a five-hundred mile front across southern Cameroons, Rio Muni, Gabon, and the very northeastern portion of Congo-Brazzaville. Until well into this century peoples were in displacement along this entire axis for about a thousand miles, tracing northeast from the mouth of the Ogooué.

The matrix of this massive movement lay in the plateau and highlands of northwestern Cameroons and northeastern Nigeria. There have been numerous attempts at mapping the routes of the various subgroups.[2] Sudanic events such as the Fulani expansion have been credited with providing the centrifugal shocks and pressures in the matrix zone which were felt as far south as the Gabon Estuary and along the Ogooué.[3] It might well be argued that Fang were only the first line of a phalanx dislodged by Sudanic imperialism into Equatorial Africa. But thus to incorporate them into this larger movement is to ignore that it was Fang who were its cutting edge, the terror of autochthonous peoples. Their success in the nineteenth century in gradually taking over the land and trade routes they wanted, coupled with the laudatory opinions of Europeans which we have examined, must have provided an exhilarating sense of self-respect for Fang themselves.

The withdrawal of this respect, brought about as the colonial vice inexorably closed about them, was a central animus in their twentieth century state of mind. Balandier has provided us with a memorable phrase "conquérants en disponibilité,"[4] to describe that state. But the phrase is not altogether exact. Fang preserved, it is true, a lively sense of superiority to the peoples upon whom they intruded. They felt themselves more active and able than those peoples, but military pride, as the term "conquerants" suggests, was only a part of this ethnocentrism. In regard to peoples to the north, Fang felt inferior, as Ze Azi confessed.

Fang were aggressive, but not truly warlike. Their warfare was sporadic and rarely well organized in any tactical sense. When men like Emane Tole occasionally appeared, they yet had great difficulty in gaining the allegiance of other clans. Often they were undone by the disaffected within their own lineages. Fang did not take much pride in themselves as warriors, and one of the few blessings of colonial life they could agree about was that it put an end to that strife, so often internecine and fraternal. It is true that there was some nostalgia. Old men in the council houses often recalled the excitement of the old days when the possibility of a skirmish was ever-present and men had at once to protect their womenfolk and be on guard lest they be betrayed by them.

The excitement remembered was not of great battles planned. It was of a state of constant uncertainty and turmoil. The autochthonous peoples of Gabon were overwhelmed not in military campaigns but by sheer numbers and the gradual sapping of their endurance through incessant harassment: ambushes, trade blockades and extortion, night assaults and bluffs, and vocal skirmishes. It was a swarming process, as Fang villages moved forward in leapfrog fashion, "saut-de-mouton," as the French call it. And it was abetted by their ferocious reputation. It is likely that the autochthonous peoples were also victims of their own propaganda, the tales they used to bear against the "terrible Pango" in order to preserve their middleman status with the European traders.

Balandier's phrase is more vigorous than accurate in another sense. We find, as often expressed in Fang legends, the view that their migration was more a flight from some greater power—variously symbolized—than a conquest undertaken toward some objective. This element in Fang folklore relates to a particular arrangement of "reference groups" running along that northeast-southwest axis of migration which they followed. Peoples to the north tended to deprecate those to the south and receive respect in their turn. For example, in the south across the Ogooué and on the coast Fang were neighbors to peoples grouped by them under the rubric *bílôbôlôbô*, onomatopoeia for the sounds made by a person speaking gibberish. This term, which was applied to all of the five principal language groups of mid- and southern Gabon—the Miene cluster of coastal languages, and the Kele-Tsogo, Shira-Punu, and Njabi groups—was used pejoratively even though Fang contact with these people had varied in intensity and duration and even though the Miene and the Tsogo peoples favorably impressed Fang and had considerable influence upon them.

On the other hand, to the north, Fang found their congeners—the Bulu, the Ewondo, and the Beti—whom they conceived to have sprung from the same loins as themselves, and whom, during much of the colonial period, they regarded as more progressive, more powerful, and more successfully adapted to the modern world. This particular arrangement of "reference groups" running from north to south is partially due to the advanced status the northern Pahouin, of the Cameroon, were felt to have achieved first under the Germans, and then as a mandated state preparing for independence, rather than as a territory integral to the French union.[5] It also must be traced to the memory, as in Ze Azi, of a concerted series of "raids" (oban) carried out by the northern against the southern Pahouin in the 1880's and early 1890's.

It was probably the Bane of the Cameroons who initiated these raids south—hence the name. But their action was part of a general predatory unrest characteristic of the period in West Africa. The Bulu are remembered for leading the assaults in northern Gabon. The raids did not proceed much further south than the Woleu. But the memory of them is widespread.[6]

This admiration for more northern Pahouin was also part of a set of related attitudes. These included feelings about the migratory flight from greater powers to the north as well as feelings by the more northern Pahouin, and particularly the Ntumu, that the southern Pahouin—Fang primarily—were descendants of dissident younger brothers who broke away in disgruntlement from their more northern family villages. While this set of attitudes was strong during the period of field work, it becomes problematic in folklore where Fang are regarded as the oldest, or the eldest brother, of the various divisions of the Pahouin. Just as Fang attitudes toward themselves as conquerors were complicated by a view of themselves as fleeing from conquest, so the north-south axis of deference and esteem was complicated by legendary evidence that Fang were the eldest and, therefore, by custom entitled to the greatest respect. In point of fact, the past as it was handed down in Fang oral tradition did not contain a simple lesson. It was susceptible to several interpretations. The past taught various lessons to Fang and each generation had to find a consistency—an interpretation of its own. Often no consistency was achieved. Old Ze Azi shifted back and forth between Fang subordination and a legendary and mythological mightiness. He no longer strove for a central view but shifted from view to view according to his mood.

ORIGIN AND MIGRATION: HOSTAGE TO MONSTERS

With Ze Azi I wanted to talk ''genealogical history'' (*minkandé meyong*) but he was only interested in giving me *nlang*. Nlang is the general term used by Fang in respect to narration and means story, account, ''histoire.'' To recount ''histoire'' (*lé minlang*) may mean an attempt to give a true rendering of facts, but usually it was an attempt to amuse, to instruct, or to be contentious—to animate, in short. While nlang could also be told about one's own clan—*nlang ayong* or *minlang mam ya okua* (history of former times)—the term for accurate accounting of such events seen with someone's eyes was *nkandé*. A recital or an explanation or an exposé of events in which the clan had been involved (such historical events as those in which I was interested) would be minkande meyong.

Ze Azi, more interested in nlang than in nkande, was more interested in accounts of the past which were just-so and not virtual. Fang themselves would frequently enough debate whether accounts of origin and migration were nkande or *nlang*. But Ze Azi in his old age had moved away from a concern with legendary representations of the past as, inevitably, men in reciting genealogical history were obliged to do. As they moved further back in the genealogy, they were obliged to move from fact to fiction.

The nkande of Fang origin, Ze Azi's and those which appear in the literature, are quite diverse, but practically all contain three important elements: (1) life in a "savanna country to the northeast" (*mfa'a ôkwi* or *ôswi ôkwi*) from which Fang were chased, (2) crossing of a great river by the supernatural aid of a chthonic being, crocodile, snake, or hippopotamus, and (3) the frustration of further progress into the equatorial rain forest by the giant azap tree.

The actual creation of man himself has never been a focus of these myths. They often began with the descent of a "spider" (*abô*) from the sky into the waters below. Out of her egg-sac, in the more traditional versions, she poured termites that began to make the earth. But man was largely neglected. Largeau's brief myth of the creation moment, collected at the turn of the century, shows this. For the creation of man turned out to be, in reality, the creation of the efficient god of this world. "In the creation he created man. This creation nobody can know of it. Such a thing we call *é zen-zam* (a mystery). It's the kind of thing in which 'God' (*Mebege*)—without man, without woman, without child, without mother, without father—is such that we can understand nothing. Mebege alone can understand such a thing. The question is in what manner did he create man. Mebege created man with clay. He made him first in the form of a 'lizard' (*a nga sum nye ane nsvie*), and then he placed this lizard in a pool of water. For five days and then for seven more days and on the eighth he went to look at him and said, 'Come out.' He came out and he was man. Then he knelt and said, 'Thank you.' Mebege asked him, 'Whence do you come?' He replied, 'I know not. I was in the water. Suddenly I stand here.' Mebege said, 'Go.' Mebege said, 'It is I that created you.' Then they went to the village of Mebege and the son asked, 'Father, what is my name? What is yours? They shall call you, Mebege who created all things; myself they shall call me Nzame ye Mebege.' In the creation Mebege created man in this way!"[7]

Missionaries, by and large, took the name of Nzame (or Zame) for God, although in most creation myths he is the son of God, and often enough, *emwan môt* (the child of man). The relative familiarity with which Nzame is treated in Fang religion may be traced to the fact that in many myths he was an ancillary deity as ignorant about the facts of creation as man himself. The identification of Nzame with man in this legend was in conformity with the genealogical custom of concluding with Nzame as the clan founder. Nzame had, therefore, a status midway between divinity and humanity.

Since Fang culture was created there, more attention was paid to occurrences in the Village of Nzame (*adzal Nzame*) well after creation. It was relatively easy to collect stories about life in adzal Nzame, and these were often related to Fang children by their elders in order to justify various customs: why young men were not allowed to hunt in the deep forest, how it was that Fang practiced agriculture and what crops they planted, what were the taboos to be observed in hunting and trapping, what herbal medicines have what power, how men must bury their dead, etc.[8] Events in this village also accounted for the differences between Whiteman and Blackman and other kinds of mankind. The most frequent theme, and not a surprising one given the schismatic nature of Fang society, was the conflict between the descendants of Nzame which made it difficult for them to live on together in their ancestral village. These accounts of life in the Village of God have an uncertain relationship to the origin legends. They often incorporate Christian myths of origin in Eden and the legends of dispersal to populate the earth.

Frequently the earliest accounts begin not with creation or with accounts of events in the Village of God but with life in a savanna country lying next to a great ocean called Endendame. Life there has a paradisical flavor. "There was plenty of gold and game." Dislodged for uncertain reasons—generally thought to be attacks made upon them by a race of "Redmen" (*mvele me bot*), the ancestors migrated southwestward through undesirable countries between the mountains and a great river which they were unable to cross. Under constant attack, they were finally able to cross over the river with the aid of a giant snake, crocodile, or hippopotamus. This creature drowned the pursuers as they attempted to use the same bridge. The river was called Yom and was identified with the Sanaga in the southern Cameroons. In some versions there were several different colored rivers to be crossed. Alexandre collected materials from the Bulu indicating that one of these rivers was white and the other black and they were traversed in that order.[9] The significance of these colors was lost to his informants but gains importance in the study of Bwiti, for colored rivers frequently emerge in initiates' hallucinations.

The crossing of the Sanaga or Yom was an event of marked importance, the first rebirth from the old life to the new. The second act of much greater salience is the penetration past the azap tree, the final barrier to Fang migration.

But what of the significance of the chthonian creatures who enabled Fang to cross over these rivers? The reptilian and river- or water-dwelling creatures, in the old religion, were associated both with creation, as in the account above of the lizard as the earliest form of man, and with protection or surveillance of the village. Tessmann pictures the mounds sculptured to represent snakes, pigs, and crocodiles that were found in the cult sanctuaries of *Dzok* and *Ngi* (both male, secret, antiwitchcraft cults).[10] Tessmann was concerned with what he perceived to be the dramatic struggle between good and evil forces as represented in these cults. He understood these chthonic beings, in their association with filth, decay, and death, as representatives of evil. It was the lizard who brought the news to men that instead of life eternal he must suffer birth and death.[11] The other chthonic beings, particularly snake and pig, represented the forces of evil, an uncontrolled sexuality and the underlying presence of death, by which the initiate had to pass as he was brought into full membership.[12]

Tessmann's notion that the saurian creatures were associated exclusively with physical and social death and destruction is too simple. They were tutelary and protective as well. Trilles,[13] whose book makes an extended search for tutelary beings, argued that the most ancient totem of Fang was found in the Cult of the Crocodile. He based his evidence, lacking any surviving ceremonies at the time, on legends from the Mvet troubadour cycles and particularly on the legend of the culture hero Ngurangurane ("the ransom which ransomed all," from *ngure*, "ransom"). Fang of that legend were terrorized by a giant crocodile (*ngan esa*, the father of the crocodiles) named Ombure. He offered Fang protection from others and from himself if they would make tribute of slaves and of youth whom he then consumed on the margins of the great river. Fang were obliged to make war to obtain these sacrifices.

> Here is what I, Ombure, order you to do and you will do it. Everyday you will bring me two men, one man in the morning and one man in the afternoon. The next day you will bring me two women, one woman in the morning and one in the afternoon. And on the first evening of each new moon you will bring me two young girls, well gotten up and decorated in red powder and shining with oil. Go, it is I, Ombure, the king of the forest, it is I, the king of the waters.[14]

Fang attempted to flee this terrible creditor and migrated south, but by his powerful magic he was able to follow them. Finally, he engendered the hero, Ngurangurane, with one of the sacrificial maidens. Become a man, this son of the crocodile was enabled to kill his own father and free Fang from their bloody bondage. A communal feast was made of the crocodile's body. Ngurangurane, as his son, was yet obliged to perform funeral ceremonies and lamentations for his dead progenitor, and these rituals were the source of the archaic cult of the crocodile, in which Fang did homage to this primordial saurian.

From this Fang terror, Ombure, who protected them at great cost in human tribute, was born a protector and culture hero, Ngurangurane, who killed the scourge and yet established a cult in honor of him. The notion of tutelary protection bound up in this legend is complex. In the framework of all the folklore on this subject one sees that the giant crocodile who provided the means for escaping the vast rivers in the origin legends is also represented as a monstrous oppressor. Tutelage and supernatural surveillance require sacrifices, and possess polyvalent potentiality for good *and* for evil. One set of ideas to be extracted from the various cults in which earth-associated animals were employed is that there is a close and problematic approximation of protection and oppression, of life and death, of good and evil.

The final and crucial event in the migration legends is the frustration of further progress by the azap tree (*mimusops djave E*). The azap is one of the tallest trees in the equatorial forest, with an impressive rufous bark and a very straight trunk. It ascends like a massive pillar eight-tenths of its length before it branches and foliates. Fang were blocked by this tree but eventually managed to pierce it and pass through to the forest beyond. Pygmies, in most versions, participated in the piercing of the tree. They have an important place in this part of the legend, for it is they who provided Fang with the knowledge and techniques necessary to life in the equatorial forest, and Fang have continued to admire the Pygmies' ability to subsist so easily in this environment.

The azap tree seems to represent the rain forest, which constituted a barrier and a traumatic problem of adaptation to these people of savanna origin.[*1] But it also represents a transformation of Fang from the unitary state which they possessed during the migration previous to azapmboga to the divisiveness which was their lot afterwards. For it is after azapmboga that Fang dispersed, forming the various tribal units and, subsequently, the multitude of clans. Practically all clan genealogies lead back to azapmboga. Since there was some indication of divisiveness in ancestral life before azapmboga, if one considers the Village of God stories, the azapmboga experience may represent unification of previous disparate tendencies followed by a return to divisiveness. It is a central and recurrent motif, but a problematic one capable of representing traumatic adaptation or salvation from pursuing forces, unification or dispersion, rebirth or disappearance into the forest.

THE EXCITEMENT OF TROUBADOURS

The most extended and most interesting genre in Pahouin folklore was that belonging to the chest harp (*mvet*).[15] The Pahouin, whether Bulu, Eton, Beti, or Fang, were famous in their respective republics for their mvet troubadours. Festivals were often organized featuring this instrument with its associated folklore.[16] Ntumu of Rio Muni, southern Cameroons, and northern Gabon were generally recognized to be the masters of the art, and most *bebôme mvet* traced their apprenticeship to some troubadour from this region. Blind men were often associated with the mvet and regarded as the outstanding performers. The blind Ntumu, Ekot Nsila, was said to have been the original creator of mvet,[17] while in the 1950's and early 1960's in northern Gabon the blind Edu Ada of Atonville, between Oyem and Bitam, was the acknowledged

---

[*1] The contrast between the savanna region and the forest belt of Equatorial and West Africa, and the contrasting opportunities they have offered for cultural elaboration and diffusion, is a dominant characteristic of the culture history of Africa. Though this history offers many examples of forest people moving into the savanna and more frequently the reverse, it was not a step easily taken and was probably always accompanied by the kind of cultural trauma that would produce such symbolizations as we get in the legend of Azapmboga.

master. The mvet songs and chants weave an epic fantasy; imagination rather than eyesight is important. The opaque eyes of blind men easily gaze into other realms of existence where dwell the warriors of Ekang in the land of Engong.

There were a variety of mvet and many cycles. Eno Belinga considers them all to be part of a genre which he calls the Chante Fable.[18] This genre was one in which an epic-tale was accompanied intermittently with songs and instruments. These were usually responsorial, since the audience was expected to animate and encourage the troubadour. The mvet recounted the adventures of a supernatural race, usually identified as Fang or as ancestral to them. The most widely known cycle was that of the immortal people of Engong. The exploits of their invincible chief, Akoma Mba, and his principal lieutenants were sung, and their mighty provocations and recurrent triumphs celebrated. The Gabonese authority, Ndong Philippe, himself a mbômô mvet, has given a literary version of one of these epics: the battle of the men of Engong against the Tribe of Flames.[19] These epics, similar to the epic of Beowulf in the Anglo-Saxon tradition, were the favorite material and the oldest form of the mvet.

But the troubadours might also sing of the War of the Chimpanzees, known by the name of their terrible primate leader, Mesi me Koro Endong, or of adventures of foolish or wise men with the dead. More recently the bebome mvet incorporated materials from recent migration and from the colonial experience itself. Thus the experiences of the Yom or azapmboga or the Oban invasion were recounted. Disputes and skirmishes between village headmen and well-known chiefs might also be sung. This led some students to argue that the mvet legends are closely related to the migration experience,[20] but there seems to be little evidence for this in the classic Akoma Mba cycle. Some troubadours, rather than chanting and singing the old lyrics of tribal defiance and exaltation, came to make up personal songs, often of courtship and sexual conquest, comparable to the goliard minstrelsy of the European Middle Ages. A favorite modern theme, not unrelated to the colonial experience, was that of "the world has gone to pot" (*sí e ne abé* or *sí e kangan éyan*).

The famous Ntumu troubadour of the 1940's and 1950's, Edu Ada, though concentrating on the classic epics, would generally begin with, and often intermix, "plaisanterie songs" (*fiang*) in which he would refer to his "miraculous talents" (*ma bô biang akyunge* or *akyunge edô da ye me wing*) or his "long apprenticeship in the art" (*nge wa kômô nyong mvet*) or "the ill treatment he had received as a stranger in the villages where he sang" (*beyung be yen mam be wôk alun*). A favorite fiang was the song celebrating his sexual desires. Thus he sang of the nubile girls who flocked to him. "They sit on my lap and I play with them (and fondle their breasts) like an old codger squeezing offal out of a slain antelope gut" (*me nga vwing ane nôm wa tô miyeh mitzit).* In the more modern mvet there was often a mixture in any one performance of various genres: personal lyrics, topical songs, and the classic epic.

But what is the meaning of the mvet cycle to Fang? Most modern observers agree that the mvet musician as a troubadour was an itinerant observer of society and culture.*[2] He was a bearer of information from other parts of Fang country. The gossip and news he brought were valued. When roads and vehicular communication became well developed, this function of the mbômô mvet lost value. But in the old days when internecine strife rendered traveling hazardous, the relative freedom with which the mvet troubadour could move made him a valuable source of information.

Eno Belinga regards the mvet as having a more important function than providing topical observation on Fang society or even epic amusement. He interprets the formula of introduction to the epic recital *okang biso elang elang* (after a forest's journey to encounter doubt, suspicion, insult) as expressing the troubadour's desire to be the guardian of secular traditions. The phrase also expressed the troubadour's impatience that this function should in any way be questioned.[21] Belinga sees these epics, as have others, as presenting to the listener all the old problems of the Pahouin world. By dramatizing these problems the epics acted as a source of wisdom or at least as a means of facing the issues.

Ndong Philippe argues for a more utilitarian function. He regards the mvet as having originated in the process of migration and as acting to revitalize Fang, changing their feeling of flight to a spirit of active conquest of the autochthonous peoples upon whom they were intruding. According to Ndong Philippe, the creator of the mvet, one Oyono Ada Ngono, returned from a vision experience with the knowledge of the mvet and the pronouncement that "we are not condemned to flee eternally. While we cannot prevail against those accursed Mveles we can in our own turn scourge and pillage the villages before us. We are strong! Let us have confidence in our power."[22] The epic struggles of the mvet were invented to give this animation and to excite this feeling of power. The mvet was, first of all, then, an "instrument excitateur," although later, with the cessation of warfare, it became simply a "distraction instructive." And while it could no longer excite the enthusiasm for conquest, it still contained "a literature, an ethic, and a philosophy of an incontestable richness and variety."[23]

That something powerful was contained in the mvet cycle could be seen in the atmosphere in which it took place. The mbomo mvet appeared in the village either on direct invitation or in the process of his itineration. In either case he was sponsored by one or another "village family" (*mvogabot*) which

---

*[2] There are a variety of troubadours that pass through Fang villages, though the mvet are the best known. The other itinerant musical specialists include balophone players with their own epic repertory.

offered him the use of one of their "council houses" (*aba*). It was filled to overflowing. Women and children clustered outside. The performer was given enough space to sit or stand and dance about in a small circle at one end of the aba. A fire was often placed in the center of the aba before him. He was dressed in the old style with a headdress of bird feathers, a loin garment of raffia, and small animal skins (primarily the skin of the civet cat, *esinga*). Seed rattles were tied on his upper arms and ankles. His face, at least around the eyes, was painted with white clay. The men of Engong looked as forbidding. Several local men kept time to the recitation and intermittent songs by tapping lightly on a "bamboo sounding board" (*ôbaka*).

Portions of the mvet were responsorial. The troubadour began singing, for example: *A se mvé, melô me baa*? ("Everything is not in order, is everyone attentive?" literally, "Are the ears alert?"). And his audience responded, *Me baa fwô* ("They are truly attentive"). During the process of the epic the assembled male audience periodically responded with a chant, *hé, hé, hô ôhh*, or by a simple affirmative *yaa* or *yoo*. Since the classic mvet concerned the recurrent battles of the men of Engong, and since the immortals were often engaged as "battle teams" (*ensama*) in their exploits, the periodic chanting in unison of the male spectators gave an impressive actuality to this epic celebration of male solidarity. It was revitalizing. And it could be enduring. The mvet generally began after dark, and often continued until midnight. There could be hundreds of verses, upwards of five hundred in the classic mvet. If there was a moon, a favorite time for the mvet, the children caught the mood of the epic events being recited and played at war in the plaza of the village.

If it was more than simple entertainment, as the African authorities argued, what was learned from it? Though the epic heroes were immortal and their exploits miraculous, the everyday village life of Pahouin was presented with much veracity: the problems of respect and forbearance toward in-laws, the troubled relationship between man and wife,[24] the problems of courtship and brideprice, and the problems, in an egalitarian and unstructured society such as Fang, of the maintenance of authority by those who had been granted it only briefly. The theme of ephemeral authority was the particular emphasis in that cycle of the mvet concerned with the war of the chimpanzees among themselves and against mankind. Fang found a rueful reflection of their own affairs in the excitable anarchy of the chimpanzees.[25]

The more obscure and more unwelcome aspects of Fang life, the devious struggle for power by sorcery and witchcraft as played out in the patrilineage, was also well represented. The murder by fathers of their own children in the womb was a frequent theme. Heroes had to resist their own fathers' maleficent forces and, even "en utero," become self-sufficient engines of aggrandizement, claiming the time of their own birth. One remarks, however, the greater importance of the mother-son relationship in the mvet. The father was usually inimical or not present.[26] Akoma Mba himself was regarded as the product of brother-sister incest and hence, in effect, fatherless in the jural sense (with genitor but without pater). His mother was finally courted by his eventual jural father, Mba, in his own adolescence.

> When Mba came to demand Bala Mendji in marriage, Msem Dzingi was already a great adolescent who terrorized his entourage by his brutalities. It was thus with joy that the Yemosomo gave their village child to Mba when he married the mother. His new father called him Mbôô Zôô Mba (Hide of Elephant, Son of Mba). But Mbôô Zôô Mba became so "méchant," maltreating his brothers and beating them on every occasion, that life became impossible for his parents. They called him therefore Akôma Mba (the creator of Mba) because it was said this child is so much more powerful than his father that one has the impression it was he who created Mba.[27]

A great deal of time in the recital of the mvet was given over to the genealogies of the various heroes. The mvet often began with the divine genealogy of God, Nzame, though the version was often more literary than the ones commonly recited in the clan.[*3] This emphasis upon genealogical matters was often so detailed that the visitor was likely to lose a sense of momentum. But such reiteration was didactic, and confirmed the crucial place of the genealogy in traditional life.

The influence of the mvet can be seen in the fact that Gabonese lycée students, in drawing up portraits of the ideal man among Fang, frequently referred to the attributes displayed by the heroes of mvet.[28] What these attributes are can be gathered from the following counsel given to the young future chief of the Tribe of Flames, Ovang Ndoumou Obame, by his father Ndoumou Obame.

> Be a chief of unapproachable authority. A good chief pardons rarely but chastises frequently. He defends his tribe but subjects other people to it. He fears neither fire nor heaven nor the anger of men. He burns rebel villages, massacres without mercy all those who violate his law. All that pleases him is given to him, all that displeases him remains with its owner. A chief spits haughtily, he roars and thunders like the storm. He overturns the government of others and provokes calamities.[29]

[*3] The divine genealogy given by Ndong Philippe is a literary one surely: "Aki Ngoss (globe de cuivre) se forma avec quatre faces. Il grossit, explosa et don a naissance a Midour-Mi-Aki (l'infini). Midour Mi Aki engendra Biyem Yema Bi Nkour (nebuleuses) engendra Ngwa Bikoko (1er esprit) engendra Mba Ngwa (2e esprit) engendra Zokom Mba (3e esprit) engendra trois esprits: Zame ye Mebegue (Dieu des hommes, de la terre et du souffle), Kare Mebegue (Dieu Ascendant des Immortels, habitants d'un monde inconnu des hommes), Zong Mbegue (dont on ignore les attributions)." "Le Mvet," no. 1, p. 8.

Of course, the Machiavellian features manifestly do not exhaust the attributes of desirable social identity nor the criteria of full manhood among Fang. They are nevertheless attributes—to recall Ndong Philippe's emphasis upon the mvet as an instrument calculated to excite Fang into a warlike frame of mind— of great value to those in a state of migration and constant strife with local populations.

Like many epics the mvet celebrates sheer miraculous power, unmitigated agression, and gargantuan appetites in its heroes. They are able to transport themselves great distances with the gesture of a finger, raise mountains in the midst of the courtyards of villages, employ magic animals such as flies, bees, and birds to enter the ears, mouths, and anuses of their enemies so as to distract them. They can bring down lightning upon their opponents and shift their own shape into countless creatures of cunning. A favorite trick is to enslave a man by turning the brains around in his head. Such powers[30] are not obtained, however, without great sacrifice. And a recurrent theme—it occurs as well in the migration legends—is the sacrifice of someone closely related to the hero, a sacrifice by which he obtains his power.

In Ndong Philippe's legend of the chief of the Tribe of Flames, it is the chief's grandfather who must die, shortly after he has magically prepared (akômnge) his infant grandson, in order to ensure the success of that preparation. In one of the favorite mvet legends of Edu Ada of Atonville, a grandmother prepares a child for success in life and subsequently throws herself into the river. But here she becomes a river monster (ebibi), in some versions a giant crocodile, who requires the periodic sacrifice of an infant of the village. This tribute becomes so oppressive that the village calls upon the immortals of Engong to destroy the monster. They do this after many years of ceaseless underwater battle.

In this association of the sacrificial grandparent with the monster crocodile, one recalls Trilles's legend of Ombure, the monster crocodile who fathers the hero who later slays him and ends the bloody tribute he exacted. These two versions of mvet are reworkings of a set of elements expressing the theme of power obtained from a monstrous possessor of that power by the sacrifice of that incumbent—it is the theme of life obtained through death, of an older generation forced to sacrifice itself for a younger, yet at one point or another oppressively demanding compensation for that sacrifice.

It was not easy to get at the meaning of these two legends to Fang. Informants' commentaries were sparse. But the central problem they seemed to grapple with was generational continuity, the incompatibility between the nurture owed the new generation by the previous generations and the inevitable self-assertion of the new generation against the rights of its elders. Thus elders raised to monstrous dimensions offered ''preparation of capacity'' (akomnge) but had to be victimized by that very capacity as they passed it on. They were both sacrificed to and sacrificed themselves. The legends expressed direct conflict between father and son—as, in fact, often arose in Fang society in the struggle over the use of brideprice monies and the establishment of the son's own line. When fathers did appear in these legends, they were often monsters who had to be sacrificed. Grandparents sacrificed themselves but were revived in monstrous form and then had to be sacrificed. The self-sacrifice of the elder generation did not solve the problem. It shifted it to a supernatural place where the claims of the ascendant generation were reasserted in the form of a specter or monstrous oppressor which exacted a newborn or a youth from its descendants until appeased or destroyed by other supernaturals. The mvet legends dealt with this problem of generational continuity in, so to speak, a monstrous manner. If they contributed either to the resolution of the problem or to the maintenance of good will in that relationship, it was, at best, only in an indirect way.

What other functions did these miraculous and belligerent epics have in the late colonial period? Had they become "instructive distractions"? It may be doubted that they had much didactic value unless one argues that it is instructive to present cultural dilemmas in a hyperbolic way. Of course, they had the conpensatory value that is found in most folklore. In a situation of comparative deprivation as was characteristic of transitional Fang society, these evenings of miracles compensated for daily feelings of poverty of accomplishment in respect to the modern world of airplanes and bulldozers. Frequently enough I was told, in the manner of Ze Azi, "Look what distances they could cover in a moment!" Towo Atangana argues, in fact, that the miraculous land of Engong, this "pays de toutes les merveilles," was identified with the land of the Whiteman.[31] More and more modern artifacts, bicycles, airplanes, European clothes, appeared in the legends to bring them up to date. But at the same time their themes remained the old ones of challenge and betrayal, cunning, deceptive villainy and stealth, cosmic combat and utter triumph and disaster.

The mvet reasserted the constant presence and imminent possibility of the supernatural. It recreated periodically a realm of existence whose potentialities greatly exceeded and thereby compensated for the practical incapacities of Fang. In the past it was no doubt a functional stimulation for a people in dynamic aggressive migration. Whether it was just the kind of "instructive diversion" Fang needed in the colonial world is another matter. A better answer to this question may be found in examining a legendary history, or pseudohistory, "the legend of Afri Kara" (*Dulu Bon be Afri Kara*), composed after the Second World War. It made every effort to be modern.

As for the supernatural world created by the mvet cycle, it may be usefully contrasted with the supernatural world of the Bwiti religion. For Bwiti, like mvet, is also celebrated in a council house (aba) and offers a vision of a reality quite different from the everyday. But whereas mvet celebrates a competitive and combative toughmindedness in an aggrandizing male group and applauds an ever-readiness to take merciless advantage of circumstances for personal or in-group gain, Bwiti[32] celebrates protective benevolence and that form of human relatedness which they call "oneheartedness" (*nlem mvore*).

THE PILGRIMAGE OF THE CHILDREN OF AFRI KARA

The Journey of the Children of Afri Kara (*Dulu Bon be Afri Kara*)[33] was published in Bulu by the American Presbyterian Press in Ebolowa, Cameroons, in 1954, though it was written by Ondoua Engutu in 1948 at the height of the "clan regroupment movement" (*Alar Ayong*). It was intended to serve the purposes of that movement. It presents a history of Pahouin from the point of view of Ntumu of the Ntem watershed (southern frontier of Cameroons, northernmost Gabon, and Rio Muni), beginning with their life beside the "great salt sea" (*mang me nku*), their traverse of the "desert" (*nkôtô si*) and the "savanna" (*bilo'o si*), and their entrance into the "equatorial rain forest" (*beta afan* or *bilé si*) through "the giant barrier tree" (*ôjambo'a* [B]; *azapmboga*). The account continues until after the Second World War. Like the genealogies, upon which it is in good part based, it begins in mythology and ends in historical actualities. *Dulu Bon* explains the origin of many of the important customs of Pahouin, but it is particularly concerned with the appearance and the branching off of the many different contemporary clans. Early versions of *Dulu Bon* were widely circulated in northern Gabon, and it was something of a Bible to the clan regroupment movement,[34] for the matrix clans which were the basis of that regroupment were clearly identified and related to each other at their moment of origin. So widespread was the circulation of this version of the Pahouin past, and so well did it fill the need for a past, that it was often difficult to obtain any other version. The colonial administrations took this book equally seriously and regarded its circulation and its contents as a sign of a clandestine independence movement.

There are three aspects of this published version of the past which are relevant to considerations of that past from Fang points of view: (1) the general progress made during the course of the history it presents, (2) the *Dulu Bon* phrasing of some of the themes, motifs, and symbolic events of Fang lore previously discussed, and (3) its development of the genealogical structure.

The account begins with the disruption of ancestral life on the edge of the salt sea, where the ancestors are victimized by the *Bivele be Bot* (the Red People) who make slaves of them to sell to the Whiteman across the ocean. The latter are given in Old Testament referent (*mvong bot Japhet* [B]).[35] The weakness of the Africans in the face of Bivele be Bot forces them to migrate. Their life is further devastated at the moment of departure by a flooding of the salt sea which swallows up much of their material culture and with it much of their knowledge—separating them, henceforth, in this respect from both the Redmen and the Whitemen.*4 But in their devastation they remember the advice of their patriarch, Afri Kara, who counseled them to follow the sun and the moon as their path until they came to where the sun sinks into the sea. There they may live restored to a full life. This injunction to "follow the sun and the moon as their path" (*mi ayinae kale jop ba ngon mbie bi ne mia zen* [B]) until it took them to the sea was reported by many early observers of Fang as the reason for Fang migration. The missionaries seem to have been told, or they interpreted this to mean, that it was the departed God that was the object of search.[36]

The bulk of *Dulu Bon* recounts this pilgrimage, the traverse of Africa east to west. In the process it gives a rich description of various customs: marriage, death and burial, the other "gods of Fang" (*Bezambe be fe*) and their associated cults, the origins of "evil" (*evus*) and the machinations of witchcraft, and the engagement in repeated skirmishes and battles. The saurian creature that enabled the children of Afri Kara to cross the Yom, though not identified at the moment of crossing, is later revealed as a "giant snake" (*beta nyo*). He is called *Ngang meja*, a play on words meaning, depending on tone, crocodile of destructive force, or respect due to destructive force, or wizard of destructive force. It is implied that he is a blessing sent by the "creator god" (*Nkôm Bôtô*).[37]

The children of Afri Kara gather confidence in their powers as their migration proceeds and they are victorious in their wars with the "autochthonous peoples" (bilobolobo). Finally, the Europeans arrive, conquer, and impose their peace. The focus of the narrative now changes from the wars of the Africans to the more awesome wars of the Europeans during which Fang are but onlookers. The German colonial hegemony is replaced by that of the French. The dividing up of Pahouin into three territories under separate colonial governments provides a concluding dispirited note. For in the final portions of the narrative a growing sense of being mere spectators of history is portrayed. The Ntumu must now go to work for the Whiteman,[38] although their migration and their battles had been undertaken to avoid domination by the Bivele be Bot. The final chapter, Chapter 61, discusses the depression Ntumu experience (*ate'e Ntumu*) at being divided into three colonial territories and thus rendered unable, without permission, to visit their brothers.[39] Such statements as these were taken by colonial administrations as having revolutionary implications for the colonial status quo. But the issue of colonial boundaries was only a focus for a more general malaise arising out of the

---

*4 The translation of the relevant passage in *Dulu Bon* (p. 7) is the following. "Those things which we have made whose ingenuity gave us such pride we ended up leaving at the bottom of the water. Much knowledge ended up perishing . . . all things ended up being left there . . . things created by our predecessors in their efforts . . . iron things, stringed instruments, flutes and skin flasks . . . those things we knew how to make so well we left there . . . the separation of the reds and the whites from us this was it."

sense of historical impotence into which *Dulu Bon* finally evolves. It was to this malaise that the clan regroupment movement addressed itself.

Though there is much more in this narrative than an account of the origin of the clans in relation to the core genealogy of the Pahouin—that genealogy founded in Zang Hamata and his "great-great grandson" (*Engurabon*) Afri Kara—the development of this genealogical structure was the most valuable feature of *Dulu Bon* for most African villagers of northern Gabon, southern Cameroons, and Rio Muni. In view of the uncertainties in most Fang genealogies, the support that any clan regroupment movement might arouse had to rest on the certainty of its genealogical evidence. Engutu's account was very clear about such matters. He not only gave precise data on the line of descent, but was ingenious in offering folk etymologies to explain the various clan names. The genealogical structure which can be abstracted from the *Dulu Bon* narrative is illustrated in Figure 2.1. This is but a portion of the entire genealogy, but it is sufficient to indicate the way in which the various contemporary clans were brought into genealogical relationship with each other. One sees that Bekoe, for example, whose Gabon genealogy will be discussed in Chapter 3, is as closely related to Ndong (a clan found mostly in the Cameroons) as are a father and son, and also to Yevó, Ewoan, and Esamvin. Ndong and Bukwé, says Engutu, are thus but one clan.[40] Similarly Yesok and Yebisob are grouped by Engutu as Yemisomo.

This genealogical reconstruction not only regrouped various local clans as in the cases just mentioned, but it also pointed the way to a much higher order of regroupment. Thus all the descendants of Mebumu me Ngbwa, the great-grandson of Ntumu Afri, were grouped together as a kind of supergroup, Mebum or Mobum. This regroupment brought together the following clans, as seen in Figure 2.1: Ndong, Bukwé, Yevo, Ewoan, Esamvin, Abaé, Azok, and Yemfek. It was just this kind of probable connection that the agents of the regroupment movement, as they circulated about in Fang country, were quick to capitalize upon in reorganizing Fang.

Engutu in his efforts to tie together Fang so that "each and each might know what man they might properly call brother" (*nde a ye bo ngule ya loene môte si môte kale na mojang* [B]) was driven by the logic of the genealogy to an all-inclusive brotherhood. "We are all related if we begin in the days of Kobata and Tamengo'o" (*bia bese bi vuman a so melu Kobata, Tamengo'o* [B]).[41] In this conclusion, the colonial administration suspected the rise of a powerful ethnic nationalism, but reason enough for such genealogical reconstruction is found in the aged Ze Azi's sense of Fang dividedness and impotence. The demonstration of Fang solidarity was quite enough for many villagers, without any suggestion of political power and independence.

Engutu, in a manner typical of Fang wordplay, provided a fertile etymology for the various clan names, not only in his creation of an ancestor, Afri Kara, but also in his names of the existing clans. The clan Esangbwak, for example,

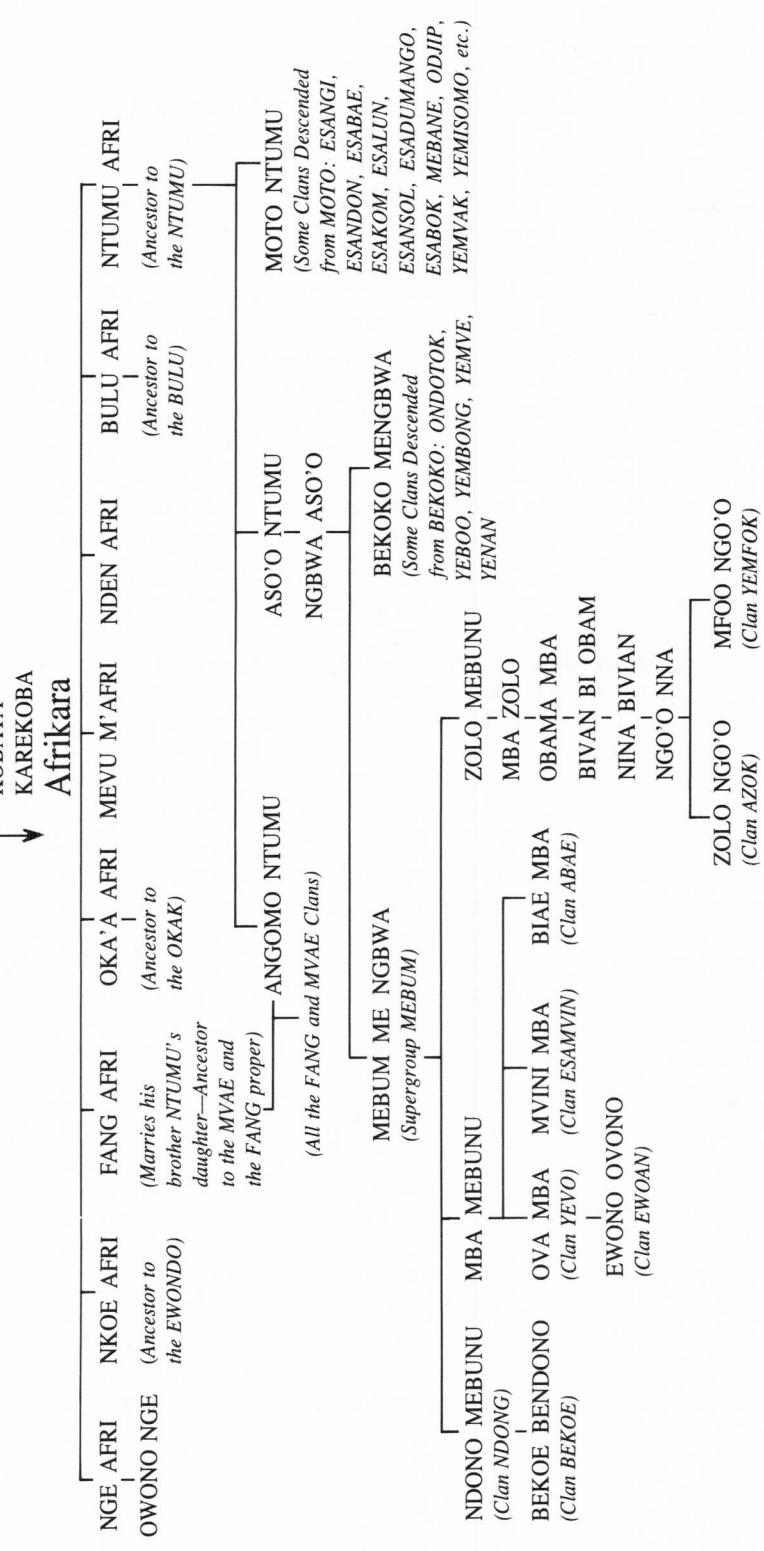

2.1 Descendants of Afri Kara (from Ondoua Engutu, 1954)

is traced to Ngbwa'a Mekomo, an ancestor given that name because it was he with his ''adze'' (ngbwak) who was chiefly responsible for chopping the hole through the azap tree.[42] The Yemayema derive their name from the fact that their ancestral *mvonge bot* (people of one seed) did not know the name of the ''elephant'' (*zok*) when they first encountered it in the savanna (from *yem*, to know). Such word play, double entendre, and punning made for an additionally convincing document.

There are a number of meaningful motifs and themes in *Dulu Bon* besides the central ones already discussed: the great salt sea of origin, the bright ocean of pilgrimage, the waterless desert between, the guiding orbs of the sun and the moon, the great barrier river Yom, the saurian bridge over the river, and the final barrier tree, azapmboga (B). Water, whether in the original flood of the salt sea, by which all Fang accomplishments and knowledge were lost, or in the form of the various rivers through which they passed to a new life free from the more powerful peoples of the northeast, is a particularly recurrent and forceful image. It is a final irony that the ''great bright ocean water'' (*mang*), the object of their pilgrimage, brings to them, at once, European goods *and* European domination.

A fundamental distinction throughout this narrative is that between knowledgeable people (*Beyeme Mam*), ''those who know things,'' and the ''simple and ignorant people'' (*Bidimi Mam*). This distinction underlies a good bit of Fang thought on the nature of social relations, and particularly on the operation of witchcraft where it is the Beyeme Mam or Beyem who are able to manipulate occult powers to their advantage. The Bidimi Mam (those who ignore things or are in obscurity about things) or *mimia* are the perennial victims of this capacity. *Dulu Bon* details the way in which the Beyem, by not fearing to employ the night for their reunions, were first able to astound and confound the innocent. The night is shown to be the source of power and clairvoyance. Out of this dichotomy between those who know and those who do not know emerges the principle of ''evil'' (evus) which, although anthropomorphized as a night creature, is the principle of exploitation and deception of the innocent by the knowledgeable.

The emergence of evil and the disparity between knowledgeable people and innocent people were very much Fang preoccupations and will recur in our discussion. Here it is helpful to observe that the relationship between the Whiteman and the Blackman is a relationship between those who know things and those who, being innocent of that knowledge, are subject to exploitation. For the pilgrimage by the children of Afri Kara from sea to sea is halted by the coming of the European, who imposes not only passivity upon them, but the status of mimia or bidimi mam as well.

This consequence of the coming of the European is not, at first, clear in the narrative, just as it was not at first apparent in the history of contact. At the earliest moment of contact the narrative shows us great interest displayed in the ntangen (ntañan), "those fortunate ones who have eaten salt regularly and have an abundance of trade goods" (besôm be nga di nku a jeé bisa).[43] Much debate ensues as to how contact might best be established with them. Finally, emissaries are sent to Rio Muni and they make contact with the government there. These emissaries return with tales of spices and gunpowder and guns and cloth of many different kinds and a readiness on the part of the European to "teach and instruct in their manner of doing things" . . . (be nga sô fe mvaman a be nga ye'e fe ane b'adô je e mange woe).[44] The Europeans must be attended to for "they bring to us many riches" (ba sô bia abui akum).

But not so long after these first moments of contact, the narrative gives news of the first fight between African and European over the very riches that had brought them together. And soon afterward colonial authority is established throughout the forest, and the mood of the account begins to drift toward that "depression and frustration" (atek) with which the narrative ends. A new social status appears in the story after the coming of the Whiteman: the nkukuma (the Richman).[45] He is able to wield authority as it has not been wielded before in this legendary history—that is by powers accruing to him through his accumulation of impersonal wealth and without reference to genealogical principles of descent and seniority. No resolution is offered of the problem of conflicting principles of authority and the newly perceived differences between wealth and know-how.

MINTANGEN: THE PEOPLE WHO COUNT AND RECOUNT

But what of the European himself? We see him in Dulu Bon as a source of wealth and as a colonial arbiter whose judgments are baffling and often demeaning to the African. All of this seems a natural enough reflection of the European views of Fang reviewed in Chapter 1. The shift, traced in that chapter, from African nobility to servility has its counterpart in the shift in Dulu Bon from the early views of the European as a source of wealth and as benevolent in parting with both it and the knowledge of its creation to a subsequent perception of his stinginess on both counts.

Whiteman appears early in Dulu Bon. He lives on the other side of the salt sea and he buys the enslaved children of Afri Kara from Bivele bi Bot. But he is not a central figure and no specific origin is assigned to him, nor is any attempt made to derive his name etymologically. And little appears in Dulu Bon of the widespread Whiteman-Blackman legends which in the twentieth century come to assume importance in Fang understanding of the colonial past.

These legends appear to have sprung up rapidly after European contact, and were known as the Ntangen ye Nsutmot tales. Trilles collected several of them under the title Noirs et Blancs.[46] They sought primarily to explain

African poverty in the goods of the world and in the techniques for obtaining these goods. In *Dulu Bon* this is explained by reference to the watery destruction of a former culture. The deeper reasoning behind this theme of goods and know-how denied was the distinction between "those who know and those who do not know" (beyeme mam and bidimi mam), and it was this distinction that was tackled in most of the Blackman-Whiteman stories. It was not so much the European's wealth, but his knowledge of how to do things, his "cleverness" (*meduk*) that impressed Fang. It was that which lay behind his wealth.

In the most frequent version of these tales told by old men in the districts of Oyem and Mitzik in the late 1950's, the efficient God, *Nzame ye Mebege*, son of the primordial God, Mebege (Mebeghe [N]), created the world and man and left them to their own devices. Soon he noticed turmoil and realized that his all-too-human creatures needed further instruction. He called them together and decided first to talk to Whiteman. Whiteman listened patiently. Then God turned to Blackman who was squabbling with his brothers. Blackman was inattentive and impatient. Before Nzame could finish all he had to say, he was called away to heaven, never again to appear in the affairs of men. Thus was Blackman left without vital information that Nzame intended to give him. He was left, as the storytellers usually concluded, unable to discover anything and unable to complete anything because he lacked the necessary "words of God."

The congruence of this tale with the aims of missionary evangelization is apparent. In fact, among Fang as in many parts of Africa,[47] there was a ready adaptation of several Biblical episodes, the sons of Noah and Isaac's blessing episodes in particular. We find tales in which Blackman's disrespectful attitude toward the nudity of his father is visited upon his descendants. In respect to Isaac's blessing, the collusion of the mother of Whiteman to deprive Blackman, otherwise Nzame's favorite son, of his inheritance results in the ignorance and deprivation which Blackman has since suffered. In both cases Fang tradition made for easy reinterpretation of the Bible. For example, Fang traditionally held that the "display of the father's nudity to a son" (*alere shéshé*) was one of the powerful sanctions prevailing in that relationship. In the second case, as a patrilineal, patrilocal society, they well understood the struggle between co-wives for the advantage of their respective sons.

Which lesson is to be drawn from these tales: that the European had simply tricked the African and subjugated him (the "Jacob and Esau" view) or that the European had justly come into possession of his impressive knowledge through the fault of the black (the "sons of Noah" view)? Fang in earlier years gave greater voice to the latter interpretation in accounting for the misfortunes and deprivations that had befallen them. In later colonial years they tended more to the idea of European trickery.

The European, in any case, was first of all the "knowledgeable one." What he was otherwise may be guessed by examining the folk etymologies offered for the term by which he was commonly called—ntangen (ntañan), mintangen. Panyella and Sabater, the Spanish authorities on the Ntumu and Okak Fang, derive it from the term *ntange* (a species of flourishing convolvulaceous tubercle very difficult to extirpate). The more common derivation was the substantive *ntang*, which is variously to be interpreted as "he who pays," "he who relates stories," or "he who is the ransom or the indemnity paid" (from *tang*: to pay, to count, to recount).[48] For those who took the view that the significance of the Whiteman arose from his having brought commerce and trade goods and having established, thereby, the cash nexus as opposed to older forms of reciprocity, the first derivation (he who pays or counts) was most appropriate.[49] For those who saw the evangelical missionary presence as the most important aspect of the Whiteman, the second derivation (he who recounts stories, relates legends) was the most apt. For those who took into account the *Noirs et Blancs* legends in which the Black was tricked out of his inheritance following a Jacob-and-Esau-type tale, the return of the European with his riches could be regarded as indemnity in reparation of a past wrong. The latter interpretation was full of the possibilities of unrequited feelings.

Conclusion: The Assertion of the Legendary Past

We began with old Ze Azi drifting off in his thoughts to the legendary past. Younger Fang were not as absent-minded. But all Fang were faced with the problem of the past, and that past was subject to various compositions. It held no simple lesson. In respect to creation itself, the relations of the gods to each other and of man to the gods was uncertain. While Fang legends told Fang that their ancestors made a great journey from savanna to rain forest, that journey could be interpreted variously as a flight from or a pursuit of— as an escape or a search. Fang could regard themselves as either conquerors or as the conquered. Various motifs appear in the migration legends, such as the pierced azap tree or the barrier rivers crossed with the aid of giant reptiles. But one cannot state with certainty how these were to be interpreted. The azap tree could represent a rebirth from the savanna into the great forest and/ or ancestral unity before the divisiveness of forest life. Remembering their mythological and legendary past could provoke in Fang, therefore, both pride in great deeds accomplished and disgruntlement over flagging energies and tribal, clan, and family divisiveness. The act of remembering could provide a sense of a search being made or a sense of something irretrievably lost, of exhilarating conquest or suspenseful flight, of advantage lost through Blackman's stupidity or stolen by Whiteman's chicanery.

Several deeper but still not unambiguous lessons seem to emerge from the lore here presented: it seems to teach that men cannot easily live with those who created and protected them; that creators and protectors must be sacrificed, made to die, for otherwise they turn into oppressors; that capacity is only achieved by that sacrifice and maintained by a ruthless exercise of power; and that life is only guaranteed through the facing of recurrent death. The lore also seems to teach the crucial distinction between "those who know" and those "who do not know." Some of these are monstrous lessons and it is appropriate that some of those figures who embodied and enacted these lessons were themselves monsters or the offspring of monsters. It is also not surprising that Whiteman, "he who kills without a dispute," shared in the ambiguities of those "heroes." He seemed to be one who knows in a mysterious way, and perhaps in a monstrous way.

But in trying to summarize the lessons of the entire range of Fang folklore one is on very uncertain ground. For in summarizing the content across genres one is bound to have to struggle with contradictory or inconsistent elements. Each of these genres is itself devoted to rather different ends. In the presence of such diverse material it is more satisfactory to speak of specific compositions made of the past by specific Fang making use of specific genres: by an mvet singer exciting feelings of power and transforming thoughts of flight into the desire for conquest, or compensating for the deprivations and debilitations imposed by the colonial situation; by a disgruntled old man using the origin legends to confirm the degenerate condition of his people; by Ondoua Engutu trying to provide a base by which divided clans might be reintegrated; by a Bwiti leader reaffirming the past by reworking legendary motifs so as to give the membership a more solid feeling of their place in time and space— giving to them, that is to say, a microcosm in which to live.

It is not surprising, in any case, that among Fang one finds various versions of the past put forth with contention. Deschamps, who collected oral histories throughout Gabon[50] remarks the frequent "polemiques" on these matters among them. There is not only the diversity. Fang history passes into myth and myth into history so easily. François Muye, the Gabonese politician, presented in *Réalités Gabonaises*[51] a historical romance recreating a typical raid of the oban invasion—a real event, it will be remembered. The episode involves the slow destruction of a village, Nong-Eki, which had undertaken to defend itself in spite of forewarning. The two leaders of the Mveles, Otoung and Medung, are in their more-than-human quality assimilated to the heroes of the mvet cycle of epic poems. Such prodigious personages are only by a stretch of the imagination to be associated with the historical events of the oban.

Comment has been made upon the passage of history into myth—the frequency, for example, with which colonial administrators were introduced into troubadour epics to the amusement of the audience. But the influence runs the opposite way as well. Myth becomes history. Testimony that the make-believe world of the mvet might be confounded with the everyday is found in the fact that young men occasionally appropriated, as "noms d'encouragement," the names of the heroes of mvet. One found villages referring to themselves by the clan names of the mvet tales. And periodically rumours circulated among the more credulous to the effect that an mvet hero had actually made an appearance. In February 1959, the southern Ntumu of Oyem District, Woleu-Ntem, heard that Ngema Nsing Bere had actually visited several council houses at widely separated villages in a morning's time. He had spoken mysteriously to the occupants about the European's oppression of Fang, and given away his identity by his stature and his accounts of just having visited far-distant villages. It sounded like the kind of mixture of mythical and historical experience that Ze Azi in his dotage might have related. But how different is it from that which occurs in the Bwiti religion, where mythological and legendary motifs are given new composition, reenacted, and made a religious reality, where genealogy is revitalized and unknown ancestors are made present? In Bwiti, as in mvet, there are sacrifices; there is a recurrent facing of death; progenitors are evoked and carefully cultivated. But there is a pronounced emphasis on harmonious living together, and new knowledge is discovered which assuages Fang ignorance and confronts the knowledge of the Whites. Bwiti is an excitement of benevolent ancestors and benign deities, but not of monsters. In Fang lore we see the roots of Bwiti, but it is a significantly new composition.

·3·

Extensions into
Social Space and Time

Elé e nga be tele tara nlem?
Mintem mi tsam mesí mese.
(Riddle: A tree grows in my father's heart. Its branches spread
throughout the land. Answer: *ndan*! The Genealogy!)

NDUTUMU IS CALLED NTOBOT

THE MEN'S COUNCIL HOUSE was a blessing to anthropological inquiry. Except
during the heaviest seasons of work, chopping down the forests for new
plantations for example, some member of the family was almost always to
be found within, making some craft object or playing on the *mbek* board with
a companion. And frequently there were many men clustered about a common
pot at mealtime, sitting moot on some family quarrel or entertaining in-laws
in some question of the brideprice. Most men, when found in the council
house, were willing to talk genealogy and what recent history they knew that
was attached to it, though many felt in recent years that they had lost much
of this information. I spent many hours in various council houses, gathering
genealogical lists, and then, on the basis of these lists, trying to establish the
relationships of various families within villages and between villages as well
as the history attached to the genealogies.

One of the most hospitable men in Assok Ening was Ndutumu Zogo. He
had brought me a chicken when I first arrived, another to my wife when she
arrived, and other gifts of food as well. Moreover, he never pressed our
reciprocal obligations upon us as some men did, and was ever resistant to
taking gifts in return. But it was difficult to tell in what council house Ndutumu
belonged for he seemed to be present in several. I was insensitive to the fact
that Ndutumu never volunteered his genealogy. One day I asked him pointedly
for it. The genealogy he gave me, sixteen names in length, seemed at odds
with others I had received in the village. It contained the name Mve Ndekwa,
apparently a brother of the Oye Ndekwa, the father of the Mba M'Oye who
had founded the "village family" (*mvôgabot*) with whom we were living.
It was a name appearing in other genealogies. Yet the deeper names in the
list did not conform to other genealogical lists. I pressed Ndutumu on this,
but he retreated saying only that this was what his father had taught him.

Muzwi Mebiame was in the council house at the time, a man always on the edge of the antagonism toward his brothers and confident of his own secure place and sure knowledge in lineage affairs. He accused Ndutumu of having forgotten or of having made up his genealogy. He then recited the genealogy of the family Mba M'Oye and of clan Bukwe as most family members gave it and, in its deeper reaches, as most men in Assok Ening and surrounding Bukwe villages recited it. Mintza Mve, who was also present and, as usual, a quiet and assuaging force in family affairs, said to no one in particular—but perhaps to Ndutumu who had gotten up to leave the council house in irritation—"These days everyone has forgotten his genealogy. But this does not mean we are not all of one stomach."

As it turned out, people believed that Ndutumu was *ntôbot*. He was a descendent of one of those persons or families among Fang that had come to stay in a village seeking protection. They took up permanent residence in a family although they were not of it. The circumstances of migration and internecine strife in the nineteenth century were particularly likely to produce ntobot. Ndutumu was not the only example, as Mintza hinted, of a man living in close fraternal relations where genealogy failed to demonstrate that fraternity. In Ndutumu's case, his grandfather, the real ntobot, had tailored or added a name in the genealogy so as to give it some resonance with the "village family," Mba M'Oye, with which he had settled. It may have been that Ndutumu was actually descended from a different clan, although his genealogy ended with the clan founder Bukwe Ndong. Although ntobot were usually of the same clan, some arrived from different clans, changing their allegiance in so doing, and altering their genealogies correspondingly. And some had changed their genealogies so completely that there was no evidence whatsoever in them of being ntobot.

The status of ntobot was not especially detrimental, for Fang were egalitarian in every visible respect, and most "house families" (*ndébôt*) were self-sufficient so that clientage had no enduring economic base. In the first generation of ntobotship, the individuals or family were recognized as refugees and were not easily admitted to the activities of the "village family" (mvogabot). In subsequent generations this special status, though not forgotten, was overlooked in most respects and discoverable only by close scrutiny of a genealogy and, perhaps, as was the case with Ndutumu, in a lingering peripheral relationship to the main village families. But, on the other hand, by a determined overhauling of genealogies and the successful production of progeny any ntobot might lose that label in two generations.

In another sense Mintza Mve was right. There had been so much turmoil in Fang past—migration and warfare—that "historical reconstructions" (*nkande*) of even the recent past were likely to be regarded with uncertainty. And this very often acted to prevent a "more family than thou" view from imposing itself. Usually the parties involved in such disputes ended up by agreeing to disagree. Or there might be general acquiescence in the view of the most influential and, usually also, the wealthiest man in the village, the *mienlam* (incumbent of the village). His success indicated that he was a man "who knows" and hence should also "know" about the village's place in social time and space. But it was possible that his ancestry at one time or another was itself ntobot.

SOCIAL TIME: THE GENEALOGICAL STRUCTURE
OF THE PAST

The major themes and convergent emphases in Fang accounts of the recent past (nkande, events seen with one's eyes) are best discussed in relation to their "clan genealogies" (*ndan ayong*). The genealogy was that list of ancestors in the patrilineal line which traced back to the founder of the clan and often back into mythological times to the line of creator deities. The genealogy was the centerpiece of traditional education, a template of instruction and a mnemonic device whose recitation brought forth associated information relevant to the past experiences of the group. The genealogy also played a crucial role in earlier times, for it carried valuable evidence of blood relationship and guaranteed, thereby, hospitality and good treatment at times when, in the highly unstable and acephalous condition of Fang political life, there were few means of guaranteeing the security of strangers.

Strangers could examine their genealogies in depth so as to arrive at common ancestry. Naturally such a discovery had real significance—much more than the declaration of common clanhood. Such a discovery was usually the basis for concluding, according to a Fang formula, "We are of one stomach" (*Bi ne abum da*) or "We are of a common birth" (*Bia nye bi ne ebial*), phrases which lent feelings of mutuality to the relationship. The ndan ayong was taught early and remembered perfectly, for not only was it the central source of identity, it had survival value. In more recent years, lacking this function, knowledge of the genealogy deteriorated.

Fang genealogies averaged fifteen generations in depth. Some ran over twenty and some offered only ten names. Northern Fang (Ntumu) had deeper genealogies, up to thirty names,[1] probably due to their greater stability. The more rapid migration and turmoil to which southern Fang were subject may have cut down their genealogies. The length of the lists might seem unusual. It is usually assumed that the longer the genealogy, the greater the sense of segmentary organization. "We might expect long genealogies to be found in these systems where corporate lineages provide the central political framework of the total structure. . . ."[2] This expectation of corporate structure was not realized among Fang in the twentieth century, though the length of genealogies as well as surviving grouping concepts at various levels may well be vestiges of a fully corporate lineage structure.

Fang genealogies contained a more or less accurate historical portion, increasingly in dispute, and a deeper portion for which there was little historical knowledge and in which mythological process took over. We can show this by examining in some detail two genealogies: that of Ayang Ndong, the observer of the action, of clan Essisis, Village Etsam, District of Medounou, and that of Ngema Mvé, the mienlam, clan Bukwe of Assok Ening, District of Oyem.

Ndong Zamé	22	
Bukwé Ndong	21	
Obwobo Bukwé	20	Sokom Mbongwé
Bewue Obwobo	19	Zui Zokom
Nso Bewue	18	Mpwa Zui
Abwokon Nso	17	Mebege Mpwa
Ndono Abwokon	16	Zame ye Mebege
Entraba Ndono	15	Mbele Zame
Azeme Entraba	14	Mvomo Mbele
Mvina Azeme	13	Edzogo Mvomo
Bé Mvina	12	Moburo Edzogo
Zogo Bé	11	Minkwé Moburo
Biwia Zogo	10	Mekina Minkwé
Nsumu Biwia	9	Ekwikwi Mekina
Mvé Nsumu	8	Ongondena Yekwikwi
Ebu Mvé	7	Wimelena Ongondena
Ndekwe Ebu	6	Abo Wimelena
Oyé Ndekwa	5	Nkogo Lena Abo
Mba M'Oye	4	Ndong Mkogo Lena
Ndong Mba	3	Esogo Ndong
Mvé Ndong	2	Ndong Esogo
Ngema Mvé	1	Ayang Ndong

In Fang custom each man bore the given name of his father, Mve, as well as his own given name, Ngema or Ayang.

The history of a clan's migrations was associated with the genealogy. But as time passed it became increasingly difficult to correlate migration stages and genealogical generations. That is, not every ancestor on the genealogical list was associated with a specific village site. More than one ancestor might be represented at one village site or one ancestor might have been responsible for several moves. Well-remembered ancestors, moreover, might not be represented in any genealogy later recited because their line had died out and they had no descendants to recite their name. Thus two names, Ekaba Nso and Mba Ngwe, well remembered in the Bukwe clan and associated, respectively, with the primordial symbolic experience of Fang at Azapmboga in the Cameroons and with defense against the oban invasion, appear in none of the twenty genealogies that I gathered from contemporary Bukwe in central and northern Gabon. Ekaba Nso's brother appears seventeenth on the list while Mba Ngwe appears through no fraternal connection. Sometimes ancestors might be remembered by a "nom d'encouragement" (eyôle mebara) rather than by a given genealogical name.*¹

In association with this genealogy, but not in direct association, the Bukwe of Oyem remembered fourteen different "village sites" (elik, belik). Four of these sites were in the Cameroons, two were in the present Rio Muni, and the eight remaining living sites were in the present Gabon. Very little, if anything, was remembered of the living sites or their inhabitants in the Cameroons or Rio Muni. The first five names in the genealogy were associated with the last eight village sites, though there was considerable debate as to the specifics of association. The difference of opinion was strongest as regards the first three living sites in Gabon.

Fifteen years may be taken as an average length of habitation of one village site, though in more recent years colonial pressures and coastal attractions quickened the pace of movement. A generation may be taken as 25 years. Clan presence in Gabon from these estimates would be some 120 years. If we include the Rio Muni sojourns, the figure for residence south of the Ntem (the demarcation line between Gabon and the Cameroons) would be 150 years. Arrival in the general area where the representatives of the clan now live would have been around 1800. In contrast to many Fang genealogies which conclude with that ancestor who founded the clan at Azapmboga, Ngema's genealogy takes us four generations past the Azapmboga experience to the founder of the Ndong clan of which Bukwe was a derivative clan. Ndong was represented as the "son of the son of God" (Zame), thus, Ndong Zame. This final apotheosis of the clan by claim upon divine establishment was a frequent conclusion to clan genealogies. In the second genealogy, that of Ayang Ndong, the last five generations were all divinities. In fact, they constituted the "genealogy ancestral to God himself" and were thus ndan Zame.*²

Except in the beginning of this long Bukwe genealogy where Bukwe, as the derivative clan, forms out of Ndong, there is no testimony as to the

---

*¹ Fang men could carry as many as five names: the name (eyole) given to them in their father's clan (those names listed in the genealogy); the name given in their mother's clan and used on visits there; a "courage name" (eyole mebara) given to praise and to strengthen the individual in the face of challenges, and a locutionary or drum name which might or might not be different from the eyole mebara. Also, a secret name could be given in the men's societies. For a brief discussion, see A. Panyella and J. Sabater, Esquema de la anthroponimia Fang de la Guinea española desde el punto de vista etnológico.

*² The more common form of this ndan: Zame ye Mebege, Mebege Nsame, Nsame Mbongwe, Mbongwe Sokome, Sokome Nkwa (J. W. Fernández and P. Bekale, "Christian Acculturation and Fang Witchcraft," p. 258). The custom of tracing genealogies back to God may owe something to Trilles (and other missionaries) who invented his own genealogy and following a biblical model, traced it triumphantly back to God (Totemism, p. 5).

formation of any other derivative clans. The genealogy, insofar as there is
any evidence, demonstrates an impressive continuity of clan identity. It carries
back, once again taking a generation as 25 years, 500 years. This, according
to genealogical legend, is 100 years before Azapmboga. These deeper time
estimates, however, are not as trustworthy as the more immediate estimates
of arrival across the Ntem river from Cameroons.

The fact remains that the continuity in this genealogy in respect to derivative
clans is unusual. In contrast, one should consider the historical testimony
contained in the genealogy of Essisis. This genealogy was fifteen generations
deep. It was associated with the recollection of twenty-one different living
sites, a significantly more detailed list than Bukwe. Four of these sites were
in the Cameroons and included Azapmboga, two were in northern Gabon,
three in northern Rio Muni, and the remaining twelve in southern Rio Muni
and north-central Gabon. As the local lineages of this clan had seen great
shifting about in more recent years, the congruence of this genealogical evidence with that of clan Bukwe as to the length of time Fang were present in
northern Gabon and Rio Muni is closer than would appear: between 150 to
175 years, or since 1800.

Bound up in the Essisis genealogy is the recollection, however, of a matrix
clan splitting into a number of derivative clans. According to the genealogist,
Ayang Ndong, the original name of this clan was Mobum.[3] At the time of
its arrival across the Ntem into the region of the present-day Bitam, Oyem
and Minvoul lineage fission produced derivative clans. This took place over
a period of years and in a series of different moves. The derivative clans were
Essisis, Essabang, Essosim, and Essanjol. Thus:

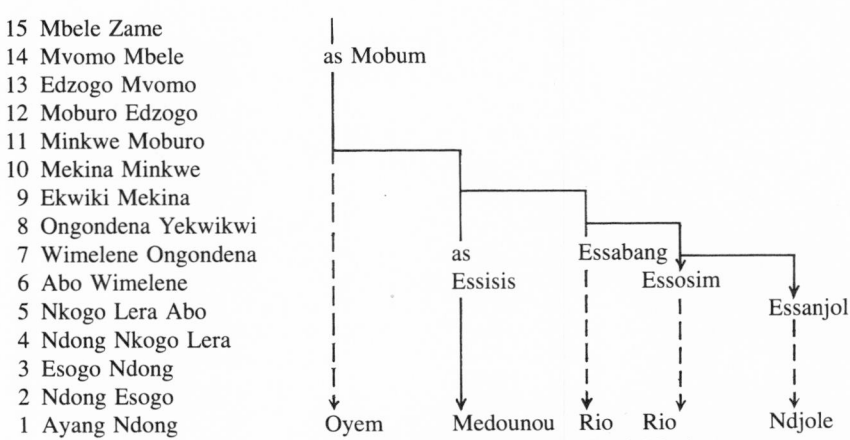

3.1 Mobum Derivative Clans

By mid-century all the derivative clans were widely separated in Gabon and Rio Muni, and they were all larger than the matrix clan, Mobum, which was found only in several small villages south of Oyem. Ayang Ndong, in looking at the past, saw a process of gradual fission of derivative clans from matrix clans. This image would seem to conform more closely to historical fact and to analytic schemes employed by other students of Fang.[4] Nevertheless, many genealogical accounts testify to a process of spontaneous fission occurring at one point in time. This account of sudden and simultaneous dispersion conforms more closely to Fang feelings about the explosive potentiality of conflict within any local group. And indeed no major dispute would have been recognized as such without threats from the parties concerned to move away from each other.

In Ayang Ndong's genealogical knowledge there were problems which were common to Fang genealogies. It was difficult for him to relate migration stages and village sites to names in the genealogy. Ayang Ndong could generally provide names for the headmen of the various ancestral villages, and he could readily locate these villages geographically (with the exception of the Cameroons sites). But relatively few of these names appeared in his own genealogy. Thus one of the principle ancestors of Essisis, a name associated with the foundation of the clan, Mebung Mba, was not found in the genealogy. Yet when the Essisis hunted or raided in the old days, they recited, at crucial moments, the name of this powerful ancestor in order to insure good fortune. The failure of Mebung Mba to appear in the genealogy, according to Ayang Ndong, was due to the fact that he had no surviving male children. His daughter Mekina Minkwe, who gave birth to several "village children," was included in the genealogy in his place. Though women were sometimes included in the genealogical lists, this explanation seems difficult to reconcile with the data.[*3] The facts seem to be that at the depth of the genealogy where this problem occurred no exact knowledge was recollected. Legendary interpretations took over. This made it very difficult to reconcile one set of images about the past (as contained in genealogies) with another (as contained in legendary accounts of migration).

These two lists may be taken as a sample of the range of Fang genealogies.

[*3] The "village children" (mwan adzal) explanation is acceptable. Fang family heads such as Ngema, should their wives give them no male heirs, might actually reject offers of marriage payment and encourage their mature daughters to bear children in the village. The children would most often be included in their own line as their own children. If the daughter was included, she would be given her father's given name as her own surname. This does not occur in the genealogy examined here for if it was Mebung Mba's daughter who continued the line by bearing "village children," she should have the same surname as he. The explanation seems, therefore, factitious. As unusual as it may seem for patrilineal genealogies to bear female names, this could sometimes happen, as Panyella and Sabater have noted (*Esquema*, pp. 78-79). There are various explanations: the customs of "village children"; the right of clan sisters to "marry" women for the benefit of their patrilineage, etc.

They suggest that the past was structured as follows: Level 1 (1-6 generations) of fairly detailed historical knowledge (nkande) of ancestry and migration events; Level 2 (6-12 generations) of some historical detail but inconsistent with other data, i.e., historical-legendary materials having to do with the origin of derivative clans; Level 3 (12-18 generations) the legendary period (Cameroons and Azapmboga), "which is less detailed, often symbolic hearsay information, nlang ayong, as to the founding of matrix clans and the principal subgroups of Fang"; Level 4 (18-plus generations) the mythological period where the primordial experiences of Fang as one people are expressed symbolically in "creation and origin legends" (*nlang Zame*). These four levels in the structure may be diagrammed as shown on p. 82.

As one retreated with the genealogy further into the past the names of ancestors were more and more likely to have drifted into symbolic forms founded upon praise or courage names, plays on words, or popular etymology. Thus, in the Essisis genealogy the ancestress Mekina Minkwe may very well have taken or been given a name by virtue of some real or putative origin from the Meke or southeastern branch of Fang.

The possibility raised in this genealogy that one ancestor was to be traced to the Meke branch of Fang brings into focus a common error in discussing Fang migration into Gabon. Practically all students treat the different subgroups, usually called tribes,[*4] as if they were discrete and homogenous entities. For purposes of presentation here, I consider Fang as having the following six "tribal" divisions: Ntumu, Okak, Fang proper or Fang-Fang, Mvae, Betsi, and Meke. But the matter is not so simple. For example, Largeau speaks of the Betsi migration down the left bank of the Como, the Fang (Fang proper) migration down the right bank and down the Abanga, and the Meke migration down the Okano, the MVoung, and Ivindo.[5] Later, however, he discusses the mixing together of Meke and Betsi as the former, migrating down the Ogowe river, pass up its tributary, the Abanga, where it flows very close to the Como and Betsi country. The Betsi take this same route to pass

---

[*4] Largeau (*Encyclopédie pahouine*, p. 658) equates the term tribe with the ayong, generally called clan. Largeau's usage is also seen in S. Alcobe and A. Panyella (*Estudio*, p. 54) who consider such divisions as Meke and Okak as polytribal groupings. Trilles (*Totemism*, pp. 15-17) initially identifies the tribe with the ayong and refers to the Betsi-Meke division as groupings of the clans (mfulan meyong). But later in his discussion, he falls into the habit of speaking of the ayong as the clan, reserving tribe for the Meke, Betsi, etc. Alexandre and Binet (*Le Groupe*, p. 44) draw the distinction made here. The question is vexing because Fang had no generally recognized concept for the Okak-Meke level of grouping. Some referred to fellow tribesmen as mvuma. In the usage here, tribe is a multi-clan grouping which possesses a name but for which no clear concept exists. The Fang clan, in contradistinction, is here defined as all those who trace descent through the male line to a common ancestor, usually the founder of the clan. As seen below, it was necessary to distinguish between matrix and derivative clans. Derivative clans recognizing common ancestry might group themselves together as ayom. The term nyiayong (mother clan) could be used for the matrix clan.

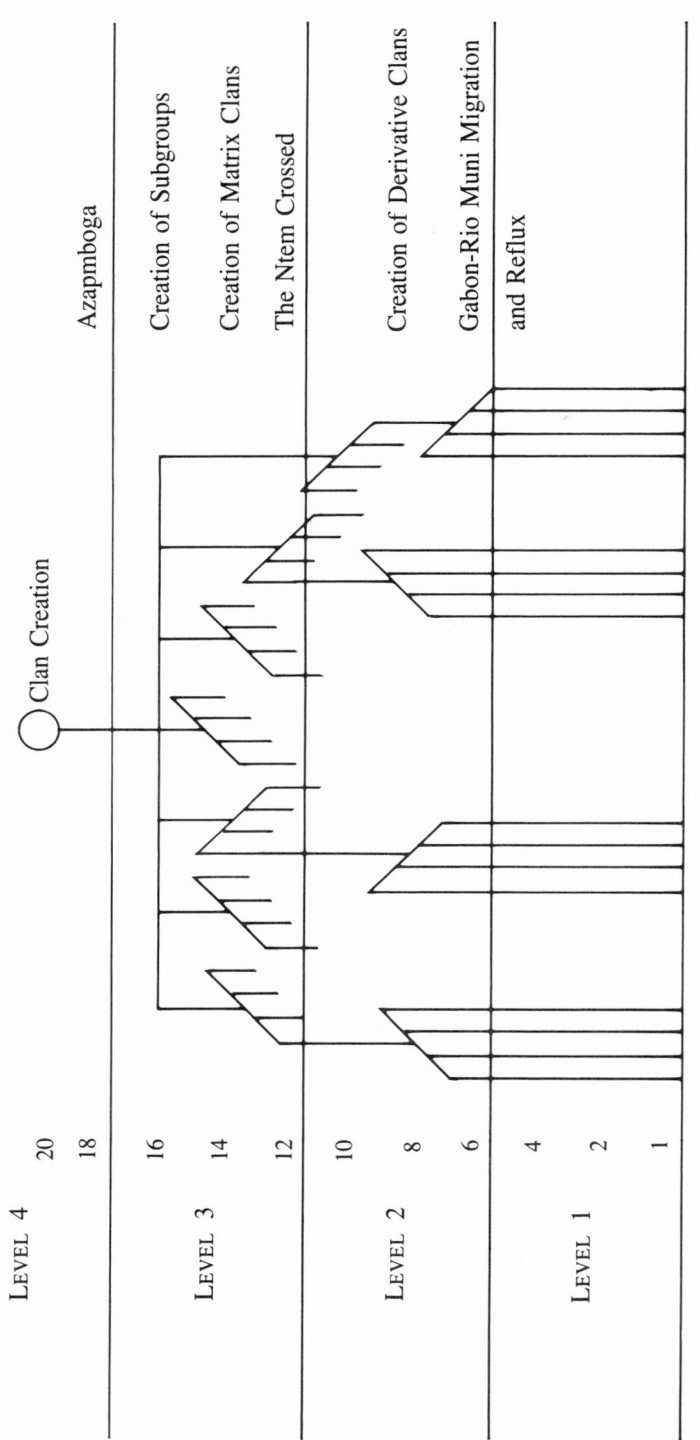

LEVEL 4   20
           18

LEVEL 3   16

           14

           12

LEVEL 2   10

           8

           6

LEVEL 1   4

           2

           1

Azapmboga

Creation of Subgroups

Creation of Matrix Clans

The Ntem Crossed

Creation of Derivative Clans

Gabon-Rio Muni Migration

and Reflux

Clan Creation

3.2 Structuring of the Fang Past

down the Abanga to the Ogowe and mix with the Meke. Largeau elsewhere
mentions villages which have migrated very long distances from one subgroup
area into another.[6]

From Largeau's own data, then, there is good reason to conclude that the
tribe was not a discrete and homogeneous entity, even though he treats it as
such. In fact, the study of genealogical histories shows how volatile and hard
to define these tribes were in respect to constancy of membership.

First, it is difficult to delineate tribal boundaries. There was usually a
penumbra zone, as in Bukwe villages south of Oyem, where as many families
claimed membership with Ntumu as with Fang proper. In the district where
the Essisis village of Ayang Ndong was located, due to the confluence of
Meke and Betsi on the Como, there were as many who claimed themselves
Meke as Betsi and Fang proper. The Spanish Guinea border tended to impose
a sharp distinction between Okak and Betsi-Meke-Fang, however, and testifies
to the influence of colonial political boundaries on tribal relations.

Second, one cannot think of these tribes as being composed of separate
sets of clans, for while there were clans specifically associated with some
tribes—this was particularly true of the Meke—most clans, due to the turmoil
of Fang migration, were widely dispersed and represented in the various
tribes. Even when clans were largely confined to one subgroup, these clans
remembered their matrix clan origins in other tribal areas. Among the Meke
who conceived of themselves as derived from the Bulu, the Ntumu, and the
Betsi, most clans, according to Galley, remembered their matrix clan of origin
in these other tribes.[7] Thus the Essensop were originally Angonemvel; Ebibam
were Esinzoi; Ebimum were Esokeng; Ebito were Esibem and Esindukh;
Ebisa were Esoden, and so on. We have seen this preserved knowledge of
the matrix clan of origin in the case of both Bukwe and Essisis. The wide
dispersal of clans is easily shown by drawing up the generally accepted tribal
boundaries and then tracing, only partially, the dispersal of the two clans
whose genealogies have been examined—see the figures on pp. 84-85.

Given this dispersal we might instead ask what Fang talked about when
they spoke of the Betsi, or the Okak. They talked almost exclusively about
regional distinctions, with overtones of invidious and ethnocentric comparison. For example, Ntumu of Oyem, when discussing Okak, mentioned differences in speech, degrading eating habits, uncleanliness, and a permissive-
ness toward brother-sister incest.[8] Reference was also made to the particular
climate or topography of the tribe's zone of habitation. When speaking of
Mvae or Betsi they might speak of a strong Pygmy influence upon their
customs and their physical type. But this tribal ethnocentrism was rarely
carried to the extreme of xenophobia because early or late in their genealogy
the speakers realized that their clan brothers were represented among the
Okak, Mvae, or Betsi. All three tribes were not only tied together by common
origin at Azapmboga, but in the turmoil of clan dispersion and in the divi-

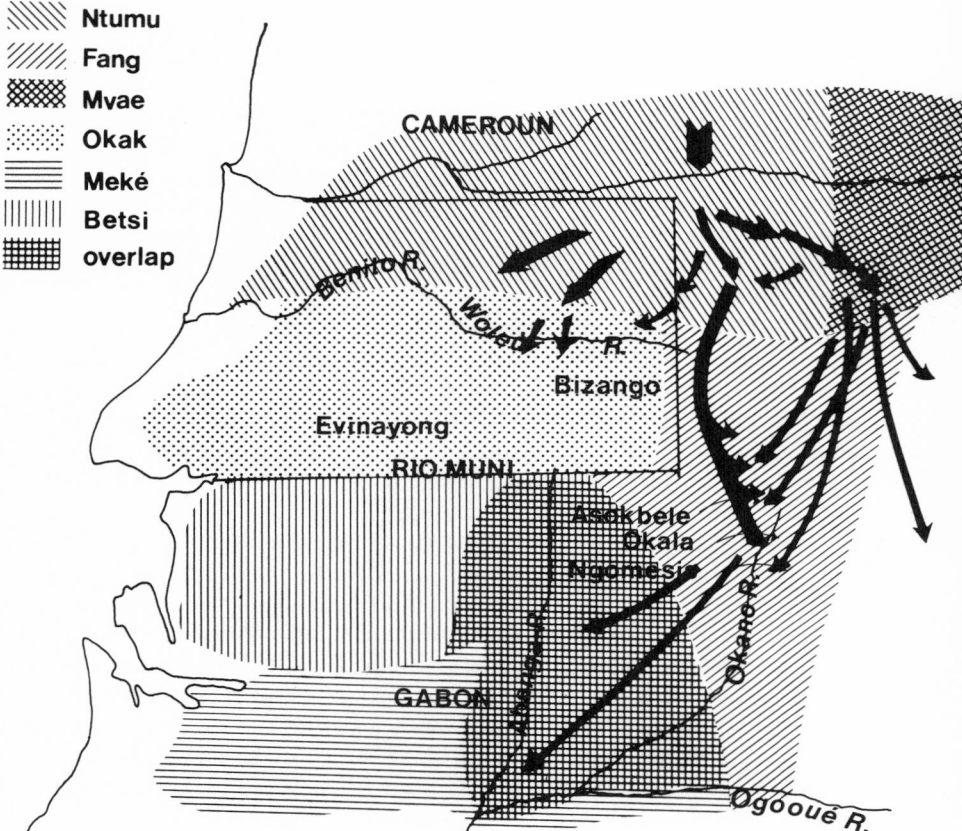

3.3 Fission of Clan Ndong Bukwe

siveness of migration they had been related over and over again. Any very marked cultural distinction was thus prevented from arising.

Whereas it is supposed that territorial contiguity is one of the basic criteria for defining a cultural unit such as a tribe,[9] the dynamics of clan dispersion among Fang meant that the insularity of their "tribes" was constantly being breached by the penetration of lineage segments from other tribes. Over time the natural process was for these enclaves to take over the cultural and linguistic identity of the tribe with whom they were living. As the riddle used here in the chapter epigraph states, the clan genealogy was a tree whose roots extended into all parts of the land.

Such facts caution against too simple a view of migration. The notion that there was a steady migration southwestward is countered by evidence of reflux and return.[10] Of course, since the establishment of the European presence in

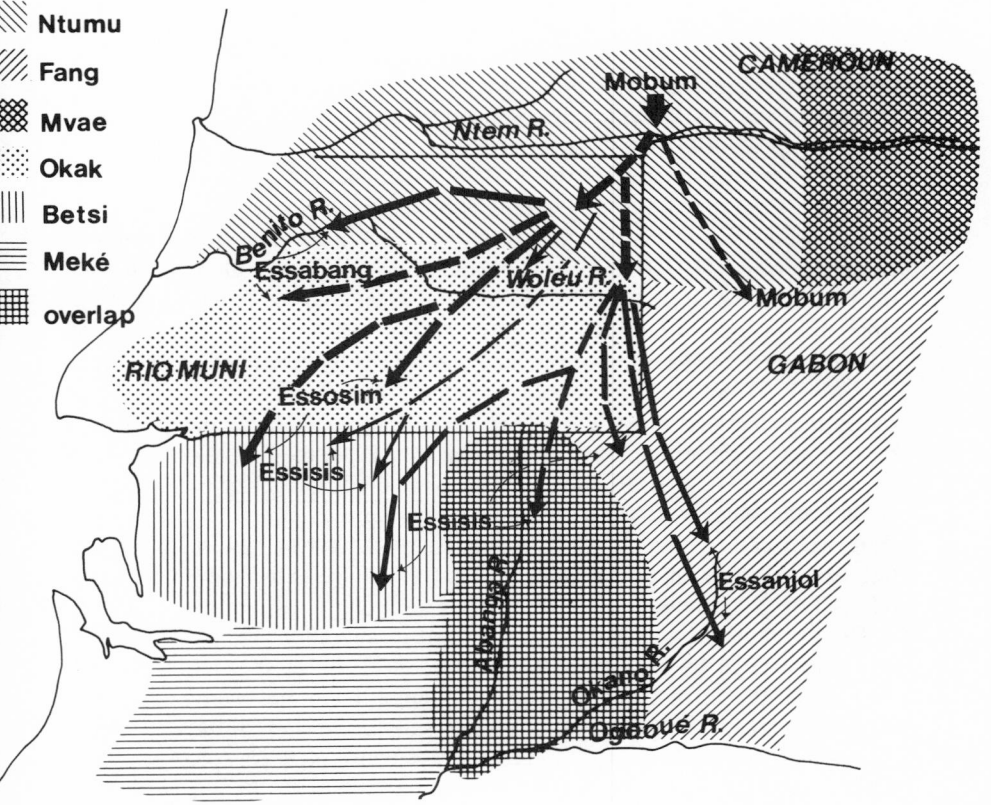

3.4 Fission of Great Clan Mobum

the Gabon Estuary in 1840, the overall pressure toward the south is undeniable. But both genealogies which have been considered here at length make reference to segments, three in the case of Bukwe and one in the case of Essisis, which had located much further south toward the Ogooué and which had then returned north to rejoin those from whom they had originally separated. Occasionally, dispersed segments would reunite, as Figure 3.3 makes clear. Evidence of a reflux north on a larger scale than individual villages and minor lineages is found after the oban raids of the 1880's and 1890's.

Here, too, the caution previously exercised with respect to the phrase "conquérants en disponibilité" is in order. To Fang the sense of the nearer past arose out of a framework of genealogical and associated knowledge which showed such constant and often confusing dispersion as to belie that overall feeling of massive clan or tribal organization implied in the term "conquérants." Asked to comment upon the reasons for migration and the constant village displacement Fang rarely gave conquest or pursuit of the conquered as a dominant motive. Many informants remembered the great famines of the 1920's which drove many villages down to the coast simply to obtain foodstuffs.

Various reasons relating to the colonial situation were given for migration and dispersion: the ability to get more for one's money and buy more things in Rio Muni than in Gabon; the absence of corvée labor in one or another colonial territory (its absence in Rio Muni during the early days and particularly during the Spanish Republic, and its absence in the French territories since the *loi cadre* of 1948). The most general reason for the migration of villages was the exhaustion of the land and forests by crops and game. More figuratively, Fang sometimes spoke of that never-ending struggle with the forest and their search for light. They periodically galvanized themselves to make a new assault upon the forests elsewhere. From the late colonial period on, administrative pressures and the commercial advantages of being located along trade routes kept villages fixed for long periods in one location. Thus Fang were denied this periodic reconquest of the forest represented in the frequent changing of village sites. In that sense, perhaps, they were aptly referred to as "conquérants en disponibilité."

The excitement and anticipation involved in migration, the revitalization, was complicated by a nostalgia for "abandoned village sites" (*elik, bilik*). For the old people, especially, whose childhood memories were attached to these abandoned villages, there was great satisfaction in returning. It was a "great blessing" (*abora be Zame*) to return because, as it was phrased, "our afterbirths are buried there" (*bekue bam ba zebe wé*). If the elik was close enough, huts and lean-tos were maintained there to provide shelter for week-long hunting and gathering expeditions. Even if there was no living person who remembered an elik, it was still regarded and visited with emotion, for "our ancestors lived here!" (*bimvama bam be nge bole va*).

In any event, Fang sense of the past, as bound up in their knowledge of a complicated, genealogically anchored history of clan and lineage fission and dispersion, was almost always disturbed by inconsistencies and conflicting versions of the genealogy. In the old days, the frequent reiteration of genealogies and discussion of genealogical knowledge not only acted to preserve and prevent drift in that knowledge but also produced a consensus version of that past. But at mid-century that knowledge was no longer certain, as my discussions with Ndutumu Zogo testified.

Even if there was accuracy and agreement about the first five generations, this left ten or more generations in the genealogy; it was here that legend and myth gave more vivid shape to the distant past. It is not surprising that as uncertainty in genealogical reconstruction increased (that is, with greater depth), there was increased reference to legendary forms. Through such dramatic representation the Fang sought to manipulate those areas of their experience which lay beyond their knowledge. By means of such devices the distant past was made a vivid arena of Fang experience.

FANG IN SOCIAL SPACE

An examination of the various concepts by which Fang social structure was labeled is a convincing demonstration of the uncertainties with which they lived. In recent years there were more labels available than there were entities to apply them to. Social realities had collapsed while a lexicon persisted. Inquiry inevitably produced debate among Fang informants about the meanings and applications of the terms. A highly egalitarian society like that of the Fang, where there were no cognoscenti to homogenize and establish opinion, would naturally show a high degree of individualism. But the differences of opinion in respect to grouping concepts were extraordinary. And Fang were discomfited by these differences. Terminological evidence that clan organization was formerly greater, coupled with present ambiguities about the application of terms, convinced many that their social affairs were in a vestigial state. Largeau noted this feeling at the turn of the century. It was a feeling of being a scattered people and of needing to reunite and reorganize.[11] Sometimes this sense of disorganization, as seen in the Whiteman-Blackman tales, was ascribed to moral failings. Other times it was regarded matter-of-factly, and pragmatic remedies were sought.

Discussion of the grouping concepts makes clear the disorganization and vestigial quality of the clan structure. One consequence of this was the emergence of the individual from within the state of corporate identity.[12] There were many forces accounting for this emergence. The introduction of cash crops, which, since the late twenties, had been extensive among Fang Ntumu of the Woleu-Ntem, and labor migration to the lumber camps among Fang (Meke and Betsi) of the Ogooué had produced an economic individualism which weakened the corporate claims of the various lineage segments. Missionaries also had as a main object the disentanglement of the African from what they felt to be the toils of fetishism. The doctrine of the soul's unique relationship to Deity was preached with the special intent of weaning the individual away from this allegiance and creating the consciousness of self as a religious subject. Also promoting individuation were the laws of the colonial governments, with their refusal to recognize corporate, that is, lineage, obligations in exaction of vengeance and the collection of blood debts.

The impact of this individuation can be seen in a scheme used by Fang, responding to inquiry, to model their kin system. This contrasts with the usual anthropological model. For example, a model most often employed by anthropologists centers ego within the expanding universe of his relatives ascendant and descendant, lineal and collateral, consanguinal and affinal. He (ego) is embraced at the very heart of the kinship structure.

In villages of the Woleu-Ntem, Fang informants employed a different convention, using straw, to demonstrate on the ground the operation of various kinship and grouping concepts. They started from themselves as ego and built a chart of relatives downward in descending generations. The past was only prologue, and these men were oriented, it would seem, to the possibilities of descendants sufficient to promote their status and preserve their name. This preoccupation with progeny may first relate to the fact that in a society of ancestor worship, descendants were the final guarantee of a man's status and, moreover, in the dynamics of Fang kin groups, the amount of authority a man was conceded depended very often on the number of children he could successfully raise—upon his biological fitness, in other words. This kinship chart convention may well express these facts as much as the increasing individualism emphasized here.

But these kinship charts laid out with straw upon the ground arose, as far as I know, only in the situation of ethnographic inquiry. A more culturally ingrained image which appeared when discussing matters of lineage and kin was that of the chest, arm, hand, and extended fingers. This was a frequently encountered metaphor of social structure. A generation among Fang, that is, all those of roughly the same age, was called *zong* (joint or point of articulation). It might be asked, for example, in tracing the relationship between lineages: "That man is mvamayong to us, how many generations (joints) does he stand to us?" (*Mot a ne bia mvamayong a nto biyong tang ya?*). Since the identification between the joints of the body and the points of generational articulation in the lineage was already made, it is easy to see how the clan itself was represented as rising in the chest or the heart (as the riddle suggests) and as spreading out through one or both arms to its contemporary representatives, the fingertips (Figure 3.5). Depending on the way of counting joints, seven to eighteen generations could be represented in this Fang metaphor of corporateness. The metaphor may seem strange, but the association between body parts and parts of the social structure was found also in traditional Europe.[13] It is not only among Fang that the body microcosm was projected upon the social macrocosm. In particular, the chest (*nkuk*) was a metaphor of social thought. Corporeally the chest was the source of human vitality, the vitality of the clan founder.

An analytic model developed for the northern Fang (Ntumu) clan structure is that of the Spanish ethnographers Panyella and Sabater[14] (Figure 3.6). It is analogous to the chest to fingertip metaphor, employing four grouping concepts to flesh out Fang social time and space. Each of these concepts expresses a gradation in the clan structure. In decreasing order of scale the authors give the following concepts: *etungabot*, translated as "estirpe" or

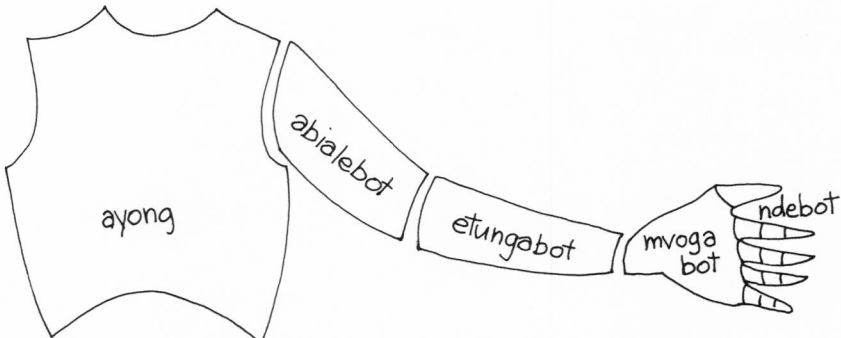

3.5 Body-Kin Category Conceptualization

stock; *ayomabot* or lineage; *mvogabot* or village family (people of the village), and the *nda-bot* (*ndébôt*) or house family. The extent of application of the terms is given as well as the founder, male or female, to which each gradation is traced.

But there was more ambiguity in this matter than the scheme makes clear. The authors say, for example, that the ndebot and the mvogabot are both traced to females, while the ayom and the etunga are traced to males. This practice, however, varied greatly, and any grouping level, with the exception of that of the clan, could be traced to a female. In our own research in ten clans in Gabon and Rio Muni, and within twenty-two different ndebot, the largest proportion of cases—nine ndebot—traced the ndebot to a female founder, the mvogabot to a male founder. Intermediate groupings between the mvogabot and the clan were traced to a female and the clan was traced to a male.

Though Fang were a patrilineal, patrilocal people in which the lineage was perpetuated by its male members, and though, in principle, they excluded women from participation in lineage affairs, still, as we have seen, female names could appear in the genealogy. So the tendency to associate the various grouping concepts with males and females alternatively, regardless of cognatic status, is not surprising. In a significant proportion of cases, it should be remarked, the filiation was complementary. The ndebot traced their key parentage to a woman, and the mvogabot to a man. Beyond that the abialebot, people of a common birth, traced themselves to a woman and the clan, ayong, to a man.

The clan concept imposed exogamy and other forms of figurative fraternity. But it was not otherwise institutionalized in the colonial era. The ndebot and the mvogabot were the crucial groupings of northern Fang patrilineages.[15] Though a number of concepts existed for groups beyond the level of the mvogabot, they were only vestigial and did not function in either clan politics

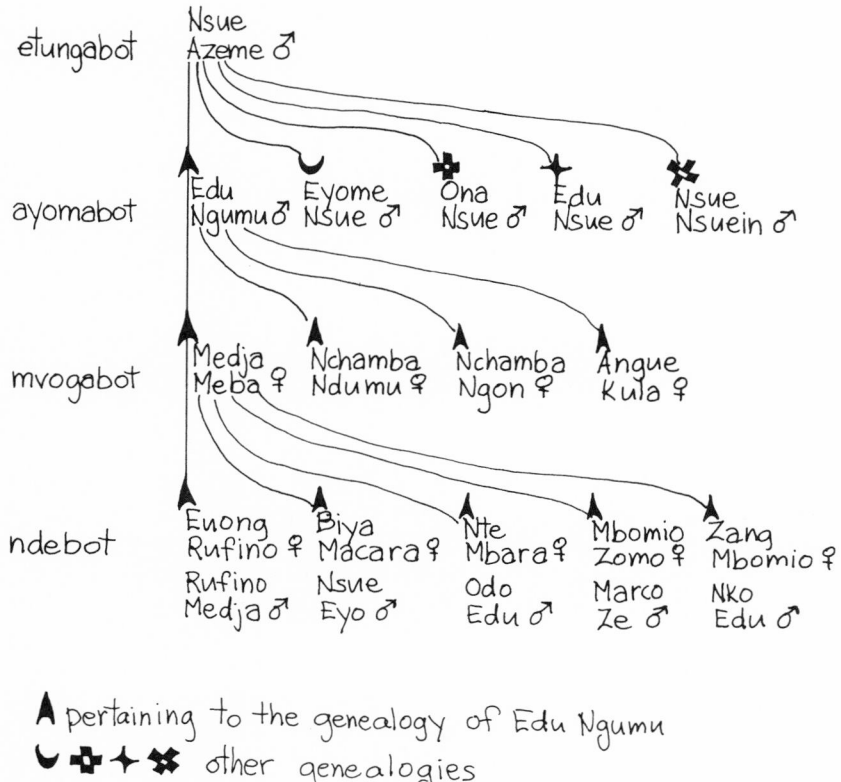

A pertaining to the genealogy of Edu Ngumu
ᴗ ✚ ✦ ✖ other genealogies

3.6 Grouping Levels (following Panyella and Sabater)

or the religious life, such as these were. The effective minimal segment of
the lineage was the ndebot. It consisted of an *ntôlmot* (senior or oldest man),
his uterine brothers and their wives and the children, sometimes married
children, or all of these. The ndebot took its name from the woman out of
whose womb it was said to have come. It was known, for example, as Nda
Ada Ndong. Its cohesion arose from this uterine origin. Thus in the southern
Woleu-Ntem, District of Mitzik, among local Bukwe villages the three ndebot
present (Figure 3.7) carried the names of women. These were the three wives
of Zomo Okuru, the founder of the mvogabot of which all these ndebot were
a part. Such women could be generationally as far removed as a great-
grandmother (*mvivimvama*) if for one reason or another, such as low fertility
combined with effective leadership, the inevitable fissiparous tendencies were
resisted over several generations. The "founder" of the ndebot, on the other
hand, might sometimes be a living old woman.

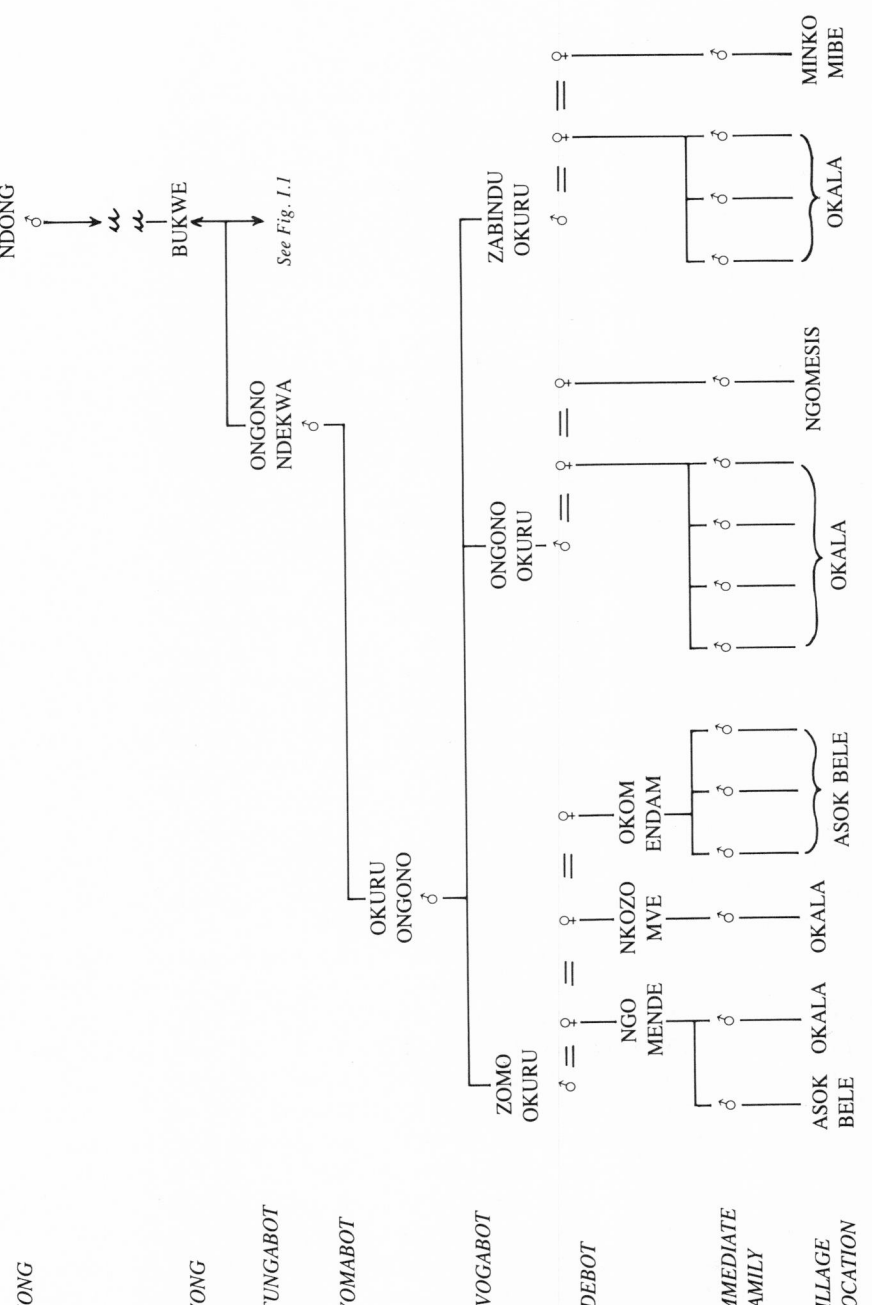

3.7 Grouping Concepts as Applied by Mitzik Bukwe

During the colonial period, ndebot sometimes lived in villages (*azal*) which were independent of each other. But characteristically they were grouped with others of their kind into a town (*nlam* or *mvog*) and into the kin grouping of next greater span, the mvogabot or "people of the town." For most purposes, this was the effective maximal segment among Fang. Towns characteristically possessed two mvogabot who lived in the two rows of huts opposite each other. The town was the natural residence context and Fang usually responded to the inquiry "*wa sô ve*" or "*wa ké ve*" ("where are you going" or "where are you coming from") by naming the town—"*me ka mvôg*" or "*ma sô nlam.*" Reference to the azal was unusual. Moreover the town, unlike the village, usually had a proper name: Akurnam (village of folly—from *akut*).

The mvogabot took its name from the man who had founded it or who, in a later generation, in a situation of fission or reintegration, could be assigned founder status. To speak of a man as a founder was to imply an intention on his part that was surely present in all fit Fang men, but it ignores the vicissitudes of subsequent fertility and family life. In the dynamics of lineage formation, a man might be chosen a generation or so later as a founder who himself perceived no such possibility. The mvogabot name was frequently employed. At the moment of circumcision, for example, it was the name of the founder of his mvogabot that was recited in the child's ear as a "name of encouragement," by the nyamoro (full member of the lineage) holding him.

Ideally, the founder of the mvogabot was the husband of the various women who gave birth to its constituent ndebot. In Figure 3.7, Zomo Okuru is such a man. The founding father of the mvogabot, like the mother of the ndebot, was thus located genealogically from two to four generations in depth, though he could have been a living old man. But once again, by virtue of vicissitudes in the rate of reproduction and solidarity in ascendents, a mvogabot might persist for many generations. One or more ndebot from within this enduring mvogabot might assert itself as a new mvogabot.

The degree to which an actual situation might depart from the prevailing structural definitions of a mvogabot and a ndebot can be shown in the village of Assok Ening itself and in respect to the family of Mba M'Oye. In the first place, the mvogabot was found in two different villages distantly separated. Thus the members of the group were not "people of the town" in any real sense. In the second place, there were only two "council houses" for all the representatives of that mvogabot in Assok Ening, although there were at least two ndebot which could be identified as descendant to Mba M'Oye by reference to his wives, and a third emerging as indicated in Figure 3.8. In the third place, the people of Assok Ening used the term ndebot variably. When they were feeling particularly united, they referred to the entire mvogabot as an ndebot. But often enough they referred to every mature man with his wives and sons and their wives and children as constituting an ndebot. In this town the ndebot was referred less to founding women than elsewhere. By a defi-

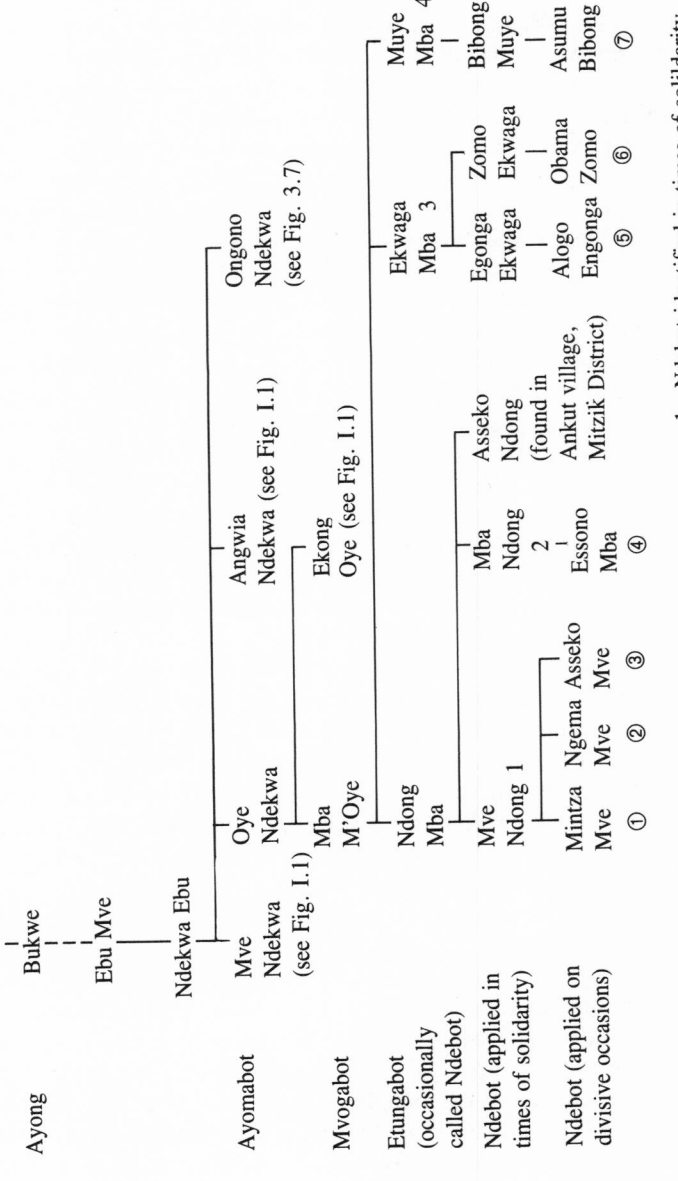

3.8 Grouping Concepts in Assok Ening Village

nition such as this which referred to every mature man as a founder, there would be seven ndebot in Mba M'Oye as seen Figure 3.8. These would be the ndebot of Mintza Mve, Ngema Mve, Asseko Mve, Essono Mba, Alogo Engonga, Obama Zomo, and Asumu Bibong.

The degree of variability in Fang definitions of these concepts makes it difficult to arrive at a settled definition for even the most salient and functional groupings, mvogabot and ndebot. Ayang Ndong of Essisis even claimed that, in the past, the term mvogabot was a term of disrespect, and that to say that someone was mvog with you implied a state of strife. The term *essabot*, he argued, was more common, for its meaning, "people of a common father," emphasized the common paternity at some point in time of all those in the town. Beyond the level of the mvogabot Ayang Ndong used other terms than the ayomabot concept singled out by Panyella and Sabater (Figure 3.6). For example, he referred to *mvongabot* (people of a common seed) and *abialebot* (people of a common birth) and *nzangabot* (people of a common origin).

The term *etungabot* illustrates the variability. For the majority of informants it was defined as that group of patrilineally related people of the same clan who had not forgotten the specifics of their relationship but who found themselves living in two different clan territories, *etun ayong* (clan segments) or *afan ayong* (clan forest). These separated brethren would describe themselves as being etunga. And yet other informants used this term to describe all the patrilineally related people who lived within the same territory, regardless of whether they were closely related or not. In this view, if they were of the same clan and if the hazards of dispersion and migration had thrown them together again, they were etunga.

And in still other contexts etunge was simply understood as those who were members of any segment of the social system the speaker had in mind. Because of increasing uncertainties in the range of application and the contextual character of these terms it is not surprising that many Fang accepted with alacrity the French rubric "famille," in preference to any of their former terms. This term had for Fang a convenient vagueness of reference which covered over the many complications of their traditional terms about whose usage there was so much disagreement.[16]

PRINCIPLES OF COMPLEMENTARITY AND VITALITY

We have treated the increased diversity that characterized the grouping concepts in some detail because it is important to understand the conceptual uncertainties of this vestigial system of Fang kin groupings. If these uncertainties put pressure on Fang thought to adopt simplified rubrics like the French "famille," they could also eventuate in such recreations of kinship between the living and the dead as occurred in the Bwiti religion. Despite the uncertainties of the complex conceptual situation we have described, there are certain underlying principles with which any recreative or revitalizing effort has to work—simplicities on the other side of the conceptual complexity. One of these principles is complementarity as seen in complementary filiation. Another principle is that of ambiguous possibility which results from the collapse of complementarity and out of which arises the possibility of fission.

The complementary filiation itself was an expression of the fact that in these unilineal descent groups among Fang, ideas and feelings of integration and divisiveness could be conceptualized on the basis of uterine and nonuterine sibling relationships in the polygynous family. Thus, immediate family experience could be extended into the entire patrilineage as a means by which its complexities could be grasped. For example, when two strangers of the same clan met, they might sit down and try to discover where their ancestry was of the same ndebot. They examined genealogy in an attempt to discover a woman from whom they both could be said to have descended. This discovery had great affective import and was the basis for concluding with the formula, "We are of one stomach" (*bi na abum da*). The metaphor grasped at an ultimate bond between men—their birth from one mother. It may be for that reason that though by complementary filiation the clan was recognized as having a paternal origin, the concept of "clan unity" (*abial*)*5 placed emphasis upon common birth. The values of Fang life might be distributed in complementary fashion in social time and space, but there was always the possibility of their assertion in contrasting if not conflicting fashion in the same time and space. The important thing was to maintain complementarity and in that to achieve a fruitful vitality.

The principal connotation of paternal origin was divisiveness, even conflict. The principal connotation of maternal origin was unity and common purpose. These connotations accorded with the nature of the various segmentary groups as they were traced to either a paternal or maternal origin. For as Ayang Ndong said, "the voices of the ndebot are quiet," while "the brothers of the mvogabot shout insults across the courtyard at each other." Any of the possible intermediate groups beyond the mvogabot, though vestigial in this century, were noted for peaceable relations. Men meeting on the level of the ayomabot, for example, seemed always ready to establish the affective bond, "we are of one stomach." The character of the clan founded in the father (*essayong*) was most evident in its division and dispersion.

Still, the ambiguous possibilities for any group must be reiterated. Even within the most solidary group, the ndebot, there was uncertainty and the constant possibility of fission. Often enough in our inquiry, men were hesitant to identify their ndebots, perhaps because of possible imminent fission. As the proverb says, "One house two beds" (*nda dza, binong bibang*). The high

---

*5 This concept of abial (common birth or origin) was often applied to all members of the same clan. The phrase was *bi ne mebiale mebot* (we are all people of a common birth).

degree of solidarity and relatively diffuse and unstructured face-to-face relations that prevailed in the ndebot could not themselves completely overcome
the latent possibilities of fission and the need to maintain complementarity
of the several unnamed groups within the house itself.

Thus, whatever the ordinary solidarity of the ndebot and divisiveness of
the mvogabot, there were latent possibilities in which the solidarity of the
ndebot was threatened and the divisiveness of the mvogabot yet possessed
a certain stability. The fact is that both the condition of uterine origin and the
condition of membership in the group that immediately derives from it were
ambivalently appraised. On one level of awareness, these conditions were
manifestly solidifying. On another and perhaps deeper level, by the very
intensity of interaction that characterized them, they provided the matrix of
division.

But while I believe that these complementarities achieved in the face of
"divisiveness amidst solidarity" and "solidarity amidst divisiveness" were
the vital realities of kin life with which a revitalization religion had to work,
yet a rather more straightforward representation of Fang lineage structure is
possible (Figure 3.9). The depth and the scale of application of the concepts
seem most aptly indicated in this way. We can also see their principal con-

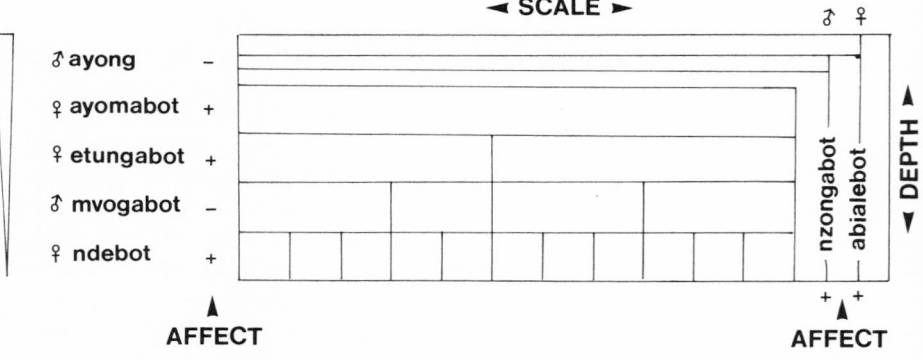

3.9 Grouping Concepts by Scale, Depth, and Affect

notations: positive and negative in respect to the solidarity of the group
described by the term, maleness or femaleness in respect to its derivation and
quality. Even if we wish, however, to assert this as an underlying structure,
we cannot overlook the surface ambiguities and ambivalences. They are the
essential element in the dynamics of lineage affairs and the real challenge to
those who would represent, if not actually establish, order in Fang society.
In the new religion of Bwiti, we will see how an order is suggested, if not
achieved, by a complex structure of images well adapted to overcoming the

uncertainties we have reviewed here: the uncertainties of both fission and fusion in social units, of both mobility and stability, of both maternal and paternal, male and female connotations of kin-group activity.

Conclusion: Familiarization of Social Time and Space

The master idea of Fang life was the genealogy, a ladder of names extending back in time and out in space—a figurative path leading from birth to death, from the newborn down through all the dead. Also central to Fang social thought, although increasingly vestigial and uncertainly conceived, was a ladder of clanship terms of increasingly wider scale of application extending into space. There was a progressive abstraction of both names and terms. The near names and terms were much more closely associated with family experience of which there was direct memory. The far names and terms were necessarily more figurative but not necessarily less vivid, for the extension of personal experience out into legendary time and space could be even more arresting than direct memory.

In respect to the ladder of clan terms, there were three fundamental experiences which Fang extended into the kaleidoscope of interrelationships which was clan life in order to grasp them, to make them familiar. First, there was the experience of their own body which was employed, from heart to fingertip, as a model for genealogy. Second, there was the experience of nuclear family life and the complementarity of maternal and paternal influences, uterine and nonuterine brotherhood, extended into clanship. Finally, there was the experience of the differences between the sexes. This last extension was at work in the assignment of values to the various levels of the clan. One sees there a manipulation of male and female associations in the genealogy which gives evidence of a kind of "experimentation or play of fashion."[17] The consequences were satisfying fictions—the fictions of the corporeality of clanship and of a commonness of birth and a complementary filiation even in very distant relations. Amidst the ambiguities and ambivalences in actual relationships, which was the reality of social life, these metaphoric extensions of primary experiences could provide for Fang some sense of familiarity and order. This was an example of the familiarizing function of metaphor.

Though there is no real proof, it appears that in former days the social order was referred to more clearly and consistently by the grouping concepts. The concepts were less numerous, less overlapping. As that structure became increasingly vestigial and ambiguous, the individual's corporate involvement with it diminished, and his sense of ancestry diminished. His individual identity became an increasing focus of his interest. We find men falling back on generic terms such as the French "famille," or otherwise burdened with a sense of uncertainty and confusion about the social order and their place in it. The names in the genealogy were remembered better than the armature of grouping concepts, but even in the genealogy there was increasing forgetfulness and argument by mid-century.

Whereas incompatible elements of social life, such as paternity and maternity or fission and fusion, had been held in complementary relation, they fell out of that relation and became ever more problematic and unpredictable. Whereas once Fang had riddled, "A tree grows in my father's heart whose roots extend throughout the land," and had been confident of the answer to the riddle, their social order as anchored in the genealogy began more and more to appear a riddle without a solution. Whereas once they had been confident of their belonging to a kin group, they more and more felt like "ntôbot," individuated, wandering men and women without family, who "just came to stay." It was in such a situation that the Bwiti religion appeared. We will see how it offers, to those who felt themselves ntobot, the centered corporate feeling of belonging to the Bwiti kin group. We will see how it provides a path uniting the newborn and the old dead. And we will see how, through the "forest of Bwiti," the religion again extends the roots of Fang experience throughout the land.

ᐧ4ᐧ

Fang Incorporated in
Built Space

Ndok dulu a ne kison mintangen a bezimbi(B).
(The passion for journeying ends in the Whiteman's
towns and in soldiering.)

MBA M'OYE BUILDS A NEW COUNCIL HOUSE

WHEN ESSONO MBA'S SON Bekale Essono came back from Libreville for a
short visit, he mildly insulted the family by telling them that the council house
was the worst of any he had seen in 500 kilometers of road. His mother, who
saw him getting out of the lorry, gave the high-pitched wail—of mourning
or rejoicing—and began a little hopping dance around him. His brothers and
sisters who were nearby, including two in the council house, ran to embrace
him. And the older men got up and went to the entrance of the council house
waiting for their "son" to come and greet them. He came shortly to embrace
them all and shake my hand. He went to put his baggage away and then came
back to tell them of his three years on the coast and his trip home.

It was during that recounting that he chided his elders for the decrepit
council house. It had been standing for more than ten years and had begun
to lean perilously. Even the *akôn aba* (the main post at the front entrance)
was awry, and the gorilla skull, which it was Fang custom to hang there, had
slipped to one side. All this had been debated before. But there had been a
fight between the prime movers in the family, Ngema and Asseko Mve, and
without their support no one else ventured to embark upon the construction.
Besides, the council house as it stood had a kind of ramshackle grandeur as
perhaps befitted the first family of the village. Men still flocked to it. Major
palavers were held there, and it remained the place in which visiting troubadours sang their songs.

But when Ngema heard Bekale Essono's criticism, he saw that the time
had come for the family to build a new council house. He noted that bushes
had been allowed to grow close to the back door. "One day soon," he said,
"the forest will walk right in on us. The family should take more pride in
itself than to allow the council house to collapse in this way. The council
house is the family that strangers see."

It took the family more than two months to lay up materials—liane strips for tying the whole together, wood poles for the superstructure, sheets of thatch, bark for the walls, raffia palm poles in halves, and quarters for benches, walls, and ceilings. The new council house was begun next to the old. The gorilla skull was carefully transferred to the new center post. When a thatch roof had been put up and bamboo benches built so that the new house would seat and protect the men gathered there, the old house was torn down and burned in an hour. Then the laborious work of tying on the walls began. All the family members lent a hand but Ngema Mve did most of the work. He remarked several times that this was the first time he had ever built two council houses in the same village. In the old days Fang changed their village site every ten years or so.

Bekale Essono helped out desultorily with the new council house. He had returned to visit the family and pay some money on a brideprice of a girl he intended to marry. But he was soon to leave for Libreville again and return to his job as a laborer on the docks there. He no longer felt really of the village and it was doubtful that he would return permanently until his old age or until he could find no further work. He intended to take his wife to the coast. Besides, people remembered that Bekale had originally left Assok Ening because of a bitter dispute with his father, who had failed to provide him with a wife from available brideprice monies. Bekale had also been accused of adultery with one of his father's younger wives. Nobody spoke of that during his visit, but nobody forgot it either.

VILLAGES IN THE FOREST

In the last chapter we saw how the social structure had opened up, and how the individual, more and more making his way by his own resources, had become subject to centrifugal influences. Having tried to locate Fang in social time and space we now try to locate them in real space. Centrifugal influences were also at work here. If Fang had an uncertain sense of their place in the social structure, so too they had misgivings about their place in space, and in particular that center space, once powerfully centripetal, of the Fang village.

Coming down from the grasslands and savanna, Fang, long since habituated to a forest life, still tended to regard their villages and plantations as portions of warmth and light that they had succeeded in chopping out of the pervading rain forest, cold and obscure.[1] They often spoke of their struggle with the forest and employed an imagery of conflict. When asked why they so frequently changed the sites of their villages, they responded that the forest which year in and year out they had beaten off had finally gotten the best of them, had crept in upon the village, and would shortly have overwhelmed it. Hence, they galvanized to reestablish themselves anew (*tu adzal*).[2]

This attitude did not preclude an accompanying feeling that they had become a forest people. The version of the tribal name to which they most often subscribed derived it from the name for "forest" (*afan*), making the Fang "people of the forest."[3] The forest as one of the crucial arenas of Fang life aroused complex sentiments. Fang men found their greatest satisfaction in economic activities in the deep forest: hunting, fishing, and wild fruit gathering. At the same time, their idea of the greatest punishment for evil was the transformation of the shade after death into some being (*engungul*) doomed to wander interminably in the furthest, darkest reaches of the forest until finally killed and thus liberated by a hunter. The chimpanzee tales, treat thematically their escape, by using their intelligence, from the dampness and obscurity of the forest to the building of their own villages. After a cold rain when the steam rose in wisps here and there out of the forest, Fang called to their children, "You see the chimpanzees are building fires to warm themselves—miserable cold people of the forest." The forest was cold and alien, a place of adventure both natural and supernatural, no doubt, but one inhabited by forces inimical to man.

The village was contrasted with the forest. It had warmth and light, and most important, it had the activity of man.[4] One of the basic pleasures and greatest sources of prestige for Fang was the production of "pleasurable activity" (*elulua*) in the village, whether by dance or ceremony or the visits of relatives or the arguing of disputes. The means was of less importance than that elulua should exist. Activity dispelled the solitude of the forest and the coldness emanating from it. This activity constituted for Fang the most rewarding manifestation of man's social nature. The village in olden times was the arena of that activity, the focus of the many euphorias of Fang social life. Later villages became backwaters, and the *ndôk dulu* ("the passion for voyages" away from them) became an overmastering impulse and source of malaise in many villages.

The traditional Fang village was a long, narrow rectangle formed very simply by two long rows of continuous raffia and bark huts (*nda, menda*) facing each other across a "cleared central court" (*nsung*) at distances ranging from 5 to as much as 30 meters (see Figure 4.1). In the days of internecine strife the courts were narrow, for the two rows of huts and the men's council house or "corp de garde" (*aba, meba*) at either end provided, with some stockade work, an effective defense perimeter. The length of the village depended on the number of "village families" (*mvôgabot*) which had succeeded in grouping themselves together. The average length was from 100 to 150 meters, but in the reports of Tessmann and other early observers[5] one reads of villages more than a kilometer and a half in length, probably a protective measure taken in very unsettled regions where strife was endemic. It was unusual for Fang to live in such agglomerations. But on the other hand, the very small and scattered villages, often the abode of a single *ndébot*, that appeared during the colonial period represented a degeneration of Fang capacity to group together.

When approached from the tangled banks of the equatorial rain forest, the

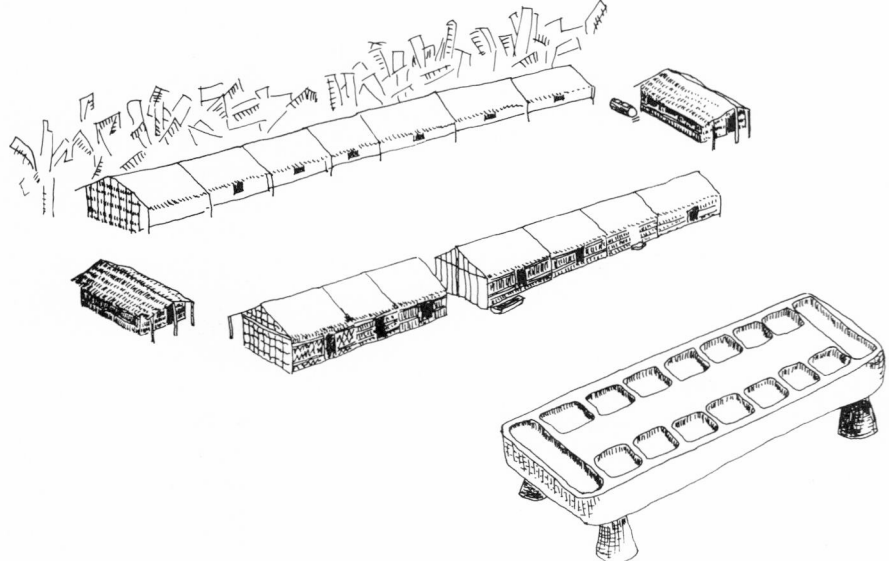

4.1 Fang Village with Mbek Board

Fang village, with its two long rows of huts facing each other across the narrow barren court, provoked in the traveler the immediate impression of opposition. In fact the mvogabot was often defined as those brothers who built opposite each other "the better to shout their insults." In conjunction with the genealogy, Fang remembered and located their former villages according to the nearest stream or river. Every possible tributary had its name, and since their country was a rain forest the watercourses were abundant and Fang mental maps could be very complex. The larger rivers had greater generality of use in most discussions, example in the context of examining migration stages. Such major confluents as the Woleu, the Ntem, the Nyie, and the Obango appeared time and again. But neighboring villages discussed their past and present events with reference to a bewildering variety of rivulets. It was appropriate that the old greeting for a stranger was: "Friend, from what river do you drink?" (*Amui! wa nyu dza ôswí?*)

Fang conceived of particular areas of the great forest as belonging to local segments of clans, but these areas were identified by fluvial coordinates. Thus, the members of clan Bukwe had been associated in the first half of the twentieth century with the headwaters of the Ngoum. Their neighbors the Essangi had been associated with the western forks of the So. To the south, the Nkojen had been associated with the Mvia and the Mekage branch of the Woleu.

Fang knowledge of where they were was largely situational. It was based on knowing at any time where any trail or stream would lead, and hardly ever upon total overviews. They rarely generalized, and this contrasts with the Bwiti religion which in its microcosmogony did take overviews of the largest order. On being asked to discuss these matters Fang would square up a model, usually by reference to watercourses. Thus Essono Mba marked out upon the earth of his courtyard a model of the various *etun ayong* (clan portions), with the major rivers running northeast to southwest to the sea and their tributaries associated with various clan portions (Figure 4.2). The clan portions lay in rectangular areas upon these tributaries with portions of forest between. This rectangular way of representing local clan portions would seem to be built upon the model of the Fang village.[6] It will be noted in Essono's map that the "etun ayong" lies parallel to its respective tributary and therefore has, like the village, an upriver and a downriver direction. This "upriver-downriver" axis (*ôswí kwí, ôswí nkeng*), which is roughly northeast to southwest in orientation, was the basic axis of Fang as they located themselves in space.

Younger men, when asked to draw maps of clan lands, almost always drew them in reference to the colonial road system running through Fang country. They strung villages and clans along these roadways. While the rivers led to the sea, these roadways had as their focus and destination "towns and trading centers of the colonial and modern world" (*kisawn*). As implied by the proverb used as the epigraph to this chapter, the coming of the roads had brought a passion for journeying to these towns.

Cosmic Space

Discussion of Fang in real space can begin, since myth and legend have been reviewed, with cosmic space. There are hazards, because one must go beyond Fang commentary. Nevertheless, the materials point in certain directions. In the creation of the earth by the "sky-spider" (*abô*) working in conjunction with the creator god Mebege, there was an important vertical dimension: above and below. The great spirits belonged to the sky. All living and dead things whose abode was in or on the earth looked ultimately to the above to negotiate their fate.[7] At the same time, as in the ancestral cult (*Bieri*), the living negotiated with the dead as inhabitants of the below—as inhabitants either of the earth or of the depths of great rivers, which was a favorite location of the "village of the dead" (*azal bekôn*). In the cosmological sense, creative and destructive powers came from below or above. Living men endeavored not to rise too high or fall too low. Height and depth constituted one essential dimension of Fang quality space. It was the spiritual dimension.

Fang migration legends give the second dimension: upstream and downstream. These were the cardinal directions among Fang and provided an axis roughly northeast-southwest. Certain meanings attached themselves to these directions. Upstream was sometimes said to be the male direction and down-

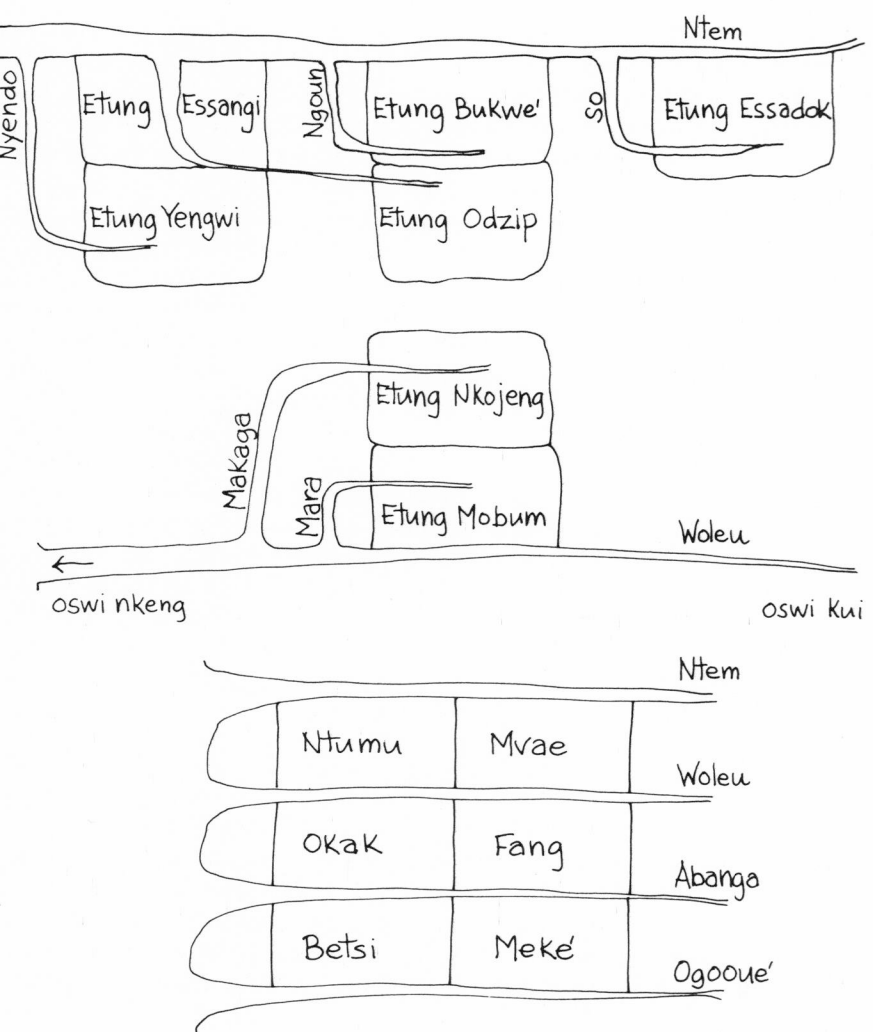

4.2 Watercourse Concepts

stream the female direction. This association arose out of several facts. The sun (*nlôdzôp*), which was male, arose in the east; and the young moon (*ngwan*), which was female, appeared first in the west. Upstream was the land of the forces which had dislodged Fang from their original home and pursued them downstream. Downstream was the abode of those peoples whom Fang had conquered or displaced in their rapid migration into the forest and toward the sea. Within Fang territory there was a tendency to seek wives from downstream clans; husbands were welcomed from upstream clans. Upstream tribes of Fang were esteemed as being more advanced. And, indeed, in terms of contact with the West the Bulu and the Ntumu enjoyed progressive advantages over the more southern Fang groups. In respect to the fissiparous character of Fang lineage dynamics it was the junior segments that generally split away from their seniors and moved on downstream to reestablish themselves. Upstream was thus associated with seniority in both clan histories and migration legends; downstream had the subservience of junior status. For a combination of these reasons, upstream was a dominant direction and downstream a subordinate direction. Dominance expressed itself against the subordinate, as did maleness over femaleness.[*1] This was the semantic of migration along the second dimension of a Fang Euclidian space.

But the third dimension was less salient among Fang. Informants spoke of front and back or head and foot on the analogy of a man extending his "right hand (*mfa nôm*), the male hand" upstream and his "left hand (*mfa nga*), the female hand" downstream. Here again the body microcosm was extended to organize macrocosmic space. Clearly, the primary experience of the body and body image was fundamental to Fang spatial architectonics, as it was in the structural order.

Progress on the vertical dimension was cyclical. Spirits rose from the earth, became men, fashioned their better selves out of the combined action of brains (*bô*) and heart (*nlem*) over against the gross visceral appetites of stomach, bowel, bladder, and genitals, rose further to negotiate with the higher powers, and were fated finally to fall back to earth, only to rise again as spirits were called to negotiate the ills of the living or to reassume mortal shape.

Progress on the other, horizontal dimension was essentially linear and noncircular. There was little notion of a return to the original savanna homeland, and the possibility that it could be regarded as a paradise was only taken up in the Bwiti religion. That the sea as final destination could represent a return to that original body of water beside which Fang first dwelt is another conceit—the conversion of the linear into the circular and the identification of the "European" ocean with the ancestral sea—of Bwiti microcosmogonizing. Such "eternal returns" were only implicit in tradition. What emerged in tradition was a progressive transformation of nature and destiny. Traditional

---

[*1] In the late fifties and early sixties this was part of the difficulty Fang of northern Gabon experienced in submitting themselves to a political control emanating from southern Gabon and from southwestern Fang. This cosmic dimension was still an organizing force in village affairs. Informants testified to a norm by which the village as well as the house structure were aligned or should be aligned on the oswi kui-oswi nke (upriver-downriver) axis. Tessmann suggests that the virtual alignment was more strictly observed formerly (*Die Pangwe*, Vol. I, pp. 56 and 73). "Even when a path is running to the south, it will bend around the village east to west and take at the other end the southerly direction again." He adds that graves were dug on the "east-west axis." This was not generally the case in 1960, despite the rule.

cosmology was more open-ended. The Bwiti cosmos, as we shall see, obtains more closure.

DOMESTIC SPACE

While macrospace was traditionally organized by reference to rivers and the sea and more recently by reference to the colonial arteries of commerce and administration, the microspace of village life was organized first by reference to the forest and the plantations and secondly in relation to the traditional structures: the women's dwellings or kitchens (*kísín*), the men's apartments (*nda* proper) where the ancestral shrines (*nsuk bieri*) were found, the men's council house, and the central courtyard. The affective contrast between the forest and the village has been pointed out. The former was cold, yet the prime arena of male activity—hunting, warfare, defense of frontiers. The latter was hot, yet the arena of women's work—the cooking of food, the raising of children. Between them lay the "plantations" (*efekh*) of manioc, peanuts, and corn to which Fang women paid daily visits. These had intermediate status between the forest and the village. The men reclaimed them from the forest by chopping and burning. The women brought the seed out from the village and cultivated and harvested the crops.

Adventures in the forest (trapping, hunting, wild fruit gathering) were among the most frequent topics of conversation in the men's council house. The forest was a foreign place[8] which has not been defined by any building activities, and what occurred there was always unexpected, adventurous. The frontier between the forest and the village was the plantations. Here the forest was defeated for the sake of village life. The felling of trees and particularly the "burning off of the plantations" (*tzige tsí*) provided moments of high excitement and real danger. These moments were frequently relived in the men's council house. One of our most articulate informants and an important local political leader in the southern Oyem district was killed while felling a tree. This event was discussed widely and was also the occasion to remember many other fatalities of the same nature. The firing of the brush was preceded by tales of men trapped and consumed in backfires.

When one passed from the village to the forest, then, one passed through various life zones or envelopes, each with its particular set of associations according to the activities carried out there. A model of the envelopes of domestic space is seen in Figure 4.3. One begins in the central court of the village, passing through the wall of houses on either side and out the "back door" (*mbí a fala*), which opens upon the "zone of small gardens and banana groves" (*fala*). The terrain of each family stretched out in rectangular fashion behind its dwellings. Crops to be closely watched were planted here, and also those crops which were predominantly the concern of men: tobacco, oil palm, and the important cash crops, coffee and cocoa. At its fringes were isolated

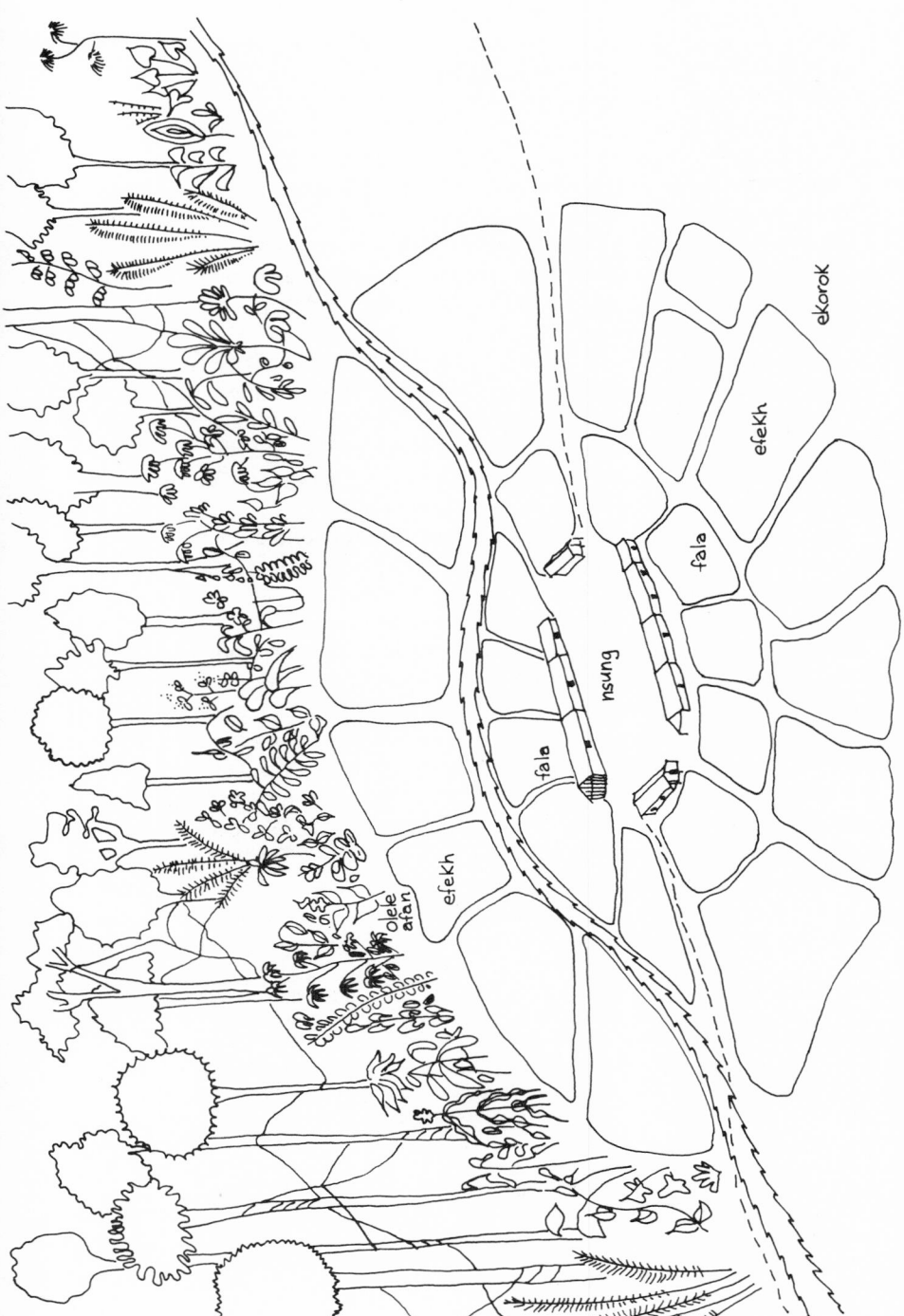

4.3 *Envelopes of Domestic Space*

stands of "forest" (ôkan) where the latrines were located and beyond which ceremonial activities of the ancestor cult and the secret societies took place. Wild fruit trees were maintained here, asas, mvut, and tôm (Pachylobus le testui, Trichoscypha ferruginas, Piptadenia africana), and during their season the okan was the scene of much pleasurable activity.

Beyond this area was the zone of the large gardens or "plantations" (efak). These plantations were of many varieties, including corn, peanuts, manioc, sugar cane, and yam, and they carried various names according to when they were planted (etutua, plantation cleared in November and burned in December), the principal crop (asan minkô, sugar cane), and their size (ekora, small plantation).

Beyond the plantations was the forest, on the frontiers of which men did their battle, slashed and burned new fields, laid traps for animals, and hunted. Deep within the forest a stream or a ridge marked the frontier with another clan segment, formerly a zone of potential hostility. But the forest itself, regardless of the societal frontier, quickened the thought. Therein men engaged in the chase, while families "camped out" (ake mvwan) on fishing expeditions of hilarity and solidarity. Therein shades of the troubled dead and other malevolent spirits wandered.

Fang made fine distinctions concerning the forest, according to its various stages. For though one talks of the equatorial rain forest and thinks of it as largely virgin, Fang and other populations at one time or another worked the greatest percentage of the area now abandoned to forest in Gabon and the Central African Republic. Thus Fang spoke of tsi-afan (abandoned plantations) just being taken over by graminaceous plants (Pospalum conjugatum, Eleusine indica, Digitaria velutine). This stage was followed by olele-afan, where relatively soft-wooded, fast-growing trees, often used for firewood, asserted themselves (also called the stage of ekorge or ekorok). The early part of this stage[2] presented a scene of dense underbrush very difficult to pass through because of the presence of the "saw vine," fefole (Scleria ovigera), which wounds and leaves sores that are a long time healing, as well as a spiny bush, asar (Fleurya aestuaus), which is equally formidable. At the end of this stage

---

[2] Six evolutionary stages in the replacement of the efak by the afan were given by informants. The stages were usually identified with the dominant plant or tree characteristic of them. Thus efak becomes avu or ekorok characterized by the various kinds of tall grasses, obut, ekang, ntobo. The next stage was eseng characterized by the aseng, the parasolier. This was followed by two stages in which increasingly useful and hard-wooded trees took over, the stage of mbur and the stage of esana. Finally came the stage of angoma in which the anguma (okoume) was the most important tree. All the concerted effort of a family was needed to subdue the deep forest to agriculture and domestic use. The southern Fang said: Ba kire dia angoma ye bôn sông (One doesn't attack the deep forest with the aid of one's father's sister's children). For belonging to a different patrilineage and themselves laying claims on other parts of the forest, they could hardly be of help.

taller trees appeared which were of more use to village industry and house-building. The overcover began to suppress the redoubtable underbrush, and finally one had the deep forest stage, *ngom afan* or *angoma*, of hardwoods and the very tall trees such as the *azap* (*Mimusops djave*), and the *enguma* (*Okoume kleineana*). In this last stage of "virgin" forest the underbrush was entirely suppressed. Within the afan it was easy to move about upon a thick carpet of dead leaves. Long vistas opened out in deep forest galleries.

The movement out from the village into the forest was not only an experience of succeeding zones with qualitatively different associations but it was also an experience of the passage beyond a threshold. One crossed a boundary from the domain of familiar and domestic activity, the village and its associated gardens and plantations, to the other realm, the deep forest with its useful trees, its game and well-stocked streams, but its alien uncertainties.

These contrasts between the forest and the village were both marked and mediated by the tangled and nettly thickets growing up in old plantations or on the forest's edge—the *olele afan*. It was a barrier between two worlds, but it also submitted to men's purposes and from it were taken not only the firewoods which heated the village and kept it "tranquil, prosperous and in good health" (*mvwaa*), but also many of the herbs and medicines that served the same end. In the same way the deep forest, so alien, was yet the source of important supplements to domestic diet: "meat" (*tzit*) and "wild fruits" (*mvut*). And from it, as well, were taken most of the essential building materials—not only the poles which provided the superstructure of Fang house construction, but also the raffia palm (*Raphia hookerii* or *vinifera*) which grew along watercourses in the forest, and the varieties of "liane," *nlôn* (*Eremos patha cabrae* or *E. heullevilleane*). These two materials together constituted the most important resources in Fang architecture. In this way the village so at odds with the forest was yet constructed out of it, and to that extent the distinction between these two realms was transformed into a close association. Men going back and forth between the forest and the village created a unity where a set of contrasting categories existed in spatial fact. This synthesis was expressed in Fang architecture itself. The houses were within the village yet essentially of the forest.

We have tried to indicate both basic Fang spatial categories and the stages in that journey which Fang experienced as they went out to the forest and returned again to the village. It was a journey celebrated in a variety of ceremonial sojourns in some of the traditional cults. It is celebrated in Bwiti. It is also architectonically formulated there.

But this village-forest round was an integrating journey of the past and of a revitalized present. It was the comings and goings upon the colonial roads and highways that more excited the imagination of the young. The new frontiers were the trading centers and cities by the sea to which individuals were attracted but in which they were decentered. For Bekale Essono and others it was hard to go home again and experience the totality which that home had traditionally provided.

THE BUILDING IN OF
CORPOREAL AND SPIRITUAL EXPERIENCE

A. THE *nda kisin*

The notion of opposition provoked in the observer by the appearance of a Fang village corresponded in some respects to social structure, for men of a common ndebot built side by side, while those of the mvogabot already undergoing divisive processes built opposite. Nevertheless, the village plan as traditionally conceived was a tight enclave which was easily enclosed by palisades and strengthening of the outer walls of the houses so as to provide good protection against external threats. The village was always planned with defensive purposes in mind. That a sense of opposition was also expressed in its layout was a "structural replication"[9] of the salience of segmentary opposition in other aspects of Fang life. The village in its very structure expressed these oppositions and at the same time constituted a self-contained enclave, a microcosm, very clearly defined against an outside world.

A further example of congruences between primary and secondary experiences—structural replications at various levels and in various arenas of Fang life—is seen in Figure 4.1. Set next to the village is the *mbek* board. The game is more widely known in Africa under the name of kala or warri. The resemblance between the village and the board will be apparent. It was clear to Fang[10] that the board was a village with a row of seven houses on each side and a men's council house figured by a receptacle for captured pieces at either end. Each "house" contained five people to begin and the object of the game was to destroy the adversary's house by removing his people. One of the key strategies—it was also a strategy of social life—was to build a house as full of "people" as possible so that one could "capture" the other side of the village. Thus were village structures and the realities of social life played out in other dimensions.

If games are understood as expressive models of greater cultural activities[11] this game will be seen as a means by which young men, who were the chief participants in the game, learned some of the essentials of their culture. It makes much clearer the competitive element in Fang society and village life. Microcosm and macrocosm shed light upon each other, and provided for some measure of cultural integration.

Within the village the notion of opposition evoked by rectangular patterning had also undergone change as, more and more, the men of the patrilineage had undertaken to build houses in the European fashion—multiroomed dwell-

4.4 Cold Houses and Their Compounds

ings with concrete floors, wattle and daub walls, and zinc roof. These houses, often called "cold houses" (*nda avep*) because unlike traditional dwellings no fires burned within, gathered around them into a compound their associated complex of women's kitchens and men's council house (Figure 4.4). This compounding effect tended to break up the common plaza and undermined the unity provided by that plaza. In the old days the men's council houses could survey the whole village, but later the council houses were often found within the compounds and cut off from each other. This development was congruent with increasingly nuclear families on the one hand and a centrifugality in village life on the other. Fang were not very comfortable in these cold houses. But such houses were a source of prestige; they were the consequence of arduous laying up of funds and materials, and they were universally desired. The traditional houses were still associated with all the major events in Fang life from birth to death. Often the cold houses were kept closed except for social occasions. They were not yet really lived in, and they remained associated with the inauspicious and sterile quality of coldness.[12]

The heart of Fang microspace in the traditional village can be understood by considering the relationship between the men's council house (*aba*) and the combination sleeping quarters and cook hut (*nda kisin*).[*3] It was the general feeling that the nda kisin belonged to the women and the aba to the men. An old tale was often put forth to account for the difference:

> Man and wife built one house to live in together. But life became so unbearable that man abandoned woman to her house (nda) and built the aba in which he might dwell with other men. Men and women can only live together, thus, by living apart. So to this day if a man's presence should bother a woman, she may always smoke up the fire and drive him out with eyes smarting. She says: "Go to your council house, you bother me. The kisin is women's sanctuary and she has her means to defend it. *Keng aba jue, wa ndugele me!*"

The nda kisin was the women's world (Figure 4.5). It was men who built these houses but it was the women and children who largely inhabited them. The corners of the nda kisin were furnished with the bamboo slat beds (*enong*), which were also employed during the day as seats and occasionally as storage platforms. Several cooking fires might be burning at once under the circumstance of more than one wife sharing the nda kisin (depending upon the presence of offspring). Against one wall various large storage baskets contained the essential products of agriculture: peanuts, dried manioc chunks, corn, cucumber seed. Chicks and ducklings might be underfoot or penned in a corner to keep them from harm's way. Drying racks including a raffia

---

[*3] Before the construction of cold houses men slept in another hut (nda proper) or in a portion of the kitchen partitioned off from the cooking and the women or the children. Sickness, however, would bring them back into that kitchen. The word kisin is a loan from the French.

4.5 Fang Kitchen (nda kisin)

foodchest hung over the fires, and usually a platform was built under the roof at one end to serve as a loft. Medicines were often kept in bark containers there, or were hung up high from the ridge pole. An older kisin was thoroughly sooted from the cooking fires so that the interior was obscure, lit only by the two doors—the one leading out into the plantations and the other opening upon the central court. This obscurity combined with the constant smokiness created for those not used to it an atmosphere in striking contrast with the bright tropical world outside.

It was a very compact world with practically every bit of space used for some purpose. Once accustomed to the atmosphere of the kisin the visitor felt a palpable coziness. It is not surprising that men who were sick or dying generally preferred to return to a bed in the kisin. They were born there, after all; they were brought up amidst its constant activity. It seemed the appropriate place to die. Thus the kisin enclosed men's most vital experiences, with the exception of sexual relations, which took place in the men's chambers adjoining.

The specialness of the space delimited by the structure of the nda kisin can be seen by reference to four rituals which occurred in relation to this building and which expressed certain attitudes towards it.

(1) In the case of difficult delivery when prolonged labor was exhausting the mother, the expectant father was encouraged to climb upon the roof of the kisin and, by carefully poking about, to discover the spot in the roof precisely above the stomach of his wife. Thrusting a hollow banana stem through the thatch he poured a medicinal water through the stem onto his wife's belly. This medicine was the same as that already employed liberally by the midwives within the hut. It was a mixture of leaves and barks from various plants, banana primarily, grown in the "inner gardens," *fala*. This same mixture or a separate mixture might contain a "crab shell" (*kara*) and a splinter from the lintel of the back doorway. The explanation of the plant items from fala was that the child was thus encouraged to be born into the human world of responsibilities, out of the village of the dead from which his spirit had come. The actual village of his birth was thus assimilated to the village of the dead and the confines of the womb to the confines of that village. The use of a splinter from the lintel of the back door had the same general meaning but assimilated the doorway, it appears, to the cervix of the womb. The crab shell was intended to work by opposites. It was added when the child's head appeared so that it should not disappear again as the crab so easily disappears scuttling under a rock.

The ritual was called simply *biang ndu* or *biang nzí* (roof medicine). It utilized the assimilation of the house to the womb. For the father, having penetrated the womb to create the child, must "penetrate" it again in symbolic form to release the child. The ritual which I observed was witnessed by perhaps a dozen villagers. Their quiet amusement at the father's poking around on the roof, their sense of the ribald, would seem to confirm the interpretation we have put upon the act.

(2) As Tessmann shows,[13] it was the custom to take the clothes, weapons and personal gear of a recently deceased man and display them on the roof of his sleeping hut at the time of the mortuary ceremonies. This was said to be done to show who it was who had died and what his sister's son would inherit, as these personal effects were by custom assigned to *nyangndum*. But it was also true that as the man's spirit had departed his skin (his clothes) so it had departed his sleeping hut. There was an equation then between a man's clothing and his hut—and a contrast made between his material embodiment and his spiritual self. Fang buildings were a material embodiment of spiritual selves and were given life by human activity within them—as in an elementary manner was the case with personal accouterments.

(3) and (4) Two further rituals associated with birth reflect upon the meanings tied up with the nda kisin and its assimilation at once to the womb and the sacred space of the ancestors. The mother and newborn remained in the house for upwards of a month without going out except for the necessary bodily functions. It was said that neither mother nor child were strong enough to leave the house. Within the house they were protected from the evil and envy of social life by the ancestors, who could not protect as effectively in the public arena of village life. The interior of the house was in some sense their space. After a month's time the child was "outdoored": brought to the men's council house where he was given a name and came thereby to occupy a place in public social space. Fang said that he was not given a name at once because it was not sure that he had really survived and the ancestors had really given him up. During the woman's confinement with her infant, special attention was paid to returning her self and her womb to normal. She underwent vaginal irrigation. She was purified by being whipped briskly with branches dipped in boiling water. This seems to have meant that the identification achieved between house and womb was shifted, and that by flagellation she was being toughened and prepared for abandoning a preoccupation with her womb, that is, a preoccupation with internal space, and emerging into public and social space.

The second, and a related, ritual was that of laying the infant upon the front threshold when his mother returned from her village (or the hospital). This was done only when he was not born in his own village. Often a woman facing her first birth elected to return to her mother and her own clan village. When returning to her husband's home, then, the infant was laid inside the threshold and the mother stepped over him and took him up again. Thus, it was said, he was properly made at home and would not be unhappy or sick in his own house. Fang informants said no more than this, but it could be well argued that if the association between house and womb continued to prevail as it did at the moment of childbirth, then by stepping over the infant the mother both welcomed him into the "womb" and gave birth to him within his and her proper house.

We should treat these interpretations with some caution. They do not rest on explicit Fang statement. But they are compatible with other data on how the house was architectonically linked with primary bodily experiences. Other customs carried the same weighting and implications: for example, the use of a heated machete when the "witchdoctor" (*nganga*) exorcised evil spirits within the house. The machete was struck against the walls and supports of the house. For just as the witchspirit was said to lodge itself upon the interstitial structures of the body and had to be dislodged by attacking that structure, so it was symbolically dislodged by attacking the structure of the house within which the patient suffered and which was assimilated to his body. Other areas in which the assimilation emerges are seen in the distinction between the front door (*mbi nsung*) and the back door (*mbí fala*) of the house, the one associated with the intaking of foodstuffs and the welcoming of guests and open social activity, and the other associated with the throwing out of refuse and secretive nonsocial, even shameful, activity.[14]

If the nda kisin was the scene of the most vital primary experiences, it is not surprising that it and its structure were assimilated to the corporeal arenas of these experiences. The assimilation may seem farfetched to the modern who dwells "in" rather than lives "into" his house and who does not choose to be born nor to die there. But it is a perfectly natural application of the penchant for analogical extensions which Fang manifested and which gave to their world a redundancy and unity it could not otherwise, in the absence of their interest in abstraction, possess.

B. THE *aba*

The men's council house must be sharply distinguished from the nda kisin. The distinction was so marked that even in the matter of those very strict dietary and behavioral laws or taboos (*ekí*) for which Fang were known,[15] it was present. One spoke of "the taboos of the house" (*ekí nda*) and the "taboos of the council house" (*ekí aba*). These were otherwise said to be the taboos of one's mother and the taboos of one's father and of one's clan. For in contrast with the nda kisin, the aba had a male identification. It was the seat of the patrilineage or the essential local segment of it. During unsettled times in former days when the villages were palisaded, the aba was the most heavily armed structure and the center of defense. Throughout the day and night men were on guard within it. It was the structure from which the whole village was surveyed. Since the suppression of warfare it came to function as a center of judicial dispute. And though it was no longer so centrally placed as to survey the entire village, it still maintained its importance in social and cultural affairs. It was smaller than in former days but it still provided sleeping quarters for men of the village or strangers. Young men and older boys still often slept there. Custom still required that strangers be first hospitably seated and received there while they were also carefully scrutinized. As a center of major ceremonies, it provided a place of concealment for the changing of costumes or for the examination of neophytes. The main supporting post of the entrance, the *akôn aba*, upon which the gorilla skull was hung, was at the center of these ceremonies. The post accumulated over time a certain power from the habit, in all those who entered and left, of laying a hand upon it.

If the village was to be ritually cleansed, the aba was the last and most important place to undergo purification. At night, as the center of story telling or of entertainment by traveling troubadours, it became an arena for the imagination and for the recreation of the past. Tessmann points out perfectly the atmosphere that could be created in the aba by the story tellers in their imaginative art.

> How differently works [the aba], which we have just considered with a deprecatory glance, when evenings the men and young people one after the other gather to hear what the stooped old Njem Ndong recounts of the uncanny configurations of the world of legends; patiently they harken however long he spins his tale, motionless they stare at him as restlessly he rubs his hands over the fire, a threatening finger waggling to and fro; he pushes the wood apart or together when it is too hot for him or he would defend his face from the smoke, softly but firmly as a man sends away a small child. It appears that he speaks with the fire and lectures the kindling. All are quiet, all hang on his lips. And now an artful pause . . ."[16]

If the nda-kisin was the arena of the primary experiences of men's lives the aba was the arena of the creative imagination.

Various ceremonies confirmed the aba as the center of the man's world. Shortly after he was born the male infant had to be ritually presented there by his mother to his father and his father's close relatives. The custom was called *abing ojeng*. When he married, his wife and mother-in-law cooked a ritual meal (*bidzi bi nengon*), and presented it to him and his relatives gathered there. It was there that he undertook the "ritual prohibitions and preparations" (*bekí aba*) for the outstanding pursuits of his manhood such as warfare and courtship. Serious concern began to be entertained on his account when in his old age, he could no longer make his way to the aba. And when he died, his male friends and relatives gathered there in "proper recognition of his death" (*ntô awu*), and as a dramatic demonstration that the group had surmounted this loss.

One aba ceremony, in particular, suggests corporeal assimilation in this structure similar to that pointed out for the nda-kisin. This was the boys' and girls' "prepubertal purification ceremony," *ndong mba* or *andé*. This was an involved ceremony, highly variable in various parts of Fang country.[17] Principally it was concerned with removing the "sin" (*nsem*) of incest between clan brother and sister. Fang were resigned to the fact that sexual exploration among young people in the village might lead to nsem but took ceremonial precautions to assure it would not affect the future fertility and prosperity of the participants or of the village. The central feature was the construction of a small hut (*ndzôm*) in the forest in which the boy or boys being initiated were confined and in which they were threatened by some forest being called Ndong Mba or Ande, unknown to them.

The girl or girls were confined to the kitchen of their mothers. In the village a scaffolding was erected next to the aba upon which an asam log was laid (*Uapaca le testuana* or *Uapaca guineensis*).[18] At the beginning of the ceremonies the youth was required to climb over the roof of the aba and to descend upon the log and to dance there while the men harassed him. He was then taken out to the forest. After his experiences there and after the forest hut was destroyed, he was brought back into the village and placed within the aba which was hung with raffia mats so that nothing could be seen within. The asam log had been now arranged in such a way that part of it was found within the interior of the hut and part of it projected out of the hut.

The girl believed to be involved was then sought by the men in the nda kisin. They pounded upon the walls of the kisin to frighten her and finally, thrusting the door aside, they rushed in and grabbed her. She was brought to the aba and caused to straddle the asam log. At the same time the boy initiate was forced to straddle the log within. They were both washed with a purifying bath. The men suddenly jerked the log out from under them both and carried it out into the forest. The ceremony was thus completed. The boy remained in the aba some time longer and the girl was returned to the kisin.

The sexual and phallic associations of the ceremony are clear enough, and in particular the assimilation of the aba to the male body. The initiate was gradually incorporated into that body while the girl was brought from the nda kisin to an engagement with it and returned to the nda kisin. The forest hut, the transititional abode of the initiates, was destroyed after the initiation for it was only a temporary extension of the body change that was being represented in the aba itself.

The aba in mid-century was no longer the arena it once was. In conjunction with the construction of European-type houses, which were generally built by and for the use of the nuclear family head rather than for extended family use, there was a movement by the younger men who held a primary school diploma to take their meals in these "cold houses" rather than in the aba. The old men, sensing the threat to traditional social organization that such a move implied, vigorously reproached their juniors for doing this. The following are the observations of Asseko Mve of Assok Ening on this problem.

> In our father's time our relationship with our women was better than it is today because our fathers didn't stay with their women in the kitchen or in a cold house. They stayed in the men's council house. They used the aba to gather together and assuage the injured feelings of another. The brothers would gather together with their fathers and they would say one to another: "My wife, if I gave her to you, you would return her very quickly, for she is one of the laziest and most intractable women that was ever created." Another would say, "I never eat except after long yelling." And a third would say he watched his wife constantly for she had an eye on every young man in the village. And then after all this complaint their father would say, "Your complaints are as nothing compared with what I had to put up with in the case of your mother." In this way each would assuage his feelings with the miseries of the other and all would gather counsel from the other, and for that reason by dividing man from wife the aba kept them together.
>
> In the aba we also examined the character and intention of any stranger. When a stranger arrived he would be regarded very closely out of the men's council house, from the moment he came out of the forest. Unless he came straightforwardly to the aba where he could present himself, and his customs and speaking could be examined, he was regarded suspiciously. If he went into a kitchen to light his pipe or search for food before he arrived, that was a sign of a man with adulterous intentions and bad customs.
>
> My father said, "*Eyong bia jímí aba bia jímí mefule mam*" (When we abandon the aba, we will lose our custom). For it is in the aba that we Fang learned our "character" (*mefule*) and in it we learned to judge the character of others.

The aba played a crucial role in the socialization of the young. It was there that Fang boys and young men learned how to act and how to speak, for the aba was fundamentally the place of talk (*adzô*). It was expected that after years of respectful and attentive observation of the techniques of dispute a man already married and with children could take a strong position in the affairs (*medzô*) of his family. The threat of abandonment of such an arena was naturally felt by the older men as a threat to the Fang way of life.

If the aba was no longer the center of village life that it once was, so the village itself was no longer the center of the universe it once was. It was this process of decentering under the influence of increasingly wide-scale relationships and easier travel that as much as anything unhinged the old cultural universe. It made highwaymen of many Fang. They looked down the roads in the expectation of the coming of riches from another culture instead of moving in regular self-satisfying cycles back and forth between forest and village as in the old days.

When we speak of decentering we should not forget that in former days all villages were periodically decentered in a very radical way. When we examined the migration stages associated with the genealogy, we noted that Fang villagers rarely remained longer than fifteen years in the same location and the average was closer to eight to ten years. This periodic relocation of the village had a powerful revitalizing effect, as attested by Fang themselves. When after the Second World War their villages were regrouped and fixed in place by government sanction, they were caused to remember vividly the challenge of chopping a new home out of the forest, the construction of new dwellings, and the transfer of belongings from the old to the new. Often, of course, new villages were constructed because of bitter conflict within the mvogabot. But the act of establishing a ndebot anew within the forest affirmed the strength and independence of the family members involved—an independence that had often been brought into question in the mvogabot dispute.

Fang mental and material culture, it should be noted, was not so complex or stratified as to prevent an extended family from breaking away and reestablishing the Fang cultural universe virtually in its entirety elsewhere in the equatorial forest. The point to be made is that these periodic decenterings ended with the recreation of the same cultural universe at the hands of the several adults involved in the shift. It was an affirmation of their powers in respect to their culture and their own incorporation of that culture. We will see in Bwiti this same confidence in recreating a universe—in microcosmogony—and a restoration of this sense of incorporation. In both bases the consequences were revitalizing and in both cases an essential part of the revitalization was found in the new constructions themselves.

The decentering of the village in more recent decades, however, was not restorative in any lasting sense. It was hardly galvanizing. In most cases it was dispiriting. As the attention of the villagers was drawn toward the towns and trading centers, their villages were coming to seem backwaters. For many villagers the most vital thing was the experience of life in the towns. Formerly centers of their universes and embodiments of the most fundamental experiences, the villages became the victims of centrifugal forces as these experiences were themselves decentered.[*4] While formerly Fang could revitalize

---

[*4] Demography documents this decentering. Age pyramids of 1960 in the Woleu-Ntem show the paucity of men to women in the young and early-middle-aged categories. This is indicative of the losses brought about by labor migration to the coastal lumber camps, mines, and urban centers. The total male-female ratio in such regions of emigration was inevitably affected—81 men per 100 women in the Woleu-Ntem. Coastal regions of predominantly Fang population— Estuaire, and Ogooué Maritime—as the recipients of this migratory labor, show complementary

themselves by recreating their old culture with new buildings in new space, in the late colonial period, as their villages opened up, they were confronted by the necessity of extending themselves to meet an alien culture in alien buildings in an alien space.

THE VILLAGE PLANNED

Fang spoke of the various "plans" (preparations) in a man's head— (akômngeh, mekômngeh). From what has been said it is not surprising that the foremost of these was usually the "plan to make a journey" (akômngeh dulu).[19] But among these one also often found the "plan to build a house" (akômngeh nda). Discussion to this point has concentrated upon the images Fang held of the spaces they occupied as a consequence of the interaction between their vital activities and these spaces. But it is as important to understand the "plans" associated with these images, as such plans relate more directly to activity itself.[20]

The plan to build a house developed very early in the young person, for traditionally he had participated by his early teens in at least one shift of village and, moreover, by the age of puberty was himself in need of his own quarters where he and his brothers could entertain others free of the injunctions of elders. He had also participated in the pleasurable construction of those "small forest houses" (ebem elik) in which the Fang sheltered themselves when sojourning at old village sites or in the deep forest.

There was thus a very positive feeling associated with the planning and bringing to completion of new structures. When old structures had outlived their vitality—their positive association with primary experience one might say—this planning and construction was revitalizing. At the same time Fang relished anticipatory more than consummatory satisfactions, and houses often

---

figures in age pyramids and sex ratios, that is to say more men than women. (Gabon, *Recensement et enquête démographique*, Chapter VI, pp. 105-130; Chapter II, p. 32.)

Mobility figures are more difficult to interpret. Gabon as a whole was characterized by an exceptional mobility of population. Forty-eight percent of men and 59% of women had changed their residence since birth compared with 10% and 24% in Dahomey and 29% and 48% in the Central African Republic (Gabon, *Recensement*, Chapters V and VI). For the Woleu Ntem, the region where this study was concentrated, the figure was much lower for men, 17%, and much higher for women, 71%. This reflects the stabilization brought about by cash crops and village regroupment on the one hand, and the practices of strict exogamy on the other. In other Fang regions except for the coastal ones, the mobility figures approached the national average. Thus in some parts of Fang country the attractions of wage labor had increased mobility and put corresponding pressures on villages. In other parts cash crops and regroupment had acted to reduce mobility. The former rhythms of village life, in either case, were subject to unwonted pressures—greater mobility in one case and greater stability in the other. In either situation the traditional relation and rhythm of the village to the space it occupies was subverted.

stood in a state of incompletion for a long period of time. In respect to the aba it was often difficult to obtain the agreement of the men of the ndebot for a new construction, and hence it was dependent upon the strength of a lineage leader (*nkukuma* or *njiabot*) such as Ngema as to whether a new aba would be constructed at all, although the need might be plain.[21]

The importance of the leadership factor in the building of the aba reminds one how important generally this factor was in Fang society. Visitors to Fang country have frequently remarked on the considerable variation in the aesthetic aspect of the villages.[22] These differences in logico-aesthetic integration were directly traceable to the powers, talents of persuasion, and sense of order of the village leaders.[23]

It is useful to consider briefly the effort and material resources involved in bringing these house plans to fruition, both for traditional housing and for the latter-day "cold houses." First, note the main verb for house construction, *along, along nda* (literally to weave, to weave a house). It was the same word employed for the construction of a basket. In fact, since the materials used in house-building—liane strips and raffia (*dzam, nlong*)—were virtually the same as those used in basketry, the common verb is appropriate. (It should be remembered as well that practically all basketwork, except the very small fishing baskets, was done by men.) A great deal of tying and interweaving was involved in house-building.

It is important to point out the association between house-building and basket-making for several reasons. First, a frequent experience of young children was to be carried to the plantations by their mothers and to be left in a "backbasket" (*nkweng*) for sleep and for protection against the elements. For a very young child, Fang said, the first "house" of his own was a basket. Second, when Westerners think of constructing a house, they think of driving a foundation, riveting, welding, or nailing up structure, and then filling in the interstices. Fang drove poles by hand for a foundation and then raised a ridge pole, but from then on the rest of the structure was tied or woven together. Third, though we have been working out a Euclidean space in this chapter and have referred to the "carpentered" world in which Fang lived— varieties of rectangular and cubic spaces—we must be cautious. Just as it has been difficult to identify the third dimension of Euclidean space among them, so it must also be pointed out that though from the Euclidean view a round basket and a square house may be entirely different structures, it is possible that much more of a homomorphism, a topological equivalence, prevailed in Fang thinking. This equivalence is expressed in the common verb, to weave, and in other ways such as the fact that basket-weaving and house-weaving were felt to be male responsibilities.

In traditional house-building, women were involved only in the muddy work of preparing the foundation. In the more modern housing, Fang adopted a Cameroons custom of bamboo wattling, then filling the walls with ten centimeters or more of mud. This mud wall, which was often finished with a cement "crépissage," was the responsibility of the women and was a task that fell to them because of the traditional division of labor in which pottery-making and other tasks involving mud and clay were their responsibility. But the consequence was that women came to have an important role in house-building, and to some extent the traditional distinction between men building the structure and women filling them with vital activity was broken down. The extension and replication of corporeal experience which was involved in the older procedure lay in Fang belief that in the creation of the infant the red drop of female blood containing the homunculus was surrounded by the protective and fostering shell of white male semen. In the adult person the male element was the skeletal structure and tissues and tendons, all white, within which the sources of vitality—the blood and bloody organs—carried on their primary activity.

Traditionally there was a frequent enough change in village site so that the plan to build a new house was almost constant.[*5] It would take two to three years to build up the new village and finish all construction to satisfaction. After the swift passage of several years, another new village site began to be

[*5] A man undertaking to construct a traditional house with sleeping chamber had to accumulate and use, on the average, the following materials:

110	wall barks (1 meter by 3 meters)	2 weeks of work
58	roof poles	1 week
8	asung logs and mats of support poles for storage platform	1 week
35	structural support poles (mvis)	1.5 weeks
12	inside poles	3 days
1	ridge pole (nfas atwing), 6 meters long, 25 cm diameter	2 days
2	support poles, 3 meters long, 25 cm diameter	2 days
900	meters of bamboo stripping outside-inside	1.5 weeks
320	raffia thatch panels 2-3 meters, 15 per day	3 weeks
	liane tie strips, nlong, 1500 to 2000 meters, 150 meters per day	2 weeks

The accumulation of the materials alone required, therefore, thirteen weeks if pursued steadily by one man. Once accumulated, construction could proceed rapidly: the ditching and stamping of the foundation might take a week and the erection another several weeks' time. But usually the materials were accumulated as the construction proceeded and as they were needed. In no case did I discover a house that was under five months in construction, and the average was six to eight months, with many dwellings lingering in an unfinished state for up to two years. Delays were much more characteristic in recent years where men embarked upon the construction of the costly and modern "cold" houses and then found themselves without the resources to finish them. The aba could be put up much more quickly once the nkukuma succeeded in galvanizing the ndebot. But in all cases the plan to build a house was not easily brought to fruition.

contemplated. By the mid-twentieth century colonial requirements and insistence on stabilization meant that this shifting of village sites and the revitalization it obtained was no longer possible. Men's animating plans for construction could no longer rest on the prospect of a new village in new forest. Plans for new construction shifted to a focus upon the "cold" houses.

These were, in some respects, a suitable replacement, for by cost and size the bringing to fruition of such a plan was a much more lengthy and laborious process. It was not unusual for men to be at work up to a decade trying to gather the resources to complete a "cold" house. In 1960 the total cost of a 3- to 5-room house, with concrete floors, cement walls, window and door frames and shutters and doors, etc. (but without a zinc roof)[24] was on the order of 80 to 100 thousand francs CFA. If a man with the then average monthly salary for the District of Oyem, Woleu Ntem, Gabon were to save half of that salary (two thousand francs), it would take him four years to accumulate this amount. The average yearly income from cash crops was less than this—between 20 and 40 thousand francs CFA. In addition he would have had to contemplate about 300 man days of work in both laying up materials and construction. So the plan of new houses was at least ten times and as much as thirty to forty times the undertaking of traditional houses. If one adds a zinc roof and carpentered interior furnishings, which were highly desired, then one had a long-term commitment and preoccupying plan not at all typical of traditional housing. Instead of the periodic revitalization and plan-realization of entirely new construction of new villages, one had a sort of ebb and flow of revitalization as one or another piece of building material, addition, or improvement was achieved in the same long-planned construction.

CONCLUSION: CENTRIFUGALITY AND CENTRALITY

In this chapter two issues have been considered. Field materials have been organized to show the relationship of Fang to the spaces they occupy. It was shown first that the villages which were the very focus and center of gravity of Fang life had experienced a decentering and centrifugality. This arose for various and often contrary reasons. Conditions and means of travel were much improved over the traditional situation of constant internecine strife and frequently inundated and badly maintained trails. There was the attraction of wage labor and urban life. At the same time, the early colonial policy of stabilization of migrant populations and a later interest among the modernizing elite in village regroupment meant that many Fang were confined within the same villages and upon the same site longer than was ever traditionally the case. In former days villages galvanized (and revitalized) themselves every decade or so by an entire change in site. Later they were tied down by regroupment and cash crops. Such forced sedentarization only added to centrifugal impulses. Fang had always had a love of journeys, and, one might even say, a love of movement, *bewulu be yen mam* (moving is seeing). They had been, after all, a people in slow migration for at least the last several hundred years and well into the twentieth century. Centrifugality was not an entirely new disposition. But it was much exacerbated. Formerly, however much Fang experienced the love of travel, the villages remained the center of life. One did not move away from villages. One moved one's villages, and in that movement periodically recreated one's world and realized one's plans in a wholly satisfying way. Village movement was an important kind of microcosmogony.

The second issue which has preoccupied us is the nature of the centrality of village life. We have sought to demonstrate, insofar as the data available in the late 1950's could make the case, that the centrality of village life lay in its architectonic integration of the cosmic, migratory, economic (forest and field), social, and vital personal experiences of Fang. The buildings of Fang space embodied meanings from myths and legend, from migration experiences, from the daily relationships with courtyard, plantation, and forest, from the social relationships of ndebot and mvogabot within the village— and, most particularly, the vital relationships between men and women and between peers in ritual, in game, and in song.

It is still difficult to demonstrate that degree of interpenetration of the various levels of Fang experience which would make for a cosmic "système de connaissance." Such demonstrations have been provided in detail in the Sudanic studies of the Griaule school.[25] Perhaps Fang in their rapid migrations out of the savanna selected for men of action rather than the speculative personages who so fully supplied the French ethnographers with their rich data. Perhaps Fang were too far removed from the great literate Islamic traditions at work in the Sudan. Perhaps it was too late in the late 1950's to get this kind of material from Fang culture itself. Acculturation often acts to break down the associations and extensions between the vital experiences of personal and domestic space and a larger architectonic. It can lead men to concentrate upon the material rather than the logico-aesthetic aspects of spatial organization. This had surely happened among Fang in their preoccupation with "cold houses."

Perhaps, however, we have been able to see enough of the integration of microcosm and macrocosm to understand what a more comprehensive and logico-aesthetically integrated "système de connaissance" might be among Fang. In the religion of Bwiti, a great deal more attention *is* paid to an architectonic integration of microcosmic and macrocosmic space. If speculation on such matters is a characteristic of many cultures of the savanna— as the Griaule school has shown—then in that sense Bwiti returns Fang to their savanna origins.

⋆5⋆

Resource Distribution and Social Reciprocities

Elulua e ne akyenge.
(Pleasurable activity [animation] is a wonderful thing.)

MUYE MICHEL TRIES TO FORM A DANCE TEAM

MUYE MICHEL always had many ideas. He had hoped to interest his village brothers in buying an old Renault truck for commerce, but to no avail. He had set his wife up with a small store in one corner of their house but she had no head for business and they lost money. So all they sold were kerosene and sardines. He had both a cocoa plantation and coffee trees, but he was so busy with the affairs of the Bwiti religion—he was building a new chapel— that he hardly took care of them and they yielded very little and of poor quality in a time of low prices. One day he decided that the family of Mba M'Oye might successfully buy and sell the mangan dance that was spreading throughout the region.

There was a famous dance team from Essangi clan teaching at Endama village. Muye asked to be taken over to Endama with his wife and several of her friends on the following Sunday, the day of the concluding dance. They would see whether the dance was worth buying. We arrived at Endama village later in the afternoon than we expected and the dance was well along. Two rows of women sat on stools facing each other, the teaching team from Essangi and the novice team from Endama. There were two teams of drummers at one end. The women who wore red tassles danced seated, shaking and flailing their heads, shoulders, and arms. Occasionally one of the leaders from the teaching team would rise and dance out into the middle calling upon her opposite number to join her. The songs and the drums of both teams were sung and played in unison as the Essangi team had spent several weeks teaching the dance nightly in the village. But the woman song leader, the *nyíabía*, also improvised songs. When we arrived late, she called out and the women responded, singing "*Ye ô sô ya ntangen*" (So you have come at last white man). We recorded more than twenty songs while we were there—a small part of the repertoire.

In the process of the dance, spectators came forward from time to time to place ten- or twenty-franc pieces in one of the small enamel basins that each dancer had at her feet. After a solo dance, men or women came forward and, waving as much as a hundred-franc note over the head of the dancer, placed it in her basin. The drumming stopped and the donor made a short speech. The Chief of Endama village put one hundred francs in the basin of each of the three female dance leaders of Essangi. He said, "We are very content with the dance you have taught and it is even more beautiful today. Hide none of the dance and its particulars from us." At a later moment, the Commandant of the Essangi team came forward and put several hundred francs into the dish of the head dancer of Endama. He said, "We have shown you everything. We see that you are now highly skilled. There only remains the making of 'medicine' (*biang*) for your own dance team. But do not count on biang to be admired and invited to teach the dance elsewhere. Count on the skills which you have learned." The hundred francs was a generous gift from the Commandant. But he would recover it. All the women carried white handkerchiefs tucked into their armbands. Whenever they made a mistake the Commandant rushed down and whipped away the handkerchiefs. They could be recovered at a cost of ten francs.

The last set of the dance was the appearance of Flanco at the far end of the village behind a raffia bark wall. We had been promised his presence several times in the song *Avion Flanco da lot ôyô* (the airplane of Flanco passes overhead). The drums of the dance stopped suddenly and the deep tones of the war drum were heard at the other end of the village. Just as suddenly, a white mask set on a white uniform was thrust up on a pole over the wall, then quickly withdrawn. There was a gasp from the crowd. The drums at the near end started up again and one by one the woman members of the visiting team got up and, choosing their opposite number from Endama, danced down the village courtyard to meet Flanco. As they danced below the wall, suddenly Flanco and his wife would appear momentarily above them saluting them and dancing themselves. Sometimes the pair of masks embraced in mock sexuality to the amusement of the crowd. Only the dancers could come down close to the wall and all spectators were kept distant. To take a close-up picture would cost 500 francs.

Muye was anxious to find out costs. He spent some time after the dance talking to the two teams. He learned that the Essangi team had known the dance more than a year and had taught it three times previously. They had learned it from a team on the Rio Muni border who had learned it from a clan Essawon team from Spanish Guinea. They had learned it, in turn, from Obuk clan in western Evinayong District, Spanish Guinea. After leaving Endama where they had been for two weeks, the Essangi team hoped to pass another week dancing in various villages. They would be glad to come to Assok Ening for a night.

The teaching team would not divulge the amount of money they had been paid for teaching the dance. This varied with the richness of the village. And Endama was a poor village. It could be as much as forty thousand francs. Muye had a relative in Endama who said the total amount was eighteen thousand francs plus some unanticipated gifts given at the concluding dance. Two thousand francs was paid to the Commandant (*njía mangan*). Each drummer received 800 francs. The head of the woman's team and caller of the songs (*nyíabía*) had received 1,500 francs and her two assistants 1,400 and 1,200 francs apiece. The Commandant said also that something had to be paid to bring Flanco from Spain.

When Muye returned to the village, he was enthusiastic about the Essangi mangan. He came into the council house the next evening full of plans for inviting the team to Assok Ening. But Ngema and Essono greeted the idea sourly. Ngema said that mangan was now an old dance. Our brothers of Medoumou bought it years ago and they did not get their money back. They made just a few francs dancing at funerals. Essono said "I can count fifteen mangan teams in the district. How do you expect to gain any money?" Muye argued that this was a new mangan dance characterized by the appearance of Flanco and more beautiful songs and dress. "Our brothers of Medounou were lazy with that dance and thus no one else wanted to be instructed by them. In our case, it would be different. Our family is already famous for the size of our houses and our concrete floors. We have an ntangen living with us. We have this market place and the school and the infirmary in our village. If we had this dance, many villages would invite us to teach them. And should we talk just of the money? It has been a long time since we have had any activity in our family. We have been very 'tired' here (*atek*). As the words of the mangan song tell us: *elulua e ne akyenge* [activity is a wonderful thing]. We need elulua in our village. Money without activity is nothing."

The family was, in part, convinced by Muye's words. But then they began to inquire as to what women would form the team. Several of the men were not sure they wanted to trust their wives or daughters to Muye as Commandant. Mintza said in his quiet way: "Muye, we have long been angry with you for taking our wives and daughters off into Bwiti. How can we be sure you will not make Bwiti with them as well as mangan?" Mintza's son, Bekale Mintza, one of whose wives had been dancing Bwiti, seconded his father. "With all your involvement in Bwiti can you really be a good Commandant?" These were telling criticisms. The family decided not to invite the Essangi team. They decided instead (it was Bibong Leon's idea) to send for Edu Ada, the famous mvet troubadour, to come and sing of the great clan of Engong. In that way the family would make elulua.

THE ECONOMICS OF VILLAGE LIFE

Whatever Muye's final motives were in trying to acquire the dance of mangan, as far as the family was concerned the economics of buying and selling the dance were foremost. It is useful to place this event in the context of the economies of Fang life—a life which had been turning more and more to cash crops (cocoa and coffee) and to a greater commitment to general purpose currency, the African colonial franc (CFA).

Fang had long had a special currency of "iron money," *bikuela*. These were originally irregular in shape, subsequently cast in the form of small pipettes and finally in the form of flat spear points.[1] Tessmann carefully noted down in three parts of Fang country the equivalents in iron money for most items of their life.[2] But bikuela was mainly a ceremonial and special purpose currency, most frequently used in the sphere of marriage transactions, brideprice, and ensuing ceremonial payments. Fang had an essentially nonmarket economy. Markets established among them in the colonial period never flourished. In Assok Ening, for example, the market was defunct six years after its founding. It is true that some goods were traded widely from the coast upcountry. But this was usually done by barter or, in the Cameroons, by a form of ceremonial exchange called *bilaba*. An elementary form of this existed among Fang of Gabon.

In economic life, as was the tendency elsewhere, the *ndébot* within the *mvôgabot* was virtually self-sufficient. Formerly some resources were given over to the head of the mvogabot for redistribution at ceremonial periods; it was in that lingering spirit that Mba M'Oye made family decisions on payments and purchases. Hunting, fishing, and gathering, not to mention agriculture in a country as sparsely populated (5 per km^2)[3] as Gabon and as rich in fish and fauna provided a substantial food supply for the family. Such supplies were consumed quickly and rarely sold except by bachelor hunters who spent most of their time hunting or by old women who sold smoked fish.[4] Most men kept traps in the forest, though some men, often older widowers or bachelors, devoted themselves almost exclusively to long strings of traps[5]—as many as a hundred—which needed daily scrutiny. At the end of the colonial period among Ntumu and Fang, fishing and hunting still produced more than three-quarters of the meat consumed. This was supplemented by tins of corned beef, sardines, hausa beef, and salt fish.[6] But these supplements were luxuries due to a pronounced taste for meat. (Fang distinguish the "hunger for meat," *wôk nzang*, from "general hunger," *wôk nzeng*.) The staple crops, peanuts, manioc and corn, were planted in sufficient amounts in normal years to supply the family for the entire year, and all had the virtue that they could be easily dried and stored. It is true that Fang remembered suffering periodic famines or "great hungers" (*zeng nen*), particularly after the First World War when the flu and then a series of very bad harvests took a great toll of the population (1920-1925). But generally Fang were confident of their ability to feed their ndebot by steady recourse to forest, field, and stream without relying on markets.

Nevertheless, the economic impact of the colonial regime was unmistakable. It brought (1) a general purpose money; (2) head taxes which acted to force Fang into a relationship with that money; (3) fluctuations in the value of that money which created in Fang a special attitude toward it; and (4) by the middle of the century, a development of cash crops that linked Fang even more closely to the colonial economy. We may obtain some idea of the economic framework of Fang life by first of all getting a sense of daily activity, secondly by getting a sense of the average income and possessions of the villages, and thirdly by following over time the changes and manipulations in the brideprice as Fang shifted from special purpose currency to the colonial franc.

Fourteen men of varying ages were followed through for a week's time in Assok Ening. This was outside the planting season, which was an exceptionally active period involving long hours of cutting and burning of forest. The tasks of the harvesting season fell mostly on the women's shoulders. One morning there was a death in the village and ten of the men were closely enough related to the husband of the deceased to avoid all work that day. On another day, six men were involved in palaver in the council house and, as usual, this took precedence over other forms of work.

The men rose early, before the sun, and walked wrapped in their night cloth around the village for half an hour. They then took a snack left from the evening meal and departed by seven for the fields or forests. If it was to the fields, they were either going to cut trees for a new plantation or clean out the margins of old plantations so as to help the women whose main responsibility was the weeding of the growing fields. When the sun rose high around 10 a.m., and it became very hot and humid in the fields, the women returned to the village and the men retired to the deeper forest to check their traps, to gather fruit, perhaps to fish or hunt or simply to rest. Young men, and those who had no traps or were much given to handicraft, returned with the women to the village to lounge in the council house, or to take up their basket-making, net-making, or woodworking. Those who stayed in the forest carried out leaf food packages for the noon meal. But more men returned to the village in recent years because the women were more and more given to preparing a hot noon meal.

Men who returned to the council house continued to shade up after the noon meal, playing on the *mbek* board, engaging in crafts or discussion. If they were building or repairing a house, as half the men were, they worked at this. When the sun was well into its decline, men went out to their cocoa plantations, often well into the forest (70% of the mature men in Assok Ening planted cocoa). They cleaned out underbrush and carried out manure swept up from animal droppings in the village plaza. As they returned, after taking a bath at a favorite waterfall or deep hole in a stream, they paused to work among the coffee trees close to the village. The hot evening meal, perhaps ground nut soup or corn soup with fish or leaves of the manyini plant (*Senecio blatrae*) fried in oil, came at dusk or early evening. It might be followed by the visit of a troubadour or a long discussion with a visitor from another clan or a new outburst of a lingering argument, or otherwise by an early bedtime.*[1]

For those men who had a love of the forest, or who could contemplate with anticipation the growing of cash crops, or who derived satisfaction from their handicrafts, this round of life offered plentiful recompense. The periodic appearance of a troubadour or a dance team and the occasional marking of the life cycle by a birth or a marriage or a death was enough to fill up the days. But the younger men had developed greater expectations. They were easily bored (*wok engil, nyôl esusula*). Like Muye Michel, they were not long happy in the forest and returned early from the plantations to the village, running about from council house to council house, playing mbek, singing, disputing, and agitating with their mothers and their sisters for a hot noon meal. The day-in and day-out care of the cash crops was not sufficiently rewarding to them. They spent more of their time than in former years off courting. And this freedom of travel ended up inspiring many to abandon the villages entirely to gain their living in the cities. The old cult activities were largely defunct and laid little claim on the imaginations of the young, hardly holding them to the slow round of village life. Some felt loyalty to the Catholic or Protestant churches, but as the major ceremonies and social activities of these religions usually took place in the mission centers they in fact contributed to the decentering process previously described.[7]

The income to be had from cash crops was not enough to hold younger people in the villages. It is true that in the northern areas of Gabon most Fang

---

*[1] There are of course marked individual differences. Ngema Mve, one of the hardest working men in the village, rose early every day and reached a distant plantation he was clearing by 8 o'clock. He worked until 11 o'clock and then retreated into the forest where he was building a small hut where the family could spend the night. He always took a leaf package of food out with him. On the way back to the village he worked his cocoa plantations. He always returned by 4 in the afternoon, usually taking part in some palaver or discussion until sunset. The twilight hours he usually spent in the kitchen of one or another of his wives. He usually ate after dark, going to bed early unless there was a palaver, for it was he who got up at first light and woke the rest of the family.

Ndutumu Mve, on the other hand, always returned at noon to rest in the council house. He was making a basket, as he always was. He spent two days until 2 p.m. checking his traps, and two early mornings he did not get out to his traps at the plantations until much later because he went down to mass at the chapel. Ngema's day was usually much different from Ndutumu's because he had nine wives to Ndutumu's one, was usually called upon to hear palavers, made no baskets, kept no traps, never went to mass and had four times as many cocoa trees as Ndutumu. Muye Michel would fit somewhere in the spectrum. He never took food with him to the plantation. He usually wandered from council house to council house playing mbek, as Ngema and Ndutumu never did. And his week was much influenced by the fact that he danced Bwiti at least once and often twice a week all night long. Though he said that Bwiti gave him strength for the next day, on the day following the next day he was likely to be very lethargic. Thursday in any case was never a day of hard work for the Bwitist, said Muye, and he stayed close to the village doing light work with a machete and walking about from council house to council house participating in various discussions.

and Ntumu men referred to themselves as "planteurs" in census inquiry and they took pride in the title. Nevertheless, the returns were insufficient to convince many of the young of the advantages of that occupation. After five years of attending to the 1½ to 2 hectares of cocoa bush most men possessed, they began to harvest between 4 and 8 sacks of cocoa weighing 50 to 60 kilos per sack. At the going price for cocoa in the late fifties, 118 colonial francs per kilo, a year's harvest was likely to produce, at the most, 50 thousand francs a year, or roughly $200. This income could easily be equaled in the towns by a shopboy at modest wages, between 4 and 5 thousand francs a month.

One might argue to the young that because of subsistence living in the villages, practically all the money made on the cocoa crop could be saved, while it was a rare shopboy who could save one-fourth of his income. Yet the number of years before a cocoa plantation was fully productive and the amount of care it needed effectively discouraged many young men. Besides, in the village one's family and in-laws were ever ready to take what sudden income a man should have. Though one might argue that unemployment was common in the district centers and coastal cities, it could be fairly pointed out that cocoa prices fluctuated very uncertainly with a general downward trend. In Gabon, where African planters were unprotected from the world market by government stabilization or cooperatives, the prices fluctuated between 175 francs per kilo in 1954 and 60 francs per kilo in 1955-1956. These fluctuations, regarded as robbery perpetrated by the traders, were a constant topic of conversation in every village. Most young men felt themselves less susceptible to victimization by having a steady salary.

Since not every man was a planter, the average yearly income in these Fang villages in northern and central Gabon was much less than the $200 to $250 a year a well-tended two hectares of cocoa might bring.[8] My own calculation of the average annual income in the villages which concern us here is between $60 and $80, which means that a significant number of villagers were living very close to subsistence. They were unlikely to find ways to obtain more than three or four thousand francs a year. For women particularly, who had minimal benefit from cash crops, the possibility of buying and selling dances— that is their own skills—had considerable attraction. In an inventory of eight houses in the village of Assok Ening, the average value of possessions of male heads of family was 60 thousand francs ($240); of men not heads of ndebot, 30 thousand francs. The average value of the possessions of women was 5 thousand francs ($20). The average value of kitchen utensils belonging to both men and women was 12 thousand francs ($60).

THE BRIDEPAYMENT

But no account of the economic situation in Fang country of the period is complete without considering the fundamental Fang preoccupation: the exchange and accumulation of resources through the bridepayment (*nsua*). For the primary resources which Fang men possessed were women. A man was considered rich and fortunate in the number of women he had at his disposal— sisters in the first place, whose bridepayment could be exchanged for wives for himself and those brothers and sons he protected; and wives in the second place, whose work in the plantations and in the kitchen could provide resources by which a man could entertain strangers and kin. An nkukuma was not measured by the amount of his possessions alone but by the scale on which he entertained others. The rich man was he whose "name is in the mouth of many others." And this was made possible by wives and sisters.

There have always existed means by which a man deprived by the facts of birth from having women at his disposal could work toward their acquisition. Old men recounted this work (*eseng*) with relish and related how in former days a man might lay up resources for a wife. He might work very hard at making baskets or roof thatch or by hunting or by raising sheep and goats or chickens and ducks. But all these were painful and lengthy ways to obtain a bridepayment. A man would be worn out before he obtained a wife, which augered ill for any marriage because women only wore out men the more. Winning many wives in this way was unlikely unless a man should be so fortunate as to immediately produce daughters with the first wife. For at a very young age, and sometimes at their birth, he could obtain further bridemonies.[9] Men could also take up the employment of troubadour or blacksmith or doctor (*ngungan*). Or they might organize an Ngi team and "sell" antiwitchcraft dances elsewhere. But these occupations either demanded a special skill of which not everyone was capable, or they were open only to those such as the leader of an antiwitchcraft team who had already demonstrated power in the village—they were already "nkukuma." It was not easy for a poor man struggling to provide himself a wife to lay claims to the powers of an "ngungan" or "nom Ngi."

With the coming of the colonial powers, there were increasing means available by which men could earn wives. Ngema, for example, was left only two sisters, but was able to parlay that inheritance, through his position as overseer on a nearby citrus plantation, into nine wives. Still, for the average man, even with the possibility of employment in the towns nearby, it would have been a number of years, if he had no other resources, before he could obtain a wife. It is not likely that he could have saved more than 1,500 francs a month working in town. At an average payment of 50,000 francs and 75 pieces of merchandise (roughly $300), it would have taken a man between four and five years to earn money sufficient for the bridepayment,[*2] not to mention the additional costs of the marriage ceremonies themselves.

[*2] Bridepayments in the region of the Woleu-Ntem during the period of fieldwork ranged between 30 thousand and 80 thousand francs CFS ($120 and $320), and between 50 and 140 pieces of merchandise. Generally the higher the payment in francs, the lower the amount of merchandise. The total value of the brideprice (calculating 3 pieces of merchandise at 1,000

The bridepayment was not something that was paid all at once, but was a continuing obligation between affines. The average payments we give— $120-$320—were those calculated at the completion of the marriage ceremonies themselves. But initial payments on a young girl may have been made years in advance, with subsequent payments continued at every death of the wife's close relatives. A man never knew in the case of a good marriage when one or another of his relatives might arrive requesting an addition to the payment. And in the case of a bad marriage, the fathers and brothers of the bride were never quite sure at what moment the in-law would arrive returning the bride and demanding payment. In such an event, both parties embarked upon a long and involved litigation. As many payments would have been made over a long period, there was bound to be disagreement on the totals involved. And generally there was debate on the merchandise returned. For the original merchandise—trade cloth, towels, blankets, handkerchiefs, etc.— had been put to use and other items had to be found. There was never, in any case, an equivalence here, for the in-laws never returned all the merchandise. It was accepted that something must be kept for the services of the bride, however bad the marriage may have been. And there was always a debate on how much must be kept. If the divorce took place after children had been born, a rarer event, there was always debate as to the value of the children in respect to the bridepayments.

An additional complicating factor since the mid-twenties, when Fang abandoned the old iron money and began to negotiate the bridepayment in colonial currency, was the fluctuating value of that currency.[10] Though earlier attempts by the Germans to turn the iron money into an all-purpose currency had some impact upon its stability of exchange, Fang remembered iron money as being very stable and the colonial currency, in contrast, as subject to unpredictable variations. Any middle-aged man recounting his own history of bridepayments had ample evidence of shifts of value. For example, here is the history of monies paid by Sima Ndong up to 1959. He had a history of unstable marriages because his wives had not been blessed with children.

Bridepayment

FIRST WIFE: My father paid 500 francs in 1939, with money from my first sister's brideprice. Three hundred francs more was paid in 1941, the year I brought her to the village. I sent this woman back in 1944 and reclaimed 2,500 francs, the amount to which the brideprice had grown.

SECOND WIFE: I married my second wife in 1945 and paid 3,000 francs for her. The money came from my first wife's returned brideprice and my second sister's brideprice in small part. I sent this wife home in

francs) was thus between 50 and 100 thousand francs—$200 and $400. Higher amounts were paid on the northern frontiers with the Cameroons, and lower amounts in southern Fang districts.

1950. The brideprice had grown to 5,000 francs, the amount returned
to me.

THIRD WIFE: I married my third wife for 8,000 francs in 1948 . . . she
was a second wife in my house at the time. I was working at that time
at the citrus plantation of Assok Ngoum and some of the money came
from there. Some came from the marriage of my second sister. I sent
this wife back in 1955 . . . the bridepayment had grown to 24 thousand.
I received that back but not the merchandise.

FOURTH WIFE: This is the wife I now have. I married her in 1955 for
35,000 francs. This has now grown to 48,000 (1959).

FIRST WIFE OF ZE NDONG (younger brother to Sima): 40,000 was paid
on her in 1957. Ze, who was working in town, provided 15,000 of
that amount. The rest came from the marriage of our younger sister
in 1954 for 34,000 and this has since grown to 46,000.

Bridepayment Received

FIRST SISTER: The marriage of this sister was arranged by my father who
spent half the "dote" for another wife and half the "dote" for my
first wife. She divorced in 1951 and I had to return 8,000 francs. She
married quickly again at Yengwi where her husband paid 13,000 for
her. She divorced again and went to Essangi for 16,000 in 1953.

SECOND SISTER: She went on marriage in 1948 for 4,000 francs. But a
considerable amount of this had been paid several years before. She
was sent back in 1950 and I had to return 6,000. The next year she
went to Odjip clan for 10,000. In 1956 she divorced Odjip and I had
to return 20,000. Then she went to Mvelmavop for 30,000 where she
now is. This dote has grown to 36,000.

THIRD (YOUNGER) SISTER: She was married in 1954 to Odjip clan for
34,000. This has since grown to 45,000. Part of this money was used
for my younger brother's marriage and part for an operation on my
leg.

THIRD SISTER'S VILLAGE CHILD: My third sister had a child in the village.
She is still in school. We took a dote on her in 1956 when she was
10 of 30,000. Now the man is dissatisfied and we are returning that
money. We still owe 20,000 and wait until the next cocoa season to
pay it. Some of that money has gone for cement floors and walls of
our house.

In this history covering a twenty-year span, we see clearly the speed with
which sisters' and daughters' bridemonies were used to obtain wives. Bridemoney was also paid out of savings from wage labor and cash crops, but the
first source was bridemoney received. Bridemonies could be put to other uses
as in the case of Sima's operation for elephantiasis of his right leg, or for
improvement of his "cold house." These expenses and his sense of respon-

sibility in marrying off his younger brother denied him a second wife and meant also that he had to delay returning monies he had taken on his younger sister's village daughter.

The remarkable fact about these histories is that the price increased from 800 francs in 1939 to between 40 and 50 thousand francs in 1959. Fang had to contend with inflation and devaluation of their currency—more than a fifty-fold decrease in the value of the franc in a little over twenty years. This inflation and recurrent devaluations acted to increase the number of contacts between in-laws, as fathers and brothers, noting the decrease in the value of their money, hastened to their daughters' and their sisters' husbands to demand increased compensation. The increase in these requests, trying to all parties concerned, was an important source of social tension at the end of the colonial period. Inflation and devaluation also acted to increase the divorce rate. For, as bridepayments rapidly increased, unsteady marriages were likely to be pushed toward divorces by fathers and brothers confident of getting a higher payment elsewhere and unwilling to negotiate higher payments from already disgruntled in-laws.

Despite currency fluctuations and devaluations, matters in themselves foreign to Fang awareness, Fang nevertheless quickly noted changes in purchasing power and acted to assure that over the long period, the real value of women remained relatively constant. Bridepayment was not only a ritual matter. These histories show us a relatively constant value of the female against declining currency. If we compare the monies paid in Tessmann's time (1905-1907) with those paid in 1959, we note this stability. In fact, slightly higher real value payments seem to have been made in former days, perhaps justifying the old men who argued that men worked harder to gain women formerly and that women, appreciating that work, remained truer to husbands. And surely with cash crops and wage labor there came a greater diversity and ease of means to gain bridemoney. But the real value of the bridepayment was relatively stable. Tessmann[11] gives a figure of between 200 and 750 marks as the range in values of the bridepayment of his time. The average figure is 500 marks. An adjusted real value for 1957-1959 dollars would be $144-$544 with the average value at $376. This is close to the late 1950's average figure for northern Gabon of $300.[12] In respect to Sima Ndong's brideprice history, though in 1949 he was paying fifty times the number of francs as in 1939, the 1959 franc was approximately one-fiftieth as strong as the 1936 to 1939 franc.[13]

Thus, though the bridepayment seemed to have increased greatly over the years, the real as opposed to the apparent value of the woman had remained relatively constant. The consequences of inflation and devaluation had been largely psychological. Fang, aware of such apparent increases in bridepayment, often argued they were paying much more for women and receiving much less. This troubled the marriage bond. This bond was also threatened by in-law demands for further payment in attempts to compensate for inflation or devaluation. In-laws were even led to try to break up old marriages based on low payments in order to form new and monetarily advantageous unions.

The awareness that modern currency was not a satisfactory representation of woman's value and man's work did not lead to abandonment of bridepayment or to token payments or exchanges in kind only. Indeed, Fang steadily resisted government efforts at limitation motivated by the desire to liberate monies bound up in brideprice so that they could be put into savings, useful to national investment. Perhaps this was because, as Fang said, the wife's father must be compensated for his loss and the husband must be assured of his control over his wife. Perhaps it was because bridemoney did represent "work" and evaluation and thus expressed "appreciation" of the woman in a society where such expressions between man and woman were rare. And perhaps it was because for an impoverished and fractiously egalitarian people these endless exchanges of relatively large amounts of money gave a feeling of importance in personal possession and position, and a feeling of permanence and order in social interaction.

The Dramatic Integrations in Monetary Exchange

The buying and selling of dances was an attractive possibility for women. With possessions worth only 5 or 6 thousand francs, the chance of earning several thousand francs on an 800-franc investment was appealing. But to most men the opportunity to earn money, an uncertain outcome at best, was not as attractive as the opportunity to escape the ennui of village life and enjoy a pleasurable activity—*elulua*. That pleasure was obtained first by inviting the teaching team into the village for several weeks, and then by leaving the village with one's team to dance elsewhere.

Fang valued periodic travel away from the village. They held a Rousseauian notion that the social atmosphere of the village—the social contract—was flawed and acted overtime if undiluted, to provoke antagonism and misfortune. Partially this expressed a fear of sorcery, but also the belief that an unrelieved village life gave rise to a "bad heart" (*nlem abé*) or a "bad head" (*nlô abé*). Tranquillity in heart and head was preserved by departing for the fields and forests every day and by leaving the village entirely several days a month, taking advantage of that network of relationships brought into being by exogamy and periodically reinvigorated by marriage payment negotiations. The formation of a dance team served the double function of providing pleasurable activity in the village and enabling escape from the village confines.

As richness was traditionally recognized in a Fang man's control over that chief resource, woman, so the men who formed dance teams derived their chief satisfaction not from payment—they usually claimed not to have received it—but from the temporary authority they exerted over twelve to fifteen women.[14] Though sexual relations were not included in the dance Commandant's powers, yet there was an illuminating similarity between dance exchange and marriage exchange. They were both exchange relationships which brought about important transformations in the social situation.

Of course Fang, no different from any other people under the influence of all-purpose money, were capable of reducing their institutions and relationships to matters of monetary compensation. They argued frequently enough that the purpose of the bridepayment was to "pay" (*tang*) for the services of the woman in field and kitchen work and in child-raising. Yet the ceremonies of marriage itself were not limited to simple compensation. In respect to the dance teams, while it could be argued that the visiting team had to be compensated for the work done in the fields and kitchens during the teaching period, and for their dance skills and "medicine," yet more was going on than simple compensation.

Though the exchange of currency and goods and services was a salient feature of these institutions, on close inspection we see they were aptly referred to as "economic dramas."[15] More values were inherent in transaction and transformation than could be represented in modern currency. In understanding the dramatic or ritual element, we see how it was that exchange relationships (the marriage of women or the selling of dances) mortgaged the divisive and self-interested tendencies of village society to relatively long-term obligations. The surfeit of self-interest, the desire for greater brideprice payment for example, was prevented from reaching such proportions as to cause a breakdown in affinal relationships. Human relationships characteristically struggle between commitment to self and commitment to system, commitment to short-term and commitment to long-term gain. Among Fang, two different clans, for example, whose interests were fundamentally opposed, yet linked themselves together systematically so as to find common interest. Self-interest was transmuted into system interest in part by dramatic and often ritualized processes of transformation.

The institution of *bilaba*, found formerly among the northern Pahouin (Bulu Ntumu and Ewonde) throws light on the problem. In this institution of competitive gift exchange, we find trade goods moving East being exchanged for traditional goods moving toward the coast, West. This exchange was accomplished by competitive activities between stranger clans. The object of these festive competitions was to gain prestige by hyperbolic openhandedness. The "potlatch logic" of transforming economic goods as quickly as possible into status and prestige acted to stimulate trade. The self-interest which might attach itself to the accumulation and hoarding of these goods, a grave threat to subsistence economies in any case, was countered by promoting galvanic expenditure. Bilaba insured continuing exchange of goods and, moreover, united alien social units in so doing, containing their implicit antagonisms by expressing them in patterned ways.

Balandier has analyzed the paradoxical process involved in bilaba as "antagonisme organisateur" and "mariage des contradictions."[16] He also suggests but does not analyze the importance of the symbolic elements manipulated in process. He points out, as has Alexandre,[17] that there was male-female symbolism involved in the polarity: the traditional goods from the South and East had a female valence; the trade goods from the North and West were male.

Because bilaba of the northern Pahouin was defunct and could not be observed, these notions could not be fruitfully pursued with this trading institution. But they can be pursued in relation to marriage ceremonies, dance team ceremonies, and in relation to a dance of gift-giving by sons-in-law and brothers-in-law at the end of mortuary ceremonies, also called "bilaba" or "lablaba," by the southern Ntumu and northern Fang. It is more properly referred to as *afa abong* (payment of the funeral money).

At the death of a member of one's family, all sons-in-law (*nôm ngwan*) were invited to be present at the mortuary ceremonies (*dzem awu*). At the end of these ceremonies—they often lasted a week—the nom ngwan had an opportunity to show respect for his in-laws and for the dead. The whole village gathered early in the morning around the family council house. Within the house at a large table called the Presidency sat several secretaries ready to write down the various amounts. The bulk of these gifts were entered into the calculation of the brideprice. Suddenly the drums started up and as suddenly quieted. Out stepped a man from the village, performing a "dance of mockery" (*afôn*) of the gathered group of nom ngwan. He danced out to the forest and then at a distance dropped his loin cloth with his legs spread showing his bare backsides and his parts. Then the drums started up again. The sons-in-law had been challenged.

Now it was their turn. The first one stepped forward to make his speech and give his money. In the late 1950's, two thousand at least was expected and six thousand hoped for. The payment was often both in money and merchandise. If the amount was large, there were shouts of pleasure from the village and the nom ngwan "danced bilaba" holding his two little fingers in the air. "You are as little fingers to me." It was a gentle mockery of the other sons-in-law and of his in-laws. But if the amount was small, there was a disgruntled silence. Men unable to give large amounts tried to engage a friend or relative in the local village to make the gift. This major contribution to the brideprice was not the only gift exacted from the nom ngwan. Other tables and other secretaries were set up to exact from him small amounts to pay for the invited dance teams, for the drinks offered to guests, etc. The Presidency of the Funeral might also "fine" the nom ngwan for some fancied slight.

The following is the record of the "nom ngwan" who came forward at the funeral of Mba Muzwi (see below, Chapter 9):

ASSUMU EYO (Clan Essangi): He gave one bottle of wine to the table of the President and 11 pieces of merchandise: 1 sheet, 1 light blanket,

1 shirt to Obunu, 2 cloths to his wife's mother as well as 500 francs.
200 francs to the table. 100 francs because he kept the table waiting.
He gave 35 francs for cigarettes for the Presidency. He was so confident of the importance of his gift he started to dance bilaba before
giving. He said, "I have no problem to speak of. I have been married
6 years to your daughter and we have never had a fight. She has
always shown good conduct and we have made children together
easily. I have come only to pay." And he then gave 7 thousand francs
and began to dance bilaba in earnest to the cheers of the crowd. The
Presidency gave him in return a chicken and a bottle of wine and said
they would later respond to his generosity privately.

BUKWE PAUL (Clan Efak): He gave a pair of shorts to Obunu, Mba
Muzwi's uncle, 200 francs to the player of the tom-tom, and two
pieces of cloth to his wife's mother. Before he made his big gift, he
caused a laugh by asking the Presidency for a bottle of wine. He said:
"For my gift you will attack me, thus I wish to be a bit drunk before
I give it." He gave 5,600 francs. The Presidency replied that there
had been four previous funerals and he had not come. They knew that
he had treated their daughter well and taken her to the hospital when
she was sick. He must give only an additional 400 francs to make
6,000. The Presidency gave to him a bottle of wine and a duck after
he finished dancing a brief bilaba. The size of his gift would have
been applauded more if he had not been absent for so many funerals.
But the family appreciated how well he had taken care of their daughter.

MBA BUKUH (Clan Odjip): He gave 3 cloths, a handkerchief and 500
francs to his father-in-law (his mother-in-law was dead). He gave 485
francs to the Presidency and 10 franc notes and cigarettes to assorted
family members. Then since he was embarrassed about his gift, he
asked Ngema Mve to present it for him. Ngema did this because Mba
Bukuh was of the village where his mother came from—he was
Ngema's mother's brother in an extended sense. Ngema apologized
for the size of the gift, 4 thousand francs, but he pointed out that the
wife had only been with Mba for two years and they were not absolutely
sure about her yet. The Presidency responded that more must be given.
"How do you expect our daughter to act well in the future when such
a small amount has been given at the death of her brother?" Ngema
responded speaking in the person of Mba. "I am still a young man
without many resources and without work at the present time. This
is all I can afford to give you—it is not because I am selfish (akuíng)."
But the Presidency attacked Ngema and Mba again and finally Ngema
gave 500 francs more. Mba, relieved, then danced bilaba.

NKEGO ESSONO (Clan Maban): He was the last of the Nom Ngwan. He was the only one to have come and sit with the family months before, the day after Mba Muzwi had actually died. He had given a thousand francs at that time. Thus his gift of 4,000 more was well received by most. But the Presidency said, "We hear you have been fighting with our daughter. We want at least 6 thousand." Nkego said, "Well you keep the daughter and I will go back and get another thousand." Since many felt Nkego's gift was adequate, Chief Essono stepped in. He was Nkego's mother's brother in an extended sense because Essono's sister was one of the wives of Nkego's father. He said, "Nkego, as you know, broke his jaw. He had to go to the Cameroun to have it fixed. He spent much money on that. He should be forgiven." Then, as was unusual, Nkego's wife, the daughter in question said: "We both went to the Cameroons and spent much money. This is all we can afford." The Presidency acquiesced. Nkego then gave an additional 10 pieces of merchandise and three bottles of wine and danced bilaba. He was given a duck and a bottle of cognac in return.

In this afa abong the sons-in-law gave 21,500 francs plus assorted small gifts to the value of another 8,000 francs. But the dramatic development is more interesting. First there was the "dance of mockery" (afon) of all the other "stranger" clans by a local family member. This mocking antagonism was then transformed into the antagonism between the various brothers-in-law and between their respective clans as they competed among themselves in giving gifts to their wives' family. If a man's gift was small, insults would be raised against his clan. And though the bilaba dance was also a mockery by the son-in-law of his wife's family, the prevailing result of afa abong was the transformation of that antagonism into a solidarity. First, other family members, as Ngema Mve or the Chief, entered in to take the son-in-law's part against the Presidency, thus showing the realities of deeper affinal bonds. And, second, at the end of afa abong the son-in-law was almost always given a gift, embraced, and brought into the private chambers of the family to be warmly received.

THE EVOLUTION OF A DANCE TRADITION

Many of the features of dance exchange like those of bilaba, and surely the monetary aspects, were the result of the peace imposed by colonial authority as well as of the resultant intensification of trade. However, old men recalled dances being traded very far back. The ceremonies of the antiwitchcraft cult, ngi, were brought by one clan and established in the village of another clan as far back as could be remembered. In fact, Fang found it hard to conceive of a dance or ceremony that had always been the property of all Fang and did not originate somewhere and become subsequently widely exchanged.

Fang remembered many "dances." Practically any Fang of middle age in the districts of Oyem and Mitzik could remember fifteen to twenty dances that originated elsewhere and came to local villages through a teaching team. This did not include many individual dances held within the old cults: dances of men or of women to prepare for war, to purify the village, to celebrate a victory, to protect the newborn, to calm the ancestors, and so on.

Here is the list of team dances, produced by Obunu, from those which he had seen or heard of: *ball, belebele, bieri, bwiti, ekota, elong, enyenge, epwak, flanco, mangan, manzang, medok, mevungu, ngwan ntangan, ebwen, efayang, olanchea, emias, ozila, nguh, ngi, ngol, nkekek, nlup.* But not all these dances had equal standing in Obunu's eyes. Bwiti, as a revitalization movement which had become widely institutionalized, was really not to be compared to an ephemeral dance form such as mangan, although the importance of the dance element in this religion was impressive to Fang and, in some respects, the spread of Bwiti was comparable to the spread of any dance.

These dances listed by Obunu must also be seen in evolutionary relationship to each other. Belebele, manzang, nguh, bieri, mevungu, and ngi are the more or less traditional dance institutions among Fang and long known to them. (Bieri, Mevungu, and Ngi were religious cults.) All these dances were until recently very widespread in Fang country, although versions of them were exchanged in the manner of the more modern dances. Ekota, nlup, emias, and epwak were regional versions of ozila, in minor ways different perhaps, but in essentials the same as the parent dance, which originated between the two wars in Spanish Guinea. We can place all these dances into an evolutionary framework (Figure 5.1) with the six traditional dances providing a cultural reservoir of elements out of which the more recent dances were constituted.

This chart, by no means a complete account of dance developments among Fang, points up the interweaving of elements from more traditional dance institutions into subsequent dances created for exchange. The Belebele dance was a night dance in which men lined up on one side of the central court and women on the other. The men and women alternatively danced across to each other mocking and calling upon the opposite sex to come out to the center. This form was reiterated in later dances in which men and women danced opposite or in relationship to each other. In elong, however, balophones entered in as the musical element and instead of a line of men facing a line of women, the men, in a circle, turned within a circle of women whom they induced to dance with them. Ball was an elaboration of elong, but more influenced by modern pair dancing. The instruments—drums, bottles, accordions, and guitar—were more important. The music dominated. In manzang we see three progressive developments of the balophone dances. Originally the emphasis was upon the balophone played by one- or two- or three-man troubadour teams. The men both played the instrument and danced around

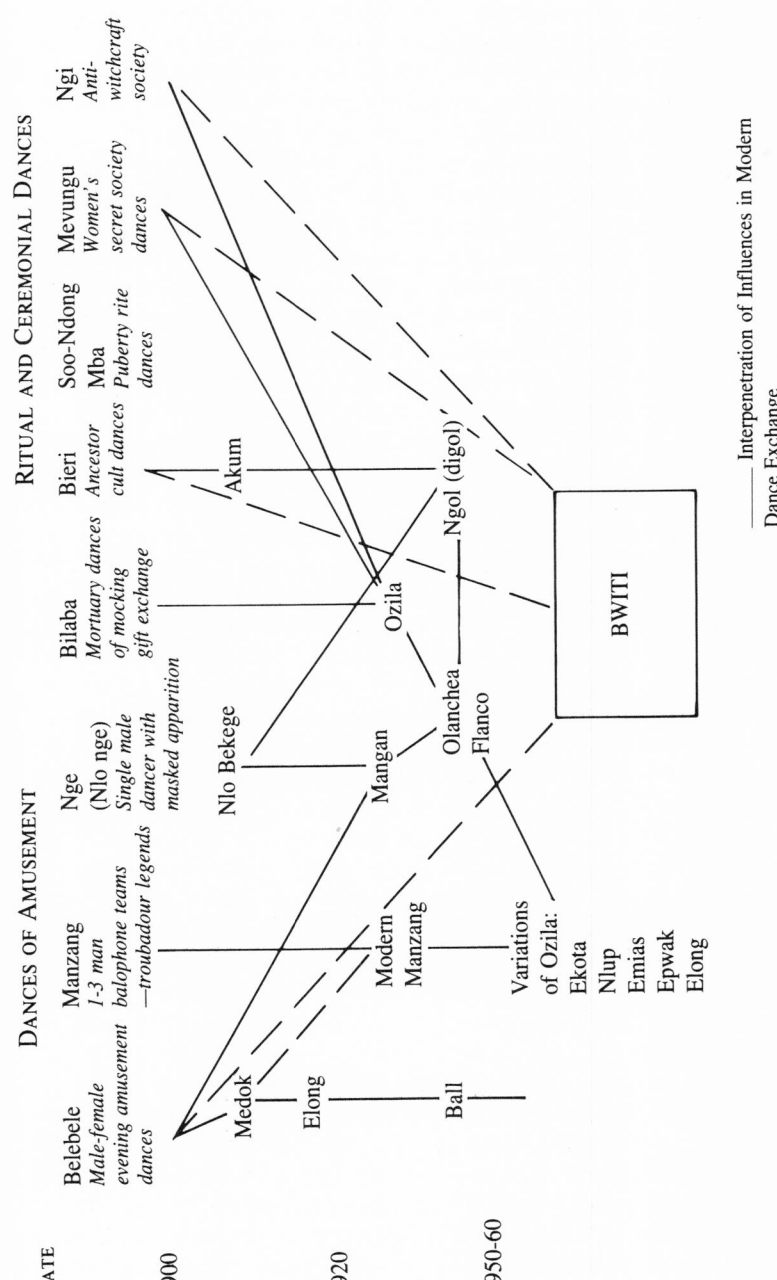

DANCES OF AMUSEMENT

RITUAL AND CEREMONIAL DANCES

DATE

Belebele
Male-female evening amusement dances

Manzang
1-3 man balophone teams —troubadour legends

Nge (Nlo nge)
Single male dancer with masked apparition

Bilaba
Mortuary dances of mocking gift exchange

Bieri
Ancestor cult dances

Soo-Ndong Mba *Puberty rite dances*

Mevungu
Women's secret society dances

Ngi *Anti-witchcraft society*

1900

1920

1950-60

Medok

Elong

Ball

Modern Manzang

Variations of Ozila:
Ekota
Nlup
Emias
Epwak
Elong

Nlo Bekege

Mangan

Olanchea
Flanco

Ozila

Ngol (digol)

Akum

BWITI

———— Interpenetration of Influences in Modern Dance Exchange

– – – – Source of Dance Patterns in Bwiti Dance Complex

5.1 Evolution of Fang Dances

it. In the second version of manzang, a woman's dance team was formed to circle around the balophone, though the instrument was still central. In the third and final version, the instruments had become peripheral and it was the woman's dance team that had become important.

In the old nguh dance, women and men from the village gathered to sing before a raffia screen behind which a male and/or a female dancer occasionally showed himself until finally, inspired by the increasing pace of the music, he rushed out and danced among the spectators. The appearance of the mask and the subsequent outrush of the masked dancer was the central element. This element was found in subsequent dances such as ngwan ntangan, in which a white female visitor appeared, and the mangan-Flanco which we witnessed above with Muye Michel. The original version of mangan, however, showed no masks and was essentially a female dance and a reworking of elements of the dances of Mevungu (the women's society). We have placed ozila and enyenge under the Ngi dance because in these dances, as in the Ngi antiwitchcraft cult, a small group of men give direction to the women and also because the dances were felt to be efficacious against witchcraft.

The ngol and the olanchea dances deserve special mention. The ngol dance, which came to Fang from the Congo Brazzaville, produced Charles de Gaulle in the process of the dance. The Fang version has some similarity to the nguh dance in which powerful, usually masked figures were induced to be present, but ngol, or digol, was syncretized with modern bureaucratic forms and will be discussed below. The dance of olanchea, active in Spanish Guinea in the late fifties, was named after a strong but fairminded and popular District Administrator, Captain Basilio Olanchea. The women wore fanciful oriental-style garb and sampan hats, but danced in a circle as in elong and produced a masked white figure behind a barrier as in nguh.

The point is that in the challenge of inventing new dances for exchange, Fang were not simply dependent upon outside influences but possessed a rich tradition of their own which they combined and recombined in various ways. One may disagree with the particular typological dynamics we have arranged for the dances given to us by Obunu, but it is evident that each of these dances combined in a different way a set of elements common to the dance tradition. These elements of recombination are the instruments (the variable use of drums, harps, balophones), the variety of relationships of dancers to instruments (are the instruments central or peripheral?), and the variety of relationships of men to women (equal and opposed as in Belebele, or women alone as in mevungu, or men dominating women as in ngi or bieri). The innovators of "new dances" had to decide whether to climax the dance with the miraculous appearance of a masked figure and whether to invent new songs. For some of the old songs of Belebele or ngi came up in the new dances. Thus, the mangan dancers still sang the love song from which Belebele took its name:

*Meking me tan, a nto oyap, a yenyen mis, a belebele nam. Me keme nye
yen; ye ba bele, ye ba duk a ntô oyap!*
The voices grew enfeebled, he is far away. Oh to see him with the eyes,
oh to have him to touch; do they tell the truth or do they fool me he is
far away.

And they sang songs to Ndong Beyene, "the man with the glasses," who
was a powerful personage of one of the more recent versions, the Ndong
Andrike version, of the Ngi cult. For as the old cults, from which many of
the elements in these dances were taken, died out, there was a tendency for
the dances themselves to appropriate, albeit in a casual and secular manner,
some of their religious functions. Thus, mangan-Flanco was felt to have some
effect against witchcraft.

The elders' argument against Muye Michel that they had seen the like of
the mangan-Flanco dance before could be repeated, therefore, of practically
any dance exchanged by Fang. Of great interest was Muye's response, for
he suggested that the money payments did not measure all the values in
question. He was sensitive to the tendency in his elders, surely a tendency
in Muye himself, to convert the values which were in play in the dance
situation to monetary equivalents, and to suppose that any values which could
not be so converted were irrelevant to the transaction. In the exchange institutions of people just moving into a monetary economy, we find, however,
difficulty in "standardizing the exchange-ability value of every item to a
common scale,"[18] and Muye was playing, argumentatively, on that difficulty.
Accepting Muye's argument, we have pointed up that what was being trans-
acted in these dances, and in bilaba, was not simply payment of money for
an aesthetic good but was much more the transformation of social and cultural
relationships on several different levels so as to achieve "marriages of contradictions" amidst pleasurable activity.

MARRIAGES OF CONTRADICTIONS

Speaking of "marriages of contradictions" implies that it was in the institution
of marriage itself that the basic elements of both bilaba and dance exchange
were found. In their way, the "bilaba" of Fang mortuary rites recelebrated
the bonds of marriage at the moment of death, just as so many songs and
dances of the dance teams, in their allusion to courtship and lovemaking,
anticipated the celebration of marriage. Marriage as Fang celebrated it was
more than an understanding reached between two alien kin groups, one of
which had suffered a grievous loss in the person of its daughter, for which
it was being compensated. It was also the playing-out of the relationship
between dominant and subordinate social units. We have reviewed the subordination of southeast to northwest and the association of the former with

femaleness and the latter with maleness. These directional and sexual biases were reiterated in marriage. Ideally the family of the bride came from the southwest. If not actually from the southwest, they might still be spoken of as *minkí me nsi nkeng* (our downriver in-laws). They were in a subordinate position for that reason and also because they were coming at the insistence of the lineage of their new son-in-law. Marriage was understood as initiated by the man and his patrilineage, and this ideal was expressed frequently in "marriage by capture" (*abôl ngwan*). Here the onus under which the bride's family labored was made especially clear and they were obliged to come to either retrieve or accept the "de facto" loss of their daughter.

What is of particular interest, however, is the way that this dominance and subordination were symbolically presented in marriage festivities and the manner in which alignments underwent dramatic transformations. In the process of the marriage, efforts were made to mask the facts of dominance and subordination. The fact that their subordination had caused the bride's family to suffer the loss of their daughter was compensated both psychologically and materially in hospitable gratuities and considerable deference and respect on the part of the son-in-law and his family. Equality was suggested in the competitiveness of the "contradote" (*biôm bí nkía*), the father-in-law's gifts advanced against the generosity of his son-in-law. But what was most suggestive was the shifting back and forth of symbolic alignments between kinship identification and sex identification. Marriage ceremonies offered an opportunity for ritual reversal in which the dominant position of the man was either mocked or reversed. Thus, at one point in Fang ceremonies, the women of the husband's patrilineage lampooned, in brief dramatic sketches, the foibles of men in their favorite occupations of debate, hunting, and war. But later, in the final act of the ceremonies, the women cooperated in serving the men the *bídzí bi nengôn* (*nyingwan*) (the meal of the mother-in-law).

There were three allegiances involved in marriage: (1) clan members to themselves, which was divisive in respect to interclan affairs; (2) men to men and women to women, relationships which were divisive as far as internal lineage affairs were concerned; and (3) the relationship of men to women in which the marriage was grounded but which was divisive as far as the patrilineage was concerned. The first two of these allegiances were played upon in the marriage ceremony in such a way as to balance each other. Thus the social divisiveness of each form of allegiance was prevented from manifesting itself disruptively. The marriage ceremonies brought together two clans whose self-allegiance was divisive to their interrelationship. Their antagonism was expressed in competitive exchange and in the dominance and subordination understood to prevail between them. It was modified by reciprocal respect and deference enjoined by the occasion. But the tugs of this allegiance were rapidly modified by being transformed into the allegiance of men to men and women to women as the men were mocked by the women. In the final "act of marriage,'' bidzi bi nengon, the men of both lineages sat together and were served a meal by the women. Their equality and allegiance to each other in dominance over women was affirmed. No statement about the relationship of man to woman or man to wife was put forth. This relationship, too warmly pursued, was threatening the lineage loyalties. But it was of course celebrated in the songs of the dance teams and to a degree in the songs welcoming the bride to the village.

What occurred, then, in marriage were transformations of allegiance by which the "marriage of contradictions" was accomplished. Cleavages were reduced by casting them into changing perspectives. We find such transformations also in operation in dance exchange. In the dramatics of dance exchange, at least for the more recent dances and, in particular, mangan and mangan-Flanco, we get lineages first being posed against lineages, later to be transformed into men cooperating with men and women cooperating with women. The women first dominated by taking center stage and mocking the men. Then they sang of the virtues of togetherness through courtship. Finally, women appeared as subordinate to men. This was the same shift back and forth between sex allegiance and lineage allegiance as was noted in marriage with the addition of the element of sexual allegiance. In dance exchange, however, the visiting lineage which was teaching the dance was dominant. This was because they possessed special knowledge. The team of twelve to fifteen women was held dramatically under the very rigid bureaucratic control of the Commandant. He blew his whistle and stamped around in the full vigor of executive responsibility. The authority of men over women seemed manifestly confirmed. That this dramatization was gratifying to the men, at least, was explained by the fact that it was precisely this control of men over women that Fang felt to have been most disturbed by colonial contact. A constant complaint of village life was the escape of women from fathers' and husbands' supervision.

While these jaunty Commandants faced each other in the opposition of lineage to lineage, the women were, however, singing songs which mocked the men, abusing their generosity and capacities of leadership. They sang:

Ma yen dzam nzen Abung evôm ma so va; befam bene bizizing ve bininga ebo ba dang bizizing.[19]
I see on the road I came to Abung village; the men in friendliness and generosity by the women are surpassed.

The fact that the women also got up from opposing teams and danced together in pairs, coupled with the fact that they cooperated closely in garden work over the three-week period of instruction, brought about a transformation— the substitution of sex allegiance for lineage allegiance.

These processes occurred in brief compass. The two Commandants began by making competitive statements about the effect and beauty of their two teams. The women sat facing each other, twelve against twelve. They alternated singing together under the leadership of the head woman dancer or singing in competition. But at the climax, when the mysterious masked dancers—in earlier times said to be the ancestors and in mangan called ngol (De Gaulle) or Flanco (Franco)—appeared at the other end of the village behind a raffia screen manipulated by the male leaders, the women were brought together in common cause against male domination. They ran down together in pairs, old team members escorting new, to do homage to the "ancestors" and disappear behind the screen to be incorporated with them. Here, as in the culminating ceremony of marriage, bidzi bi nengon, the antagonism of lineages was played down in favor of the symbolic statement of the adhesion of men to men dominant over women adhering to women.

Conclusion: A Sense of Overarching Allegiance

The family expressed skepticism to Muye Michel that his proposed dance team would be economically viable. And would he adequately protect the virtue of the women who would accompany him? Muye countered that the family needed the "pleasurable activity" a dance team could bring. This argument was telling, and the family agreed to invite a troubadour though not to support Muye's team. Many could agree that the accumulation of monies was not an end in itself. They could agree that, as Muye implied, the hoarding of resources was dangerous and open to the accusation of witchcraft. Dramatic expenditure was required.

Despite the introduction of cash crops and wage labor, the transactions involved in the bridepayments were still the major economic preoccupation of Fang. There was, therefore, a connection in their minds between monetary transactions and the relationship between the sexes. But the one could be too easily taken to represent the other. The exchange of money was only a salient element in a deeper drama. More enduring social values surrounding the relationship of the sexes were in play. Money itself was an inadequate representation of the woman in marriage negotiations, just as it was an inadequate representation of all that occurred in dance exchange. Despite very great fluctuations in colonial currency, the real value of the woman had remained about the same over the years although the fluctuations had tended to conceal that fact to many Fang. Similarly, despite the many new dances invented and exchanged by Fang, these were, in large part, recombinations of persisting traditional elements. There were thus more enduring motifs and thematic values behind the busy buying and selling which took place.

What we have seen exchanged in the "economic dramas" we have examined—marriage, bilaba, team dancing—was more than money. It was dominance for subordination, lineage allegiance for affinal allegiance and sex allegiance. The consequence of this "exchange," in addition to the relationships established by purchase, was the tying together of social units which were ordinarily in opposing or contradictory relation. It was an important transformative process, a "marriage of contradictions."

Of course colonial life had an effect upon these economic dramas. There was an increasing tendency to reduce the values and qualities present in situations of exchange to the lowest common denominator—the all-purpose colonial currency. The result of this tendency was to particularize those involved in a transaction, confirming their opposition and separate interests rather than knitting them together. Such a reduction of marriage was not only one important cause of the alienation of the sexes among Fang, it also meant increasing alienation of men from men and of clan from clan. The same consequences flowed from the reduction of dance exchange, in the minds of many Fang, to the simple purchase of an aesthetic good.

Fang of Muye Michel's disposition, money-minded as on some occasions they were, yet preserved a more traditional feeling that it was as unsatisfactory to reduce the ritual aesthetic and magical accomplishments of these dances to simple monetary exchange as it was distasteful to let a daughter or a sister be purchased solely with money without establishing reciprocal relationships and carrying on exchanges at other levels of social and cultural life in the process. They recognized, if only in moments of argument, that the direct purchase relationship with all-purpose money was too barren an affair. It did not allow for the dramatic celebration of antagonisms and their transmutation into solidarities. It could not effectively tie together disparate allegiances and bring about that "marriage of contradictions" amidst "pleasurable activity" so essential to a harmonious social order. They recognized in money a fluctuating agency of self-interest that threatened the enduring interests of men and women in the social system to which they belonged. They recognized that there was a "tradition" to these dances, expressive elements, that offered the possibility of transmuting self-interest into system interest. Muye failed to persuade his fellow villagers to involve themselves in dance exchange. It is not surprising that he began to devote himself, more and more, to the Bwiti religion, a religious system incorporating many traditional dance elements, which was expressly dedicated to the transmutation of the self into an overarching cosmic order.

❧ 6 ❧

The Relations between the Sexes

Mininga a ne ana nsinga lam ntangan.
(A woman is like the wick of the European lantern.)

NGEMA TAKES A NINTH WIFE

FOR SEVERAL MONTHS Ngema and his wives had been busy making preparations for his marriage to Ada. She was already living with him, as the bulk of the brideprice had been paid. But the marriage had to be concluded by the formal visit and the entertainment of her family. Several things happened that made Ngema wonder aloud in the council house why he was taking a ninth wife. For one thing he suspected that Minkpwe, the third youngest of his wives, and formerly a favorite of his, was having adulterous relations with a man of a neighboring village. Ngema had discovered the "good man," Bikuh Oyono, in her kitchen on several occasions in the evening. Bikuh said he was visiting relatives.

A day later Ngema went off in the forest early in the morning. He overheard two women speaking in a nearby plantation. They said, "Everyone knows that Ngema has a wife off 'in marriage' (to a man) in Medouneu." A week later Ngema found Bikuh again in the kitchen. Bikuh went out immediately saying he wasn't going to be insulted by a jealous husband. When Ngema again demanded an explanation, Minkpwe answered that Bikuh was a son-in-law (*nôm ngwan*) of Ngema's first wife, Nana Michelle. This was true in a distant sense, as Bikuh's older brother was married to the younger sister of Nana Michelle. Then Ngema demanded an explanation from Nana Michelle, his respected first wife. She said, "I told Bikuh that I am now staying in the kitchen with Bibong's wives and the new child, and he ought to find me there. If he comes to this kitchen he doesn't come looking for me." At that Ngema was very angry and moved to strike Minkpwe. But she dodged and said she had told Bikuh that he shouldn't visit at night because all the food prepared during the day had been eaten. "Why did you give him any food at all?" said Ngema. "He is not related to you."

Since his marriage was approaching, Ngema decided not to raise palaver against either Minkpwe or Bikuh. He would simply try to keep her under close surveillance. Then about a week before the marriage his wives were involved in a fight with a wife of Chief Essono and the wives of Ngema's older brother's son's family, the family of Mintza Mve. Efop, the wife of the Chief, had gone out to her chocolate nut tree (*ndok, Irvingia gabonensis*) to find that the nuts had been gathered. This tree had belonged to her husband's eldest sister. There had been many disputes about the tree, which was a long way off in the forest near an old abandoned village. It angered Efop to walk all that way to discover that most of the nuts were gone. She had her ideas as to who had taken them. When she returned to the village she found Ngema's women gathered in Bibong Leon's first wife's kitchen. She came to the door and asked: "I am looking for the person who has taken the nuts from our ndok tree." Nobody answered. Efop then said, "I will ask you one by one until I find the person who has stolen the fruit of that tree." Marie, Ngema's daughter by his second wife, Zang, was in the kitchen. A strong-willed woman in her twenties, she had been kept in the village by Ngema to give birth to "village" children, two sons as it turned out, to strengthen his family line. Marie replied, "Are you calling me a thief?" Efop said, "Why didn't you answer when I first spoke?" And Marie said, "I wanted to see what you would say about me!"

Efop then said, "I know why you rob from me. You have the wives of Bekale Mintza who always take your part!" By this time these two young women had come up and were standing behind Efop. One of these women was Efop's sister of the same village and clan. This woman, Mfum, said to Marie, "If you didn't steal how is it you went and harvested those fruits when we weren't present?" Zang, Marie's mother, said, "My daughter did not steal. That tree belongs to her too for it was her great-grandfather's tree." Efop said to Zang, "You yourself steal and that is why you have taught it to your daughter." Marie was so angered at this that she rushed at Mfum. Four of Ngema's wives rushed to help Marie, while Marie's mother rushed at Efop.

Only Mve Essono and Ngema Pierre were in the council house at the time. They ran out to stop the fight. But although they were strong boys in their late teens they were soon lost in the pile of flailing women and retreated. Bibong Leon, who was in another part of the village, hurried up upon hearing of the fight. He was very angry. He placed himself between Marie and Mfum and said, "Why do you fight next to this kitchen? This is where my wife has just given birth to a child [the child was two months old]. You know my wife has lost many babies. In the kitchen of a newborn all ought to be happiness and tranquillity and especially for a woman who has just given the first live child in six births. Get out!" The women were ashamed and retreated, but not until after further shouting and a brief flurry of fighting further on. Essono finally came and pulled his wife away. Ngema then arrived and calmly told his daughter and wives to return to their kitchens.

The affair was little discussed in the council house, though it was on every tongue in every kitchen. "This is not a palaver," Ngema said, "for it is between the women only." Among the women it was said that Marie was not at fault for picking the fruit. The tree belonged to her great-grandfather too. But she was at fault for not having responded to Efop's first question. She did not give the good answer (*mbamba nyalan*) that turns away wrath. The older women said that fighting was a bad thing that women had learned from the men. In the old days the women married into a village, lived and worked well together, and did not fight.

THE MALAISE BETWEEN MEN AND WOMEN

In the transitional period the malaise between the sexes became an even more fundamental theme in Fang culture than that between the generations. Thus it was said that the first worry in any man's mind was likely to be the whereabouts and "whoabouts" of his wife or wives. The second worry was likely to be whether or not they respected him enough to provide him with his next meal. Lack of hospitality among Fang—a rare event—usually arose from the dour demeanor of hungry men, or men caught up in a connubial contretemps.

A full man (*nyamoro*)—and a nyamoro should be a well-fed man—was in part judged on the fairness (*sôsô*) with which he treated his wife or wives and the harmony (*mvwaa*) that he was able to make prevail in his household. Young men in conflict with their wives were repeatedly advised to act with the patience (*nzong*) characteristic of maturity. I learned this in my first days in Gabon. Across the aisle from me on the DC-3 flying from Libreville to Bitam in 1958 was a young couple returning to the husband's village in northern Gabon. The man's older sister, he explained, had given him a plaintive farewell at the airport. "I do not find myself well now," she said, "and you may not find me here when you return. You would please me if you would remember that you are going to our village and if you are to be a man you must treat your wife well. The village will judge you as the city does not." And yet most villagers recognized that the relations between men and women had also deteriorated in the villages. This meant, in part, a shift from a sexuality well controlled by society for its purposes to a libidinous sexuality in which amorous adventures and infidelity were widespread.

The traditional attitude toward women was ambiguous. In part it depended on whether one considered woman as sister or woman as wife. Balandier understood the fundamental ambiguity surrounding Fang women. She is, at once, the element in Fang social life which is "the most constrained, causing her to say following the proverb, 'I am nothing before a man, I am as stupid as a chicken'—and the element of which one demands the most."[1] Indeed she was the chief agent of agricultural production and clan reproduction. The patrilineal line was nothing without her fecundity. Marriage to her guaranteed a man the means to offer hospitality to people outside his household, which was the main source of his prestige and renown (*nsem y duma*). Marriage enabled him to establish the network of cooperative relationships between clans which had survival value in a decentralized society. Women gave rise to many disputes, but that was because she was primordial. It was said, "The palaver is not the village, the woman is the village" (*Etom e se mvôk, mininga nye a ne mvôk*).

That woman, withal, remained exasperatingly elusive was seen in axioms with which fathers often counseled sons: "Woman is like a shadow. When you run away from her she runs after you, and when you run after her she runs from you." And though woman held the village together she could also "destroy the family" (*mininga ajum etunga*). She was the path to both prosperity and conflict.

Attitudes surrounding the bridemoney (*nsua*) give some understanding of the increasingly conflictive and ambiguous relationship between male and female. Fang men were generally frank about the many services that women performed which justified the high bridepayments prevailing in the late fifties and early sixties. Thus Essono Ebang of Endama told us, "A man marries a woman with the bridepayment so that she should cook for him, provide entertainment for his friends and relatives; and if a child is born it will be his."[2] At the same time men testified to the malaise between the sexes by insisting that without the bridepayment there would be no fidelity in the women. They would wander without regard for any male attachment. Madang Sima of Assok Ngoum remarked, "If the men did not employ the bridepayment, they would have no women with them for any length of time. Women are incapable of staying with men who have not paid the bridepayment."[3] The bridepayment held the woman in obedience to her husband. She respected it and it prevented her from "vagabondage and laziness" (*ndende ye atuk*). There was the sense, then, of women's potentially labile sexuality and the need to attach it to its socially appropriate object by means of the bridepayment.

In this situation of malaise the bridepayment came to seem less a compensation to her family for her loss or a "purchase" of her affection than a guarantee of her good behavior. For it was given to her fathers and brothers—those men of her own clan with whom she had the closest and most enduring affective ties and who, it was hoped, could most influence her behavior. She might develop such ties with her husband, but that took a long time and was increasingly rare.

That such hopes should be concentrated, at least by men, in the bridepayment rather than in the women themselves was already, perhaps, testimony to the growing fragility of the bond between men and women and the instrumental way that it was regarded. The stereotyped attitude of men toward women as such became increasingly deprecating. The following are the dismal views of the married men of Mba M'Oye:

> CHIEF ESSONO MBA (age 50): Women are truly human but their heart does not support impatience and they think like "one who has been struck foolish for transgressing a taboo" (ane mesisok eki).
>
> ZOGO EBU (age 60): Women have bad customs. They are very cruel and act like animals or children. We can say that they won't care for their husband when he is sick. They won't listen, and they are stubborn.
>
> ASSEKO MVE (age 42): Women are people but very ignorant, like a child or an animal. Men don't put much hope in women. Thus we marry women as children so that our mothers can teach them in our village. When a woman behaves well we say she acts like a human being. When she acts badly we consider her a bushpig or a chimpanzee.
>
> SIMA NDONG (age 35): The woman is like a child. The thing that most bothers us in her are her bad thoughts. For example a woman has no concern for her child and her husband. She does things according to her own ideas. Many women abandon their children in their first married situation. Women are a constant care to men.

These dour opinions of the immature and untrustworthy character of women were widespread. They might be modified, however, to reflect a more traditional appreciation of the services women rendered.

> ONDO NDONG (age 25): Woman is to man as a child of the same mother because she does all things for him, cooking his food, washing and pressing his clothes, everything. I can say that the woman is a workman for the man. She is like the "boy" or the laundryman that works for the Whiteman.

Those who took a less emotional and more utilitarian view of women often argued that Fang women performed a function for Fang men equivalent to that performed for the European by his many servants and his machines. It was often maintained that until Fang had such servants and such machines at their disposal, they were fully justified in their polygyny. The "fullmen's" attitude toward women was concerned with women in their roles as wives. It would be another thing to have men discuss women in their roles as mothers, sisters, or daughters. Yet some of these stereotypes tended to be carried over and generalized. Thus, boys too young to have contemplated marriage might readily reflect adult male stereotypes. They picked these up, no doubt, in the council house during the interminable debates on bridepayment, adultery, and divorce.

> MVA BIBANG (age 13): Woman is like a child. I say this because her actions are like those of a child.

NDONG ASSEKO (age 11): Women don't know how to do things. Women are disorderly. They are ill-tempered. They are not strong and cannot strike their husbands.

Even Bibong Ngema (age 8) was sure that women were not like men. They do not have the same spirit (*nsisim*). Some act like men but others know nothing at all. "They act like fools [*akwan nlem*]. They always look for reasons to be struck by their husbands." It was hard for even the very young to escape these stereotyped views of women, even though the women they knew were their cherished mothers and their nurturant sisters.

It is illuminating in this regard that one of the most positive things that could be said about women was that they could be like siblings (*mwan nyang* or *mwadzang*) in assisting one.[4] In one sense it was indicative of the failure of the role ideal for the wife (*nga*) that it tended to be conceived in other terms. In another sense it was not surprising that sibling likeness should be seen as the ideal role, for it was precisely the wife's quality of being alien to the lineage that was a cause of the mistrust and deprecating attitudes she inspired, just as it was a source of her unpredictability. By suggesting that she might best learn to act like a sibling one suggested that the best wife was one who had developed consanguinal loyalty. This suggestion deemphasized the sex differences in the husband-wife relationship otherwise featured so starkly in the kinterms for wife (*nga wum*) my female, and husband (*nom wum*) my male,[5] and was probably a response to the fact that sexuality was increasingly posing problems of control.

The underlying dilemma was the dilemma of exogamy: sexuality was expressed and indeed only appropriate between those who were socially alien. It was infused with that danger. Patrilineality posed a problem for the woman. She had to shift from her well-appreciated status as sister and daughter to the uncertain status of wife and daughter-in-law in an alien patrilineage. Some of the ceremonial events designed to face these dilemmas and effect that change of status are examined below. Here it is enough to remark the difficulty of the passage, and how the accommodation it aimed at was vulnerable to the changes of modern times.

Ngema Mve, by reason of his nine wives, had long been a student of the struggle between the sexes. He, like so many Fang men of a reflective turn of mind, swung between blaming external agencies for what had happened to Fang women to blaming the women themselves. The intransigence of the women, he often argued, was provoked by the European and particularly the missionary.

They are always lecturing us about our women. In any palaver they always side with the women, although there are many who simply abandon a man because he is poor and can't buy them things and will not work together with a man to get good things for the family. My mother lived happily with my father a long time and when he died she was happy to be given to his brother. Now the Europeans call that enslavement.

But on other occasions, as on the eve of that palaver with his wife Minkpwe about the suspected adultery, Ngema delivered himself of stronger opinions. He remembered in the old days that Fang used to take the women who were disobedient out to the courtyard and strip them naked under the sun and march the other women by them. If it was a case of adultery the elders went off and killed the man responsible and brought the cadaver back and placed it over the woman's body. "See here, the cause of this man's death is you and your adultery."[6]

The preoccupation with adultery in mid-century was very great among Fang men and particularly among polygynists. Of Ngema's nine wives, only two had not been involved in talk or accusations of adultery. A third of the cases argued in the men's council house concerned adultery, but this included only those cases which could not otherwise be arranged. There is no measure of how much adultery had increased over former times, though Ngema, like many Fang men, maintained that it had. Tessmann's observations belie this. "Faithfulness in marriage presents itself rarely . . . although one must recognize that there are women who live with their husbands without wandering, it is about as rare as white ravens."[7] Fang men generally spoke matter-of-factly of this problem and even pointed out that the fines an adulterer had to pay for his "privileges," if divulged, could adequately compensate or even be a source of income to the offended husband. The fine (*ntang abwan*) in 1960 could amount to 5,000 francs.[8] But Ngema pointed out that the evil in adultery was that it led to the "bad head" in a woman: a reluctance, even a resentment on her part to carry out responsibilities to her husband and his family. Fang said, "If a man would only keep his mouth closed in adultery it wouldn't be a bad thing" (*Nge mot a nto bo ebwan adzip anu ebwan e sa ki abe*). "But the adulterer always says things that give ideas to women and break the marriage apart."

The malaise in the relationship between the sexes to which the preoccupation with adultery attests can be otherwise demonstrated by taking the divorce figures for the 85 married men in Assok Ening. While adultery may not have increased significantly, it seems clear that divorce had increased, due to the greater freedom with which women themselves were able to exercise that option. These 85 men, in any case, had, in their lives, set about to marry 424 women. They got little beyond the stage of *edza ngwan* (requesting the girl) and making a token downpayment in 100 cases, but in 324 cases they had paid enough of the brideprice to have brought the girl or woman to the village. Of these women, 186 were divorced (*avar*) after full or substantial bridepayment. Fifty-seven percent of all marriages thus ended in divorce. The figure would be 67 percent if one were to take the token ''propositions'' and include them as engagements and dissolutions. Moreover, of these 85 men 50 had been divorced at least once in the sense in which we are examining it (after payment of bridemonies). Divorce was admittedly difficult to define in Fang society, as it was in many African societies, where it was a family matter and not a social event which had to undergo jural sanction and, moreover, where it took place in the stages of the lengthy process of establishing bridepayment. But the 50 percent or above figure of the proportion of marriages ending in divorce was congruent with the pessimism most Fang men felt as to the permanence of their bond with any woman.*[1]

The Fang situation would seem to accord with the general observation made by Binet on family stability in francophone Equatorial Africa: ''The rupture of marriages, formerly very rare, has become very frequent to the point that morality and the demographic situation are placed in peril. In certain groups one can only with difficulty find a woman who is living with her first household.''[9] Binet's contrast is perhaps too starkly drawn but it is clear that the men were increasingly dissatisfied with their spouses, and women were increasingly availing themselves of newfound rights of repudiation not only of their original husbands but of any other man the levirate might formerly have prescribed for them.

As for the women, they rarely regarded the men as having changed drastically from former times, and they spoke of male habits in marriage with more of a sense of the immutable in male character.[10] But women often recognized change in the situation of marriage and regretted the loss of the patience that men in former days used to display in counseling their wives when they did wrong. This, they said, was because they were marrying men much younger than formerly and these men had more of the quality of *nduman* (impatience and braggadocio), and less of the patience of maturity. Women

---

*[1] Fang figures are on the high end of those assembled for Africa by Barnes, ''Measures of Divorce Frequencies in Simple Societies.'' They are less than those of the Fort Jameson Ngoni where 65.6% of all marriages not ending in death ended in divorce. The divorce ratios we give here are very simple ones based exclusively on responses of married men. The women were resistant to this inquiry so we do not know the degree to which the high ratio reflects the circulation of sterile women. My observation would be that it does not. Moreover, the analysis was not age-specific and does not give us, as would have been desirable, any indication of change in divorce rate over time, as between the young men and the older men, for example. The tendency, in recollecting the past, to remember only long and fertile marriages is likely to be a bias at work in Fang insistence upon increase in divorce. As it is, we have to accept Fang views that men of all ages currently were suffering higher divorce rates than men formerly. This is true even though the Gabon census of 1960 returns a figure ''relativement faible'' of Fang respondents divorced at the moment of inquiry: 3 to 5% of men and 2 to 3% of women. But this picture of present marital state is of little value in answering questions of frequency. By combining the dynamic turnover in spouses we have noted with these figures of divorce rates, we get an indication of how acceptable divorced people were as spouses.

often claimed they worked as hard as they ever had but the men were striking and insulting them more.

Also, they said, men were intruding more and more into women's provinces. Men and women, folklore had it, were never able to live close together without palaver. This was because men who had swallowed their anger in the courtyard or the council house would later spit it out upon their wives who had nothing to do with it. A common retort by women in conflict with their husbands was "Go to your council house and leave me alone" (kung aba jue). The legend was, we know, that men and women long ago had tried to live together but their relationships soon became so embattled that men were forced to build the council house for themselves. The paradox was that men and women could live together only by living apart, and women did not hesitate to smoke up their kitchens and burn men's eyes if their presence became too overbearing.

It was a vicious circle. Men become increasingly suspicious of their wives and were trying to keep close watch over them. Women felt the increasingly overbearing presence of the male and tried to escape this watchfulness. This circle has been given a spin by at least two other forces: (1) the change in the structure of the village from the long street village to the family compound, which meant that women were subject to much greater male scrutiny, and (2) the increasing sense of their own rights and deprivations communicated to them by administrators and missionaries concerned with their "enslavement" by brideprice.

CEREMONIAL CELEBRATIONS AND
SUBVERSIONS OF MALE-FEMALE RELATIONS

Whatever the malaise between husband and wife, one cannot neglect the satisfactions that existed in the relationship. Satisfactions were bound up in a proper discharge of reciprocal responsibilities. Men derived satisfaction from the respect (efongla) with which their wives treated them, and the women derived satisfaction from the fact that out of their respect for their husbands they became the object of a particular affection or affectionate care (nlugha).

It was easy to obtain from Fang men a list of responsibilities of husbands and wives. Men must first of all build and outfit a kitchen for their wives. They must clear the forest and provide their women with adequate fields. They must hunt and trap and bring home ample supplies of meat. They must provide salt and iron goods and cloth for dresses. A polygynist must regularly include each wife in his connubial attentions. A woman on her part must prepare clean food for a man in such a way that he may eat three meals a day: a big one at night, a smaller one in the early morning, and a snack wrapped in a leaf package at midday. The wife must also provide guests with food. She must keep the fire in the kitchen and provide fuel for it. In the first

four or five years of life children were entirely her charge and she must train
them not to disturb or soil the village. She must give the "good answer"
(*mbamba nyalan*) to the questions and requests of her husband. She must not
wander unduly in the village or elsewhere. She must plant, weed, and harvest
her several gardens: manioc, peanut, and corn. She must not refuse her
husband in bed. Her responsibilities to her children seem to have been taken
for granted. It was not surprising that with all these duties she must not be
lazy (*ndender*).[11] But it was also not surprising that there were marriages
among Fang in which obligations were discharged and in which satisfactions
were fully received. It could produce a "still deep pool" of mutual satisfaction.

The marriage ceremonies themselves (*avak mbôm*, reception of the bride)
tried to point the couple toward such satisfactions. Though given over to
several days of the kinds of dances and rejoicing characteristic of many Fang
ceremonial occasions, the marriage ceremonies were also an occasion for
integrating the bride into the collectivity of women within her husband's
village and for demonstrating reciprocal respect between in-laws which would
be a stabilizing element in their future relationships. In respect to the first
objective the new bride (*mbôm*) was isolated and closely accompanied by her
"mothers and sisters-in-law" who washed her from head to foot and instructed
her in the responsibilities within the husband's patrilineage. They provided
her with a new bark apron and rubbed redwood powder on her body. She
was visited by the women of the village, who sang welcoming songs of advice
and encouragement (*bía bi mbôm*).

These songs ranged over a wide range of topics and included the song we
have used as the chapter epigraph. "A woman is like the wick of the lantern."
That is, if you raise her in your respect she will shine upon you, but if you
lower and deprecate her she will leave you in the dark. This song, as others,
was intended as much for the ears of surrounding men as for the mbôm. Most
songs concerned the bride and her relation to the women of the village. Many
songs simply complimented the beauty of the bride. "What a beautiful thing
I see here" (*Za awale mbeng dzam me teh di na*), or "Little fruit where did
you buy that fine bottle [i.e., your fine figure]?" (*Ebuma mwan o wa kus
mbeng ndak-wové?*). Many songs were meant to encourage the bride's proper
comportment in the village or the respectful humility with which she should
approach her in-laws. "What kind of a mysterious person with dark glasses
is this bride who looks her mother-in-law in the face instead of looking
down!" (*Ah! Ndong Beyene aval mbom di da dege nkia asu ka dege osî*).
The women sang of the bride's need to keep her body free from dirt and
parasites. "A woman walking with sand fleas in her toes makes of a plain
a great mountain" (*Aso ônyu mbembe nya nkol*), or "Women of other towns
have a clean face but their head-cloth hides dirty hair" (*Ebininga be ye minlam
ba bo na; asu mfuban eyak mvin nol*). The mbom was told that she was there
to serve her husband and his family and no one else and to make no foolishness

with other men. And she was reminded again and again that beauty was no substitute for hard work: *mvé e se ekop, mve e ne biyem o se ki mbeng bikop nge o ne biyem abe, mvé a na zeh-e-zeh* (beauty is not the skin, it is one's habits, you are not beautiful if you are of bad habit, beauty is nothing). The majority of songs, therefore, while complimenting the beauty of the bride and encouraging the husband to provide good treatment, put major emphasis on the respect due the in-laws and the satisfactions of hard work amidst the collectivity of women married into the village.

The second phase in the integration of the bride with her in-laws occurred in the meal of the mother-in-law (*bídzí bi nengon*). The bride and her sisters cooperated in this meal. It was an occasion for the bride to come out from isolation (*akulu ngwan*), and was composed of game and domestic meats (goat meat, mutton, and sometimes pork) provided by the groom's family, together with agricultural foodstuffs (manioc, corn, peanuts, cucumber) and dried fish brought by the in-laws. It was served first of all to the groom's male relatives in the council house.[12] The meal was intended to represent, as did the marriage itself, the bringing together of the two main categories of Fang foodstuffs provided by male and female respectively, as well as the division of labor in respect to the gathering of these foodstuffs. It signified the obligation of the wife to prepare food for her husband and his male relatives. It demonstrated her probable skills in this matter as seen in the skills of her mother who taught her. After the meal all men shouted their praises of the mother-in-law (*minkí*) and deposited a 10 franc note as a token of appreciation in front of their plates. The new bride came and collected the dishes.

As a final phase of the ceremony, the bride and groom sat down together in the courtyard under an umbrella while the women's groups danced in front of them. Generally the words sung at this juncture were of mild challenge and mockery between the two clans. In Ngema's marriage to Ada, the women of her clan (Essangi) sang, "Ngema have you the resources to entertain a team like ourselves?" (*Ngema a ne bele nsama te?*) The women of Mba M'Oye, some thirty strong, responded, "Who is poor?" implying, "We will show you our generosity" (*Za enya a ne ekukut?*).

The demonstration of reciprocal respect was made, therefore, in the atmosphere of a ceremonially competitive exchange of goods. It was a delicate balance. After a half-hour of the above kinds of songs, Bibong Leon stepped forward and sang, "Let the clans listen to my name" (*Meyong me wôk meyôla*), implying, "Through my gifts you will know my name today." The women of Essangi responded joyously to this boast singing, "Joyous action takes its place here" (*Elulua e ntô va*). At the conclusion of this song Leon presented the Essangi family with a gallon bottle of cognac. Essono, on the fringes, fired off a shotgun in jubilation, as was the custom.

After this gesture the competitiveness gradually built up between the two teams until it threatened to exceed the occasion. Ngema himself then stepped in and presented his gift to the father of the bride, a man of his age. He made a long speech declaring his high respect for the good man and his inability to give gifts commensurate with that respect. He then had substantial quantities of wine, cognac, dried fish, rice, and other store-bought items brought forward. He also made a personal gift, to the father of the bride, of a thousand francs. Once again Essono fired off the shotgun.

The Mba M'Oye women took up the singing again, demanding, "Father-in-law, what can you respond to us?" (*Esa minkí ye ô ne kat bía?*). Minki then took up the challenge. He apologized profusely for an epidemic in his village which had killed off many animals, "You, Ngema, a rich man must have pity on my poor gifts." He then gave three goats, five ducks, two chickens, three bottles of palm oil, one basket of peanuts, one basket of smoked meat, and one basket of dried onions. The Essangi women sang proudly of these gifts saying, "We swell with pride at this child of ours so open in his ways" (*Bia tem angombe mwan wum ayô*). But the Assok Ening women took exception to their pride. They began to count the items missing in this gift. Finally Ngema had to halt their counting. It was all he could do with a final word of thanks to avoid having the exchange end on a sour note.

Much more in these ceremonies was made of the relationship between the two clans and their adult representatives than that between bride and groom. The former, after all, was confined for several days to a hut while festivities proceeded, and the latter was often elbowed aside and, in any case, usually played a secondary role to his father in the welcome and demonstrations of respect. Yet while the marriage ceremony seemed primarily intended to establish strong bonds of mutual respect between the two clans, there was plenty of advice and many examples offered to the young couple to start them off correctly in their marriage.

Despite the good counsel they provided, some explanation for the high divorce rates may be found in the exchange songs themselves which, in boasting of gifts, sharpened the woman's desire for the material advantage of married life by pointing her toward the pride of possession (*menguma*). This pride in possession was traditionally interpreted as modest pride in the domestic things that were the product of the women's world. But more recently it led to a covetousness that was unsettling to domestic tranquillity. During these exchange songs the women often brought forth the gifts they would be giving one after another, singing, "Cucumber seeds these they are pride, pride. Peanuts these they are pride, pride" (*Ekwan edzí dzí e ne menguma, menguma. Owônô enyí le ôwônô e ne menguma, menguma*). This pride in possession was easily associated with the affectionate care (*nlugha*) that women looked for in their husbands, with the result that this latter came to be exclusively recognized through the giving of gifts. Many young married women took the paucity of possessions in which they could take pride as a reflection of their husbands' affection for them. Husbands with few resources found themselves pressed to demonstrate their affections materially before they had good evidence of their wives' respect for them. The dilemma of unrequited reciprocities was indicated in that song which appeared so frequently in the bia bi mbom, "A woman is like the wick of the lantern, you turn her up and she gives a bright light." Couples often descended into an impasse, a vicious circle, on this matter. The reciprocal satisfactions of married life (nlugha and efongla) were subverted before they could establish their claims.

DEMOGRAPHIC PRESSURES ON SEXUALITY

Among the forces at work in disturbing the relationship between the sexes, perhaps the most important was the demographic factor: population decline through declining birth rate and the high incidence of infertility, and an imbalance in sex ratios. Vital rates in Gabon as a whole were long recognized as low even within the African context. The growth rate was suspected to be a negative figure in the thirties and forties, and though the much improved prophylaxis after mid-century brought back a slight measure of population growth, the footnoted table based on a corrected estimate of vital rates in French-speaking Africa[13] shows that the situation remained serious. The birth rate and the growth rate, still only marginal, were among the lowest in Africa. The death rate had, however, decreased markedly.

In the Gabon census done in 1960, at the time of this study, this general picture was confirmed and it was further pointed out how high was the percentage of sterile women in the Gabonese population, surpassing 30%, compared with other African countries.[14] The fecundity rate correspondingly was the lowest in the francophone countries, 116 births per year per 1,000 women of childbearing age. Fang had about average rates among ethnic groups of Gabon for the measures we are considering here,[15] and, thus, were well represented by the overall figures. The situation in the region of the "estuaire" where Fang predominated and where Fang Bwiti has flourished has to be contrasted, incidentally, as even more depressed in every one of these rates than the region of the Woleu-Ntem, the northern part of Fang country, the country of family Mba M'Oye.

In addition to the above facts of birth rate, growth rate, and total fertility, the imbalance of sex ratios between bush regions of emigration and coastal regions of immigration was also notable. These demographic facts were not ignored by Fang. In truth the infecundity of their women was painfully perceived. It could hardly be ignored that more than one-third of the women were barren. Time and again villagers complained of this fact which was so threatening to them as members of a decentralized society. The size of the extended family had been one of the main sources of security, and the number of a man's progeny was one of the chief sources of his prestige, the guarantee of the preservation of his name, and the assurance of his spiritual status in the ancestor cult.

The direct cause of this infertility seems to have been a very high endemic venereal disease rate—gonococcal infection primarily—emanating from the longstanding lumber camp operations in the Gabon Estuary.[16] The men, however, did not customarily assign the fault to themselves and to their own gallivanting outside the village during their youth. Rather they blamed the profligacy of the women's lives and the contamination they underwent by their acquiescence in adultery—their easy accessibility to any traveler. The married women experiencing their infertility firsthand were just as likely to blame their husbands and to seek the possibility of conceiving through adulterous relationships with other men. When the desire and obligation to bear children was coupled with the anxious prospect of old age without children to care for them, the woman's acquiescence in adultery, quite aside from the attractions of sexual intrigue, was understandable. As the village became decentered, and communications opened it up to strangers and encouraged the women to leave more frequently for family gatherings, ceremonies, and markets elsewhere, women's resistance to solicitation was much taxed.

It cannot be forgotten in this discussion of "new freedoms" that occasionally in former times either clan-sisters—who had remained in the village or returned after divorce or widowhood—or women married into the village could achieve significant status. Such women could play important roles in decision-making, whether in conflicts in the council house or within the ancestor cult. Village women staying on in the village to bear children had the double advantage of motherhood and its esteemed contribution to the lineage, as well as membership in that lineage.[17] In Assok Ening there was the case of Ada Mve, a daughter of Ekong Oye, who left in her late teens for Libreville and returned in her late twenties a well-to-do woman. She did not then marry but provided brideprice out of her earnings for a brother. She supported a Bulu man as a consort for herself in her natal village. Though she did not take part in council house discussions, she was frequently consulted by the men of the mvogabot. Villagers were not surprised at this turn of events. It had happened before in living memory.

For unmarried girls the opening up of the village had exacerbated the solicitation to which they were subject even if they did not leave home. Fang expected nubile girls to have a period of sexual experimentation with a variety of suitors unless the girl were spoken for by some initial payment on the brideprice. And, of course, one reason for offering brideprice for prepubescent girls was to assure the sexual rights of the future spouses and avoid this adolescent experimentation, with its possibility of venereal contamination. But, even so, this period of sexual experimentation was not meant to be a long lusty one and girls were under considerable pressure to socialize their sexuality soon by accepting a chosen suitor to marry. Girls were often in contention with their families because they were prolonging this period of experimentation.

On the other hand, girls could be victims of the high rates of infertility, for their fathers—themselves conceiving few children—would often encourage them (as Ngema with his daughter Marie) to stay unmarried longer and bear children in the village. Also the widespread infertility led to the view that a girl increased her marriageability by proving her fertility and bearing children in the village during adolescence. Thus, the opening up of the village and the freeing of the individual from close identification with the group had its impact upon women's sexuality. These changes, coupled with a high rate of venereal pathology in the countryside, tended toward the libidinalization of women. The challenge to be strong and serviceable—the challenge which was laid down for women in the symbolization of marriage—was a challenge more and more subverted by the awareness of themselves as objects of covetousness and solicitation, as provocative forces in the relations between men.

PURIFICATION AND POWER THROUGH SEXUAL INSULT

Fang men felt that women had certain advantages in sexual affairs. There is a tale, with some Christian influence perhaps, which accounts for the difference between men and women. It was told with an increasing sense of aptness in northern Gabonese villages in mid-century.

> Long ago men and women went naked. They fell to fighting. Women said I am going to hide from you and you will never find me. Man said hide! Woman made for herself a "cache-sexe." Man hunted all around for her but couldn't find her. He said, "I cannot find you." He was tired. Woman said, "Hide yourself." Man made himself a "cache-sexe." Woman took off her "cache-sexe." She walked slowly past man. He had an erection. Woman said, "Aha, I see you! You cannot hide from me, even though you are tired."

Obunu, whose characteristic ironic observations on such deeper attitudes in Fang life we have heard before, observed that this tale showed why men were always angry with women. He gave the following aphorism to explain the tale: "The naive vulva, the penis comes to it angrily (with determination), but the vulva is quiet with surprise."[18] Thus did women, in Obunu's view, make light of men's most serious intentions. Men, too, were like the wick of the lantern.

During the marriage ceremonies the women's singing groups often mocked men and men's societies. But it was in the women's secret society of Mevungu that the female tendency to mock male potency was institutionalized into open raillery. This society, the female counterpart of the various exclusive male cults, acted to create solidarity for women displaced from their original clans by marriage. Daughters of the village were not ordinarily offered membership. In the battle between the women of Ngema and Essono which we have reviewed, many villagers bewailed the disappearance of the Mevungu society, a society that created among women a strong esprit de corps. At one point in Mevungu ceremonies this female solidarity was achieved by openly insulting the men. The women exited at dusk from the cult precincts and streamed through the village. They carried machetes in their hands and sang insults against the men, who, for their own welfare, were best hidden within their huts or deep in the forest. Otherwise they risked cruel wounds from the women. The women during these ceremonial days were without pity (*nget mininga*). They sang as they came into the village,

(*Awu a soang oh. Nget mininga mevungu a soang oh.*
Mevungu a so, a va so, a va so.)
Death has come oh. The cruel woman of Mevungu has come oh.
Mevungu has come, it has come, it has come.

The members beat upon the walls of the huts where the men were hidden and they sang mockingly of the size, strength, heat, and endurance of the masculine member, both in general and in the particular. "Look at that large member (or large scrotum)." (*O dege nye moro nkon*, or *Mora abin.*) "Look, he is impotent as the leaves of taro in the pot." (*Teh e ne eyeh ana lome mvi.*) Or they sang, "You remain lying with a woman but you can only take possession of her making love with your hands (instead of your member)." (*O lighe zoghbe mininga ô nga van nye ebon ye mô.*) The woman whose role in Fang sex behavior was characteristically passive and demure nevertheless sang, "Worn-out lance of a penis come bury yourself. I myself will cause to stand erect the rootless tree (that which is rootless)." (*Ondor nkon za bembe ma mien ma sôang munubu.*)

In respect to potency, reciprocal obligations were stressed. "If a man is impotent," Ayang Ndong warned, "he will have nothing to eat, for what wife will prepare food for a feeble husband?" (*Nkukuma ka bô eseng . . . ka zí.*) "Even the rich man who doesn't do his (connubial) work won't eat." Thus it was that the frequent complaints by Fang men about not being properly fed were often tied up at a deeper level with sexual relations. These concerns were reflected in the act of circumcision. An iron spear point was fired red hot to cauterize the wound. As this was done the circumciser (*nkik*) said, "Man never dies in the woman's portal—like the iron, like the iron and the fire." (*Fam da wuwu mininga mbí été—ékieng, ékieng ndwan.*) The nkik also chewed hot pepper and then spat it on the wound. As he did so, the nyamoro of the family who was holding the child sang, "Strong pepper, it is strong pepper, it is as fire." (*Ondondo ngu a ne ondondo nya na a ne nduan.*)

The sexual insults of the Mevungu ceremony were not, despite their dramatic interest, ends in themselves. They, and sexual insults generally (*ongômô*) which took place on other occasions, intended the purification and the obtaining of good luck for the village. If the village was overcome with filth and bad luck which had no evident source in witchcraft or ancestral displeasure, or which could not be controlled by the male antiwitchcraft society (*Ngi*) or the ancestor cult (*Bieri*), then women were called to make Mevungu or dance Ongome. Their cult, whatever particular functions of female solidarity it served, was still performed for the general good. The women were often asked to dance Mevungu in order to obtain good luck for the men in warfare or other arduous masculine activity (*abwia*). Nevertheless, in more recent years, as the forces we have examined were brought to bear on the relationship between the sexes, the sexual antagonism and the insults were more likely to be remembered for themselves than for the overall purpose of purification and the obtaining of good luck.

While the attitudes expressed in Ongomo or Mevungu may have been transitory, emerging only for regenerative purposes, yet enough suspiciousness remained in respect to women's sexual proclivities and powers as to make warnings in this regard part of the folklore of father-son relations. Fathers offered cautionary similes or metaphors such as the following from Essono Mba. His comments are paraphrased:

> *Mininga a ne nzen*: The woman is as the trail in the forest. Many men can pass to and fro over it, some of them die and others trip and stumble, but the trail remains (*nzen e ne mbembe*). So you can fornicate with a woman all night until you are nearly dead but she remains the same route as ever.[19]
>
> *Mininga a ne olam*: The woman is a trap. Man is as the game caught in the trap who struggles and struggles to escape but cannot and only breaks the member that is entrapped. So are men that act the animal with women, make violent movements with her and think they are accomplishing something. All they do is break their member.
>
> *Mininga a ne etutua elubiga*: Woman is a sieve that cries out for water while that water given to it runs away. Meanwhile that barrel (*ntegha*) from which the water comes is quickly emptied.

Such analogies were compatible with the general warning given to young men about marrying women who had circulated too much and known too many men. They will never be satisfied and will always seek to excite a man anew. In this way men quickly become old by "destroying their vertebral column" (*a wing nka'ale*). The old Ayang warned the young Mve Essono, "Do not go with your wife more than once every five days, do not let her tickle your testicles" (*nang be abing*).

Conclusion: The Hands
on the Wick of the Lantern

Fang increasingly struggled with that anomaly widely noted in Africa: though the productiveness that women so demonstrably achieved was highly esteemed, they were assigned low status. Though disputes which involved women took up an increasingly large part of men's time in the council house, disputes *among* women themselves were not deemed worthy of discussion there. The assignment of low status was rationalized by stereotypically associating women with children or the creature world—with the unsocialized. Women had always had some room for maneuver in this situation, despite male dominance, and had thus been able to resist, in part, full subjection to that low status. A few women had been able to achieve striking prestige. And women could count not only on the esteem felt for their role, but on beliefs as contained in the physiological philosophy of Fang. In that philosophy the actual contribution of female blood to creation and the place of the female element in the social life-style of mature men and women were given their due. The incompatibility between women's status and the esteem accorded them had its counterpart in conflictive attitudes toward sex. The sexual dominance of the male over the female was not at all clear, and always coexisted with the possibility of female manipulation of that dominance. The woman's hand also rested upon the wick of the lantern.

The Mevungu ceremony, with its mockery of the male sex, dramatized in a number of ways the freedom of maneuver that women possessed. Mevungu in the old days, as a ritual of reversal, was intended primarily to obtain supernatural blessing for the community. As such it may have tempered the anomalies of the woman's role by offering momentary compensation and catharsis for the inconsistent status which she was assigned. In recent decades, under conditions of pressure toward increased female sexuality, such celebrations of female power acted more to exacerbate the situation, by playing on men's anxieties in regard to females. Such rituals of reversal functioned most satisfactorily where the Fang social order had strong allegiance, where there was no exaggerated libidinality, and where there was no serious pathology affecting the birth rate and women's productiveness as in recent decades. One might argue that the Mevungu ceremony was part of the internal dialectic—the alternate stressing of contradictory values found in any society—of Fang life. If so, the confidence that there was any overall moral order in which these values might be suspended (dialectically or otherwise) had been so weakened that the old patterns of ceremonial resolution were more threatening than resolving. It was not surprising, in any case, that the Mevungu ceremonies had been generally abandoned and that marriage ceremonies more and more stressed competitiveness in personal and clan relations rather than the complementarity of man and woman and of clan and clan that should have

been brought about by marriage. As the architectonic of Fang building tended
to be reduced to material concerns, so marriage itself tended to be reduced
to material interests.

In Tessmann's discussion of the sex life of the Fang, he contrasted a plain
lustiness on the one hand, with an aversion to sexuality on the other. The
prevailing attitude which mediated between these two tendencies, he argued,
was reticence or shame (osôn) as regards sexual relations. He saw this shame
(which is not to be confused with simply an aversion to sex) as being inculcated
by cult life which, in his interpretation, inveighed against the sinfulness of
sexual activity and tended to associate woman with evil. But cult life also
aroused attention to sexual matters, and some cults gave the women their due.
It is more exact to argue that shame was a social strategy—a demeanor or
comportment—designed to handle the contraries embodied in women (to some
degree produced in the cults themselves) and to protect Fang from an unwelcome exposure to them. Oson was shown at the time of the marriage
ceremonies by the bride, and was meant to protect her against the severe
contradiction she faced of undergoing familiarities in a quite alien situation.

Oson demeanor fell upon both men and women. Men, too, as regards their
cross-sex in-laws, were constrained to show a prudery verging on avoidance.
But there had always been an unequal distribution of the burdens of oson.
And failure to maintain a balanced comportment in the face of contrary
tendencies has always been more suspected of women. Hence it was more
incumbent upon them to manifest oson. Tessmann felt that oson would be the
first casualty of contact with the West. This contact would undermine the
religious views which activated the feeling. Fifty years later many Fang men
would agree. Women, normally expected to carry a heavy load of reticence,
were felt to be casting it off not only through a scandalous libidinality but
through active disparagement of male status and even male sexuality.

This led in more recent years to the appearance of the Delilah complex.[20]
In Fang this tendency arose out of unaccommodated inconsistencies in sex
relations. In face of the unaccommodated fact that high esteem was found
with low status, and that by exogamy women were alien familiars, there was
a tendency to focus upon their low status and their alien quality rather than
upon the esteem due them and the fact that they were the essence of familiarity.
They came to be seen as weakening rather than confirming. They were suspected of betrayal. And women themselves were not immune to these changing
views. There were inroads upon their relationships with each other. The old
solidarities celebrated in marriage ceremonies, in the women's cults, and in
common agricultural labor were on the wane, as were these very ceremonies
and cults, before increasing economic independence. Suspicion and competitiveness emerged among women, producing the kinds of strife which Ngema
experienced among his wives.

In the Bwiti religion we will find marked effort to accommodate the sexes. There is a male-female dualism in the ritual structure whose consequence is to emphasize a productive complementarity in the relations between the sexes. Bwiti attempts thus to restore reciprocal satisfactions by means of ritual—to enable men and women, so to speak, mutually to turn up the wick of the lantern. At the same time this is done while restoring the sense of "oson." This development of a ritual dualism combined with sexual circumspection is not surprising in an adaptive thought system such as Bwiti. For the conflict that developed between the sexes in recent decades surely called out for such a solution. Though effort was inevitably expended on male-female relations in traditional cults and cosmology, we do not find in them this sharply dualistic ordering of the universe. And, in any case, the old cults in which this enduring human problem was cosmologized had long been moribund, leaving Fang caught up in that vicious circle in which the sexes turned down the wick of the lantern upon each other. Bwiti faces the fact that the materialistic, the libidinous, and the dominance-subordination aspects of the male-female relationship were coming to be stressed at the expense of the complementary satisfactions that used to exist. Women, formerly always the path to prosperity, were coming to be more the path to weakness and conflict. Bwiti attempts to set men and women once more upon the path of birth and death.

⋆7⋆
Authority and Benevolence in the Life Cycle

Ma tup ntia a se biang atuk (N).
(I turn away from the quarrel. But it is not
that I am tired.)

The Rise and Fall of Bibong Leon

Ngema Mve worked for many years as an overseer on a nearby citrus plantation. It was the money he earned there that enabled him to become the richman (*nkukuma*) of Assok Ening. But he was also persuasive in oratory and wise enough in judgment to be what Fang call the incumbent of the town (*mienlam*). Except in times of warfare in the old days when commanders (*njia*) were temporarily put forth, the mienlam was the closest that Fang came to recognizing an overall authority. The recognition gave few if any arbitrary powers. Fang habitually negotiated everything in long drawn out discussions. Or they burst out in sudden and heated quarrels.

As Mintza Mve passed over into old age he gave leadership in the family to Ngema who was still close to the peak of his powers and the fullness of his faculties. Mintza still had his strength and went to the forest to cut down trees for new plantations. But, always a soft-spoken man, he was rarely heard in the *aba*. More and more he slowly walked the courtyard holding his infant grandchildren in his arms. But Ngema could be heard speaking daily on a multitude of issues. He moved briskly here and there. He was the epitome of the full man. It is they who held sway in Fang affairs. Though Ngema had held leadership in the *mvôgabot* for a number of years by means of rhetorical powers of influence and the wealth he had achieved, he was not unchallenged in the life of the *ndébot*, let alone the mvogabot.

For example, Alogo Engonga, who was rendered passive in mvogabot affairs by a locomotor ataxia associated with tertiary neurosyphillis, was at the instance of his own son, Muye Michel, separating from Ngema. As nkukuma and mienlam, Ngema was chiefly responsible for mvogabot solidarity. Alogo Engonga's people, acting in his name though not in his clearly conceived intention, were on the verge of moving entirely into the other council house. There were also acrimonious exchanges between Ngema and

Muye Michel, who stood as classificatory father and son to each other. Ngema referred to Muye as "my little one whom I benevolently protect." But since Alogo Engonga was ill there was little that could be done to persuade his "offspring" to a continuing solidarity. Alogo could not himself play a part in the discussion of the council house, in which divisiveness was definitively expressed or solidarity renegotiated. And Muye Michel, though in his late twenties, was still a "little one" in that house. Thus Alogo's people "were drifting away into an mvogabot of their own and Ngema was perplexed as to how to deal with it. He was a master of oratory which often knit such nettled matters back together again. But he could not squarely engage the sick man with this talent nor deal freely with his "little one."

Another "brother" still firmly integrated in the mvogabot but almost as removed from Ngema as Alogo was the Chief, Essono Mba. As a gesture to his dignity, Essono had been put forward to the administration, on Ngema's urging, as Chief of the Village. He was thus the public representative of the mvogabot and of the village itself. His external formal authority, however, had little enduring effect within the mvogabot. One says enduring effect because the influence men wielded by reasons of wealth, wisdom, and persuasiveness fluctuated. Men alternated in acting as counselors and intermediaries (ntebedzang) to each other, often in situations posing a serious threat to the integrity of the mvogabot. Ngema was subject to such fluctuations as well.

When I first arrived in Assok Ening, Ngema had been for some weeks acting as intermediary between Essono Mba and Essono's younger brother in respect to the use of bridemonies. He had talked to each brother separately and then brought them together until the dispute had been settled. But six months later Ngema himself was involved in an outburst which came to blows, blood, and nearly to firearms. The dispute arose with his younger brother Asseko. The occasion was an insult offered to Ngema by Asseko's teenage daughter Germaine for which her father would offer no excuse or apology. Ngema had attempted to counsel her about her promiscuous entertainment of strangers and her refusal to marry.

The incident brought into focus the tensions in the relationship between younger and older brother. Such tensions were bound to exist in a society where the privileges of primogeniture were palpable and profitable, but weakly enough sanctioned as to be easily resented. Asseko shared the feelings common to Fang younger brothers who resented the management of their affairs by their older brothers. Ngema in his turn, besides feeling the insecurity that was normal to a Fang in respect to increasingly elder status, had other reasons for resenting his younger brother. For Ngema, with nine wives, had produced only three children, all girls. And though one of these girls, Marie, had produced two "village children," both boys, his younger brother Asseko, and three wives, had produced six children, of which two were boys who had a strong claim on leadership in the future of the lineage. Ngema, as most Fang, recognized that the venereal infection from which his people had suffered in the late colonial period has something to do with sexual promiscuity. His motives in correcting his brother's daughter were thus altruistic. In any case the rebuff he encountered in trying to prevent the contamination of his brother's daughter must have reminded him all too well of his inability to control the infection he suspected had wasted the fecundity of his wives.

The dispute was a surprise to the village, for these two brothers, the most well-to-do in the community, had maintained a stout fraternity heretofore in all affairs of the mvogabot. The first sign of the event was the sudden appearance of Ngema's wives out in the courtyard. They shouted to the children playing there to run and intercede with their fathers who were fighting behind the huts. Even the children of the patrilineage may be called in as ntebedzang, intermediaries, in an attempt to halt violence. The other men hearing the uproar rushed in from the forests and fields to separate the two brothers. Ngema was soon constrained to sit in the council house by six men holding his arms. But he kept breaking out the rear of the house shouting great oaths and making for his sleeping chamber to get his shotgun.

This was a change from the measured and courteous family head we had known. Ngema demanded and kept demanding that his "little brother" leave the village and remove his belongings from the various "cold houses" which he had provided for him. He added insult by proclaiming that all that Asseko had in wives and wherewithal he, Ngema, had provided him. "Had he ever failed in his benevolent protection?" As for Asseko's errant daughter, "What kind of an animal is this that the wife I have given you has spawned? She sleeps with any stranger who comes to her door but insults her 'father'?"

This affair was eventually settled by the intercession of Bibong Asumu Leon and by Chief Essono Mba who had been the subject of Ngema's counsel in a similar dispute not so long before, and by the two angry brothers' elder sister who was called back from her village of marriage to counsel them. Leon enhanced his authority in mvogabot affairs by being the effective intermediary and by pointedly reminding Ngema that it takes *zong* (maturity of patience) to hold a family together. If Ngema and Asseko split apart, he implied, it would be plainly for lack of that quality. Ngema meanwhile had begun to argue that even if Asseko did leave, he lacked the force to hold a family together, for he was ruled by his women and children and that was what had caused all the trouble.

Ngema had been recently sick and Asseko was fighting an infection in his leg. The view was that illness had made them both irritable. But some suspected that Ngema had been worried about his position in the mvogabot largely because of the threat to it posed by Leon, a younger and more vigorous man than Ngema, though not as powerful a speaker. Under these threatening conditions he was likely to feel any insult to his authority more deeply than would otherwise be the case. This would be so, quite apart from the relevance of the issue of promiscuity to Ngema's own problems of family formation.

Leon was at an age when a man could well assert his dominance in the mvogabot. His position was enhanced by his effective intermediary role, but he was also gaining stature through his work with the nationalist political party, the USDG, for which he was the local representative. In many villages men much younger than Leon had been gaining a precocious authority in this way.

But Ngema was still wily and strong, and bided his time. A year later Leon was discovered in adultery with one of Ngema's wives. Ngema very patiently prepared a case against him for the council house. Now it was Asseko's and Essono's turn to act as intermediaries. In the council house Ngema's oratorical skills were used to great effect. Already Essono was inclined in Ngema's favor since Leon had previously insulted him in the fight between Asseko and Ngema by suggesting that he spoke badly when he took up the role of the intermediary. Essono as Chief of the Village was also distrustful of Leon's authority gained through politics and not from the administration.

Ngema's statement swept all before it. He recounted the many ways that he protected Leon, his "little one." He had gladly taken him in charge when Leon's father died. And here Leon was "eating" one of his wives. At one point Leon broke out in tears. In the end this turned out to be an occasion in which the assembled mature men could deal with the growing influence of Bibong Asumu Leon. "He must not only compensate Ngema, he must leave the village for a year or more to allow the anger to die." A good excuse was available. Leon had suffered for years from a crippled hip. "He must go to the coast for an operation."

Some months later I visited him in the hospital in Libreville. Ngema and the others had sent him some money. When he returned to Assok Ening he would again be their "little one," indebted to their protective benevolence and in no special position. Ngema would continue as the chief elder (*ntôlomot*) and incumbent of the village (*mienlam*) for some years to come.

BEING A FULL MAN BY EVEN-HANDED TRANQUILLITY

We see in this chain of events a slow turnover of influence in village life. Most Fang, in their egalitarianism, expected that all men would sooner or later be involved in mediating among and counseling all others. The man who suffered the embarrassment of the counsel of another could expect that sometime the opportunity would arise for him to provide counsel. As Leon had earlier said to Ngema: "Why is it now that you will not listen to my counsel when it is you who have counseled me so many times?" Even the oldest man and the incumbent of the village could expect to endure the mediation of others. Where, as among Fang, there existed no enduring authority structure[1] and no effective sanctions in the hands of the ntolomot or mienlam, the stability of the village rested in great part upon the willingness of mature men to undergo mediation and counsel from others regardless of age, wealth, or closeness of blood relationship. The sister of Ngema, when she was brought in to counsel the two brothers, had said, "The family is more than 'friendship,' it is of a common seed and birth" (*ndebot a dang "amitié," e so azô, e ne ebial*). "Men," she went on to say, "must lay aside their pride for its sake. This palaver which has brought about a great threat to the existence of our family can nevertheless be an occasion for giving it a new life" (*mfefing ening*).

But the virtues that could make for this accommodation and resultant re-vitalization were not in plentiful supply. And for that reason Fang history was characterized by the breakup of villages and kin groups. Reintegration was the less usual case. Man went off in a huff. It is not that Fang did not emphasize the virtues that would provide for social stability. A theory of physiological development often put forward by them points toward such a virtuous maturity. Though this was not a subject easily brought to light, the basic outline was clear enough. It emerged around such key terms as balance (*bipwe*) and even-handed tranquillity (*mvwaa*) and upon the differences between blood and sperm. Many Fang believed that a man received his essential forces and powers (*ekí, bekí*) from the blood of his mother (*mekí nyia*) and the sperm of his father (*meyôm esia*). There was an attendant belief that the woman possessed within her a homunculus, itself made of blood, which could be brought to gestation by the influence of male sperm.*[1] The maternal element

---

*[1] Fang regularly practiced autopsy (esal) to determine cause of death. They had therefore a relatively detailed knowledge of the internal organs. They made distinctions, for example, in the stages of the foetus: kigile abum (first three or four months before movement), ndue abum (fourth and fifth months after first movement). Fang were particularly anxious about the possibilities of early miscarriage—at the kigile stage—as a consequence of the improper coming together of the male and female element.

In folklore there were the "kigile ki stories" about beings not fully human born in these early months. These shapes were monstrous and were usually defined as balls of white tissue with some distinguishing human features—perhaps teeth. They were said to be particularly powerful beings with the capacity to go bouncing around the world creating havoc. There may be medical facts at the base of these tales. They may refer to dermoid cysts—encysted or tumorous embryonic tissue which may have hair or teeth. Since a cyst or tumor would not give any evidence of movement, it would be properly referred to, when aborted, as kigile. The point to be made here, however, is that antisocial power resulted from the improper union of male and female elements (ki is the root for power or capacity).

Fang said that proper union with a woman should take place in the first week after the menstrual period had concluded. This is after the woman has seen her taboo—a yen eki. It was said that all the bad blood had then departed leaving a drop of good blood which was the essence of the female principle of creation. It was this drop of blood that was sometimes said to contain a homunculus. In any case, it was the essence of female creativity and unlike menstrual blood it was fertile when in contact with the surrounding sperm (meyom). Both female blood and male sperm could be very destructive commingled in inappropriate circumstances. For example, should

went to make up the flesh, blood, and bloody organs of the body cavity, particularly the heart. The paternal element went to make up the bones, sinews, and brains. Just as the creation of the child was dependent upon the harmonious working together of blood and sperm, so the full power of the adult was dependent upon the working together of the body members which the two essential substances of coitus had brought into being.

A man with strong brain, bones, and sinews but with weak blood, organs, and heart would confront life as inadequately as he who possessed strong blood but weak sinews. The brains and bones and the sinews were the center of the will, the driving force, the determination of a man (*ngul, ngul abô*, "power to do"), while the blood and the heart were, at once, the sources of life (*ening*, "that which gives life to determination") as well as the sources of reflection or thought (*asiman*, "that which gives direction to determination"). In a nyamoro both of these sets of attributes should work harmoniously. They should be in balance (bipwe). That harmony was an essential quality in the strength and tranquillity (mvwaa) of men. Young men were too willful, too much under the influence of meyom. Old men were too reflective, too much under the influence of meki.

There was an impressive neatness to such physiological philosophy. But it was not without its inconsistent or alternative interpretations. Despite its being socially desirable that mature men be seen as working out a harmonious, balanced and tranquil, physiological synthesis, such a desirable fit between physiology and social activity was not always admitted. For many Fang such physiological premises demonstrated that men's fundamental sinewy and seminal nature was potentially dangerous. It too easily gave vent to violent emotion and energetic undirected action. Men, not just young men, were too hot. Ngema's outburst was an expression of that more essential masculinity, even though in his role as nyamoro he should have been more balanced. Here social solidarity was in struggle with essential nature. Women, it followed, had a cold nature. They could be too easily influenced by the blood of their nature. Their potential was for passivity and inaction, scheming and calculation. This stereotype was put forth by men despite the fact that blood was the source of life itself and despite the fact that blood was the vehicle of reflection, deliberation, and thought.

It is not surprising that such elementary physiological elements as blood and sperm had polyvalent usage in respect to social situations. Some saw in these sexual substances the source of fundamental differences between the sexes and turbulent uncoordinated elements in the inheritance of each person. Such interpretations helped explain the endemic conflict and fission of Fang family groups. But other men, persuaded by the ideals of mature balance and

---

a man have intercourse with a menstruating woman or with a nursing mother or with a girl before puberty (the view on postmenopausal women is not clear), the result would be undesirable if not disastrous.

by even-handed tranquillity, formulated what it is not too much to call a physiological philosophy in respect to blood and sperm. We will see the results of this persuasion more markedly worked out in the Bwiti religion in its search for spiritual tranquillity through the balancing of physiological images of being.

Further insight into these matters is gained by listening to the counsel given by fathers to their sons in the interest of their achieving a full manhood. There were many stages that men passed through from the moment they quickened in the womb (*abum mwan*) until, long since dead and satisfactorily dispatched by mortuary ceremonies, they had spiritual status among the other ancestors. But Fang reached their peak when they became nyamoro, and it was upon this status that greatest interest was focused. It was not a status that was ascribed at a certain age. It was achieved within the kin group by showing capacities of patience, of judgment, of oratorical persuasiveness, and finally, of the capacity to forgive. All these qualities were evidence of a fully tranquil state. Outside the kin group the capacity for calculated cruelty and summary revenge was esteemed. The problem in the presence of these contrary values was to distribute them appropriately—and primarily to prevent cruelty and revenge from erupting within the clan. For such emotions often did erupt even at the most intimate levels. And this threat became acute in the colonial period when their outward expression was suppressed.

All of these virtues were intended to act positively in the interests of the kin group. Since a nyamoro was judged according to his capacity for service to the ndebot and mvogabot it was necessary that he be married and have a family. No bachelor had an influential place in the council house. As Ayang Ndong said, "What value has a bachelor? What can one expect of him? What food or hospitality can he provide? At night when he goes home he will stumble around in his hut trying to get to bed because he will have no wife to light his way! He may speak in the council house but what weight can his words have [*medzô me se ki eban*]? He has neither children nor wife whose demands have given him a strong and dignified heart [*nlem nseghan*]." Ayang and other nyamoro pointed out that all the demands of marriage—the bad-headedness of women, the demands of in-laws, the intransigence of children—went into the making of the character of the nyamoro. If the fecundity of a man's family showed that he might lay a strong claim on a future place in the lineage then he would surely have a place in the council house. It was just the lack of this kind of family prosperity that deeply worried Ngema, who otherwise had all the attributes of the nyamoro. His contribution to family affairs was currently very great. But what would he leave behind him?

Fang represented these differences in nyamoro by speaking of two kinds: *nyamoro nsôm* (nyamoro of the hunt) and *nyamoro ôzem* (nyamoro monkey; *Cercopithecus talapoin*) The reference is to the domain of man's most pleasurable activity, hunting, and it contrasts the nyamoro who is the "hunter" and the nyamoro who is the "hunted." The *ôzem* is, moreover, a monkey with a small beard who is born looking old and wizened. So it is that though many participate in the life of the council house and all look like nyamoro, some are the masters of the life of the council house and others are the mastered. They chatter and are not heeded. They are nyamoro only in appearance.

Ayang Ndong's father, whose counsel to his "son" on matters of sex we have encountered earlier, gave what he called instructions of the council house (*melua m'aba*). These were concerned with the comportment of the full man. His father advised Ayang to show calmness (*lonbe*) in the presentation of himself to others in the aba. He should avoid emotion (*ôlun*). There were other situations in which a full man might show his violent capacities for cruelty (*mvô*), but in family life, in the life of the lineage he must be justice (*sôsô*) itself. Toward his youngers he must endeavor to show protective benevolence (*mvam*).

The Balancing of Qualities and The Ephemeral Exercise of Authority

The virtues urged by Fang upon their nyamoro—"tranquillity," "justice," "forgiveness," "protective benevolence" toward those younger—were all guarantees of the life of the lineage. But men did not follow them impeccably. They erupted, like Ngema, from frustration. They did not balance their various qualities and were cruel within the lineage. Others had then to counsel them and urge virtue upon them. They had to remind them that they were nyamoro. So it was that in day-in and day-out relationships there was a turnover of influences, of unbalancings and rebalancings. And this turnover occurred even if over the longer period of time one or several men like Ngema were more influential and more respected than others.

The vicissitudes of the nyamoro arose mainly at the two thresholds of that status: the threshold at which the young men (*nduman*) were pressing to become nyamoro and that later threshold at which the nyamoro relinquished his claim to be the perfect exemplar of his culture and the arbiter of its conflicts and confusions.

There was uncertainty about the term *ntôlomot* and the exercise of the rights and duties associated with this status. The greatest uncertainty was at the upper threshold of nyamoro status. The term ntolomot embodied the principle of seniority. It meant the older or eldest man. He should be the personification of "protective benevolence." It was the ntolomot who should represent and speak for the ndebot in the various disputes in which its members were involved. The ntolomot was the head of the ndebot. No dispute should be discussed in the council house without his presence. In the ndebot he should be the receiver and dispenser of all marriage payments and he was responsible for providing the marriage payments for his sons and younger brothers. He should exercise strong influence in their selection of wives and he should negotiate the ensuing matrimonial compensation. He was the one who allocated agricultural and hunting lands.

But who was he? For age alone was insufficient. Activity of mind and body was the determining attribute. The rights of the ntolomot, the actual elder brother, could be and usually were subject to the manipulation of younger men of personality, talent, and personal power. The conflict between the principle of seniority on the one hand (Mintza's right, for example) and the authority given by competence (Ngema's or Leon's claim) on the other, was especially acute at that boundary between full manhood and old age. The ntolomot was an agnatic leader and his authority was parental and moral in character. But with noticeably old men this reversed itself and it was the younger brother or son who, in effect, took parental authority over the elder or the father. Fang recognized that the child was eventually father of the man. And this was why very little children and infants were called *ata*, "little fathers."

Where did the authority of the ntolomot lie if it was so readily contested? The answer to this question involves principles underlying the ancestral cult, Bieri—the supernatural extension and justification of the lineage. But let us first consider other kinds of authority that appeared in Fang life. Corresponding to the ntolomot whose authority should prevail at the level of the ndebot was the mienlam whose authority was exercised at the level of the mvogabot. The authority of the ntolomot merged with that of the mienlam as the ndebot merged into the mvogabot as a section of it at some moments and identified with it at others. To the degree that the mienlam was powerful in his village, and this depended on his wealth in wives and his verbal talents, the authority of the various ntolomot of the constituent ndebot was diminished. The mienlam, in this case, might be invited to intervene in disputes over land, and in domestic disputes within an ndebot that was not his own. Though he did not hold the marriage payment funds, he might be consulted on marriages, since the parties involved could count on his aid with these payments. It was the mienlam who took over representation of the mvogabot in litigation with other groups.

As leader of the mvogabot the mienlam exercised rights that derived from his position as ntolomot of one of the extended families. But his authority as mienlam differed from the moral energy bound up in parental authority and seniority which was the authority of the ntolomot, in scope as well as kind. Most obviously he was confronted with a larger group further removed from him in kinship relation and therefore less susceptible to the moral authority he might exercise over those more closely related to him. Central to his exercise of authority was his wealth. For a wealthy man had the capacity, based on the productivity of his many wives, to tide his neighbors over in times of scarcity or need, and hence to command their allegiance. He could also entertain strangers. The ability to provide hospitality confidently (*so beyung*), as we see in the remarks of Ayang Ndong above, was one of the most telling marks of a full manhood. Such a man was in a good position to "own," in the sense of possess, the village, the literal meaning of the term *mie*. For the mienlam had a proprietary right which arose from the way his wealth brought people under economic obligation to him.

The obligation, however, might not be simply a personal one. The village as a whole might feel itself in debt to the mienlam because as a rich man, nkukuma, he brought renown. He "lifted" or "carried" the village up (*a bere adzal ôyô*). Through his entertainment of strangers he made the village a livelier place in which to live. His presence made for pleasurable activity in the village (*elulua*). His village would be hot (*ayong*). He defeated boredom (*e bengle nzuk*).

The interdependence of the roles of mienlam and nkukuma is such that Spanish administrators in Rio Muni mistakenly took the name nkukuma as the Fang word for a man of authority, and until independence they continued to call their local chiefs nkukuma, richmen. The chiefs did not hesitate to capitalize on the confusion. But Fang distinguished between the idea of wealth and the idea of authority, however often the two tended to go together. Wealth was only one aspect of the honor or respect (*engang*) shown a leader. In matters of respect oratorical talents also bulked large since these talents, as in Ngema's palaver with Leon, could be used to obtain justice and exert moral suasion. While wealth was important because it gave a man the capacity materially to aid others and thus be more influential in their lives than was otherwise possible, the effective exercise of authority depended upon a combination of oratorical talent and the moral persuasion that comes with its proper use, and wealth.

Beyond the mienlam, who could at most be the leader of a collection of mvogabot grouping themselves together into a town, there were several positions of potential leadership recognized by Fang, though evidence that they were ever filled is scanty. One of these positions was that of *njiayong* (he who commands the clan). The more northern Pahouin peoples, the Bane particularly, had such leaders, and their invasion of Gabon in the late nineteenth century testifies to it. Fang claimed to have recognized such leaders in times of warfare. But it is probably to diffusion from the north, from the once German-administered Cameroons, that we must trace references in Fang oral narrative to an *njiabot keza* ("kaiser commander").

Thus we come back to the ntôlomot and the mienlam as the essential authorities. Principally their authority was exercised in the interests of maintaining a pleasurable activity amidst even-handed tranquillity in the kin group and village, over against the ever-present possibility of ritual sin (*nsem*) and social disorder (*ebiran*).[2] The authority of the ntolomot was the authority of kinship and it emanated from a long-term desire on the part of all members of the patrilineal kin group to preserve, protect, and strengthen the viability of that group. Authority was granted to the ntolomot because by using it judiciously, by opportunely restating ritual conventions or applying moral suasion at the first signs of disorder, he could guarantee this viability. The authority of the mienlam on the other hand derived from a more immediate desire on the part of all those living in the same locality to preserve coherence and order in the affairs of their several kin groups by avoiding boredom and privation. Authority was granted to a rich man of the locality because it was felt that he could give coherence by preventing privations. He could give a quality to village life that others could not provide. The authority of the ntolomot was rarely as great as that of the mienlam. But by virtue of its appearance in a temporal rather than a territorial context—namely, the patrilineal line—it was more permanent. About the rich and their power Fang said, playing on the alliterative sounds of words, "The rich man who commands the hill (today) tomorrow is going to fall off the mountain" (*Nkukuma wa jia nkôl okiri a ke ku kum*). They said, "From wealth to misery less than a moment" (*a koro kuma y'ake ôkukut ka awala zing*).

Ritual Authority and Cult Solidarity

The ntolomot and the mienlam were granted authority from their kin and territorial units for practical reasons. If the consequences of their actions were generally regarded as beneficial to the group they became charismatic—associated with the ancestors who were the ultimate source of protective benevolence. One occasionally saw gifted old men who maintained their authority despite the decline of their physical powers. They had a moral balance and tranquillity and an intellectual vigor which were truly impressive. Their extended families surrounded them, ever heedful of their needs and mindful of their views. Tessmann was drawn to them[3] as the epitome of the Fang version of human nature. Indeed they attracted anyone who came searching for wisdom among Fang.

These paragons of Fang culture were inevitably centrally involved in the ancestor cult, where the ultimate qualities of Fang life reposed. The full men who were members of that cult were called *ngômalan*, meaning those who had eaten a decoction from the root bark of the *alan* bush (*Alchornea floribunda*). The bark is psychoactive and aided passage to the realm of death and contact with the ancestors. The nyamoro who could combine in himself the attributes of an ngomalan, an ntolomot, and a mienlam was the epitome of male achievement in Fang society. His status as ngomalan gave him claim to supernatural qualities. His status as ntolomot gave him the powers of accumulated experience and lineage leadership. His status as mienlam implied the very temporal powers—the wherewithal to bring about marriages and liven things up.

The ancestor cult will be considered at greater length below but mention should be made of other ritual authorities. In the antiwitchcraft societies of Ngi and Nzok or Dzok, leadership was usually given over to the physically strongest and most energetic man, called *nôm Ngi* or *nôm Dzok* (the old of Ngi or the old of Dzok).[4] This leader was rarely an old man and was usually a young and vigorous nyamoro who commanded, while the rituals were in session, with harshness. In the old days he had the powers of life and death, for he was eradicating evil. During the height of antiwitchcraft society activity such leaders were much feared. The nôm ngi was the only person, Fang said, before whom men fell on their backs and begged for their lives.

Important though transitory ritual leadership flourished within two other societies. In the Soo cult, held for the initiation of young men and women at puberty, a man from another clan was called to lead the rituals. His membership in another clan was mandatory since he was purifying the sin of prococious sexual relations which might have contaminated the entire clan and its members, disqualifying them from ritual leadership. He was called *ande* or Ndong Mba and in his purification of the group of older boys he too was peremptory in his commands.

The women's purification and initiation society (Mevungu) acted under its leader, the *nget mininga* (the cruel woman) to preserve the community from sickness and infertility and to guarantee success in such dangerous undertakings as hunting and warfare. She might be consulted by the men of the village (although she was only a woman married there and not of their clan) because her ritual and moral support was important to the success of their most uncertain ventures. In the course of Mevungu cult ceremonies, we remember, the authority of this woman was such that men hid from her and her assistants. Like the nom Ngi they carried machetes and might wound anyone who was nonchalant in their presence or who was judged inimical to cult purposes.

What is clear about these ritual leaders is that though great authority was exercised in ritual situations it was of brief duration. The power they possessed was not significant in the long-term problems of village life.[5] Mevungu was a temporary ritual of reversal, and the women carried little authority over from it into everyday affairs. Here as elsewhere in Fang life such authority as manifested itself followed the formula: the more powerful the less permanent, the more permanent the less powerful.

The ancestor cult, Bieri, was concerned with the quality that resided in the lineage principle—a quality that tied together the living and the dead. The term which comes closest to capturing the binding quality of patrilineality is *mvamayong* ("providential benevolence" of the clan). That lineage principle was constantly reinvigorated by the learning and the recitation of genealogy which was the foundation of traditional education. The power that lay in that concept of lineage bondage is seen in the strongest ritual sanction a father could employ against a recalcitrant son. When he became sufficiently exasperated by endless disobedience and when all else failed, he could show his sexual parts to his son (*alere shéshé*). He might call the young man out to the courtyard and suddenly drop his loin cloth before him. "I remind you from whence you came," he would say. This was an extreme form of the power to curse which elders hold by virtue of their place in the lineage. In effect, the son was removed from the protective benevolence of the patriline. This could bring disastrous consequences. Expensive ritual purification was demanded, including the washing of the craniums of the ancestors on his behalf with the blood of the "goat of forgiveness" (*kubn abong*).

In the old days Fang worried about the capacity of fathers to cut sons off, even inadvertently, from the "protective benevolence" that flowed down the patrilineal line. Sons feeling themselves in a condition of misfortune might ask their father at any time to "lift the weight of the malediction" (*ava meteng*).[6] If at all possible, fathers on their deathbeds would call their sons together and offer them a benediction and blessing (*abora*) by "lifting the malediction," inadvertent as it might have been.

The power to curse was the reflex of the more natural tendency of the ntolomot to protect (*akôm*) and benevolently to promote (*mvam*) the interests of his juniors and his lineage. Often that protective benevolence was clouded by an uncertain sense of rights and prerogatives among nyamoro, as we have seen. Very old men who had given up competing in Fang life, however, should have had these sentiments in abundance. For that reason the name for grandfather was *mvama* ("he who acts benevolently and providentially in the interests of his lineage").[7] It is no wonder that Fang said of the old that their "ears go to the place where the benevolent man has gone" (*melô me ke evôm mot mvam a nga ke*). For, like the ancestors, though the old no longer had an imposing physical presence, yet they possessed a moral presence to be listened to and followed.

At the same time, however much they might gain in feelings of benevolence toward their juniors and descendants, the fact that Fang men lost their place as they grew old brought ambiguity and suspicion into the social order. If they did not actually resent those who replaced them, it was readily suspected of them that they did. The old men, it is true, could present a picture that inspired sentiment. For as society turned away from them, they spent their days in quiet contemplation of the ongoing affairs of the village, smoking reflectively in the council house, nodding off, awaking suddenly, swatting a fly with the raffia fly swatter—a remnant of their former prestige. They were seen more and more in the company of their grandchildren. One saw a return to childish ways. Fang in Bwiti, ever ready to play on words, point out that the term for the old (*nôm*) exactly reverses the word for the very young (*môn*), child.

Whatever hopes could be platitudinously expressed about their increased benevolence and whatever tolerant sentiment might be attached to their return to childhood, however, the lot of old people was uncertain, particularly if they did not have children to care for them. They might be accused of sorcery (*ngwel*) with impunity. Frequently enough the disease or death of children was blamed upon old men (*envalen*), who were supposed to have taken advantage of their proximity to children in attempting, by witchcraft, to regain their dwindling vitality.[8] The more good-natured sentiments entertained of the old then underwent a rapid change and their renewed interest in the young was turned against them.

Even if they were never suspected of sorcery, their burdensome presence in a society on the narrow margin of existence might provoke hostility of which they could not fail to be aware. Obunu was the author of an ironic commentary (*fiang*) that had much currency in Assok Ening in late 1959. His wife's people had been a burden to him recently with demands on his hospitality and for additional bridepayment. He said, when they left, that he should go to their village and convince some of the old men there to die. Nobody over there had died in a long time and the village was full of useless people who were causing problems for their in-laws. "People have to die," he said, "if a village is really to prosper (*ntô mvwaa*)."*[2] Though this pronouncement was put forth with jocularity, a cheerless truth lay behind it. People who could no longer make a contribution in the gardens, plantations, forest, and council house might easily feel themselves the object of social accusation, covert or overt. It was not surprising to hear the old people themselves comment ironically upon their condition.[9] Their will to live could be affected. They might abandon themselves to their demise, for they, as it was said, "belong with the ancestors and their craniums can be of use to their descendants in the reliquary."

It was often, thus, no happy condition the nyamoro could look forward to when he was forced at last to abandon his status. He would not often find the "fruits" of his old age. And, moreover, men, in more recent years under the pressure of precocious youth, could find themselves old before their time.

---

*[2] When Sima Ndong chided Obunu for the harsh attitude he was taking toward old people, Obunu asked him to consider how his life had been burdened by the fact that Sima's parents had lived so long. "My parents," he said, "died early and that 'certified' me. Write your old people into the book." Such shocking talk was typical of Obunu. But it testified to what may be called a Fang law of "the conservation of matter." In some sense for the satisfactory progress of those born and living, there had to be an appropriate number of dead and dying. However feared, death brought a certain relief and even a cleansing. It freed the village again for prosperity. This seems to be what Obunu meant.

This heightened the anxiety of the nyamoro, increasing the tendency, as we see in Ngema, to overreact to perceived threats to their status. They more and more quickly abandoned that patience and sense of balance, the essential virtues of that status. Growing old gracefully had always been a problem for Fang, but with so much that was new in Fang life elders were more easily replaced by youngers who could pretend to a knowledge of changed conditions.

We are not sure in old Fang society how often elderly men could parlay their proximity to death and the ancestors into a prestigious position in the general society. That very proximity has been a rationale in many societies for granting to old men an authority they could not physically justify. It is probable that the unsettled state of Fang culture in recent centuries—their rapid migration through changing ecological zones and culture areas, the constant internecine strife that characterized clan relationships—placed a premium upon physical vigor and upon a pragmatic flexibility that would prejudice the status of the old even with the support of the ancestor cult. Priority seems long since to have been placed upon traits which could respond vigorously to the challenges of an unsettled culture passing through changing environments.

In any case there was, because of the emphasis on middle age, a marked difficulty in dealing with death and the afterlife. Eschatological views, in my experience with most Fang, were neither clear enough nor of sufficient weight to give to old people the respect or sanctity due them because of their imminent demise. While one must point up the this-worldly and pragmatic emphasis in contemporary Fang character, so as to understand better why the heights belonged to ever-younger nyamoro and old age had become a plight, the potential of the ancestor cult cannot be entirely overlooked. In taking up the Bieri cult in Part II we will see ultimate concerns which invigorated the elders' role. Whether Bieri at one time made the lot of the old substantially better than it has been in recent decades we do not know. But we do know that Bieri institutionalized concerns which the contemporary religious movement of Bwiti was able to pick up again and utilize in shifting the attitudes of their members away, not only from money-mindedness and the consumer orientation of the colonial world, but also away from a youth orientation. This orientation tended to lead to embittered, even malignant and hostile, relations in the lineage. It led away from the principle of protective benevolence in relations between brothers and between fathers and sons upon which the lineage was most surely founded. It was a "short path," as the members of Bwiti say, and not the long path of birth *and* death.

Conclusion: Reflections and Suspicions

In this chapter we see the revolving quality in the exercise of authority within a general tendency to grant greatest authority to those in their vigorous middle age. In the long run the father became the son and the son the father; the child became the man and the man the child. They reflected each other. In the longest run, as we will see in Bwiti, the living and the dead reflect each other. In village life, it was expected that the one who had counseled me today—the one in whom I saw wisdom—would be the one who tomorrow would be in a situation to accept my counsel and see wisdom in me. This revolving quality of life, perhaps the keystone to Fang egalitarianism, was less true of those in vigorous middle age (like Ngema) who could maintain their authority longest if, paradoxically, they could at the same time control their vigor and manifest the nyamoro's virtues: patience, balance, and protective benevolence toward all members of the lineage. They had to remember above all that which Ngema forgot under provocation: the "good answer" (*mbamba nyalan*). They should say, "I turn away from the quarrel but it is not that I am tired."

But more and more, as the vigor of presumptuous youth educated in alien customs pressed in upon them, and as the specter of the unrewarding tiredness of old age rose up before them, nyamoro tended, like Ngema, to be easily unbalanced and to focus narrowly upon their rights, their authority, and their power to curse and cut others—principally those younger than themselves—off from lineage solidarity. In the figurative if not the actual sense they "showed themselves naked." They let slip the mature capacity for balancing the different physiological qualities of the person so necessary to tranquillity in self and society. They forgot the lessons that were so important to youth and which young men should learn to reflect in their own actions.

Lack of balance and attendant suspicions increased in the twentieth century. No doubt there was always an ambiguity associated with passing into old age in a migratory society which emphasized full manhood. This ambiguity could foster a suspicion that the old would seek to recapture their lost powers by corrupt means. This was a suspicion, however, that could be counteracted by actively participating in the ancestor cult with its dedication to protective, if authoritarian, benevolence in village affairs. And the ancestor cult, even though it was still the most vigorous men of middle age who were its leaders, was also a means by which the aging could retain a sense of relevant activity and of esteem as they approached ancestral status themselves.

Another ambiguity surrounded the richman, nkukuma. Part of Ngema's problem as a nyamoro was bound up in the fact that he was also the nkukuma, the richman of the village, an object of resentment and suspicion. For though he had worked hard as a foreman on a local citrus plantation and thereby put aside the bridemonies for some of his nine wives, yet he had also been particularly fortunate in family circumstances and in the availability of marriageable sisters out of whose bridemonies his other marriages were made. Such good fortune provoked suspicion of the presence of *evus*—of aggrandizing witchcraft. The richman might effectively counter that suspicion by working to redistribute the advantages of his wealth. For example, he might foster entertainments such as visiting dance teams or troubadours. Or he would aid with other bridemonies in the mvogabot. In later years there was much less of this redistribution, and as a consequence the suspicious attitude toward the richman was much heightened. To this situation the Bwiti religion makes a response, although largely in figurative ways. It provides for redistribution and it allows for growing old. For it places all generations on the "long path" of birth *and* death and in so doing promotes reflection on the revolving (and reflective) relation of men to men and of women to women and of men and women to each other.

❧ 8 ❧

Coming into Manhood

"Medang," Medang enyi a ne nlem ose—
edô ô ntô avit-zang.
(The desire to exceed is in every heart,
and the heart is such a small organ.)

ANTOINE THE NIGHT FOOL

THE FIRST that anyone realized that Ngema Obama Antoine might be "sick in his heart" (*nkukwan nlem*) was when he began to pile stones on the edge of the Oyem-Bitam road. He said he was going to build a house of stone like the Europeans. People then remembered that Antoine, who was still a young man and not married, had gone around asking villagers for money—twenty francs apiece—in order that he could have a postal box in Oyem. He said he had important letters to receive. The next day, after he piled up the stones, an old Renault arrived in the village. It was owned by an African trader. Antoine had hired it in order to get more stones. He climbed into the cab to direct the driver to the stones down the road by Ngoum. After about two hours they returned. The driver was very upset. He said that Antoine kept telling him to drive on and on until he had gotten into Oyem itself. Antoine had hopped out at the post office and inquired after his mail. Then he had ordered him to return. The driver angrily demanded 1,500 francs for the use of his truck. Antoine peremptorily threw 500 francs at him. "That," he said, "is all such a broken down truck is worth." The villagers had to restrain the visitor. They reminded him that men should be patient with those who are "sick in their hearts."

If many villagers were still uncertain that they had a young fool on their hands, ensuing weeks made that quite clear. He began to say on every occasion that he no longer needed a postal box, for he was receiving his communications in other ways. "I receive them at night after making my prayers. The letters from Paris reach me in bed." He would regularly proclaim, "You see me in black skin, but actually I will become as rich as a white man."

Antoine went down to the other end of the village one night and into a kitchen. He asked a woman to wash his hands with water. As she did so, he said, "May all my palavers and bad luck be left with you" (*Bitom bisese bi lige wa, mbea maa wum a lige ebe wa*). Then he asked the woman to sleep with him. She cried out to her husband.

Antoine sometimes confessed he was a fool, but he blamed his older brother, Ondo Obama, who was keeping all that was rightfully his away from him. Antoine began to go into people's houses and take out things he said belonged to him. He hauled out the teacher's trunk in mid-morning when the teacher was in the school room. When the bus stopped in the village he would try to climb and take down the roof-baggage which he said had been sent to him. Until the drivers came to recognize him he would flag down buses in order to do this.

As we were the only Europeans in the village, Antoine often demanded of me that I produce the goods that had been sent to him from Paris. He knew me, he said. I was the dead blacksmith, Eye Zolo, who had died after the war. I had thus suffered and paid the sins of the black man, gone to Paris, and returned in my present form with all this wealth. Where was Antoine's share of that wealth? "I am no longer a poor black man," he said, "I am prepared to suffer."

Proposals for confining Antoine in a wooden stock began to be debated seriously after a week of his climbing on people's roofs in the middle of the night, or pounding on their doors and demanding their "goods." Ngema, who considered Antoine his "little one," led a debate in the council house on the issue.[*1] On three different occasions Antoine woke us in the small hours by rattling our door and demanding that we bring out our goods (*biom*).

But not so long afterward he abandoned that tactic and launched upon the night talks which continued on and off for six months. Meanwhile, he had moved out of his elder brother's house into the market—an open, tin-roofed, brick structure with a concrete floor which the administration had built for the village as an inducement for them to regroup. He set a table in the middle with a checkered tablecloth and a flower vase. He slept in a corner. Antoine took every opportunity to contrast the opulence of this establishment with the miserable quarters in which his brother had forced him to live. The interior of the market had a pronounced acoustical effect upon his voice and boomed his pronouncements out upon the sleeping village in an arresting and disembodied way.

Antoine's notion (which was not his alone) that black men died into a salvation of goods and that white men, all of them rich after all, were these black men who had suffered yet were saved, led him frequently down to the village cemetery in the evening.[1] He was checking on the progress of his relatives' salvation. These visits always excited him, and he could be heard

---

[*1] At one point Antoine was tied up and confined. He had begun to swing a long stick at people. Once tied up, his brother carried him back to his bed. Antoine broke down in tears and implored him in the name of their dead mother to release him. Though the older brother had been gentle, a sister's son who was in the village accused him of being too harsh with a sick brother. He gained his release in the evening.

singing sections of the mass in a fine baritone. He then came back up to the market and began his night talks. These were long rambling affairs in which he recounted his supernatural adventures, regularly ridiculed his older brother, and often commented with acuity and sardonic wit upon village affairs and village notables. Many were the men and women who chuckled in their beds one night at a neighbor's discomfiture only to find themselves held up to scrutiny on the next.

Antoine was very democratic in his ridicule, as Fang were inclined to be. He did not spare the Chief. He described him in his fine uniform running in a sweat to Oyem at the beck and call of the administration. He did not spare Ngema Mve, the "incumbent" of the village. Antoine proclaimed his admiration for his many wives, but so did others in the village, and so it was understandable that Ngema was anxious over their fidelity. Antoine did not spare the ethnographer. He imitated his clumsy Fang speech and spoke roundly against his stingy ways. He castigated the profligate ways of the local teacher so "clearly" the superior of any villager. He thus produced a veritable catalogue of the backstage of village life and the foibles of villagers. The inclination of many inhabitants to silence him was stayed by a consuming interest in his future chronicles.

Antoine spoke regularly of witchcraft and of the night flights (*mbwôl*) of his witchcraft demon (*evus*). He described his own efforts to ruin the harvest of his brother and blast the fertility of his sheep. No normal villager would think of thus confessing. But Antoine spoke with impunity. He always pointed out, as well, how measly and corrupt was the mbwol of the black man as compared with that of the white. "They go from Paris to Libreville in a night. All we do is eat away at the substance of our brothers." "Now I, Antoine," he said, "am studying this 'grand sortilège' (*mbwôl nden*) and will soon show you the consequences of it. In fact, I have become such a whiteman that I can marry my sisters in this village!" At other times Antoine's desires to appropriate the powers of the white man were tempered by his distaste for what he called the odor of white skin. The several villagers working with us were told that they were already beginning to smell bad, to smell of "la politique" which was all the white man knew.

Early on, when the state of Antoine's heart became known, his brother had engaged a woman herbalist from a nearby village. The woman determined that his witchcraft spirit was twisting his heart, and she treated him with a concoction to calm it. She beat him with leaf branches dipped in hot herbal infusions. But sometimes Antoine refused her ministrations and, in any case, the medicine was a long time taking effect. Finally Antoine abandoned his midnight forum. He left for Oyem to take up again his tailor's job. Though he regularly visited the village of his mother's brother, he was not seen in his own village again for a year, at which time he returned apparently normal.

CLASSIFYING THE ILLNESS: THE "HEARTSICK ONES"

What was wrong with Antoine? The villagers were by no means certain. Everyone could accept that Antoine's was "a sickness of the heart"—the Fang organ of perception, intellection, and balanced judgment. Antoine was "heartsick" (*nkukwan nlem* [N], *Nkôkôm nlem* [F]): the concept of general application to those disturbed in their thinking about themselves, about others, and about the visible world in which men lived. But the more detailed classification to be assigned was in dispute. It was given out by Antoine's family—as well as by the woman herbalist who had been called to treat him, a choice made necessary by Antoine's covetous antipathy toward the men of his patrilineage—that he was the victim of *eluma* (a secret, malevolent attack by magic pellet or an invisible arrow thrown by a village enemy—said to lodge in the chest and attack the heart). But some villagers maintained that Antoine had, indeed, attempted to launch his personal witchcraft being against his fellows—an event which he had frequently alluded to in his night talks. But the intended victims had defended themselves well. Antoine's demon had been stricken. It had returned to its abode in Antoine's chest, and he was stricken in return. His heart and bloody organs were being eaten away by his defeat. It was a sickness of his witchcraft (*nkukwan evus*).

It was more generally maintained that Antoine, well known as a careless young man and a good tailor, had failed to observe one of the prohibitions (*ekî*) given to him when he was prepared (*akômnge*) with witchcraft during his childhood. The demon was aggravated by this breach of "promise" (*akyage*) and was strangling his heart in return. It was a sickness caused by his failure to live up to the commitment of his childhood preparation. Ngema Mve, who had little respect for his "little one" nor for the family line from which he derived, felt that Antoine was to be classified simply as a simpleton or good-for-nothing (*ôkukut* [N]) or an ignorant one (*nzam*) who had no natural or supernatural powers. He was simply taking advantage of the village to get himself a reputation that his capacities did not deserve. Of course Ngema had been particularly insulted by Antoine's night remarks. Finally, there was some opinion abroad that Antoine had been playing with white man's medicine (*biang ntangan*), and had failed to control it.

Though there was uncertainty about what exactly ailed Antoine, Fang easily provided a detailed disease terminology in such situations. This is not surprising in view of the equatorial diseases which afflicted them.[2] Diseases which others and they themselves might suffer were of surpassing interest to them. Inquiry among Fang men usually yielded more than twenty types of diseases and often more than thirty. Always among the first diseases recited were those which had to do with witchcraft, either involving aggressive or reflexive attacks of the evus or failures to observe the *eki-akyage* complex of prohibitions and promises. Fang made a major distinction between sick-

nesses of the heart and sicknesses of the body (*nkukwan nyôl*). As for sicknesses of the body, they made a distinction between those caused by accident
(*njuk*), those caused by deleterious internal worms (*nson*), and skin eruptions
or lesions caused by epidemic infection (*abyen*). While any illness could be
attributed to the maleficence of unseen forces, there was a category of sicknesses and suffering which was directly traced to this maleficence without
recourse to intermediary explanation by reference to contagion, worms, or
accident. Diffuse or sudden and acute pains of the chest or upper viscera (the
nkuk) and of the head were likely to have that immediate attribution, while
piles or swellings of the spleen or of the joints were credited to unseen powers
only after lingering affliction.

"Sickness of the heart," that is to say, of the chest and upper viscera, was
always of great concern to Fang. This was the first area that came under attack
from the aggressive witchcraft of others. And if the individual himself possessed the demon he would first have a sign that it was acting up against him
in the upper trunk, for it was there that the demon was usually lodged. The
center of the trunk was the heart, considered the most likely focus of the
diseases of that region.*² When a man felt himself under attack from the
demon or had disobeyed an injunction which was laid upon him in obtaining
the demon, he was likely to feel his chest grow tight or his heart pound, and
this could lead to bizarre psychic states, thus confirming the affliction of his
heart. But whatever the prodromal conditions, behavior which was bizarre
and unusual by village standards was, in contrast to most explanations for
body sickness, first referred to some action of witchcraft: either aggressive
(by action of *eluma* or *evus*) or reflexive, by virtue of some confusion in the
eki-akyage complex.

The general term for those afflicted with these disorders was *nsok eki* or
nsusok eki, "those who hallucinate and act foolish by virtue of the turmoil
in them of having broken taboo." It is uncertain from which root nsok eki
derives: whether from *sok*, "to drink like an animal," and, hence *nsok*,
drunkenness—or from *sok*, "to search out hidden truth" as in *nsok angang*.
In the first derivation it would mean "he who is drinking like an animal and
thus failing to observe the proprieties and injunctions of his preparation" (the
taboos most often pertained to food and drink), "has been struck inebriate
by the power of taboo." The second derivation would give us "he who has
for some reason penetrated to the unseen power of the taboo and been struck
foolish by the confrontation." The second derivation would help explain better
that mixture of exasperation, wonder, and anticipation with which fools (such

---

*² Fang had many terms for states of the heart and hence states of the person—hot heart, cold
heart, hard heart, tranquil heart. The term for delirium or vertigo was nlemda. Though most
Fang understood that the brain was the organ of thought, these terms were in general use during
the period of inquiry.

as Antoine) and their actions were regarded. They might, in fact, be bringing forth wisdom from the unseen.

When faced then with this young fool, Antoine, villagers asked themselves various questions. Was his heartsickness the result of the aggressions of others, or was it a failure in his own aggressive designs? Was it the consequence of the failure to keep promises made during his preparation, or was it simply a case of stupidity and malicious foolishness—as Ngema believed?

It might give us a reference point in assaying Fang thinking on "heart sickness," to consider Western psychiatric categories.[3] These categories, however, have a relatively narrow vision of social order, and do not allow much room for foolishness. They do not easily grant it significance. They are like Ngema's judgment in that regard.

We need to know about the way the villagers represented Antoine's illness to themselves. A more dynamic account of a Fang theory of mental illness emerges by reference to the lexicon of individual and social states. Such a lexicon suggests stages of illness as well as notions of actions that push the individual or the village beyond harmony (*bemle*) and into discord.[4]

In the social life of the village and in the life of the individual, Fang recognized a range of behavior which was characterized by habits of "orderliness" (*ngomge*), by "an orderly preparation in the discharge of all things" (*akômnge*),[5] and by "a general integrity of feeling and thought in human affairs" which they called *nlem mvore* ("oneheartedness"). This normal range was characterized by a fluctuation back and forth between "states of tranquillity" (*mvwaa*, calm, "even-handed," well-being in every sense) and pleasurable and appropriate activity (*elulua*). We note in Figure 8.1 Fang

---

[3] H. H. Leighton and A. T. Lambo, in *Psychiatric Disorders among the Yoruba*, particularly Chapter IV, contend with the application of the diagnostic categories of American psychiatry to an African situation. They recognize not only the inapplicability of some categories, and the cross-cutting of others, but also some special African disorders such as periodic psychotic excitement which are not on the American list. Antoine seems best described in their terms as a schizoid personality (rather than a chronic or acute schizophrenic) who, under the pressure of young adulthood, adopted temporary behavior typical of paranoid schizophrenia. That is: "Autistic unrealistic thinking with mental content composed chiefly of delusions of persecution and/or grandeur and often hallucinations. It is often characterized by unpredictable behavior with a fairly constant attitude of hostility and aggression, excessive religiosity may be present with or without delusions of persecution. There may be an expansive delusional system of omnipotence, genius or special ability" (Leighton and Lambo, *Psychiatric Disorders*, p. 67).

[4] Bemle, to provoke or push into excess, to excite. The radical here, "bem," is of interest. Pronounced in high tone it means to go up, to remove one's self in an upward direction. Pronounced in low tone it means to ground, fix, or push something down below, "enforcer" in the French. These radicals are of interest because they relate to the convention, employed in Figure 8.1, of excessive behavior as falling either above or below a line.

[5] The radical in this term, "ko̱m," is a key one in both this chapter and in the entire study. For the central term in the discussion, akomnge (preparation in the demon), also rises from it. It means "to form or shape."

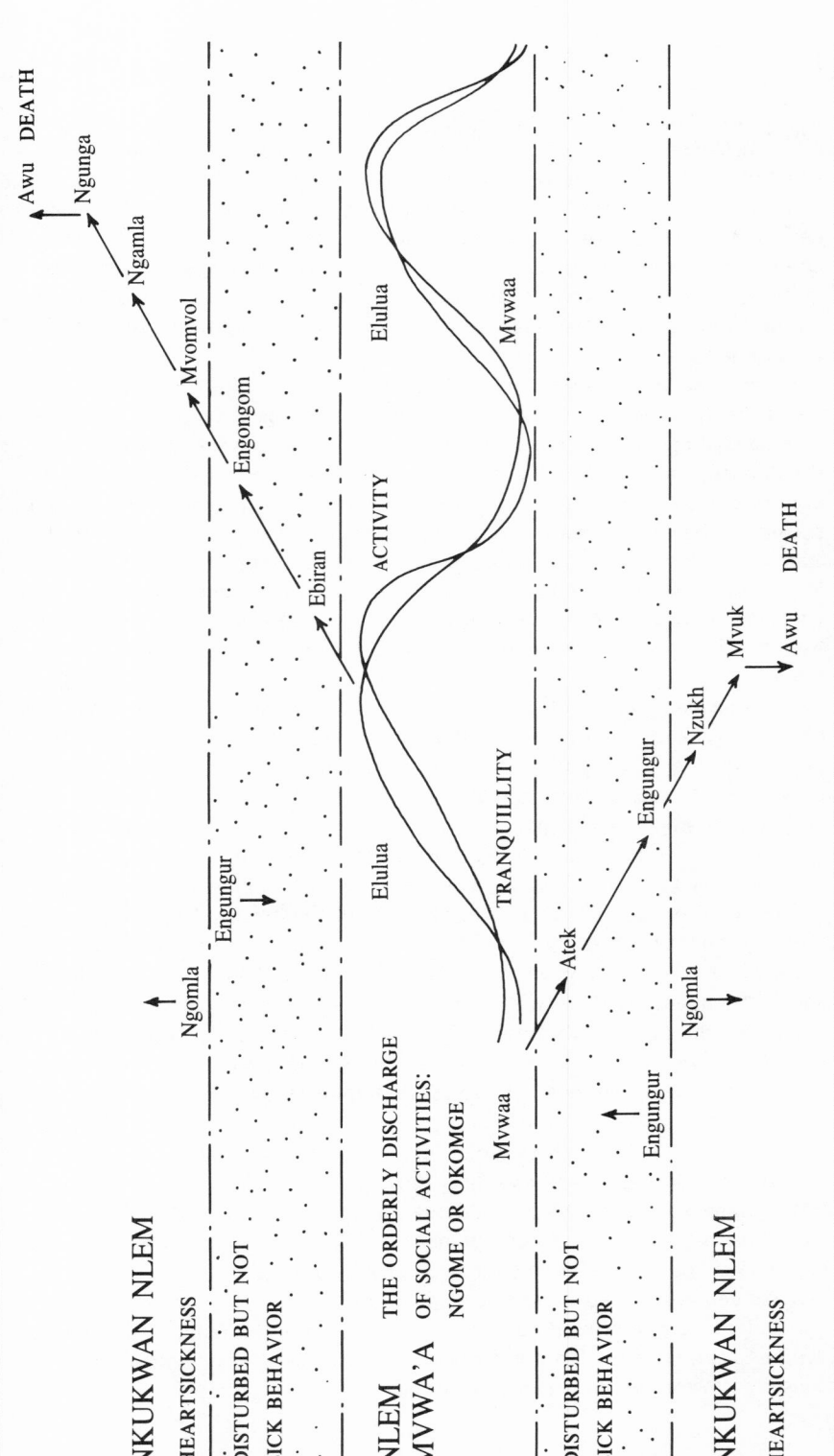

8.1 Vicissitudes of the Heart

notions of maturity or wisdom as lying in a "proper balance" (*bipwé*) between different states—male and female in the case of their physiological philosophy, and activity and tranquillity as regards social and mental orderliness.

Men departed from this expected range in two directions—toward greater and greater activity, noise, disorder, hotness, aggressiveness, and finally, tempestuous violence on the one hand, and toward greater and greater tranquillity, lassitude, disorder, coldness, dumbness, stupidity, and unresponsiveness on the other. The stages of these developments were well represented in Fang lexicon.

From elulua men passed to *ebiran* (action which was unjust, self-interested, and destructive) or *ôdon* (an inconsequential foolishness of action in which men danced and sang, shouted and laughed in a manic way). These actions, if extended, brought the village to the state of *engongom* (disordered agitation). Driven by their demon or some unrequited spirit, men thrust on and became *mvomvol* (violent transgressors of other's rights), and this led to the state of *ngamla* (pell-mell disorder), if not *ngunga* (tempestuous mutual violence and reprisal). The inescapable consequences of the continuation of those latter states were death and the "dispersion" (*ngomla*) of the kin group. This was the ultimate worry provoked by any sign of mental disorder in a fellow villager.

From *mvmaa*, on the other hand, men were liable to fall into a condition of *atek* (weakness and docility). If this continued they could become progressively *angungur* (presenting a slovenly and unkempt appearance) and pass, hence, to the state of *nzukh* (a general malaise or sense of overbearing affliction compounded of pain and ennui) till they finally fell *mvuk* (dumb and unable to communicate or participate effectively with others).

The theory that lay behind these notions was that while men in their transactions with others and with themselves might be expected periodically to pass beyond the range of the expected, if they passed far beyond or chronically engaged in behavior beyond that range, then some classification had to be sought for them. If there was no obvious physical evidence of disease, it would be said of those dwelling outside the range of "tranquilheartedness" that they were "heartsick." The further beyond the normal range the more the village and its various healing and disciplinary agents might be called upon to act.

Rather different rationales were offered for the two sorts of excess—excess of activity and excess of tranquillity. But it was generally felt that men who had demons were driven to destructively self-interested and violent disorders. And those who had no demons (*mimia*) had their substance consumed and dissipated. They fell below the range and tended toward weakness, persistent malaise and ennui, and more dire states of affliction. Still, the etiology was ambivalent, and men with demons could fall below the range by action of demons against them. Doctor diviners (*ngungan* and *nsok ngan*) had to be consulted to resolve the vagaries of causality.

Fang notions of mental (heart) order and disorder have very much to do with the effects these conditions produced in village affairs. Fang were prepared to offer men considerable leeway in their actions—as they offered Antoine—if the consequences for the village and kin group did not seem to be leading to breakdown (*ngomla*). But, in the end, both individual and village responded to the sense of disorder with treatment aimed at *engungun* (reunification, knitting together, the making as one). Such treatment was ultimately aimed at returning men, and the village affected by their actions, to appropriate activity or tranquillity by calming or animating demons or ancestral spirits, whichever might be involved. Antoine, too docile (atek) during the day and too ngongom or mvomvol at night, eventually regained his balance. But some men never did and chronically dwelt on the margins of the normal fluctuations of everyday life.

Much more than this taxonomic information is needed, however dynamic it may be, to explain events like Antoine's night foolishness. There was more meaning to Fang sickness and treatment than simply the loss and reestablishment of a kind of homeostatic order. There was more to Fang suffering than categorization could cure. We need to examine more closely the concepts of the soul, of the demon. We need to know more about the socialization of children which put heavy pressures on Fang young men and which led Antoine to struggle to fulfill himself in such a bizarre manner. Finally, we must consider (in Part II) those rituals, vanished or only vestigial in village life, which acted formerly to organize and to insulate and balance young men against and amidst these pressures.

The Youthful Search
for Renown and Sexual Property

Antoine's affliction was not unknown in Fang experience with young people. In recent decades there had been a number of young fools in the villages.[3] A favorite device with which they sought to draw attention to their plight was to set up a very tall pole with a colored banner at the peak. Various reasons were given for this pole: that it announced to the spirits the abode of their devotee or that it warded off evil spirits. For as Antoine himself was preoccupied with appropriating something of the material wherewithal of the European and the colonial world, so these other "heartsick" young men made a bizarre search for other features of that lifestyle that had impressed them, such as its panoply of power. Just as the commandant of District or Region discharged his functions behind the flagpole of the Republic, so these young men actualized their fantasies by erecting flagpoles in their courtyards. A young man of Koumassi on the Bitam road who stopped the cars of white men by setting up fences (as white men do) had a different strategy. By doing the things of white men the Fang could chase the whites from Africa, he argued. These young fools not only appropriated objects of the colonial world as symbols, they also appropriated from their own tradition objects and behavior that belonged properly to full men. Thus Antoine's night sermons were an appropriation of the ''night talk'' (*nkôbô alu*) that senior men might avail themselves of when the village was fully settled for the night—in order to provide important counsel for all ears.

These young men were victims of very contemporary uncertainties. For just as the threshold between full manhood and old age had broadened out and created anxiety in full men about their status, so, at the other end, the threshold between young men (*nduman*) and full men had also broadened out and created uncertainties. Old men frequently complained about the presumptuousness of the young and about their wandering and profligate life. Said Ndong Engonga with impatience, ''As soon as a young man has a wet dream (*aku nka enong*—ejaculate bed), he thinks he can debate his elders in the council house.'' In the old days the constant threat of warfare kept young men at home until they were of age to defend themselves. Courtship and marriage was supervised by the village. ''But now,'' complained Ndong, ''young men carry on promiscuously, picking up with any girl that interests them even before they can grow a beard.'' It was more than simply ''youthful presumptuousness'' (*afam* or *angwek*) that Ndong decried. There was a deeper source of generational conflict which concerned sexual property. For the young girls just past puberty who were swept up into this supposed promiscuity might well be, it was feared by the nyamoro, those for whom the older men had already offered some bridemoney and fully expected to make their wives.

The contemporary presumption of the young consisted not only of being able to gallivant freely throughout the village, but also of having imbibed enough elementary education to feel superior to their unlettered elders. If the nyamoro felt that the young were unbearably presumptuous and insulting, the young in their stead felt the old were oppressive, ignorant, and selfish. This range of feeling was often expressed in the idiom of sexual rights and duties. In my discussions in Libreville with young men from Oyem District about their reasons for leaving their villages, I found that following close behind the desire to adventure and see the world was the refusal of fathers or older brothers to provide bridemonies to enable the young to marry. This deprivation was felt very strongly by the young bachelor Antoine. Since his father's death, however, it was his older brother who had become the head of the family and who had replaced his father as ''the selfish and deceitful one.'' It was thus that Antoine in the expression of his fantasies laid claim—like any ''European''—upon his own village sisters as wives.

The presumptuousness of the young of which Antoine's foolishness was a bizarre extension was not exclusively the product of modernization. The very word for young men was usually derived by folk etymologists from *duma* (glory, renown, reputation) and the nduman, hence, was understood as ''he who was unduly preoccupied with his reputation and his glory in the mouths of others.'' In the same way the physiological philosophy we have reviewed shows us the nduman (as opposed to the nyamoro) as operating excessively under the influence of semen (*meyôm*) and, hence, too willful and unreflective in his social relations. There may have been an increase in "heartsickness" in recent years, but there was evidence that the problem of the young was an enduring one.

THE PREPARATION OF THE CHILD FOR ADULTHOOD

In discussions of the raising of children, Fang commonly stressed the immutability of nature against any efforts of nurture. Inherited propensities were stronger than any instruction (*ayugele*) or parental advice (*alibiguh*) in a person's behavior. A man's fundamental character was inherited in the blood and the sperm, though Fang usually referred to the blood alone (*mefulu me sô meki*). One spoke of the blood of the patrilineal descent line (*meki me nzangabot*) or the character or influence of patrilineal descent (*tchiga me nzangabot*). Still, there was no anticipating the source of a child's character, and that is why fathers so often asked: "Where does that bad character come from?" (*mbeafulu da so ve*).*6 Elders sighed, "Inherited character is surpassingly strong, fathers can advise, advise, advise . . . no result." (*Mvuan a ne dang ngu . . . essa a ne liba, liba, liba . . . ke dzum!*)

Some took more considered views. Chief Essono, for example, hazarded that strength, intelligence, capacity for work, and ability to exercise authority over others were inborn. But the instruction the individual received in childhood was crucial in determining whether these capacities would be exercised in prosperous tranquillity or would instead be frustrated and lead to heartsickness and disorder. Such Fang had clear notions of maturation stages and watched their children alertly, hopeful that they would reach these thresholds in good time. They realized their responsibility in facilitating or frustrating the achievement of these stages.

This process began in the womb and proceeded regularly, if all had gone well at conception, and if neither the woman's menstrual blood nor the father's semen had been unduly influential.*7 Fang talked about four stages in the womb. Each stage depended upon appropriate observances by the parents. The first stage was that of *kígíle* in which the fetus was a potent ball of matter.

*6 This question need not deny the patrilineal source of one's habitual behavior, for often the father was implying that the child might be the product of adultery—and possessed thereby of the blood of another man (meki mefe).

*7 Intercourse too close to menstruation or after the child had moved in the womb could have bad results. A child who had moved in the womb might swallow the semen and would be born sick in the chest (okwan nkuk) all his life. The association for this belief was probably the calcification that resulted from tuberculosis. At the same time, there was also a belief that at an earlier stage of foetal development the father's semen was important in surrounding and protecting the homunculus as it grew.

The second stage was that in which the fetus resembled a small lizard (*nshia*). From this stage it passed into the condition of an ogre being (*akôwô mot*). This was a delicate stage, and if the parents committed sin or broke a taboo at this time, their offspring was considered likely to be born a disfigured monster. Finally, the fetus became fully formed and moved within the womb. It became *abum mwan*.

When the child was born the dangers for him and the anxieties of his parents did not diminish. For a time, during the first year—which was one of high infant mortality[4]—they increased. As the child passed from being an infant in arms (*nkenle mwan*) to a toddler (*etun mwan*), through childhood (*môn*) to puberty when he finally became an nduman, he had to be protected, given a name, prepared, and circumcised, as well as put through a set of rituals which implicated the community as much as himself.

For several weeks after his birth, while his mother was undergoing purification and fortification for her reentrance into the life of the village, the child would not be given a name. Was he going to survive? Had the ancestors really given up this child? No name could be assigned until the ceremony of immersion (*dzok*) or "boiling" (*etok*) took place, generally in the second day of the infant's life. A basin of leaves was prepared in the mother's hut, and herbs and symbolic objects were placed in it. The water was allowed to cool and the infant was bathed. Dzok was a ceremony of protective cleansing. The objects added to this bath strengthened the child in respect to the activity with which they were associated. Formerly Fang iron money (*bikuela*) was placed in the basin, and more recently currency was placed there. It was said that wealth would be washed into his blood. A pencil or ball point pen has come to replace an iron spear in the basin (of a boy baby) to bring the child intelligence and success in his schooling—perhaps a place in the bureaucracy.

The dzok was really a preparation for life, and some informants argued darkly, since the idea of akomnge raised in people's minds the thought of the demon, that even at this early stage of infancy a child could be prepared with witchcraft. An old man of his family, powerful in witchcraft, an envalen, could come forth and, by placing a piece of human flesh in the basin, quicken the witchcraft spirit in the infant, giving him an early taste of acquisitive power. But the akomnge came more safely at a later time when the child could take some cognizance of the requirements of preparation. The preparation with witchcraft power was very dangerous in one who did not have the strength to support the demon. Since at an early stage little could be told about the infant's strength, to prepare him might be to endanger him.

After the child was cleansed and strengthened he would be given a name. He was not considered a real person belonging to the family until he had one. The naming invested him with the honor (*ewuma*) of his patrilineage and particularly of the man or woman who had carried the name before. There was no general belief that the spirit of an ancestor reincarnated itself, but it was recognized that one ancestor in particular might have shepherded the child to his birth. The character of this ancestor might be evident in the child, so he would be studied for evidence of it. Men in any case wanted to honor those dead who were of pleasant or powerful memory. "In giving a child a certain name," said Obunu, "we are trying to keep before us the image (efônan), or likeness, of him who carried that name formerly." Since the child would later have the character of his namesake extolled to him, it could influence his behavior.

At the time the infant received a name the mother could exit from the birth house. She went down to the stream to bring back fish and ceremonially present them in the man's council house. This presentation was regarded as a "payment" to the men of patrilineage so that they would allow "her child" (male or female), which had been so much a part of her in the confines of the birth house, to enter into the patrilineage and into the council house.

This was one of several ceremonial observances that women alien to the patrilineage made toward its men gathered as a group in the council house. Another example already discussed (Chapter 6) was the ceremonial meal presented to the men in the council house by the bride's mother at the time of marriage (bidzí bi nengon). In both cases the ritual presentation of food integrated alien flesh and blood to the patrilineage. The mother ritually contributed to the patrilineage so as to gain its benevolent protection of her child. She nurtured the patrilineage that it might nurture her child. The principal object of bidzi bi nengon was to assure the bride's well-being. The principal object of the mother's gift of fish—called "the capture of the antelope" (abi ôjen)[5] was to assure that the patrilineage would incorporate and protect the child, which although belonging to it, was yet born of her, of an alien clan. After consuming this meal in silence and building up some suspense, the father finally announced publicly the name for the child.[*8]

As the child grew and after he had left the breast in his third or fourth year, he was watched for signs of forcefulness in expressing his desires. Was the child nkukut, gentle to the point of laziness or passivity (craye)? Were there signs of self-indulgence and gluttony (ndawk)? The elders' expectations here were well read by the child. This close observation ascertained whether he could be prepared with the witchcraft spirit and whether he could be given a name of encouragement (eyole mebaran) at the time of circumcision.

Formerly circumcision was the last dramatic act in the male child's preparation before puberty. Occurring from his eighth to twelfth year, it came well after any preparation he might have received in the powers of witchcraft. In more recent years, however, circumcision was practiced in infancy. We have discussed the potency that circumcision sought to promote. Fang felt

---

[*8] The name need not always be the one borne by the ancestor. It might simply reflect a present circumstance—bekale, "he with many sisters" and hence with the promise of many marriages.

that the foreskin was an encumbrance as well as aesthetically unpleasing. "Women laugh at it," said Obunu. Hence circumcision was an act of preparation in the sense that it freed the child for full achievement of his sexual identity. It was understood as Fang usually understood "preparation"—as a freeing of a child's nature from encumbrances so that it could fulfill its potentiality. It was in this context that Fang could maintain that nature was everything and nurture of little importance.

But circumcision late in childhood was an act of character-building as much as an act of release of potentiality. This was particularly so if circumcision was accompanied by a "name of encouragement" which was spoken into the boy's ear by males of his patrilineage as he was cut. This name was intended to be used at any future moment of trial, whether in hunting, warfare, or debate in the council house. The names evoked qualities of resistance to attack, of cunning and stealthiness, or of dauntless force.

> *Bidu bi koro akawk* (*"bidubi"* for short): "the rats flee the stone (untouched)"—the reference is to the grinding stone in the kitchen. Rats ravage anything in a kitchen, but they cannot attack the grinding stone.
>
> *Nguraben ôngongor* (*"nguongo"* for short): "half elephant hide shield strong child"—but also in word play it can be shortened to *"engurbe,"* he who waits in hiding to surprise others.
>
> *Akoro abang*: "the otter has fled"—reference is to the arrival of the fisherman at his traps. He finds the otter has fled with all the fish.
>
> *Asang mefa*: "[he] slashes [with many] swords"—the name of encouragement of Emane Tole, the Fang leader of the turn-of-the-century uprising.

These names in reiteration had an influence on a man's performance if not upon his character. But the frequent circularity of the nature-nurture debate was indicated in the characteristic Fang response. "A child did not receive a name of encouragement until it was clear that his nature was such to deserve it." The name thus confirmed and did not shape nature.

THE "GOLDEN AGE" AND ITS BOUNDARIES

Fang gave the child a long period—the first two or three years, or as long as nursing continued—of ready nurturance and indulgence. He was nursed on demand and handled affectionately by his mother's co-wives and by his grandmothers. This "golden age" was brought abruptly to an end by the appearance of pepper on his mother's breast or simply by her disappearance from the village—leaving him to a more diffused nurturing group. He was already eating solid food in any case. It was not a painful rejection. He was then turned over to his elder siblings who continued mostly to indulge him.

Young children had their noses or ears tweaked when they misbehaved, when they took something that did not belong to them, or continued to annoy their elders. Older children were sometimes disciplined by being hung up by their heels for a brief time (*akele mwan*). But this was generally remembered with amusement. Fang said that one should be strict with children so that their natures were not corrupted. But they were actually quite lenient, and children were rarely beaten. Fang children, though not regarding their parents as harsh, considered them unpredictable and swift to punish, largely, perhaps, because elders did not spend time explaining things to small children, and hence felt obliged to enter in unexpectedly to change direction when things were going wrong. Rather than punish the child physically, they might suddenly remove or destroy that with which he was playing. The quality of parental discipline accords with later adult attitudes toward the supernaturals. Ancestor spirits were unpredictable and rash, but not especially cruel or hostile in Fang thought.

Parents and elders dramatized the existence of dangerous supernatural forces. From very early in the child's experiences, parents might hush him by speaking to him of the "forest monster" (*kôkaw ebíbî*) who ate children and knew how to discover them by the sound of their crying. Usually some playful man in the village took the role. In the evening he would come to the hut of a whiny or disobedient child and beat against it with the flat of his hands, making gruff noises and grunting or swinging the bullroarer (*avuntra*). Occasionally he would appear during the day covered with a cloth and chase the children through the village. The children learned early that the forest was full of potential dangers which could intrude into village life and that the inside of the huts could be a refuge against these hostilities if one behaved properly there. They would also have been inside the huts during various ceremonies when men or women came in groups and beat against the walls pretending they had come to kill all those within. From very early in the colonial period, it appears Fang mothers used the white man and his reputed taste for the flesh of young children as a threat to quiet their wailing youngsters. This no doubt energized the "supernatural" qualities of the white man as these are expressed in various mythologies and legends. Harmful supernaturals were all created for the child external to the family and projected outside it. The child was warned that weakness on his part—crying, gluttony, self-indulgence—would allow these dangers to enter into the mvogabot itself.

In his seventh or eighth year, the young boy became the object of stronger physical discipline, not only from his older brothers who might beat him, but also from his parents who demanded compliance from him. The informal solidarity group of age mates (*nkôabot*),[6] those within two or three years of each other, now made its appearance, while the next older age group in their early teens would exercise their new-found sense of importance as very young nduman by bossing their "little ones" around. It was in late childhood that Fang developed an antagonism toward their older brothers. That was part of the resentment that went into the rivalries and suspicion between brothers that was characteristic of adulthood.

Boys in these years played separately from their village sisters, but already a certain intrigue was apparent which resulted around puberty, and after, in a warm joking relationship. Incest was something which village adults worried about, partly as a projection of their own preoccupation with adultery. One suspected sex play in the forest. The Ndong Mba ritual was devised to deal with that, and to make sure the young understood what the social boundaries of sexual activity were.

Men and women remembered their childhood with pleasure. It was a golden age. Women experienced a re-creation of that golden age at the time of the birth of a child for they were again indulged in every way by mothers, mothers-in-law, and co-wives. They enjoyed pleasures of command over these other women (during the early nursing period). As for men, they frequently reflected on their childhood. They commented nostalgically at the first heavy downpours of the rainy season when children stripped off their clothes and went splashing and rushing about under eaves and in the puddles of the courtyard.

Children's games were especially remembered, and at the time of the full moon, when children were most active at them, adults came out to watch with enjoyment. "Little goat" (*mwan kubn*) particularly attracted attention. One of the stouter boys or girls became a leopard. He rushed around outside a circle of children who danced round and round. Their hands were clasped tightly and they tried to prevent him from breaking into the middle where the "little goat" roamed. Should he break in, the goat was permitted to dart out and the children tried to hold the leopard within. Finally, the leopard found a weak spot and caught the goat.

Defending boundaries against hostile (external or internal) forces was also represented in the game of "civet cat" (*nsing*). Here a boy hid outside in the banana bush while the children formed a chain and snaked around in the courtyard to the clapping of spectators. Suddenly the nsing rushed in. The children rushed immediately to crouch around the leader, "the mother hen." If the nsing could catch them before they did, they were dead. It was a lesson in the benefits of solidarity in the kin group as well as a lesson in external dangers and in the importance of maintaining boundaries.

Adults might be involved in these games, or at least offer apt comment while they were being played. In "the head of the line" (*efak nlong*) the children lined up from the biggest to smallest. They passed under the out-stretched arms of two older children, each of whom represented a notable of the village, one a Catholic, the other perhaps a Protestant catechist, or one a leader of the progressive and the other the leader of the conservative village political faction. First the end of the line was trapped as they passed under the arch (the smallest children), and each was asked to which faction he chose to belong. These lined up behind their leader, whether progressive (UDSG) or conservative (BDG), to help him hold the larger boys and girls if they escaped the trap. In the end the object was to ensnare the larger group for one or the other side, and in this way a commentary was made on the adult power structure of the village. Adults watched this play, just as they listened to Antoine's "night playfulness," with more than unalloyed amusement.

A full feeling for Fang play is given by Tessmann's compilation of games at the turn of the century. He gives six different categories of children's and adults' play.[7] Of these categories, play that was imitative of adult crafts, occupations, and rituals and games of mental agility, such as memory games (Gedächtnisspiele) and puzzles (Geduldspiel), loomed largest in his experience. The social or group games (Gesellschaftsspiel) that we mention above are hardly considered at all, and late-nineteenth-century mission schooling may have been influential in promoting them.

Tessmann was impressed with the variety of games of mental agility and treated them in detail. In more recent years the imitative play continued, though less elaborately, with boys making trucks, mammy wagons, and airplanes out of raffia wood rather than drums, spears, and ancestor cult figures. Girls made their little kitchens out of tin cans rather than mud pots. But puzzles and memory games were much less in evidence. Perhaps they had been upstaged by the more concentrated "Gedächtnisspiele" and "Geduldspiel" of village schooling. In any case there was more emphasis on physically active group games such as the soccer and the "moonlight games" we have considered.[*9] There was an increase in games which added to the competitive atmosphere of village life and which emphasized maintenance of boundaries rather than group problem-solving or theatrical creativeness. Tessmann early remarked that Fang play was often accompanied by raillery of group by group, but this spirit much increased.

In more recent days there was constant observation of Fang children, particularly during games, for signs of their capacity for the demon evus. From very early on this was a concern of adults (and even more, it is supposed, of old people) who wanted to prepare these young people in a manner beneficial to the child and perhaps to the adult as well. Children were surrounded with talk of "preparation" (akomnge) and with incidents in which there was some failure in ekí-akyage. Then they might find themselves in a situation in which there was a strong hint of "preparation." This watchful parental

---

[*9] The former emphasis, if we are to accept Tessmann's sample, on problem-solving games of mental skill rather than upon purely physical games of group competition relate, perhaps, to an increased divisiveness in Fang life and a greater tendency toward spontaneous and emotive rather than composed and calculated attempts at problem-solving. The latter is cold-spiritedly emphasized in the mvet cycle (see Chapter 2). The earliest reputation of Fang was of a wise and reflective people, though coastal peoples emphasized their unpredictable violence. For the general theory of the relation of games and other expressive activities to culture, see the work of John M. Roberts, summarized in Roberts and Ridgeway, "Musical Involvement in Talking," pp. 223-246.

atmosphere and the recurring evidence of the presence of the evus made a strong impression on children. In recent decades it was one of the experiences most remembered from middle and late childhood.

Fang in the early colonial period seemed promising from the point of view of performing productive and intelligent work in the colonial enterprise. Yet for several reasons this expectation of achievement was thwarted and in ways indicative of the several "binds" in which latter-day Fang found themselves. For while Fang waited anxiously to see what the character of children would show, most believed too much in the fixity of nature to endeavor in a positive pedagogic way—as opposed to ritual preparations—to shape that character. They sought mainly to prevent the child from being spoiled through self-indulgence. The kind of mind-training that once occurred in Fang folklore and which parents could avail themselves of was in sharp decline. That which did occur was compartmentalized into the rote training of the schools and was alien to most of the problems Fang faced in maturing; in any case it was not available for parental use.

There was another restraint on achievement. Fang had a strong notion of what may be called the "conservation of matter."[8] In the spirit of the hunter egalitarianism with which they identified on the one hand, combined with the parsimony of rain forest agriculturalists living on the narrow margin of existence which they were, on the other, they kept a sharp eye out for those too anxious for excessive place, power, or possessions. To encourage children openly to obtain by independent effort goods which were in limited supply was, in effect, to encourage them to appropriate selfishly from others. It was an act of ebiran.

The role of Fang youth, then, in this "atmosphere of expectation" was ambiguous and conflictive. One was prepared for success but one was not encouraged to succeed nor given, any longer, training in that crafty lore by which in an oral society success was best secured. They were often left, like Antoine, in a competitive and avaricious atmosphere without the tools of competition. They saw that for Fang "the good" was, indeed, very limited, yet in the colonial world it was obviously abundant. It was hard for them to obtain a sense of the limits of acquisitiveness. As Fang they knew that men were, over time, fundamentally equal, yet they saw all around them in the colonial world enduring hierarchies. Antoine's bizarre activity was, no doubt, one way of working out the uncertainties of this situation—of fulfilling the expectations laid upon him without, in actual fact, fulfilling them. It was imaginative fulfillment only.

Surely the remembered "golden age," those intimations of omnipotence from recollections of earliest childhood, was also a part of adult character. It was celebrated in the mvet legends of the miraculous powers of the men of Engong. It was manifested in the belief in the demon, whose capacity to go anywhere and do anything in self-interest resonated with that primordial omnipotence. Released from customary constraints, the demon often enough, like Antoine, knew no bounds. But imaginary as its activity may have been, its boundlessness had a depressing effect on the relationships between men.

Indeed it would be true to say of ancestral Fang wisdom about the nature of mature character that such character lay in the apt maintenance of boundaries. What was important was to maintain the boundaries of the self and the boundaries of the kin group. The true nyamoro not only balanced the incompatible elements of inheritance, they were also strong enough to prevent inimical external forces from penetrating their own person and their own social group. They were strong enough, on the other hand, should they possess the demon—as nyamoro almost always did—to prevent it from exiting from their person to wreak havoc in the kin group and village. They were strong enough to control their demon and use it only defensively for self and society. There persisted out of the "golden age" of earliest childhood a tendency to extend the boundaries in megalomaniac fashion. This tendency was exacerbated by the demon evus which could act to terribly efficient effect as the agent of that extension. The "preparation" of the child, intended simply as a strengthening of boundaries, could result often enough in later years in aggression and aggrandizement. It could result in the destruction of boundaries: of one's own, of one's kin group, and of one's village society.

In Fang society of the old days, we must assume, it was not only games which taught that boundary maintenance; the lessons were also taught by ceremonies of puberty, Ndong Mba and Soo, and by ceremonies of adulthood, particularly by the ancestor cult. This cult took initiates inside secret forest arenas to show secret powers which lay inside the reliquary. These ceremonies counteracted the megalomania implicit in infant indulgence and the aggrandizement too easily excited by "the preparation." Rituals kept eyes focused upon the corporate good and upon the social body and its component bounded parts. The declining lore of strategic argument, of repartee and proverbial wit, rather than being a means of advancement was most often, like the epigraph of this chapter, a counsel of acquiescence to the social good and a repository of wisdom about human foibles and pretense.

But the abandonment of these ceremonies and wisdom in colonial times coupled with the acquisitive character of the European mercantile milieu, not to mention the abundant possessions of Europeans, led not only to the increasing importance of preparation in its aggressive and aggrandizing sense but to a consequent breakdown of boundaries. The environment of expectation became excessive; the old "golden age" of indulgence foreshadowed a new golden age of consumerism. When the ancestor cult and the antiwitchcraft cults disappeared, the demonic powers easily exceeded themselves and their appropriate boundaries. In exceptional cases this precipitated delusions of grandeur and megalomania. All this was seen in such troubled young men as Antoine and in his night foolishness. His "heartsickness" was as much as anything a matter of collapsed or vague boundaries in an ambiguous "atmosphere of expectation."

THE PROMISES MADE TO HIDDEN CAPACITIES

Though one may speak of a child's or a man's character, in fact Fang conceived of men and women as having several natures which could respond to the various situations in which they found themselves. The demon itself was not *the* man's character—though it could take him over—but only part of his character with which he had to struggle. This plurality of natures is seen in the variety of names a man received. First—and here there is an obvious relationship between name and character—was the "name of encouragement" (*eyôle mebara*). Then a person carried both a name given by the father (*eyôla esia*), the name by which he or she was generally known, and the name which was assigned in the council house at the time of his presentation there. They were also given a name by the mother (*eyola nyia*) which did honor to one of her relatives and which was used in her family and in the company of her brothers. A child or a youth, it was recognized, was a rather different person in the mother's village compared to his role in the father's. Different possibilities of character also lay in the physiological philosophy and in the different possible balancings of semen (male) and blood (female) natures.

In Fang doctrines of the soul and in their conception of unseen power, we see other sources of belief in the diversity of nature and the necessity of balancing parts of the self. Tessmann conceptualized this diversity by referring to the transitory visible part of men (korper), the actual body; its being, animating principle or essential, though still transitory nature (korperwesen); the enduring invisible part of man's body, the soul (seele); and the soul's being or essential nature (seelenwesen).[9]

Reference to Fang terms shows three underlying spiritual entities that could belong to a man: the evus (called here the witchcraft spirit or demon), the nsisim or shadow or incorporeal form of the body which missionaries took up for the translation of soul, and the kon or shade which subsisted after death. Both the body and the evus which invigorated it disappeared at death.*[10]

---

*[10] Fang sometimes said that the evus might persist in dangerous wild animals after the death of its possessor. They also said that the evus was passed on from an old man to a young one and could thereby gain an immortality beyond the life of its original owner. And more; a truly evil evus when its host's body was moldering in the grave would tear the network of veins and tendons loose and install itself in some wild animal.

In extended discussions with Fang one arrived at various kinds of evus: good and bad, aggressive and defensive, social and antisocial. One might even use the Lévi-Straussian categories: the evus of nature over culture and of culture over nature (Mallart, "La Médecine traditionnelle"). Fang could conceive of many kinds of evus. And while some might argue that a man's nature inescapably followed and was to be identified with the nature of his evus, the reality I perceived and that I emphasize here is that (1) one was never sure of the nature of one's evus and (2) all evus tended to be aggrandizing and antisocial and men had to struggle to control

The nsisim, or the essential though incorporeal form, persisted after death and roamed the village until finally laid to rest by a mortuary ceremony. This left only the shade of the dead which was dispatched by this ceremony to the village of the dead. The point is that men's characters were compounded of different mixes of these "essential natures."

In the ancestor cult Fang were preoccupied with kon—that truly perduring element of a man which could be brought by cult activity into an invigorated relation with other bekon in the land of the dead. But in the daily life of mid-century and in the raising of children, Fang were more concerned with the evus. True, in the period after death, the nsisim might wander and create difficulties for the living. And the kon was susceptible to shade-brought disease and anxiety. But the demon was constantly present, living in the body of often envious and untrustworthy neighbors. Or perhaps it was present in one's own body where it had to be constantly kept calm. The nsisim had become the concern of missionary Christianity which sought to focus Fang upon the fate of this soul. The ancestor cult focused on kon, but this cult had collapsed or been suppressed and with it had gone much of the reality of the shade concept which it cultivated. The evus thus swelled, into the vacuum left by this collapse. A grandiose mythology of evil was produced, as we see in the next chapter.

One incident can show how the suspected presence of the demon galvanized emotions in mid-century villages, particularly among the young. On a gray, overcast, typically cold-season day in 1959, I was called from work in the Bwiti village of Efulan seven miles south of Medouneu by an agitated informant who would say only that a young boy nearly dead had been rushed down from the adjacent village of Nkolayop and into the hut of the woman who was the head of the local MBiri curing cult. He had been carried along by his father's brothers and followed by his wailing mother. The young informant, probably because of his own preparation, would not speak on the subject of eki akyage and no further comment could be obtained from him.

The hut of the female ngungan was so crowded that one could hardly find standing room. A thin boy of about ten lay cradled like an infant in the lap of an older woman, who, it became clear, was his paternal grandmother. His eyes were large and gazed at the crowd in fright. His mouth was open and his tongue trembled within. His breathing was very shallow. The mother was crying in a corner. Soon another woman came rushing through the village, wailing, and threw herself down on the threshold. Someone calmed her and helped her inside. This was a paternal aunt. The father, a man of about thirty-five, stood to one side giving signs of extreme anxiety. He occasionally left for the council house to communicate his agitation there.

---

them. The results of the failure of this kind of control produced the many different kinds of evus. In any case, the whole area of demonic capacity was an area of ambiguity in Fang thought, and very often circular reasoning prevailed. A man's character followed the nature of his evus. How did we know the nature of his evus? We knew it from his character and his actions.

When the boy had first been brought in, the ngungan had blown explosively over his heart and had fastened a red strip of cloth around his chest. Now she called for an egg and broke it into a pot in which leaves and herbs were mixed. She mixed this with water. Then, with her back to the boy, she handed the cup around to him in her right hand. He drank some of it. The fact that he could drink was a good sign. The evus, if it was there, had released some of its stranglehold upon him. She then drank a mouthful and, holding another mouthful, turned and spat a part on the boy's head and another part, explosively again, against his heart.

Shortly, the brother of the child's mother arrived and tapped him attentively about the chest and stomach—particularly around the right side—asking for the source of his pain. Various women had gone out and returned with leaves. A medicine pot was brought to a boil with the leaves, short pieces of liane, and pieces of rosewood. The boy was stripped naked and with some difficulty removed from his grandmother, for he was obtaining solace by playing with and occasionally mouthing her nipples. The ngungan took a bundle of leaves and, dipping it into the pot, swatted the boy gently all over the body. He sneezed and this caused a ripple of anxiety to pass through the onlookers. It was his heavy breathing that had first created the flash of despair for his life. Any sign of chest distress was a bad sign. Hiccups were, however, a sign of the accommodation of the evus. As the swatting continued, the boy began to perk up, and when he was taken back to his grandmother's lap he was much changed. Things gradually relaxed in the hut. The onlookers began to drift away. The child remained lying on the bed until the next morning. He was periodically doused and swatted with leaves. On the third day he was back playing but still wearing the red cloth about his chest.

It was believed that this was a case of a preparation of the child with the evus, akomnge evus, and was a sickness arising out of some failure in the coalescence of that constellation of powers, prohibitions, and promises known as the eki akyage. The consensus was that the father's older half-brother had invited the boy to his hut for a meal of soup in which a piece of human flesh was concealed along with a portion of this man's demon.[11] The boy, though thin and not particularly forceful in the affairs of his peer group, was of a type with tendons and muscles on the surface of his body. Since the demon, when it dwelled in the body, dwelled upon the sinews, tendons, and arterial structure, a sinewy person was often associated with its presence. This may have encouraged the father's brother to believe his demon could be introduced and multiplied, as it were, in the child's body. But as it turned out, the boy, probably suspecting the event, immediately began to choke and feel very tight

---

[11] Fang usually said that a piece of human flesh, often the dried flesh of someone recently dead, must accompany passage of the evus from one person to another. In fact, this was not mandatory. The envalen could hold a special leaf in his mouth with a hole in it. The evus could take its place in this leaf. The leaf was then deposited on the soup and this effected the passage of the evus.

in his chest. Some suspect that he did not start to choke until the envalen informed him that having ingested the evus he would be obliged to cooperate in "eating" one of his relatives so that both demons could be strengthened. It was true that the evus could be given in benevolence and with no obligation to cooperate in feasting upon other members of the family. It could be given only to increase the child's powers and his chances of a prosperous life. Yet collusion was most often feared. The general impression in this case, since one of the father's closer brothers was suspected as the envalen, was that the boy's nature could not support an evus. He was a simple boy. Hence the demon stirring around in his chest to secure a place for itself was killing him.*[12] It was a case of *etun biang* or *etun akyaga* (half-medicine or half-promise). The result could be the death of the recipient or chronic suffering from a never fully accommodated power.

Whatever the case, the boy's terror was real and so was that of his family. News of his affliction spread rapidly and was especially impressive to other children. In such an atmosphere, there could be little skepticism about the reality of the evus. The rush to the house of the ngungan swept up the whole village. The ngungan's great care in treating the disease added to the impressiveness of the event. Her offering of the egg and herb mixture with her back turned—the soft front of the body was more susceptible to the attack of the demon than the rear—confirmed that this was a serious business. In the end, it was decided that the evus had entered only briefly and had departed again. Some, however, believed that the egg and herb mixture had satiated it, and that it was no longer strangling the heart. If so, the boy still possessed the evus. The outcome was ambiguous.

In spite of the fright provoked by such incidents, preparation in the demon was widely accepted or even coveted by Fang. In the decades of mid-century it had become the most significant supernatural being, and it was believed, although the belief was mixed with a sense of affliction, that the evus was the best protection against evil and best guarantee (for it could strengthen all one's capacities), of one's achievement of the good things of life: riches, wives, children, authority, prestige. Fang estimated that more than half of their people had the demon, though few were sure who had it or how it really operated. Even those men who remembered clearly their preparation and the eki akyage that accompanied it were uncertain as to the actual nature of the evus and as to what evils, through mbwol, it might be effecting nightly in their name. Only a few Fang, convinced of the nature of their demon, were content to identify themselves with it and look to it for support and definition of self. Such men, the real sorcerers, instead of struggling with the evus, tried to exploit its powers with cold-spirited intent. They took this imaginary com-

---

*[12] One of the reasons for giving the evus when the child was young was because the child's bones and sinews were not hardened. Hence, the evus could accommodate itself with less insult to the recipient's body.

panion to heart. Antoine seemed to be one of these—and was self-confessed as such. But one could not be sure. Perhaps he was just a pretentious fool!

THE EVUS AND PSYCHIC CONFLICT

What can the evus be understood to be? I had many conversations with Fang who participated in two cultures and who offered many analogies. "The evus is our airplane because it enables us to go long distances quickly." "It is our science because it enables us to know difficult and hidden things." "It is our book because it tells us of things when we are not present." "It is our rifle because it enables us to defend ourselves against enemies." More and more there was the tendency to speak negatively of the evus: "It is our devil and the curse of the black man."

With the uncertainty with which the evus was regarded and its unpredictability in Fang eyes, it is not surprising that Fang developed a system of prohibitions or taboos (*ekí, bekí*)*[13] which one engaged oneself to observe in undertaking preparation in the evus. This system of compulsive observances gave one some control over this powerful and aggrandizing yet inchoate force. It is true that the demon could be transmitted without these prohibitions, and that the akomnge could take place without eki-akyage. But in most cases prohibitions were given. This is why one waited until the child's heart had

---

*[13] The radical "ki" was a central one in Fang and expands into a crucial domain of meanings in their thought. This has to do with the force or capacity one should manifest in life, ki, as well as with the abstinence one ought to show, ki, to certain things and the respect (kia, to respect), or even veneration (kiba, to venerate), that one should feel toward these things. Fang said of themselves that they were "able to do" because they "had the force"—*me ne ki* (I am capacity) or *ki e ne me nlem* (capacity is in the heart). They said they "could not do" because such a thing was a capacity or force prohibited to them—*a ne me eki* (it is a prohibition to me) or *Me ki kubn* (I am prohibited to eat sheep).

Taboos were taken up to maintain appropriate amounts of capacity or force. While force in itself was neither good nor bad, its possession or lack of it was. It was the object of preparation to appropriate ki in the form of the evus. Contrarily it was the object of antiwitchcraft rites to defend against the abuse of ki. Like radicals generally in the Bantu languages, ki entered into many combinations by affixation. One could compile a long list of these and in pondering them gain some insight into this central domain of Fang concern. A few terms will give an idea of this centrality: nkia, father- or mother-in-law; meki, blood; aki, egg; kik, cut or judge; king, voice. Alexandre (*Le Groupe*, p. 22) takes ki as a typical Bulu-Fang example of the Bantu radical at work.

There are many prohibitions that were not attached to the evus, for Fang accepted the efficacity of taboo quite apart from the question of witchcraft. Tessmann has a long list of Fang taboos (*Die Pangwe*, Vol. II, pp. 184-193). Some of these taboos rest upon close observation of nature and intrinsic properties of species and plants—crab was prohibited to pregnant women because it scuttles and hides itself sideways and so might the foetus—but others were assigned quite arbitrarily, for the mere exercise of restraint was efficacious. In Lévi-Strauss's reading of Tessmann (*The Savage Mind*, p. 99) he suggests the existence of a "system of significance" in these taboos which I was unable to discover.

descended into the stomach and until he could count on both hands. He had to remember his taboos.

The eki were of many varieties, but most often they concerned food. In general it was the common foods from the plantation that were prohibited as a test of willpower rather than wild fruits, which were only an occasional part of the diet. Game such as wild pig or various species of antelope might also be prohibited. Some taboos were singular. The child might be told not to bathe in rainwater, not to look at a rainbow, not to marry more than so many women, not to have sexual relations until a certain age. In fact, outside the category of food taboos—the largest category—prohibitions affecting sexual relations figured prominently. Occasionally one heard that an eki grievously affecting a man's destiny had been assigned: "You will enjoy great prosperity and success with women until the age of twenty-five when your evus and yourself will weaken and die." Fang, as other peoples remarked, took these taboos with remarkable seriousness.[10]

The compulsive and unrelenting character of these taboos was confirmed over and over again while I was living in Fang villages. A man suddenly rushed from the council house in deep fear of sudden seizure in the chest. He discovered that at the bottom of the pot from which he had been eating were the remains from a previous meal containing the leaves of the manioc plant—"It is taboo to me!" (*A ne me ekí!*). Or a man suffering from some chronic infection or malnutrition felt himself weak and listless. He reflected and came to the conclusion that at such and such a time he violated a taboo—had drunk river water, or committed adultery during a prohibited season or time of day. His demon had been offended and was attacking him.

On such occasions the ngungan was called in. The man confessed his transgressions. Blood was poured, whether of sheep or chicken, for blood was the crucial element in calming an agitated or rampant evus. If the relative (envalen) who originally prepared the victim was still alive, he was called upon to administer the medicine, for he had particular influence over "his evus" and thus over the welfare of the person he had prepared. Ngungan and envalen together could restore the victim to his proper destiny as implied in his preparation.

Any discussion of destiny must be based upon the three character types which Fang recognized: *mimia, engôlengôla*, and *nnem*.[11] The mimia was a simple man entirely free of the evus. He lived quietly in his village in good relations with his neighbors. Lacking the evus he lacked force and would have little chance to gain wealth, wives, or influence in village affairs. Should he acquire such things, he would be subject to the jealous or aggrandizing attacks of those possessing the evus. Without the demon, and no longer able to depend upon the ancestors or antiwitchcraft cults to protect him, he lacked satisfactory means of defense. Whatever he had accumulated would be quickly appropriated by supernatural means. The mimia was vulnerable to sickness and death. It was dangerous for him to provoke the desires of witches by a personal search for good fortune.

The engolengola was a man who possessed the evus to protect him and aid him in the search for fortune. His evus was for the most part quiescent, small in size, and had no taste for human blood. His evus served the engolengola without need for sorcery. Neither the engolengola nor his evus, therefore, was evil. It might be that the evus simply lacked aggressive power or that the engolengola had enough force of character to master the appetites of the entity within him.

It was the third character type among men, the nnem, which posed real danger. He was the "complicated" man. His demon was accustomed to make the "sortilège" whether through its own ravening powers or the weakness of its possessor. It subsisted on the blood and hidden flesh of men—and many were the mimia who wasted away under its anthropophagic onslaught. Fang recognized very well the unfortunate irony, often a tragic fact, that the most successful and fortunate men among them, by the terms of these character-ological distinctions, were almost obligatorily nnem. Hence, however much they were social paragons in one sense, they were potential outcasts in another.

It would be a mistake to suppose that men could give themselves up to the character they obtained through the evus without having constantly to undergo a more public struggle to establish their identity. It is true that here Fang talked of being "guaranteed"—they used the French "garanti" to translate the phrase *me ne nkoman*, "I am prepared." But they were constantly having to negotiate that private guarantee with society's expectations and arbitrate between the very egocentric desires embodied in their demon on the one hand, and the desire to be a well-accepted and a trusted, cooperative member of the larger society on the other. Fang, particularly in recent years, tilted that balance toward individualistic and egocentric solutions. But the conflict was still there. They had to struggle to master their evus, for only the most depraved resigned themselves to its propensities with an easy fatalism, saying, "As my evus so am I."

CONCLUSION: THE PREPARATION OF THE HEART

What then of Antoine the night fool? This chapter, scrutinizing the influences important in explaining his actions, may seem to have carried us far beyond his own delusions and his suffering. But we have been trying to raise the extremes of his personal experience to their value as an expression of the dilemmas of his people. For his experiences were characteristic of his culture at a certain time, when the desire to exceed was so often instilled in small hearts. No doubt anxieties and fantasies of a more universal nature, charac-teristic of young manhood in many cultures, are also present in the discussion and embodied in Antoine's disorderly and excessive behavior—his grandiose fantasies of acquisition and achievement and his resentment of elders.

A key term here has been preparation (akomnge), by which Fang meant "the opening up of one's nature for the fulfillment of its potentialities." But the situation was never easy and was full of ambiguity and contrariness. One was never sure what another's or even one's own nature really was—one could have various natures—and whether that nature was demonic or not. For though Fang tended to argue that nature was immutable, they recognized various natures in a man or woman. And insofar as it was a matter of demonic nature, they watched its unfolding with high interest and sought to prepare that nature. Though they might argue for a balance of activity and tranquillity in village life, yet they became ever more fascinated in the colonial period by demonic determination in the acquisition of power and goods as such determination flowed from men's unconscious which they called evus. Perhaps this occurred in part because of the "spectacle of the European's creative force" which seemed demonic.

The relationship between a man and his evus was similar to that between his society and himself. As Fang society both encouraged and repressed aggressive aggrandizing and hateful tendencies in him, so he treated his evus in the same manner. It is not surprising that both Fang society and Fang individuals found themselves increasingly threatened by exaggerated personalities in every way a violation of their egalitarian tendencies. Out of the "atmosphere of expectation" grew an atmosphere of frustration or intimidation. It was the kind of atmosphere in which Antoine would recurrently ask himself whether his miserable bachelor existence eked out among hundreds of tailors of the town was what he was prepared for. The evus had laid in him the seeds of excess and of fantasies which the barrenness of his actual existence pressured him to act out. And many were the Fang so deprived by comparison.

But Antoine's disorder is not explained only by the evus, the Fang representation of the psyche of most current interest at the time. Antoine was also motivated by frustration provoked by his older brother, who, since late childhood, had laid restrictions and constraints upon him. This brother was preventing him from getting married. He refused to share with him. Antoine openly fantasized aggressive actions against him. He was also motivated by frustration with the Europeans of the colonial world, for he knew from his life in the town how much of their wealth they preserved for themselves. On the fringes of his fantasy Antoine turned from the power of the evus to the power he might gain in being a European.

From earliest childhood Fang learned to represent the self as a balanced entity—a boundary between external and internal forces—and frequent were the rituals and games that taught that representation. We have seen the same thing in the associations between Fang dwelling structures and the male and female body. Antoine's frustrations arose in part from the fact that his boundaries contained, he thought, a potent demon—yet circumstances were forcing him more and more to define those boundaries narrowly or to confuse them. They seemed to be excluding him from the good things in life, from his patrimony. His night foolishness was in part an attempt, unbalanced to be sure, to expand those boundaries and lay claim to women and goods in megalomaniac fantasy.

In a deeper psychological sense, one might speak of Antoine's fantasies of self and evus as an attempt to recapture the omnipotence of the "golden age" of childhood in his unrequited young adulthood. Antoine would have his every wish the villager's command. He would treat the evus as his omnipotent public agent. His trips to the cemetery and his midnight invocations remind us that he was motivated to come to terms with his dead predecessors as well. He sought them out, and in seeking them out he sought out his patrimony. He even tried to join them by proclaiming himself a dead man returned to the living.

Just here we recognize that Antoine's "heartsickness" was very much a phenomenon of Fang society in transition. For Antoine was approaching the age where, had the ancestor cult been in existence, he would have been ritually brought into contact with the ancestors in a way sanctioned by the entire village. He would not have had to acquaint himself with the dead and with the powers of death in an egocentric manner. His patrimony would have been offered to him under the aegis of the principle of "protective benevolence." The entire village would have applauded his "death and resurrection."

And the threshold between young manhood and adulthood would have been more clearly taught. Had Antoine undergone initiation into Ndong Mba, he might have gained a more philosophic view of good and evil. At the least it would have offered him relief by showing how his inadequacies and indecencies had their source, not in his own nature or natures, but in nature itself and how, in any case, they could be relieved by ritual purification. Antoine had never passed through these ceremonies and thus was not prepared to counter or resolve the discomfiture of his failed "preparation." In the end he attempted to deal with these things by a microcosm of his own manufacture.

In the same village, however, in which Antoine acted out the frustrations of his "preparation," the Bwiti religion, in which he would not participate, celebrated its own microcosm. It was a microcosm in which a "nightwisdom" argued against pernicious "nightfoolishness" and in which "heartsickness" was transformed into "oneheartedness." It was a microcosm with clearly drawn boundaries and with multiple thresholds of experience in which the participant's fundamental nature was at once "broken open" and changed and given a new Banzie "name of encouragement" while at the same time it was made receptive to a balanced plurality of subordinate natures predicated upon it in the ritual process. Above all, it was a microcosm that emphasized instruction and learning, although it was a learning that leaned heavily on the old lore and its "argument of images."

‹ 9 ›

The Occult Search
for Capacity

Abe ye mbeng ba wula nsama.
(Good and bad journey together.)

THE DEATH OF MBA MUZWI

IN THE EARLY MORNING HOURS not long before sunrise of a September night
on the threshold of the long cold rainy season, Muzwi Ekwaga came slowly
wailing through the village. Villagers were already in that deep and final stage
of sleep of which Fang spoke.[1] But Muzwi's cry as he passed through the
village sank ominously into our reviving consciousness. We awoke struggling
to understand what he was saying. He sang keening: "I have lost my son!
. . . The only son that was left to me . . . the son that would take my place
in the family. I am an old man. Who shall take up my work? I am an old
man and he is dead." Finally the wail passed away as the old man entered
the forest on the other side of the village with his lantern. He was on his way
to Assok Bele to cry the death there. Everyone knew now that Mba Muzwi
was finally dead. He had already lain three days as a dead man, refusing all
food and drink.

Mba Muzwi had fallen sick the Friday before. By Saturday he had lapsed
into a dumb state in which he heard what was said with his eyes but would
not speak. Very little food and drink could be forced through his lips. The
ngungan was called but, studying him a minute, resigned the case saying it
was an illness brought on by white magic. Everyone suspected the truth of
his remarks because Mba Muzwi had long been trafficking in occult literature
which he ordered from France. He had many of the little pulp pamphlets in
his room. It was whispered about that he had engaged himself to a White
Spirit but had disobeyed the terms of his engagement.

When the ngungan resigned the case, I was called down to see whether
there was anything in our small bag of medicines that we had been sharing
with villagers—aspirin, aralen, antibiotic ointments—that could be of use.
I found Mba Muzwi perfectly healthy of appearance, breathing normally, but
impossible to arouse in any way. He stared fixedly at the ceiling and gave
no sign of recognition. I offered to take him to the District Hospital. But such

cases, I was told, always died in the hospital. While I was in a hut, a disciple of Ndende arrived. He was the local representative of a Bakota man, the Great Ndende, who had passed through the village the year before eradicating witchcraft. Before he left, Ndende trained local men to fight all kinds of magic in his name. The disciple prepared a medicinal broth to drive the torturing spirit out. He believed, as did many villagers, that Mba Muzwi had tried to engage himself to the spirit known as Mademoiselle—the white lady with which the Great Ndende himself worked.

When the disciple of Ndende could not get Mba to drink the broth, Muzwi Ekwaga knew the situation to be desperate. He sent a boy into the mission to call the priest. The priest, Père Dominick, came in the evening. He asked Mba from what he suffered and if he could talk so that he might confess himself. But Mba would not answer. When after an hour or so nothing could be elicited, the Father said sadly, "This boy is in no way physically ill. He suffers psychologically. He has a sickness of the soul from working with the devil. He believes absolutely in the fetish he has acquired and fear of that fetish makes him dumb. If he could speak we could return him to life. But as he can't speak, nothing can be done. I have seen this many times before. The European professors who sell you these things fool you tragically. Why do you not place your confidence in God?"

When the priest went out the men murmured to themselves: "Voilà, here is a boy who is certainly dead!" Early on Sunday Mba Muzwi's father's brothers came to carry him to Medoumou, the next village. Perhaps he could be brought to drink and confess there. A man might always be afraid to confess in his own village for fear of his brother's anger. But Mba was already very weak when they carried him to Medoumou. His mother, who accompanied him and sat by his side, already cried as one bereaved. Early next morning he died.

The day dawned overcast and chill. No one went to the fields. The men sat around in the council house in Medoumou, occasionally going out to console Muzwi who had retreated to his quarters or going out to look at the cadaver in the kitchen. The women of the family sat quietly around the corpse there. The mother and Mba Muzwi's sisters keened next to the bamboo bed. Behind the kitchen two men were nailing together a coffin out of rough boards. The men were discussing the affliction of White Magic in Assok Ening. The village had seen three similar deaths in the last several years. Discussion was occasionally acrimonious. Some men from Medoumou accused Assok Ening of giving their young no proper preparation. There was too much pride and ambition in Assok Ening. "You have a school, a coffee mill, a marketplace, an infirmary, you even have a white man living with you. You want everything and your young people want everything. In such an atmosphere of desire witches flourish and kill our sons!"

The Chief of Medoumou village arrived midway through the morning. He

had been on a visit to district headquarters. He complained to the gathered
men that they were sitting the death in the wrong council house. They should
be in his council house as Chief of the Village. The men from Assok Ening
responded with a proverb. They said, *Nung a yim song mbias*. (The stranger
makes no distinction between the tombs of twins.) The Chief then chided his
brothers for offering no wine to ease the pain of the mourners. The Chief's
brother, whose council house it was, responded tartly. He said he would be
glad if the Chief would bring out the wine so he might learn hospitality from
him.

Someone suggested that they disperse to eat and return in the early afternoon
to bury the boy. Some of the men went down to look at the cadaver. There
was a dispute as to whether to apply white kaolin clay to its face (*fim*) or to
apply red padouk powder (*baa*) or to apply both. Some said it was not
Christian to apply anything. Others said white powder would make Mba look
more like a Christian. The older men said that red powder should be applied.
The Chief of the village said it was the custom in the old days to apply both
white and red powder to the body—half and half. The issue was settled by
the dead boy's mother who applied kaolin.

The men gathered again at three. This time the discussion turned to Mba
Muzwi's supposed impotence which, it was generally believed, he sought to
counteract with this magical amour. Ndutuma of Medoumou argued that men
naturally die when they could no longer have relations with women. But
others challenged that. As Obunu put it, "We all know that going with women
destroys the backbone and brings bad luck." Bibong Leon said, "When I
was a chauffeur in Bitam, I once took a woman in the cab of my truck. Next
morning the motor wouldn't start." The Chief of Medoumou entered and
chided the men for disrespectful talk. He returned to the problem of who was
to provide money for the costs of the burial and the entertainment of the
guests. Various friends and relatives of Mba Muzwi offered a total of 2,800
francs. Some wine was bought with that.

Then the women called up to the men. It was time to take the casket down
to the grave. It was carried by Muzwi's brothers from Medoumou down into
the forest behind the village. Most of the villagers followed the coffin singing
Catholic songs. The Catechist was present to say the last words. The coffin
was lowered into the grave with Muzwi's feet pointing toward the village.
Some of the old men muttered and after the burial complained that the corpse,
as in the old days, should be laid with its feet to the west; when it got up it
would walk to the village of the dead and not come back into the village. Just
at the moment when the last earth was being tramped down an elder of
Medoumou broke out and said: "How is it you young men hang your heads
and carry a sad air? You ought to rejoice. You will soon join your brother.
We lost Fabian and Mbong Mbwe and now Mba Muzwi and all through
meddling with "white magic." Soon you will all be gone!" One of the young

men replied: "Do you mean young men did not die in the old days?"[2] The old man replied: "Of course, but not in such a mysterious way!"

THE FLOW OF POWER AND THE USES OF CAPACITY

Villagers shared Père Dominick's belief in the importance of confession (*atu minsem*, "to break open, pierce, the sins"). The ceremonies of Ndong Mba and Bieri sought confessions from initiates as part of the ceremonial preparation. In Ndong Mba a confession of incest between brother and sister was elicited so that the rituals could better act to liquify the engorged sin. A medicinal potion was poured over the initiates. Fang represented the bodily consequences of sin as a tumescence or engorgement of a part of the body, in particular that vital region, the chest. Finding no exit, the sin began to inflame one's character and then one's health. In giving blessings, the action of spitting, *atu menden* (to break open the throat), was employed for it was a guarantee that any engorged condition of the throat or chest, possibly associated with sinful intentions, was relieved and without effect upon the blessing. In sicknesses involving the *evus*, whose principle place of residence was the chest, it was feared that the evus would close off the flowing processes of the chest and bring about death. This was why hiccuping or any other sign of congestion was regarded seriously. Fang medicinal ritual sought to break open or pierce engorged or stuffed-up conditions.

This representation of sickness as an engorging or clogging and curing as a piercing and releasing was frequently seen in curing rituals and particularly in a rite called *ngang* (basket hanging from a circle). The basket of leaves and vines in this rite was hung from a tree and the sick person placed on a stool beneath it (Figure 9.1). Into this leaf basket a medicinal concoction of various barks was poured.[3] The ngungan, dipping from the basket with a branch, swatted the sick person over the body. Then with a pointed stick he pierced the bottom of the basin, allowing the medicine to run down over the patient's body. Thus, by sympathetic means, clogging was released and bodily processes brought again to flow properly. This medicine was particularly effective for sicknesses caused by one's own demon.

Engorgement of the normal processes of life flow led rapidly, as in Mba Muzwi's case, to dumbness (*mvuk*) and death or to increased agitation, aggressiveness (*ngamla*), and finally a fatal bursting. In the autopsies (*esal*) which Fang practiced regularly, the elders looked for burst or swollen organs as signs of blockages, as well as for signs of the evus in paracardial tissue. The belief was that these blockages were caused principally by the action of demons and that they were best treated sympathetically by running water and the flow of verbal confession.

Thus it was ominous for Fang who were present when Mba Muzwi not only refused to give verbal confession but could not be brought to take any liquids nor evacuate any. From the first moments of his illness, he was blocked

9.1 Curing through the Use of Medicinal Fluids (nket)

up, and various efforts to break open this blockage were fruitless. True, there was something inexplicable for the villagers in this! But it was not that they were unaccustomed to such hysteria and to such a precipitous fall from good health. Fang characteristically suffered drastic reactions when they believed their pact with the evus had somehow been violated. This reaction, most often a hysteric shutdown of life-acquiring processes, had long been of concern to doctors who served in the Gabon colony.[4] The manner of Mba Muzwi's demise was not really alien to villagers. What disturbed them was that they were not sure of the agency responsible. What was this white magic with which the young were meddling?

Villagers understood well enough that evus in itself was not an ultimate or final cause. Its character was not absolute. It was an agency.*[1] The men of Medoumou, it will be remembered, accused the men of Assok Ening of desiring too much, of trying to appropriate too much of the things of the world for themselves. In such an atmosphere of desire the worst agencies of witchcraft, black or white, could only flourish. The desires of the individual or the collectivity could exacerbate the search for power over others and for the goods of this world that that power brought. The desires of individuals or collectivities had an important influence upon the nature of the agencies they worked through to obtain power. And if the life flow of individuals could be blocked up by mischance in the search for power, so could the life flow of collectivities. That was what the men of Medoumou were implying about Assok Ening.

There may be a theory of power here, but caution is in order. Tessmann, in his constant search for the philosophic basis of Fang action, suggested that they believed in an "organisationskraft" which came from God and which inhered in all things.[5] Some things had more of this "kraft" than others: bones, for example, because of their endurance, had this and hence Fang worshiped them. Earth, sun, moon, water, and fire were worshiped for the same reason. They were ever-present elements in all things and, thus, repositories of "organisationskraft."

These matters cannot be discussed without reference to at least two Fang words: *kí* and *ngul*, both of which were translated as force, power, and sometimes as virility. Both terms had to do with the capacity to do things. Kí was located especially in the thorax, *nkuk* or *nlem*, and the phrase *kí nlem* (force of the heart) was a Fang concept that comes closest to the English "capacity or efficacity." Fang did not have, as Largeau pointed out,[6] a term for the French "pouvoir" (to have the power to do something), but under acculturation quickly adopted the phrases, *me ne kí e bô* [F] or *me ne ngu ye bô* [N], to express the English, "I am able" or "I can" or the French, "je peut."[7] *Kí*, pronounced in low tone was the verb to abstain from doing something, not to exercise capacity, not to put into effect. The potency of this root in Fang thought was shown in its emergence in many key terms: *nkí* (in-law), *mekí* (blood), *ekí* (taboo), and *akí* (egg).

---

*[1] The circularity of reasoning which prevailed in many informants' minds in this "area of ambiguity" was present here as well. "The evus is an agent of men's intentions but men's intentions are a consequence of the nature of their evus." It was true that men giving in to the struggle with evus became simply its agents.

Alexandre argues, like Tessmann, that ki is a force which exists exterior to the individual. It is impersonal; it pre-dates and survives the individual. Ngul, for Alexandre, has to do rather with the capacity to utilize ki—to dispense it, augment it, or control it.[8] Mid-century inquiry did not yield evidence that older Fang conceived of ki as a cosmic energy or electricity of which men availed themselves, although it is a logical enough extension of the belief in a realm of the unseen. A more apt understanding of their views was that the struggle of life (Tessmann's "kämpfen des lebens") revolved around the capacity (ki or ngul) to organize persons and things for specific purposes. The highest exercise of this capacity was in the interests of the social order and an optimum mix of activity and tranquillity.[9] Such exercise of capacity could only take place in a constant flow of social and economic reciprocities and redistributions. Just as individual life was a flowing through, so social life had to be a flow of exchange and distributions. And just as the flow of life could get blocked up in certain parts of the body to the detriment of the individual, so the flow of goods and persons could get blocked up in certain individuals or collectivities to the detriment of the body social. Such individuals or groups had to be dealt with in such a way that they released that with which they were engorged.

Fang, in other words, represented the healthiness of flow in the body social by extension of their understanding of the importance of flow in the body personal. In both realms evus could create blockages. But the evus was simply a way of representing to themselves hidden or uncertain aspects of capacity. The matter of capacity was very important to Fang. That was why they watched their children so intently and created that "environment of expectation" we have discussed. But they also asked the question: capacity in the interests of what? It was evident to all that Mba Muzwi did not have the capacity to deal with the agency he was invoking, ironically, in order to gain capacity. But more, for the men of Medoumou, his incapacity was the product of a swollen collectivity, Assok Ening, which was putting its capacities to antisocial uses.

THE ANTIWITCHCRAFT CULT AND ITS EVOLUTION

Another word as crucial to the discussion of power as it was frequent in everyday idiom was *biang* (medicine). Insofar as men did not have any empirical way to relieve their afflictions or control their destinies, and insofar as they had not been "prepared," they turned to biang. Biang, then, may also be translated as "remedy" for the lack or surfeit of capacity. It gave influence over things unseen and otherwise uncontrollable. Fang often said that biang gave capacity to do—ngul—and though there were many kinds of biang, they all acted to increase or decrease the capacities of whatever they were applied to, whether inanimate objects or living beings. Biang was applied to seeds, making them fertile; to spears, making them accurate; to fishhooks, to traps, to gardens, to musical instruments; to girls' faces, making them pretty; to warriors making them invisible. The use of biang in respect to the evus, whether to calm it or remove it or increase its capacity, was one of the most important uses of medicine.

Most Fang knew biang and had their own stock of remedies. But three specialists in biang were recognized: the *mbôbiang*, the *ngungan* and the *nsôkngang*. The mbobiang (the maker of medicine) was one who, by strength of memory, possessed knowledge of remedies beyond the ordinary. Except in extent, his knowledge did not really differ from that possessed by any man. To the ngungan and nsokngang belonged knowledge of more powerful biang— of the "magie supérieure." The ngungan (one powerful in hidden things) possessed knowledge of the diseases of the evus or of the other spirits that burdened man.[10] His biang was powerful enough to protect him against the evus. Still, the ngungan had his limitations for it was generally believed he did not know enough of the evus to contend with it without the patient's confession. And this was why the ngungan so quickly abandoned the case of Mba Muzwi.

It was just here that the nsokngang demonstrated his superiority. The medicine he knew enabled him to search out and reveal (*sôkh*) those things which were hidden (*angang*). He was a diviner. He knew how to read signs (*ndem, mindem*) which indicated the nature of things unseen. More than that, he could set various proofs and ordeals for men so that they themselves should give signs. In recent decades, because of administrative pressure against them—divination was formerly accomplished by trials and ordeals often with fatal consequences—and because many Fang had turned elsewhere for knowledge of the unseen, very few diviners were found in the villages. Mbobiang and ngungan continued to flourish.

The most powerful biang and the most penetrating nsokngang that Fang formerly possessed for use against dangerous concentrations of capacity was the antiwitchcraft cult of *Ngí*. Ngi and Dzok and other antiwitchcraft cults were very much alive in Tessmann's day. He devotes many pages to their description.[11] Since Ngi was not as ritually complex as the Bieri or Soo Ndong Mba cults—and therefore did not provide as much of a cultural patrimony for subsequent reworking—we need only discuss some features of the cult, emphasizing its evolution. For while Bieri and Ndong Mba were slowly abandoned, Ngi, probably in response to a Fang sense of increasing witchcraft, progressively developed. This is the case even though Ngi was subject to the same administrative suppression as these other cults. As Fang reflect on Ngi, they emphasize that its purpose was to protect children and those innocent of witchcraft (*mimia*) from witches. Ngi killed witches. And the impetus to celebrate the cult was often the death of a child attributed to the witch, evus.

The most interesting and enduring features of Ngi were the earth mounds and the tunnels and pits dug as a means of access to them. These mounds, which measured as much as 8 by 4 meters, represented a man-animal (a gorilla), an elephant, or some other chthonic or saurian creature. The mounds were decorated to be attractive to witches and at the very heart of them substances were buried that would kill the witches once attracted: reptile fangs, spiders, leaf poisons, and sometimes the fortified body of the young child killed by the witches. Long after the ceremonies had been abandoned, it was felt, the mound preserved its power.[12]

Important biang found in Ngi mounds were stones and waterlogged wood from bottoms of streams. The waterlogged wood had a particular efficacy against witchcraft.[13] This was the efficacy of earth against evil spirits. For evil spirits were things of the air and good spirits were things of the earth or the bottom of streams—the locale, in the old view, of the village of the dead. If the bad evus could be brought to earth or water it could be destroyed. In a similar sense, the leader of the Ngi cult (nôm Ngí—old of Ngi) spent much time in the pit constructed at one end of the mound of earth. It was constructed in such a way—with boards covering it—as to give a booming sound to his voice and a deep penetrating tone to the boards as they were struck. These intriguing cavernous sounds were employed periodically during cult celebrations to attract witches and to frighten young men being initiated into the cult.

The nom Ngi, after building his strength in the hole, made periodic and rapid sorties into the village seeking witches. If the leader of the cult was strengthened against evil spirits by dwelling in the earth so were the initiates strengthened by having to crawl through the mound tunnel during initiation. Naturally these earlier Fang notions of the atmosphere as the abode of evil spirits and the earth as the abode of the good conflicted with Christian notions. An intellectual readjustment became necessary and is seen in the idea of God Below (Zame así) and God Above (Zame ôyô), latter-day religious conceptions embedded in the Bwiti religion.

A detailed account of an early Ngi initiation (1908) in the area from which much of our data comes (Oyem District) is that of Captain Maignan, French District Administrator, who spent successive evenings observing the establishment of Ngi among the Nkojeng, the clan closest to his headquarters.[14] Two children had recently died in one of the Nkojeng villages. The ceremonies took place in the evenings preceding the full moon and were under the direction of a team of teachers (called by Maignan "une compagnie du ngil") from clan Essangi. The proceedings lasted each evening from the rising to the setting of the moon. In these ceremonies, a young boy of about ten acted as a kind of acolyte and "bouc-émissaire" for the witches. He carried a cranium covered with redwood powder. The nom Ngi himself had his body painted half white and half red. The village was divided into two parts by a liane. The red cranium was placed on the earth behind the liane on one side and the young acolyte behind it. Before this cranium other biang was placed. All along the liane resin Okoume torches were lit. On the other side the nom Ngi danced and then pulled the head of a chicken. The blood from this sacrifice was dripped along the entire liane. The purpose was to attract the witches to the boy.

Meanwhile, the "compagnie du ngil," together with villagers, danced and sang on the other side of the liane. Then suddenly they rushed out and made a tour of the entire village. Assistants of the nom Ngi periodically ran out and hurled sharpened slips of bamboo into the air. No one alien to these ceremonies dared be present, we are told.

The ceremonies proceeded each night until the full moon. Then the two teams departed for the forest to construct the Ngi mound. After the construction, the first person to penetrate the precincts through the tunnel and into the hollow at the head of the Ngi was the boy with the red cranium. Only the nom Ngi and the acolyte now entered the Ngi enclosure. Maignan was impressed with the power of Ngi. On the final night under a full moon, the barriers were pulled down and all the villagers were required to file past the Ngi mound and thrust a sharpened bamboo wand into its body, exposing their possible witchcraft to its power.

> In the case I report, one Abesolo Ndong of the village of the Chief Okan Mvele was taken with a sudden failing at the moment of thrusting in the spear. He fainted and had to be helped home in the arms of his brothers to his village. Two days later he was dead. There could be no doubt. His family had to pay the death of the two children.[15]

Abesolo Ndong suffered, it seems, the same kind of shutdown of life-acquiring processes as Mba Muzwi.

Already in Tessmann's and Maignan's time there was a diversity and dynamic in the Ngi cults. Maignan comments on this and limits his comments to Nkojeng clan and the Essangi version of Ngi being taught there. And Tessmann noted the many types of Ngi mounds and the way a new variety of Ngi was spreading among southern Fang. It was changing to such a degree that even women were being admitted.[16] While we should be cautious of speaking of any Fang cult, including Bieri and Ndong Mba, in a static sense, we have particularly good evidence of the evolution of Ngi.

Ngi ceremonies seem to have been "bought" and "sold" in much the same way as the dances we discussed in Chapter 5. A new version of Ngi rises somewhere and spreads from village to village. A village feeling itself afflicted by witches invites an Ngi group (*ensama Ngí*) from another village. Maignan points out that clan Nkojeng felt itself victimized by sorcerers and hence invited their clan "enemies," Essangi and Yengwi, to come and establish a new Ngi.[17] Only alien clans could mount a truly ruthless crusade against witches, since one suspected collusion between witches and one's clan brothers. Part of the fear provoked by Ngi arose from the fact that an alien or enemy clan was leading the ceremonies.[18]

The following are the Ngi cults remembered in the districts of Mitzik and Medounou (Woleu-Ntem Region) and the southwestern borders of Spanish Guinea.

Mfum Ngí	Ndong Andrike Ngí
Avaziba Ngí	Abam (Ndende)
Amvam Ondo Ngí	

Fang differed as to the dates to be assigned to these successive forms of Ngi, but most agreed that Mfum Ngí was the original ngí—"the Ngí of our fore-fathers." The nom ngi went around painted entirely in white kaolin clay, giving the cult its name, *mfum Ngí* (white Ngí). All male children of the village were initiated. The very young ones were carried around the mound and the older ones crawled in through a tunnel to the mound. All these initiates had white powder applied to their bodies. This was a dangerous Ngi. It killed many sorcerers.

After the First World War and around the time of the flu epidemic and the subsequent famines of the mid-twenties, Avaziba Ngí swept through the villages. This Ngi came from the west and was associated with a special dance. The nom Ngi was only spotted with white kaolin clay as were the initiates learning the dance. The cranium of the dead child or a recently dead child where witchcraft was suspected was taken up and filled with medicines and placed at the head of the Ngi mound. Fires were lit around it to attract witches. It was then carried around the village to combat them. Children were also passed around the mound to protect them. There was no wild dashing through the village on the part of the nom Ngi and his followers looking for witches.

Amvam Ondo Ngí was known in the early 1930's. The leader was called Amvam Ondo and not nom ngi. All able-bodied men and older boys had to become members. It was a particularly vicious Ngi. In an initiation reminiscent of Ndong Mba the younger boys were maltreated—swung by the arms until senseless, placed in a dark hut for a day, taken out the following dawn and thrown on their stomachs in the Ngi sanctuary where Amvam Ondo tattooed them on the small of the back. He also rubbed medicine in their eyes, ears, and nose to make them strong enough to see Ngi.

The mid-century form of Ngi, other than the Amvam or Ndende movement discussed below (Fang often argued that it was a form of Ngi), was called Ndong Andrike in the French territories. It was active during the Second World War and the decade of the forties, having originated in Spanish Guinea as the Don Enrique movement.[*2] There it had been vigorously suppressed by the government not only for religious reasons, but because it appeared to set up a separate police and judicial institution.[19]

[*2] We do not know to whom this name referred: whether it was to a powerful Spanish colonial official or simply to a visionary person. More than in the French territories the names and representations of Spanish officials entered into cult life and dances. Spanish administrators

Ndong Andrike was often called the Ngi of women because they had equal membership with men and because the cult came with an origin legend in which the founding of the cult was credited to a woman. The Clan Essangi version of this legend, as told to their clients of Oyem District, was the following. Obunu relates it:

> There was a woman in Okak country who lost a child to witches. No one did anything about it. One night she had a dream. A voice told her to revenge the death of her child. She responded, "I am but a woman." The voice said that it made no difference. The woman went to the council house the next day. But the men said it was a dream, not a vision. They would wait and see. Later the woman went fishing in a certain hole. She heard the blast from the antelope horn trumpet. Digging there she found an antelope horn and a thighbone buried in the sand. Suddenly a voice said, "Take this horn and thighbone to the village if you wish to avenge your child." When the men saw this they knew immediately it was Ndong Andrike or Ngi and they took the bone and dug up the head of the child and made an Ngi with all the poisons. The only difference was that women could be present.

The emphasis here upon the origin of cult sacra in the depths of water courses repeats that old emphasis in ngi upon waterlogged medicines.

In the Nkojeng version of Ndong Andrike that came to Assok Ening the teaching team was composed of nine men and nine women.[20] The women's chore was to cook up the plantain they had carried with the powder of a human thighbone. This meal provided protection against witches. In older forms of Ngi the thighbone was the chief weapon wielded by the nom Ngi. Here it was reduced to an ingredient in a medicinal potion. In other ways, the direct menace of the cult was softened. No one was struck as in the old Ngi.

The visiting team of Ndong Andrike also constructed an Ngi mound, but they had two particular weapons. The first was a series of beautiful songs and dances which attracted the witches to the mound where they could be killed. The second weapon was a decorated skull—usually of a child—in which pieces of glass were buried in clay within each eye socket. This gave the impression of glasses (*beyene*). This skull, called Ndong Beyene, was hung around the neck of Ndong Andrike. Behind the clay powerful medicine was placed. This, together with the eye glasses, enabled Ndong Beyene to see the witches day or night.

At the end of the training period, in the late afternoon, the teaching team went off in the forest and blew on the antelope horn. The home team gave

---

seemed to create more charismatic paternalism in their dealings with Fang. We have already discussed the mangan-Flanco and the olanchea dances. But there was also the Ngol dance in Gabon.

chase and, catching them, took their weapons in a mock battle. Their own weapons might have been contaminated by their local sorcerers. That evening the new team held a dance, singing Ndong Beyene songs. The male members of the cult faced the female members in dances reminiscent of the *belebele* dances of moonlit nights. At a given moment, Ndong Andrike blew on the antelope horn. The dancers suddenly broke out into the crowd swinging their machetes over their heads. Many witches attracted by the dance were thus killed.

Two points arise in respect to the evolution of witchcraft movements. First, as the more elaborate Fang rituals—Bieri and Ndong Mba—collapsed, some of their elements were syncretized into succeeding forms of Ngi, particularly in a developing emphasis on initiating both males and females and on blessing the village—not simply eradicating witches. In response to increasing threats of witchcraft, successive forms of Ngi turned to other resources in the Fang cultural patrimony than those that belonged strictly to the old antiwitchcraft cults. Second, we note that as with dance exchange, these Ngi cults spread rapidly by buying and selling to many parts of Fang country, virtually to the point of saturation. But there was never, as was characteristic of Fang, any overall political control of this spread and hence there were often marked differences in these cults from village to village.

THE APOTHEOSIS OF EVIL

If Ngi tended to persist in recurrent forms, this is because sorcery was an increasing problem for Fang. The abuse of the knowledge of the unseen grew, despite the spread of Ngi cults and, perhaps, because of the preoccupation they instilled. A situation developed in the decades of the mid-century which one can call the "apotheosis of evil." The disappearance of the old cults like Bieri, which served, in part, to control the untoward concentration of power in antisocial appetites, contributed to this. But so did the increasing frustrations of changing colonial life: the breakdown of the family under the pressure of cash crops and economic individualism, the concentration of populations through the regroupment of villages, the sense of deprivation and the decentering brought about by mass communications, and the new awareness of "paradisical" life-styles elsewhere. These elements of frustration, widely noted in the colonial world, were bound to have their impact upon that supernatural agency which had always been the chief projection of Fang frustrations—the evus. Instead of being an entity of uncertain though highly suspect capacity lodged in individuals, it became more and more an impersonal power[21] in the universe, often identified with Satan and totally evil in character. This was a violation of traditional Fang belief, a tendency in African thought generally, which regarded nothing as entirely good or entirely bad. "Good and bad walk together."

Bekale has shown this "apotheosis of evil" very well.[22] One says "apotheosis" because in his manuscript, "Du Mal ou de la sorcellerie noire," the worldwide activities of the Grand Society of Evus are shown as much more potent than the divine forces of "the Eternal." Bekale gives a detailed and anguished account of the world society of sorcerers meeting under the aegis of Lucifer-Evus. He shows it choosing the souls to be served at its bloody repasts, the fine dishes on which the human flesh is served, the goblets of blood, and the other appetizers—"toutes sortes de denrées africaines, le tout dans une présentation surnaturellement appétissante."

The manuscript shows how much evil forces had gotten out of control. Bekale decries a great affliction among Africans requiring special measures. While sorcerers, practicing their sorcery, were often thought to work together in former times, no tribal-wide society of sorcerers was conceived of by any evidence available. The individualistic, anarchic nature of Fang society was projected into the unseen, and sorcery was thought of primarily as a collusion between a living man or woman and the witchcraft being with which they struggled. But under the influence of the political and social structures of the colonial world, not to mention the influence of the Europeans' own ideas of the universal nature of demonic evil, Fang possessing religious imagination changed their projections upon the supernatural.

Among Fang of northern Gabon, the struggles of the 1950's between the two political parties—the BDG and the UDSG—were often cast in the idiom of witchcraft. Partisans of one party accused the other of being a cabal of witches.[*3] The following highly animated discussion occurred in the marketplace in Assok Ening not long after the De Gaulle referendum of late summer 1958. De Gaulle had offered independence to the African territories. It shows just how manifest and public this projection was becoming that the Chief of Medoumou marched into Assok Ening asking why none of the sorcerers of the village had volunteered any information on the Congress of Sorcerers of Africa that had been held the same time as the referendum. The results of this Congress, he said, were more important than the referendum. His own evus had been there and had been charged with passing on the results to the local village. Why didn't the sorcerers of Assok Ening speak?

The local Chief, Essono, offered his colleague a bottle of cognac if he would tell those things. Meanwhile, many men of the village had gathered

---

[*3] It has been a frequent enough occurrence in political struggles in African states since independence for witchcraft to be imputed to one's adversaries and for these accusations to be published in the press. When the first president of Gabon, Leon Mba, was in his last lingering illness and left for France for treatment, it was reported he was in a struggle with, but had triumphed over, a local sorcerer. After Nkrumah's downfall, it was reported in the local press that he had been in collusion with a powerful sorcerer in Guinea, Kankan Nyame. In his last days in power, the Equatorial Guinea dictator, Macias Ngema, was supposed to be closeted with witches in his home village of Mangomo. This was in 1979.

in the market pavilion, for the rumour had spread that "things of the night" were to be spoken of during the day. Conspicuous by his absence was Ngema, who later called the gathering a "mass of the lazy."

The Chief began by describing what sorcery was like. "When you are in 'sortilège,' " he said, "you cannot recognize yourself. You are as if in a cloud. You 'feel yourself but you do not see yourself' (ba wôk ka yenebe)." The Chief then complained that no one else would speak out, for many from Assok Ening had participated. Obunu then agreed to speak. He said: "Let me tell you the good things we voted. We voted a new life (mfefé ening) for all. We voted a rise in the price of cocoa. We will eventually obtain 200 francs a kilo instead of 90. We also voted many more children. We saw at the Congress a DC4 taking back to heaven all the recently dead children. We know God sent more to the poor but the bad sorcerers have prevented it from arriving. These children will be returned to their fathers." As Obunu counted off the good things voted, he tore off pieces from a large leaf and placed them before him in a row. He emphasized that the good sorcerers had triumphed at the Congress. He pointed to the leaves to demonstrate it. Still, all these things would come to pass more quickly if it were not for all the bad sorcerers left in the villages. "Instead of using the evus like the European," he said, "to make airplanes and trains and cars and guns, we use evus mostly for evil against our brothers to destroy children and crops. That is why we are lost in perdition. Our fathers used evus to advantage. They forged iron! But today the evil evus has triumphed."

These are only parts of a long rambling presentation by Obunu on the Congress of Sorcerers. Obunu was at his best. He illustrated the nighttime action of the "evus." He crouched and jumped. He chirped like a sinister night creature. Then he roared out like a leopard. He held the crowd spellbound. Was he serious? Only Obunu really knew. Afterwards some said this confession was a good thing. But others shook their heads. Ndutumu said: "It is all very well to talk about good sorcery, but the bad ones will only take advantage of all this information." Muzwi M'ekwaga said: "How can we know that a bad sorcerer does not speak to us of good things." Ngema added later that the village was full of foolish talk these days. Indeed Ngema was at the time suffering from the night talk of Antoine the night fool.

There is a similarity between the night talk of Antoine and these daytime confessions of the Chief of Medoumou and Obunu. They all three gained, if not the respect, at least the attention of others by laying claim to special contact and control over powers of the unseen. And although in most cases villagers listened carefully, there was much ambiguity as to how these disclosures were to be weighed. The village was much surer that Antoine was a fool, yet there was also something foolish in Obunu's confession. But practically everyone still had sufficient belief in the powers of the unseen, whether the ancestors or the evus, that they had to listen. The fact was that

Fang beliefs were changing, and men were not really sure of the shape of those beliefs. Surprised as they were to hear a young fool lay claim to contact with the ancestors or men in plain daylight confess what should only be confessed to the ngungan in private, they were still bound to listen. The supernatural was inchoate. And men of religious imagination, like Bekale or Antoine or Obunu, filled in their projections a need for a new constellation of religious beliefs.

THE TURN TOWARD THE OCCULT POWERS OF THE EUROPEAN

In one sense, this "night talk" and this "day talk" about witchcraft, by making repeatedly public what was formerly private and sinister, led to a decline in the energy of these beliefs, particularly among the young. For them, all the talk of evus bloated this agency to such an extent that it collapsed of its own weight. Though men might continue to argue that evus is "our rifle," "our airplane," "our radio," others would reply in bad humor: "If the evus is so powerful, how is it that it never taught us to make the most insignificant thing such as a match or a kerosene lantern? It has left us living in darkness." Some young people drew, as Ngema had drawn, the appropriate lesson that hard and practical work in the world was the only antidote to the "sad life" (*ening engôngôl*) of the African. But others, continuing in the belief in manipulation of the unseen by magical means, but losing confidence in evus, became susceptible to European merchants of occult literature. Mba Muzwi was one of these.

To understand the sources of Mba Muzwi's fatal affliction, it is important to be aware of an antiwitchcraft movement of the mid-fifties that swept through Fang country and that many Fang considered the most recent form of Ngi: it was variously called the Ambam, Ndende, or Mademoiselle movement. The leader of this movement, Ndende, was much influenced by European occult literature. He combined the combat against witches which was the essence of Ngi with an attempt to bring Africans into relation with the occult powers of the European. Ndende spoke particularly to those who had experienced the "Apotheosis of Evil" and who believed that extraordinary measures were needed if that evil was to be combated. At the same time, there were those who yet believed that the agency of power bound up in that evil— evus—was an outmoded and degenerate force and that the European offered other agencies for the control of the unseen of greater consequence. Ndende spoke to them too.

The Bekale manuscript is itself a forceful appeal for new forms of combating evil. It ends with a promise to the reader of a specific and imminent extermination of evil. It promises that in view of the onrushing cataclysm brought about by sorcery, "Africans are finally turning to the Immaculate Virgin, the Queen of the Universe, for her aid against the sorcerers." "The Mother of

1. The Chief of the village of Assok Ening, Essono Mba, posing before the collapsing Council House (aba) of Mvok Mba M'Oye. Assok Ening, Oyem District.

2. A newborn child, still with the whiteness of the land of the ancestors from whence it has come, is placed on the back of the next oldest sibling, as a sign of the continuity of the genealogical line. Assok Ening, Oyem District.

3. The close relationship encouraged between the infant and its next oldest sibling. Assok Ening. Oyem District.

4. Young village boys and girls play together until, approaching puberty, their interests diverge. Assok Ening, Oyem District.

5. The boys' earliest interest in courtship is expressed in the dancing male and female bamboo figures going a-courting on a string (see Chapter 6). Assok Ening, Oyem District.

6. Boys practicing spear throwing. Assok Ening, Oyem District.

7. Striking small stones as accompaniment, girls gather to sing the rhythm songs particular to their sex. Assok Ening, Oyem District.

8. Young men (nduman), escaping the ennui of their decentered villages, leave on a courting expedition. Azok, Mitzik District.

9. Young men playing mbek in the Council House. Assok Ening, Oyem District.

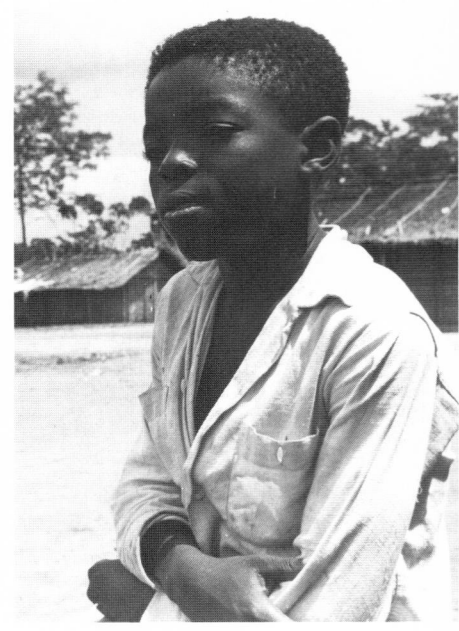

10. Young girl on the margins of puberty (ngwan).

11. Young boy (mon).

12. Young married woman (ekoma mininga).

13. Young husband (fam).

14. Man at the height of his powers (nyamoro).

15. Another nyamoro.

16. The tiredness of the old (nom mininga).

17. Old man (non fam).

18. Ndebot: a house of people. Evinayong, Spanish Guinea.

19. Mvogabot: people who look across the courtyard at each other. Kougouleu, Kango District.

20. Preparing the leaf package of pounded food (zom).

21. Leaf packages of pounded manioc prepared to be sent to male relatives in the lumber camps around Libreville.

22. Tying together the house. House-building in a modern regroupment village. Assok Ening, Oyem District.

23. Burning the forest in preparation for gardening at the beginning of the long, cool, rainy season. Assok Ening, Oyem District.

24. Another view of forest-burning.

25. The newlyweds, but particularly the bride, are addressed by the head of the Women's Society (Mevungu) of the husband's village.

26. An elder woman of the Women's Society takes a male role, chiding a "young bride," played by a local woman, for her "bad habits" and carelessness in feeding her husband.

27. The elder turns upon the ethnographer's wife and disciplines her for her "bad habits."

28. The women of the husband's family (ndebot) bolster the pride of the family in their possessions (menguma) by competitively lavishing gifts of food upon the bride's family (see Chapter 6).

29. The two mothers-in-law embrace and resolve the tension building up over the competitive gift giving.

30. A daughter of the village is "imprisoned" because her husband has been making inadequate bridepayments (see Chapter 5).

31. A villager whose mother is of the same clan as the delinquent husband pleads his case and obtains the release of the woman.

32. Another husband, always faithful in bridepayment and considerate in his treatment of his wife, makes an impressive payment.

33. This husband and his wife dance "bilaba" in jocular mockery of the villagers.

34. The visiting team, giving instruction, prepares to begin the final celebratory dance of mangan. The learning team is on the other side of the arena, not shown (see Chapter 5). Koomassi, Oyem District.

35. Solo dancing in front of the great drum. Woman dressed in civet cat skins (esinga).

36. Another view of the same woman.

37. Visiting team members dance out to show the local team some fine points of style. Koomassi, Oyem District.

38. Another view of the dance.

39. The leaf curing basket (nkat ngan) being pierced so that its fluids will flow over the afflicted person. Efulan, Medouneu District.

40. A local lieutenant of Ndende (the eradicator of village evil) and his assistants before the "fetishes" they have discovered and destroyed in the village (see Chapter 9). Ayol, Mitzik District.

41. Ndende listening to the voice of the female spirit, Mademoiselle, through the magic wand. Ayol, Mitzik District.

God and of men will not fail the blacks," we are told. This, in fact, was
what the Marian cycle proposed by Pius XII was all about. It was a periodic
attack against sorcery directed by the Virgin herself. As early as 1945, Bekale
relates, a Fang from Makokou, northeast Gabon, Jean "Bon Coeur" Emane,
had understood how to take advantage of the power of the Virgin to combat
sorcerers. Similar but even more powerful movements, he says, are now at
work in the same area.[23]

Bekale seems to be referring here to the Ndende movement which arose
in Makokou about the time he was writing. Ndende himself, the leader of the
movement, was not a Fang, but a Bakota. And the Virgin in his movement
had been generalized into a white female spirit called by most villagers
"Mademoiselle." This Mademoiselle spirit, moreover, was strongly syncretized with female water deities very common among the coastal and Ogooue
River peoples of Gabon and familiar up the coast of West Africa as Mamywateh. In Gabon these female water spirits, Mbumba among the Galwa and
MPongwe, were associated with the rainbow and with cults for the obtaining
of wealth and fecundity. The Mademoiselle of Ndende promised the spiritual
solace and protection of the Virgin, together with the hope of material and
fleshly well-being bound up in the water spirit cults. It should be emphasized
that interpretations of Mademoiselle differed from locality to locality. Fang
of Oyem District believed Mademoiselle was a spirit that came to Ndende
from Paris. They held to the following myth, where once again we note the
beneficial power of watercourses in the eradication of witches. This is the
version related by the old man in Assok Ening who assisted Ndende, Alogo
Zogo:

> Ndende was just a lowly Bakota fisherman. One day while he was out
> alone working a trap in the river, he suddenly saw a white woman rise
> up before him. She drew a baton out from her dress. It was made of
> ebony with a cap of ivory. She told him that this baton had a special
> magic power and that she could be called from Paris to dwell within it.
> Her power and the power of this baton could have beneficial effects for
> the whole country. Ndende returned to his village and, with the aid of
> this baton, was able to divine, to the amazement of his fellow villagers.
> He was able to tell how many bones and skulls they had in their pos-
> session. Later Mademoiselle came and told Ndende how to build a shrine
> to protect villages and replace the dirty bones people were keeping. That
> shrine is called *ambam*.[24]

As was typical of Fang dance exchange, the Ndende movement spread very
rapidly in Fang country. The original Ndende taught his methods to many
men, some recruited and others inspired to his banner. They, in turn, taught
elsewhere, inviting the original Ndende for final ceremonies. None of these
subordinates had the original's force of character and clairvoyance.

Ndende operated in the following way. He came to a village only when invited, for he said "my methods are unrelenting and unless I am invited, complaints could be lodged against me by the government." A man from the local village was chosen to assist Ndende as his secretary or his substitute. This man would later become the "Ndende of the village." Ndende's reputation preceded him and villagers flocked to see him perform, becoming themselves vulnerable to being called out of the crowd. In Assok Ening only Ngema and his branch of Mba M'Oye did not come forward to be scrutinized by Ndende. That part of the family saw the invitation as a plot on the part of poorer villagers to convict them, because of their prosperity, of sorcery.

After several days in the village acquainting himself with its problems,[*4] Ndende gathered the villagers in the courtyard. He reminded them that they had invited him because of the ills they suffered. He proposed to cure these problems by removing all the filth of fetishism that caused them. Singing and dancing, his face white with kaolin, Ndende summoned Mademoiselle. Then he sat down and, placing one end of his baton in his ear, pointed the other toward the villagers. For a time he chanted in tongues. This was the voice of Mademoiselle. Then, calling his assistant and speaking through him, Ndende, now possessed by Mademoiselle, began to scrutinize each villager for fetish. Sometimes "she" would talk in generalities and other times with astounding specificity. Some he would release as "simple ones." Others he would hold a time until he was convinced by the steadfastness of their denials. Others he held regardless of their denials. If these last could not be forced to confess and bring forth their fetish, Ndende would summon them the next day or keep them standing long hours in the sun. He would threaten. If nothing could be done, he would tell the assistant to write the fetishes on a piece of paper. Several drops of his magic perfume were poured upon it. Then Ndende spat into the paper, crumpled it, rubbed it against his forehead and threw it at the man or woman. "I wish you a bad life," he would say, in this case not speaking for Mademoiselle. A man might establish his innocence and escape this curse by going to the ambam shrine with the paper. Tearing it up over the shrine, he would say: "Mademoiselle, it is you who must judge this issue."

It is instructive to consider several of the divining interviews among the 50 or 60 that Ndende held in Assok Ening. For over half these interviews exploited or exacerbated axes of enmity already present in the village.

> MBA AKOMO (a man with elephantiasis, a man much disliked for his slovenly habits): "When one looks at you you appear poor. But you are a king of sorcery. By day a beggar, by night a king. Mademoiselle says this swollen leg, elephantiasis by day, at night is a rubber boot that enables you to make great strides in doing your evil work. You

---

[*4] It was at this time that Ndende obtained information from villagers on the basis of which he was able to make convincing, even astounding divinations.

destroyed the European plantation that brought so much work to the
village. You will die a painful death. Bring me your fetishes, you
have many.'' Mba brought him a rock saying that was what he had
used to destroy the plantation. Ndende accepted that and as was his
custom sprinkled white powder upon it.

EKOGO MVE: ''Why are you such a bad family head?'' Ndende asked.
''It is regrettable that you head a family. You have the root of a tree
in your home. Whenever a youth of this village or your family goes
seeking work, you wait until the moon rises and then you go out late
at night and, in the courtyard, you draw this root across your forehead.
You make a mark on the ground and look at the moon and you curse
that youth. Why has your son failed so often to obtain his driving
permit?'' (The son had previously gone to consult Ndende about his
misfortune.) ''You do not wish your sons to succeed and replace you!''
Ekogo steadily denied these things and had a ''convocation'' thrown
at him.

NDONG NKULU: Ndende startled everyone by telling Ndong Nkulu he
kept a portion of the rainbow. ''Bring me that. This rainbow is to
protect you against sorcery. You also have a woman's collar bone that
you have kept to marry off your children easily.'' The villagers nodded
in agreement for Ndong was famous for marrying off his three sons
for trifling bridemonies, much under the ordinary. Ndong produced
a thighbone which Ndende accepted. But he could not produce the
''rainbow'' or the collarbone. Ndende let him go after he went back
and brought an ancestor figure which he had hidden and which had
a piece of bone in its stomach. Neither of Ndong Nkulu's other fetishes
were ''eating people,'' Ndende said.

MUNGEH OBIANG: Ndende accused this woman of keeping medicine
against her husband. The woman denied it and Ndende called her
further forward. He took her by the arm and asked her gently why she
would not confess and come forth with it. Then he looked at her inches
away, leaned forward and rubbed his face against hers and stood back.
The woman stood like a stone without moving or speaking. Ndende
asked the spectators what should be done with her. No one answered.
Ndende tapped her on the forehead with his baton and told her Mademoiselle would deal with her. A year later when this woman began
to go blind it was credited to Mademoiselle.

In these interviews we see Ndende capitalizing on existing rumors and
resentments and concentrating, as did the ngí cult before him, upon the sick
and the unfortunate whose misfortunes might be taken as signs of their evil
natures. He also acted in the interests of one brother against another or father
against son or vice versa. The effects of his activities, on balance, tended in

the direction of exacerbating social disorders rather than resolving them. Villagers, a year after, noting a continuation of ill-feeling and sorcery among them, looked back with misgiving upon his visit. Obunu reminded them that Ndende had forced him to dig up the skull of the child that had been used in the last Ngi, Ndong Andrike. As was his custom with all the fetishes brought to him, Ndende had sprinkled white powder upon it and thrown it away.[25] Obunu had also been forced to give up the cranium of his great-great grandfather. At the time this had caused heavy-heartedness in the village. It was a well-known skull and many felt that great power and good fortune for the entire village had come from it. Obunu asked the men of the village: "Does the ambam shrine which Ndende left us protect us as well as those skulls?"

The last act of Ndende's visit was the making of the ambam shrine. A hole one foot in diameter and one foot deep was dug in the central court of the village. As with the Ngi mound, various poisons, plants, and insects were placed in this hole. Small bamboo spears were set carefully upright. Then Ndende's own perfume was poured in. The hole was closed up. Ndende sang and danced over it, calling Mademoiselle. Mademoiselle was now "in" the village and would protect it against evil. "No brother shall eat another, nor will wild animals destroy your crops. Nor will any boy be able to have intercourse during the day." A large stout stick was then stuck upright in the center of the shrine. This was the stick of Mademoiselle with which she would strike the evildoer. Any villager who suffered unjustly at the hands of another could come to the shrine and denounce him to Mademoiselle. A year later the shrine was largely forgotten in the village.[26]

In part the death of Mba Muzwi arose out of Ndende's success in compelling villagers to render up to him the various biang they possessed, including the bones of their ancestors. Mba Muzwi was an intense observer throughout the Ndende trials, though he himself never came forward. Later he was one of the few to come and make prayers at the shrine of Ambam. It had long been known in the village that Mba Muzwi subscribed to occult literature peddled from Paris and Monaco.[27] Before the arrival of Ndende, Mba had concentrated on the Secret Psalms of the Old Testament which were drawn up in such a way as to guarantee the supplicant protection against the evils of others. Two of his favorites, 54 and 58, marked in his own copy of the *150 Psaumes de David*, show his preoccupation with protecting himself against sorcery.[28]

Psalm 54: Psalm of Appeal Imploring Divine Help
and Complaint against Men.

Lord listen to my prayer and supplication. My enemies menace me and would do me in. They pursue me with anger and plot my misfortune. I fear the jaws of death and my heart is troubled. I desire the wings of the dove to take me to a place of repose. Confound them Lord and lead them to perdition. For discord and violence are in the village. There is nought but injustice and oppression. But you are my counselor and my friend. You eat at my table. I desire that they should be taken living to the land of the dead. Because their hearts and their dwellings are full of evil.

Psalm 58: Psalm Against the Evilness of Enemies.

My enemies rise against me. Deliver me Lord. Save me from these bloodthirsty men. My enemies are assembled to throw themselves upon me and they seek my perdition. Yet I am not guilty nor have I sinned. I have never practiced injustice and have always walked the straight road. Rise, Lord, come and chastise these evil men. My enemies return every evening and make the tour of the town. They look for their victim like famished dogs. They menace and their mouths hang open and they pretend God cannot hear them. But you laugh at them, Lord, and you will reduce them to nothing.

After the departure of Ndende, it appears that Mba Muzwi shifted his attention to prayers directed to the Virgin and to the Mother of Heaven, and to a chaste Mademoiselle which he fashioned for himself and who arrived nightly to him from Heaven or from Paris.[29] No one knew what subsequently occurred or what precise relationship Mba had with Mademoiselle. Perhaps, as some suggested, it was a secret sexuality of the unseen. Others thought Mba was negotiating for riches and overreached himself. Perhaps he had been enticed into some village affair which offended his tutelary spirit. All that was known is the context in which Mba Muzwi fell into a deep stupor from which the masters of neither black nor white medicines had the capacity to retrieve his doomed spirit.

THE SEPARATION FROM DEATH

The discussion to this point helps explain Mba Muzwi's death but it has not separated us from him. Fang emphasized that separation is comprised in the three stages of their funerals: *ntômbim* (sitting by the cadaver); *dzembim* (the separation of the cadaver by burial); and *dzemawu* (the separation from the death at a mortuary ceremony). The mortuary ceremonies took place at a later date for plans had to be laid so that all important relatives would be present. As we know, it was particularly important that sons-in-law be present to, quite literally, pay their respects in *afa abong* and to dance *bilaba*. The separation from the death came later for a second reason. It could not be expected that either the *nsisim*, the incorporeal form of the body, or the *kôn*, the spirit or shade, after such long residence in a village would be able to leave it quickly. Their ties had to be allowed gradually to fall away.

Fang attitudes toward death were in part a result of their beliefs and in part a result of the frequency with which they, as any kinship-oriented society, had to confront the fact. In a family such as Mba M'Oye with its 65 members (and with an annual death rate in Fang country of 30 per thousand)[30] members could expect to participate ritually in two deaths a year. But, in fact, all deaths in the village, averaging between 10 and 12 a year, evoked strong response as seen by the attendance of members of Mba M'Oye at the funeral of Mba Muzwi. If we include in-laws, we come close to 15 deaths a year each of which laid some burden upon a person's awareness.

Fang had a certain insouciance in the face of death.[*5] When Ndong Engonga died, life in his son's wife's kitchen—for men, born in the kitchen, returned to it to die—went on as normal. Women cracked peanuts and ground them up, and children and ducks ran in and out. Engong had given up eating and drinking. When I came down to see him he said, in a faint voice, "Friend, I come to the crossroads, but am prepared to pass over. I blessed my sons last night." While we were talking, an assistant to the local catechist came in and, sitting for a moment, suggested a prayer. Ndong's daughter-in-law hooted. She said, "No! There is nothing like a prayer to hurry a man on his way." Even Ndong cracked a smile.

Fang struggled very hard, in ways we have seen, for the capacity to resist forces working against their survival. But once convinced they were on the road to death, they resigned themselves with remarkable composure. Père Briault stated this very well, though he takes the colonial view of the African imagination:

Death angers the black more because it interrupts the ordinary course of his days than for the mysterious perspectives it places before his imagination; ordinarily his imagination does as he does—, it reposes . . . we Europeans have become éligiaques. The convention of secrecy dominates us and we have lost the habit of reasoning simply on the most simple subjects. It is here that the primitive is superior for he has preserved his simplicity. He fears death. He cries at the danger. He seeks to punish those who would afflict him with it. But when he sees it is inevitable, he resigns himself without our terrors. He regards the supreme passage with placidity."[31]

[*5] The anxiety surrounding death promoted in many religions by thoughts of judgment in the afterlife was not present in Fang with whom I worked. The kon goes on eventually to the village of the dead regardless, though inadequate death ceremonies may cause it to wander sorrowfully in the deep forest—a kind of damnation. Generally a man suffers in this life for his evil, not in the next. Largeau's informants, however, told him of three kinds of judges in the afterlife: Oyem Bot (Scrutinizer of Men); Oka Bot (Partitioner of Men); and Oyile Bot (Classifier of Men) (pp. 18-19). He admits, however, that their notions of hell are very uncertain (p. 287). This was my experience. Allegret (p. 6) tells us, however, that Fang believe in a second death of the kon, if it has led a bad life, sending it to a terrible place from which it can never return. One can protect oneself against a troublesome spirit, he says, by wishing it this second death!

The phrase "hysteric reaction" has been used to describe Mba Muzwi's rejection of all further relations with the world. But we might as usefully refer to it as an extreme form of that composure Fang showed before the fact of death once convinced they no longer had the capacity to survive. To be sure, the mystery of Mba's death, coupled with the speculations about the unseen we have recounted, was acting to disturb the equanimity of villagers more than Briault could have suspected.

It should also be pointed out that this composure, the old composure at least, rested in part on the firm belief that portions of the self, in particular the kon, would be passing beyond the crossroads to another life in the village of the dead. While there was disagreement on where that village was and the nature of life there the quality of the belief was not impaired.

While Fang preserved a certain confidence about the afterlife they had little confidence about the dead themselves. The various phases of the funeral were designed primarily to separate the living from the errant dead. The dangers of the dead were seen in the attitudes toward the corpse. Men with pregnant wives did not look upon it. It could destroy the conception. Children too were prohibited from looking upon it. They are not strong enough. The corpse, however, was buried soon enough. It was the death that lingered and that had to be confronted.

In the first days after the burial the wives of the deceased (if unmarried, his sister) bore a particular burden of mourning called *nkus*. They had to remain a week in a dark chamber sitting on a mat on the ground. It was important that the mother's brother, *nyang ndum*, be present to shave the hair off these women and take their good clothes in exchange for rags. For the mother's brother was the only man free of suspicion in the death of his nephews. His genuine grief was in part compensated for in nkus and materially assuaged by gifts of chickens and money from his nephew's family. The hair and the clothes of these women were taken and buried in the forest.

Several reasons were offered for the imposition of this mourning upon women. First there was the belief that women weakened men's backbones and hence contributed to their deaths. There was also the belief that women practiced witchcraft against men more than the reverse. But women sat upon the ground for another reason. They were felt to be closer to death—perhaps to life and death—than men. Their closeness to death was seen in the fact that it was they rather than men who clustered around the cadaver bathing and tending it, making it more difficult to separate them from the fact. For them death was confronted by their sitting upon the ground until their attachment to the dead fell away as the ragged garments themselves. And both death and their own emotional involvement was neutralized by the earth.

Fang also said that women were more vulnerable to a dangerous feeling of loss—*enyuyung*. Sitting upon the ground protected against being overwhelmed by this emotion. Sitting on the ground changed the unstable state of their bodies from a bad state (*nyôl abé*, bad body) to a clean state (*nyôl nfouban*).

The separation from the spirit was also dramatically enacted in Assok Ening and other Ntumu villages in the dance called *nyas* in which a dancer painted white or with white spots hid under the rafters of the house in which the man or woman had died. Upon the starting up of the death drum (*nku awu*), this dancer began to pound the roof from within, lifting the thatch up and down. Suddenly he would slip out between the sheets of thatch whose raffia ties had been cut, slide down the roof to the ground and begin a rapidly whirling dance. After a time, a man came out from a banana thicket on the edge of the village with a peeled banana stalk. He struck the dancer on the back who, at this signal, wheeled and whirled out into the forest. This dance, was said to have represented the spirit (kon), leaving the place where it had lived and upon the call of other spirits departing for the village of the dead. Some informants said that the man who came out of the thicket represented the kon calling the nsisim and whipping it away from the village, while others maintained it was the nsisim that has been wandering lost in the thicket who came back to collect the kon spirit and depart with it. In some villages, the white-daubed dancer returned at the end, taking the dead man's clothes onto the roof and dancing with them out to the forest.

The final separation of Mba Muzwi lasted seven days. It began with a mass in his name. There were dances every night and on the final day, all day long. After the mass on the first day, an *esulan awu* (reunion at death) was held in the house of Muzwi Ekwaga. Five bottles of wine, 1 bottle of gin, and 7 bottles of *malamba* (corn beer) were opened as well as 25 leaf packages of food. Many speeches were given, mostly concerning the generosity of the family and its hopeful future. Nothing was said of Mba Muzwi. On the evening of the seventh day, the day in which dancing was continuous, the mother's brother was shown the inheritance—that which had been left by Mba Muzwi in addition to his clothes which had been displayed on the roof. This was called *enving mekawk* (the leftovers from the chewed sugar cane). The name was appropriate, for very often things were hidden by the dead man's brothers. The mother's brother was shown these things so that he might make a selection if he wished. There was nothing of any consequence in Mba Muzwi's inheritance except the few pulp books of occult literature. Nyang ndum chose nothing.

On the final day the death drum spoke early. All the men of the family then came and danced in front of the drums. The sisters' husbands were also gathered but they did not dance. The moment came for *afôn*. Mendame Simon with his fly whisk in his hand started dancing further and further away from the crowd, shaking his fly swatter at the heavens and at the ground. Suddenly he bent over and flung his loin cloth over his hips displaying his backside and his parts. A great shout went up from the crowd. The sisters' sons raced out into the village, running into kitchens to steal food and pounding on walls. Other men danced out to where Simon was recomposing himself to congratulate him and dance with him back into the drums. After this "scandal" the payment of respects by the sons-in-law could begin. If the spirit of Mba Muzwi had not departed by this point, he had certainly been shaken loose from the thoughts of the villagers. The week's events had effectively removed them from his death.

Conclusion: The Isolation of
the Religious Imagination

In mid-century Fang religious imaginations were in an unsettled state, uncertain of the shape and aptness of old beliefs, yet still convinced that whatever it was in the unseen that these beliefs represented—power, knowledge, capacity—it still existed and had enormous importance in human affairs. Fang religious imaginations were in search of new representations of "the unseen." Mba Muzwi was one tragic casualty of that search, for the new spirit he took up, Mademoiselle, was, as most villagers recognized, a highly volatile agent of the unseen with whom no one had the knowledge or medicine to deal. When through some violation of his proper and respectful relationship to her, and perhaps through his own search for too great a capacity, she began to "strangle" him, no remedy could be discovered.

Representations of the unseen can take shape for many human purposes—consolation, benevolent protection, social and personal discipline, the philosophical satisfactions of final principles. In the next chapter we will describe Fang rites of former days that sought to represent and enact the unseen to such purposes. But for many decades these rites had been moribund. The cult with which Fang had lately been preoccupied was the antiwitchcraft cult, Ngi, which has sought to give, in its evolving reenactments, capacity to deal with the unseen represented in its most hostile and aggrandizing form—the diabolic evus. It was designed to provide protection against the most disturbing loss of all: the death of the young. The result of the continuing concentration of this cult on a definition of the unseen as evil was an "apotheosis of evil." This was not surprising since Ngi ceremonies, unlike those for the ancestor cult which was very much a domestic cult, were brought and enacted by alien, even enemy clans. Though Ngi evolved and in some respects tried to take over the representational functions of these other cults, its principal definition of the unseen as hostile and alien remained dominant.

The definition of the unseen as predominantly aggrandizing coupled with the exacerbation of material desire and the encouragement of economic individualism during the colonial period led to evident excesses. More and more for Fang the healthy and normal flow of personal and social life—the revitalizing exchange between men and women and the environment and the recurrent invigorating and transforming exchanges between social units—was becoming blocked up, swollen, and eventually strangled by a surfeit of desire. The restrained use and balanced control of supernatural power which the engolengola—the most desirable character-type—evidenced, was increasingly rare. Men—unbalanced and unrestrained men—were giving themselves over too much to the agency of the evus or some other vehicle of self-interest and aggrandizement rather than to community. But it was not only men such as Mba Muzwi who could fall into that mortal, and in the end self-imposed, dumb state (*ngím-mvuk*); communities themselves could be swollen. This was the view of the men of Medoumou in regard to Assok Ening—that it was a regroupment village bursting with pride in its prosperity yet strangling its young. The family, in short, may have separated themselves from the death of Mba Muzwi. Many felt they had not separated themselves from some new and deeply troubling problems having to do with death itself, which had risen out of the isolation of individuals (such as Mba) in relation to very particularistic representations of the supernatural.

PART II
INTERPRETATIONS

⁓10⁓

Ritual at Work
in Two Old Fang Cults

A Baa So!
(The fathers come again!)

ONE LATE SUNDAY AFTERNOON when Ngema had returned from his coffee trees he got into an argument with his older brother Mintza, who reproached him for not stopping work on Sunday out of respect for God. Mintza had been known to try to take Ngema forcibly by the hand down to Mass. Ngema replied, as he often did, by asking Mintza if he really knew who God was and what he wanted. "I work like my ancestors did every day of the week." Mintza misunderstood him and thought that Ngema was referring to the work done for the ancestors in the ancestor cult Bieri, for cult activity was known as work (*eseng*). Mintza said, "I know you used to work hard as *ngômalan* [initiated member of the ancestor cult] but now you have the good news brought by the missionary. Why don't you work hard as a Christian? That good news means you only work one hour a day on Sunday and the rest of the day you stop work out of respect for God." Ngema replied, "You respect Sunday now, but soon it will also be Thursday like the members of Bwiti. And the white man brought us also the autocar and we have to respect it and wait to see it pass at 8:30 every morning before we go off to work in the forest. All this is just an excuse not to work!"

Muye Michel was in a corner of the council house at the time, making a bamboo fish trap. He was sensitive to how often the members of Bwiti had been accused by other Fang of being shiftless and good-for-nothing with their all-night dancing. "It is true," he said, "that Christianity is no form of work. It is just an excuse to sit down. We used to work hard for the ancestors and now in Bwiti we continue to work hard for them and for God too!"

But neither Ngema nor Mintza wished to accept Muye's mediation in their argument. He was no interpreter. They both sat down together to belabor "the foolishness" of Bwiti. Muye Michel, who had been building a new

Bwiti chapel in the village, finally convinced his "fathers" to stop criticizing their "little one." He gave a "good answer" by inviting them down to visit the chapel. We all got up and went out of the council house down to the new building. Everyone, that is, except Ngema, who said he had to repair a bed in his first wife's kitchen.

THE INTERPRETATION OF FANG RELIGION

What was the meaning of the old religion to Ngema? What was the meaning of Christianity to Mintza? What was the meaning of Bwiti to Muye Michel? *Da yile dze*? (What does it mean?) It is a question that can be put too abstractly either for Fang of the old culture or for the materials which are available. Allegret maintained in his brief work on the religious ideas of the Fang[1] that there were two errors to be avoided: "One should not give too much credence to the responses of the natives to such abstract questions as we are accustomed to ask, and one should avoid classifying their ideas following our modes of thought. Natives do not see the utility of such questions and classifications and are of a tendency to hide their interior life when asked to confront it directly." Perhaps the problem to which Allegret alludes is bound up with the word "religion." The question in Fang would be: What does your confession (*nyibe*, acceptance, agreement) mean to you? Since a religious person is called an *mbune* (he who believes), one might also ask: You are a believer (*mbune*), what does your belief (*mabun*) mean to you?

But even these questions apply best to the evangelical religions. The old cults were not matters of a decided acceptance. They did not so much mean, they were![2] It was better to ask: What did the old cults represent? Consider the Fang verb *yile* which was usually translated "to mean." The better translation was "to conclude."[3] Thus, *da yile dze*? ("What does one conclude? What is the consequence of it?"). Of the old Fang religious practices, one thus asks: What were the consequences of them? What did Fang conclude from their religious work? And more: What penalties did their evolving culture pay when it no longer offered such "conclusions" to the open-endedness of their existence?

Inquiry concerning meanings often proceeded from fixed ideas. Despite Allegret's warnings, he himself, because of his own religious categories, slighted Fang ideas in respect to the dead, to good and evil, to sorcery and purification, and to "preparation." He concentrated on Fang ideas of God, a relatively weak category. Perhaps the most instructive example, however, of an overdetermined search for religious ideas was that of Tessmann, the author of the basic Fang ethnography. He set himself the objective of finding the philosophic base behind Fang practice. But more than that, he was interested in confirming his conviction, much in the air in German intellectual circles at the time, that there were a set of primeval ideas ("Elementarge-danken" in Wundt's phrase and "ursprünglichen Ideen" in Tessmann's) that lay behind all primitive religions ("Religion der Naturvölker). In discussing Fang cults, he emphasized how "primitive thought" was revealed in them. He was also influenced by the psychoanalytic interpretations of the period and concentrated his descriptions on the various sexual representations in cult objects and actions: snakes, fruit, etc.[4] His informants could not always give him the kind of commentary that would suit these interests. He had to inter-polate. This led him to complain that "the earliest ideas survive unrealized in the Fang and only through incidental, unconscious expressions can their coherence be grasped."[5] He treated with impatience explanations that did not meet his needs. Often he was forced to draw his own conclusions, for "the Fang will not split their heads over such matters."[6]

Part of Tessmann's difficulties was the diversity of explanations for any action or image. Fang were egalitarian, and establishing a consensus among them was difficult. The temptation was to make one's own interpretation. It was a matter of recognizing a range of beliefs, and a range of possible interpretations depending on the particular situational interaction of ethnog-rapher and informant. Out of our particular interaction, then, we shall seek an interpretation here of the two central cults of the old Fang religious life: Soo Ndong Mba, the initiation cult, and Bieri, the ancestor cult. We shall use Tessmann since after all, his accounts are detailed and he was there. But we shall compare his accounts and also those of Père Trilles to what we were told by Fang men and women who had participated in these cults. In an interpretation emerging out of this comparison we will argue for a continuity between the preoccupations of the old cults and the religious movement of Bwiti.

SOO-NDONG MBA: THE VILLAGE PURIFIED
AND THE YOUNG ACCOMMODATED TO THE HUMAN CONDITION

Fang practiced clan exogamy. Sexual intercourse between brothers and sisters of the same clan produced "monsters" (ebibi) or "miscarriages" (kigile) and could destroy the good luck (maa) experienced by clan villages. Incest was the act against nature par excellence, as Fang understood it. It was a ritual sin (nsem) and in fact the most important of these, nsem nden.[7] Yet sex play between older children on the verge of puberty was inescapable in village life. Children's games such as shale had marked sexual overtones.[8] And boys would often be seen playing bidzang, an amusement in which two puppets were suspended on strings held taut between the big toes or the thumbs. As the string was tensed and relaxed the puppets danced toward each other and finally met. Since one of the puppets was male with a large member and the other female with a pronounced vulva, the sexual element was inescapable. (Tessmann pictures the puppets with an obscured member.)[9] The boys sang:

Bidzang be sô ôkwin	The courting ones come from upriver
Bidzang be sô nké	The courting ones come from downriver
Bidzang bia bidzang	Courting ones, our courting ones
Be sia kakak, be lumiang.	They abandon themselves to each other intensely. They have done battle.

The cult which attempted to sanction Fang sexuality was Ndong Mba. It was often linked with the Soo cult among the Ntumu and Fang proper. From our inquiry, it appears as a collection of not fully integrated rituals which served a set of diverse purposes. Though Soo and Ndong Mba were two cults among northern Pahouin, in the south they were often indistinguishably mixed, and one can speak of Soo-Ndong Mba. Parts of these ceremonies derived from the Pygmy and from neighboring patrilineal peoples to the south. Still other parts were autochthonous. Both Ndong Mba and Soo sought the purification of the village and its protection against incestuous sexuality. The precipitating cause was the pregnancy of a daughter of the village when there was reason to suspect sibling incest. If the pregnancy was the result of quite legitimate courtship with a boy of another clan there may yet have been such sin (nsem) in the past, and this had to be purified and washed away (*atunba*) so that the birth might move forward satisfactorily. There was also an element of rite of passage which strengthened boys for the dangers and opportunities of hunting and fishing in the forest.

TESSMANN'S INTERPRETATION: GOOD AND BAD ORDERED BY TRANSFERENCE UPON NATURE

Fang discussed these rituals with us and demonstrated them. But they had been abandoned for some years. Our commentators struggled to integrate diverse remembered elements. Tessmann observed Ndong Mba and Soo among the Yaounde and the Ntumu. He found an overall rationale and a sense of coordination of parts.[10] I shall summarize his views, correcting his observations on the basis of information later obtained. Soo-Ndong Mba was as rich as any ceremony Fang had, and its elements lingered in Fang minds as a significant inheritance.

Tessmann interested himself first in what Fang religion seemed to say about sin. He recognized that Fang did not carry the personal burden of sin familiar to him in the Christian West. Sin seemed to exist in the nature of things, and the religious cults existed to enable man to come to terms with that nature.

Tessmann took note of and explored with Fang a creation legend similar to the biblical one (perhaps a diffusion) in which there appears the first sin (*nsem ôsua*) between men and women (brother and sister). His informants regarded this sin as God's will. "The snake is itself a part of God."[11] Fang, he felt, recognized that death and suffering resulted from sin and excesses of various kinds, but while one might be ashamed for not controlling these, one could not be guilty about the existence of the conditions.[12] Nsem was inevitable and therefore death and suffering were too. Tessmann saw Fang cults, therefore, as shifting guilt onto nature[13] and establishing its origin there rather than in mankind. Since, from the male view, woman was the most inescapable and intractable part of nature, men's cults were preoccupied with shifting guilt over upon women. Women's cults returned the compliment in respect to man's nature. In short, Fang cults such as Soo Ndong Mba served principally to accommodate Fang to good and evil by postulating these as the natural condition, or at least the condition of the opposite sex.

Tessmann observed these cults, then, with an eye to how this "transference" was achieved. He looked for the symbols of good and evil, and since for him good and evil were inextricably tied up with sexuality, he looked for the representations of that element. He found few social functions in these cults. They seemed rather to work against solidarity. By conveying to initiates and participants their culture's fundamental religious beliefs they acted to protect against the facts of death and misfortune. Since the natural condition was that men must die for their inevitable sins, so all the Fang cults brought their initiates through some kind of "innoculatory" death in the process of protection. The focus upon death in these cults was shown, Tessmann believed, in the general name for Fang cults, *awume*, in which the radical wu (*awu*, death, to die) was central.[14]

Tessmann pursued the Fang "elemental thought" further. Given that good and bad existed in nature, where in nature did they lie? The Fang, he says, took their answer to this[15] from the natural and orderly oppositions of night and day, moon and sun, earth (water) and heaven (fire), etc. Earth and water and moon and night and men's bodies (*nyôl*) and their soul bodies (*nsisim*, from *si*, earth) were all representations of bad. Fire, sun, and sky were all elements of good. There were, however, four elements ("Grundstoff") which were venerated in the Fang cults: moon, sun, water, and fire. The various cults could thus be talked about as a moon cult (cult of the bad), sun cult (cult of the good), water cult (cult of the bad), etc. These four elemental representations of supernatural powers categorized specific animals and plants that were venerated with them in their cults. These animals and plants often came to stand by association for the elements themselves. Thus the black-backed horned antelope *sôô* (*Cephalophus dorselis*), the only truly night-living West African antelope, came to stand for the moon (horned creatures in any case were associated with the equatorial crescent moon), the elephant stood for water, the gorilla for fire, and the cock for the sun.[16] Tessmann's pursuit of the "Elementargedanken" yielded the following organization of good and bad Fang cults:

BAD	GOOD
Soo—cult of the moon under the image of the antelope	*Ndong Mba*—cult of the sun under the image of the cock
Dzok—cult of the water under the image of the elephant	*Ngi*—cult of fire, under the image of the gorilla

In his description of the Yaounde (Northern Pahouin) Soo cult, Tessmann had little problem with his interpretations. The phallic elements were very obvious. The boys as they were initiated mounted a tree trunk carved with figures of elephants and pigs or snakes, symbols of sexual impurity and the bad. This trunk, often erected projecting from the men's house, represented the erect penis. The accompanying dances represented the sexual act, while the young man emphasized their sexuality by wearing a "penis cap" decorated with the red tail feathers of the African gray parrot.

At one point a goat was killed whose horns represented the moon. It was dismembered in a great melee. The goat was a stand-in for the antelope, and his dismemberment was supposed to represent the silent dying of the moon which disappears piece by piece. The initiates then underwent "death" in the forest after which they were daubed entirely in white clay with the striking exception of the red tail feather of the parrot. "Symbolically," Tessmann tells us, "it is quite clear. White is the color of death, for the moon in its waning phase is white and the bones of the dead are white. The penis cap covers their sexuality and indicates that after death one is sexless." The initiates slept in the forest, the abode of the dead, although they returned to the villages during the day. Gradually after some time in the bush they returned from the dead. This was represented by gradually painting less and less of their bodies in white clay.

The Soo cult among the Ntumu and Fang posed more of a problem for Tessmann because it was integrated with Ndong Mba—thus bad and good, moon and sun, antelope and parrot were intertwined in a more complex way. In Tessmann's day the Ntumu and Fang ceremonies were three days in length, beginning with a long evening dance in which the master of the ceremonies, Ndong Mba, made his appearance. Tessmann found the dance quite sexual in portrayal, leaving little to the imagination. Even less was left in the songs which insulted the sexual parts of the women.[17]

It was during the evening that the masked figure of Soo[18] appeared, followed about by attendants covered with cloth (*bisis*). They crept and crawled in a curious way upon the ground. What shall they represent, asks Tessmann, cats or bats? No, their groveling on the ground appears to him appropriate, for the bad is being celebrated. The masked figure represented the moon and the cloth figures the bad spirits of the dead which were left to wander in the forest after their soul essence had departed. They lunged at the initiaties—several boys aged between six and ten—and grabbed them. They tried to take them away to their kingdom of the bad.

The next day belonged to Ndong Mba.[19] An older man carrying that name came forth without disguise to give the young instruction in their corporeal nature and in their relations to the sun. Tessmann points out that mental disorder (Geisteskrankheit) was regarded differently among the Fang than in Europe. Fang associated it with the vertigo or dizziness produced by standing a long time in the sun. Since mental disorder had this sunstruck quality, it was, he believed, associated with the good. It had a quality of lifting up to the heavens, of initiation into a godlike state. Also, the sun itself going down at sunset shimmers and seems dizzy.

In Tessmann's account Ndong Mba then danced and sang to the assembled village. He demonstrated his soundness of body by grasping each body member firmly; then he fell down in a faint after shaking and twitching. He went to the hut where the initiates were confined and led them out, gesturing to the heavens and in the general direction of the sun. Tessmann could obtain no confirmation from Fang that the sun was being shown, and mid-century inquiry indicates that the object of attention was the giant bird, Ande, to whose imminent arrival the initiates were being alerted. Ndong Mba then sat down with the initiates and sang and played to them on the kazoo. Without giving us the texts, Tessmann says that Ndong Mba was telling the initiates of the dawn and rising of the sun and associating that phenomenon, as a lesson in transference, with their own birth and growth.

Ndong Mba again examined each of his parts and had the initiates imitate him. He showed them how each part awoke as the sun arose and was slowly put together to form the whole body.[20] (In the Soo cult the dismemberment was portrayed.) Then suddenly Ndong Mba shouted "War is come!" and led the initiates in a run out in the forest. They pursued honey, and when it was found the initiates endured the sting of the bees to obtain it. In the forest Ndong Mba was careful to point out the nest of parrots. For during the time when all were sitting around in the courtyard Ndong Mba had imitated the parrot, leaving his nest and climbing by use of his beak far up on a branch to greet the sun. Tessmann had already remarked that the parrot was a creature of the sun. Its gray body from which the red tail feathers thrust was like the rising of the sun in the morning.

For the following two days Tessmann's descriptions parallel those obtained later. On the third day one side of each of the boys' bodies is painted with padouk powder. They are brought to dance back and forth one after another upon the log which is erected from the council house or simply on a support of poles against a wall of bushes. In mounting upon the pole, in any case, their sins were eradicated, for the men sang:[21]

Mon a ne Bebae, Tsea	Child is from Bebae without sin
Mon a na Makomo, Tsea!	Child is from Makomo without truth.
Mon a ne Ebangon, Tsea	Child is from Ebangon.
Tsea, Tsea, Tsea, nge.	Sinless, sinless, sinless, truly.

These references to other villages and clans affirm that the pregnancy was not the result of clan incest but arose from courtship with another clan youth, from Bebae, from Makomo, from Ebangon. At the same time the boy who danced was cleansed. If he danced well the assembled village cheered him. He was then carried off on the shoulders of a man to the council house.

FANG REFLECTIONS ON SOO-NDONG MBA

In later inquiry (among southern Ntumu, Fang, and Okak) informants emphasized that Ndong Mba and Soo (most did not recognize these as distinct cults intertwined) were celebrated to combat misfortune occasioned by incest between brother and sister. The cults purified the village. Since they were held preferably at the end of the long dry season in September just before the major planting of crops, they also acted upon crop fertility. The initiation of the boys, though focal, tended to be secondary in these later accounts. Initiation depended upon which boys were available when a pregnancy occurred that needed purifying.

The first night of the ceremonies was remembered much as Tessmann describes it. The initiates were warned that they would suffer and might die. They were isolated, naked, in the men's council house. The shadow figures (*bisis*), the night antelope (*sô, Cephalophus castaneus*), and masked man all came forth. No mention of the moon was made or could be elicited.

On the second day the tree trunk was carried into the village and set up projecting from the men's council house. But instead of sitting down with the initiates, Ndong Mba led the men over to the kitchens where the women were all shut in. Beating against the walls they demanded the girls who had sinned with their brothers. The pregnant girl or a girl suspected of nsem was thrust forward. She was taken to the council house and put under or astride the log. The boy initiate straddled the log either directly above her or within the council house where he could not be seen. Accusations were directed against the girl. Finally a purifying mixture of herbs and leaves was poured first over the boy and then over the girl. The girl was returned to the kitchen. One side of the boy's body was painted with white kaolin clay and he was asked to dance first upon the trunk. Then he was returned to the council house. After the initiate had danced, the women carefully swept up refuse in the courtyard and kitchen and deposited it in a corner of the village.

On the dawn of the third day the leader of the Ndong Mba ceremony came and blessed the village. He blessed the men's council house by ritually anointing the principal supporting pole (*akôn aba*). The refuse gathered by the women was thrown into the bush, after which they retired to the cooking huts. Each initiate was then brought out accompanied by an adult and began a period of endurance tests under the hot sun. They were warned that a giant bird, Ande, would come out of the sky to attack them, and occasionally the adults looked into the sky and warned them. After this the initiate was flogged with branches, caused to crawl through a miniature hut full of biting ants, and forced to eat offal. Finally, each initiate mounted again upon the log and danced to rapid drumming. In an effort to make him fall he was distracted by warning about the coming of the bird from the sky. After these dances the log was removed and thrown on top of the other refuse.

On the fourth day before dawn the initiate was taken to the edge of the bush, given a bamboo shoot, and told to follow a narrow path and to spear the first animal he saw. All around him in the bush he heard the menacing sounds, made by village elders. At a turn in the path the initiate saw, by dawn light, a portion of banana trunk set upon wooden legs simulating a gazelle, at which he threw his spear. Immediately the men rushed out of the bush and seized him, dragging him through a pit of mud, leaves, and urine. This pit was located in a small clearing in the forest along with mounds of earth sculptured to represent snakes, pigs, and elephants. They threw him face down while Ande, screeching in a falsetto voice, straddled him and with a small knife made three incisions on the back of his neck (*bewu*, "the marks of death"), rubbing mud into them. Finally padouk powder was dusted on the left side of the boy's body and the ordeal was over. The initiate had to spend another night in the hut away from the view of women. On the fifth day he was taken down to the stream and washed.

The fourth day, in Tessmann's view, was held under the sign of the bad. It took place in the very early dawn and the initiates, he felt, did not rise above their sins but were, literally, swamped in them. It was not life which was celebrated, and the good things of sky and atmosphere, but death. The initiate descended among the crawling things of mud and earth. But this interpretation was difficult to confirm. Contemporary Fang focused on the problem of incest and the purification obtained in Soo Ndong Mba. If the initiate was brought through the swamps he was also finally washed at the river.

AN EMERGENT AND PRAGMATIC INTERPRETATION

Whatever the direction of Tessmann's interpretation, his account is detailed and may be usefully combined with more recent views. It is now recognized that mythology is best understood when all available variants are studied. In the same way culture may perhaps be best understood in the interaction of variant interpretations of it—each a selection out of a richer set of images. One might argue, indeed, that culture is a repository or inventory of images and ideas, selections of which are taken up and given a narrative form, whether as myth or as an interpretation of a culture. This underlying inventory or wider set of images may well be available to those who create new religious movements in their acts of narrative composition. Bwitists, for example, can be aware of a range of issues probed in one of their oldest ritual complexes, Soo Ndong Mba, without having seen all of these issues explored in any given instance in a particular village. The ethnographer ought to have the same awareness.

Thus there is much in Tessmann that justifies treating his interpretations, even though they may appear forced and are hard to confirm. For while some of his interpretations tell us more about his reading of the Solar Mythologists of his day and his fascination with the "elementary thought" approach, yet his work resonates, both in general and specific terms, with some of the liturgical formulations to be found in Bwiti. For example, the sun and the moon are regularly figured in Bwiti and often divide the chapel into spheres of influence. The moon, however, becomes the good and propitious orb while the sun is the orb of death and destruction—of negation. The painting of participants and cult objects half white and half red is also present in Bwiti, as is a tendency to focus upon elementary images, fire and water for example, and to expand them in various cosmogonic ways into an overarching sense of order. Indeed, animals and plants come by synecdochic association to stand for the elements themselves. One animal, the African gray parrot, and one plant, the red-trunked azap tree, have become leitmotifs of the religion.

More generally, though the resolution of the existential problem of the relation of the good and the bad is not a marked concern in Bwiti, one of its central problems is the relation of life to death. And the Banzie might well agree to speak of these as the kingdom of the good and the bad. Banzie seek to overcome the unwelcome contradiction between the living and the dead by ritually passing over to the land of the dead where, paradoxically, the dead become the living and the living, the Banzie, become the dead. By "dying" while living out their most lively performances, men and women are made stoic about death which is, for Banzie as for Tessmann's Fang, a chief focus of attention. Finally, where Tessmann speaks of the resolution by transference of good and evil over upon nature, we should rather speak of the use of nature and natural analogies to make more concrete and graspable—and thus resolvable— what is inchoate in human experience and human relationships. What Tessmann seems really to have been talking about is the use of nature to bring about order and organization in Fang society and culture. Here he insightfully anticipates subsequent anthropological views on the use of nature to organize culture.[22] In Bwiti as in Soo Ndong Mba nature is a macrocosm by which the human microcosm, and particularly the human body, can be put together.

Despite his intellectual predilections, then, Tessmann lived long enough with Fang to be well attuned to those processes of analogic reasoning by which they tied their world together. He knew their associations. Notice him as he explains a song which has appeared in Soo Ndong Mba and in which a kola nut is mentioned.[23] The refrain of the song goes, "Hemisphere of the heavens like the kernel of the kola nut." Tessmann recognizes that the kola nut, which is pinkish red, appears like the half-risen or half-sunken sun. It is the same kind of association that is made between the horns of the antelope and the crescent moon. That the kola nut can stand for the sun, he points out, is seen in the proverb, "Will I die lost in obscurity when there is a kola nut in the shoulder basket" (*Ye ma wu ndzime, aba a mfak*). Kola nut refers here to the tools with which fire is made. Kola nut stands for the sun in small. Very close observation of the details of Fang life, then, underlies Tessmann's accounts. Such observation is important because it is this detail that is taken up and reworked in imaginative acts of cultural creation such as Bwiti, even though mid-century Fang, in situations of ethnographic inquiry and at the point of a question, did not recall much of it. They focus rather upon the thematic preoccupations with incest and purification that were embodied in the cult. Such detail lives in performance and not usually in question-and-answer sessions. It is better recalled when new performances have to be created out of preoccupations with purity and efficacy. Such preoccupations energize fabulation and provide narrative structures with apt images from the past.

This later, more restricted or thematic interpretive commentary is helpful, however, because it enables us to identify enduring themes in Fang culture and to identify Tessmann's own particular preoccupations. He saw the problem of good and bad in sexuality generally, whereas it is more accurate to say that Fang were concerned not with sexuality as such but with one uncontrolled form of it, incest, and the impact of this on the access to the flow of ancestral protection and benevolence.

BIERI: THE RECIPROCAL FLOW
OF PROTECTIVE BENEVOLENCE AND HONOR

CLEARING THE LINES TO THE ANCESTORS

The ancestor cult (*Bieri*) sought to assure the flow of ancestral protection and benevolence and put the uninitiated, *abin*, into effective contact with the shades of the dead (*kôn, bekôn*).[24] They maintained the lineage and the village under their benevolent tutelage. Ritual gestures were periodically necessary, for the dead had two wayward tendencies. They became preoccupied with their own affairs in the village of the dead, or they manifested themselves in uncontrolled ways. The dead should naturally feel a protective benevolence toward the living. At the same time they may be jealous of them. They might resent the living who might have hurried them on their way to the grave. Thus they might afflict the living with disease or even kill them by calling them to the land of the dead. The dead rejoiced when someone died (*nge mot a wu, bekôn be yen mve*). The ancestor cult dealt with these uncertain attitudes of the dead and tried to stabilize them around their most desirable expression, protective benevolence and maintenance of oneheartedness in the living. In Bieri, then, Fang dealt with the unseen (*engang*)[25] in the interest of increasing benevolence (or *nlem mvé*, goodheartedness) and mitigating malevolence (*nlem abé*, badheartedness). The Bieri elder (*ngômalan*) was concerned to make contact with hidden things (*asok engang*) because the ancestors were hidden and not palpable in the light of day.

Fang referred broadly to the practice of the ancestor cult as *biang* (substances and techniques having to do with the gaining of capacity over unseen forces). The carved figure that sat on top of the reliquary was the child of medicine (*mwan biang*). The relations established with the ancestors could thus appear manipulative, with the dead frequently called sharply to account for their neglect of the living. Tessmann argued that the ancestor cult was just that:[26] another kind of magical technique (biang). There was little piety or even respect for possible ancestral vengeance. In Tessmann's view, the ancestors were coerced by imprecations, solitary confinement, or even purposeful neglect. Such treatment was then pointedly reversed with gifts of food, following which the bekon were pointedly reminded of their reciprocal responsibilities.

But there were deeper lessons in Bieri than that of simple coercion of the dead. Joking with the dead was not necessarily a sign of disrespect. Having essentially the status of grandfather (*mvama*) they participated in that joking relationship that arose with the cult members, their grandchildren. That they were sometimes treated as children was compatible with the turnover of influence and readiness for role reversal in authority relationships that we have discussed. Fang fathers often called their infant sons *ata* (the familiar form of father). This custom indicated a belief that a man's ancestors could re-create themselves in his offspring. At the least it was congruent with the fact that as men grow old their sons must care for them, as they once cared for their sons. It was one of the "saving circularities" of Fang life.

Whatever the views on transubstantiation there was a strong association between ancestors and infants—between ancestry and infancy as it were. This was appropriate since one of the prime responsibilities of the ancestor cult was to maintain the fertility of the kin-group. This association was visually represented in the carved ancestor figures which combined the awesomeness of age together with an infantileness of proportion.[27] This paradoxical combination of respect for age and indulgent paternalism toward the aged was represented in cult activity, and was seen in both the awe with which the craniums were looked upon and the paternal indulgence with which the reliquary was treated once the craniums were nested within it. The cranium was taken up and cradled in the arms of the ngomalan. He rocked it and sang to it, particularly during his trips back and forth from the sacred precincts of the cult. The song was almost a lullaby:

Bekeh be Ningwan[28]	Bekeh be Ningwan
Azak yen misuk mi bieng!	Come see the containers of medicine
A ne ne	There it is
O Yô Yôlô Yôôô!	Yoo Yolo Yoo
Ehhhh (explosive)	Ahh!
A Baa Sôôôô![29]	The fathers come!
Tege! Ebiang tara lige!	Look the medicine father left.
Ohhh	Ohhh
A Ba Sôôôô!	The father comes!

Obunu, who demonstrated the entrance and sang the song, remarked, ''The Bieri comes softly, unlike Ngi who comes with a rush, cruelly, fiercely shouting, wounding and killing people!''

Bieri, then, though concerned with clearing the lines of communication between ancestors and men so that a protective benevolence could flow along them, demonstrates that the flow goes both ways. In a sense this identification of ancestry and infancy establishes an ultimate communication. The protective benevolence was circular, reciprocal. For their part, the ancestors had need of the honor (awume) done them. The dead had need of the vitality of the living.

One asks how the image ''clearing the lines'' related to Fang representations. The metaphor of the ancestral line may be a convention of ethnographic inquiry, embedded in the analytic notion of lineage organization. The Fang conception was of men and women attached to their ancestors and ultimately to God himself (Zame ye Mebege) by a string of umbilical cords and male organs. This was the meaning of ''showing oneself naked.'' For the father showed the son whence he came and suggested in so doing that he would choke him off from the seminal flow of benefits that derived from that tutelary string into which were tied all the names of the genealogy. This line of ancestral beings was thus represented in its essential parts, cords and organs, the perpetuating parts of its continuity. These body images made concrete and corporeal the abstraction of lineal descent.

This incorporation was also seen in the ''lifting of the malediction'' (*ava miteng*). Its literal meaning of ''removing the saliva'' derived from the view that the father, rather than spitting out and ridding himself of his distaste for his son's actions, had swallowed the saliva and thereby poisoned his body against his son. This blocked the son off from the protective benevolence that should come down through that body to him. He was left without support or protection and an easy victim of malevolence. The dead, like living elders, could act in the same way to impede the flow of that protection.

A positive form of blessing, *abora*, employed by elders to youngers was accompanied by the expression "rest always well" (*mbembe ntôô ntôô* [N], or *seseghe ntô entô* [F]). The elder blew upon his cupped hands and pressed them directly upon the recipient's body or upon his head. There was a direct passing of the blessing from body to body—the ultimate realization of the meaning of lineage membership. The blessing prevented the unlucky state called bad body (*nyôl abé*) or dark body (*nyôl envin*). Behind the abstractions of lineage descent and genealogy, then, were corporeal facts in which those abstractions were embodied. As one recited genealogy, the vulnerable and unprotected body of the individual was incorporated into a larger body. Ancestor cult was fundamentally the rejuvenating interaction between microcosm and macrocosm.

THE SACRA OF THE CULT: SIGNIFICANT IMAGES

Ancestor cult was also a relating of opposites. This was seen in the sacra of the cult. Bieri rituals were of two kinds: the initiation of new members and the reestablishment of ancestral benevolence in village affairs. The first was called *adzi malan* or *aku malan* (the eating of malan, or the falling under the influence of malan). The second was called variously *akôm adzal, akôm Bieri*, or *akulu malan* (the preparation and strengthening of the village, or of Bieri, or the coming forth of malan). The sacra around which these rituals were organized were the craniums of the lineage ancestors and the reliquary figures. The craniums were kept in a bark drum (*nsuk Bieri*) found at the corner of the bedchamber of the *ntôlomot*. The reliquary figures, called "child of medicine" (*mwan biang*) or simply the Bieri figure (*eyima Bieri*), were set on top of the bark drums to warn away women and children and to provide focus for periodic offerings of food.

Fang said that every council house has its own reliquary. One never took the skull of one who had not sat in one's council house and with whom one was not in good relation. Such a cranium would be untrustworthy and self-interested (*alet*).[30] On the average each reliquary contained eight to ten skulls, the number normally assembled over several generations by an integrated ndebot. Craniums, like the ancestors they represented, lost their identity and their power after several generations and were buried again. Fang did not negotiate with all the ancestors on a corporate basis but as far as possible with particular ones about whom something was known.

The scale of the ancestor cult as represented in its collection of craniums was a replication of the scale of solidarities that prevailed in the social structure. When the minor lineages split apart they also split the reliquary. On the other hand, the reliquary collection acted to keep the kin-group together by representing its solidarity in the unseen.

European attachment to saints' statues led to the notion that the reliquary figures were powerful in themselves. But only in recent years, after the decline of the ancestor cult and when pieces of cranium were buried in the figures, were they invested with power. The statues were part of the dramatic enactment of the ancestor cult but were not the objects of expectant adoration. In their austere yet penetrating gaze, in their unelaborated simplicity and dynamic symmetry, and in their striking combination of age and infancy they presented fundamental truths. They were significant images which associated the responsibility of mature men and the ancestors to guarantee vitality and prevent chaos by holding opposites in balance.[31]

This same significance inhered in the cranium itself, for it was taught that the maturing cranium was gradually knit together at the cranial suture as a man knits his fingers together. Thus the cranium held the two sides of the person together—the *efa mayôm* (the male or sperm side) and the *efa meyal* (the female or blood side). A headache was really a sign of the two sides of a person in conflict. Fang locked their fingers together and strained them back and forth. A child, they taught, had a hole in his head, *ndagba*, where one could see the heart beating. But the older he got the more the two sides were knit together. Wisdom came with that knitting together.[32]

These observations conform to Fang physiological philosophy,[*1] particularly to the belief that mature men held opposites in balance. The configuration of the cranium was compatible with that deeper reference to the essence of maturity. But the cranium had additional significance. The brain and cranium which composed the head were thought to be the first elements created during the growth of the child in the womb. They were both white elements and therefore associated with the male sperm as an essential expression of it. The craniums, therefore, were an enduring relic or concretion, as it were, of the essence of patrilineality. In coming into proper relationship to them one came into relation with the capacity inherent in clan and lineage membership. The brain was also the organ of effort and willfulness. The choice of the cranium as the object of devotion was congruent with the main purpose of the cult. For the protective benevolence extended by the ancestors gave capacity to obtain fulfilment in life.

Fang explanations of these matters were often not so detailed. Many were content to say with the practical-minded Ngema, "If we had the bones of our ancestors they could not entirely leave us and go off to the village of the dead.

[*1] The temptation to dogmatize this philosophy is again to be avoided. Fang, with a speculative temperament, took different approaches to the main principles involved: male and female sidedness, the nature of maturity in a situation of almost constant family conflict. Some Fang, unlike Essono, used as a point of departure for their speculations the idiomatic observation that when a child was wise enough to run errands and converse sensibly, "his heart has descended into his stomach"—(*nlem o nto abum*). Behind this idiom lay the view that when a child was born the heart was in his head. This view rose in turn from the belief that in both mythical phylogeny and individual ontogeny, a headlike mass, kigile, was created first and all other parts of the body were added to it. In any case, early in life the infant and child were confused in the actions of heart and brain—willfullness and thoughtfulness were confused. Eventually the heart fully descended into its appropriate and complementary position, the chest (nkuk) or the stomach (abum), where it could act in concert with the head and, more particularly, the brain (boo), and not at cross purposes.

The bones kept the dead interested in us.'' Nevertheless there was more significance to the sacra than that. They were images of the capacity to hold opposites in balance.

For example, though the ancestor cult was predominantly a male activity, the reliquary figures were often female. Why? Tessmann remarks the presence of several women in the cult he observed[33] and credits it to accident or curiosity. The women had inadvertently looked upon the craniums and had to be initiated to protect them against ancestral wrath. But since the reliquary itself could carry the name of a woman, accident alone does not explain their presence. The explanation lies rather in recognition of service to the lineage, and beyond that in recognition of the paradox of patrilineality. For despite its exaltation of maleness, the patrilineage depended upon women for pro-creation. That paradoxical dependence was often recognized in ancestor cult. The craniums of women (called *nyiabiang*, mothers of medicine) who had made outstanding contributions to the lineage by number of living children, by hard work, and by force of personality could be included, a balancing recognition that the perdurance of the lineage was not a product of men's activity alone.

Deep lessons, then, reposed in the sacra—the reliquary figures and the craniums. They bodied forth the nature of ''capacity'' and they struggled with paradox. These lessons were more powerfully contained in the craniums for, unlike the figures, one could be brought to a mortal illness by looking upon them. The craniums, and the ancestors they represented, were the mysteries themselves. The ancestor figure was only their simulacrum, just as men's visible bodies were only the tangible representation of deeper mysteries they contained. The ancestor cult was not only a putting of initiates into contact with ''protective benevolence,'' it was, as well, an opening up to deeper lessons of human capacity. These were mysteries of both the internal and external world. As the reliquary was opened up, eviscerated, and the craniums displayed, so would the initiate find his corporeal self opened up and its panoply of elements—blood, sinew, and bone—displayed and comprehended. As the ceremony took place in a forest arena which was external to the village, so he would be opened up to realms in which relevant forces other than those of village life were present. In Bwiti, as in these sacra, we will see a knitting together or at least a balancing of opposites. We will see a continuing preoc-cupation with the paradox of women's place. We will see a continuing search for the plenipotentiary self that lies both within and exterior to the visible body.

PROCESSES OF INITIATION:
SELF TRANSFORMED INTO COMMUNITY

Initiates into the ancestor cult were usually young married men who had need, by the fact of their marriage and its potential responsibilities, of ancestral surveillance. The impetus to initiation might be a spell of misfortune (*abwia*), but the fact of marriage promised children for the patrilineage and hence a need on the part of a prospective progenitor to come to terms with those for whom he was now to be an extension. Initiation might occur even though there was no new cranium available to contribute to the reliquary. But often enough an influential "father" would have died not long before. The young initiate was then brought into the cult together with that respect-laden relic, a guarantee of his domestic well-being.

Initiation involved falling "dead," senseless, under the influence of the rasped root bark of the *alan* bush (*Alchornea floribunda*), an alkaloid with a moderate effect on the central nervous system.[34] Prior to the initiation a forest enclosure was prepared (*ngun Bieri*) with a forechamber and a hidden afterchamber.[35] The reliquary was taken out to this enclosure and the craniums were lined up, in the middle chamber, upon a platform of banana trunks (Figure 10.1). Depending upon the social solidarities of the moment, as many as three or four ndebot might participate together with their reliquaries. Meanwhile in the village the initiate sat down upon a banana tree trunk in the courtyard. He had fasted and had no sexual congress during the preceding day. As he ate the alan root villagers danced around him to the company of drums, xylophones, and harps. They bent over him and shouted in his ear. This rhythmical activity acted to mesmerize him as much as the drug itself.

The songs of this phase were in effect, funeral songs, for they anticipated the "death" of the initiate. A song of emotional power given by Trilles as a funeral song[36] was characteristic of the early phase of malan, particularly if a new cranium was being "shown" to the reliquary. Ayang Ndong gave the following version of this song.

Ô tara, ye, ye wa kura zi	Oh father when you abandon the hearth
Nsisim ô ke lot efa ayat	Your spirit passes to the other side
Ô tara, wa kura zi, akal ze, tara	Oh father, why do you leave the hearth
Dzôp da yen ndendang, mis me vineang	The sky clears but the eyes darken
Medzim me sugla ele eyô, efo za kuang	The water drops from the tree, the hollow seed shells fall
Ta! Nda tara	Look at the "house" which was our father
Akolga bilok	Gather the medicinal herbs
Efa meyom, efa meyal	[Sprinkle them] to the right side and to the left side
Fam a yen minsobe	A man now sees hidden things.

The hearth referred to is both the fire which burns within a man's own being, giving it vitality, as well as the fire of the hearth. This association is strength-

10.1 Forest Precincts of the Fana Ancestor Cult (Bieri) and Display of Craniums

ened by the phrase, "Look at the house which was our father," and it accords
with the microcosm, macrocosm identification which has frequently emerged
here. That fire, it is said, goes out of the eyes and they darken, but they
impart their former brightness to the sky. Trilles argued that Fang take life as
a flame that lights the eyes and when life departs that light is transferred to
the atmosphere giving it its brightness. I could obtain no such account from
Fang. But the Banzie of Bwiti say the stars are the souls of men and that
falling stars indicate a birth, or a taking up of residence of the fire of life in
a new being. When a person dies, his fire goes back to heaven, a return to
an older idea explored by Trilles.

The reference in this funeral song to the water dropping from the trees is
an allusion to the misty dawn in the humid equatorial forest when the spirits
are most actively returning to their abode. This kind of dewdrop imagery is
recurrent and we shall see it in a Bwiti sermon. Spirit departure is also implied,
for the image connotes the flight of a large bird (the soul) out of the tree (the
bodily superstructure) where it has been perched. The flight shakes the dew
from the leaves. The *efo* (the nut of the *ewomi* tree, *Coula edulis*) was most
often found as a shell-casing rather than as the nut entire, which was distressing
because the nut is almondlike and quite edible. This is another reference to
spirit departure seen as the departure of a vital substance which leaves a shell.
The sprinkling about of medicinal herbs was characteristic of Bieri rites. But
it should be pointed out that in Fang parlance this was literally a sprinkling
to the right side which was the "side of the male" or the "side of sperm,"
and to the left side, the "side of the female," or the "side of the blood."
This spatial differentiation by sex is carried pronouncedly into Bwiti.

As these songs of death and desolation were sung to pulsing accompaniment
the Bieri initiate consumed malan. A piece of cranium from the reliquary
placed in a cavity dug in the banana tree trunk on which he was seated caused
the initiate to lose consciousness before he consumed a toxic dose of the
narcotic plant. To this same purpose a member of the ancestor cult was
assigned to watch over him as his *essamalan*, his father of malan. This
guardian rubbed his back and massaged his arms and shoulders so that the
malan would work upon his whole body and not only settle in his heart.
Finally, when the initiate seemed on the verge of collapse he was tapped on
the chest with a bark wand containing medicine. To wipe "the last light"
from his eyes, a feather dipped in a mixture of the latex from the *ayang* bush
(also *ayang beyem*, *Elaeophorbia drusipere*) and oil was rubbed across the
eye. This had a painful, burning effect and, acting on the optical nerve,
produced bizarre visual impressions and a sense of dissociation.[37] The initiate
collapsed shortly afterward. The ancestors had taken him up the road of
death.[38] He was then carried out into the forest to the outer chamber of the
forest precinct, accompanied by the simple chant *A ba soo*! (the fathers come
again).

The initiate was laid upon a mat and his face was washed with an infusion of medicinal herbs. If there was concern that he had eaten too much malan, a scourge of branches was prepared and dipped into a basin hollowed in the earth and lined with leaves. The initiate was whipped on his body until the point of revival. This moment was feared for it was said that many die, taken permanently by the ancestors to the land of the dead never to return or, not welcomed by the ancestors, left to wander as malevolent shades in the forest. The villagers thus waited anxiously for the sounds of the forest drum. It would tell them whether the initiate had recovered his life or not.

Folk wisdom also dictated that a "complicated man" (Fang often used the French *homme complique* to translate *nem beyem*, that is, those with an aggressive demon evus) took much longer to "die." Since the evus was an egotistic principle generally attended by secretive self-serving, it was resistant to and a contaminant of the communal principle on which the ancestor cult was based. By reducing men to senselessness they were purified because in that state they ceased complicated preoccupation with themselves. Until a man had "died" one could not be sure that his sins had left him. Unless he was "brought low" in this way, his self-interest, his hardheartedness (*nlem alet*) would make him impervious to the influences of the ancestors. This emphasis is seen in the Bieri song recorded by Trilles[39] in which both the initiate who sings the solo and the mingomalan who respond as the choir recognize the softening of the heart and the humbling effect of eating malan. Here are the pertinent verses:

INITIATE: *Me mana kom nlem wum*   I have finished disposing my heart
    mbeng. Me mana kom.   well.
CHOIR: *A mana kom nlem wé*   He has well disposed it. He has
    mbeng. A mana kom.   finished preparing himself.
INITIATE: *Dighe, me ne nsil Dighe,* Look, I am humbled (brought low).
    ka nlem alet.   Look, no (longer) the hard heart.
CHOIR: *Dighe, bia ne nsil Dighe,*   Look, we are humbled.
    ka nlem alet.   Look, no hard heart.

This emphasis on a well-disposed heart is called "oneheartedness" in Bwiti. The religion likewise emphasizes "communing"—the abandonment of "egocentrism" to the community interest.

COMMUNING WITH THE ANCESTORS

When Fang were asked why it was necessary to eat malan and "die" they responded similarly to Ayang Ndong who said, "The ancestors being dead and on the other side can accomplish the miracles (*akyunge*) of things unseen. Men who join the ancestor cult should die and know something of that akyunge. They should have their heads opened (*akwia nlô*) so that they can stand between (*ntôbô ezizang*) the life of the village and the life of the ancestors." It was clear that though Fang used the term *awu* (to die) they did not mean it in the physiological, irreversible sense. One died in stages, and the apparent cessation of bodily functions was only the first stage—a cessation accomplished by the consumption of malan. As the shade (*kôn*) passed over to the land of the dead in stages it was more than a year after the halting of bodily functions and after mortuary ceremonies that villagers could be assured that the recently deceased were finally separated as the dead. In a malan ceremony properly conducted the initiate did not lose the kon. He made only half the trip to the land of the dead. But having made that, he could, thereafter, continue to make contact with the ancestors.

Accounts differ as to whether men had important dreams and visions under the influence of the malan itself. Some said men saw their ancestors in their "death." But others said that nothing was seen. Most agreed, however, that the evening after the ceremony one expected to receive signs (*ndem*) from the ancestors. The newly initiated slept with the bark barrel containing the craniums at the head of their beds. The cult members anxiously queried the initiate the next morning. Did he dream the death of someone? Did he dream he was wandering cold and alone in the forest? These were bad signs (*ndem abé*). Did he dream of the killing of an animal, of a marriage festival, of eating in the council house? These were good signs. They affirmed the benevolent intention of the ancestors and particularly of "his" ancestor.

But we get ahead of the events themselves. While the initiate was recovering in the front chamber of the forest precinct the members were refortifying the craniums. A sheep and a chicken were sacrificed and their blood was poured into another basin of banana leaves in which the bark of several powerful trees, the head of a viper (*Bitis gabonica*) and boiling water were mixed. The craniums were washed in this mixture and set upon the banana stem platform in a row. The new cranium, if such was present, was washed last and placed in front of the others. The cult members began to dance in circles before the skulls and around them. Occasionally they would pick them up and dance with them held low over the ground, as pictured by Tessmann.[40] The skulls came from the ground. It was an impertinence for man to raise them high.

The initiate, now revived, was taken down to the stream to be washed carefully.[41] It was forbidden to appear before the Bieri covered with dirt and perspiration. When the initiate was clean, Ayang Ndong related, the essamalan applied the red padouk powder to one side of his body, the left side, and raffia palm oil (*mbon djuing*) to his other side. The palm oil signified cleanliness and the padouk powder joyfulness at his recovery. These were the same substances applied to clean the reliquary figure, thus making another association between the initiate's body and the accessory paraphernalia of the reliquary—the barrel and the ancestor figure.

In the hidden chamber of the cult precincts the skulls were packed into the barrels and the members, in the company of the initiate, danced into the village holding the reliquaries in their arms. Once again they sang, "Fathers have come." The barrels were taken to their respective chambers, with the exception of that of the initiate's own family. It was placed at the head of his bed. The "medicine child" stared down upon him. He prepared for his dreams and for an ancestral message. As a concluding act, the elder of his ndebot made a departing prayer before the reliquary.*2

THE PREPARATION OF THE VILLAGE

On the second day the initiate was shown the skulls of the ancestors and passed from his state of ignorance (*ebin*) to a state of newly acquired secret knowledge (*mvon*). When his dreams had been interpreted he was taken once again to the forest clearing. Already the reliquaries had been brought out and the skulls set in their rows, but screened from view. Before the craniums were shown, the reliquary figures appeared over the barrier in the clearing, while voices from behind threateningly demanded the initiate's name, his genealogy and what he had dreamed.[42] There were various ways the craniums could be shown to the initiate. Ayang Ndong told us that the men of clan Essisis sat the initiate upon the ground so that his back was to the hidden arena of the clearing. A mirror was placed before him on the ground. He was told to stare into it. The mirror was then gradually shifted so that the skulls on the banana trunk came into view behind the parted barrier. Obunu says the initiate stood before the raffia curtain, which was whisked away revealing the skulls. In either case, the object was to startle the initiate with the "miracle of the craniums" (*akyenge minkukweng*). The man has never before seen the craniums of his relatives. It would be a shock to him. The initiate was then queried following the formula noted by Trilles.[43]

Dzam ete, ba le dzo na ze!	And this what is it called?
Me a yim.	I do not know.
Me ke yegele wé. Melô.	I will teach you. Be attentive.
Melô.	I am attentive (lit. "ears").
Dzam eté a mbe ôsu, etô a ne,	This thing was in the past. It is and
dzam eté a ke tobo.	it will be.

*2 Ayang Ndong gives the following common prayer of the ntolomot before the reliquary. "*Betara ya bimvama me zo mine na . . . mine mi nga lik me azal. Edô zal te e ntô envin. Ka tzit, ka bwan, ka mimbôm! Me vora zia ka mina va. Edo ma so bier abon di bekubn ye mitam. Me zo mine naj mi ve me abore abui amu azal e wulu mbung!*" The prayer has that contractural coerciveness of early Old Testament prophecy. "Father and grandfathers I tell you now. You left me the village. But that village is dark—no game, no children, no brides brought here. I am tired of counting the ways you have not given [from your side of the agreement—zia, to calculate, used primarily in respect to marriage payments]. But now I bring you (an offering of) sheep and cooked food. I tell you to give me much blessing so that the village will go well. You must tell me what I must do that the village will go well."

In this way the instruction of the initiate was begun as to the family identity of the various crania, and preparation was made for the recitation of the genealogy in relation to the skulls. "This is your grandfather," it was said. "You will work together (*wa seng nye*) and you will care for each other. When you go on a journey bid him farewell. And ask his blessing. When you kill an antelope give him the best part. Do not let the woman touch it. Keep him clean. Come to him from time to time and wash him."[44]

Tessmann was not impressed with the gravity of these instructions nor with the accuracy with which the skulls were identified,[45] but he appears to have attended rituals already in decline. The songs which Trilles preserved testify to a more profound religious quest for solace and understanding. The cult may have seemed to Tessmann crassly coercive and too devoted to amusement. But the following song[46] was sung when the skulls were displayed to the initiate, and it testifies to deeper concerns with "ultimate things" within the cult:

Weni, Esa, wa yem dia awu	You, Father, who knows not death
Wa tôbô ka yemeyem awu,	Who rests impervious to death,
Wa nying ka yeme fe ening.	You live on, knowing life no longer.
Ka wok avô, ka wok ôyô	You feel no cold, no sleepiness
Ebô bia da man sô va.	Your people have come to you here.
Ba sulan esama wé.	They assemble themselves your group.
O ke ve bia eki zia, weni, Esa.	O give to us your capacity, you, Father.
O ke tobo né bot bwé né nsisim.	O remain to share with the people your spirit.
Weni, Esa, wa yem ka yem awu.	You, Father, you do not know death.
Weni, Esa ayong die.	You, Father of our clan.

The concluding events of the third day led Tessmann to his low opinions of Bieri, for they included a kind of puppet show; the carved ancestor figures were shown, often to the whole village, above the raffia barrier. They danced and frolicked and embraced one another, and if male and female statues were involved they engaged in mock intercourse. They leaned over, and with those brass eyes characteristic of many Fang figures, gazed down piercingly upon the villagers. They disappeared and reappeared in company to the drum and the xylophone. They listened to the appeal of the villagers and threw sticks and stones at them from behind the barrier. There was considerable hilarity.

But it was intended primarily as a grace note and relaxation from the previous engagement with death.

When this show was over the ceremonies were concluded. Single file again the membership of the ancestor cult marched into the village singing "A Baa Sô!" The reliquaries were again cradled in their arms. Now, however, the reliquaries were placed in front of their respective council houses. Persons, weapons, animals, tools, seed, anything in need of blessing, were laid before them. Now that the ancestors' interest in their former villages had been reawakened, they were ready benevolently to prepare the village (protect by constructive action, *akôm adzal*). As for the initiate, he had further obligations before becoming a full member of the cult. He had to go out and kill an antelope and lay the choice parts before the reliquary. But he did not again have to eat malan, nor attempt the "road of death" until his own demise. The villagers, in final place, hold a dance of rejoicing for which the women prepared much food. These final moments, like the final early morning moments in the Bwiti religion, were moments of high euphoria—of collective sentiments of solidarity.

THE BREAKUP OF THE RELIQUARY AND
THE COLLAPSE OF THE CULT

Fang were quite emphatic that the ancestors were invoked for the good of the entire cult-group—at the least for the entire ndebot if not the mvogabot. Attempts to appeal to the ancestors for personal needs were considered an abuse of the cult. Initiation into the cult intended to purify by softening and opening up the heart to other than its ("complicated") purposes. The very presentation of the reliquary itself suggested the values of social solidarity. For the ancestor skulls rested tightly accommodated within the confines of the reliquary. As the ancestors were thus bound together so ought their descendents remain united in order to obtain their protective benevolence. In a society such as Fang, where there was no political hierarchy of any significance, there was a tendency to be suspicious of the strong and to take precautions against them. One set of precautions was found in the antiwitchcraft institutions. Another precaution against personal aggrandizement was found in this emphasis in Bieri upon an "uncomplicated" protective benevolence in the interests of the patrilineage. One aspect of the apotheosis of evil lay in the fact that, as the ancestor cult collapsed or was supressed, the bones in the reliquary were sequestered by individuals for individual purposes.

Fang, playing on words, said that the *nkuk* had replaced the *nsuk*. The craniums which had been maintained as a group for collective purposes passed into individual hands. To protect against missionary or administrative expropriation, pieces of cranium were introduced into the ancestor figures. Very small reliquaries were constructed to be hidden in dark corners. Attention to these was called nkuk.

But this brought crucial changes. In the process of Bieri ritual an identification was established between the reliquary and the body of the initiate.
By means of this association, the ritual evisceration of the reliquary taught
that at the heart of his matter, so to speak, lay the craniums—the concretions
of the perduring patrilineal element in human experience. The Bieri cult was
directed toward the head as its revelatory principle. This was the principle
of will and endurance and protective benevolence which lay in the lineage
itself. In the increasingly private use of the bones there was a shift toward
preoccupation with matters of the nkuk—of the chest and of the thinking,
calculating heart that inhabited it. This was a shift away from an emphasis
upon the enduring ''headfelt'' lineal principle of allegiance to a preoccupation
with the ''complicated heart-thought'' matters of interfamily resentment and
struggle. The personal obeisances of nkuk dealt with the ancestor spirits, not
in the spirit of communing with them the better to face ultimate circumstances—above all the fact of death itself—but compulsively, compelling
them and controlling them for purposes of personal protection and acquisitiveness.

Already in his time Tessmann noted an affliction of inimical supernatural
powers promoting selfish and aggrandizing purposes in Fang life. For him it
was the task of the colonial mission to rescue the African from the vicious
circle of witchcraft. He ignored the degree to which the colonial situation had
created the condition. Tessmann was led to speak of Fang existence as a
''Kämpfen des Lebens,'' a battle of survival.[47] But the main thrust of the
Bieri cult was against the development of excessive antisocial forces in Fang
affairs. In the decline of the cult these forces grew in aggravated measure,
and it cannot be doubted that Fang were well aware of their affliction and
that the Bwiti religion was a response to it.

Conclusion: The Fathers Departed— The Inertia of Their Descendants

Had the cults of Ndong Mba and Bieri been active in the lives of Antoine the
night fool or the departed Mba Muzwi, they might have been of benefit to
them in their troubles. Insofar as the problems of these two young men were
problems of sexuality, the cult of Ndong Mba would have dramatized the
parameters of their sexuality, showing them its obligation to society, projecting it into the cosmos, transferring it, in Tessmann's phrase, over upon
nature. It would have helped them confront the feelings of impurity which
arose from excess or inadequacy in this domain of their corporeal experience.
Insofar as they both felt excluded from the protective benevolence of the
patrilineage to which they belonged—they were both socially isolated individuals—the ancestor cult ceremonies would have helped them to feel included
in the flow of that benevolence and to feel an obligation to it.

If we emphasize "elementary movements," and not "elementary ideas" as Tessmann did, we recognize that neither Antoine nor Mba Muzwi had been dramatically moved in their lives. The two old cults had largely collapsed before the Second World War. These young men were seeking their own dramatic movement. Take, for example, the movement to both ends of the night from evening to dawn and the movement into the forest that took place in Soo-Ndong Mba. Its four-phased initiation began in the early evening, proceeded, in the second and third phase, in full day and ended in the early morning at dawn. It moved its initiates through the evening, through the day into the dawn. In a similar way the cult moved the initiates from the familiarities of the village to the terrifying mysteries of the forest, which leapt upon them and scarified them and which they finally mastered, back into the village. What, for example, did the mock image of the antelope, so,[48] after which the cult was named and which the initiates speared, represent? It was the animal that had an easy familiarity with, a mastery of, the nighttime forest. The French, noting its large eyes, call it the "antelope nocturne."

The initiate appropriated this mystery by spearing. We note, as well, movements from the earth and the chthonic creatures that crawl there to the sky and the great bird, ande, and back to the earth and river courses. The dramatic movement here was from earth to sky to earth to water. These are all elemental movements central to Bwiti which moves its membership from dusk to dawn (though not through the day), and from chapel to forest and back again.

There were other elemental movements in these two old cults: from life to death to life, from one painted side of the body to the other, from the front of the body to the back, and from the feet to the head. All these movements tied together not only the various parts of the body but also tied together into a larger whole the various domains of Fang experience. It is in the Bwiti religion that we will find the dramatization of these elementary movements par excellence—not only the "saving circularities" of the old cults (earth to sky to earth, or village to forest to village) but progressive movement, the passage from the below to the above and from the savanna to the forest to the sea.

The difficulties of Antoine and Mba Muzwi were problems of inertia, of the absence of saving circularities, of the lack of passage, of the uncertainty of active belonging. Neither had properly passed into maturity, and both sought means to make that passage—the one through the proclamations of a very public delusion, and the other through intense commitment to a very private one. Antoine's delusions made him an exceptionally vocal member of a large group, that of the entire patrilineage, living and dead. Mba Muzwi's delusions made him a member of the smallest of groups, that of the secret connubial pair. Had they passed through Soo-Ndong Mba and Bieri, both young men would have achieved a stronger sense of membership in the patrilineage. They would have confronted socially approved mysteries instead of having to elaborate their own. They would have been moved by these mysteries in the confidence that this movement was in keeping with the momentum of their world and served the public good. Bieri and Soo-Ndong Mba moved to accommodate men and women to some of the persistent contradictions and paradoxes of their culture. The contradiction found in the status of women was, to some degree, accommodated in the, albeit token, role given to female sacra in Bieri. Other contrasting qualities of life such as potency and dependency, obligation and capriciousness, and life and death were celebrated and accommodated in these cults. The ancestors were not only the living dead; they also accommodated in themselves features of all ages and thus summarized the paradoxes of the life cycle. Visually this accommodation was shown in the age and infancy of the reliquary figure. It was dramatically shown in the awesome manner in which the skulls were displayed combined with the frolicsomeness of the reliquary figures in the "Punch and Judy" enactments atop the raffia palm barricades at the forest's edge. And surely Ndong Mba with its dramatizations of birth, growth, and death, with its paradoxical emphasis on sexual potency and sexual purity, gave similarly ultimate if complex—mysterious—overviews.

It cannot be overlooked, however, that, while these rituals accommodated, even celebrated, troublesome contraries in Fang life and death and set paradoxes at relative rest, they could also exacerbate problems of social solidarity. The reiterated paradox of potency and dependency in the ancestors encouraged an unstable attitude which swung between coerciveness and pious compliance in relation to them. They thus contained the seeds of their own abuse.

The evidence is that in the old days the ancestor cult knit together contraries as the cranium knits together its two opposing sides. It moved men about in such a way as to plumb the profundities and knit together the domains of human experience effectively, as we have seen in its songs and commentaries. It legitimized the participant's condition. In the reliquary itself, there was a consoling statement about the permanence of patrilineal potency represented by the craniums, which yet were contained within a fragile corporeal shell, the bark barrel and its figure.

There is also evidence, especially Tessmann's, that such accommodations did not occur and that the ancestor cult, by his time, was shallowly conceived. It was treated as an opportunity to coerce unseen forces and self-interestedly obtain goods, and to provide mere entertainment. There is evidence that the ancestors were merely abused and the village amused. The fathers, as such, had essentially departed from the cult. It is also clear that Soo-Ndong Mba became, more and more, mere ribald entertainment—an opportunity for the old to harry the young rather than a ritual opportunity for the young to gain perspective on the problems of sexual purity and potency, of birth, growth, and death. In other words, these cults no longer worked, and Fang came into profound disagreement about the nature of religious "work."

Still, Fang like Ngema or Essono Mba did not abandon all respect for these old cults even though they no longer practiced them. There were attempts at reinterpretation. One such attempt may be seen in the distinction between Bieri as Zame asi (God Below) and Christianity as Zame oyo (God Above).[49] While those who continued to practice Bieri were known in the deprecating words of many Christian converts as "believers in bones" (*mbune bives*), there were many who recalled that there was more in those old cults than bones alone—and more in the bones than bone alone. If Zame, as they were coming to learn, was a word for an ultimate accommodation, then there was something of Zame in these old cults even though it was a God of the Below.

⁓ 11 ⁓
Reinterpretations
of Mission

Mezô ba fômle afan me vale anwan.
(Words cast out in the forest start up many birds.)

NINE CHRISTMAS ALLEGORIES

FROM THE EARLIEST MOMENTS of evangelization, missionaries sought to convey the "good news" by parable and allegory. They thus personified what might otherwise be arid casuistic counsel. It was an effective mode of representing Christian comportment. But these devices for representing the Christian message—ancient techniques of religious persuasion, to be sure—were also subject to misinterpretation. What was gained in dramatic statement risked being lost in clarity of understanding.

Contrarieties and misinterpretations were seen in the pre-Christmas skits organized by the Protestant catechist of Assok Ening, Ondo Mba, in the local chapel in the forest just east of the village. Though the catechist intended the dramatic presentations to convey useful biblical lessons of Christian comportment, all were cast from a Fang perspective and most escaped the catechist's intentions. The final skit, in fact, took a surprising turn and had to be peremptorily concluded. It was largely the teenage and young adult members of the congregation who acted in the presentations. And it was that age group in the audience that registered appreciation or opposition to the performances.

There was a rapid movement in the presentations from a solemn emphasis on evangelistic pieties to the assertion of a Fang sense of what was problematic—and humorous—in the human situation. This was pretty well foreshadowed from the beginning in the mock figure of a rotund "missionary" amply stuffed with pillows around the waist who welcomed the audience one by one with lofty formality and then continued as a busybody master of ceremonies. His ministrations were received with that exaggerated respect combined with mockery which Fang usually showed toward the "Europeans" they created as dramatic presences in their dance and cult activities.

The first skit directed by the catechist himself was from Matthew 25: the story of the rich man (*nkukuma*) who went on a journey and left his servants with talents of money according to their ability. It is the parable of the worthless servant who buried his talent instead of investing it fruitfully. He was therefore consigned by his master to "outer darkness where men weep and gnash their teeth." While this might be taken in Europe and particularly in Calvinist culture as a lesson in the proper management of money, the Fang audience had a different interpretation. First of all, it was made clear that the poor third servant was given only one talent while the others were given three and five. Second, it was emphasized that the third servant, aware of the tightness of his master, did not wish to risk his money. So when the master returned and banished this servant for not respecting him enough to invest his wealth properly, there was strong empathy with his plight rather than with the "good and faithful servants" who had risked their master's goods. The Fang audience must surely have felt that in the distribution of largesse by their colonial masters, it was they who had been left with one talent without confidence enough to invest it properly. And it was they who had been banished to outer darkness. The difference between what was intended and what was interpreted—the catechist seems to have been animating his congregation to take advantage of the "wealth" of the colonial world—may have accounted for the silence of the audience after the skit.

The second skit reworked the old Fang tale of the "original child of incest," Kigile Ki. Kigile, born as a ball of gristle and bone, was given limbs by a great King. But ignoring the source of his salvation, he neglected the King's requests. The King peremptorily returned him to his original and hopeless state. The moral drawn was that humans are like Kigile, in need of everything from God. "Let us not forget all the blessings provided to us who are otherwise helpless," said the master of ceremonies. Much pleasure was provided by the actor who played the "ball of gristle and bone." He gradually unfolded and discovered his limbs one after the other. At the end when he was cursed again, he collapsed instantly back into a tight ball. It was reminiscent of the discovery and integration of appendages that took place in the Soo-Ndong Mba ceremonies.

The third skit pictured two married women washing clothes at the stream. A young man (*nduman*) tried to seduce them. The first woman, a Christian, told him off tartly, while the second, the pagan, went off with him into the woods. Given the problem of adultery among Fang this skit held great attention. The Christian woman was cheered. But since the part of the seducer was taken by a young woman in shorts and a chic blouse, "his" leering role was most appreciated. It reminded the audience of the capacity of worldly women among Fang to "marry" other women for the sake of lineage increase.

The fourth skit was an old Fang joke of a village of sick people who call a specialist in medicine (*ngungan*) to cure them. He proposes to kill the sickest of the patients and distribute the ashes among the rest. With alacrity, all the invalids stood up and the village was cured. There was also an undercurrent of reference to anthropophagy as a means of restoring and maintaining power and good health.

This skit was followed by another in a more Christian vein: a rich man said he had no need of God but then, suddenly falling sick, he professed Christianity. The remaining skits were more and more Fang in content. The sixth skit was the Fang tale of the husband lost in the forest who begins to play on the "balophone" he carries with him. His wives, hearing the music, are excited and dance a path out to him which he then follows back to the village. The pleasure here was in the balophone playing and also in the reversal of several bits of Fang conventional wisdom: "the good husband is a path to his wife," and "the adulterous woman is a worn path for many men." Here the good wives wore a path to their husband.

The next skit also employed the balophone and the same actor. This time he played the role of the blind troubadour, Edu Ada of Atonville. He was singing mvet legends among strangers, *bílôbôlôbô*, who understood little Fang. He sought to explain to these people that the audience sings only the chorus of the mvet. Instead they repeated all his words, effectively blocking his recitation. This statement about contemporary language problems drew applause.

The eighth skit was a shortened version of the dance, *bikege*, like *belebele* a dance in which all Fang, both men and women, participated. A young man had organized the dance to celebrate the mortuary ceremonies of his father. He warned the crowd that he had a taboo (*ekí akyage*) against hearing the woman's high-pitched scream of pleasure, *ôyenge*. Unfortunately, the men and women danced so well together that a woman screamed in pleasure and he fell "dead." To be revived he had to be given an unmarried girl. In the process of the dance he was "killed" three times and thus obtained three wives. This reworking of the "miraculous boy" and the "dead revived" motifs in Fang folklore was appreciatively received.

By this point the momentum of these dramatic representations had turned so much to traditional Fang preoccupations that the catechist became uncomfortable. When the ninth skit, by teenagers, began to present the recent visit of Ndende, the white-faced eradicator of witchcraft, it was too much even though the visit was done mockingly. He called a halt to the skits and moved on to the banquet.

The Momentum of Village Culture: Changing Missionary Interpretations

If Fang interpretations of their own religion underwent change, so too did the interpretations placed by missionaries on Fang and Fang religious sentiments. These changes were true of both Catholics and Protestants but are more available for scrutiny in the voluminous Protestant literature. Initially we see

Fang described, usually by comparison with coastal peoples contaminated by long contact with the European, as a people of moral vigor fully conscious of their shortcomings and their need for spiritual truth. "Never," says the missionary Allegret on first arriving at his post, "have I better understood the basic human distress than in discovering among these cannibal Fang an ardent desire for truth and life mixed with the lamentable cry as of an abandoned child who would never again discover his father's house.[1] That sprightly hopping dance and cry of joy that Fang women usually reserved for kinsmen returned from long journeying is offered to missionaries as they appear out of the forest. "Zing, zing krikading, za za krikadikading, za za krikading."[2] Fang express devotion to the missionaries as to parents who will teach them God's love.[3] They convince the missionaries that their migration to the west was actually a search for their Father God who had abandoned them in the early days of their migration. The missionaries, not surprisingly, perceived a profound "besoin moral," an "élan instinctive vers Dieu."[4]

But already at the turn of the century Fang began to refuse to supply food to missionaries.[5] And not so long after penning the above hopeful words, Allegret changed his mind. He found himself mocked by a villager with whom he had prayed in unison, "Je suis un pecheur." He wrote that "the Fang know what is wrong but they are not bothered by it." "I may be mistaken perhaps, but it seems that the sense of sin, the sense of culpability before God is lacking. I don't expect any real conversion among them despite their amiable dispositions. They think of God only as a powerful chief with whom it would be desirable to establish a treaty of friendship."[6] Most missionaries followed this change of view. The migration to the coast, once seen as a search for salvation, was reexamined. It was now perceived as a search for trade goods—for wealth.[7]

Allegret's turn-of-the-century work on Fang religious ideas was representative of a then current position that much was to be said for the African point of view. It was worth careful study and attempts were made to depict it fairly. Perhaps the constant itineration through the bush conducted by the early missionaries gave a more realistic view of village life. Later the establishment of mission stations tended to separate missionaries from everyday life. In the early thirties, at least, we get from the missionary and agricultural engineer, Felix Fauré, a very baleful account of life in the village: *Le Diable dans la brousse*.[8] This was one of a series of caricatures put out in the decades between the wars by the Paris Mission Society: for example, *Obam et son fetiche*,[9] *Sauvons les paiens du Gabon*.[10]

It is not that one could not take a highly critical view of village life and still report it insightfully. Fernand Grébert was a missionary critic of Fang domestic life who yet wrote perceptively. Serving in Gabon in the first three decades of the century, between Allégret and Fauré, his writings, intended like Faure's to explain the mission enterprise to the French public, yet captured accurately the form and feeling of village existence. No missionary understood better the difficulties facing Fang who converted to Christianity and remained in the village. His brief books for young readers, *Avema* and *Ekomi*, are fair portraiture not only of these young Fang converts but of the constant strain they found themselves under by virtue of their Christianity. Grébert's major work, *Au Gabon*,[11] shows in ethnographic detail the complex web of village life from which previous missionaries had thought too easily to detach their converts. He shows, for example, how the ramifying obligations of the bride-price are subject to unscrupulous manipulation by fathers-in-law to the exhaustion of naive young husbands seeking to marry in a Christian fashion. He shows how persuasive Fang taboos (*ekí*) could suddenly become for even the most willing convert. He knew how powerful a center of gravity the culture of village life could be, and the relatively slight penetration of the missionary influence.[12]

Grébert provides good counsel to the missionary effort but he is pessimistic because the Fang "migratory impulse"—"oiseaux migrateurs" he calls them—is an enduring impediment to effective evangelization. Evangelization might be more effective if Fang would stay put for their lessons. But their momentum is a problem. "Next week, next month, next year they are off again for another part of the forest and their good will and interest evaporates. The lesson is lost."[13]

If the villages were changing, they were changing in a way contrary to missionary intentions. After the war, in the twenties, Grébert notices a malaise in the villages. *Sí e se fe mvé*, "the land is no longer good," he is told. Before the war Fang had admitted that they felt they were living in "chicken coops" (*menda beku*) compared to Europeans. Perhaps the "good news" of the evangel could change all that. After the war, they seemed to have lost that hope. It was a time of disease, the flu epidemic of 1918-1919, and a time of the famine, which ravaged Gabon during the early twenties. And instead of improving, the villages were coming to seem more and more peripheral to colonial realities. A new doubt entered the relationship with the European. Where were his promises? For some missionaries this discontent betokened moral failings in Fang.

Various strategies were followed in the face of this malaise, this failure to bring the spiritual "good news" to bear effectively on the conditions of life. The most pronounced sign of failure in missionary eyes was the increase of material demands on the mission. In the nineteenth century, many missionaries shared Mary Kingsley's view that African "spirituality" contrasted with the materialism of the European. By the twenties, it was common for missionaries to remark on African materialism: a people whose only "salvation" lay in trade goods and whose only hope of the missionary was that he would share some of those trade goods.[14] There was a return to the discussion of African "fetishism," a material rather than a spiritual religion, more exterior than interior.[15] Missionaries with perspective, like Schweitzer and Grébert, realized how much African materialism and money-mindedness were a reflection of just those values in the colonial enterprise. The qualities that later missionaries "discovered" in Fang were those their predecessors had sought to defend Fang against. Clearly, Fang and missionary interpretations were evolving in relation to each other. Villagers were undergoing a frustrating and untoward "conversion" of their own. The momentum of village life, and finally its loss of momentum, worked counter to missionary interests.

MENTALITIES: OLD TIME AND OLD TESTAMENT

These evolving and interacting interpretations were often provoked by feelings of unrequitement. The missionaries were not producing the "goods" which Fang had expected of them and missionaries on their side were disabused of the high hopes for the Fang "moral impulse" and spiritual search. But behind these unrequitements there was a struggle going on over the mind—a struggle between mentalities. This struggle ranged from such matters as "time sense" to the population of the supernatural. In the colonial literature, for example, we find recurrent deprecation of the African time sense by both missionaries and administrators. The African preference to live time as periodically intensifying rather than as predictably regular frustrated both these groups in their efforts to mount organizations with specific time requirements. As far as the Fang supernatural was concerned, from the missionary point of view it was too overpopulated with spirits of various kinds and particularly with evil ones.

The Gabonese missionary Père Briault[16] discussed "time sense" and the missionary pressure upon it. He noted African reactions such as the importance to youth of wristwatches as signs of acculturation. He might have included the growing emphasis upon exact timing of ritual events. In the clan federation movement, Alar Ayong, a mock bureaucracy used time coercively on the members. Dances were held to a strict time schedule. In Bwiti, alarm clocks are kept in many chapels to control events. Leaders frequently carry clocks with them. In their passage through the equatorial forest they are periodically brought to their knees in genuflection by the sound of the alarm—an action which was surely the result of pressure put upon Fang thinking.

The main sources of these influences upon Fang thought and feeling were the Bible and the catechisms and missals associated with it. Missionaries made very early efforts to bring the pressure of this "good news" to bear upon Africans.[17] As more of the Bible was translated and as the distinction between the religious cultures of the Old and New Testament became clear, Fang reacted in favor of the Old Testament. It was not only that Fang found their own rigid taboo system reflected in the Book of Moses. The patrilineal extended family and the polygyny and exogamy of the Old Testament was also congenial. Particularly for Protestants, with their focus upon the Bible rather than upon catechism, this unexpected preference posed a problem. Grébert complained in 1919 of this difficulty in evangelization—how to pass from the "mentalité juive" to the "mentalité greco-latine." [18]

What was occurring was an unforeseen misinterpretation of the missionaries' own message. The counterproductivity of evangelization was noted often enough by missionaries themselves. [19] The same thing occurred in respect to scientific thinking. Presumably missionaries as representatives of modern rational-technical societies would have moved Fang toward more scientific thought. But here too evangelization often worked counterproductively.

To understand this we need to make distinctions among three different types of representation of experience: enactive, iconic, and symbolic. [*1] Experience is represented, first, in habitual action, in our muscles, as we single out and learn to chain and thus reproduce certain sequences of action in recurrent situations such as tying a knot, building a trap, playing an instrument, typing. It is hard to speak much about these representations. We enact them according to a complex system of signals, often nonverbal. Second, experience can be represented by certain mental images—sign-images or icons—that we preserve out of the past and that we employ in order to recognize and confront or relate to a new experience. Out of our childhood we are, in our adult years, enabled to recognize a male figure of benevolent authority as a father. Finally, experience can be represented in abstract symbolic models. Here experience is represented in a set of explicit rules. Reference to these rules and the procedures they describe serves to solve problems presented by future occurrences of similar experiences. One states or codes the rules in one's language or metalanguage—the rules for integration in calculus, for forming the past tense in French, for employing the astrolabe or sextant—and then one applies the rules when confronted with a problem in Paris or a missed landing on the equatorial coast. All these modes of representation are employed by all peoples of all cultures. But different cultures put different emphases on different modes.

In the West the symbolic mode is emphasized. Scholasticism and the scientific method have produced academies and laboratories and other "think tanks" by the thousands. The sheer magnitude of experiences contemplated and problems posed for solving have resulted in self-conscious emphasis upon

---

[*1] These three modes of representation correspond to those singled out by Jerome Bruner, "The Course of Cognitive Growth," p. 2. From another perspective, we argue a distinction between signal interaction, sign interaction, and symbol interaction as the three modes of experiencing social and cultural life and obtaining social or cultural consensus (Fernandez, "Symbolic Consensus"). Signals are the elements of enactive representation, signs of iconic representation, and symbols of symbolic representation. In this book we are mainly interested in signs or sign images.

abstracting rules of operation—on genericizing. Traditional cultures on the other hand, like Fang, which are not under such problem-solving pressure, tend to use enactive and iconic modes of representation. They prefer to assess their successive experiences concretely by analogies found in habitual activity or familiar images rather than by abstract analyses.

Traditionally, then, Fang relied primarily on actions or images of experience previously represented to handle new experiences. Their approach to problem-solving we may call proverbial. The proverb is a good example of iconic representation. A former experience is recalled as an image or set of images and exploited to provide direction in understanding a present experience. The reference of proverbs is usually the picture of an everyday domestic happening which contains some truth applicable to an experience one is currently struggling with. For example, an apt proverb heard frequently in Fang "palavers" was "gravel thrown in the forest kills birds" (*bikôk be ake afan bí awing anwan*). It was usually used as an admonition to suggest that "wild accusations will eventually find a target" or in the sense of "wild accusations will surprise you with their results." Sometimes, since practically all proverbs lend themselves to multiple interpretation, it was taken to mean "one's case must be presented with greater diversity of argument if results are to be obtained." But in any case, no abstraction of rule for application in the argument was required. The similarity in the experiences compared by choice of proverb spoke for itself.

There is surely intelligence in the proverb. It parsimoniously though implicitly codes several different wise observations (we may abstract them as rules) about experience in general within an innocent domestic observation. As with all use of analogy, however, the rule to be applied is ambiguous and dependent upon context and inclination. In this tolerance of ambiguity it defeats analysis. And in its iconic nature, as opposed to symbolic representation with its abstracting response to a situational dilemma, it summons up imagery which is itself exciting to the consciousness whose dilemmas it appears to resolve. It provides corroboration and it has dramatic possibility.

The point is, however, that missionaries, rather than working to inculcate in Fang Western symbolic habits of representation, adopted the modes of representation preferred by Fang. This is understandable. They had a message to convey. And they wished to convey it dramatically and with ease of comprehension. Naturally they sought local idioms. It is not fully accurate, of course, to say that missionaries "adopted" Fang thought. For the Bible itself generally relies on iconic thought. It is closer to the truth to say that in morality play, in preaching, in parable, and in proverb missionaries reinforced traditional thought styles. But at the same time, without changing Fang preferred modes of thought, they introduced new icons and images which put pressure on some aspects of the Fang worldview.

Missionary Metaphors and Explanatory Models

We have examined certain of the images, or organizing metaphors, which were central in Fang experience and with which they approached their round of life: the image of the full man, the legendary images of migration and entrance into the Equatorial Forest, the image of the European, the images of the witch, the personal images of the future contained in one's preparation, the image of the village with its component buildings and central courtyard, the image of the forest. We have also noted changes in these images.

We can learn from these constructs by comparing them to Western ones. Consider, for example, Horton's comparison of the prescientific thought systems of Africa with the scientific thought systems of Europe. He argues that while the two systems are similar in many respects,[20] they employ different models. "Scientific thought tends to choose things rather than people as the basis of its explanatory models while African thought systems by and large tend to make the opposite choice." This arises, Horton argues, because any model must have familiarity and order and regularity in its behavior. Nature is better understood and has more regularity in technologically advanced societies. Traditional societies with little control or understanding of nature look to social life for their models. It appears to be the more orderly area of their experience. While it is doubtful that society is always more orderly than nature for prescientific people (there is good evidence from Fang religion, for example, that an order was sought in nature which society did not possess),[21] and while it is too easy to suppose that a change in model or organizing image will bring about a change from prescientific to scientific orientation (the crucial shift is from enactive and iconic to symbolic representation), still Horton points us toward the question of the differences in the models and metaphors of Western and African culture. And these differences in the colonial situation where the flow of information ran perforce from European to African constituted an important pressure upon Fang thought.

Are there any changes in Fang models? In respect to scientific thought and natural models such changes are not likely to have occurred in the villages prior to formal education. For neither missionary nor administrator was a particularly forceful advocate of this kind of thought. Missionaries were professionally committed to a religious view of reality resting on a personal model of the universe.[*2] In other respects, however, new models and images appeared inevitably as a consequence of the expanding horizons of Fang and of the new organizations, documents, and directives circulated in the "civ-

---

[*2] Cf. J. W. Fernandez, "Fang Representations under Acculturation." For many centuries in Christendom, of course, there has been a stable dualism, or compartmentalization, as between religious and scientific understanding or, in terms of our discussion, as between personal and natural explanatory models. Missionaries, naturally enough, rarely bothered to communicate that intellectual modus vivendi to Africans, though it was the source of much misinterpretation.

ilizing mission." We have seen a shift in Fang thought from a model of the various streams and tributaries as the crucial interstices of their landscape to a representation of the colonial road system with its thoroughfares and feeder routes. In social life, we saw a shift from an image of the universe as an agglomeration of widely separated segments of clan lands with villages as their centers and multileveled lineages as their structure to an image of the "mvogabot" (village of people) as the maximal social unit and of the village as an entity decentered and peripheral to the trading centers and great cities. We saw a blurring of the image of the fully mature man and of the benevolently protective ancestor.

While missionaries could hardly have put pressure on Fang personal models of the universe, they brought more specific pressures on the Fang supernatural. Fang believed in too many spirits and gave too much credence to everyday evil spirits (*evus, beyem*). One main task of the "bonnes nouvelles" was to curb this supernatural overpopulation as well as to invigorate and make central what was to most Fang either an otiose creator deity or simply a philosophical first principle useful in laying inquiry to rest.

"UNE SCIENCE DES CHOSES CACHÉES"

But missionary intentions, conveyed as much as possible in local idioms, had many inadvertent results or were counterproductive. Inadvertently, for example, missionaries fostered a false notion of science. Missionary reports are full of accounts of African "émerveillement" before some gadget or other of European daily life: matches, collapsible drinking cups, bicycles.[*3] Many missionaries succumbed to the temptation to credit these marvels of material culture to the Christian way of life, the "bonnes nouvelles" they were preaching. The compartmentalization between science and religion that had long prevailed in the West was overlooked as was the Western skepticism about religion that sorely tried and perhaps invigorated Western faith. The word "science" seems to have entered the Fang vocabulary early and it came to be associated with the theological perspective of the missionaries. Thus Cadier writes enthusiastically of the thirst of young Fang for more and more knowledge of the Word of God, "an astonishing zeal, always eager to penetrate further this mysterious science that gives this power to the white man."[22]

There may have been some missionaries who actually believed that this "mysterious science" had theological or even "Protestant ethic" origins. But the consequence for Africans was that they labeled as science what was actually nonscientific thought and set themselves up for the inevitable frustration inherent in the belief that pure piety and faith would be materially

---

[*3] Thus in the *Journal*, 1911, Vol. I, p. 93, M. Cadier reports "une des femmes qui m'ont apporté de l'eau et des bananes me demande avec vénération si c'est Dieu lui-même qui m'a donné cette belle machine . . . ma bicyclette."

productive. Many villagers, while increasingly convinced that the "bonnes nouvelles" was in some respects a fraud because it yielded no material benefit, were yet persistent in trying to penetrate that "mysterious science" which the whites possessed. Even in the Bwiti religion there were those who described it as a "science des choses cachées" whose purpose was to penetrate to those hidden sources of power in the afterlife which the whites had hidden from them.

For these Bwitists, as for most Fang, religion was not a matter of faith, of "belief in spite of" or "willing suspension of disbelief." It was a very pragmatic technique for understanding, predicting, and controlling—in short a science or pre-science of hidden things. To believe in something despite lack of evidence or evidence to the contrary, which is the Western religious condition, was foreign to their attitudes. Fang had always had good evidence for their beliefs. That is why they gave up the ancestors when it became evident that Christian beliefs were more powerful. By indulging the notion of "a mysterious science," missionaries inadvertently exacerbated the frustrations implicit in mission, while at the same time they impelled many Fang toward occult practices "scientifically" designed to control and predict the unseen.

In a certain sense, there is a "science" to religious evangelization. It consists in finding ways to talk about nonempirical matters—about hidden things. It is a "science" of apt use of analogies, parables, metaphors. Where different cultures are involved, it is a matter of talking about these things in local idioms. Missionaries often displayed an impressive sensitivity to these matters. The Fang, for example, are great hunters in the forest. Thus, the image of "la chasse" appears again and again in the missionary record. A newly converted Christian who is yet reluctant to return and spread the news to his brothers is asked what he would think of a hunter who had killed a fine antelope and, instead of returning it to his village, hid it in the forest to eat of it alone, day by day.[23] Trees of various kinds appear to have been important vehicles of missionary thought. The *oveng* (*Guiboutia tessmanni*), one of the giant trees of the Equatorial Forest, subject, however, to being strangled by the parasitic *ekekam* (*Ficus hochsteteri*), is compared with Christianity, that ancient institution towering above all other life but always threatened by the suffocating encirclement of evil.[24] The oil palm (*Elaeis guineensis*) and the hard battle it must wage against birds, goats, grubs, and ants in order to reach a fruitful maturity is compared to the life of a Christian who must ceaselessly combat all kinds of impediments to his spiritual growth.[25]

This last image, developed by Samuel Galley, the Fang lexicographer, is more suggestive than it might appear. Not only was it used at a time when both Fang and French were struggling to make oil palm cultivation a paying enterprise, but Galley's mention of the invasion of the palm by certain kinds of birds was bound to suggest to Fang a witchcraft spirit (evus) often represented as a bird "à l'oeil féroce" taking up residence in the human body.[26] It is not surprising that missionaries like Père Trilles who spent much time with Fang prided themselves on their grasp of figures of speech—on what Trilles called "la métaphore juste."

But, naturally, such subtle matters were often misinterpreted or counter-productive. When Cadier argues[27] that replacing the old Bieri practices with Christianity is like substituting a ham from a wild pig for a tired mush of manioc leaves, he should have been aware that he was deprecating a staple of the Fang diet in favor of a rare treat unpredictable and not to be counted on. The conclusion which must naturally have suggested itself to Fang from this metaphoric argument—a conclusion which accorded with the strategy they adopted—was to take advantage of the windfall of missionary evangel-ization while continuing to hold on to traditional beliefs as the more trust-worthy staple. A kind of compartmentalization and opportunism in beliefs is suggested in Cadier's metaphor which was hardly part of his intentions.

Sometimes the images suggested by missionaries were just too recondite or bound up with European culture. Thus, in the *Journal* of the Paris Mission Society for 1919, H. Perrier tells us how he used an eclipse of the sun as a parable—the moon of sin hiding the sun of justice and salvation.[28] He had first tried, valiantly employing his travel lamp, a man, and a boy, to make for his auditors a natural model of the event. But interest quickly flagged in such a conceit and he then turned the affair into a parable which, he tells us, created a great stir in his audience. But whether the stir was of understanding or of surprise because of a violation of the associations customarily attached to sun and moon is another question. Sometimes the images were just too recondite, as when the action of the "evus" is compared by Cadier to radium: it mutilates those who work with it.[29] On other occasions, metaphors were employed which were no doubt dead for both French and Fang. Over and over the "bonnes nouvelles" was presented as "food for souls" without reference to particular categories of food or to the fact that the image was likely to evoke for Fang sacrificial presentations to the ancestors at the reli-quaries.

It is not surprising in any case that missionaries began to develop the idea that Fang tended to understand things in a countersense, to understand things from the exterior rather than the interior,[30] or not to understand things at all. For while playing to Fang preferred modes of representation of experience, missionaries also had to risk the basic ambiguities involved in analogy and metaphor coupled with the difficulties of translating such modes of thought directly from one culture to another.

Two Edifying Images

Fang misconstructions of the missionary message were yet constructions and had their consequences. The missionary use of proverb and parable, if anything, increased Fang dependence upon these ambiguous modes of thought and encouraged their inclination to present things indirectly. The constructive consequences are best seen in religious movements, such as Bwiti, where the missionary message had its greatest resonance even if it worked by opposites. In two respects, particularly, missionary arguments challenged Fang to new constructions of their religious worldview. The missionary concentration on the reality and fate of the individual soul challenged Fang notions of the corporate group as the greater reality. And the missionary emphasis upon permanent redemptive conversion from a former sinful state to a subsequent state of salvation challenged Fang notions of the saving circularities of ritual and the essentially restorative function of religion. The constructive response in Bwiti, as we shall detail in Part III, was to meet these challenges with adaptive images.

The challenge to traditional African views of these two evangelical arguments has been widely noted by historians of mission. Kwesi Dickson, the Ghanian churchman and historian, asks with some concern,

> are we in danger of preaching with too great an emphasis on individual involvement . . . the doctrine of justification by faith is, for example, the most missionary of doctrines, but we distort the gospel if we preach this to the absolute exclusion of corporate salvation through the Body of Christ . . . let us practice fellowship evangelization!

"Religion," Dickson argues, "knows no individualism." The Moslems, he feels, are much more effective in making the corporate appeal to brotherhood. Christian missionaries should remember, he urges, the metaphor of the body and the vine and its branches. In fact, Protestants could learn much about "the corporate metaphors of religious experience" from Catholic evangelization. He speaks admiringly of the Catholic employ of symbol—the *signum efficax*.[31]

The missionary tendency to choose images that concentrated religious experience upon the individual rather than upon the group was naturally open to counterproductive interpretation. For the isolation of the individual in a singular relationship with supernatural powers was for Fang a characteristic of sorcery. The Fang reliquaries, though generally served by one or several men of the family, were repositories of the bones of many ancestors and represented the interests of many descendants. It was a misuse of ancestral power to appeal to them separately and solely for individual ends. One of the misfortunes of the suppression of ancestor cult in the colonial period was that parts of the bones fell into individual hands and were used for egocentric purposes. This egocentric use of the supernatural contributed to the "apotheosis of evil" which we have discussed.

We see a constructive response to this religious individualism in Bwiti. Individual prayers, as we shall see, are discouraged unless undertaken in the presence of the entire membership. Prayers are usually undertaken by the entire worshiping group. At the same time, in a more imaginative vein and in an effort at "corporate salvation" as Dickson calls it, Bwiti has constructed rituals in which the individual microcosm is projected into the macrocosm as part of it—certainly an edifying response to excessive individualism.

The second missionary argument for redemptive salvation was also subject to misconstruction. Williamson's observation among the Akan is apposite for Fang.[32] He argues that the Christian need for salvation evokes no significant response among Akan. "The Akan approach is to see human life in need of vitalizing rather than of changing from a sinful or fallen state. A summum bonum was bequeathed by the ancestors, evil and wrongdoing are a retreat from this state, and religion exists to appease the offended forces. Thus, there is no concept of individual spiritual progress, but rather one of obedience to a traditional pattern." Though it is not true that Fang regarded the past as an unqualified summum bonum (their folklore gives plenty of evidence of past imperfections), nevertheless they did not entertain the hope of redemptive conversion. Keeping in mind their notions of the "flow of power," the object of religion was that of restoring, "opening up," the human vessel to the flow of beneficial forces and the elimination of constrictive, choking, or inhibiting forces. Naturally, the missionary image of the redemption of the vessel itself was not well understood, or at best was understood as applying to exceptional people—the witches.

Yet here as well missionary images had constructive consequences. For the Bwiti religion has made, as we shall see, elaborate attempts to restore its members to the saving circularities of the overriding cosmos while, at the same time, it has emphasized a ritual progression from one state to another by means of a recurrent "path" metaphor which leads ritually from life to death, or, more exactly, from death in life to life in death. Of course, this metaphor had traditional antecedents in such notions as the genealogical path of descent from clan founder to living member, or the legendary notion of the path of migration of the Children of Afri Kara from savanna upland to seaside. But the emphasis upon the path and upon the qualitative transformations of the membership as they ritually tread thereon is unique. It is a constructive response to notions of redemptive conversion—to the "straight and narrow path" of Christian salvation.

Conclusion: A History of Creative Misinterpretations

The communications between Fang and European led, in many ways, to unrequitement. For Fang, the "good news" brought some unexpected and unfortunate consequences—an "apotheosis of evil." For missionaries, the very vehicle of that news was coming to be misread or worse—the wrong parts appreciated. We have emphasized here the imaginative sources of this unrequitement, looking at some of the volatile and easily misunderstood images in which the two parties expressed themselves. At the same time, while missionaries lent themselves to misinterpretation in their efforts to explain scripture there was also some condescension in these explanations. This condescension ranged from amusement over Fang interpretations[33] of scriptural episodes to a plain deprecation of Fang culture—and particularly those aspects which made the Old Testament so attractive to Fang.[34] These misinterpretations, combined with condescension, led to Fang suspicions that missionaries were not fully candid in their explanations. The suspicions in turn led to the search for other sources of insight into this "mysterious science" of the European such as might be found in occult literature, in Black Bibles, and in imaginative cosmologies of their own creation, notably Bwiti.

There is a kind of intellectual history to these evolving misinterpretations and evolving attitudes—a double intellectual history, in fact, which has to be drawn from both the European and the African perspective. From the European perspective we may note the following phases:

1880-1900: The Golden Age of Missions and the period of the "manifest destiny of the civilizing mission." Fang and European seemed to be coming into earnest communication. Fang were perceived as theologically naive but as a people of estimable religious and moral sentiments to be defended against administrative and mercantile attitudes.

1900-1920: Increasing disgruntlement with the turbulent and ephemeral commitments of Fang. Awareness of the decreasing hospitality for mission. The entanglements of village life for those who convert now sensed, the momentum of African culture now appreciated. An African mentality, inadvertently reinforced by missionary modes of communication, is perceived.

1920-1950: It is recognized that African "fetishism" runs deeper than suspected. The "superficiality," the "materialism" and "exteriority" of African religious attitudes are emphasized. The loss of European "moral authority" that occurred during and after the First World War is projected upon Fang, and the depravity and barbarity of village life come to be singled out. There is increased awareness of counterproductive communication, of misreading, and of African "literal-mindedness" of interpretation.

1950-   : Animism comes to be recognized as an authentic religion. Dialogue seriously undertaken with African thought. African forms are incorporated into Christian architecture, catechism, and liturgy. The incompatibility between the two world views becomes apparent: the Christian ideal of celibacy confronts the African ideal of procreation, Christian eschatology confronts African vitalism and pragmatism, Christian passive piety and religious individualism confront African contractural and corporate worship, the striving for redemption confronts the striving for "restoration."

Fang also underwent their phases of reaction. While the long-term reaction of the majority of Fang, that 70 to 80 percent who are nominally Christian, may be termed compartmentalization with a dominant and public commitment to Christianity, coupled with a recessive commitment to animism, the actual evolution of Fang reactions to mission is more complex.

1818-1900: Period of conflict with administrative culture but of hospitable acceptance, even enthusiasm, for the "bonnes nouvelles" as the secret to Western power and as a more closed religious system than Fang possessed. A tendency to identify Europeans with the supernatural and to express dependence upon them. Lack of common language makes communication of more than earnest mutual interest difficult.

1900-1925: Acceptance of administrative control and beginning of disillusionment with evangelization and suspicion that the "good news" was not being fully imparted. Dependence shifts from missionary to administrator and merchant. Local revitalization movements appear. Each party now knows the other's language well, but misconstruction or creative misinterpretation is typical of Fang.

1925-1950: Increasing tendency to cultivate Europeans for material ends. Strong attachment to Old Testament. A baffling increase in witchcraft, "the apotheosis of evil." Social disorganization opens Fang up more to revitalization efforts such as Bwiti or MBiri or Alar Ayong, the knitting together of the clans. Mistrust of missionary message leads to increasing occultism and use of occult literature in search of the "science des choses cachées." Attempts at syncretism of the two world views by architectonic construction, by edifying images, and by adaptive conversion.

1950-   : Much greater confidence in African belief and practice makes Fang culture more open to syncretism. New confidence leads to pressures toward indigenization in religion and independence in politics and administration.

We have concentrated here on Fang-missionary interaction because missionaries, in their constant itineration, made the strongest cumulative impact on Fang thinking until after the Second World War, after which there was widespread establishment of primary education. But it should be remembered that there were at least four cultures in interaction: the secular, organizational culture of colonial administration: the production-consumption oriented mercantile culture of the merchants and traders; the Christian culture of the missionaries; and Fang animist culture. Of course there was interpenetration of these cultures. Many an administrator was an exemplary Christian or espoused mercantile views. In the two-sided meeting of Fang and missionary, three possible Fang reactions have been noted: complete conversion, a Christian-animist dualism or compartmentalization, and an effort to syncretize cultures, as occurred in Bwiti or in the Alar Ayong movement. If we add the other two secular colonial cultures to this mix, additional permutations and combinations become possible. In every village there were men like the *mienlam* of Assok Ening, Ngema Mve. He had turned skeptical about religion of any kind and was attempting to master the mercantile culture. And, of course, any syncretism such as Bwiti, though largely in dialogue with missionary culture, also incorporates elements from mercantile and administrative culture.

Early in the colonial experience of Fang, their own culture underwent a devaluation in their eyes. Missionaries promised so much and raised so many expectations that traditional life came to seem poor by comparison. The power of the administration was overwhelming. The trade goods of the merchants seemed greatly superior to anything of Fang manufacture. It was not long before these immediate things came for many to substitute for the ultimate things offered by missionaries. Still, the missionary-Fang dialogue continued in many minds and, though each side was subject to misconstruction and misinterpretation by the other, had enough impetus to reassert itself in various ways against the more secular colonial cultures. The most interesting and creative reconstruction to come out of this dialogue was the Bwiti religion to which we now turn.

PART III
A PLEASURE DOME

⌐12⌐

Administered Morality and Moral Movement to a Fuller Self

Ntang, bi atang mesem esi nyi.
(A payment, we pay the sins of this earth.)

A DYNAMIC STRANGER

LATE ONE EVENING about three months after I had taken up residence in Assok Ening—and when my presence was no longer such an object of attention—there was a loud knocking at the door. Surely there had been an accident or sudden sickness. Most of the villagers were long abed. The open door revealed in the light of the pressure lamp a man of about 35 with a beard, a long flowing robe, and a red cord about his waist. "Monsieur," he said, addressing me in French, "I am Metogo Zogo, Nganga Bwiti, and I must speak with you." He fixed me with an unrelenting gaze. "You seek the truth here but you will not find it." As I stepped back, he made a dramatic entrance, sweeping himself and robes into the center of the room. "You do not know me but I am no stranger. I am a child of this village just returned from a long spiritual journey. I have been following the truth! You will not find it in this village talking to these old men. You must come to the Bwiti Chapel in my father's house. Zogo Ebu."

The nganga could not contain himself but paced back and forth, stopping to pose dramatically on a point. "You want to know the 'old things.' But none here know them. They have not seen them. We Banzie see them when we eat eboga. We see the 'old people' there. We know the 'old things' through them."

"Now you want to know why the condition of this village and of the Fang is desperate. None of this village except we Banzie can tell you that. The people here are lost in sin. They have not paid the price of those sins. They have not died for their sins. But we Banzie have died and paid the price. We die and return, die and return, each time more purified. As the whiteman has died and been purified, so have we. He, has paid the earth. That is why he is white. And the blackman must die in Bwiti."

Suddenly the nganga grabbed my left hand and lifted my arm. "Don't be too sure of yourself. You are not free of all your sins. Look at this arm. You are not without blemishes." He pointed out freckles and pigmented spots. "These are your sins! You should dance with Bwiti. You have heard the harp at night? While all these villagers are asleep we dance and journey far. They go nowhere here. They wander around in confusion. They don't know where to go. But we go far." He took hold of the red-woven cord around his waist. "You see this cord? This is the Path of Birth and Death. We follow this path. We know life. We know death."

Metogo was much the most dynamic visitor I had had—a voluntary informant of such personality and volubility that I despaired of keeping track of the rush of his observations and dramatic claims. He began to sing me some of the songs of his religion, volunteering to fetch his harp for accompaniment. But I did not wish to wake my neighbors to an interview already grown overly loud and self-directed. Under the excuse of the lateness of the hour, I postponed discussions for another day. The nganga taking his leave turned a handshake into a blessing by cupping my two hands together and blowing into them. "You are not such a whiteman as not to need the blessing of a Banzie."

Reversions, Revivals, and the Doubling of Personalities

The invention and diffusion of religious cults for purposes of protection and revitalization in Africa is, particularly in central and equatorial Africa, a very old phenomenon antedating European contact.[1] But the pressures of colonial domination and missionary evangelization coupled with the relative inertia, the ennui, that came to prevail among such a previously turbulent people as Fang created particular needs for revitalization. Chief among these motivations was the constriction of "native" personality[*1] which was often a consequence of the colonial enterprise. For administrator and missionary alike sought definitions of local peoples with which they could work or turn to their own advantage for purposes of conversion. In response to these constrictions many Fang multiplied their personalities in unruly ways. They sought greater potential of personality, greater movement and transformation in qualities and feeling states than the colonial condition permitted.

A strong impulse to this kind of revitalization lay in the missionary enter-

---

[*1] This constriction has been frequently enough observed by students of colonialism. In French colonization, and in Gabon, Balandier discusses the African reaction to the attempt to turn them into "simples machines à produire" (*Afrique ambiguë*, p. 247). And the Chief of Research for ORSTOM in Gabon, M. Laurent Biffot, points up in his survey of Gabonese workers the "sentiment de n'être qu'un outil." *Facteurs d'intégration et desintégration du travailleur Gabonais à son entreprise*, p. 13.

prise itself. Often enough there were African catechists or pastors-in-training, for such had been Metogo Zogo, whose conversion had failed them at crucial junctures of their lives, and who returned to their cultures energized with a double vision—and with the makings of new and separate communions.

As early as the 1860's the American mission on Corisco Island off the Muni Estuary—a bare twenty years in place—was confronted with Ibia J. Ikengue, a Benga pastor, who criticized a fundamental disorder in mission itself—missionary failure to adopt a mode of living corresponding to Christian piety. Ikengue raised questions as to the aim of mission. Was it to maintain the African in perpetual tutelage?[2] He was probably responding to the pressures of the Uruku religious movement among his people, the Benga, at the time.[3] Its object was to restore the vitality of the traditional religion in the face of missionary pressures. Ikengue's critique and perhaps the pressure of the Benga Uruku led to "a great awakening" in the mission on Corisco Island.[4] This was the first of a series of revivals experienced in the mission church during the colonial period.

The missionary literature and unpublished correspondence repeatedly refers to African mission personnel falling back into paganism. Often enough these "backsliders" were trying to reach some orderly accommodation between the two religious perspectives. The French missionary Cadier mentions a Fang Catholic mission pupil, one Koule or Bekoune, who claimed to have achieved special powers over the dead in his training.[5] While he abandoned the mission, he tried to preserve what he had learned there. He set up a special cult of the dead which syncretized some of his Christian teachings with elements of the Fang ancestor cult.

Grébert, with customary wisdom, recognized from the first that "double personalities" were being created out of the missionary enterprise. "After communion with the resurrected Jesus," he says, "the Africans naturally search for communion with their own troublesome spirits. They become easily victimized by those who promise to resuscitate their own dead."[6] Such a promise was fulfilled in the double personality of Koule who, under the influence of the ancestors, became Bekoune ("man of the dead"). Grébert noted that these resuscitations by ecstatic alienation and doubling of personality were an old technique in Fang religious practice. But he also noted that the phenomenon was much on the increase, particularly among those who had had substantial Christian instruction.

The Antonian Movement led by Doña Beatrice in the early eighteenth century in the Congo reminds us how long these reinterpretations had been going on. Like Bekoune, Doña Beatrice had "died" and had been resurrected in her Christian training, obtaining thereby special communion with the saints, notably Saint Antony of Padua, as well as with the Bakongo dead. She extensively reinterpreted church teachings and was burned at the stake.[7]

Within the mission itself there was plenty of dissatisfaction as to results achieved. Revivals from within the fold, such as Ikengue's on Corisco Island, were recurrent. Both Catholics and Protestants in Gabon underwent well-remembered revivals in the 1930's. Father Hee revived the Catholic mission and brought scores of new converts among the Adouma in 1936. He baptized upwards of five hundred people at a single mass.[8] Among Protestants there was the Vernoud revival of 1935-1936. Converted to Pentacostalism (Assembly of God) on his vacation to Europe in 1934, Vernoud, returning to Gabon and still remaining with the Paris Evangelical Mission, traveled widely, announcing, "l'esprit va venir."[9] Thousands of Fang are said to have come to Easter services in 1936 expecting accession to and protection by the Holy Spirit. Vernoud's master metaphor, recognized by hundreds of Fang, was "soif" (thirst). He sought to convince Fang of their "spiritual thirst." Hundreds came forth to be quenched. Many miraculous cures were claimed, though enthusiasm rapidly ebbed. Vernoud soon left the Paris society to form a small Pentacostal mission in the hills above Medouneu (Woleu-Ntem District) with only a handful of members.

The thirst metaphor and its slacking in "spirit" resonated with Fang conceptions of bodily flow and health. No doubt many Fang felt blocked by the contrarieties working within them between traditional religious requirements on the one hand and the missionary message on the other. The "coming of the Spirit" offered catharsis to such a clotted communion. A spark of recognition even flashed between Bwitists of the period and Vernoud. The pastor testifies to his effect upon a young member from this "complicated sect dedicated to dead spirits that employs poison."[10] The young Bwitist, he says, exclaimed that this was the first time he had understood a European.

It is doubtful that at this mid-thirties date many Bwitists came forth to accept the Spirit or the agency of Jesus. Pronounced Christianization of Bwiti came after the Second World War. But Vernoud's enthusiasm may have had some influence. Particularly in Bwiti chapels around Vernoud's station in Medouneu, the figure of Christ as the Child of Man was brought into ritual focus. One also noted in these chapels a Protestant-like emphasis on Bible study and biblical events in recounting myth and history, an emphasis not everywhere present in Bwiti. Both Vernoud and the Bwitists sought a new order of things. Vernoud was trying to cleanse the cosmos with Spirit and return to primary relationships between man and deity. Bwitists were cosmologizing too, though in a more thoroughgoing way.

THE REACTION TO COMMANDMENTS

Despite these sparks of understanding, and the fundamentalist search for world view which they represented, there was among Fang a reaction to the moral order put forward by missionaries and administrators with their emphasis on codified pieties, on commandments, and on compliance with bureaucratic rules and orders. For Europeans that compliance was a measure of African response to the "civilizing mission." Indeed, when one thinks of the Western "moral order" as embodied in the "civilizing mission," one thinks of rules of various kinds—everything from the Ten Commandments, the Apostles Creed, the Sermon on the Mount, to the Pledge of Allegiance, the Oath of Office, the bureaucrat's table of organization, and the Scout's Pledge. One thinks of what can be enumerated and thus appealed to in guiding conduct.

Though they recognized "social sins,"[*2] Fang had a much stronger feeling for ritual obligation than for moral enumeration. They did not readily recite codified moral rules. Indeed, it was difficult to get Bwiti leaders to list their "commandments" or otherwise enumerate or codify their moral position. The crucial moralities are bound up in the nature of the cosmos and these rights and wrongs are adhered to as they are achieved over and over again by ritual celebration. Whereas Tessmann argued that Fang energetically tried to transfer the "good" and the "bad" over to nature, it can just as well be argued that that transference was the result of a breakdown of cosmology only reparable in cosmogony. The "moral integrity" of cosmogonic ritual, is different from that imposed by moral rules, which raise the question of dissonance in a pointed way. It is an integrity achieved, rather, in the face of "doublings" and dissociations which are, in the end, accommodated and reassociated in the overall "microcosmology" of ritual metaphor and symbol. The "moral order" in ritual, if it may be called such, is an overarching system of associations produced out of "doublings," incompatabilities, tensions, and contrarieties of all kinds. Moral rules, as such, are too constricting.

What the missionaries were interpreting as an unfortunate "doubling of personalities" was, as often, in the Fang view an attempt to escape from the tedious constraints of a moral-bureaucratic order—that of Christian piety and administrative rules—that was tying down their personalities to a too sober colonial civility. Many Fang (not all of course, for men such as the Benga pastor Ibia Ikengue held Christian morality up as a mirror to mission) understood such "doubling" as an escape from religious tutelage and administrative directive. The doubling of personalities was, therefore, an attempt to return to a more polyvalent personality—a personality that could relate, as their effective and authoritative personalities have ever had to do, to the realms of both the living and the dead, the seen and the unseen.

[*2] We have discussed the distinction between ritual and social sin above and in "Christian Acculturation and Fang Witchcraft," p. 260. The much greater sin was the ritual one, for it had cosmic implications. Social sins—the rights and wrongs of social life—were much more commonsense requirements. They emerged in the observations, usually proverbial in form and not didactic or codified, of wise men and women faced with social disorder in council house or kitchen. Of course this wisdom was passed down from the ancestors and so enjoyed their sanction. But it was not really a supernaturally derived morality as were the Ten Commandments. Wisdom about social sin emerged out of men's attempts to maintain harmony amidst the heated passions of village life, and not out of a burning bush.

There was doubt on the part of many Fang from very early on—a doubt fully articulated in Bwiti—that Christianity could effectively relate to and make personally relevant the ancestors and the realm of the dead. The doubling of personalities restored this contact and reestablished this relevance while, at the same time, it enabled Fang to escape being exactly what missionary and administrator wanted them to be. This "escape" and this "restoration" are shown in two quite contrary reactions to the colonial moral order: first, Fang "celebrations" of its peremptory nature, and second, a reaction much influenced by Bwiti but going much beyond it, to restore a full range of moral realms of existence, realms of right action, to the African.

Administered Morality: De Gaulle and Franco

Albert Schweitzer frequently remarked that Europeans lost much of their moral authority after the First World War. Nevertheless, certain European personalities who were much in the news were used as dramatic "points de repère" in new rites and dances. Though no cult, rite, or dance appeared featuring Adolf Hitler, plentiful was the folklore still remaining in the late fifties which recounted his secret visits to Gabon or the Cameroons—a harbinger of a new order of things, a liberator from the yoke of French colonization. Informants heard of those who had heard of those who had seen his plane.

At more local levels there were administrators and other colonial personages who discharged the civilizing mission with such force and even-handedness as to become dramatic moral presences. Practically every district had at some time an officer of such quality that his long-departed presence is still recalled in the names of children born during or just after his tenure. The dance of Olanchea of the 1950's was named after a tough and paternalistic, though fair-minded and popular district officer of that period at Ebebiyin in Spanish Guinea. Likewise, the Ndong Andrike dance seems to have been named after a Spanish administrator—Don Enrique—of the thirties. There was also a lingering presence in folklore of the fair-minded de Brazza.

During the Second World War, Charles de Gaulle inevitably became such a moral presence in Equatorial Africa where he first organized the Free French Movement and where many administrative centers—Libreville, Oyem, Bitam, Medounou—saw battles between Free French forces and the Vichyites. In the late forties and early fifties the dance of Ngôl (also known as Digôl) swept through Fang country. Balandier regarded ngol as a simple and amusing ritual innovation compared to such thoughtful syncretisms as Bwiti or any of the challenging messianic movements of the Congo.[11] Its simplicity enabled it to spread readily across political frontiers and from one tribe to another. Alexandre,[12] on the other hand, saw the ngol dance and its attendant rituals as a variety of cargo cult playing upon themes from the Whiteman-Blackman legends. He understood the cult to be the dramatic enactment of a powerful White presence returned to restore material benefits and supernatural blessings lost in the original contest between white brother and black brother.

It is true that ngol was much more of a dance or festival celebration than a movement. It also celebrated a restoration of material blessings and a new accommodation of Whitemen to Blackman. More than this, however, it also celebrated, in a complex way, powers of the European moral presence and its administered morality. Fang appreciated the ngol dance on several levels. It is not enough to see it only as a slavish imitation of administrative mannerisms, though that feature is most striking. It also held up a mocking mirror to those mannerisms. Earlier, in the forties, of course, the ngol dance may have seemed more threatening to administrators. It may have seemed less mocking and imitative and more of an attempt to appropriate administrative prerogatives.

In any case the playful versions witnessed in Ndjole district in 1959 seem to have maintained their character throughout the fifties, for they were similar to the version described by the missionary Ochswald in 1950.[13] A large arbor or hanger of woven palm fronds is the scene of the dance. In the center behind a low raffia barrier are the drums. The dance is attended in Western dress with women in skirts and blouses or cotton dresses and the men in pants and shirts, sometimes ties. In contrast to practically all other Fang dances and in contrast to Bwiti, shoes are required. Around the wall of the hanger are found "stalls" or "loges" with chairs and tables. These are the bureaucratic pavilions for various of the male dignitaries, the "President," the "Customs," the Justice of the Peace. A French flag is draped over the principal entrance.

The women gather at one side of the dance arbor, commence the dance, and carry the major burden until the later appearance of "de Gaulle." He is one of the dance organizers and appears, usually with white kaolin on his face, dressed smartly in *kepi* and in a uniform with weighty epaulets. He may be accompanied by other dignitaries—the "Governor General Eboue" and even "General Pétain." All participants stand at attention when his arrival is announced, for he is to make an inspection. During this inspection some may be fined for disarray of dress. The General and his aides and confidants now enter their pavilion and the dance resumes. His subordinate "officers" enter next and with other men choose their female dance companions. "De Gaulle" and an assistant look on with attention, continuing to levy fines from ten to a hundred francs for missteps and awkwardness. A good deal of small change may be collected. Finally, after several hours, the General takes his leave, once again circling the arena and making a final inspection. This concludes the formal part of the dance though the drummers may continue until the small hours. This depends upon the regimen of the dance team which has come to teach the dance locally. For ngol in the 1950's, like all dances flourishing at the time, was taught by a visiting dance team.[14]

Ochswald regarded the de Gaulle dance as a manifestation of the clan regroupment movement (*Alar Ayong*) which had begun in the Cameroons in the forties. But while that northern movement was effective in leading Fang to greater cooperation and mutual aid, the de Gaulle dance, in his view, was simply a sterile and costly diversion pandering to the bureaucratic preoccupations of "evoluées." In point of fact the organization of the dance chamber into bureaucratic pavilions was similar to the way Alar Ayong itself organized its forest precincts.[15] Moreover, Alar Ayong, at least toward the end of its career in the fifties, had similarly evolved into a "costly diversion in part pandering to and in part mocking bureaucratic procedures."

But whatever satisfactions, these imitations of bureaucratic routine and governmental power had for Fang, they served in a situation of transitional disorder to promote a transitory discipline and create a singular moral personage around whom ceremonial events could be focused. Digol was not the only example of this sort of ceremonial focusing upon an administrative presence. There were also the *Flanco* dances which came out of Spanish Guinea in the late forties and early fifties and which featured, at the end of a long afternoon or early evening of dancing by the women's team, the appearance of Flanco and his wife as two life-size figures[16] with headgear and uniforms thrust above a raffia screen. This was reminiscent of the way the ancestor figures were danced above a raffia screen at the conclusion of ceremonies of initiation into the ancestor cult. The scenarios differ, but in both Digol and Flanco the dance ceremonies are brought to focus on a powerful alien personage who confers discipline and blessings. He also does not hesitate to exploit his authority to monetary advantage.

We may speak of a novel element in this "administered morality" but the sudden production of an august "presence" in dance and ceremony was an old element in Fang culture. In the Bieri cult the ancestors, or their cranial semblance, had to be produced suddenly for initiates while the rest of the villagers were shown them in the dancing forms of the ancestral figures. In the nineteenth-century dance of *nlô bekege* ("the head of the man who turns the situation upside down"), a white Janus-faced mask suddenly appeared above a raffia barrier and then, accompanied by thunderous drumming, the whole dancer, dressed in raffia costume, rushed out to dance through the crowd.[17] He flung himself to and fro and frightened children and women. A later version of this dance, *nlô nge* ("the head of he who will seize and carry away a victim") was still being danced in the mid-twentieth century.[18] Here also the object was to frighten the spectators by means of a white-faced helmet mask. Thus the Flanco mask and others similar to it such as *ngwan ntangan*[19] are reinterpretations of an old Fang dance motif by which in the process of dance a returned shade or forest spirit is suddenly produced. In the later, acculturated versions this spirit became a miraculously summoned European— the association between Fang dead and the European is at work. In both cases, the traditional and the acculturated, the apparitions acted to impose discipline upon an unruly crowd.

Digol appears, however, without a mask and in this he is more like the white-faced dancers that emerged out of forest precincts in the Bieri cult— or the *nom Ngí*, the chief dancer of the Ngi antiwitchcraft cult. These represented either the ancestors or powerful shades, so that the transition from the Bieri or Ngi dancers to ngol is also apparent. We see the same transition in the Metsogo ancestor cult of Bwiti where it was the claim of cult leaders that they produced the miracle of direct contact with the dead. The "dead" (disguised dancers) would actually appear at the edge of the forest in the process of the cult. In mid-century, among other impressive miracles produced by various chapels of this cult, was the appearance of a white district officer.

Mademoiselle, ngwan ntangan ("the daughter of the European"), Ndong Andrike, Flanco, and Ngol or Digol, then, are all recent reinterpretations both responding to and reflecting the pressures of colonial bureaucratic authority. But they also carry on an old Fang interest in sudden ceremonial apparitions which could, in such an egalitarian society, exercise a transitory discipline. The tutelary powers which lay behind the Mademoiselle of the Mademoiselle cult were more enduring than these other figures who made their appearance only in the dance context and were not part of repeated ritual activity. They had no ritual context in which they might be recurrently revivified to their followers. They were ephemeral also because in their authoritative administration of order they did not really speak to the diverse potentialities in Fang personality. That is what was humorous about them. There was a puppetlike one-dimensionality to them.

THE SECRET BIBLE OF THE BLACKS: THE DISSOLUTION AND COAGULATION OF BEING

If Fang, Metsogo, and other Gabonese peoples could reinterpret their traditional, momentarily powerful, apparitions and make of them a European presence, so could they in the other direction take such an authoritative European document as the Bible and turn it to their own use. An example of this is *The Secret Bible of the Blacks According to Bwiti* published by the Etshira, Prince Birinda de Boudieguy, in 1952.[20] One in a series of short occult works published in France at the time, it had begun to circulate widely in Gabon by the end of the decade. It reflects Gabonese Bwiti doctrine of the forties but it also possesses imaginative elements of its own and an overall breadth and integration of perspective not often found in local Bwiti leaders.[21] For example, Birinda's treatment of the female principle, *Dintsouna Muata Benga* (Spiritual White Woman), is a more elaborated notion than was given in the forest chapels themselves. Birinda presents Dintsouna as the luminous princess, daughter of the night, who was created out of the breath of the first of the creator gods, Mukuku Kandja. In her right hand she bears the sun and in the left the moon which she brings together to form the solar prince whom Birinda calls "the Eternal Verb." From Dintsouna's right breast flows a torrent of blood and from her left breast a torrent of milk. It is Dintsouna who fills out and stabilizes the tumultuous night, and it is only through her that devotion can be expressed to the supreme being.

Some of these elements are present in Fang Bwiti ideas about Nyingwan Mebege, the Sister of God and the Female Principle of the Universe, but not in such concentrated measure. For example, the issue of Dintsouna's color is more artfully presented by Birinda. We are told by the author that this daughter of the night is black as the night but has a luminous existence for, like the dark moon itself, she dresses in a white robe with a diadem of stars. That is why she is called "Femme Blanche, Princess of Light."[22] Her sex is ambiguous. He treats her as feminine in some places and in others seeks to relate her to the "Great Androgynous One" of cabalistic and alchemique literature.[23] Though the theology put forth in equatorial chapels of Bwiti is also the product of acculturation—the syncretic intertwining of traditions—the forest gods are not as polyvalent of personality as Birinda's Dintsouna. Her shifting shape is very much the product of Birinda's expatriate intellectual odyssey. There is plenty of similarly creative thought in the Fang Bwiti of the equatorial forest. But Birinda's long Paris sojourn exposed him to influences which complicated his discussion of Bwiti doctrine.

There is also a more pronounced animus in Birinda to "remove the veil that has covered the wisdom of Black Africa and to furnish an argument against the disdain of which it has been the object." "Is it because our skin is black that our spirit must also be shadowy and our practices pathological?" he asks. "In the view of Europeans we are obedient to sorcerers and we practice only black magic." But the doctrine of Bwiti, Birinda shows, reveals a profound wisdom.[*3]

Whatever Birinda's metropolitan sophistication, he shows insight into the way Bwiti works to "dissolve" and "coagulate" (his terms) the mental states of its participants through the process he calls "initiatory dissolution" (*dissolvants initiatiques*). This may be compared, I think, to what I have elsewhere discussed as "progressive ritual predication" and "the performance of ritual metaphors."[24]

Playing upon the macrocosm-microcosm distinction Birinda argues that every person is a universe in small, for every person synthesizes the universe at large.[25] Bwiti, therefore, provides a liturgical method by which the person

---

[*3] His argument is reminiscent of Mary Kingsley's defense, based on her Gabon experience, of the "wild African idea" in favor of spirituality as opposed to materialism (*West African Studies*). Birinda de Boudieguy argues that the black's sense of reality is spiritual, not material. The black seeks to understand the beyond in order not to have fear. "Il refuse d'abdiquer en faveur de la materie qui, trop asservie, se venge en prenant le sceptre" (*La Bible secrète*, p. 122).

can come to learn what the universe is made of through a ritualized exploration of what he himself is made of. The whole world has gone through various creations and every man contains and can recapitulate each of these existences in himself. The "seed and tree" metaphor carries an important burden of that discussion.[26] Just as the tree is found potentially in the seed so the universe is found in the individual man. "Man is the seed of God."[27] It is the object of Bwiti to take souls drowsing in their fleshly cells and make them conscious of their universal existence—to enable them to sing in unison the harmony of the spheres,[28] . . . to grow into the universe.

Birinda makes concentrated use of the sacred number three. He discusses the Theosophique Trinity (to which Dintsouna provides a fourth unifying and stabilizing principle), the nine states of creation and existence, and the three spheres of every stage.[29] Here again Birinda shows conceptual interests that do not preoccupy most practicing Bwitists in the Equatorial Forest. Nevertheless, it can be said that every Bwitist without exception, as Birinda argues, desires to show initiates, members, and himself other realms of existence be they only, as is often the case, the realms of the living and the dead. The desire is to enable men to dwell profitably in these realms, thereby escaping the somnolent and powerless monotony of the merely material colonial existence. Essentially Bwiti offers, as Birinda penetratingly suggests, the power of extending oneself into other realms, other domains of existence—an extension that capitalizes upon metonymic and metaphoric correspondences between microcosm and macrocosm.

> Man can enter into relationship with whatever entity of the universe of whatever region by putting into action that portion of himself that corresponds to that region and the nature of that entity. The Art (of initiation and celebration) consists of heating up the interior faculties with the object of leading them to different states . . . of the occult anatomy of man which is analogous to that of the Universe.[30]

In Birinda's Bwiti cosmology man possesses nine bodies, regions, or realms where this micro-macrocosmic extension can take place. Such multiple potentiality of personality extension is also greater than any transformations offered in any practicing branch of Bwiti known to me. But the fact remains that the Bwiti of the Equatorial Forest, in place of seeking to unify doubled personalities by either conversion to Christianity or nativistic rejection of that message—or even by celebrating an administered morality as in the case of Digol or Flanco—seeks to accustom its members to a much more polyvalent existence by offering them extension into a variety of realms of being.

THE BWITI MORAL ORDER AS "MOVEMENT TOWARD"

If we mean by a "moral order" an easily volunteered code of rules or commandments, these, at the time of research, were still difficult to obtain from members of Bwiti. One says "still" because as various branches of Bwiti become more and more Christian, commandments, the fundament of Christian casuistry, will become more a part of the public culture and of easy access to initiates and strangers. The difficulty of obtaining them in the 1950's is seen in the village of Ayol (Woleu-Ntem), for example, where, though I received very willing and gratifyingly extensive exegesis of ritual matters, I created consternation by asking for the commandments of the chapel. This provoked a long silence. Then one of the younger *yemba* (knowledgeable ones) proposed to answer, but he was immediately disputed by an elder. After some heated discussion among them I was told that the commandments would be provided the next day. The hammering out of these commandments provoked further lively argument in the chapel well into the evening. First I was told that Bwiti was founded on two principles of right action: love for others (*nyuge bôt bevôk*) and mutual aid (*evwalevwalen*). Upon these two principles the following twelve articles of faith were established.

ARTICLE I: Every Banzie must respect authority and cooperate with the Government.

ARTICLE II: It is forbidden to speak badly of another religion.

ARTICLE III: The Banzie must be clean in every area of his life.

ARTICLE IV: Every Banzie accepts the justice of the punishment meted out to the guilty by the Government.

ARTICLE V: Every Banzie recognizes the good deeds of the European and is grateful for them.

ARTICLE VI: Every Banzie must be polite.

ARTICLE VII: The love of work is paramount. Laziness is not permitted in the Church.

ARTICLE VIII: Every Banzie must fight against sorcery.

ARTICLE IX: Every Banzie speaks only the truth, avoids lies, and sees the criminality of stealing.

ARTICLE X: Banzies do not employ hemp.

ARTICLE XI: The Banzie refuses intercourse with others' wives.

ARTICLE XII: The Banzie does not enter into disputes with others.

Clearly this exercise in the listing of commandments was provoked by my inquiry. Indeed, it seems to reflect a concern—many of the members of this chapel had fled from government persecution of Bwiti in Spanish Guinea— that government might be privy to my work.

A more authentic source of a moral code might be found in the visionary experiences of cult members and particularly of the founders of new branches of Bwiti. We have cited the visionary journey in the twenties of the Fang, Bekoue or Koule, though we have no evidence that he returned with new moral rules. We do, however, have evidence of just this consequence in the 1938 account of the visionary death of one Jacques Ngoya, probably a Teke of Okandja, who journeyed several days to the land of the dead.[31] The consequences of Ngoya's journey were twofold. First, his dead brother appeared to him and taught him many dances which he was to teach to people on earth for their salvation and well-being. Second, this dead brother carefully enjoined Ngoya to follow a set of rules: "Do not eat salt, do not have sexual relations for four months, do not kill or steal, come to the aid of all those who are sick and provide food for all those who have hunger." As the district officer who interviewed Ngoya points out, the first four rules are traditional and similar to the prohibitions or taboos that attended individual strengthening rituals (*ekí akyaga* ceremonies among Fang). The last two injunctions, however—to provide food and succor to all in need—are universalistic principles that show the effect of Ngoya's Christian education in Franceville.

Fang Bwiti visions—Ngoya was not a member of Bwiti—rarely produce a set of moral rules. Indeed, they are mostly filled with encounters with the dead ancestors and with the various spirits and gods.[32] While these ancestors may give general advice on the need for the visionary to change his lifeway, to join Bwiti, or to work harder in it, they are rarely more specific. In the midnight sermons like those to be considered below, however, we see four stylized injunctions which initiate the sermon or conclude it.

Mina ta dzi môt.
You shall not eat of men.
Mina ta bele eves emôt.
You shall not keep the bones of men.
Mina ta kuing ngwel.
You shall not go out in sorcery.
Mina ta zu biom bôt bevôk.
You shall not steal others' belongings.

These four injunctions are said to have been brought from the grave by the founder of the Commencement of Life (Asumege Ening) branch of Bwiti, that branch in which we are mainly interested in this analysis. These "moral rules" of the founder, Ndong Obama Eya, give us greater insight into the dynamics of the cult than the decidedly Western commandments that one obtains by direct interrogation. For these rules express preoccupations about the increments of sorcery (the "apotheosis of evil"), about lingering customs which have come to be regarded as degrading (the keeping of the bones of the ancestors in particular), and about the narrow margin of existence and the limited good of their lives which makes the appropriation of others' belongings painful and threatening.

Still, to search for the Bwiti moral order in codified form, although it may gratify a Western need for abstractions of that kind, yet misses the Bwiti moral order where it reposes: in the images and actions of Bwiti myths and legends, in the night-long rituals and accompanying song cycle, in the architectonics of the cult house, and in the midnight "évangiles" of cult leaders. The moral order is more acted out than spelled out, more ritualistic than didactic. It is a set of images of pathos and despair countered by a set of images of rightness of situation in relation to which one acts and which one seeks to approximate. It is as much as anything a kinesthetic order that is gradually *exposed* to the membership in the process of their worship. It is much less an *imposed* authoritarian or administered morality posted in codified form in every public arena and drilled into the head of every initiate.[33] It is probably these differences that the missionaries had in mind when, after their first deception in Fang moral sensibilities, they said of them that they were a people "more religious than moral."[34]

To say these things is to say that the new Bwiti moral order can fully emerge only in discussions of myth and legend, ritual and song, architectonics and evangelization. Still, we may suggest a general context by which to approach Bwiti feelings of worthlessness and "worthfulness" and we can comprehend in a general way where they want to move—the conditions they seek to escape and the conditions they seek to achieve. We must remember that a central image in Bwiti is that of the road—*zen*—and that Bwiti worship itself is conceived by the Banzie as a movement along a road. The issue of moral order is best discussed in terms of that image and thus in terms of the "moral movement" of the Banzie from one condition to another.

We may begin with a recurrent phrase in the Bwiti song cycle, and in the évangiles: *O Tara Zame bi ne engôngôl* (O Father God we are in a state of despair and misfortune). It is that despairing sense of disarray, misfortune, and disorder that first energizes the Banzie in their worship. For while the religion makes many promises to its members, fundamental among them is the promise of escape from the state of despairing sinfulness and the achievement of a state of grace (abora)—essentially a state of satisfaction in one's situation and confidence in one's enterprises.

For the Bwitist, the qualitative state of abora[*4] is achieved by many different and distinguishable movements. First of all, it is achieved by escaping the condition of bad body (*nyôl abé*) or obscure or black body (*nyôl nsut*), a very concrete and corporeal feeling of being unclean. That feeling lies behind the Bwiti emphasis on personal cleanliness, upon the careful washing of ritual garments before services, and upon ablutions before and after ceremonies. And that undesirable quality no doubt provoked the visionary injunction with which the founder of the Commencement of Life cult, Ndong Obam Eya, returned from the Land of the Dead: "Remove the filth from our lives" (*ava efufum e ne bia*). While this injunction is understood specifically to speak

---

[*4] Traditionally this was the main word employed in the invocation of the ancestors by the elders before hunting, fishing, or warfare expeditions. It was the state of cleanliness and clear-sightedness brought about by ancestral beneficence and was probably related to the set of verbs bora and bore, to besmirch or be besmirched with mud.

against keeping the bones of the dead, it refers more generally to the feeling of living in filth. This is no new notion to Fang, for in various traditional rites and particularly in the ceremonies of the women's cult, Mevungu, the debris and rubbish of the village were periodically gathered together and disposed of ceremonially.[35]

One basic "moral movement" in Bwiti, then, is away from the quality of bad body to the quality of "clean body" (nyôl nfouban) or cleanheartedness (nlem nfouban)—a movement which, with caution, can be understood as that from blackness to whiteness. One says "with caution" because there has been a tendency in the literature to treat bad body as being mainly "black body." And there are many instances in the interchange between European and African where jocularly or in earnest there are allusions to the desirability, the possibility or impossibility, of changing skin color from black to white.[36] This, often unseemly, commentary had an effect upon Fang and upon the Bwitist in particular who made much of color transformations. Bwiti makes much of "paying the earth" (atang asi) or "paying the sins of the earth" (atang mesem asi nyi) as the white man has done, thereby escaping blackness and obtaining both his whiteness and his control over the earth.*5 Nevertheless, black remains a peripheral color in Fang ritual, for red and white have the central role. Moreover, filth is not only to be associated with a surfeit of blackness but also with a surfeit of whiteness. The unclean state of excessive whiteness is called efufum.

One primary source of "bad body" was sexual appetite and indulgence. Here also Bwiti makes a moral movement to the state of ôkan—abstention and purity. One of the most beautiful of the concluding songs, ma bô ôkan (I am sexually pure) celebrates the achievement of this state by the membership. And it is regularly put forth by cult leaders that one of the purposes of the all-night dancing is to sacrifice to God and to the ancestors the sexual pleasures of the bed (although at the metaphoric and symbolic level of cult activity there is plenty of sexuality being represented). Here we are dealing with a moral movement fully comprehensible to more traditional Fang. For it was forbidden to men before hunting or trap-tending or warfare to cohabit with their wives. Also, it has always been conceived, and not only in Bwiti, that the state of okan guaranteed successful enterprise. Okan is an important component of the state of grace.

To say that one of the moral movements in Bwiti is toward "cleanheart-

---

*5 There is a complicated and typically Bwitist conceit here. Bwitists playing on the word for European (ntangan) will say that the European lives on the earth but is not of it or in it because he has "paid" (atang) the earth. He has paid God for the earth God made him, and thus rather than being "earthy" or besmirched with earth like the African, he dominates the earth. We note that this conceit relates to the notion of grace as escape from earthy contamination. Bwitists promise that in their ceremonies Fang "die," pay the earth, and are revived in a state of grace, abora, such as the European regularly enjoys.

edness'' is to recall the importance in Fang notions of health and disease of the concepts of heartsickness (*nkukwan nlem*), balance and integrity of conception and behavior (*nlem mvwaa*, tranquil or orderly heart), and *nlem mvore* (oneheartedness or wholeheartedness). Though abora is the state toward which the Bwitists mainly aspire, yet they could not be Fang and not offer to their membership the qualitative feeling of ''tranquil-heartedness'' or oneheartedness. Indeed, a central Bwiti ritual of midnight and first light celebrates the obtaining of oneheartedness for the membership. Otherwise Bwiti leaders frequently emphasize ''even-handed tranquillity'' and an orderly dignity as one of the main components of the state of abora. And they as frequently refer to the destructive disorder (*ebiran*) and violence (*mvômvôl*) of Fang life outside the religion. Their high valuation of orderliness in cult affairs is seen in the careful clocking of ritual activity on the part of leaders as well as their distrust of the alkaloid drug *eboga* for fear that overconsumption will lead to ungainliness in ritual practice.

The qualities of orderliness and tight organization are not highly emphasized in Bwiti alone, of course, for we have seen the strong emphasis on bureaucratic order in various of the revitalization movements we have considered: Alar Ayong, Ngol, and so on. And here as in the matter of color categories—in fact, as in practically every one of the moral movements we consider—the pressure of the colonial presence, ''the spectacle of European orderliness and creative force,''[37] is important.

This spectacle is also in part responsible for the great emphasis on ''work'' (*eseng*) as an important element in the ritual achievement of abora. From the first, missionaries sought to impress upon the African the importance of the ''work of God'' (*eseng Zame*) in which they were engaged.[38] Fang, for their part, although they did not have the Calvinist belief in the purifying possibilities of ''work,'' had always taken pride in work as they defined it—men in men's work and women in women's work. But the European disparaged Fang work habits.[39] The pace and rhythm and the sex-role distribution of Fang work were different from the colonial culture which, in imposing its peace and administrative tranquillity, often left Fang, the men particularly, with little to do.[40] In response to these tensions Bwitists propose to replace the quality of laziness (*ndender*) and lassitude (*atuk*) into which Fang have fallen—they appear to have accepted European views—with the hard ritual work (*eseng banzie*) of the cult. By that hard work abora will be achieved.

Missionaries emphasized redemptive love in their evangelizing. At first they believed that Fang moral sensibilities were provoked by this Christian message or at least by its superiority to clan- and family-centeredness. Later the missionaries came to believe that Fang were incapable of real forgiveness and charity and were hopelessly caught up in exacting debts and balancing off vengeances. There may well have been a former preoccupation with debts and vengeance but in Bwiti there is frequent mention of the importance of forgiveness and of pardoning the wrongs of one's fellows. The sharpest verbal discipline I saw administered by a Bwiti leader (*nima na kombo*) was to a sullen member who had been ceaselessly complaining of the money owed him by another. He was told, "*Wa nyuge wa kun . . . wa nyuge ki wa dzama ebô bevô*" ("You love only vengeance, you have no liking for the forgiveness for others"). Bwiti thus transformed the old deathbed custom of *ava meté* (the lifting of the curse) where there was embodied a notion of forgiveness— the relieving or eradication of bitterness and resentments nursed by elders toward youngers.

In general, however, it is not so much forgiveness as tranquil patience that is encouraged in the face of the assaults of others. It is movement toward an old quality of maturity that is urged upon members of Bwiti[41]—enough tranquillity and even-handedness of spirit (*mvwaa nsisim*) so as to be able to return the soft answer, the good answer (*mbamba nyalan*) in the face of injury, and thus effectively turn one's face away from the quarrel. Tranquillity of spirit in the individual promotes tranquillity of spirit in the group and that is why in most branches of Bwiti careful control is maintained over prayer so that wherever possible it be made for public good. And if it is made for private and personal ends, at the very least it must be supervised so as not to disturb public tranquillity. Bwiti seeks to move its members toward personal and public peace and away from the preoccupation with vengeance.

Fang, like so many people in the colonial world, have felt themselves dwelling in obscurity (*zibe*) and ignorance (*nsugbe*). Therefore Bwiti leaders promise that through initiation and by the taking of the alkaloid plant eboga members will have their heads broken open (*abing nlô*) and their understanding flooded with illuminations from the world beyond (*ndendang Zame*). They will come to the knowledge of how things really are, based on journeying to that world. The more difficult question is whether this "breaking open of the head" is intended to bring about success in this world as well as access to the next. Most commentators upon the Fang have remarked a "materialism" in them and an impulsion to obtain riches (*biom*) in this world. Missionaries came to feel that Fang religious activities served mainly material ends, as in fact in the eki akyage ceremonies they usually did.

Most Bwiti leaders and, indeed, all the leaders in the Commencement of Life tradition, which is the largest branch of Bwiti, promise just the opposite. They promise that members of Bwiti will come to see that the riches of this world are no longer important and are insignificant in relation to the riches of the next world. Such leaders promise to "break open heads" not only to the illumination and knowledge of the next world but also to a sense of proportion about the goods of this world. Of course some immediate riches must be promised. There are two riches of this world that all Bwiti leaders do promise as a consequence of abora: fecundity (and hence the birth of children) and good health.

Another difficulty in this matter of breaking open heads so that members can "see" is its consequence for what Westerners usually understand by intelligence: grasp of complexities. Bwitists are, as are Fang generally, mistrustful of one kind of complexity—complicatedness (*meduk* or *medo fuk*) in persons. For such is a characteristic of the witch (*nem*) who is always too clever by half. While Bwitists will give complicated explanations of their activities as demonstrations of their knowledge of the unseen, they also stress that Bwiti moves men away from the attractions of complicatedness. It moves men to recognition of simple and fundamental truths which include the acceptance of complexity as something which belongs to the unseen rather than to the world of man. By telling its members that they will pass over to the beyond, Bwiti promises that they will experience a transformation in the nature of things such that the simple uncomplicated person (*mimia*) without witchcraft (traditionally a person under constant threat) can feel safe in this world and confident of his place in the next. He will be brought under the protection of complicatedness without fearing it or desiring to emulate it. Bwiti thus leads from complicatedness to awareness of fundamental and strengthening simplicities. It leads to the recognition of mysteries for what they are—supernaturally ordained complexities which can be cultivated but which surpass human understanding and intention.

Bwitists often refer to the regret (*azôba*)*⁶ Fang feel for the way they and their ancestors have been living. In Bwiti they promise to make a fundamental transformation (*afôlan*) in that life. The term afolan refers primarily to transformation occurring in things, in physical things, and not in feeling states or states of mind or spirit. For there is an undesirable sinfulness in things, and especially in bodily things, which must be eradicated or controlled if a spiritual state is to be achieved. Bwitists speak of a sinfulness in corporeality and that, in good part, is what the bad body notions and the emphasis upon purification are about. But they are more specific, for they also identify three sins of the body which Bwiti counteracts: the sin of birth which is the sin of violating or even rupturing the mother's bodily integrity; the sin of lactation which is the cannibalistic sin of eating at the mother's breast; and the sin of fornication, a further sin of violating another's bodily integrity. These three corporeal sins—violations of another—are inescapable insofar as one is bound to a corporeal existence. The only salvation is the transformation of corporeality into spirituality. The phases of this transformation, which we will not comment on here, are seen in various aspects of the liturgy and the evangelizations. They are exercises in shape-shifting, that is, corporeal transformation.

*⁶ This term was taken by missionaries to carry the notion of Christian repentance, which implies some sense of responsibility for a previous condition. The more traditional usage does not carry this notion of personal responsibility. Generally this "regret" for the traditional lifeway is coupled with a blaming of the ancestors for having produced it.

We may now summarize the set of movements in the qualities of the membership which are promised in Bwiti as a kind of moral ordering. The overall transformation is from the state of despair (*engôngôl*) to the state of grace (abora) which is coterminous with the shift from corporeality to spirituality:

MAJOR SHIFT
engongol (despair) to *abora* (grace)
nyol été (corporeality) to *nsisim été* (spirituality)

The subordinate shifts which together achieve these major transformations are the following:

bad body (*nyol abe*) to clean body (*nyol nfouban*)
turbulence (*ebiran*) to orderly tranquillity (*mvwaa*)
sexual indulgence (*mvyo*) to sexual purity (*okan*)
vengefulness (*akun*) to acceptance or forgiveness (*azame*)
disorder (*ngamla*) to orderliness (*okomge*)
sloth (*atek*) to industry (*nseng*)
obscurity (*zibe*) to clarity (*ndendang*)
complexity (*meduk*) to simplicity (*nkula*)
cupidity (*ndindi*) to satisfaction (*mvom*)

CONCLUSION: THE PROMISE OF ONEHEARTEDNESS

We have sought to capture here the movement in Bwiti morality, the movement away from one set of quality states and toward another set of quality states which Bwiti promises its members. Regularly the leaders of Bwiti regret and name certain quality states in which their ancestors and Fang outside of Bwiti have lived. By "breaking open heads" and "washing bodies and hearts" they work to bring about a transformation in the claim of things corporeal so that men may "die" and come into the knowledge of "the land of the dead," "the land beyond."[7] This knowledge is embodied in the visual and verbal metaphors of ritual and sermon, and it is the most efficient cause of the change of state in the Banzie—his becoming an angel. These enduring hopes for transformation make the Bwiti religion redemptive in nature and not simply therapeutic as is the case with its sister cult, MBiri. We may also identify in Bwiti a predominantly expressive orientation seen in its endeavor to bring about a transmutation in the instrumental claims of the material things of the real world. Of course there are instrumental and practical orientations in every

---

[7] Herein lies one of the main appeals of the alkaloid drug eboga, for in suppressing the fatigue and organ distension alarms of the autonomic nervous system it actually brings about corporeal change.

branch of Bwiti—as in every human institution—but the religion is remarkable for its rejection of the material world when compared with the geocentrism— the practicality—of the more traditional Fang religious view.

Bwiti morality is not well summarized in a set of moral rules. Bwitists, like Fang generally have difficulty making any such recitation. Moral rules smack too much of the "administered morality" imposed upon Fang in the colonial situation. While Bwitists, like most Fang, have an admiration for the orderliness created by colonial administration and seek to approximate to it in many aspects of cult life, they reject the one-dimensionality of personality and the constricting civilities implied by that morality—civilities more calculated to serve a colonial purpose than to make "the obligatory the desirable" in Fang society itself. The bureaucratic civilities of colonial administration were as often mocked as adulated in the new dances Fang were constantly exchanging. Fang may have admired the efficiency of that administration, but they recognized, as they imitated in the dances, the puppetlike personality it could produce.

The desire to escape an administered morality and to open up the potentialities of the personality is seen most strikingly in the *Secret Bible of the Blacks*. It offers, first, means toward the dissolution of personality into the many energizing and potentiating domains of the cosmos, followed, second, by a recoagulation into a much more powerful and poly-potential self.

The terms dissolution and coagulation, terms used by the author Birinda, remind us of the master metaphor of "flow" to which the missionary metaphor of "thirst" is so well related. It reminds us that our best clue to Bwiti morality is a careful consideration of the images in which it is embodied. The student should be interested in the way that Bwitists obtain to the desired quality states by extending themselves into various images from diverse domains.

For another reason it is unsatisfactory to consider Bwiti morality as a set of rules rather than as a set of projected qualities. Rules suggest problems of analytics and the need for logical congruence and consistency. This compunction is not felt by members of Bwiti for whom, as with other Fang, "good and bad walk together," however the good may outwalk the bad on the "path of birth and death." Just as there are inconsistency and contradiction in Fang life—cultural dilemmas[42]—so there is a dwelling with these in Bwiti. In Bwiti, however, these contrarieties, by inspired word and ritual act, are bound into a larger narrative whole, an orderly flow of images. It is useful to recall here the Fang distinction between ritual sin (nsem) and social sin (ebiran), for if there is a congruence and consistency in Bwiti it is in ritual matters. Ritual sins, awkwardnesses, failures of observance, etc., are more important than social sins. Bwiti leaders speak frequently of the "sin" of bad performance. For the performance of man's ritual relation to the cosmos subsumes the performance of his social obligations to his fellows. Indeed, the practice of Bwiti is expected to improve, and does improve, the quality of social relationships. But to say this is to say that the cosmos is a moral order to whose orderliness man has fundamentally a ritual responsibility—which he fulfills by ritual.[43]

Unsympathetic observers may make light of this cosmic responsibility which Bwiti discharges through its ritual. Projecting a Western European materialism into the religion they may tend to see it as an institution of expediency rather than morality—of activity whose object is immediate advantage in the goods of this world rather than cosmic order. But, in fact, this predominantly aesthetic notion[44] of the cosmos as a moral order is fundamental in the religion and outweighs practical-mindedness or expedient thinking, however prevalent they may sometimes be. Though the Fang, from the viewpoint of missionary morality, became over the years a disappointment to their teachers, early missionary appreciations of their "moral sensibility" were more likely accurate. They had great "moral sensibility" if we understand by that phrase the desire that the cosmos and man in his relationship with it *be in order*. However frustrated and vitiated this sensibility became under the strains and blandishments of colonial life, it reemerged with special vigor in Bwiti.

This moral order was not absolutistic. Neither Bwitists nor Fang felt they could eradicate ritual sin or evil in the world. This incapacity explains what men have to celebrate. Good and bad walk together. As Fang frequently enough told missionaries, "We have two hearts, good and bad."[45] Early missionaries, aware of these self-confessed contradictions, evangelized with the promise of "oneheartedness" in Christianity. But Fang by and large did not find it there. For many, Christian oneheartedness was a constriction of their selves. While "oneheartedness" is celebrated in Bwiti, it is a oneheartedness" which is coagulated out of a flow of many qualities from one state to another. It is a goodness achieved in the presence of badness, an aboveness achieved in the presence of belowness. It is an emergent quality energized in the presence of its opposite. Indeed, Bwiti ritual arenas are those quality spaces in which the flow of qualitative states occurs and in which coagulations, emergent qualities, appear. There is a certain aptness when Banzie speak of "paying the earth" for their sins, for colonization has made them, as Fang, particularly aware of their "earthly qualities," their association with things below. But at the same time the "quality space" of Bwiti really "pays the earth" by creating a new earth, a new world in which Banzie can dwell and in which the sins into which they have fallen can be mitigated by incorporating them into a larger whole.

⚔13⚔

The Origin and Re-creation
of Gods and Men

Akua, Tara Zame, a zu vele bia akua.
(At the forge, Father Zame, comes to fashion us
at the forge.)

CREATION OUT OF NOTHING

THE NGANGA METOGO pressed us to visit Bwiti. At dusk on the next Saturday, he and Muye Alogo Michel came to the door. They were dressed in the white robes with the red braided cords—the "path of birth and death" they taught and also, as Muye Michel was to explain, the replica of the succession of umbilical cords that attaches mankind though all the ancestors ascendant to the female deity, Nyingwan Mebege, the Sister of God. The two men insisted that we come down to the chapel, for the *engosie* was about to begin. Muye Michel would explain all that occurred. We were caught up in the momentum of their invitation.

When we arrived, the chapel was being swept out and the sweepings thrown into the forest. It was reminiscent of the old Fang yearly custom of *va adzal* in which all fires were put out, followed by a sweeping of the entire village. The trash was dumped in the forest. The fires were then relit and things begun anew. So in Bwiti after the sweeping of the chapel the fires are relit. But this Bwiti "beginning anew" occurs weekly and not yearly. And more than just beginning anew, the engosie, the night-long ceremonies of Bwiti, celebrates the creation of the world and the creation of mankind. In each engosie there is cosmogony.

The first fire of the evening was lit far outside the chapel at the creation or origin spot, the *njimba*, otherwise called the *ekat nganga*, the priest's circle.[1] This gathering place of three logs laid upon the ground opening toward the chapel, said Muye, is "the place of Mebege," the creator god, and it is "far and on the other side" (*vôm ye Mebege—ôyap ye ayap*). He called attention to the actions of the Banzie at this spot. One of the guardians of the chapel lit the fire, and the members, called together by a sounding on the antelope horn (*nlak mvu* or *tchiga*), seated themselves on the logs. After some

minutes and on a signal they arose to gather in a circle. First they made the
Bwiti sign of the cross. With their right forefinger, they touched first the
forehead (the father), then the heart (the son), then the stomach (the Holy
Spirit), and then they reached down and made a cross upon the ground (the
grave to which every man descends). Finally they rose up and pointed their
fingers to the sky with a shout: "*Aye yôke!*" Now taking their dance instruments, the brush, *biwia*, in the left hand and the rattle, *tchôke*, in the right
they began to shake them above their heads, arms outstretched. Again they
crouched down with the rattle and the brush almost on the ground, extending
their arms toward the fire. After a moment's humming, *ebubu bu bubu*, and
again on a signal, they suddenly straightened up with a shout, throwing their
arms over their heads: *Aye yoke!* Finally gathering closely in rows of three
the Banzie began the series of entrance dances, *minkin*,[2] each accompanied
by its song. In very close order and often with arms interlocked, they began
a slow and soft singing. First they circled the fire at the origin spot. Gathering
momentum and singing louder, they made another circle in front of the entrance, at that spot where the ancestor spirits were received, and then finally
in full voice they entered into the chapel for a further series of circles. (Figure
13.1)

Each minkin—there may be as many as three or four—is made up of a
sequence of songs and dance entrances which celebrate various aspects of the
Bwiti origin myth. Although there are a number of different minkin in Bwiti,
Muye Michel began to explain the songs of that first minkin, the Minkin of
Creation: *minkin mi ye môs ye abiale* ("the minkin of the coming of day and
birth"), which is most closely tied in with the Bwiti myth.

The squatting and the rising, said Muye, represent the cycle of the spirits
and the essential movement in life itself, which is brought down from above,
passes into the ground, and then is saved and brought back to the above
again. "So the spirits come down to us from above, live in our bodies, descend
with our bodies to the grave, and are released to return to the above." This
represents the three stages of spirit: in the sky above, intermediately in the
flesh, and in the ground below. Not only the vertical dimension is being acted
out here, but also the horizontal. For they move from "far out and on the
other side" into the chapel. The njimba or the origin spot is said to be the
deep forest from where men begin. "We are cold there and slow, unable to
really sing or move. But gradually as we dance toward the chapel we warm
up, become more active, and find our voices." The movement is from a
desolate and lifeless spot "out there" where one is barely warmed by the
creation fire to the lively and orderly place, the "forge" of the Bwiti chapel,
where one is heated and "forged," as it were, by many fires.

These shifts in quality from space to space have something to do with the
"moral movements" we have discussed from disorder to orderliness, from

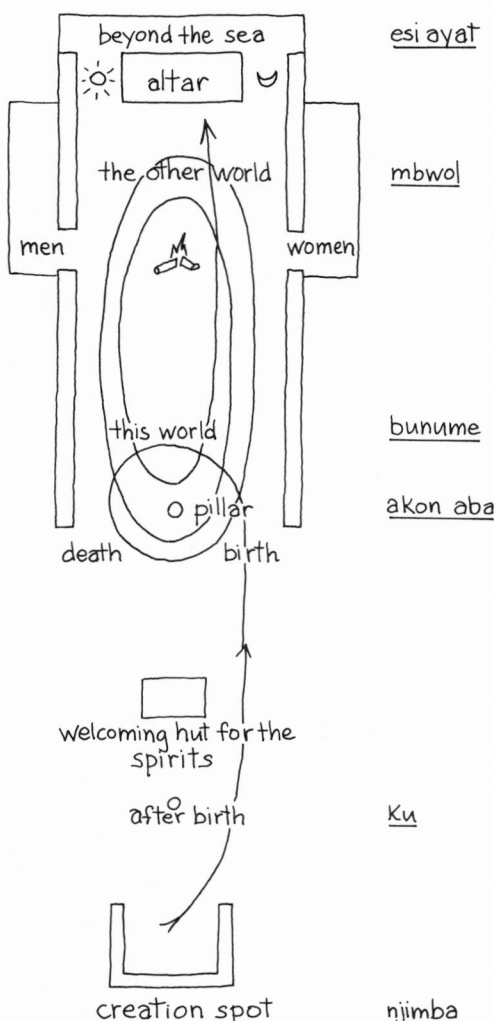

13.1 Minkin Entrance and Chapel Dance Pattern

obscurity to clarity, and also from coldness to heat. The rituals are complex
kinesthetic events in which the various senses are experiencing different but
often complementary things.

On the first dance of minkin, the Banzie entered the chapel singing:[1]

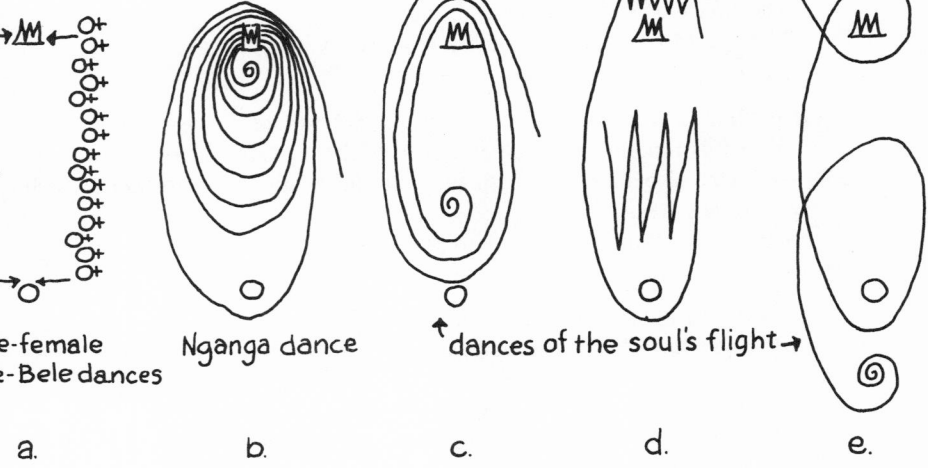

male-female
Bele-Bele dances

Nganga dance

↑dances of the soul's flight→

a.   b.   c.   d.   e.

1. *Mfonga mfonga o bele ening ase oh!*
   (R) *Oh, Oh, ening ase oh, oh.*
   The wind, the wind. It has all of life.
   (R) Oh, Oh. All of life. Oh, Oh.

Bwiti creation songs begin with wind and water and the creator gods. Life,
movement, is contained in the wind which is the essence of movement. The
word *mfonga* (wind, air, breath) is associated with "spirit" in the Western

[1] This sequence of songs of first minkin is typical of the Asumege Ening branch of the religion
and most particularly of the chapels in the Woleu-Ntem region. The sequence corresponds closely
to that given in André Mvomo Asumu and Henry Schmald, *Medzo meye Nfefe Enig, Biere
Gnigome Mebeshe: Angome Ebogha Fang*, p. 1. But this sequence here was taken from Ayol
chapel in Mitzik District. While there is an overall order to Bwiti ceremonies, there is considerable
variability from Chapel to Chapel and even from one week to another as regards the ordering
of songs. The upwards of two hundred Bwiti songs constitute a highly detailed oral tradition
susceptible to considerable variability of interpretation. This is not to consider the variable use
made of elements of Bwiti Latin (Popi Fang) taken from the Tsogo and Myene languages. We
give the Fang version here typical of Asumege Ening Bwiti. Other branches sing more in Popi.

sense and hence with the Holy Spirit. Thus Banzie interpret this song as referring to the Holy Spirit which was, primordially, the principle of life.[3]

The Banzie we were observing returned to the origin spot and began the second song of entrance:

> 2. *Nkôbo ôsua na, "etam e se mvé"*
> *Mebege a kôm wô, enin nzen, ve mfonga, mfonga.*
> (R) *Ve mfonga mfonga.*
> The first words: "to be alone is not good."
> Mebege formed the road of life from wind, only wind.
> (R) From wind only wind.

In the beginning were words, said Muye, and these words were lonely. And because of this loneliness the creator god, Mebege, created the path of life. This was later to become the path of birth and death, the path upon which all Bwiti rituals tread.

The group of Banzie returned to the origin spot for the third song of entrance:

> 3. *Nkôbô wa kane yan, o ntô ngap élé.*
> *Mfonga esa, edo e ne monenyang menzim*
> (R) *Menzim e ne monenyang.*
> The words have divided up things, there are three divisions.
> The wind is the father, the older brother of the water.
> (R) Water is a brother.

The "three divisions" referred to here are the three persons within the Cosmic Egg which the creator god Mebege, through the agency of sky spider, lowered to the water: Zame ye Mebege (God), his sister Nyingwan Mebege, and his brother Nlona Mebege. They become the effective supernaturals of this life. The fact that the wind is presented as the elder brother of the water is an instance of the genealogical idiom by which creation in its various phases is grasped.

Now came the fourth entrance song. Muye here joined the dancers. They sang:

> 4. *Ñkôl ô bele ening, mfonga ôyô, menzim asi.*
> (R) *Ñkôl ô bele ening.*
> The filament (cord) holds life, wind above, water below.
> (R) The cord holds life.

The reference is to sky spider's filament as it lowered the egg containing "life in three persons" to the sea. But this song in other contexts refers to the line of umbilical cords which are imagined to attach the worshiper genealogically through his ancestors ascendent to the great gods. This song, like many Bwiti songs, is sung in various ritual contexts.

It was time for the fifth entrance song:

5. *Mvelane bot, ebuma nzea ho.*
Mebege a vele mintol mi bot, ve mfonge mfonge
(R) *A vele mintol mi bot, ve mfonge mfonge.*
The creation of men, in a sphere very full, ho!
Mebege created the elders of men out of wind alone.
(R) He created the elders out of wind alone.

The spider's egg is here referred to as a very full sphere or as a ball, its natural shape. The sixth entrance sings of the heavenly bodies:

6. *Nlôdjop ye ndulngwan (ngômendan) bébé ho.*
(R) *Minzô mise mi ntô yang, hô!*
The sun and the full moon, two together.
The brilliant ones are fortified (take power over creation).

Muye here left the dance group. The sun and the moon in Bwiti are, he said, the son of god, Zame ye Mebege, and his sister, Nyingwan Mebege, respectively. They also represent the male and female principles, the two forms of being to which the songs refer. As will emerge, it is one of the main objects of Bwiti to bring these two forms of being into ritual coordination.

In the seventh entrance song, the two heavenly orbs are turned into the two ancestors:

7. *Bemvama ba bebe be vos ye mane.*
Osiman mvé ô dzingele yan.
(R) *Osiman mvé o dzingele yan.*
Our two grandparents are ripe and ready
The good thought of creation is now lost.
(R) The good thought of creation is now lost.

The reference here is to the readiness of Zame ye Mebege and to Nyingwan Mebege, the offspring of the Creator God Mebege, for fornication and for giving birth. But in the sexual urge, Muye explains, the "good thought" upon which creation was based, namely, to create sociable and pleasurable activity and to escape loneliness, was lost in lustful self-interest. "That is why we Banzie prohibit play between male and female in the "engosie." We seek to return to the good thoughts of creation."

The final song of the first minkin shifts to a "paradise lost" theme:

8. *Tita-Nzambi-Apongo Nkôme bôt amane yoghe ebon bé.*
Abialé ye awu da sô ebe bia, Nkôme bôt a mane yoghe ebon be.
(R) *Abialé ye awu da sô ebe bia.*
Father God of the Wind the Maker of Man has cursed the (his) two children.
Birth and death have come among us, the Maker of Men has cursed the two children.
(R) Birth and death have come among us.

This song as well as its predecessor anticipates the "creation of man" sequence which occurs in later songs of entrance. The title that Mebege is given here, translated by Muye as Father God of the Wind, is Popi Fang, that is to say a Fang mixed with elements from either the Miene coastal languages or from the Tsogo group of languages.[4] In this case Apongo is probably taken from the Miene term *omponga* meaning wind. But also in Tsogo, the first-born god of this world is Ndjambe a pongo—God of the airy firmament or "valut."[5] Because of the influence of southern Gabonese Bwiti upon Fang Bwiti many Bwiti songs are sung in a language unknown to Banzie themselves.

After the first minkin Muye was caught up in the dances. We saw no more of him. But he would come another day to tell the origin myth. It would "explain all." As it turned out, the myths do not always explain the songs and dances. They are not perfectly congruent. But if the myths do not always "explain," they always provide an additional dimension to the Banzie experience of origin.

A SHIFTING OF THEMES

The main themes of Fang folklore emerge in cosmic myth, migratory legends, and historical tales. A central theme is the Paradise Lost[6] theme referring to the savanna uplands and the former and ancient seaside existence of the ancestors of Fang. That former existence merges into a subsequent though still distant past in which Fang fly from cruel and exigent powers represented in the giant crocodile, Engurengurene, who holds the tribe ransom to his voracious demand for young men and women. Engurengurene is not a simple figure to describe. He and other chthonic creatures also act as protectors and as facilitators of the savanna passage. Various colored snakes appear to offer bridges across impassable watercourses while at the same time laying claim to sacrificial offering of Fang as payment.

These legends and tales figuratively explore the unwelcome contradiction that those who give origin and protection to men are also likely to be their oppressors. Sometimes this contradiction is embodied in monsters of various kinds and sometimes it is referred to its real locus in social life—that is, to the struggle between generations, between elders and youngers, in which olders sacrifice themselves for youngers while at the same time oppressing them. This lore explores an ambivalence in the "protective benevolence" of the old.

In the mvet cycle of tales, in recent years more popular than the savanna legends and the tales of tutelary but exigent animals, the predominant theme is the violent struggle to obtain and exercise power. But though some imaginative Fang may find a veracity in this genre and model their behavior upon it, for most it is only a folkloric amusement—a compensatory pastime—portraying events that really never happened.

After the savanna experience Fang come in their migrations to the Equatorial Forest, a milieu so different that they were initially unable to enter it. This impenetrability is represented in the giant azap tree which blocks their entrance. But here the Pygmies come forth to help them chop the tree and adapt to the forest. This adaptation is not without its penalties. The tribal unity which flourished on the savanna breaks down in the tangled forest into strife and separation into subtribes, clans, subclans. At the same time Fang discover a new dynamic impulse in the forest, an attraction toward the sea and the goods of European contact. In the savanna Fang were fleeing from greater powers. In the forest they become transformed into the "Pango," a turbulent and aggressive people scattering the autochthonous people before them in their drive toward the ocean. This is a transformation which is reversed in Bwiti visions. For though this transformation partakes of both history and legend it has historical reality to Fang for whom the Azapmboga legend is deeply meaningful.

In the colonial period there were various attempts by Fang and their Pahouin congeners to gather these myths and legends together. The most notable result was *Dulu Bon be Afri Kara*. (The Journey of the Children of Afri-Kara). This eclectic legend, published in literary version by one man but gathered together by many, emphasizes the malaise of separation and the impotence of the children of Afri-Kara, an emphasis compatible with the intention to use it as a motivating document in the clan regroupment movement, *Alar Ayong*. *Dulu Bon* ends up by reworking the paradox that givers are oppressors. It is the European that becomes the unwelcome embodiment of this contradiction.

Another version of this theme which is very old in Fang culture is the oppression of the innocent and unenlightened (*mimia* or *bidimi mam*) by the knowledgeable and enlightened (*engôlengôla, nem,* or *beyeme mam*). In recent times this theme has been also rephrased—in the Whiteman-Blackman stories where it is the white man who is the knowledgeable one and the black man, whether by accident, ignorance, or trickery, who is fated to play the role of the innocent and unenlightened.

The myths, legends, and tales of the Bwiti cult show us both a reiteration of older folklore and its themes and some transformations and expansions. For example, in Bwiti as in the ancestral cult, Bieri, we find emphasis upon genealogical pieties, upon reestablishing bonds with the ancestors, and upon eliciting their tutelage and protection. But we do not find in Bwiti a recurrent exploration of the repression that lies in the powers of creation and protection. Nor do we find the notion that tutelary beings either demand sacrifice or must necessarily be sacrificed. Where sacrifice occurs in Bwiti lore it is compliantly accepted by the victim who has previously given no evidence of being oppressed but is victimized by circumstances rather than by monstrosity of character. It is self-sacrifice.[7]

The recurrence of oppressiveness in generosity (in the Latin sense of the term *genere*, begetting or passing on of status or condition) from generation to generation in Fang legend has a typological character. That is, the same problematic relationship is presented over and over again by changing actors in different legends. But there is much stronger emphasis on typological transformation in Bwiti. Here the same characters, notably the Old Adam and the Old Eve, reappear in new guise as Cain and Abel, as Mary and Jesus. As they reappear the typology is transformed while new aspects of their relationships are explored. Still this typological couple are always protective and benevolent as regards their offspring. Bwiti lore seeks to emphasize giving without oppression, sacrifice without coercion. In part, no doubt, this change is stimulated in Bwiti by the Christian missionary emphasis upon *agape*, the celebration of a selfless brotherhood. Practically every missionary sought to convert Fang to this state.

In a similar way, while the traditional lore, particularly the mvet cycle, is full of violent struggle and strife, Bwiti lore emphasizes mutuality, fusion rather than fission, "oneheartedness" and "tranquillity" rather than clan struggle and endless turbulent activity (*ebiran*). In the Bwiti version of the legendary past also, men are no longer driven as on the savanna or driving as in the forest. As we study their architectonics we will discover the celebration of a calmer vector of movement along which nodes of centripetal activity are clustered.

While Fang lore, particularly in its latter-day versions, the Whiteman-Blackman legends, features loss of knowledge and the decline of Fang into a state of ignorance, in Bwiti lore the gaining of new knowledge is stressed. In Bwiti heads are broken open and people come to "see" the "science of hidden things." Bwiti promises that "those who do not know" can become "knowledgeable ones." And as opposed to traditional Fang thinking where early "preparation" makes men inescapably "knowledgeable ones" or "innocents," in Bwiti the path to knowledge, though hierarchical, is open to all at any point in their careers.

Three Genres of Origin

The tales told of the past in Bwiti are of three kinds: (1) those having to do with the origins of the religion of *eboga*, (2) those having to do with the origin of the cosmos and of man, and (3) those tied in very closely with Biblical events such as Noah and the great flood, or the virgin birth of Jesus. These latter events are reinterpreted in significant ways. There is some overlapping between these categories, particularly the latter two. In the liturgical cycle, songs and rituals pass quickly from the representation of cosmic creation and the creation of man into the celebration of events which are Biblical in nature. Frequently enough the account of the discovery of eboga is introduced into the quasi-biblical accounts. One justifies division into these genres because when Banzie tell tales of the past and of origins, as opposed to acting them out in all-night ceremonies, they generally concentrate on one or another of these genres and do not mix them together. The first genre, the account of the origin of eboga, is only rarely acted out in Bwiti rituals. Perhaps this is because the account of the origin of the religion of eboga contains an account of sacrifice[7] which is embarrassing to Banzie and was a cause of administrative repression between the two wars. Secondly, at the time of this research the emphasis was upon the syncretization of Christian elements. The "origin of eboga" tales are too traditional.

We have had to choose between various versions of these myths and legends. As is always the case in oral narrative there was variation from one narrator to another according to talent, experience, and interest in the materials. We have tried to choose versions of these genres which, though more elaborate than those obtainable from the average Banzie, are yet not so idiosyncratic as to be unacceptable to them or incompatible with the ceremonies.

THE DISCOVERY OF EBOGA BY THE PYGMIES

Versions of the discovery legend are found in every branch of Bwiti. Its constancy throughout the religion is shown in the fact that Veciana obtained a version similar to the one given here in 1954 among the coastal peoples of Rio Muni, the Kombe, and the Bujeba.[8] We collected five versions of this legend. The one presented is that of Ona Pastor, an Okak tribe member originally of Spanish Guinea but who had spent more than a decade in Bwiti chapels in Gabon—first in the estuary and then as a harp player (*beti ngômbí*) in the Kwakum Chapel outside of Oyem (Woleu-Ntem Region). It will be noted that he ties this legend in with the Blackman-Whiteman legends.[9]

God asked himself why he had never seen a black man in heaven. Was it because they had remained in their sinful ways? He took pity on them. He remembered he had created two peoples, black and white, but the prayers of the blacks no longer arrived in heaven. How could he help the black? One day he looked down and saw a Pygmy high in an Atanga tree (*Pachylobus balsamifera*) collecting fruit. He caused him to fall and die, and he brought his spirit to heaven. He cut off his right finger and right toe and scattered them in the forest. These became the eboga plant. He said to the Pygmy: When your people eat of this plant and pray to me I will hear it and when you die, having eaten eboga, you will come to heaven. God then took the Pygmy's bones and put them in a stream. The Pygmy's brothers looked for him but could not find his body and they made a funeral without it.

One day the Pygmy's wife, Akengue, went fishing deep in the forest. She left her companions and hearing a moan in the water upstream dug in the water and found the bones of a man. Thinking they might be the bones of her husband she washed them and placed them at the stream side intending to take them home. But while she was fishing a wildcat came along[10] and gathered the bones and took them away. In perplexity she started to return home but suddenly a voice spoke to her calling her through the forest to a cave (*nda akawk*). There in the back of the cave was the pile of bones on a wildcat skin.[11] A voice like the voice of her husband asked her who she was. And it then asked her to look to the left at the mouth of the cave. There was the eboga bush. The voice asked her to eat of its bark. To the right the voice showed her the mushroom *duma*. It asked her to eat of that.[12] The voice then asked her to turn around. Suddenly the fly, *olarazen* (he shows the route) flew into her eye, blinding her.[13] When she had wiped her tearful eye and turned around the bones were gone and her husband stood before her. He told her he had been with God (Zame) and had come back with the religion of the blacks. He renamed her Disumba, because she was the beginning of Bwiti. It was the plant eboga that would enable the blacks to see their dead ones. But payment (*okanzo*) must be made. So the woman returned to the village and came out daily with food and offerings.

Meanwhile her dead husband's brother (her husband by levirate) became suspicious and followed her. He surprised her at the cave. But she would tell him nothing. Then her dead husband spoke to her saying to give his brother eboga. When he had eaten eboga he saw his dead brother. Immediately the dead asked for payment (okanzo) for the powers they had bestowed. What can I, a poor man, give you, said the living brother. Give me your wife said the dead brother and forthwith the living brother fell upon her and strangled her so that the willing woman passed on to join her first husband.

Among the various elements in this legend that deserve commentary the one that most provokes comments from the Banzie who tell it is the sacrifice of Akengue-Disumba by her levirate husband. The explanations range from regretful observations[14] on the "sinful" nature of the original form of Bwiti—the presence of many sorcerers in the earliest forms of the religion—to a more artful explanation: that Akengue's death represents the necessary "death" that all eaters of eboga (*ndziebôka*) undergo in order to commune with the ancestors. My own tendency is to regard this element in the legend as a rephasing of that basic theme in Fang folklore—the necessity that those who give to others be sacrificed lest they be a source of oppression or because they have become so. But there is an important difference, for Akengue-Disumba is never represented as an oppressive figure and, in fact, she is a willing victim of self-sacrifice in the Bwiti account—a notable transformation of the traditional theme.[15]

As provoking as the sacrificial element is to Banzie, it is the Pygmy origin that needs extended commentary.[16] It is probable that eboga as a deep forest plant would have been part of the Pygmy pharmacopeia before it was discovered by Fang or other Bantu. Fang credit Pygmies as the source of many of their medicinal herbs,[*2] and in the azapmboga legends Pygmies help Fang to enter and adapt to the equatorial milieu. Bwitists even when not recounting myths credit Pygmies with the discovery of eboga.[17] Moreover, some aspects of Bwiti ritual are reminiscent of Pygmy ceremonies—the "molimo" and the "elima" as discussed by Turnbull[18]—and this connection is also recognized by Banzie.

Thus the appearance of Pygmies in this origin legend may represent nothing deeper than a recognition of the historical experience of Fang with Pygmy. Yet to have the religion of eboga begin with these mild-mannered little people is in striking contrast with the giant personages and the struggles with giants and monsters which appear in the traditional legends, not to mention the mighty men and mighty deeds which appear in the mvet cycle of troubadour tales. Instead of passionate, egocentric conflict this Bwiti legend begins with those familial emotions of protection and nurturance (*akam* and *mvam*) fundamental to the ancestor cult. The strong emotions here are Zame's desire to help the black make contact with him, Akengue-Disumba's search for her husband, and her readiness to be sacrificed in the interests of establishing a link between the living and the dead. The only turbulent emotion is her levirate husband's suspicion of her motives, her possible adultery. But this legend focuses predominantly upon the restoration of communication between the living and the dead rather than upon the escape from oppression and the struggle for power.

In respect to the psychological burdens of colonial life which have afflicted Fang and which Bwiti has sought to escape, the Pygmies are also apt founders. In contrast to the enforced stabilization of villages and the rigid imposition of a limited set of social categories which Fang experienced in the colonial world, the Pygmies are free spirits with the volitional movement of hunters and gatherers never tied down to any locale. Moreover, they are an egalitarian people, little given to categorization and surely without the social hierarchy of domination and subordination which Fang, fundamentally egalitarian them-

---

[*2] There is an uncertainty as to how much of their culture Fang owe to the Pygmy. Panyella in his *Esquema* (p. 17) argues that despite the racial admixture with Pygmy demonstrated by Alcobe, Fang have adopted relatively little from the Pygmies. Certainly in material culture he says it is limited to hunting nets and a variety of three-legged stools. Père Trilles, on the other hand, in his book *L'Âme du pygmée de l'Afrique* suggests a much more extensive spiritual influence of Pygmies on Fang and other Equatorial Bantu. He argues this for cosmic symbolism—the milky way as the path between God and man. But Trilles is mainly concerned to confirm the work of Pater Schmidt and the Vienna school of religious anthropology. He wants to prove the primal and pure religious insight of the Pygmies—an insight rapidly obscured by Fang materialism and fetishism. This impulse is too obvious in Trilles, but no one who has written on the Pygmy, including C. Turnbull (*The Forest People*), is entirely free of it.

selves, were experiencing under colonial rule. The values of the Pygmy way of life could not help but be appealing to Fang in colonial circumstances. There is one final attraction in Pygmy life. From a Fang perspective, preoccupied as Fang are with "bad body" or "obscure body," the Pygmies living in the forest are a pure people. They do not have the sins, either ritual or social, of the village. The Pygmies regularly inhabit those desolate and abandoned areas of the forest where troubled and impure Fang have always gone to sit for days and nights (*dzobege efun*) confessing their sins and obtaining purity of body (*nyôl nfouban*).[19]

The appearance of little people at transitional moments in myth and legend is a widespread motif in world folklore and recurrent in western Equatorial Africa.[20] Quite apart from their marginality as forest inhabitants, which gives them valence at transitional moments, Pygmies, more particularly, derive power from a paradox in their physical presentation. The transition which this origin legend describes from a state of spiritual isolation to intercommunication—the principal transformation aimed at in Bwiti—is effectively accomplished by little people who combine in themselves, paradoxically, a neoteny reminiscent of childhood and infancy with the actuality of full adulthood. Pygmies and other little people are good physical representations—a living condensation—of what the ancestor cult is all about: the establishing of a link between parents and child, grandparents and grandchild.*[3] Indeed, the Fang reliquary figures are sculptured "little people" which have aspects of both infancy and old age (ancestral status)[21] and thus artfully represent that linkage. For reasons of physical presentation, then, Pygmies are appropriate figures in this legend and assist effectively at the transition to that spiritual intercommunication the religion tries to bring about. This is in addition to the example they provide in the transition Bwiti seeks from aggressiveness, at best oppressive benevolence, to nurturance and protectiveness. For the Pygmy, both in Fang legend and actual fact are benefactors, providers of meat and forest knowledge, who are not oppressors. Pygmies are apt harbingers of the new dispensation in Bwiti.

THE COSMOS CREATED AND DESTROYED

We speak of a new dispensation brought about in Bwiti, and practically all Banzie regard their religion as a new dispensation. The name of the branch

---

*[3] One recalls the "child is father of the man" motif in Fang culture—the belief that every child is in some part the embodiment of an ancestor, and therefore to be addressed as "little father"—ata. Also consider the fact that in Fang patrilineal kinship and in the Omaha-type kinship system they use, practically all relatives are either parents or children. Older siblings of one's own sex are either "little fathers" or "little mothers," younger siblings are "children." Collateral relatives are, depending on whether they are traced through the father's or the mother's side, either "little fathers" or "my child." The parent-child axis is central and crucial. It is also in recent decades the axis most troubled by problems of communication and most in need of such figurative collapse or association as is accomplished in the figure of the Pygmy.

of Bwiti which most interests us here, Asumege Ening (The Commencement of Life), embodies that notion. But it was difficult to obtain from Fang or Banzie any clear notion of succeeding dispensations such as are so marked in many religions and which MacGaffey and Janzen have shown for the Congo.[22] For those Fang who take the mvet cycle of troubadour tales as veridical there are implicitly, at least, two dispensations: that time of the race of Engong when men were giants; and the present when, to say the least, they are not. Other Fang and some Banzie regard life on the savanna as one dispensation and life in the equatorial forest as another, followed by life under Bwiti as a third. Still other Banzie speak of each god in the genealogy of creator gods as providing a successive dispensation. The son of the final god, Emwan Zame or Eyene Zame (He who sees God) provides the final dispensation. So the matter of dispensations is not clear and dogmatic. At the most one can say that Fang looking back at their mythological, legendary, and historical past see a succession of different ways of life. For the Banzie Bwiti is the newest and the best.

Banzie give major emphasis in their liturgy to cosmic creation and, unlike "the discovery of eboka" legend, the creation of the cosmos is richly represented in their song and dance. We see this in the opening section of this chapter. In both their attention to cosmic creation and in their attention to the creation of man Banzie are distinguished from more traditional Fang who have little interest in these matters—showing at best a matter-of-fact attitude. An elaborate and typically Bwiti account of the origin of the cosmos and man was given to me by Muye Michel of Assok Ening (Oyem District, Woleu-Ntem), a man already central to the ethnography of Part I. We give it with reference to other versions both within the Asumege Ening communion and outside it.

Muye's account begins as Fang narratives usually do, with the work of Mebege, the creator god, who created Nzame or Zame, the God whom men know and worship. Mebege had his predecessors—Nkwa, Sokome, and Mbongwe. Mebege is often referred to by all these patronymics as Mebege me Nkwa Sokome Mbongwe. It was Nkwa, according to Muye, who declared that life should be created and who created fire which is at the base of life. Sokome had the intelligence to show how life could be created and how it would be organized. And it was Mbongwe[23] who carried life to the vicinity of the great waters of earth where it could be created. Finally, it was Mebege, through spider (dibobia), who created the earth and all its living things and who, in particular, created the three siblings, Zame ye Mebege (God), Nyingwan Mebege (the Sister of God and the Female Principle), and Nlona Mebege (the Brother of God, a tertium quid and an engine of evil).

Mebege was very lonely. He had only spider (dibobia) hanging below him above the water. Neither Mebege nor any of his ancestors had succeeded in creating more than one offspring to relieve the "eternal." Dibobia hanging motionless between sky and sea stirred restlessly on his single filament. He said to Mebege, we are alone (*etametam*) and there is no pleasurable activity (*elulua*). We must create the earth, where there may be activity and where there may be descendants whose activity we may watch. Mebege agreed. He pulled out from under his right arm underarm hair. He reached into his head and pulled white substance from his brain. He dipped far down into the sea and found a smooth white pebble such as are found in rivers. He put all these things in his right hand and blew upon them and a beautiful and perfect egg was formed. He gave it to spider who wrapped it in a filament and lowered it gently to the sea.[24] Mebege said, "Gradually that egg will become hot. When it does, come and tell me." Dibobia climbed back up to Mebege, for the egg was hot. Mebege descended at that moment and poured sperm upon the egg. It split open and there were the three persons: Zame ye Mebege to the right and Nyingwan Mebege to the left and in the center Nlona Mebege. These were the three children of Mebege—the God in three persons of which Christians speak.[25] Mebege and Dibobia now withdrew to regard their creation from a distance. They were satisfied with their handiwork. They left the world in good hands. Zame was to have power over it.

Zame looked around. Nothing but sky and water and a small tangle of raffia floating on the water. Zame knotted one of the strands into a cross with the knot known as the dog's paw which we still use in Bwiti. Holding that cross in his hand he looked up to his departed father. What should he do in all that desolation? Then Mebege sent to Zame the inspiring thought (*mbamba osiman*) which Christians call the Holy Spirit (*nsisim eki*). Zame then understood that each branch of the cross represented the four parts of the world. He reached under his right arm and under his left arm for underarm hairs. He reached into his head for the lining of his brain. He rolled these into a ball and blew on them. Thus he created termites and the worms of the earth. He then flung them out to the four corners. They sank to the bottom and began to eat and with their droppings they built up the earth. The earth grew in the sea. At first it was soft and marshy. Zame couldn't step off the eggshell. Then it grew hard. Zame and his brother and his sister stepped off. The first thing Zame did was plant the raffia cross. It grew into the raffia tree. Now the idea came to him to create man.

At this point in his recital Muye broke out into the eight entrance songs (minkin) found in the introduction to this chapter, although not all elements of his myth were represented in the songs he sang, which introduce other elements. For example, the cosmic wind is primordial in the songs yet it plays no part in Muye's account. On the other hand, though the songs mention the spider's filament, no mention is made of either the spider or termites so central to the myth. In short, neither myth, nor song, nor ritual actions alone are sufficient if we are to interpret matters of Bwiti thought and feeling. These modes are often in complementary interaction.[*4]

Before considering the next stage of Muye's cosmology and giving his next set of songs, we should note several features of the narrative. In all Fang versions of the myth, creation takes place from the firmament above to the sea below. In Veciana's coastal version, however, the creator God, Mwanga, emerges out of the water with earth to form the land. He creates the four sacred trees of Bwiti and plants them in the four corners of the world.[26] He then creates spider to weave a web between these trees and bring them into communication, creating a spidery network and a weaving together of the four corners, a weaving that occurs in many Bwiti chapels. In this coastal version Mwanga goes on to create the various animals preparatory to man. Veciana's version is closer to traditional origin myths which have this ''just so'' quality. The coming of god out of the water rather than to the water from above is a difference in cosmic imagination natural enough when we compare those living deep within the equatorial forest and those living on the edges of the sea. The difference also reflects the importance in Fang Bwiti of the tension between God Above and God Below—a distinction not so marked on the coast.

When we compare Muye Michel's version with another account, that of Paul Bekale,[27] we find an absence in the latter of Nlona Mebege, the intermediary sibling who, while the source of evil, also solves the problem, for Muye and other Banzie, of three persons in one God. In Bekale's version Zame and Nyingwan are created each in their separate eggs and not through the agency of the spider, which does not appear. There is a marked dualism in the Bekale account. This dualism also asserts itself in the songs which Muye sang us. For Nlona Mebege and the tripartition he implies, though mentioned in song three, are rapidly replaced by a concentration on the two figures Zame and Nyingwan and the two modes of being they represent. Bwiti in its ritual structure is predominantly dualistic, with only the occasional interjection of a mediating third element. But Nlona Mebege, however infrequent reference to him may be, is not a negligible figure in Asumege Ening.

[*4] There is also much variability from chapel to chapel and even from one night's liturgy to another as regards ordering of the songs, though one may speak of a general progression. The eight songs first sung by Muye are typical of first entrance in Asumege Ening chapels of the Woleu-Ntem but are not always sung in that order (cf. Asumu and Schmald, *Medzo meye Nfefe Enig, Biere Gnigome Mebeghe: Angome Ebogha Fang*). The upwards of two hundred Bwiti songs constitute a highly variable oral tradition. This is not to consider the choice for Asumege Ening members between singing the song in Bwiti ''Latin'' (Popi Fang) or in Fang, for in many songs there is both a Fang version and a Tsogo version.

He carries over the old Fang belief in the evus, the power of witchcraft, whose father he is said to be, while he also embodies the Christian Lucifer (suddenly brought into being without explanation in the Bekale version) in the more Christian portions of the liturgy. The evil he represents to Banzie is disturbance of communication between the two modes of being: male (Zame) and female (Nyingwan). In his central position he is a turbulent source of "noise" in the channels of communication between male and female, though his name suggests greater threats.[28]

One further important point is Muye's reference to the thought (*osiman*) which occurred to spider and which motivated the creation. A thought in English and in most historic languages, perhaps, has an element of originality—a new synthesis of a new situation. But the Fang term has much more the meaning of a recollection of a former state, situation, circumstance, or technique that can be applied to solve the recurrent problems of an ahistoric and essentially cyclical society. It is true that the myth gives no hint of a previous creation which Mebege and spider recollected. Yet we know there were antecedent creator deities. With Zame and Nyingwan, Cain and Abel, and Jesus and Mary, Bwiti shows in its myths an archteypal, repetitive creation, with each new instance of the relationship between male and female recalling the former. Thus when the leaders of Bwiti call upon their members to "think" about the troubled relations of man and woman they are asking them to recall successive creations of these modes of being which are celebrated in the religion and which provide a model by which to approach present problems.

THE INTERWEAVING OF CREATIONS

After he had sung the eight songs of first entrance Muye continued with his version of the origins.

Now Zame looked around and even though he was in the company of Nlona and Nyingwan he still felt lonely, so he reflected and made a hole in the earth—a smelting hole—and he made the Fang bellows, *nkôm*, and he took the fire from the sun which belonged to him. He gathered together a ball of earth and he shaped it, for the body comes from Zame. Then he turned to Nyingwan who reached into her heart and took out the last drop of blood that always remains in the heart of any living thing even when it is dead and she placed that drop in the center of the body of earth. For our blood is of Nyingwan Mebege. Then he turned to Nlona who reached into his brain and took out the white substance, "*meyôm*"[29] and placed it in the earth. Now the ball of earth was placed in the fire and Nyingwan Mebege began to pump the bellows while Zame turned the earth. Finally when it was red hot Zame reached in and removed it and struck it with his hands. It cracked open and out stepped Adam who resembled Zame in every particular.

While Muye was recounting these events he was animatedly going through the actions of forging iron, as, in fact, these actions are often simulated in Bwiti ritual. The forging of iron was an old craft among Fang[30] and one that excited much interest and respect. Although in the Asumege Ening branch of Bwiti there is not an elaborate ritual representation of the forging of men by the gods, in other branches this is a more central event.

In a chapel of the Disumba branch of Bwiti (Clan Essobang) at Bifun on the Kango-Lambaréné road, for example, early ritual is focused around the central circle, *ezizang nkat*, of the chapel and the fire that burns constantly beneath it, *nduan*, or *mewuba* in Popi Fang. Early on in the evening the long clay pipe attached to the double sack Fang bellows is placed in the fire. As these bellows are pumped by one member representing Zame, another member on the opposite side of the flaring fire, bending slowly forward, lights a bundle of raffia slips. When these catch fire he jumps over the fire itself, runs around it holding the torch high, and finally, running and whirling, passes out of the chapel into the night. He eventually comes to rest facing the chapel at the far end of the njimba, the log arena of first gathering where the minkin entrance songs are begun. All this represents the creation of the first being by Zame. The first being, Adam, is frightened by all the noise of creation and that is why he flees and takes his place at the quiet origin spot of the religion, the njimba.

Muye did not at once break into songs to complement his telling of the second part of the origin myth. He was satisfied to accompany himself with the kinesthesia of creation. It was only later that he sang the second set of songs which have to do with the creation. These are not a part of the minkin, the entrance songs. These are sung after the membership has fully entered into the chapel. Since these are accompanied by the harp, *ngômbí*, they are called songs of the Road of the Harp (*zen ngômbí*). They have two subdivisions: the road of creation and birth, *zen abiale*, and the road of death and destruction, *zen awu*. There is some overlapping between these creation songs of the harp and the minkin entrance songs. But redundancy and restatement and interweaving of themes is the Bwiti style.

The Road of the Harp: Commencement Songs. Muye sang two songs:

1. *Tara Zame, ening, Tara, a sumeang. A sumege. Ta Taroo,*
   a sumeang. A Nyingwan Mebege a sumeang. Koboge!
   Asumege! Ening Nen.
   Father God, the life, Father, has begun already. Let it begin.
   O Father it has begun. Nyingwan Mebege the life
   has begun already. Let it speak.
   Let it begin. The great life.

2. *Taro. Mot ka wí mot, awu e bele ening. Mebege a zô na, awu e bele*
   ening. Bot bese be semege Tare Zame ye Mebege. Betara ye Benana
   awu e bele ening.

> Father, men do not have to kill each other for death is now in possession of life. Mebege said it, death now has life. Let all men cry out in astonishment and praise to Father Zame ye Mebege. Fathers and mothers death has life.

These two first songs of the ngombi take place after the creation of Zame and his siblings when the responsibilities of creation have already devolved upon Zame. As is typical of Bwiti there is ambiguity and play on words. For example in the phrase *"awu e bele ening"* (death possesses life), it is unclear whether the "death" of a previous eternal existence is broken by the creation of life or whether we are anticipating the first sin of Adam and Eve in which they are expelled from Paradise and confront death, that is, death takes over life. Also the word *"seme"* not only means "cry out in astonishment and praise" but also "to suspend." The reference can thus be construed as the suspension of all creation from the spider's thread. Muye then sang:

> 3. *Zame a sigleang, ma ke yen. Zame Mbembe. Zame a sigle ebe Nganga. Zame a sigleang oh!*
> God has now descended. I (we) will see. God forever. God has descended to the land of the priest.

The reference here is to the descent upon the spider's thread to the land below, which is the land of the priest (*nganga*—the traditional expert in seeing through to hidden things). In the land below men have lost knowledge of the land above and hence need experts, nganga, to penetrate the now hidden things of the land above. Of course members of Bwiti regularly make that penetration without help of nganga, although the chief dancers in the night-long rituals are called nganga and in their dancing lead men from this life to the next. In the more Christianized branches Jesus is referred to as nganga— he who enables men to see beyond this life. He is also called Eyene Zame, he who sees God. Spreading his hands out over his stomach Muye next sang:

> 4. *Dibakaka Nyambi, Nyambi Tara Zame me lakeang akí.*
> *Oh Nyambi nganga, nganga ma myambi, a lakeang akí Manyambi.*
> A striking hollow sound God [Nyambi—the Tsogo name for God] makes, God
> Father God they burst it open, the egg.
> Oh God, priest, priest, priest God, it bursts now the egg!

This song steps back and refers to the bursting of the egg of creation. It also picks up more words from the Tsogo language such as *dibakaka* from Tsogo *bake*, to beat upon something hollow. Also, the Tsogo word for God, Nyambi or Manyambi, is used in place of the Fang Zame (or Nzame).

The next two songs in the series are *ôbangô* songs. Muye did not sing them. The obango are the vertiginous dances interspersed in the general ritual in which drums and the bamboo sounding staves, *obaka*, replace the gentler songs of the ngombi harp. Practically all the obango songs, abbreviated in any case, are sung in Popi Fang, that is, with Tsogo words or words interpolated from the Tsogo. It is not surprising that the obango songs should be in Tsogo, since it was the vertiginous dancing of Metsogo Bwiti ceremonies which, as we see below, caught Fang attention and was influential in Fang Bwiti.

Following these two early obangos the ceremonies return to the quieter songs of the ngombi harp. Muye accompanied himself upon the harp.

5. *Betare ye benana nkôl ô bele ening engura, ô singele ndende,*
      nkôl ô bele ening, o tsingele ndende.
   Tara a Zame wa kobege akal minsutmibot.
   Ndende nkôl ô bele ening, wa tsingele ndende.
   Father and mothers the thread holds all of life, it weaves it together.
   Suspended the thread holds life, it weaves it together, suspended.
   Father God speak in behalf of the black man.
   Suspended the thread holds life. You weave it in suspension.

The theme here, enlarging on the creation event, is that life is uncertain, fragile, suspended by a thread. It is recurrent in Bwiti. It is a theme that argues for dependence upon Father God, Tara Zame, to maintain this suspended and fragile life.

6. *Sí a sí, zôp ayô, sigebem e ne nyamoro ening oh!*
   Tara Zame wa wok. Eyong mot â ne sigebem, mot a bô ngul.
   Sigebem za yan yane nye.
   Zame ntol sigebem avôl avôl e bere Tara Zame.
   Tara Zame wa wok oh, Tara Zame ma wok.
   The land for the land, the sun above, termite is the predecessor of
   all life. Father God you understand everything. When man follows
   the termite he is strong. The termite precedes and guards over him.
   Zame is the oldest of all but termites come quickly after. You
   understand Father God, I understand Father God.

This song introduces another theme that appears frequently in the midnight sermons (evangiles): man should study the termite and learn from his constant and hardworking ways. The next song was not in Muye's repertoire although it is frequent in the Bwiti cycle.

7. *Akua Tara Zame a zu vele bia akua.*
   Nganga a nga kuang, nganga a nga kuang, nganga a nga kuang.
   Nkom wa kom mot, mam mese ening me sô akua.
   At the smelting pit Father God came to prepare us at the forge.
   The priest came then, the priest came then, the priest came then.
   At the forge, the forge, He (God) forged man, all things
      in life come from the forge.

In fact this song relates closely to Muye's version of the origin myth. It was collected at the mother chapel of Asumege Ening, Kougoulou village, Kango. The knowledgeable leader at Kougoulou, the Yemba Michel Bie, emphasized the way that the men gathered around the smelting pit. The smelting of iron was a sociable event in the way that Bwiti was a sociable event. There is word play in this song, as the word for smelting pit (*akua*) is reworked into *a nga kuan* ("came then"). The next song is one of the most popular in Bwiti. Muye sang it with gusto!

> 8. *Nlôdjôp ye ngômendan ebo be bele ening si engura.*
>   Sun and moon they held life everywhere.

This song is virtually the same as song no. 6 of the first minkin. It is repeated in similar forms several times over in the process of the night-long engosie. The sun and moon are emblems of Zame and Nyingwan. The former has command over the day and the latter over the night, the time of Bwiti celebration.

THE SUCCESSIVE CREATIONS OF MAN AND WOMAN

Muye returned now to the final phase of his account of the origin of man. He takes us from the forging of Adam to the expulsion of Adam and Eve from paradise.

> It was Adam that fell forth as Zame cracked the mound of earth which had passed through the forge. Though he was perfectly formed he was motionless and without life (*eyima*). Try as Zame would he could not bring him to life. Nyingwan Mebege laughed at her brother. "There are three of us here," she said, "so why must you do this alone. It will not live unless I breathe into it." Zame tried one last time and failed. He said ruefully, "Perhaps I should not be called Evangavanga Akombo (he who arranges and creates all things) but just Zame son of Mebege." Then Nlona took a bone of his body and placed it in Adam and said to Zame, "Put him back in the fire." And Nyingwan Mebege breathed on Adam and when he came out of the fire again he lived but he was not complete.
>
> Nyingwan said that Adam must have a partner created in my image or I shall not bless him. So Zame took her rib and packed earth around it and placed it in the fire. And when it came out and was cracked open, out fell Eve. Now Nyingwan came forward and stood over these two so that blood dropped from between her legs onto their heads and disappeared. This was the beginning of the path of birth and death (*zen abiale ye awu*). She stepped away and said, "Now they have life." And Zame set them on their feet and they awoke and lived. Adam asked Zame about Eve and he said, "She is your child and was made from you for you. And she is named Eve from the Fang word *evele* or red because

of all life begins in her blood. And you are named Adam from the Fang word *adang* (to surmount, be head of) because you came before all men (*a dang bôt bese*). And I am Zame who was Evangavanga Akombo." And Zame sent them off into the forest which had grown on the earth.

Now Zame is the sun and Nyingwan is the moon but Nlona is the secret power men have that is not seen. He is the *evus*, the source of all witchcraft. And he resented having no heavenly orb for his own. So he went off into the forest and climbed a tree. And as Eve went by he threw nuts at her. And they struck her chest and breasts swelled out. And Eve felt herself a woman. And she returned and looked for Adam. But he was off in the west. Nlona had taken Adam's shape. He allowed her to play with him. And he threw her to the ground and had intercourse with her. That was the first sin and it was not Adam's sin. Later when Adam returned from the forest he was startled to see that Eve had breasts. "Where did you get these?" he asked. He was even more startled when she began playing with him and he had an erection. He had shame (*ôsôn*). And he had intercourse with her. This was the second sin. As Adam looked up from the ground he saw Nlona like a snake in the *azap* (*azô*) tree and he understood what had happened. He shouted at Nlona to go away but Nlona threw a kola nut down which lodged in Adam's throat and is there to this day. All this happened at "Azoemboge."

Muye's pronunciation provoked laughter among his auditors because it was a clever word play. The azap or azo tree (*Mimusops djave*) is the tree which stood in the way of Fang migration and is the symbolic tree which occurs again and again in Fang legends and in Bwiti. But *zôe* means to be violated and *nzôe* (low mid-tone) means a violated non-nubile girl in whom a hole has been made.

Now Adam not only had the kola in his throat which excited him but he had the taste of Eve and they had intercourse over and over again. And they felt naked and hid themselves in their nakedness. When the sun came up Zame saw they had sinned because they had shame (oson). And he went and warned all the animals and fishes. He said I give you to Adam to play with. But he has sinned and now he will want to kill you. Go to the deep forest. Go to the deep waters. Now he returned to Adam and Eve. He said you have sinned. You must now suffer in blood. You must die but before you die you must give birth. And you will suffer in that birth and there will be blood in that birth. You will die in that birth. And you will not eat easily from the forest. And you must hunt for your food. And I shall leave you and you shall not see me again. Then Adam and Eve knelt down and sang their lament.

Oh Tara Zame, Vwalege bia, nyange bia. Bia ne engongol.
Engongol, engongol, Tara Zame vwalege bia.

Oh Father God, Help us! Take us! We are in despair.

Despair, despair, Father God help us.

Then Nyingwan Mebege rose as the moon in the sky and had pity. She said, ''You shall not suffer always for you shall sleep and your sin shall not be a pain to you.'' And she sent down red powder (*baa*) to them. And Zame heard their song and he sent down white powder to them (*fim*). And these represented the blood and the sperm by which Adam and Eve would create those who would replace them. And Eve looked down and saw blood running down her legs and thought she was dying. I am bleeding to death. And she sang

A Tara Zame me yeneang eki.

Oh Father God I see now the taboo (which I have broken).

But Adam looked and said that is but the red powder which Nyingwan sent you and he washed her in a basin of leaves from which sprang the redwood tree—*mbel*. That night was a night of storm with thunder and lightning, which they had never seen. Adam dreamt he had intercourse with a woman and woke with sperm on his leg. Eve said that is the kaolin powder which Zame sent to you. And then they had intercourse.

Here Muye sang, in Popi Fang, one of the most popular songs of Bwiti. It is usually sung in the Njimba or foregathering.

Ngadi naduma metombo ye. Ma kombwe, me nga tombwe, ngadi na duma me tombwo ye.

Lightning and thunder and young women. I am possessed by young women. Lightning and thunder and young women.[31]

Muye followed with a second verse which makes clear that lightning is a sexual metaphor. This song is predominantly in Fang with Popi words.

Ngadi a nga nyingle metombo, ma kombo mage metombe.

Lightning has entered the young woman. I create in (the fork the crossroads) of the young woman.

Now Eve became pregnant and gave birth to a white ball of gristle and bone (*kigile*). It was without arms, without legs and it died immediately. At first Adam was ashamed of this ball of bone. But then he saw it was sent by Zame. So he said let us enclose this ball in a bark container and consult it when we wish to consult God. For it knows the way to God. And that was the origin of the ancestor cult. Thereafter Eve had many children, the last of which was Noah who was born with the ngombi harp in his hand.

This section of the origin myth takes us to the expulsion of Adam and Eve from paradise. There is no notion, however, of a paradisical locale; there is simply the notion of the change in the quality of relationships between man and nature and man and woman. This section also takes us to the establishment

of the ancestor cult by Kigile Ki,*⁵ the monstrous product—a miscarriage—
of the sin of Adam and Eve. This explanation is in keeping with the marked
ambivalence about the ancestor cult and about the keeping of bones in contemporary Bwiti.

In most branches of the Bwiti religion the equal place of men and women
is emphasized in ritual activity. This is in striking contrast with traditional
Fang rituals which were largely exclusive to one sex or another. In the Asumege Ening version of Bwiti there is also a striving to obtain, by the pro-
hibiting of sexual or even sensual relationships between the sexes during the
rites, that quality of male-female relationship that obtained before the intervention of Nlona, the serpent. So the origin myth gives a rationale, as does
the Christian origin myth which is so influential in it, for ritual puritanism.
It also provides a rationale for the evenhandedness with which men and
women are treated in the religion. This is present in the account of Zame's
inability to make Adam by himself without the intervention of Nyingwan.*⁶
The myth points to the major role, virtually to the exclusion of Zame, that
Nyingwan Mebege plays in Bwiti.*⁷

We should be alert to the fact that Muye emphasizes the close relationship
and certain power over animals held by Adam and Eve before their sin. These

*⁵ The reference is to the kigile stage in the development of the fetus. The fetus born through
miscarriage at that stage is known as Kigile ki—the result of the breaking of a taboo. Nevertheless
Kigile ki appears as a powerful though bodiless monster in Fang folklore. He rolls about rapidly,
unpredictably. The resemblance of this globular miscarriage to a skull is marked, and hence the
explanation that Kigile was the first "skull" in the reliquary. In the Fang view of the stages of
the foetus ontogeny recapitulates phylogeny. The stages are: egg, lizard, monster or kigile, and
foetus proper or child. In some Bwiti origin legends Eve first gave birth to a lizard and then a
kigile before giving birth to a child.

*⁶ At the same time older views, as biblical as they are Fang, of women being created out of
man and for his service are also present. So the myth does not escape that enduring contradiction
Fang have always faced between the crucial role assigned to women in recreating the clan and
providing the wherewithal for "joyful existence" and "pleasurable activity" in the village on
the one hand, and the strict subservience demanded of them on the other. Thus while Nyingwan
Mebege has a central role in creation, the woman she insists on creating only passes through the
fire once. Adam has passed through twice and becomes, thereby, the "toughened being."

*⁷ In the Bwiti origin myth gathered by Veciana from coastal peoples in Spanish Guinea (La
Secta del Bwiti, pp. 21-22) we find interesting contrasts with the Fang Bwiti myth which show
the variability of reinterpretations. The Zame figure in the coastal myth also has difficulty in
creating man but instead of turning to his sister he turns, in his frustration, against his father,
Mwanga (the equivalent of the Fang Mebege). He is thus cast down from heaven to become the
God of the earth. Mwanga then goes on to create Christ to replace his first son—a Christ,
however, who plays little part in subsequent action. It is Mwangadikaso, the tempter, who is the
most dramatically interesting figure. There are other contrasts. Mwanga (Mebege) maintains his
omnipotence over creation whereas in the Fang Bwiti myth Mebege turns control entirely over
to his descendants, Zame, Nyingwan, and Nlona. Insofar as Christ is present it is He who
mediates between his father God on High, Mwanga, and his older brother, Mwangadikaso, the
Lucifer-like second God of the Earth. In the Fang version there is a tripartite creation of new
Gods replacing the old God. There is also a virtual absence on the coast of the female principle,
Nyingwan, so central in Fang Bwiti.

intimations of a Golden Age of communion with the animals do not emerge in Bwiti rituals though communion with the purity of the forest is emphasized. Such ideas are more typical of hunting and gathering societies or societies with totemic beliefs. And this idea is present in Metsogo Bwiti ceremonies. One of the highpoints of these ceremonies, in fact, is the dancing of the members out into the deep forest and their return in disguise, transformed into animals. The emphasis in Fang Bwiti is upon the loss of communion with the ancestors and not with the animals. Yet communion with the ancestors cannot be separated from communion with the forest which is their abode. Thus in Asumege Ening Bwiti the members file out at midnight into the forest with candles in hand. Led by the harp in soft strumming they follow narrow paths cut into the undergrowth. The stated purpose is to find and show the way to any lingering ancestor spirits who have not come into the chapel. But at the same time this rite offers the members communion with the forest. And though they do not come back like the Metsogo, dressed as animals, they do come back having partaken of the forest. There is also the custom in Asumege Ening of the leaders spending their time like the early Adam, in the deep forest when not otherwise engaged in Bwiti activities. This is the case of the leader of the Kougouleu Chapel, Ekang Engono, who, in his forest sojourns, is said to be in profound thought, osiman, and recollection of the dead.

These midnight paths into the forest are one expression of that organizing metaphor which is so fundamental to Bwiti liturgy: the path of birth and death (*zen abiale ye awu*). In the case of the midnight paths the members are said to be going out to make contact with the abandoned dead and to be bringing them back to be reborn into the chapel. We are introduced to this ''path of birth and death'' in the myth, for it begins in the blood of Nyingwan. It is thus conceived of as a red and bloody path. Banzie argue that only in the practice of Bwiti can one tread that path successfully and move from engongol, despair, to abora, the state of grace. The myth not only introduces us to despair, it also introduces us to oson (shame, sense of inappropriate behavior) which Bwiti recognizes as a widespread feeling among Fang and which it seeks to replace with harmonious tranquillity (mvwaa).

In Fang Bwiti and its myths, transformations of archetypal figures are fundamental. We can anticipate our review of further episodes of this myth in subsequent chapters by giving Muye's version of the birth of Christ. It shows the way that Jesus and Mary are a transformation of Adam and Eve who are a transformation of the archetypal male and female, Zame and Nyingwan.

It was after the great flood and the souls of the dead had gone to

Paris[32] and were reborn there . . . a great crowd of them. Zame called Adam and Eve from the grave to see the unfortunate condition of his descendants. Another flood must come again, said Zame, unless you are prepared to save your descendants from their sins. But know this, said Zame, that to save them you must yourselves perish in a horrible way. Adam said he was ready to die for them. Eve, who was at his side, encouraged Adam . . . it was actually the greatness of her heart that saved the world. Then Zame sent Adam to the earth in order to be born as Jesus by the Virgin Mary. Zame left Adam at the edge of the sea, Metsuge, and the land, Tsenge, where he changed into a baby. Then Eve came along and took the baby Adam and placed him under her robes next to the stomach. In those days everyone dressed as the Hausa women today. Thus Jesus and Mary heard from others the real fact of his birth. Even her husband Joseph thought she was pregnant when she returned from the sea. When the time came Mary reached into her robes and brought out the new Jesus.

This sequence of archetypal transformations appears even more strikingly in the origin myth given (to Binet, Gollenhofer, and Sillans) by Paul Bekale.[33] In Bekale's version Mebege me Nkwa-Sokome-Mbongwe creates Zame and Nyingwan in heaven, and then at their request provides bodies of clay which they can slip into on earth. Consequently, the heavenly brother and sister become an earthly man and wife who are subsequently betrayed by Lucifer into sexual relations. The archetypal transformation is more direct in this account (although Bekale's version has its loose ends as the creation of Lucifer is not accounted for) and here also the one god Mebege maintains his creative omnipotence. In Muye's version Zame and Nyingwan become creators in their own right and they pass that power on to their descendants. They transform themselves by their own act of creation and are not transformed by the creator. In any event this archetypal progression expresses a sense of continuity in relationships between male and female as well as important transformations in that relationship.

THE THEOLOGY IN BWITI ONTOGENY: THE OLD ADAM

From very early on in the contact period Fang interested themselves in the missionary God. Persistent inquiries on this issue helped convince the early missionaries of the religious nature of Fang. In the second phase of missions most missionaries came to the view that Fang had no real theological interests. As Allegret had stated it earlier, they "think of God only as a powerful chief with whom it would be a good thing to establish a treaty of friendship."[34] But Fang thoughts and attitudes on this issue were more complex than that, and this complexity is reflected in Bwiti.

Of course Fang could be expected to inquire after the Christian God. The missionary message was bound to pose problems for a people to whom ancestor cult and witchcraft activity defined the major supernaturals and to whom the creator god or gods were either figures of folklore or of philosophic speculation—endpoints of inquiry as it were. At the least Fang had the problem of determining whether the Christian God actually was a powerful chief or not. Accepting that he was, as was self-evident in the European presence, the next question was whether He was One or Many. This is a question to which the missionaries with the doctrine of the Trinity could only provide a subtle answer—an answer that the Fang came to call "subtle or miraculous talk" (*nkôbô akyenge*). But we see in Bwiti generally, and surely in this origin myth of Asumege Ening, that Banzie could be equally subtle in solving the problem of one in three. Origin myths show us the three in the egg emanating from the one creator god. Thus three in one or one out of three.[35]

The question as to whether God was One or Many may have bothered the missionaries in their contacts with Fang more than Fang themselves. Holding Christian beliefs in the "Uncreated Creator" and "Unmoved Mover," missionaries were challenged by the "infinite regress" of the genealogical model employed by Fang—their belief that the God of this world is one of a long line of gods and like man has his own genealogy. Some missionaries took all the ancestors of God as simply aspects of God: God in Three, God in Four, or God in "n" persons as the genealogical case might be. In fact, Binet, Gollenhoffer, and Sillans in their presentation of Paul Bekale's version of origin take just such a position. They take the three ancestors of God together with Mebege himself as the four aspects of God: Mebege the water principle, Nkwa the fire principle, Sokome the intelligence principle, and Mbongwe the wind or movement principle. But this conceit, like Prince Birinda's in *The Secret Bible of the Blacks*, goes beyond Bwiti thinking. We can learn from it but it is an overly learned speculation. This is not to underestimate Bwiti alertness to inventive exegesis and syncretism.[36] But insofar as the creators are concerned, they are usually seen as different descendent gods and not as manifestations of different elements of the same gods. Each god is a distinct person and power who brought about an important transformation of his predecessor. The principle inherent in distinct divine personalities is emphasized much more in the case of Zame ye Mebege and his sister Nyingwan Mebege, the one the male principle, exigent and animating, the other the female principle, nurturant and the embodiment of evenhanded tranquillity.

The genealogical model persists in Bwiti in another important way, and that is in respect to what we have noted as "typological transformation or transubstantiation"—the tendency for the same personages to appear over and over again in succeeding myths and legends. The notion that certain typical events and persons of one dispensation, say the first creation, foreshadow or are reiterated in a second dispensation is nothing new to historians or philosophers of religion. The science or art of discovering prophetic events or symbolic constellations in the Old Testament which adumbrated the person of Christ and the events of his life was once a lively enterprise in theology. It is surely of lively interest in Bwiti where we have seen a typological transformation of Zame and Nyingwan into Adam and Eve who become Cain and Abel (Obolo ye Biom)[37] understood by Banzie as male and female. They in turn become Christ and the Virgin Mary. But whereas Western theological typologists felt that their discoveries testified to the continuity of revelation and the divine unity of scripture, the Bwitists feel that these typological transformations testify to the reality of genealogical identity—the fact that to an important extent one is what one's ancestors have been before one.[38] One's own identity is very much incorporated into the genealogical line and the group defined by it.

But at the same time these typological transformations as Bwiti develops them contain a deeper wisdom than simply that of genealogical constancy. For there is a progression, a degeneration and a regeneration, in this typological relation between male and female. The spiritual-fraternal relation of Zame and his sister is converted into the carnal relation of Adam and Eve which degenerates into the materialistic and divisive relation of Cain and Abel which then is regenerated as the immaculate and filial relationship of Mary and Jesus. Brother and sister become man and wife, become worldly antagonists for limited goods, and finally become mother and son. Instead of referring to succeeding dispensations in history, the wisdom in this progression may well refer to developments in the life cycle where the sexes pass through fraternal, sexual, material, and maternal-filial relationships.[39]

Finally, typologizing of this kind is an exercise in the propensity to discover analogies—to note through the powers of reflective thought (osiman) the allegorical in the particular. This propensity is very strong in Bwiti which is anxious to knit the world together into a cosmos where the relationships of things are manifest and where one can escape particularity.[40] Similarly, a strong allegorical awareness can show everyman in each man. This is important in Bwiti. The religion desires to restore their humanity to Fang isolated from their ancestors in the collapse of the ancestor cult, from their families in the breakdown of the extended family, from their wives in the face of high divorce rates, and from their children in the face of intergenerational conflict. The religion desires to include them in a humanity which attaches to divinity in reiterated genealogical bonds.

Historically, over created time, then, the theological implication of these myths is the attachment of man to deity by a genealogical bond which shows typological recurrence of male-female persons (we refer to the problem of the tertium quid, the devil figure, below). These personages undergo transformations which are understood less as new historical phases and dispensations than as transformations necessary in Fang life process. So the myths contain wisdom about social relations.

But the more striking personages of these myths are the figures of Zame asi (God Below) and Zame oyo (God Above). The origin of this God in Two Persons (above and below) is not accounted for in Bwiti songs or explanations, though they appear there. The two gods appear to be a syncretic response of Fang to the challenge of heavenly Christian monotheism to their earthbound

ancestor cult. It is likely that missionaries helped Fang to this resolution, for
from very early on dictionaries compiled by missionaries distinguished between Zame asi, God Below (the old god of Fang folklore with many wives
and children and ever engaged in great demonstrations of martial, marital,
and economic prowess) and the true God of the Heavens of whom missionaries
spoke.[41] The God of the Below is often called by both Fang and Banzie,
Okuma or Kuma Zame asi, the God of wealth and material well-being, while
the God of the Above is a God of spiritual abundance but material poverty.
Whereas missionaries tended to identify Zame asi with the chief heroes of
the mvet troubadour legends, in our experience both Fang and Banzie identify
Zame asi with the powers of the ancestor cult, the Ngi antiwitchcraft cult,
and other traditional evocations of a more immediately accessible, even local
supernatural. Naturally missionaries labored to obtain the allegiance of Fang
to Zame oyo and were repeatedly disappointed by a continuing allegiance to
Zame asi in his various manifestations and to the materialism that he fostered.

Fang took various views on these two Gods in One God. Some talked of
the European and his powers over material things as being the true God of
the Below. This also occurs in Bwiti where the European is regarded as a
blackman who has died and obtained the powers of the beyond for use in the
Below. As regards the theological dilemma of mixed allegiance to the below
and the above there is no clear resolution in Bwiti. The vector of movement
is toward the above and the God of the Above but an interesting ambiguity
and tension in the cult is provided by the reality and vitality of the God of
the Below. For he may be sung to and celebrated even when a search is being
made for the One above. Fang do not easily abandon their pursuit of material
well-being and the gods that provide it. Members of Bwiti who, from a
missionary perspective, would be called enlightened speak of *nsisim asi* (spirits of the below) and *nsisim ôyô* (spirits of the above). By that they mean
spirits who have finally obtained communion with the God Above by means
of Bwiti and those, largely the long dead of the ancestor cult, who continue
to live in the deep forest and in the streams and whose hope for reunion with
the above lies in their invitation to and participation in Bwiti.

THE PERSON OF JESUS:
HE WHO HAS BEEN SACRIFICED AND SEES GOD

On the face of these myths Jesus is the Old Cain who is the Old Adam who
is the Old and ever-present God of this world and the Above, Zame ye
Mebege. Jesus is also and at once the son, the brother and the husband of
Mary who is the Old Abel, the Old Eve and the Old and ever-present Nyingwan
Mebege, the creative matrix of the world and primordial source of wisdom.
Jesus is thus a personage of many parts who always has the potentiality of
transformation of character. Because of this multivalence Jesus is understood
as having the capacity to intermediate between men and the gods and he is

often referred to as Eyen Zame (He Who Sees God) or simply as nganga, the term for the traditional holder of supranatural powers of healing and clairvoyance. The nganga was the traditional Fang figure who could see unseen things and was also a plenipotential personage with powers of transforming himself.

In the myths we have reviewed here Jesus does not have a dominant character but is just one manifestation of Deity absorbed by the genealogical model into Fang ancestry. In more contemporary liturgies of the Commencement of Life chapels, we find in both songs and ritual acts a celebration of Jesus (nganga's) career of suffering and self-sacrifice, a celebration which gives him much greater centrality in the religion. In both the ritual road of birth and creation (zen abiale) and death and destruction (zen awu) the birth, life, and crucifixion of Jesus have moved to a central position. In these liturgical contexts Jesus is given a very human presence and is frequently referred to as *emwan mot*, "the child of man."[42] It is his humanity that is featured, for in his self-sacrifice he showed men how "to suffer," how to face the state of despair (engongol) which is a constant preoccupation of Bwiti, and how to tread to completion the severed path of birth and death. In that sense Jesus is a Savior in recent Bwiti.[43] He saves Banzie by showing them how to tread the path of birth and death in order to reach God.

It would be a mistake, however, to assume that this centrality is sufficient to label latter-day Bwiti theology as Christocentric and to type Bwiti as a separatist or independent form of Christianity.[44] Communication with the ancestors and not simply with Christ and through him with God remains the central object of Bwiti. Banzie even of the Commencement of Life chapels say that all men search for God but most men commit the sin of searching too far for him. God is first of all close by in the presence of the ancestral dead. He is not simply to be found in far-off Jerusalem, much as one can learn from Jesus. And even when Christ is in focus it is not his specific personality and history that are central but rather his "everyman" status as a ritual figure engaged in a playing out of men's basic life experiences and basic moral challenges.[45]

If we are searching for a central divinity in Bwiti it would be, in any case, not Jesus but his mother, sister, and wife, Nyingwan Mebege, the sister of God and universal matrix and source of knowledge. The ritual figure of the nganga, from the moment of his appearance in the circle of origin outside the chapel and throughout his leadership of the sequence of dances, has as his primary objective the relating of men to the ancestral dead and through them to the Great Gods and principally the Sister of God.

Conclusion: The Re-creation of Continuity

We can only impose theological consistency in the origin myths of Bwiti. Fang theology was embedded in diverse lore and was not clear to begin with.

There was little interest in the topic. Bwiti, itself under the pressures of evangelization, has been too much in the throes of syncretizing diverse elements, Fang, Tsogo, Miene, and European, to have achieved a consistent dogma. Moreover, the theology does not emerge from recitations of the origin myths alone. Much is contained elsewhere in the liturgy and in what is being sung or danced about. We have to consult many interwoven modes of experience. And there is even one genre of origin myth concerned with the discovery of eboga by the Pygmies' ancestors which is altogether ignored in liturgy though it virtually gives privileged theological status to the "little people."

Since Banzie for all their exegetical powers make no formal study of their theology it is only by indirections that we can suggest it. Once again central figures of thought and speech, their metaphors, are revealing. A basic metaphor throughout is that of the genealogical line. Just as every Fang clan tracing upwards in its recitation of genealogy eventually arrives at the "this world" God as the founder, so this time-binding metaphor gives a sense of divine continuity. As we move forward in time represented in genealogy the past is not lost but is reflected upon and repeats itself. The genealogy binds time together in a fundamental way, for the living are reflections of the dead and vice versa. Indeed, the metaphor enforces a characteristic and preferred mode of thought for Fang: osiman, that reflective thought which takes the present occurrence and projects it against the past in search of likenesses, similarities, analogies, allegories.

While there is repetition, similarity, and recurrence, at the same time there are notable transformations. We see this in the archetypal couple, male and female, in various representations, who are the "two persons" of the Bwiti genealogy. In the ontogeny of gods and men there is, thus, both continuity and discontinuity, although the continuity is mainly diachronic, historical, and the discontinuity celebrated in these myths is synchronic or atemporal. The discontinuity concerns the necessary changes imposed upon the individual in the dynamics of his life's career in the kinship system. Insofar as the typological transformations of Nyingwan Mebege and her brother Zame into Adam and Eve, Cain and Abel, and Jesus and Mary are concerned, these transformations speak of contemporary challenges, of changing personal identity in the life process more than of succeeding dispensations in history. Nevertheless, the fact is that the myths suggest both continuities and discontinuities, a difficulty embodied and overcome in the genealogical metaphor which is a continuous line of discontinuous personalities.

We may obtain another view of how these myths and associated liturgy deal with the incompatibility of continuity in discontinuity or vice versa by considering vertical and horizontal elements. For example, we have the vertical discontinuity between God Above and God Below. This discontinuity provides an enduring tension in Bwiti even though there are various attempts to synthesize the two or even identify the God Below with the Devil. One means of obtaining continuity is to postulate, as Banzie do, the soul's excursion from the Above to the Below and back to the Above—making a discontinuity into a circularity. This intellectual device is very similar to the more traditional Fang device of mastering the discontinuity of death by postulating for the soul a "rebirth" into the afterlife and a subsequent "death" of the soul in the afterlife and a "rebirth" into this life. There was thus achieved a continuous circularity to the soul's apparently discontinuous career. We shall see how in Bwiti this vertical circularity is embodied in the central pillar—the *akôn aba*—of the Bwiti chapel.

Though the sin of incest (the primary sin to Fang) committed by Adam and Eve, or Zame and Nyingwan, is featured in the origin legends (Cain and Abel represent the secondary sin of covetousness and gluttony), we have not emphasized it in our discussion directed, in this chapter, primarily to the typological transformations. Nevertheless this "sin" is what causes, first, the discontinuity between the creator gods and man and, subsequently, in the form of uninhibited sexuality, the malaise between men and women. This sin is overcome, incidentally, in the filial and asexual relationship between Jesus and Mary, the transformed primordial couple. Banzie, in fact, are highly conscious of Fang sinfulness both in sexual and material matters and frequently speak to it. Cult leaders speak constantly against the overweening materialism of the modern world and justify the all-night dancing as a sacrifice of excessive sexual nature to Bwiti. In any case, in respect to the vertical dimension, it is man's sinfulness that condemns him to remain confined to the below in the ground, wandering forever in the deep forest, or sunk in the depths of water courses without the capacity to rise again. It is man's sinfulness that condemns man hopelessly to discontinuity and death—that denies him the saving circularity.

In respect to the horizontal dimension—also to be more fully discussed in relation to the spatial organization of the Bwiti chapel—it is man's sinfulness that has produced discontinuity and the migratory search from the northeast (the land of origin) to the southwest (the seaside and the sea which is the promised "land" of reunification). From very early on missionaries and other sojourners among Fang saw that Fang understood their migration as some kind of search for continuities—between themselves and the gods and between themselves and what they had lost. The missionary Allegret, in inquiring after the religious ideas of Fang, turned up time and again the notion that Fang had through their sinful nature lost contact with God. At sunset one evening an old man asks him poignantly, gesturing toward the failing light over the sea,

Isn't it there that God departed? God is surely there, for all the rivers run that way and the sun disappears there. God is surely behind the sun. You have seen him; tell me the truth.[46]

Further inquiry reveals that Allegret's interlocutor has an idea of a happier time before the tumultuous migration when men were united among themselves and with God and the animals and when nobody died. "In the beginning we were all united and we all trod the same road between two trees with God. But we didn't want to obey him and he said, 'You are of willful and bad intentions,' and he departed and left us alone."[47] Later in the colonial period, of course, the Whiteman-Blackman legends give a more detailed and, from the colonial view, a more apt account of how Blackman lost his communion with Deity.

Allowing for a Christian interpretation of what Allegret was told, it nevertheless seems true that Fang thought of their migration as, in part, a search for lost continuities once possessed in a former paradise by the sea, to be discovered in the future once again by the sea. Bot Ba Njock[48] puts it succinctly: "Le Fang, visiblement chassés de ce 'pays d'adoration' d'après la tradition, avaient eu la promesse de retrouver la securité, la paix, dans un autre pays situé vers l'ouest, c'est-à-dire vers la mer, mfa'a ya mang (direction de la mer). Ils ont donc eu la promesse de retouver leur Paradis Perdu." There was thus a notion long held by Fang that despite the separations of migration society would in the end circle back upon itself and be restored to a continuity. This circling back to a lost paradise, this restoration of seaside continuities is certainly an important promise made by Bwiti to its members. On both the vertical and the horizontal dimension Bwiti promises through its microcosmogony a restoration of continuities, a reunification of men with each other and with their gods.

Still, we must reiterate that these promises are never pressed compulsively in Bwiti for they are never stated as analytically as we have put them here. They are embodied in the indirect statement of metaphor and metonym in sermon, song, and dance, and in hallucinatory revelation. Thus discontinuities remain amidst continuities: the God Below along with the God Above, linearities alongside circularities, Good walks with Bad, and just when a dualism appears to be dissolved it reasserts itself again. There is, to be sure, the suggestion, in the intermediary deity and principle of evil Nlona Mebege, of a tripartism. But this third deity hardly holds out the possibility of resolution of the basic opposition between man and woman. He is, if anything, the creator of discontinuity, exacerbating sexual turmoil and material acquisitiveness. Tessmann is probably right that there is a fundamental dualism in Fang religion which is in constant and unresolvable interplay.[49] But we should not overinterpret that dualism in Bwiti. For it is the nature of Bwiti microcosmology as achieved in myth, legend, song, dance, sermon, and vision to appear to dissolve the dualisms and then again immediately reassert them. The microcosmos created in Bwiti promises to be one but is recurrently experienced as two if not many.

·14·

The Dynamics of Bwiti in
Space and Time

Asumege Ening, bi nga sum mféfé ening.
(The Commencement of Life, we have begun a new life.)

NEWS OF A NEW LIFE

IT WAS just after the Second World War that Zogo Ebu returned from more than a decade working at a lumber camp on the Libreville Estuary with the "good news" of Bwiti. He and another villager, his half-brother Ndutumu, who had danced Bwiti in the twenties in Libreville, began dancing Disumba Bwiti in their house on Saturday nights. As the late forties was still a time of sporadic suppression of Bwiti, they were warned several times by the Chief of the village to stop dancing. Once the Chef de Terre came by to threaten them as did a local mission catechist.

They would go months without dancing and then they would take up the religion again. Then their neighbors would complain and they would stop dancing again. Usually it was the visit of some itinerating nganga from the Libreville region who would animate them to dance again. Or they would offer hospitality to some returning laborer passing through on his way home from Libreville. If he had danced Bwiti they would dance Bwiti with him. But the group that danced locally was very small—Zogo, Ndutumu, their wives, and several members of their immediate families. Often they would leave the village to dance Bwiti elsewhere where there was a more active chapel, at Kwakum close to the regional seat, at Oyem, or even further. There was a loose network of relationships between Bwitists and frequent itineration back and forth between chapels although people tended to visit the particular branch of the religion to which they belonged.

In the fifties affairs in this small Assok Ening chapel were enlivened by the return of both Muye Alogo and then Metogo Zogo from Libreville. Muye Alogo had danced in the Asumege Ening chapel of Ndong Obam Eya and sought to convince Zogo Ebu to shift from the practices of Disumba Bwiti to Asumege Ening. "It is time to begin a new life," he argued. But Zogo Ebu stood fast and so Muye agreed to dance Disumba while in the village, although he often went elsewhere to follow the Commencement of Life path.

Metogo Zogo, who returned several years later, had danced in various chapels, including Asumege Ening. But he was an eclectic and willing to dance Disumba. Besides Zogo Ebu was his father.

After Ndong Obam Eya died at Libreville, it was uncertain who would replace him as head of the mother chapel of Asumege Ening. Finally Ekang Engono of Kougouleu established the most successful chapel and attracted the most people. He became the successor. Ekang then sent emissaries to other Asumege Ening chapels telling them of the succession and advising of new things which he had "seen" or had "heard" from Bwiti and which the other chapels ought to put into practice. Zogo Ebu resisted these innovations when advised of them by Muye Alogo. Then news came from Ekang Engono that all villages which did not have chapels should build them. The pressures upon Zogo Ebu became very strong. It was the mid-fifties and Bwiti was free to follow its path.

Zogo Ebu agreed reluctantly to look around for a building site. When the Chief of the village, Essono Mba, heard of this he took up the matter with the Chef de Terre and the Chef de Canton. For he anticipated problems with other villagers. The three chiefs agreed that the French administration should be told. But while in former days, through the 1940's, the administration might have found reasons to prevent the construction, the current Administrator, M. Pasquier, could only say that if the Banzie had land on which to build their chapel, they could build it. Was there any question of land?

The chapel was to be constructed directly behind Muye's *ndébot* dwelling, apparently on family lands. But on subsequent inquiry the Chief of the village discovered that a portion of that land was in the name of Muye's uncle, Muzwi Mebiame, the local catechist. This man, on being informed of the claim, called a meeting at the council house. The religion was of the devil, he said, and if not of the devil at least it was a religion of strangers (*bílôbôlôbô*) who were not Fang. "This religion and those who practice it," he said, "have just come to settle in the village [*ntôbot*]. It has no family!" Besides the Banzie shouted all night and were otherwise tired and good for nothing from all their dancing. Muye responded angrily, for quite beside the question of Bwiti there was a slur implied about the rightful place of his part of the family in the village. It was frequently said of the Banzie that they were ntobot, wanderers without families who just came to settle and live like parasites, ingratiating themselves into established families.

Muye said that neither his family nor he was "ntobot" and much less was Bwiti. He also said that the only way that Zame, not to mention the ancestors, would ever be attracted to the village was through Bwiti dances. Finally the elder who was to decide the affair, Essono Mba, instead of "slicing it" sent the two parties off again to the District Court. At the weekly court session Zogo, Muye, and Metogo were ordered to remove the chapel. They had already begun to dig some holes. So the site was abandoned. A year later, when Muye and Metogo finally split away from Zogo Ebu, they were able to build the new chapel of Asumege Ening some twenty feet behind this old location.

THE TAKING UP OF BWITI BY FANG

The Bwiti cult among Fang takes its name from the Bwiti (or *Boeti* or *Bwete*) ancestor cult of the peoples of southern Gabon, particularly among the Metsogo (Apinji), Massango and the Baloumbo.[1] The proper name for the ancestral cult among Fang, a cognate form, is Bieri. Banzie recognize the Metsogo ancestor cult to be the source and stimulus of many of their practices and much of their ritual vocabulary. Because of its dramatic rituals and "miraculous" apparitions Metsogo religious culture impressed observers, and not only Fang, from the time of earliest contact. Apinji Bwiti impressed the adventurer-explorer Paul DuChaillu as early as the 1860's.[2] Administrators also recognized its motivating powers. Le Testu, discussing the Leopard societies and other anthropophagic cults which were making their appearance in the twenties and thirties throughout southern and central Gabon, blamed them all on the Metsogo, "la race la plus fetishiste du Gabon." He credited this influence to the central position the Metsogo occupied on the middle Ogowe and between the Ogowe and the Lolo in Gabon. Equally influential was Metsogo Bwiti—"one does not speak to Bouiti, it is said, except in Itsogo."[3] Le Testu's perception of Bwiti as a disorderly anthropophagic cult—a cult which in the confirmation of its fetish required the sacrifice of a human life[4]—was characteristically that of administrators between the wars who generally ignored the cosmology achieved in the religion. But, in any case, the powerful and enduring religious tradition of the Metsogo people was not ignored nor was their energetic attachment, unlike Fang, to their traditions and the authority of the religious leaders who preserved it.[5]

The exchange of various cults, like the widespread exchange of dances, is a very old process in Equatorial Africa. The search for revitalizing rites from without one's own group was recurrent. In one of the earliest reports we have, that of Bowditch of 1808, reference is made to a Libreville troubadour and his songs which seem particularly syncretic in character.[6] The man played on the ngombi harp and sang cosmological tales of the "arts by which the sun gained the ascendency over the moon, who were first made of coeval power by their common father." He sang songs to a mother figure and he also sang Handel's "Hallelujah" to the strumming of the ngombi. Bowditch describes the man as an albino, "a white negro" whose countenance struck him as having an air of insanity but which may have been showing the effects of drug-taking. In any case the troubadour's presentation and his cosmic subject matter is reminiscent of a Bwiti harpist of the twentieth century, often daubed in white kaolin clay and singing of the intermittent dominion of male (sun) and female (moon) elements in the universe.

In respect to the Bwiti of this century it is difficult to establish just when Fang took up and modified the more southern ancestor cults, particularly those of the Metsogo and Massango, that impressed them. It may have happened as early as the turn of the century, for missionaries make mention at that time of the appearance of new Bwiti chapels in the region of the Lower Ogowe where Fang and Galwa were intermixed. But this early evidence is only of the adoption of Bwiti by the Galwa,[7] and whether Fang participated at this date is not known. It is generally held that Bwiti had appeared and begun to flourish among Fang by the First World War. Missionary reports for 1914 discuss complaints by Fang elders that their young people no longer listened to them because they had taken up Bwiti (Mfwiti) from the Galwa.[8] Missionaries also feared the susceptibility of young Fang in the lumber camps to this "fetish sect." They regretted the imposition of corvée (a wartime measure) on Fang along the Ogowe, for this caused families to flee back up the Abanga carrying with them the seeds of this "religious disease."[9]

BWITI AND THE COLONIAL ENTERPRISE

For reasons discussed below, the period of the First World War and its aftermath led to a rapid extension of Fang Bwiti. In the 1920's Bwiti provoked regular comment in the missionary journals as well as in the territorial press of both the French and the Spanish colonies.[10] By the late twenties and early thirties the movement began to preoccupy administrators and in 1930 the Governor of Gabon, M. Vuillaume, devoted five pages of a brief manuscript on Fang customs to this "dangerous religious manifestation" which "terrorizes the Pahouin."[11] As Bwiti attracted more and more Fang there was, in general, increasing antagonism on the part of those (missionaries and administrators largely) who bore the burden of "the civilizing mission." But from the first Bwiti also attracted interested observers and even occasional members from the European community. In fact, our interest in Bwiti in the late fifties did not surprise Banzie who recited to us the names of other Europeans who had "eaten eboga" and "danced" for the ancestors.

It was, however, Europeans not directly responsible for the success of the colonial enterprise or the civilizing mission who entered into Bwiti: traders, merchants, lumbermen, contract supervisors, and skilled workmen often living with or in very direct relation with Africans in the forest camps and work sites and in trade.[12] Trader Horn, in his enthusiastic interest in all things African, sets the style here. But he was not the only trader to delve into local practices and, as Mary Kingsley had recognized (this was one of the reasons she defended their interests), the laissez-faire philosophy of the traders was often extended to the practices of other cultures, however bizarre. One cannot generalize, therefore, about *the* colonial attitude to Bwiti. Not only were there various echelons of the colonial enterprise with distinct attitudes (administrator, missionary, trader), but the attitude of each evolved over time.

European presence and participation in Bwiti was usually ignored by the administration, however deplored by missionaries. In the agitated times of the late thirties and forties, however, the participation of Frenchmen was strongly discouraged by certain district administrators in their local fiefdoms.[13] The climax of this administrative antagonism occurred in the case of one Roger Benoist, a road construction supervisor, who was convicted of being present at a Bwiti initiation in Libreville District at which a member died. It was claimed that the individual involved had been tortured. Later, in a letter to his lawyer, Benoist claimed that the initiation was undertaken in a friendly way only to "protect" him on the eve of his transfer to the Ngounie District. At the time he was living with a Fang woman and knew well the local chapel head who was a relative of hers. He had frequently attended Bwiti ceremonies out of curiosity. He makes no mention of any deaths but comments ruefully that the initiation, during which he was shown the skulls of deceased Bwitists, ended on an ominous note of impending misfortune.[14] And, indeed, five years in a Gabonese prison of the time was a considerable misfortune. Benoist seems to have been a victim of the political excesses of the immediate postwar period.

THE POLITICS OF BWITI

Muye Michel was fond of saying, that "Politics is the way of searching for God and religion is the way of worshiping him once you have found him."[15] Though Banzie are rarely political persons themselves (they are too much involved in building their microcosm), they recognize the political implications of Bwiti. Governor Vuillaume's manuscript, indeed, indicates that Bwiti had been a matter of concern to the administration of the colony since the late 1920's. Later Bwiti was very much involved in party politics.

Vuillaume formulated an administrative view which was to endure until the early 1950's. This view is that Bwiti was "noxious" to the well-being of Fang because human sacrifice was demanded in its initiations. Whenever it appeared, it was argued, there was population decline because of the disappearance of its victims. The Fang, he felt, were "terrorized" by it. Vuillaume recognized that the keeping of the bones of the dead was a Fang tradition, but Bwiti intensified that interest to the point of human sacrifice. Moreover, the consumption of the drug "eboka" rapidly led to "the depletion of all willpower" and "the brutalizing of the race."[16]

Vuillaume's views were, in part, a reassertion of a lingering view of Fang savagery and cannibalism. In part the Governor was responding to the interest that Bwiti leaders showed at that period in communicating with the dead through their disinterred bones which gave the impression of sacrifice. In part the Governor was looking for a cause of the population decline Fang were then suffering. It was, of course, more accurately to be blamed on the venereal infection rife in the lumber camps. It is ironic that this was blamed on Bwiti, for Bwiti leaders sought precisely to restore fertility to their members. In part the Governor was reflecting the difficulty experienced by the administration between the wars both in stabilizing Fang and in organizing them in the interests of the colony. He was also reflecting the wariness of any colonial administrator toward any self-sufficient organization which might carry the case for independence or change of status to the League of Nations. Whatever the cause of Vuillaume's antipathy—it may have been only his distrust of drug-taking—it set the stage for persistent administrative suppression and persecution, forcing chapels into secret reunions. The experience of Leon Mba, who later became the first president of Gabon (1960-1965), indicates the problems then posed for those in any way associated with Bwiti.

In the late 1920's and early 1930's Mba was a young and rapidly rising "evolué" in the administration. He was Chef de Canton in the Libreville Region and a man with a reputation for wisdom in judgment, ambitious to raise the living standards and prestige of his people. His demands upon his people antagonized many Fang and his politics of African advancement unsettled the administration. It is uncertain whether Mba was ever actually a full member of Bwiti although in the fifties there were Bwitists in the Libreville region who claimed him as a member of their chapel. But it is certain that he was sympathetic to Bwiti and elicited votes in his canton from Bwitists. In 1932, a Fang woman disappeared in supposed connection with a Bwiti ceremony. Mba was accused of complicity in her disappearance (her body was later recovered) and of engaging in ritual crime. His antagonists combined to engineer his conviction on the charge. He was sentenced to three years of prison and ten years of exile in the Oubangi-Chari.[17]

We will come back to Leon Mba's political career on his return after the war because the political role of Bwiti is closely tied up with his subsequent political fortunes. But it is of interest to mention the situation in the late thirties under the Popular Front government. Whereas one might expect from that government a liberalizing effect as regards the practice of the Bwiti religion, in point of fact the administrators who were appointed, many of them anticlerical socialists and others Freemasons,[18] tended to regard Bwiti as retrograde and obscurantist and allied, in fact if not in intent, with the missionaries and the laissez-faire merchants. In fact, though Bwiti was then still excoriated by missionaries, it was beginning to move toward the incorporation of Christian elements and, indeed, would have proved resistant to any secular or anticlerical view of government. This suspicion of Bwiti as secretly or openly sympathetic to the reactionary forces carried over to the

Vichyite struggle in Libreville where Bwiti members, if they made any response at all, aligned themselves with those who fought the Free French.
Paradoxically, Banzie found themselves between two fires: missionaries on
the one hand and anticlerical administrators on the other.

At the end of the war the fortunes of Bwiti began to change, in part because
of administrative reform[19] and in part because Leon Mba, returned from exile,
was taking an increasingly strong stand against tribalism in Gabon politics.
In this battle, the intertribal nature of Bwiti, its mixture of Southern Gabonese
and Fang practices, could serve as a symbol for the "mixed politics" Mba
endeavored to practice. He had founded upon his return a quasi-political party
called the *"Comité Mixte"* (later the Bloc Democratique Gabonaise—BDG)
which emphasized intertribal membership. Indeed, in an interview held with
Mba in July of 1958 he emphasized Bwiti's promise as a religion of national
integration, a view that he never espoused publicly out of deference to the
established missionary religions.

Among his own people Mba's party was well in the minority until the
middle of the 1950's. Both he and Bwiti were held in disrepute by the majority
of Fang, who often associated the two.[20] Most of the emerging Fang elite
regarded the religion as retrograde and unprogressive—a ceremonial sink for
the energies of the villagers.*[1] After the war this progressive elite began to
formulate plans for Gabonese and Fang development. Their interests corresponded with those of the colonial administration concerned about the decline
of Fang population and the difficulties of organizing Fang to any effective
modernizing purpose. These concerns resulted in the Congrès Pahouin of
1949. Although the administration hoped to keep this Congress under control
and in the hands of the Chefs de Canton appointed by them, the more progressive elite skillfully outmaneuvered the more conservative. About Bwiti,
however, there was agreement. The conservative chiefs saw in it a threat to
their authority while the progressive elite saw it as a hindrance to material
progress and reorganization.[21] The fact that Bwiti was singled out for attention
in the published results of the Congress shows its significance in Fang life
of the period.

*[1] Practically all administrators, French and African, took this view. M. Lecuyer, who attended
Bwiti rites in Mitzik and Medouneu and generally defended the cult against charges of criminality,
nevertheless felt that Bwiti provoked "une diminution de l'assiduité au travail et une baisse du
rendement." (*Archives of the District of Medouneu*. Année 1949-2ᵉᵐᵉ semestre, 15 fevrier 1950.)
And the first African to fill the Medouneu post, M. Mbunge Simon, argued similarly. He said
to us that while he recognized that Bwiti might be interesting for a professor, for an administrator
the main problem was work and Banzie built no roads and dug no wells. Later when we confronted
the leader of the Efulan Bwiti chapel, Nzameyo Ngema, with these remarks, he replied, "We
do God's work and not the work of the administration. Our road is the road of birth and death
and not the road to Libreville" (a projected link which had been stalled for many years). "Our
wells are those in which the spirit is baptised and which satisfy the thirst for God and not those
which slake the thirst of District Chiefs."

While the preponderance of delegates looked to village regroupment and new forms of communication to repair Fang disorganization, some, like Leon Mba, saw in Bwiti a chance to link Fang together anew. The more balanced view is seen in Leon Mba's expert testimony in 1953 in the case of the poisoning and death of a young initiate to Bwiti by reason of overdose of "eboka." The death occurred in the District of Mitzik in 1951. The fact that Mba, then "Conseiller Territorial," was called upon to testify and agreed to do so indicates how much less antagonistic the situation had become for Bwiti by that period.

The case, which was first argued at the regional level,[22] involved a 13-year-old girl who died after prolonged initiation into Bwiti. The leaders of the chapel were accused of rape and ritual sacrifice by poisoning. But the medical report revealed no poison other than eboga as well as the enlarged liver characteristic of morbid malaria. The fact of rape was considered moot because the girl's parents had already received child price and the girl was in the process of "getting familiar with" her husband who was one of the Bwiti leaders. In regional court the accused were condemned to thirty months of prison and seven years of forced labor. The case was appealed to Libreville.[23]

Here two expert witnesses were called. The first was Père Gilles Sillard, the priest at Mitzik at the time of the case, who had since been transferred to Libreville. It was he who had brought the case to court. The second witness was Leon Mba. Père Sillard advanced the view that human sacrifice was necessary to advancement in Bwiti. The girl was one of those sacrificed. Leon Mba responded that though he did not know how Bwiti was practiced in Mitzik, in Libreville there were no ritual crimes. He pointed out that the cult had come to the estuary region about 1918 from the Ngounie. If it was secret, so was every religion of the blacks. It was a cult of the dead which had simply replaced the more traditional cult. To become a member one had to eat eboga but there was very little hierarchy in Bwiti and certainly no central organization as had been implied. "The elders teach the youngers. I have never heard that human sacrifice was demanded in initiation," he said, "nor have I knowledge of any crimes committed by Bwiti. It is because non-initiates are ignorant that they think there are ritual crimes." Père Sillard responded that Mba was a part of the sect, encouraged it for political reasons, and therefore was "un temoin interessé."[24] "On the contrary," responded Mba, "I have been against Bwiti because its members no longer wish to work!" Because it appeared that the girl was already married and may actually have died of malarial complications and not of eboga the Regional judgment was reversed and the men freed.

This is not the only case involving Bwiti in the judicial archives. There are other cases as well as many complaints about Bwiti activities.[25] But this is one of the most significant cases because it brought together a missionary and an African leader. The fact that Leon Mba declared himself against Banzie because of their resistance to work shows the impact of his increasing administrative responsibilities upon him. Throughout his subsequent career, however, including his time as president of the Republic, he continued to defend the right of Banzie to practice their religion and was assured of Bwiti loyalty in elections.[26] His political opponents, up to the establishment of One-Party Government in 1961-1962, continued both to denigrate Bwiti and associate Mba with its "retrograde and criminal practices."

MISSIONARY PRESSURES

Though one must be cautious in generalizing over the diversity of communions, it is clear that missionaries, more consistently than administrators, regarded Bwiti as inimical to their interests. They recognized that this new religion, even more as it began to incorporate Christian elements, was directly competitive with their own evangelization. They also recognized that many of their African pastors and priests in training—often enough their village catechists—had been attracted to Bwiti as the more attractive "evangile." Frequently they took an aggressive view toward Bwiti, either encouraging the administration to suppress it or taking an active role themselves. Incidents were frequent enough that various chapels of Bwiti bear the names of their martyrs who are recalled annually in special ceremonies. At Kougouleu, the mother chapel of the Commencement of Life branch of Bwiti, they hold "Blood of the Martyrs" rites once a year in which they recall all the Banzie, including the Gabonese President Leon Mba, who have suffered at the hands of administrator or missionary. Ten or more names are usually involved. The largest chapel in Medouneu District, Tamamanga of the Disumba branch of Bwiti, carries the following sign above the entrance:

> Mission Saint Martir Ngema Bibang dans
> le Tribunal M. Pompignant a Jugé de
> Construir une Chapelle
> TAMAMANGA

This refers to the martyrdom of the Bwiti leader, Ngema Bibang, an uncle of the present leader of the chapel. In April and May of 1934 a Libreville priest, L'Abbé Jerome, made a systematic sweep north of Libreville as far as Medounou. With a team of assistants he entered Bwiti chapels, destroying the cult harps and other religious paraphernalia and arousing the Banzie against him. In Abogotom, close by Efulan, he was assaulted and wrestled to the ground by Ngema Bibang as he sought to enter the chapel. An armed escort of the Abbé promptly shot and killed the assailant. The Abbé fled to the district headquarters which had to employ an armed force of Gendarmes to rescue the priest's escort from the villagers and convey the Abbé back to Libreville.

The case was brought to judgment, though no record remains in the judicial archives. Banzie recall that the judgment was favorable and that they were not only given the right to defend their chapels but were encouraged to build a new chapel to replace the one partially destroyed in the incident. District archives yield only a reference to the armed escort provided for the Abbé and to "a grave incident" at Abogotom caused by him. The report is sympathetic to the villagers and forwards their complaint to Libreville.[27]

Abbé Jerome was not the only missionary to attempt to eradicate Bwiti at its source.[28] Often enough missionary enthusiasm in this respect brought them into conflict with the administration. On other occasions administrative heavy-handedness would be regretted by missionaries. By the 1950's, when a more relaxed attitude prevailed in the administration, a number of district officers openly attended Bwiti ceremonies, much to the regret of the missionaries.[29] In any event the repressive attitudes and actions affecting Bwiti in the 1930's and 1940's not only provided Bwiti with an uplifting sense of struggle, martyrdom, and triumphant survival but also created in the religion the custom of worship in small familylike groups not easily brought to the attention of administrators and missionaries. It was only in the fifties and sixties that the size of Bwiti congregations grew substantially. The irony is that it was just this dispersal that administrators criticized in Bwiti. The administrator at Medouneu, Lecuyer, remarked in 1951 that "Bwiti villages are the smallest and the worst kept" at the same time that he alerted his superiors to the recent increase in the number of adherents.[30]

THE PRESSURES OF A DECLINING POPULATION

There were other, often more significant, pressures than those of administrator and missionary that had consequences for the acceptance and growth of Fang Bwiti. The growth of Fang Bwiti in the teens and twenties coincided with epidemic and famine conditions and the beginnings of a decline in Fang population. The missionary letters of that period testify, for example, to the high mortality rate caused by the influenza epidemic of 1919 and 1920. Sautter reports that this epidemic was responsible, in two years, for the death of 4,000 people out of a population of 17,000 in the area of Mitzik.[31] While Fang recognized that, like the war, this evil had its origins in Europe[32] and reflected European moral impotence, at the same time its grievous impact upon them brought into question their own relationship to sources of super-natural power. It created in them an attitude of independent search for grace justified by their growing sense of European moral inadequacy.

The highly unsettled conditions of the war years,[33] particularly in the southern part of Fang territory around Libreville and the Ogowe, were followed by the devastation of the influenza epidemic. The resulting losses in turn had an impact upon agriculture—a significant decrease in hectarage cleared and cultivated. A season of late rains in 1923 produced the famine of 1924 which had a much more massive impact upon the population than any of the previous, periodic famines to which Equatorial peoples were accustomed—for example, the famine of 1902—by reason of fluctuations in the intertropical front.[34]

The famine was made worse because the 1920's was a period in which the growing lumber industry in Gabon—based on the Okoume tree—had recruited many of the Fang men who had survived the influenza epidemic into forest work. Since it was the men who traditionally cut new fields out of the forest this recruitment also led to the abandonment of established fields and to an important change in the traditional economy. These lumber camps were important arenas for the spread of Bwiti at the time—many an old Banzie of the 1950's had first danced Bwiti in a lumber camp. But because prostitutes flourished there they were also arenas for the spread of veneral disease, one of the chief causes of population decline.[35] The lumber camps thus favored the growth of Bwiti in two ways: first, by providing an arena for its practice and second, by favoring the spread of the disease that had much to do with the reduced birth rate. Bwiti has long promised to its membership a restoration of fertility.

The strong impression among Fang that their population was in decline is difficult to support in precise demographic figures; the Gabonese archives yield only sporadic data from which to develop reliable statistics. We have already noted that in the 1960's Gabon shows by far the lowest growth rate, 0.3%, of any of the Francophone countries. This figure for Gabon, if applied to Fang, means that their growth rate has remained constant at this low figure for more than thirty years. Indeed, Le Dentu, the Doctor General of the colony in the thirties, gives a rough 0.3% figure (2.3% birth rate and 2% death rate) for Fang in the 1930-1940 decade.[36]

Though it was frequently enough argued, as at the Fang Congress at Mitzik, that Fang were losing population—were a dying race—and though this impression was widespread among Fang of all degrees of education, the figures show only an abnormally low rate of increase. The psychological impression of decline seems to have been the result of other factors operating upon this low figure. First of all, in the Fang segmentary social system, however vestigial it was, a prime value was increase in family size—numerical strengthening of the *ndébôt* (house of people) and *mvôgabot* (village of people). A slow rate of population increase frustrated that goal. Secondly, the dramatic loss of population suffered during the epidemic and famine stayed in Fang minds as a negative image not effectively countered by a modest rate of increase. Thirdly, labor migration of men and migration of families to the coast was experienced by interior villages as vitiation—the decentering we have discussed. Fourthly, whatever the actual rate of increase, Fang were most struck by the number of infertile marriages (largely due to the venereal disease rate). This manifest debility and frustration of the purpose of the bridemonies was transformed into the frequent lament: "Our women are no longer giving birth, the bridemoney has grown but we have no children." Naturally it was an attractive feature in Bwiti when its leaders promised to recreate conditions in which the ancestors and the great gods would send down children again.

THE EVOLUTION OF THE BWITI POPULATION

The evolution of Bwiti membership is no easier to establish than that for Fang generally. In most general terms, however, it seems clear that Bwiti membership never exceeded 8 to 10% of the gross population, whatever impression administrators gave of its taking over the countryside. The most reliable figures come from our roadside sampling of Bwiti chapels and their membership in 1959-1960. On the very northern fringes of both Bwiti influence and Fang country, on the Minvoul-Bitam road, for example, a 115 km stretch of road running east and west on the borders of the Cameroons, we registered six villages with chapels. This road had a total of 78 villages and a roadside population of 3,500-4,000. A total of 50 Banzie were associated with these chapels on a permanent basis—28 men and 22 women. In this fringe zone of Bwiti, then, 7% of the villages had Bwiti representation and 1.4% of the population were permanent members of Bwiti.

In the very center of the Woleu-Ntem, on an 80 km stretch between Oyem, the regional capital, and Ngomessis, 8 villages out of 56 had Bwiti chapels with a total permanent membership of 117 (58 women and 50 men). The total population on that stretch is estimated at 2,500 so that 14% of the villages here had Bwiti or Bwiti-MBiri chapels; 4.16% of the population were Bwitists. Six of the eight chapels were Asumege Ening (Commencement of Life) and two were of the older, Disumba persuasion.

In that part of the Woleu-Ntem closest to the Estuary and to the capital (Libreville), the Mitzik-Medounou road, there were nine villages with Bwiti chapels with a permanent membership of 185. On that route there were 68 villages and a population of approximately 3,000. Thirteen percent of the villages had Bwiti chapels and 6% of the population were members. Three of these chapels were of the Disumba branch of Bwiti and six were Asumege Ening.

The heartland of Bwiti is in the Estuary region around Libreville. Figure 14.1 presents the detailed census along the route from Kango at the mouth of the Estuary to Libreville. In that stretch of 105 kilometers with a roadside population of approximately 3,000 distributed in 70 villages (the villages in the Estuary region are smaller—more often a single ndebot—than in the Woleu-Ntem) there were 25 villages with chapels, or 35% of the villages. The total number of permanent members was 382 or 13% of the population.

A number of extrapolations may be made and some caution expressed with respect to this census. First, we see that the percentage of villages with chapels

Figure 14.1 Chapel Census: Kango to Estuary

TOWN NAME	CHAPEL NAME	KILOMETERS FROM LIBREVILLE	BRANCH AND DATE OF FOUNDING	MEMBERSHIP MALE	FEMALE
Esi Akang	Katele	103	Disumba/1930	5	8
Abing	Ngadi	90	Asumege Ening/1950	8	11
Kougouleu	Awa' Minsisim	61	Asumege Ening/1950	38	48
Esu Asang	Engaeng	55	Asumege Ening/1958	8	7
Mvumayong	Aba Esilayo	50	Asumege Ening/1957	5	3
Evworedun	Nda Ngombi	47	Ebange/1920	8	10
Dzoberimin- tangan	Ndong Obam	40	Asumege Ening/1947	4	3
Dzoberi II	Nlem Mve Maria	39	Andea/1946	3	
Mekonanam	Nangi Misengue	39	Asumege Ening/1948	2	2
Bingung Bisobinam	Eduta	37½	Asumege Ening/1958	25	12
Ebamayong	Mbanzie Bengonga	35	Asumege Ening/1952	3	5
Nkol- ntangan	Engaeng Mitogo	33	Asumege Ening/1956	5	4
Metena Ovono	Kanga Nangounya	30	Asumege Ening/1955	2	2
Nkawk	Divoba	27	Asumege Ening/1950	6	8
Nzong- mitang	Mibanga	24	Disumba/1925	8	10
Nzong- mitang I	Nana Nyepe	23	Asumege Ening/1950	3	3
Nzong- mitang II	Nzangi	22	Disumba/1933	2	2

(From kilometer 22 to kilometer 15 there are four MBiri curing chapels but not Bwiti chapels.)

TOWN NAME	CHAPEL NAME	KILOMETERS FROM LIBREVILLE	BRANCH AND DATE OF FOUNDING	MEMBERSHIP MALE	FEMALE
Bikete	Mowuba	15	Asumege Ening/1952	4	5
Adzebe	Awu	8	Disumba/1920	6	4
Afanmendom	Eduta Menzane	7	Disumba/1938	2	5
Tchibanga III	—	6½	Ebawge	6	3
Tchibanga I	Ening Asumeya	5½	Disumba/1945	2	2
Adzebe II	Mayanzambia	5	Disumba/1930	2	4
Adzebe I	Atonda Simba	5	Andeanari Sanga/1937	28	32
Nkolayo	Sainte Marie	3	Andea/1951	6	4
				184	198

is always higher than the percentage of the Banzie in the population. In part this is due to the dynamic tendency in the religion to shift the locus of worship from chapel to chapel according to personality and changing doctrine. There is also a tendency to construct family chapels. In any case the physical presence of Bwiti seems greater than the actual facts of membership and this may explain the impression gained by administrators and missionaries of rapid increase. Second, the membership figures given are for people in permanent attendance at the ceremonies who have passed fully through initiation. In almost all dynamic chapels there are many more persons in attendance and participating in the dances than have been fully initiated. For example, while the Kougouleu Chapel of Asumege Ening registers a membership of 86, as many as 115 participants will be present for major ceremonies such as those at Easter time. Some of these are Banzie who have come in from surrounding chapels, but many are "aficionados" who are not formally Banzie.[37]

If we can take this roadside membership as representative of general Bwiti membership percentages,[38] we come out with three zones of membership:[39] the heartland zone with membership at the 12% mark; a transitional zone with membership at the 6% mark; and peripheral zones with membership at no more than 2% of the adult population over 15. Figure 14.2 is a map showing these three zones of Bwiti membership. The first zone includes the Estuary, Kango and lower Ogowe regions. The second zone comprises the southern Woleu-Ntem and the Ndjole regions. The third peripheral zone comprises the northern Woleu-Ntem and the Booue-Mekambo regions. (We could develop no figures for Rio Muni [Spanish Guinea] where the religion was suppressed.)

The total Fang membership of Bwiti resulting from these figures would be between six and seven thousand (6,369 to give the exact calculation)[40] or 6.7% of the total number of Gabon Fang over 15 (94,196). If we add to this figure "aficionados" who in roadside chapel or forest camp participate frequently in Bwiti and eat eboga but who do not call themselves full members, then the figure would approach 8% of the Fang population—our rough estimate in the field.

Little can be said about the evolution of Bwiti membership in the fifty years since its appearance among Fang during the First World War. There are no estimates of numbers of Bwitists published or in the archives. To have become a problem in the eyes of missionaries and administrators it is likely that at least 10% of the population participated in the late twenties in the region around Libreville. Bwiti membership in those regions may have reached 20% until missionaries and administrators took repressive action against the religion in the thirties. This figure of 20% seems probable, for this was the period just after the abandonment of their own ancestor cult when traditional Fang were looking for substitute rites. In the twenties, then, there must have been rapid growth to perhaps the 20% figure, followed by decline in the thirties and

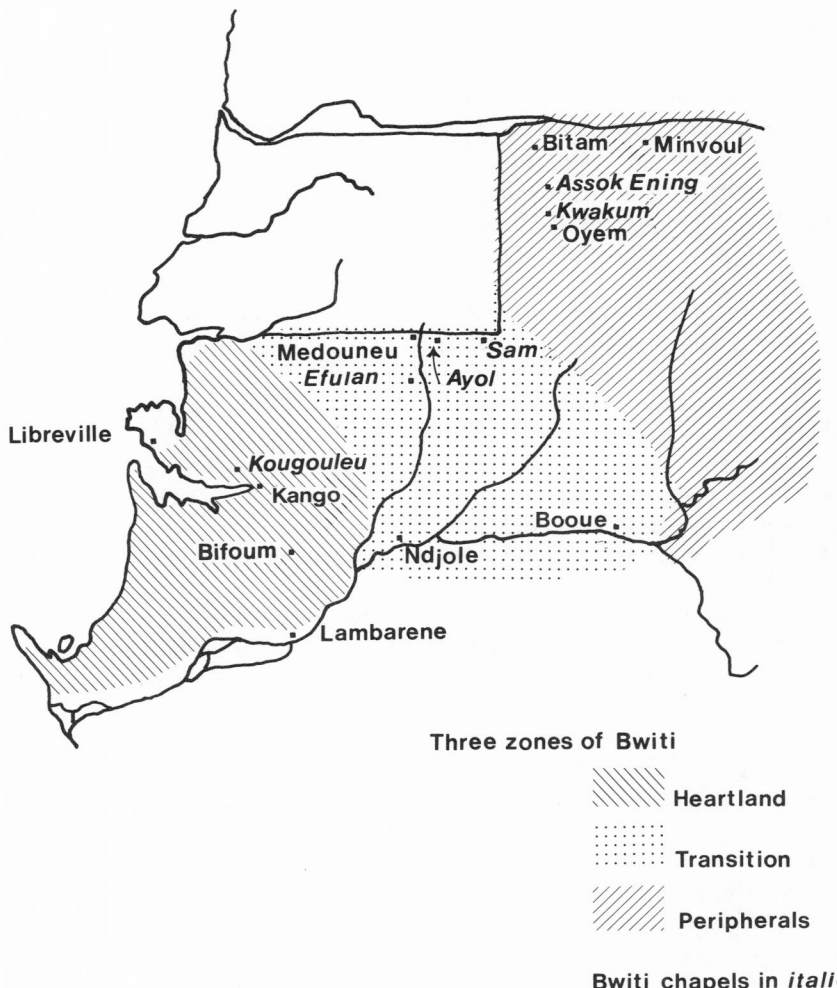

Three zones of Bwiti

Heartland

Transition

Peripherals

Bwiti chapels in *italic*

14.2 Three Zones of Bwiti Membership

forties to perhaps the 5% figure. After the Second World War Bwiti began to grow again to the figures we have given for 1959-1960. This was abetted by intertribal politics and by the malaise experienced by some African catechists and priests and pastors in training. Their entrance into Bwiti gave it a doctrinal sophistication and a Christian orientation that it did not have before the war when it was more strictly a reworking of two ancestral cults.

The Evolution of Bwiti Subcultures

In a village by village census of Bwiti chapels and membership one is made aware of dynamics and evolution—that dynamic which is evident in the struggle for establishment seen in the introductory narrative to the chapter. For example, on the Oyem-Mitzik road we noted two abandoned chapels and in Nkolabona a large chapel with twenty-one members who had been recently converted from Bwiti to its sister curing-cult of MBiri. The Bwiti practiced there had been of the Disumba variety, but the founder and leader of the chapel had died and a woman member, Soeur Berthe Marie, herself cured of illness through MBiri, had led the members over to the sister cult. On the Mitzik-Medoumeu road two chapels had recently shifted from the Disumba to the Asumege Ening branch of the religion.

Looking again at the chapel by chapel census (Figure 14.1) of Bwiti on the Libreville-Kango road we note not only that six different branches of Bwiti are represented (the majority, thirteen, are Commencement of Life as would be expected along the road where the founder of this branch worked), but more than half of these chapels were in existence before their conversion (1945-1955) to Commencement of Life and were not constructed especially under that stimulus. Most interestingly, the mother chapel of Ndong Obam Eya at Zoberi Mintangan, which had a large membership during his lifetime, was reduced to only seven remaining Banzie. The thrust of Asumege Ening had passed to chapels elsewhere on the road: at Bingung Bisobinam close by where 37 Banzie were in attendance and at Kougouleu some 20 kilometers away where 86 Asumege Ening Banzie gathered about the Nima Na Kombo Ekang Engono. Both of these leaders claimed that they and their chapels were the true successors of Ndong Obam and were in active competition for membership.

A census of chapels, then, reveals dynamics of old fissions and new foundations. This is as revealed in the histories of the Banzie themselves. Of fifty Banzie biographies taken in various chapels from Oyem to Libreville 32 men had been in the religion over ten years. Twenty-seven of these men had changed branches of the religion in those years and only 5 men had remained in the same branch of the religion with which they started. Of the 27 men, 8 had taken eboga twice (that is, undertaken the long and arduous initiation with massive doses of the plant each time they switched to a new persuasion in the religion).[41] It is possible to encounter chapels of Bwiti in which the members have been under the same persuasion for many years. But it would be accurate to say that between 50 and 75% of all Banzie remaining in Bwiti over a decade change from one branch to another. Particularly after the Second World War and under freer conditions Bwiti has undergone fission and proliferation of branches.

As we see below when we consider the problem of religious leadership in

Bwiti, a successful chapel and a growing branch of the religion are grouped around and energized by one or several religious personalities. These "knowledgeable ones" have powers of communication and evocation of the sacred that create order and significant feelings in their followers. When Ndong Obam Eya was alive and communicating the Commencement of Life to his followers, his mother chapel in Zoberi-Mintangan was full of worshipers and activity. When he died the chapel died and the activity of this branch of Bwiti passed into other hands.

Of course his presence and the coming of Asumege Ening meant very significant change in religious activity along the Libreville-Kango road. We see from our chart that he effected the conversion of thirteen chapels from a former branch of Bwiti, most usually Disumba (Mikongo or Mikongi) as well as the creation of new chapels. But however wide their influence during their lives, such Bwiti leaders rarely establish religious organizations which can survive the passing of their own personality either in time or space. Bwiti, like Fang social organization, is very much tied to personality and personality dynamics.

There are no useful observations in the archives from European observers on the various branches of Bwiti and their development.[42] We must formulate this dynamic from the Bwiti point of view. This point of view is crucial, of course, in understanding the different attractions of the branches and, as well, gives us insight into reasons for fission. It is also reasonably accurate as to the time scale for the dynamic.

In any event, Banzie say that the oldest form of Bwiti—the form that appeared first among Fang after the First World War—is Disumba or Mikongi (alt. Mikongo). The terms are used interchangeably. Disumba[43] is the name of the legendary Pygmy woman who discovered eboga and was then sacrificed for the good of the people. The meaning of the term Mikongi is uncertain and is variously translated in Bwiti (it is a Metsogo word) as derived from the first black man, the father of all men (*Kongi* in Metsogo) or from the land beyond the dead (*ekongi* or *ebongi*) to which Bwiti carries its members. The actual origins of Bwiti among Fang are almost always tied into Bwiti origin legends. Nzameyo Ngema of the oldest Disumba chapel in Medouneu gives the following account.

The Pygmy husband of Disumba, once she had been killed, returned to give the religion to his village. From there it passed to all the Pygmies. The Pygmies gave it to the people of Esidi-Kama, the Esidi Kama gave it to the Mesake, the Mesake to the Simaka, the Simaka to the Bevobi, the Bevobi to the Etsira, the Etsira to the Messango, the Messango to the Mitsogo. And it was a Messango named Mbomba who brought the eboga to the Fang. God thus created three religions, Suma-ism, the "beginning" which is Bwiti and the first he created, Catechism which is Christianity, and then Maraboutism which is of the Hausa and the Arabs.

Practically all accounts of the origin of Fang Bwiti credit it to the evangelization by this Metsogo, Mbumba. *Mbumba* as a word is derived either from the Tsogo word for the central pillar of the Bwiti hut—the *ebandja*—or from the container (literally stomach) holding the ancestor bones (*abum* in Fang). While there may very well have been a proselytizer to Fang from the Metsogo in the teens and the twenties*2 it is clear that Metsogo Bwiti came in multiple currents up the coast, up the rivers, and from lumber camp to lumber camp. The assigning of origin to one man is in keeping with the personality orientation of the religion but does not reflect the facts.

The Disumba form of Bwiti of which there are many remaining chapels was an adoption and adaptation of the Metsogo ancestor cult by Fang in lieu of their own failing rites. Both traditional cults emphasized the establishment and maintaining of contact with the dead by means of their remains—skulls in the case of Fang and the entire skeleton in the case of the Metsogo—and with the aid of *malan* (*Alchornea floribundia*) in the case of Fang and eboga (*Tabernanthe iboga*) in the case of the Metsogo. Early Disumba was an exchange by Fang of their own ancestor cult for the more dramatic and interesting and apparently effective ancestor cult of a neighboring people.

It was this typically "ancestor cult" use made of body remains, cleaned bones, dried flesh, or the entire skeleton and the ingestion of what was thought to be a poison (eboga) that provoked the hostility of missionary and administrator. Governor Vuillaume emphasizes these things in his 1930 report on this fetish movement. He describes how, during initiation, the "stomach" of Bwiti (abum Bwiti or ebumba Bwiti) was untied and the skulls or dried body parts tumbled out to the amazement of the initiates.[44] What he describes is similar to the sudden, dramatic display of the craniums of the ancestors that took place in Fang Bieri.

Vuillaume's account accords with Banzie accounts of pre-Second World War Disumba which Banzie generally accept as being similar to their own or Metsogo ancestor cults. Banzie emphasize, however, that they abandoned the *abum Bieri*, the stomach of bones, and substituted the *abum ngômbí*—

---

*2 The accounts of Mbumba's coming are most vivid around Libreville. Here is an account from a chapel at 5 km from Libreville: "Mbumba was a Tsogo and he was with de Brazza or so he said. He came with three assistants. He said he had something to show us which we must hide from the administration. He commenced to eat eboka and dance around the fire. His assistants beat upon a drum and a bamboo stave. After dancing a while he began to speak in Popi Fang. We didn't understand him but we knew he saw hidden things. He said if we saw what he saw we could defend ourselves. He and his assistants then made many miracles. He planted a banana tree at the beginning of the evening and at the end we ate the bananas. He produced a canoe that floated out of the forest on one side of the village and disappeared on the other. Those things convinced us that eboga was something to follow. He also taught us many songs."

the stomach of the cult harp which contains the "sacred voices" rather than the bones of the dead. In any case the European view that the bones and dried body parts were obtained by poison or other criminal means made much trouble for Bwiti of the period. And under such pressures many Banzie came themselves to believe that Disumba Bwiti was unclean and fetishistic. Consequently, the branches of Bwiti that appeared after the war almost all demanded that such "filthy practices" be abandoned and the bones thrown out of the chapel.

In the development of Bwiti subcultures five main religious cultures have been influential: Fang Bieri, Tsogo Bwiti, Miene MBiri (the curing cult and cult of wealth), and the two forms of Christianity. All contemporary branches of Bwiti will be found to present varying combinations of these religious cultures. Figure 14.3 shows on a time scale the relationships and influences among the various branches of Bwiti. Though there are many more branches than are discussed here—it is characteristic of Fang individualism and separation that one or two chapels could declare themselves a separate branch— these are the significant branches of the late fifties and sixties. In general there is a movement toward greater Christianization of Bwiti.[45] Though our interest is mainly concerned with the religious cultures syncretized in the Commencement of Life branch, a thumbnail sketch of the orientation of each of these branches and some of the details that distinguish them is useful.

DISUMBA: The original Bwiti syncretizing Fang Bieri and Metsogo Bwiti but much more under the influence of the latter as regards songs, dances, miraculous apparitions, drug-taking, and method of making contact with the dead. The originator said to have been an itinerant Metsogo called Mbumba. At first women were not admitted and then gradually included. Also called Mikongi.

MODERN DISUMBA: Though not recognizing any revolutionary personality bringing about its present form, modern Disumba has abandoned the use of bones. It continues to concentrate on obtaining contact with the ancestors and upon improving the material condition of its members (curing their impoverishment and sickness). For the latter purpose, it encourages the integration of the curing cult MBiri into Bwiti or encourages the proximity of the MBiri chapel to the Bwiti chapel.

ASUMEGE ENING (Commencement of Life): A reaction on the part of the founder, Ndong Obam Eya, to fetish practices and the keeping of bones in old Disumba. Begun in 1947-1948 it has since spread widely. It emphasizes the complementarity of the sexes in ritual and in the spatial organization of the chapel. It emphasizes the eradication of the sins of the membership and the obtaining of grace (abora) in this world and the next. It considers Christian deities as the Great Gods and focuses principally upon the Sister of God, Nyingwan Mebege. It

Main Influences

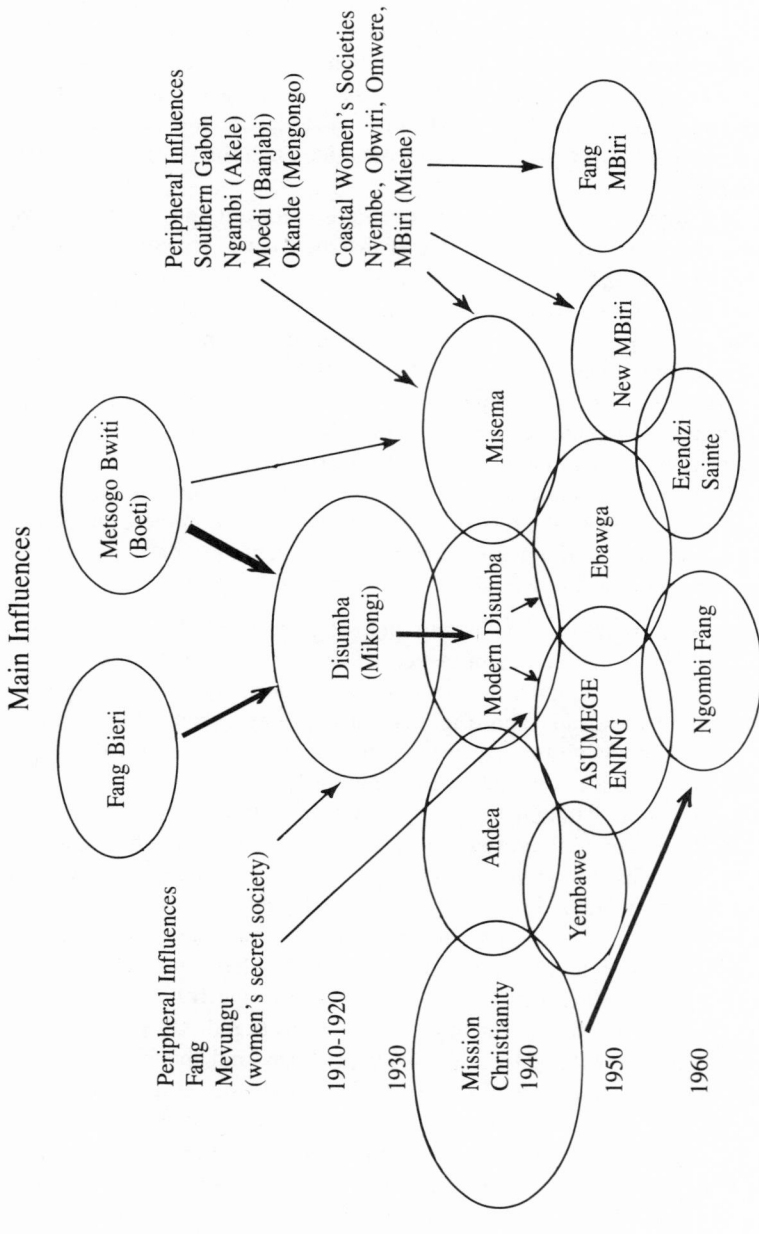

Peripheral Influences
Southern Gabon
Ngambi (Akele)
Moedi (Banjabi)
Okande (Mengongo)

Coastal Women's Societies
Nyembe, Obwiri, Omwere,
MBiri (Miene)

Fang
MBiri

Metsogo Bwiti
(Boeti)

Fang Bieri

Misema

New MBiri

Erendzi
Sainte

Disumba
(Mikongi)

Modern Disumba

Ebawga

Ngombi Fang

ASUMEGE
ENING

Andea

Yembawe

Peripheral Influences
Fang
Mevungu
(women's secret society)

1910-1920

1930

Mission
Christianity
1940

1950

1960

14.3 Evolution of Bwiti Groups

emphasizes harp music and regards the harp as the sacred voice of Nyingwan Mebege. The harp is kept in a sacred precinct. It emphasizes using Fang in the liturgy rather than Tsogo (Popi Fang).

NDEA (Andeanari Sanga): Also called Sainte Coeur de Marie. It consists of a small enclave of chapels close to Libreville (northeast) and also on the forest road to Medouneu. It was founded by Ndutumu Nkombi Georges in 1945. It is more strongly influenced by Marianism and Catholicism than any other branch of Bwiti. It arises from a vision of the Virgin with her heart dripping blood and combines hemp smoking (banga) with the taking of eboga. Its members regularly sleep in the chapel to obtain blessings.

MISEMA (from *eseme*, cry of astonishment at seeing wonderful things): It was founded by Emana Obama Louis who first learned Disumba from Mbumba in the 1920's. This branch has remained localized on the Libreville peninsula where Mbumba first worked. The founder quickly abandoned the *abum Mbwiti* and replaced it with the ''stomach'' of the ngombi harp. But he has maintained high dependence upon the Metsogo language. Singing and dancing are notably quiet and subdued compared with other branches of Bwiti. Women participate but have a clearly subordinate role in the liturgy.

MEKOMBO-KOMBE (from *kombo* [Tsogo], to be possessed by spirit): This is an energetic branch of Bwiti started around 1938 by Nzameyo Mba (a native of Spanish Guinea) in the Cocobeach District with chapels found also on the Muni Estuary and along the Noya River. It incorporates the Fang xylophone in the liturgy and members dress in baggy yellow and white satin garb. It emphasizes the Holy Spirit (*kômbô* or *kubu*) rather than the ancestors or the Great Gods. Purification takes place by Spirit rather than by contact with the individual ancestral spirits. In terms of symbolism it ranks with Asumege Ening as one of the most inventive branches.

EBAWGA NGANGA, EBAWGO or EBOGA NZAMBE: The name of the branch comes from an interesting play on words between the drug eboga (high tone) and the verb ebawga (low tone)—''skillfully to pick the essentials out from the mass''—referring both to the skillful playing of the cult harp (picking out essential music from the strings) and to the religious insight of the religion. This small branch is an early reworking of the Asumege Ening variety of Bwiti and was started by a woman (1949-1951) named Abung Sala Essono. It spread from her village, Ntoum, on the Libreville-Kango road into the forests between Libreville, Cocobeach, and Medouneu. This branch does not employ either fire or the central pillar. It emphasizes quiet harp music and singing rather than dancing. Men and women are kept much more strictly within their separate halves of the cult house. There is a ''road to heaven'' constructed along the center of the cult house, a raised platform that inhibits the dancing which takes place on the open floors of the other branches. The cult harpist has a much more prestigious position here. He is virtually the ritual leader, nganga, hence the alternate name *ebawgah nganga*. Women are influential in this sect and tend not only to take southern Gabonese religion seriously, as is true of Bwiti generally, but also to adopt the matrilineality of the south. The sect emphasizes birth as the primary experience rather than death.

YEMBAWE:[46] The name is translated as "brotherhood" by the members. This branch of Bwiti was founded by Evung Etughe in the 1940's. At that time he had close relationships with Ndea Kanga but later split with that cult because of its orientation toward a Catholic liturgy and calendar. Yembawe rejects such Christian elements as candles, the cross, and images of saints. But while it rejects the Virgin it has made a deeper syncretism of the sacred female by incorporating Nana Nyepe, the Tsogo mother of life, beauty, embellishment, and goodness, into the liturgy (from *Nyepa*, the Tsogo verb, "to beautify, to know how to live in beauty and goodness").

A narrower focus would reveal other branches of Bwiti than those listed in Figure 14.3. In almost every chapel of any size there are the disgruntled who would found a new branch if they could. Three of the most interesting of the smaller sects are Erendzi Sainte, Ngombi Fang, and Nouvelle MBiri. Ngombi Fang is an incipient branch developing out of Commencement of Life in the hands of the imaginative head of chapel at Kwakum, Oyem District, Mvomo Asumu André (Mbomo Obama or Mvomo Mendame) whose views on Asumege Ening Bwiti and its liturgy are frequently referred to in this book. These views are also presented in the vernacular text edited by him and Henry Schmald.[47] In the 1960's André began gradually working toward his own version of Bwiti. He had the religious creativity to form his own chapel though he seems not to have had the force of personality to attract a large membership. André is interesting because his independence of mind and his own elaborations of the Asumege Ening doctrine as it reached him distantly from Libreville are typical of many peripheral chapel heads.

The two other sects in Figure 14.3 show various returns to the therapeutic orientations of MBiri. All sects of Fang Bwiti are concerned with the state of health and mind of their members but practically all eschew direct involvement in healing in the manner of MBiri. They keep MBiri at a distance. But in the case of new MBiri at Nkolabona on the Oyem-Mitzik road and Erendzi Sainte at Okolassi on the Libreville-Kango road we see attempts at cooperation and syncretism with MBiri. These two chapels move Bwiti much closer to a healing function and away from the microcosmogony which is the central character of the religion.

The Banzie themselves are aware of the various tendencies in the religion and frequently comment upon them. Their critiques are illuminating as, for example, the critique of other branches by Ekang Engono, the leader of the present mother chapel of Asumege Ening at Kougouleu. Of Andea, he says that "it is too Catholic." "They are Catholics who commune with eboka and wish to read the breviary in a straw hut. They are disgruntled seminarians." Misema, on the other hand, "is not much different from the old Tsogo rites from which we took Bwiti. Ndong Obam Eya showed us such practices were unclean." "Ebawga," he says, "is too much the woman's cult. Ndong Obam showed us we must not inherit from women even if we take a religion from such a people. He showed us that we should confront and step across death rather than celebrate life."

WANDERERS AND BABBLERS

Itineration of Banzie back and forth from chapel to chapel is constant. In this they follow that Fang love of visitation of relatives' villages. Most engosie will be conducted with the presence of members of other chapels. Usually the visitors come from the same branch of the religion. Also Bwiti has been particularly attractive to the young, unmarried men working in the coastal lumber camps and factories. In returning to their up-country villages or returning again to the coast they use Bwiti villages as stopover sites, taking advantage of the hospitality of their coreligionists. But even without this presence of migrants there is much visitation. There has always been competitive creativity in Bwiti; in this it is like the exchange of dances practiced by Fang, so that Banzie have a lively interest in novelties being practiced in other chapels and, hearing of something new, often go off to visit.

There is, therefore, much communication between chapels, and innovations, or at least the knowledge of them, spread quickly. At the same time, in conformity with the egalitarianism and decentralization of Fang life, there is no effective Bwiti administrative structure beyond the chapel level. Banzie recognize those who are the founders of the branch of Bwiti in which they dance, they recognize the founding of mother chapels, and they are otherwise particularly alert to the religious practices in the "mother chapel." The leader of the "mother chapel" can take advantage of this preeminence to send advice and counsel to other chapels. No doubt political opinions pass along these channels as well and at certain moments in the colonial period they may have been effective in organizing the vote. But such communications rarely have the force of directives nor do any significant resources flow along these channels. For all practical purposes each chapel is as autonomous as the Fang villages in which they repose.

The going to and fro of the Banzie coupled with the provenience of much of the religion in southern Gabon led to the frequent charge in the villages that it was a religion of strangers (bilôbôlôbô). Since much of Bwiti language is foreign to Fang ears the more exact translation of the Fang term is appropriate—a "religion of babblers." The further and more telling accusation was that the Fang who practiced Bwiti were "ntobot," wanderers, client peoples without families of their own who had come to settle in the village seeking to insinuate themselves. And it is true that many chapels have one or several members who have no local family and who are thus true "ntobot." But no Bwiti chapel could be established in any Fang village unless it was supported by men and women fully integrated into the local mvogabot. Bwiti may have been a "religion of strangers" but strangers could never establish it in a Fang village.

Nevertheless, this charge of "ntobot" was particularly irritating, as witnessed in Muye's angry response to the accusation. This may be because Bwiti often draws its converts from families or family members who are peripheral to the main and prosperous line of descent, or lines of descent, which "hold the village" (*mienlam*). In the case of Assok Ening the prosperous mvogabot was that of Mba M'Oye only one of whose members, Muye Alogo Michel, had joined Bwiti. Both Zogo Ebu and Metogo Zogo were members of mvogabot that were impoverished in wives, buildings, and lands by comparison to Mba M'Oye. And though Muye Alogo was a member of the mvogabot of Mba M'Oye, his family (ndebot), the descendants of Ekwaga Mba, was peripheral to the main decision-makers in the prosperous ndebot of Ndong Mba. Thus, though neither Metogo Zogo or Muye Alogo were in any true sense ntobot, their lack of a central position in village affairs made them susceptible to the insult.

CONCLUSION: A TREE SPREADING OUT

Past suppressions and hostilities caused many Banzie to isolate themselves from the colonial world. The microcosmogony of the religion shows this. Eventually, however, practically all have had to negotiate, as the Banzie of Assok Ening negotiated the building of their chapel, with administration and local representatives of the missions. And in many instances they have simply had to conform to pressures which ranged from prohibition of activities to active destruction of chapels. Banzie, despite their inclination toward self-isolation, have had to develop a politics over the years, however uncertain this usually was and however they might prefer their politics to be, as they say, simply the search for Deity.

These external pressures were never so great as to prevent the rapid spread of Bwiti among Fang even in the thirties when it had to take clandestine form. And in any case the really telling pressures were not the occasional confrontations with missionaries or administrators but rather the more harrowing threats of periodic famine, disease, and population decline with which Fang have generally contended. It is an important attraction of the Bwiti microcosm that for those who shelter under its dome there will be a cessation of disease and a return to fertility. This attraction is felt even though the promise is made indirectly. Bwiti is rarely directly therapeutic. That is to say, its leaders do not directly lay on hands or pronounce benedictions to cure infertility, to heal syphilis, to eradicate tuberculosis. Rather the promise is made that in Bwiti things are in order with the universe and people participating in this order will be free of the disorders of disease and infertility.

Though we speak of the rapid spread of Bwiti, it has never been more than a minority movement. At maximum, 20% of the population of certain regions may have been involved. The average figure was in the neighborhood of 6 to 8%. And that membership has fluctuated. In the first flush of interest in Bwiti in the twenties it attracted many members of whom a large number left, however, in the thirties under administrative and missionary suppression. As the arbitrariness of local colonial rule was lifted in the forties, Bwiti grew once again and even enjoyed indirect patronage from an emerging political party which emphasized in politics a "mixing" or pooling together of tribal interests—a mixing already well represented culturally in the Bwiti syncretism of northern and southern Gabonese religions.

In these fluctuations in membership over time and in the often subterranean spread of Bwiti into the land it has become a polymorphous religion. In the fifties and sixties there have been at least half a dozen sizable branches and numerous smaller ones. This polymorphism, a product of Fang egalitarianism and the old assumption that every village, every chapel in the case of Bwiti, had its own life, is based on a variable mix of the cultures to which Fang have been exposed. Some branches of Bwiti are much more influenced by the Metsogo ancestor cult and sing songs in that dialect. Other branches like the Commencement of Life religion have sought to return to the Fang language and ritual practices more typical of traditional life. Branches are distinguished also as to the degree to which they are influenced by Christianity—some, for example, paying much greater attention to the person of Mary in syncretism with the Female Principle of the Universe, the Sister of God. In other branches that syncretism is entirely submerged, if it exists, and Nyingwan Mebege, the Sister of God, is an autochthonous figure. Christian liturgy also has had variable influence. Prayers in one branch adopt, for example, a very quiescent Christian posture while in others they are highly kinetic. Even administrative and merchant culture have had an uneven influence. Some branches expressly denounce the acquisitiveness and material-mindedness fostered by traders and merchants while others make, usually implicitly, promises of material benefits to their followers. In respect to administrative culture one notes differences in the degree to which bureaucratic compulsiveness is observed in organizing the intricacies of worship and the echelons of worshipers. In short, though we may speak of the dynamics of Bwiti in space and time, the religion is a phenomenon of considerable complexity drawing variably on a diverse set of cultural influences. For this reason, rather than focus our attention on Bwiti as a whole we have concentrated on the ordering of this diversity, the microcosmogony, in the Commencement of Life branch only.

☙ 15 ☙

The Bwiti Chapel:
Architectonics

Efa nôm, efa mininga, bi tôbe nlem mvôre.
(The male side, the female side, they become
as one heart.)

SETTING UP THE PILLARS OF THE CHAPEL

THE MOST IMPORTANT MOMENT in the building of the chapel is the raising of the central pillar, the *akôn aba*. This pillar, the axis mundi of Bwiti, is the fulcrum of their sacred space around which is enacted the architectonic of the religion. The pillar is lodged in both the below and the above, in both birth and death, and by rooting activities in both heaven and earth it gives a permanency to Bwiti which the recurrent building and abandonment of chapels would otherwise deny. Often an especially carefully sculpted pillar will be moved from chapel to chapel. Sometimes an abandoned chapel will have collapsed yet the pillar, if not removed, will remain standing amidst the encroaching vines and creepers of the returning forest. Made of the most durable wood, padouk, the pillar alone remains as archaeological evidence of the microcosm that once flourished around it.

When Muye Alogo and Metogo Zogo finally decided to separate from Zogo Ebu and build the Commencement of Life chapel they still did not come to full agreement between themselves as to basic forms. Simply in setting up the framework of the chapel, they disputed over the second main pillar in the rear. Although the pillar of the front entrance, the akon aba proper, is given much more attention both in the detail of its carving and in the ritual surrounding its erection, the rear pillar, called the male pillar (*akôn fam*) cannot be ignored. It is the pillar of Zame ye Mebege. It is said to watch over and protect the chapel. The ngombi harp is played close to its base. This back pillar is called by Muye, *akôn mebongo*. This is because the music of the chapel is played there and because Mebongo is the name of the completely white spirit of Nyingwan Mebege which is sent by her into the ngombi harp enabling it to play sacred music. Metogo, on the other hand, calls this pillar the *akôn mensunga*, that is, the place of salvation or final judgment (from the Tsogo word *sungea*, to save by judgment), for the Banzie soul progresses from the entrance pillar to that rear pillar in the process of the evening.

The dispute arose over the tree from which this pillar was to be made. Metogo argued for the *ôsa* tree (*Pachylobus edulis*) and Muye for the *ntôma* or *mbilinga* (the equatorial acajou, *Sarcopcephalus esculentis*). These are similar trees and have the desirable characteristics of yellow or reddish-yellow wood, edible fruit, and leaves and bark which in infusion are thought to be highly effective in treatment of sickness and in the divinatory practice of the priest (*nganga*). For this reason the osa is often called *ôsa biang* (the medicine tree). Metogo gave the following reason for the choice of the osa tree. "It is a tree," he said, "which enables the nganga to see the unseen. It is the tree of the *engôlengôla*."(Metogo meant the pure people who know hidden things and who have the power of witchcraft but who do not use it in evil against others [*mvôl*]). "It is a tree which has good power and sees." He implied that it was a good tree to have at the end of the chapel to remind Banzie of what they should become: wise in the ways of the unseen but good to men. The color of these trees also was important and entered into the dispute. Both trees are reddish in bark and this recalls the redwood of the front pillar. Metogo argued that the wood of the osa was yellow-red and much darker, even black, when it was old. Thus it was a wood which would remind the Banzie of the cycle of his life in this world and the need through Bwiti to make contact with the next.

Muye did not argue with Metogo's interpretation of the suitability of osa wood. He pointed out that the ntoma was much yellower while the osa was often reddish-white or even white. He argued that the ntoma was a more beautiful and a heavier and more enduring wood. It was a wood much coveted by Europeans and therefore a wood, while just as rich in meaning to Banzie as the osa wood, more likely to inspire respect for the new chapel. He also argued that the leaves of the ntoma were more efficacious in curing illness than those of the osa. This debate became acrimonious. Each felt his interpretation reflected his understanding of Bwiti. After a halt of several days it was agreed to go ahead and erect the osa pillar which in fact had been long cut. The substitution of the ntoma would have produced a much longer delay.

Muye's acquiescence was in part gained by following his suggestion to add some peripheral supporting posts of *eyen* (*Distamonanthus benthamianus*). In fact his suggestion followed the practice in many Bwiti chapels. The use of this tree in chapel construction accords with the attraction to trees whose substances, bark, leaves, fruit, are held by Fang to enable nganga to see the unseen. The eyen is also known as *élé bengang* (the tree of hidden things). Bwiti emphasizes seeing the unseen. If the wood of the chapel can aid in that, so much the better. This is also a good wood, said Muye, because "it sees God." He was playing on words (*Eyen e yen Zame*).

There was no dispute about the central pillar of the chapel which is always carved of the redwood or padouk (*Pterocarpus soyauxii*). Everyone knew that this tree stood for the red path of birth and death and that it was also, as was the red path, associated with the female cycle (*Pterocarpus* exudes a thick, dark red sap which has a direct association with menstrual blood for Banzie). Such details are closely attended to by the "knowledgeable ones" of Bwiti. They are the crucial elements out of which the microcosm is constructed.

Having decided on the woods of the various pillars, the Banzie of Assok Ening prepared to carve the main pillar of the chapel. It is usually the only pillar that is carved. Two holes were first cut in the lower extremity of the padouk pole and carefully smoothed. These were the holes of birth and death. Then other designs were debated. It was decided to call upon KaBiYen, the ethnographer's wife, who had often been seen sketching around the village, to design the sky spider, *dibôbia*, at the very top of the pole. She was also asked to suggest other designs. She did not wish to influence the design but, when pressed, suggested an Adam and Eve figure seen on a pillar at a chapel in Mitzik District. It shows (Figure 15.1) Adam and Eve on a pure white field with Eve impelled by the first sin reaching out into the red of the pillar which represents the path of birth and death upon which their sin would soon propel them. But the members did not wish to imitate another chapel.

Finally, it was agreed that Muye and Metogo should suggest the designs and KaBiYen should draw them. They would also explain the designs. On the side of the pole facing out (Figure 15.2) were designs to be read down. On the very top was the sky spider dropping the egg of creation and below that the three persons of the egg. Below that, below the death hole, were the three persons again but one of them, the principle of disorder or evil, Nlona Mebege, was lying dead on the ground through the action of Bwiti. Below this was a half-moon with an animal upon it signifying the old Fang animal sacrifice which made a stain upon the moon, the orb of the Sister of God. At the bottom of the column, below the birth hole, the eboga plant was figured, as if rooted in the ground.

On the opposite side of the pole, the interior side, and to be read up, was first an alarm clock between the birth and death holes. This was to remind Banzie of the exactitudes they must observe in ceremonies and in every aspect of their lives between birth and death. The hands stand at 9 o'clock, the moment of the beginning of the *engôsie*. Above the alarm clock a figure was pictured flying over the ground, for the Banzie attempt to "fly" over the path of birth and death in their ritual. Finally, above that and just below the death hole were the three roads to the land of the dead such as are seen in *eboga* visions. Above the death hole the three persons were figured again, this time in descending order of importance according to Banzie attention to them, the Sister of God being the most important. These three persons become one person in an ascending arrowlike figure who returns to the sky spider of creation. These figures sculpted upon the pole represent the career of the soul from the above to the below and back to the above. They also represent the career of cosmic creation from the sky spider down to the earth of the eboga

15.1 Adam and Eve on the Pillar

plant back up again to the original creation. KaBiYen put her initials on the very top of the pole together with the date to indicate that she had collaborated in the design.

Even though cut, carved, and fully designed, the central pillar was still "dead." It had to be made to live by the members in a series of ceremonies. First it was rolled to the center of the new dance floor. A hole some four feet deep was dug for it. In that hole were placed *sôkh-zome*, the riverine wasp with the powerful sting that lives in the trees, a piece of flint (*akokh*), and the red tail feather of the African Gray Parrot (*kos*). The wasp was placed in the hole because his sting heats the body as Bwiti heats the body and because his flight, after circling three or four times, is straight as an arrow, as straight as the soul of the Banzie on the path of birth and death. The wasp's association with the riverine forest is also evocative, for these trees and the river are important in Bwiti ritual.

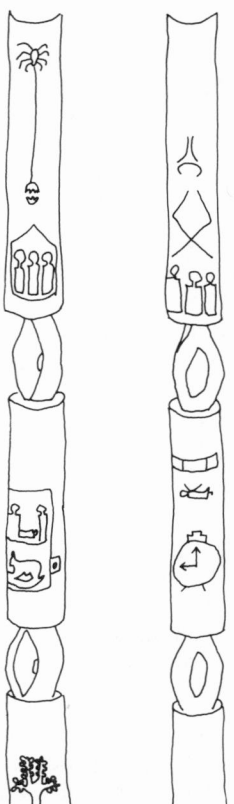

15.2 The Central Pillar of the Chapel (Assok Ening)

The flint is placed in the hole because that is the rock with which fire is made and the purpose of Bwiti is to heat up, to give life. The pillar of birth and death should be grounded in flint. Finally the parrot's tail feather is added because it is the parrot who first flew the red path of birth and death from beginning to end. This is why his tail feathers are red. Also he nests in the tallest trees, and particularly in those of red bark and wood. He nests at the final point where the soul, climbing the red path, leaves this world for the next. By placing his red tail feather in the ground and at the beginning, as it were, of the path of birth and death, the soul is reminded of the end of its journey.

When the hole had been prepared it became time to bless the pillar. First the entire membership stood spread-legged over the pole placing the flats of their hands upon it. This is reminiscent of the purification ceremonies of Ndong Mba in which the sinful adolescents straddle the pole. But in this case, the pillar, rather than taking away sin, gives and takes blessing. The antelope horn was then blown to alert the ancestors in the forest to come and aid in the raising of the pillar. In the raising of the rear pillar both men and women participate together. But the main pillar is raised by men alone.

The pillar once in place with the earth tramped down must be purified. A wad of pitch was placed between the birth and the death hole and burned. Its black smoke carries away evil spirits with it. Now a man, the nganga, was called forth to place a smudge of white kaolin (fim) in the birth hole. After this a woman, yômbô, placed a smudge of red padouk powder (baa). Finally a needle was placed in the hole. This represented the penis and its eye is the true size of the birth and death hole. Thus do men and women together prepare the central pillar for the coming of the spirits. Finally the head of the chapel, Muye, came forth and sprayed the pillar with perfumed water. This is done to make the post especially attractive to Nyingwan Mebege whose pillar, after all, it is.

Finally at the base of the pillar seven balls of pitch were placed in the configuration of Tolo (the constellation Orion) and burned. As they burned, prayers were said inviting the spirits to come and bless the pillar. The constellation Orion was chosen because it is associated with ancestral blessing and with the origin legend of Bwiti. Also it was said that dibobia, the spider, constructed her web between the four stars of Orion. Metogo explained further that Tolo represents the First Person, Mebege, and each of the outer stars represents the four elements of which man and woman are made: fire, water, bones, and wind. "All men are made of all these elements. Not one suffices. In the same way the central pillar of the chapel, or any pillar, is but a bone and that is why we take fire and water and wind in planting and dedicating the pillar in order to give it life."

The wind was given to the pillar in the final "one-legged" dance held in circulation around it. The one-legged dance generates good wind in the chapel and in the Banzie. It causes the dancers to breathe heavily as they hop around. The chapel receives and the Banzie receive the blessing of the mbamba mfongah, the "good wind" in which the Holy Spirit is contained. But the one-legged dance also represents the way that Banzie who have followed the path of birth and death properly enter into heaven. For in a lifetime of following that path with exactitude and ritual rigor men become as one-legged, a pillar themselves. They are no longer confused in having both a right leg with its waywardness and a left leg with its waywardness. Whereas Fang said "good and bad walk together," Banzie say "the left and the right become as one" or, what is the same thing, "the male side and the female side become as one heart."

Different chapels practice different ceremonies of dedication though all consider the preparation and raising of the central pillar as crucial to the establishment of the chapel. The ceremonies at Assok Ening were normal in detail. The detail is very rich. Many different aspects of Fang experience are being accessed at once though at different levels: experiences of cosmic origin, of legendary and genealogical migration, experiences of village and forest, of colonization and evangelization. There is multiplicity of meaning in the Bwiti chapel, an architectonic, and that meaning is not adequately understood by reference only to architectural structure. By architectonic we mean the significance and feeling tone that a structure has by virtue of the enlivening activity which takes place within it. In a manner of speaking familiar to Banzie we are interested in the way the mere bones of wood and thatch are quickened by the fire, water, and wind of the Fang equatorial experience as it is ritually represented. In that process a one-legged whole, as it were, is created out of a pronounced sidedness, a multipartedness of the chapel. For the overall Bwiti experience, "oneheartedness" as they call it, is a unity achieved in the face of multiplicity—an achievement never more clearly evident than in the unity in multiplicity which is expressed both in the central pillar and in the chapel itself.

A REVIVED COUNCIL HOUSE

In discussing the relationship of Fang to their cosmic and domestic space we have shown the decentering which has occurred in Fang life. Cosmic and domestic spaces have fallen out of kilter, resulting in a disturbed architectonic. The pervasive microcosm-macrocosm associations of the men's council house (*aba*) and the women's kitchens and sleeping huts (*nda kisin*), that is to say, the reverberance of that body house-structure association, have also been much vitiated in modernization with its increasing emphasis upon the construction of "cold houses" with concrete floors, stucco walls, and zinc roofs. These "cold houses" cost so much in time and resources that they deflect the meaning of Fang architecture away from the primary and vital experiences of life with which the traditional structures were associated and overemphasize the material component. Moreover, as we have pointed out, the new houses tend to cluster their accessory structures, including the aba, in compounds about them and thus break the essential "unities in oppositions" of the classic Fang village. Finally, the complementarity in traditional sex roles, where men built structures for women to inhabit is much confused by the important contribution of both sexes to the construction of the cold houses. Centrifugality, in short, is replacing centripedality in village life, and the resonance and reverberance among corporeal, domestic, and cosmic planes of existence has tended toward a tone-deaf and house-proud focus upon the material aspect of living.

In the larger progression of Fang over the centuries the centripedality of village life was a transitory pose, of about a decade in duration, in the long-term linear migration northeast to southwest. Periodically Fang were galvanized in their battle with the encroaching forest to move out and on, to slash from the forest, in an act of galvanic revitalization, a new village site. Thus Fang villages episodically moved out and onward in their progressive migrations to the sea. And these establishments of new villages restored, as well, some sense of wholeness to Fang life. The circumstances of the colonial world and of modern times have changed all that. On the one hand the villages have practically all been stabilized for administrative purposes so that the periodic revitalization of new village settlement is no longer possible. On the other hand the attractions of the cities, towns, and trading centers have decentered this stabilized village life. It is an unsettled world.

In Bwiti, however, we find an architectonic return to centripedality which features a harmony of progressive in-turning spirals in space. The *aba eboga* (council house of eboga) is an architectonic response to the various dissolutions, decenterings, and dampenings that have taken place in Fang spatial and social order. In most Bwiti villages the aba eboga occupies a central place at one end of the village: the same place occupied formerly by the aba (Figure 15.3). This is one reason that the Banzie have chosen the name aba although the aba eboga is more imposing than any traditional aba and, moreover, opens out upon the village plaza as the aba rarely did. Indeed the Bwiti village often focuses upon the aba eboga which by its position channels the life of the central courtyard into itself. A number of Bwiti rituals, in fact, extend out well into the central court so that the chapel structure itself periodically, by ritual action, opens out upon the entire village and involves it fully. The plaza is thus restored to its centrality of place and the aba to its surveillance, spiritual in this case, of the entire village.

But other reasons make the choice of the name, aba, an apt one. Most relevant perhaps is the fact that the aba as the male building was the local seat of the patrilineage and of the clan. The objectives of the Bwiti cult are many, but chief among them is the reestablishment of contact with the ancestors, abandoned under the influence of Christian evangelization. The aba was the structure in which the living representatives of the patrilineage gathered to celebrate their community of descent. It is appropriate that the religious arena in which Fang are trying to reassert that communality be called the aba. A second apt reason that this religious arena be called the aba arises from the fact that those who participate there come to dwell, like those who participated during the evenings in the myth-telling and legend-singing of the old aba, in other realms of being—in realms, as we have said, of the creative imagination.

In less lofty ways the naming of the chapel is appropriate.[1] Traditionally the council house was the arena of debate and judicial settlement of quarrels. So in the aba eboga men's hearts are ritually brought into union and, more than that, quarrels are actually heard and settled. This is done in the chapel itself by the leadership in the morning hours. They take advantage of the relaxed and often euphoric atmosphere that follows after the all-night rituals.

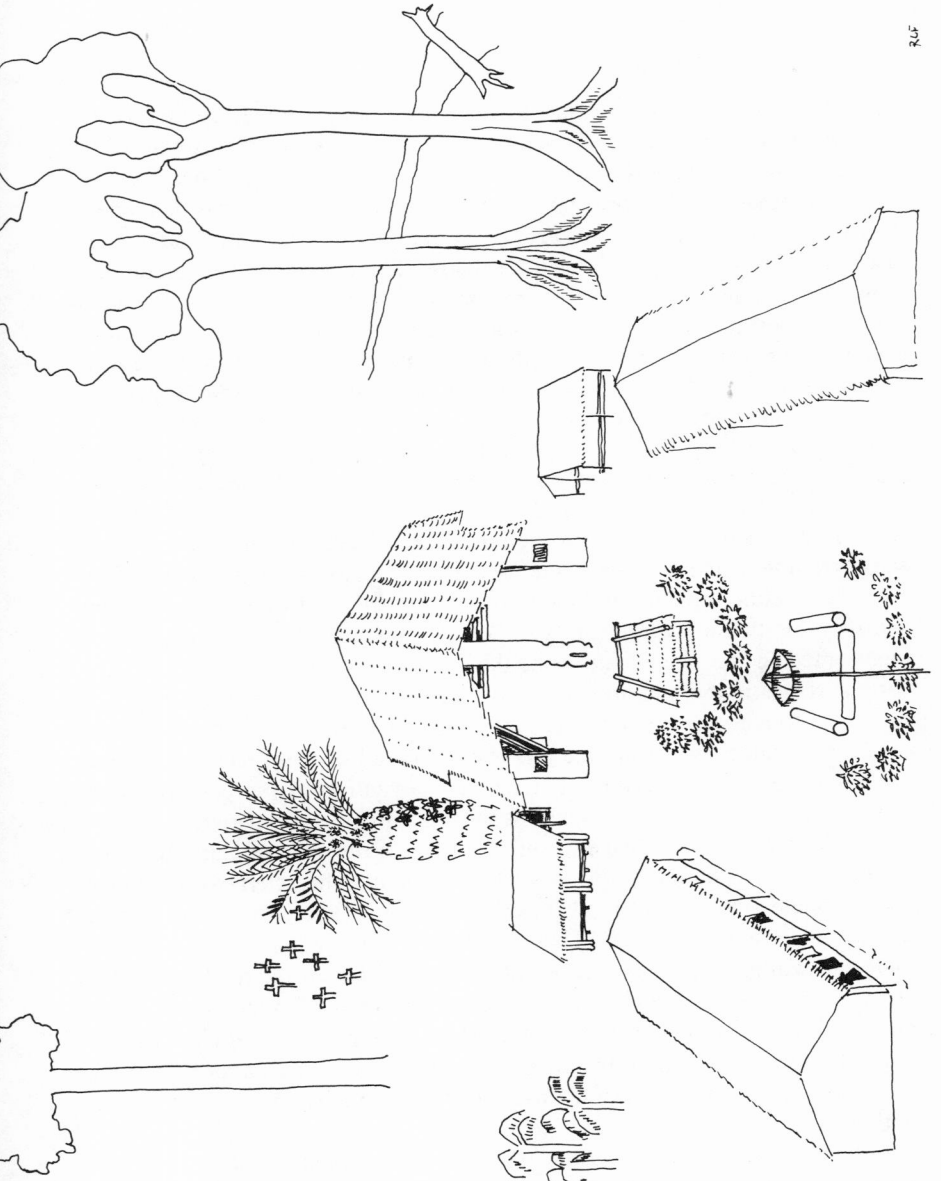

15.3 The Chapel Set in the Village

The chapel thus becomes an arena not only for maintaining integrity and harmony by ritual means but for holding council and judiciously restoring harmony in the members' affairs.

THE BASIC STRUCTURE OF THE CHAPEL

There is an underlying structure to all chapels of Asumege Ening Bwiti, although each[2] branch of Bwiti has a characteristic and distinguishing architecture. Disumba chapels, for example, do not have separate chambers for male and female. In this branch the sacred and private chamber is that where the ritual paraphernalia is kept. From this chamber, in back of and above the altar, the *ngômbí* is handed down to the harpist at the beginning of ceremonies at twilight and handed back up by him at the end of ceremonies at dawn. In Ebawgo Bwiti the sexes are more strictly separated, in contrast to Asumege Ening where there are many mixed dances. In Ebawgo chapels, moreover, a raised platform in the center of the chapel limits that area as a dance space— its crucial function in all other branches of Bwiti. Ebawgo is also the only branch of Bwiti which does not argue the centrality of the akon aba, the axis mundi of the chapel, and which may build a chapel entirely without it.

Despite these differences the aba eboga is for all branches of Bwiti the heart of the cosmos, whose construction and recurrent revitalization by ritual activity is the essential cosmogonic act. The structure is, as the Banzie say, both their cradle (crèche) and their coffin (cercueil), for they are born there and they die there. All relevant parts of the universe, past and present, are represented in the chapel: the sun, the moon, and the sea, as well as the various stages in the migration experience of Fang from the savanna through the forest to the sea. It is true that important ritual events take place outside or some distance away from the aba eboga, but all of these end up centered upon the chapel itself. Within it Banzie are revitalized by surpassing themselves in a locale artfully worked out for that surpassing experience.

The Asumege Ening Chapel (Figure 15.4), a structure averaging between 20 and 30 feet wide and 40 to 60 feet long, is first characterized by a male and a female side which are also said to be a sun side and a moon side or a white side and a red side. These respective sides, female-moon-red and male-sun-white, are, as one stands at the altar looking out, to the left (*meyal*) and the right (*meyôm*) respectively. The proper entrance to the chapel, from that position, is on the left, to the left of the central pillar, and the proper exit is on the right. We follow the Banzie in giving these orientations from the altar looking out of the chapel. That orientation follows the position of initiation.

Entrance into the chapel in ritual dance is the equivalent of being born into Bwiti. It is thus also said that the left-hand side of the chapel is the birth side or the soft side, the tranquil side (*evuvwe*). The right side, on the other hand,

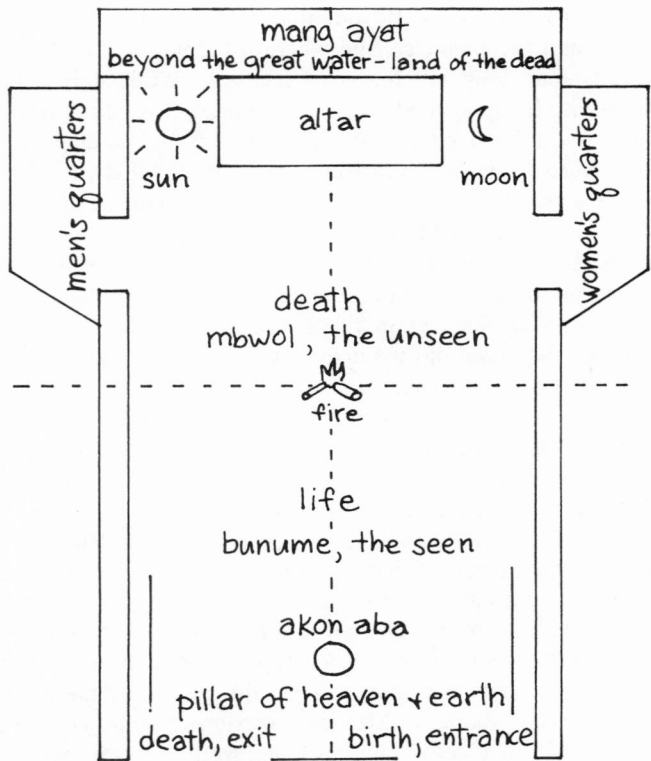

mang ayat
beyond the great water - land of the dead

men's quarters

sun   altar   moon

women's quarters

death
mbwol, the unseen
fire

life
bunume, the seen

akon aba
pillar of heaven + earth
death, exit | birth, entrance

15.4 Ground Plan, Asumege Ening Chapel (Kougouleu)

is the hard (*nget*) side, the side of agitation and death. The right-hand portal correspondingly is called the death exit. As one leaves the chapel, it is said, one "dies" out of Bwiti back into this world.

While the chapel is first organized on a left-right axis it is also organized on a front-back axis. At the center of the chapel, the focus of these two axes is the "fire of the life of the chapel" ("ta mwanga" [*otsa mwan*]—the fire of the child), either a small fire of wood or a pitch torch. The front half of the chapel is known as the life half, the land of *bunume*, that which can be seen and touched and believed. The rear half of the chapel is the land of the unseen, *mbwôl*, and it is known as the death half. One main purpose of Bwiti is to be born into the unseen and thence to come to know death and the land beyond. In Bwiti ceremony ritual progresses from the front of the chapel to the rear and thus accomplishes the movement from life to death.

At the extreme rear of the chapel behind the altar is the space called *mang* or the sea. There is also a chamber there called *sugha tsenge* (the last earth).

It is the abode of many spirits. Beyond that lies *mang ayat* (beyond the sea) where the sun and the moon go and where the great deities, God and his Sister, may be found along with the saved ancestors. While at the altar Banzie communicate with mang ayat, the land of the dead beyond the ocean.

This scheme with its sidedness, its pillar in front and its altar in back, its large central dance space, is the matrix or template in all Bwiti chapels. But practically every chapel leader elaborates this basic scheme in an idiosyncratic way as a testimony to his own creative powers and his visionary understanding of the way things are really done in the land of the dead. For the chapels of this world are said to correspond to the chapels danced in by the dead in mang ayat, the after life. Differences in chapel elaboration also act as a point of attraction designed to hold old members and attract new members to a particularly intriguing architectonic.

An example of these local idiosyncrasies is the chapel as conceived by the Nganga Metogo Zogo Vincent, much involved in the construction of the new chapel in Assok Ening. Metogo refers to the area between the main pillar of the chapel and the entrance as the grave (the *sông*). This is because it is the place where men leave this world and embark for the next. His color scheme is also different. The lower left-hand quadrant of the chapel he conceives as white. The lower right-hand quadrant is black, the place of the hovering of unburied and turbulent spirits. The entire rear of the chapel is red, for that is the color of both the sun and the moon (upon rising) and it is the color of joyfulness—the joyfulness of coming to know the unseen and the great powers and deities that reside there. In Metogo's version of ritual activity Banzie dance through these three colors, not back and forth between two—red side, white side. The "dancing through" of colors is, as we see below, an important synesthetic experience in Bwiti.

It is in the wall paintings and decorative hangings of chapels that greatest individuality is achieved. Many chapels figure the sun and the moon to the right and left of the altar. At the Efulan Chapel of Disumba Bwiti, a human figure variously described as Mebege Himself, or Eyen Zame or Jesus Christ is painted high up on the wall squarely to the rear. He is handing down the sun on the right hand and the quarter moon on the left.[3] (Figure 15.5.) The leaders of this chapel say that the two orbs are placed there because they are the celestial bodies of life and death. It is the moon which provides fertility in women and enables them to give birth. It brings souls to this world. It is the sun that gradually dries up the bodies of men and women and thus gradually "kills" them, bringing their souls back to the next world.

At this chapel there is a long red line painted high up on the side wall which leads directly into the heart of the sun and moon figure to the rear. This is the red path of birth and death upon which all men embark and which leads them to the land of the dead if they follow it well. If men do not follow this path well, then when they die their souls will be left to wander interminably

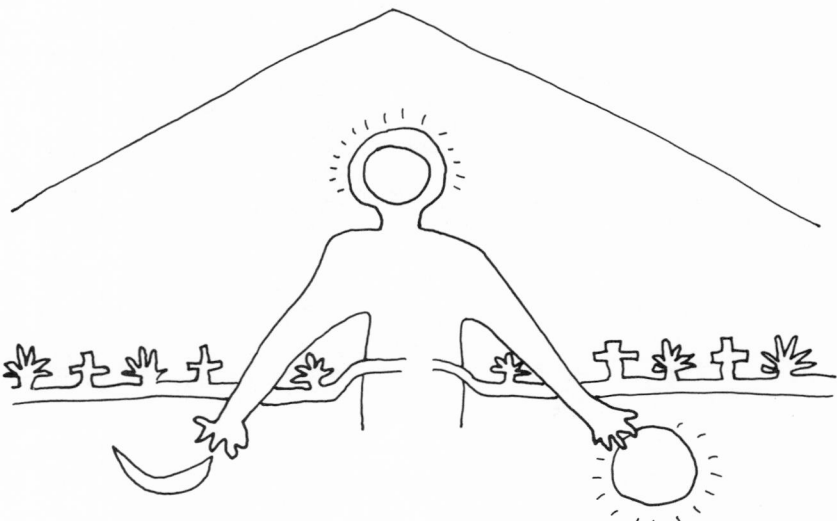

15.5 Deity Handing Down the Celestial Orbs (Efulan Chapel)

15.6 Red Path of Birth and Death: Detail (Efulan Chapel)

in the darkness of the deep forest. This happened to many an ancestor and
to many contemporary Fang who have not joined Bwiti. Bwiti ritual keeps
men's souls on the right path by periodically, through eboga, reorienting them
toward the land of the dead. For the object of the all-night ceremony, the
engosie, is to bring Banzie over to the land of the dead and to return them.
These notions of periodic contact are depicted in many "red paths" by a
sequence of crosses and eboga plants (Figure 15.6).

It is characteristic of Bwiti that there is a thickness in the representation
of their main ideas which is obtained by the replication of them in different
mediums.[4] Thus, as we know, the entire engosie is conceived of as a path
of birth and death along which men dance. But the central pillar of the chapel,
of the red padouk wood, is also conceived of as a path of birth and death,
as are the cords which are strung around the ceiling of the chapel and from
which raffia strips are hung as well as the various woven "circles of grace"
(*ekat abôra*). From these "paths" blessings and good luck descend upon the
membership. This network of cords or small forest vines (*okome* [Figure
15.7]) is variously conceived of as the tendons, nerves, veins, or arteries

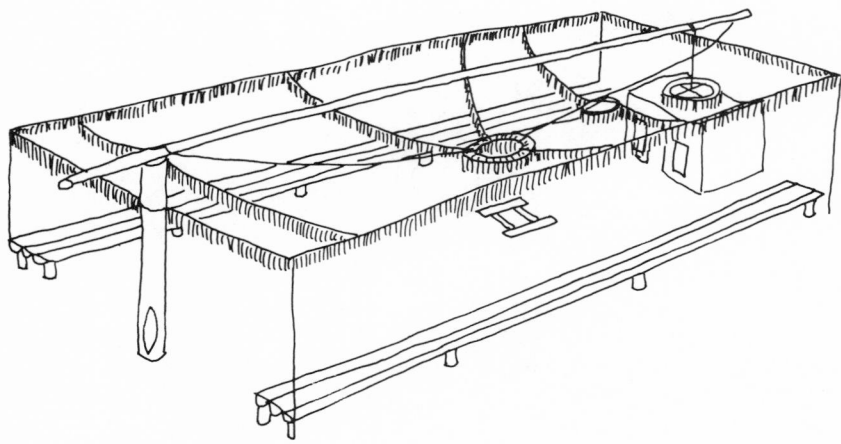

15.7 Raffia Network of Communication (Ayol-Bifoun)

(*nsis, minsis*) of the chapel. They act to hold the chapel together. Along these vital cords spiritual influences flow.[5] The totality of this network constitutes, and here the Banzie play on words, the soul (*nsisim*) of the chapel, which is to say its essential structure.[6] This network of cords is also called by Banzie of a more imaginative bent, the web of Dibobia, the sky spider who brought creation and thus blessing from above to below. Banzie of a more modern turn of mind call this network their spiritual telephone system.

The important elements in this network are the raffia "circles of grace." The network both carries that grace out to all parts of the chapel and, as well, concentrates it from the participant ancestor spirits gathered along the upper reaches of the chapel. As to the circles which concentrate the grace there is variation in their explanation and in the numbers employed. There are usually two. There is one at the center of the chapel over the central fire and one over and just to the front of the altar. The central ekat is where the spirits and the supernaturals pass their blessings down and where the dead send power to the living. This ekat is also said to be the birth circle. The circle to the rear, in contrast, is where the living send their requests, at times of prayer, to the dead. It is also through this circle that spirits of the living go to mingle with the dead. Thus this circle is called the death circle—where the spirits of the living pass over into the land of the dead. The two hanging circles replicate the birth and death holes in the pillar of the chapel. In some chapels there is a third circle (in some there are as many as five or six) directly above the harp player: the *ekat ngômbí*. The Holy Spirit and the blessing of the Sister of God shower down through this circle and give power and beauty to the harpist's music. This circle is found in chapels that lay particular emphasis on music and song or upon Nyingwan Mebege as the principal supernatural. It is treated in such chapels as the commanding circle.[7]

Banzie recognize that these circles relate to the old hanging medicine baskets (*ekat engan*) used to restore men and women to a state of good luck (*ôkan*) after committing a sin. A mixture of leaves, water, and the blood of a sacrificial animal were placed in this container. When the person had confessed his transgressions the container was punctured and the contents showered out upon the patient, cleansing him. The flow of his life was restored to him from the clogging caused by his sins. In Figure 15.8 the two circles are compared showing the literal and figurative "showering down." The Bwiti ekat is hung with red, white, and black streamers said to be the three routes to the land of the dead. Banzie pass over the red route, Christians over the white route, and the unconverted and unregenerate Africans over the black route, a knotted path and difficult of passage.

The Chapel as Body

The hanging medicine basket brings to mind Fang notions of corporeal malaise—that it is a result of clogging and blockage. One main object of therapy is to return the body to flow by various acts of sympathy and homeopathy, and by contagious coercion. In the case of the engan, the body, clogged by sin, is brought to flow again by puncturing the bottom of the hanging container, itself clogged with detritus of various kinds. As its liquid content is released and sprays out upon the patient, so is the clogging of his own chest released. An association is established between the clogged chest of the patient (*nkuk kwan* or *nkukwan*) and the hanging basket as a surrogate "chest."

In a much larger sense the Bwiti chapel is also a therapeutic "container" in which the clogged communications between the living and the dead can be made to flow again through dance and song. In Bwiti ceremonies the weaving back and forth between life and afterlife, birth and death, male and female, sun and moon—this "saving circularity" as we have called it— reestablishes communications between these isolated entities and domains in the macrocosm, making of them a flowing whole again. So the participant's own body, the Banzie microcosm, is returned to a fuller self by enabling the spirit to be released from unseeing and unfeeling entrapment in its fleshly cage. That release enables the parts of the self to come into fuller intercommunication. The Bwiti chapel, in short, is a spiritual body in which the afflicted real bodies of Banzie can once more find flow and can return to the whole.

The notion of the chapel as a body is readily volunteered by Banzie. It is not a surprising notion for Fang who in their old cults, Ngi and Dzok, mounded up large earthen images of chthonic animals and practiced their rituals in and

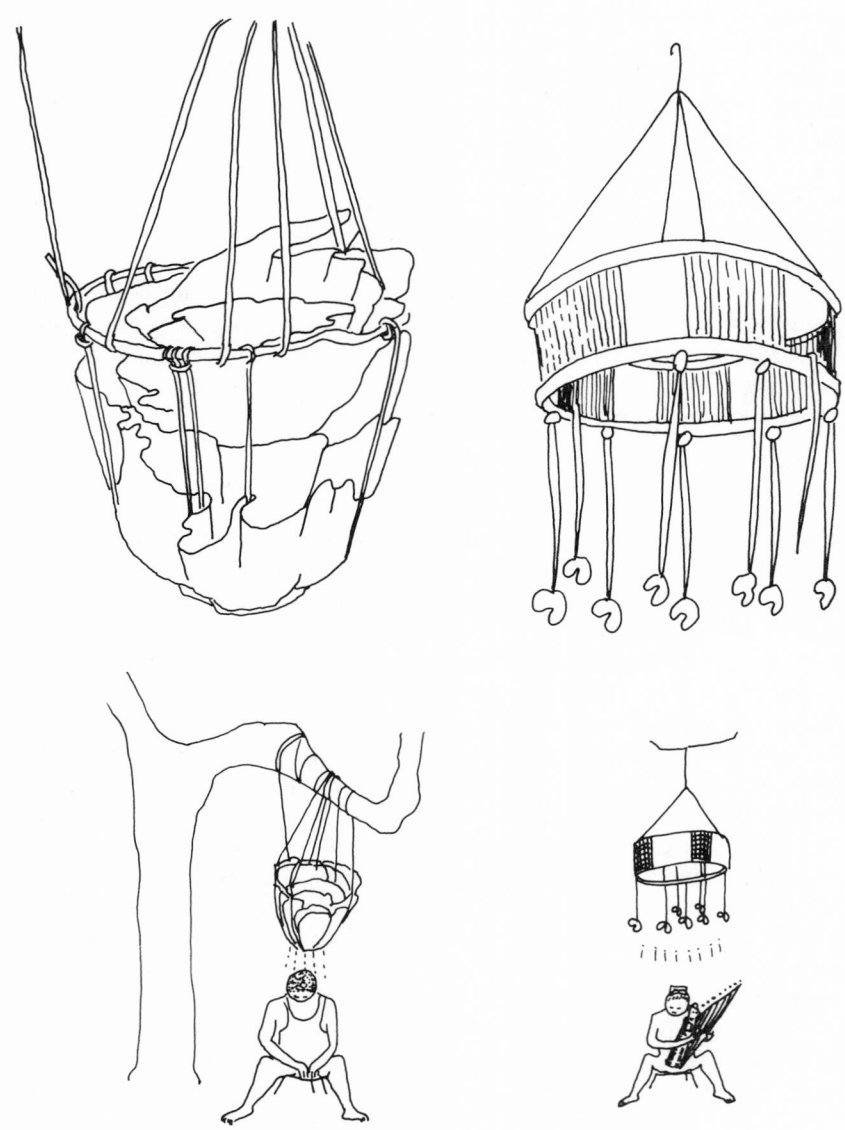

15.8 The Circles of Grace

around and under these altar mounds. We have seen this association in Bwiti in the notion of the hanging cords and circles as the veins, arteries, and tendons of the chapel. But this association is often presented by Banzie in more direct terms. Here is the comment of Mosingi Eko Obama of the Ayol Chapel. (Since Fang does not make gender distinctions the English "her" is not in the original, which is rendered without gender. It is important to note this because the chapel as body is at least androgynous though more often conceived of as a female than a male.)

> The chapel is a person crucified. On the right hand the men's chamber, on the left the women's chamber. She lies on her back. Behind her is her life and death the earth. Before her is the figure of her spirit. On the right the sun and on the left the moon. The head is the *sugu tsenge*, the supreme (first) mystery from which we depart to know death. In the center of the chapel is the fire which is the heart. . . . The fire protects the chapel against evil spirits but we replace it with a lantern when dancing begins in earnest. The fire is too strong for the spirits. We replace it with a more "douce lumière." The *akôn aba* is sex organ. It is of the man and the woman.

Banzie like Mosingi Eko Obama describe the chapel as a body lying on its back, though this body is not cruciform as in the common representation of the body cruciform in cathedrals in Europe. Mosingi, in fact, described the body chapel with its hands crossed at the chest in the manner of a Fang reliquary figure (Figure 15.9). This crossing of hands he described further as *ekat mwan môt* (the "circle of grace of the child of man"). Such a corporeal configuration expresses to him spiritual completeness or wholeness. Other Banzie, however, superimpose a man cruciform upon the outline of the chapel with right and left hand extending into the male and female 'chambers. The following is a description taken at Efulan and repeated at Abangoyo. We see that it is a description of an older Fang body mnemonic used to represent the relation of clan segments to each other, although the description is very Christian in tone.

> The Chapel like Eyen Zame is a man on a cross. We Banzie in our two chambers are the fingers of God. The five fingers are the five races of man bound together in God. The dancing arena is the chest of God, of this man (*nkuk*). In the engosie then the fingers of God who are the Banzie come out and dance upon his chest, upon his body which is the chapel.

This imaginative conception has led to the reference to the chapel as *nkuk Zame* (the chest of God). Indeed we saw in Figure 15.5 how the paths of birth and death pictured in the chapel walls lead directly into the chest of the Eyen Zame figure on the back wall. Whether drawn upon the wall or not

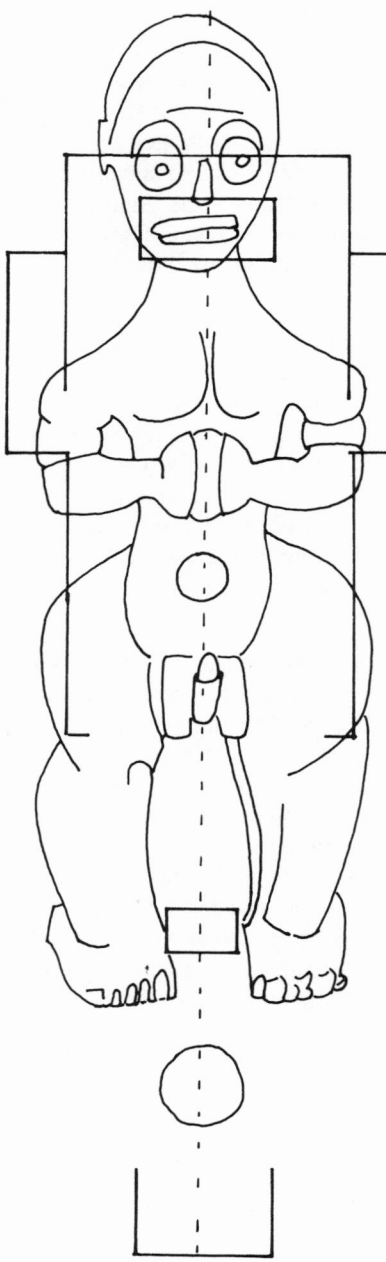

Head of Chapel
Tsugu Tsenge

Circle of Life
Ekat Mwan Mot

Trunk of Zame
Heart of the chapel
Nkuk Zame

Place of Procreation
Pillar of Heaven and Earth
Akon Aba

Welcoming Hut of the ancestors
Nda Mvama

Afterbirth
Ku

The Origin Spot
Njimba

15.9 Body-Chapel Association

Banzie believe that by following the ritual path they not only restore their own bodies to flow but they also, if not produce, at least imitate the flow going on supernaturally in the chest of God.

Though we shall reserve for another chapter the way that ritual activity enlivens and gives meaning to the chapel structure we may confirm here the corporeal association of the structure by reference to the dances of entrance (*minkin*). The description is based upon events at the Asumege Ening mother chapel at Kougouleu. We refer to the entrance dances that take place after the gathering for personal prayer and supplication at the *njimba*. In the entrance dances previous to njimba prayers men and women dance together into the chapel. Afterwards men and women divide into two dance groups. The women enter first. The three senior female members of the chapel, Yombo, are clothed in white and precede the rest of the female membership who are clothed in the regular red and white garments. These women, candles in hand, dance into the chapel bringing a small reddish stone found in a clear sacred pool in the forest. This stone, sent to man by Nyingwan Mebege, the female principle of the Universe, is the essence of creation—the "stone of birth" (*akok abiale*). It is deposited at the altar and will make possible that ritual inducement of fertility which is a main purpose of the religion. The white garments of the senior women are worn for two reasons: in their purity they protect this sacred essence and they also represent the gestation of the child in the womb. For Fang conceive of each woman as possessing a homunculus (also conceived of as a drop of blood) which the semen of the male gradually surrounds and makes viable.

But the assimilation of the chapel itself to a body is seen not only in the placement of the "sacred homunculus" within it but more clearly in the men's entrance dances from the njimba. The men, following the women, arrive at the birth entrance of the chapel and halt there. The leaders place their hands on the thatch or the lintel piece above them. Then the entire group in close-packed formation backs up and comes forward again. At each successive surge forward they penetrate more deeply into the chapel. This continues until the male group is entirely within and ready to begin the circle dances. These ritual actions at the birth entrance are explained in various ways, but predominantly they are explained as (1) the difficult birth of men out of this life into the spiritual world of the ancestors, and (2) the entrance of the male organ into the female body. The first explanation confirms the assimilation of the chapel space to the spiritual world and the second explanation confirms the assimilation of the chapel to the female body in ways similar to the traditional assimilation of the women's cook house to the woman's body. In this multilevel explanation for the men's ritual entrance we have an association between the primary processes of sexual orgasm, birth, and death—for the entrance dance represents sexual entrance and the dying out from this world and birth into the next. Overall, it is the female body that is assimilated to the chapel. This is because of the birth and fertility themes in worship and because Nyingwan Mebege is a main object of worship. But the traditional male association of the aba is still woven into the architectonic of the chapel.

ONE HOUSE, TWO BEDS: ONE CHAPEL, TWO CHAMBERS

In examining the various extensions, representations, and replications of microcosmic and macrocosmic experience which occur in the Bwiti chapel we come to appreciate how complex the architectonic is—how difficult to reduce to any simple principles. Things happen in the chapel on many levels, corporeal, social, spiritual, cosmic, and others. Nevertheless there is one principle of organization that asserts itself again and again. There is a pervasive dualism in chapel organization—even a system of binary oppositions. It is tempting to regard these oppositions as the dominant mode and the organizing principle of Bwiti ritual. Indeed the presence of the body metaphor as extended into the chapel would seem to argue it. For where the body experience is extended to understand other more complex experiences, dualistic organization often follows suit. Ogden's study[8] of the very ancient preoccupation with dualistic oppositions in Western thought argues the body to be the experience of reference, the basic metaphor, for the crystallization of dualistic oppositions as a form of understanding. The body offers both the opposition of right and left, the basic spatial cut as it were, as well as the opposites of the extremes of a scale from head to foot. It also offers the opposition of behind and in front or before and after. The dependence of representation of opposition upon the symmetry of the human body becomes evident when one considers the oppositions available to a jelly fish who has, it would appear, only up and down.

In any event it is easy, when talking with Banzie about the chapel, to draw up a list of binary oppositions that are distributed directly or indirectly in the chapel or in the associated ceremonial activity.

right hand	left hand
male	female
white	red
death	life
hot	cold
day	night
sky	earth
bone	flesh
sperm	blood
speech	silence
activity	tranquillity

The readiness of Banzie to come forward with these sets of oppositions and in fact their presence in the chapel suggests an "institutionalized dualism" in Bwiti. It seems, once again, to confirm Tessmann's views formulated at the turn of the century that there was a fundamental, unresolved, dualism at play in Fang religion. The situation is, however, more complex. First of all, except in the area of aesthetics,[9] it was difficult in our work with older Fang informants to discover any deep underlying dualism as marked as that which appears in Bwiti between the various quadrants of the chapel or between God Above and God Below. Secondly, there are examples of tripartism in Bwiti, not only in the idea of the three persons of creation, a notion influenced by missionaries in any case, but also in such notions as the three paths of life and the three stages of existence.

Still there *is* a marked dualism in Bwiti. We may well regard it as an intellectual and an aesthetic reaction to the disturbance of traditional modes of being—their redistribution brought about by acculturation. Bwiti is an attempt to restore coherence in Fang culture. In any culture, we recognize, there is a reservoir of many potential modes of being and ways of valuing. These are not necessarily consistent or compatible with each other. They may be contradictory.[10] Despite such incompatibilities men seek to maintain an image or system of images of themselves and their cosmos in which there is some coherence. One of the most elementary kinds of coherence is achieved by such "institutionalized dualism" as we see in Bwiti.

It is instructive in this regard to look at the older Fang culture where, by a process of what may be called value distribution,[11] complementarity was achieved between inconsistent, even contradictory modes of being and acting. This was accomplished by systematic structural distribution of these modes of being in time and place so that they did not make conflicting demands. Since there seems to be a clear opposition in Bwiti between male and female sides of the chapel we may ask how male and female modes of being were distributed traditionally. Anthropologists have plentiful data on celibacy, the "berdache," "make man" ceremonies, and the like to make clear that the distribution of these modes is not guaranteed biologically.

Here our discussion of complementary filiation in Chapter 3 is relevant for it shows us how Fang, though staunchly patrilineal, trace themselves alternately to a male and a female ancestor as the social structure is considered in increasingly wider perspective. Succeeding levels of grouping are seen as alternately having the sanction of either common maternity or common paternity. An interesting fact here is that the associated qualities or modes of being of maleness and femaleness tend to be characteristic of these various grouping levels. The ndebot is said to be stable, placing emphasis upon cooperation and mutuality among its members. The mvogabot is characterized by competitiveness and divisiveness between its component parts. These interpretations are compatible with stereotypic male and female modes of being as emphasized by Fang: males are competitive, aggrandizing, turbulent. Females are tranquil, cooperative, nuturant. Most of the woman's day, for example, is devoted to cooperative agricultural activities and the preparation of food while the men, if not in solitary hunting or in attendance upon their cash crops, are engaged in discussion and debate in the council house over matters of bridemonies, marriage arrangements, and land use.

The qualities attached to these modes of being are just those attached to the sides of the chapel according to whether it is a male or a female side, a death or a birth side. In any event this distribution of maleness and femaleness in the social structure achieves complementarity. Conflictive contrast is avoided, for the individual should sense what qualities to manifest by virtue of the context in which he is acting, the level of grouping that characterizes the specific social relationship of the moment. The code of behavior—the specification of the appropriate mode of being or acting—insofar as one might be abstracted has, thus, a situational orientation.

Fang culture, we see then, achieved in its traditional form some coherence, some freedom, from inconsistency and contradiction by means of systematic complementarity. In one context it was appropriate that one follow female modes of being and be tranquil and in another follow male modes and be active. In ritual relationships with the ancestors it was the value of paternity that was foremost; in strife with other lineages, it was the principle of fraternity. Thus was the satisfying fabric of social life woven together. The consequences of acculturation, however, were the redistribution of values and the creation of "cultural dilemmas" as inconsistent modes of being and acting were brought together in the same time and place, making for situations of difficult choice.

In respect to the values of activity and tranquillity we see the consequences of redistribution particularly clearly. Here the introduction of cash crops and corvée and migrant labor greatly redistributed old patterns. Older Fang complain that "we no longer have tranquillity in village life—always activity—and the result is *ebiran*, "social disorder!" Bwiti attempts a harmonious redistribution of active and tranquil modes—a distribution and an integration contained in the male and female sidedness of the chapel. What the colonial situation precipitated out of complementary suspension, Bwiti seeks to restore to an orderly distribution.

Whatever may have been the status of dualisms and binary oppositions in the older Fang culture—values were mostly distributed in systematic complementarity—in Bwiti they assert themselves repeatedly in the chapel organization. A range of modes of being and acting are brought into coherent association on the basis of opposition and interassociation—that is to say, such modes of being and acting, such qualities, as maleness and femaleness, activity and tranquillity, whiteness and redness, hotness and coldness are brought into simple systematic association.

We do not learn a great deal, however, about the actual experience of the Banzie in identifying such dualistic principles of coherence. First, there is a problem involved in identifying the male-female opposition as the basic one

around which all the others cluster. This opposition would seem to be basic
because the turbulence between men and women, the high divorce rate, the
low fertility rate, are constantly on the minds of Banzie. And it is also true
that, most often, Banzie talk about the male and female sides of the chapel
rather than, say, the sun side and the moon side and the red side or the white
side. In Asumege Ening in particular, male and female sides are emphasized
because this branch of Bwiti builds separate male and female chambers. More
than any other branch it emphasizes male-led rituals on the one hand and
female-led rituals on the other. But the opposition is still situationally determined. At certain cosmogonic moments of the ritual, the sun and the moon
are the basic oppositions in mind—at other moments activity and tranquillity.
At the least it is not true to say that Banzie simply vacillate back and forth
between male and female modes of being. By interassociation of sets of
opposition, ritual activity recurrently brings other opposing qualities, albeit
associated with the male and female opposition, into focus.

There is another important sense in which the oppositions are not the
ultimate reality of the chapel or of ritual experience. "As a child cannot be
created by man or woman alone," Banzie say, "so the world of Bwiti [*esi
ebôga*—literally 'the land of eboga'] cannot be created by dancing on just
one side of the chapel or another." It is by dancing on both sides, across
domains, that the whole religious universe of Bwiti is created; that the flow
of intercommunication is established; that the "saving circle" of grace is
achieved. Thus the more basic experience in Bwiti is the bringing together
of the sidedness of experience, the bringing together of incompatible, even
opposite, values. But we shall leave for further discussion, when we consider
the Bwiti song and dance cycle, a closer examination of the way in which
this conjunction occurs and the way in which dualistic conceptions are brought
progressively into play by the interassociation of sets of oppositions.

The bringing into conjunction of the oppositions manifest in the chapel
layout is seen most instructively in the case of the two chambers of men and
women.[12] These act as robing chambers or as resonating chambers where
women, for example, sing their part of the song cycle, the yombo songs.
Separated as they are in actuality, these chambers are also united by a ritual
event which takes place over a pool, a concrete basin of water found in each
chamber. This water represents that sacred deep forest pool where the Sister
of God sends down on a moonbeam the new soul to be born to mankind.[13]
Thus the two chambers are united by the water of the same pool. They are
also united, though in complementary fashion, by the poolside rituals within
each chamber. Periodically, during lulls in action in the chapel (particularly
at midnight), a man will grind away on a block of white kaolin clay and a
woman on a block of red padouk wood. As they grind fine dust of white
kaolin in the men's chambers and red padouk dust in the women's chambers
these powders are deposited upon the water. This represents the substances,

blood and semen, out of which children are conceived. As in the coordination of the dances themselves the chambers are brought together cooperatively adumbrating that fertility which is such a desired consequence of Bwiti.

However the conjunction between the sides of the chapel is brought about, it should not be forgotten that what is truly exceptional in Bwiti is its bringing together of men and women in the same arena. For in former times it was exceptional that women should take any part in men's rituals, particularly those of ancestor cult, just as it was exceptional that they should fill any place in the council house. In contrast they participate fully in Bwiti rituals and hold virtually equal place in the chapel.

THE PILLAR OF THE CHAPEL

Close study of the chapel reveals its many distinct parts which stand in meaningful relationship to each other. In the case of the akon aba (the main pillar of the chapel), though ostensibly a unitary configuration, we also have many parts and meanings. The akon aba is often so complexly explained by adepts of Bwiti that some students[14] have founded Bwiti religious philosophy upon it. Like the chapel itself, the pillar provides an opportunity for creative Banzie to express the virtuosity of their religious understanding. Explanations of the akon aba also confirm, the special vision of Bwiti leaders. Thus there is a range of styles in the construction of the pillar, in its elaboration and explanation.

The akon aba of the Bwiti chapel, like the aba eboga itself, has its origins in an important feature of Fang architecture—the entrance post of the men's council house. A gorilla skull was often hung on this post and quasi-reliquary figures might be sculpted upon it (Figure 15.10). It is of interest, since various holes are carved in the pillar in Bwiti, that Tessmann shows an old council house pillar with a hole artfully cut into it.[15]

The pillar of the old council house was touched for good luck (*maa*) by men coming in and out. It thus "absorbed" and could be used to express the force of the male community. Ceremonies of village cleansing and of purification of neophytes in rites of passage, the *ndong mba* ceremonies, took place about this pillar. The old council house pillar as a central feature of village life was thus apt for reinterpretation in Bwiti.

First and most important, the pillar no longer has exclusively a male association. At least one of the two holes worked through it is given a female association.[16] When the "chapel as body" is being discussed the pillar is generally given androgynous status. In some chapels of Bwiti, in fact, those particularly devoted to Nyingwan Mebege, a representation of her as *Nana Nyepe* (the Mother of Beauty and Bounty), is carved into the pillar (Figure 15.10). The main pillar is understood in such chapels as female while the main supporting pillar at the back of the chapel behind the altar is said to be male. It is a replication of the male-female opposition of the two sides of the chapel.

Practically all Bwiti pillars are carved from the redwood of the padouk tree (*mbel*) and have two holes carved in them. The pillar is carved out of redwood because it represents the vertical dimension of the red road of birth and death along which Banzie proceed. The two holes of the pillar represent the birth hole through which the spirits are born and the death hole through which spirits depart.

While these are the simple facts of practically every Bwiti pillar the particular explanations given by chapel leaders are usually more complex. Here is the explanation of Zame Nduma Obama of the Asumege Ening chapel at Abangoyo (Medouneu District). In his chapel the two holes instead of being waist high are separated at the extreme ends. The "birth hole" is low and large. "After all one is born close to the ground." The death hole is much smaller and at the top of the pillar. "That hole must be as close as possible to heaven." It is a small hole because, "as the Europeans say, the true way to Zame is as of the eye of the needle. Only the spirits of Banzie are sure to find that hole. Fang who are not Banzie never find it and are condemned to wander as vagabond spirits in the deep forest."

The old custom of touching the pillar is also found in Bwiti dancing but only in the vertiginous dances of the obango—those dances accompanied by drumming and not by the harp. "These are the dances," says Zame Ndumu Obama, "in which we try to shake the spirit free from the body. In order that it should 'die' right we touch the pillar so that the confused spirit following the path should find the death hole." Zame Nduma went on to compare the pillar to the women's kitchen (the nda kisin). He made this comparison because, he said, "In the nda kisin as in the aba eboga we are born and we die." "Red is the color of the kitchen, the blood of birth, the blood of death, the blood of women. It is the color of the pillar." "The chapel is our council house but the pillar is our nda kisin." Zame Nduma's thought makes, in this way, an entire village out of the chapel. It also expresses the opposition in village life between the council house (principally male in association) and the nda kisin (principally female in association).

Not only is the akon aba touched during the obango to help provide the spirit with a proper death, that is, assure its passage through the death hole, but in the obango dances during the early part of the all-night ceremonies when the path of birth is being followed a dancer may mount the pillar upside down five or so feet above the ground. He then slides down and out between the legs of the head dancer, nganga. He is "born" in the chapel. This particular use of the central pillar replicates the entrance dance of the men into the chapel at the birth entrance.

There is frequent debate between different branches of Bwiti, as well as between different chapels, as to the proper placement of the birth and death

15.10 A Comparison of Central Pillars

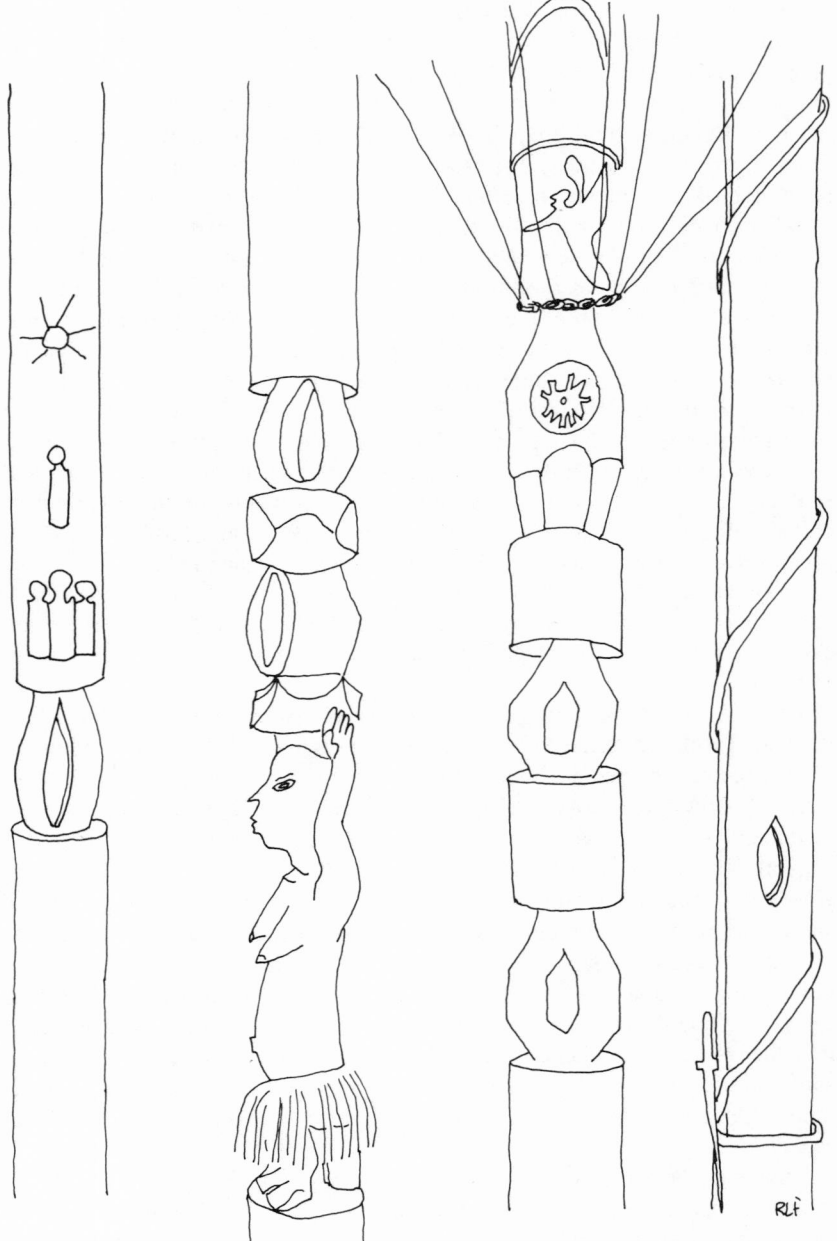

holes. Should they be transverse or in the same plane? In Asumege Ening it is assumed that one dies as one is born and hence the holes are in the same plane. In Disumba chapels the holes are in opposite planes. This occasions the observation in rival branches that their spirit is twisted or has to learn to twist to die. In several chapels of Disumba, however, three holes appear. Two, in the same plane, are for those Banzie spirits that have followed the path of birth and death correctly. The third hole is for the twisted spirits which have refused Bwiti. There is also argument, as we have seen, as to how the pillar is to be decorated. Some pillars are painted all white because it is the route of the dead.[17] In other cases the pillar is left a natural red.

Accessory decoration of the pillar is rare, but some chapels weave a forest vine around it (Figure 15.10) to represent the umbilical cord which attaches all men through the sky spider to Deity. At the bottom a sword is plunged in the ground—the "sword of anger and negligence" that can cut men off from the blessing of Nyingwan Mebege. In chapels in the southern part of Fang country more strongly influenced by water spirit cults of the coast and southern Gabon a python skin is hung on the pillar. In southern Gabonese cultures the python skin is associated with prosperity and fertility. In Bwiti it is more often associated with the rainbow-python which led Fang ancestors to azapmboga and the equatorial forest and which facilitated the crossing of the various torrential rivers by stretching his body across them. The python skin in Bwiti is not so much an image of riches as an image of fruitful migration.

This reference to azapmboga points up a Bwiti-wide meaning of the pillar. It stands for the azap tree of Fang legend through which Fang, with the help of the Pygmies, gained entrance to the equatorial forest. The use of the python skin is supportive of that main meaning. While this legendary migration is associated with the main pillar, the principal path found in it is the path suggested by its division into three parts: *djôp* (heaven), the land of the spirits; *si ye ening*, the land of life between the two holes; and *sông*, the grave, the earth, the portion of the column below the death hole and descending into the earth.[18] The members of Bwiti say that the spirits of the newborn descend down the akon aba and pass through the birth hole into corporeal existence. They continue down through life on this earth, pass through the death hole into the grave from whence they rise again in two transformations back to spiritual life in the sky. Thus there is a circulation of spirits on this "axis mundi" both descending and ascending.[19] Life is a descent and death an ascent.

Whatever the vital excursion of the spirits may be, Fang have also experienced in myth, legend, and genealogical history a dramatic migration northeast to southwest in which azapmboga is a central image. It is characteristic of the layers of meaning present in the architectonic of Bwiti that the migration experience is also present in the ritual and referenced in a number of ways, especially in the pierced pillar of the chapel which is otherwise the path of birth and death. A sense of that larger architectonic can be obtained by looking at the various structures and the ritual space outside the chapel itself.

THE LARGER ARENA OF RITUAL ACTION

The larger context of the Bwiti chapel consists of the various surrounding structures: the village in which the chapel is found and the surrounding forest and watercourses. Bwiti leaders often say that their religion is a religion of the forest. It came from the people of the forest, the Pygmies. It depends upon eboga which is a plant of the forest. It is devoted to reestablishing communications with those ancestors who wander in the forest. And the greatest pleasures Fang have are the forest pleasures: hunting for the men, fishing and wild fruit gathering for the women. It is no wonder that the azapmboga legend is richly meaningful, for it represents to Fang that crucial transformation in their lives from a savanna to a forest existence. Nor it is surprising that the central pillar, itself a focus of transformations, should be associated with the legendary azap, the locus of that aboriginal transformation. Nor is it surprising, finally, that many leaders spend, outside of ceremonials, much of their time hunting in the deep forest.

The relationship of the chapel to the forest is reciprocal. In its various pillars and subordinate structure the chapel has taken the forest unto itself. The pillars of the chapel made from at least three trees themselves constitute a "forest" of meaningful images. In Figure 15.11 we list the "forest" of these sacred trees of Bwiti.[20] This "forest" includes both the carved and shaped trees which have already become pillars of the chapel and sacred trees still growing but which are sources of ritual substance or constitute locales of ritual activity. All of these trees—we note incidentally that redness of bark or wood is one main criterion of their selection—possess medicinal properties and are important in Fang pharmacopeia.

There is often debate about specific trees and woods in Bwiti. We noted the debate as between osa and ntoma as the correct wood for the rear pillar. Generally the Banzie recognize eight sacred trees. This number accords with the eight strings of the ngombi harp. Both the eight strings and the eight trees bring blessing, and both trees and harp strings are locales for sending and receiving blessings from the unseen. Since the ngombi harp is in some part, usually the key bridge, carved out of mbel (padouk wood) and since it also has a birth hole and a death hole and is painted red and white there is a linkage and a replication of themes between harp and central pillar.

Though the forest is present in the chapel, at the same time the chapel goes out into the forest. It illuminates it. In Asumege Ening Bwiti narrow trails are cut into the deep forest at the edge of the village. There, at midnight, all members, in single file, and preceded by the Bwiti harp, move out into the

Figure 15.11 The Forest of Bwiti

BWITI USE	ACCEPTED OR COASTAL NAME	LATIN NAME	FANG NAME	APPEARANCE	TRADITIONAL USE
1. Front central pillar (akon aba).	padouk	*Pterocarpus soyauxii*	mbel	Imposing tree. Red wood, secretes a red "bloody" resin.	Powdered wood used to solidify bowels and bodily processes after dysentery, or flux of blood after parturition.
2. Used psychoreactively in initiation and to highlight all-night ceremonies.	eboga	*Tabernanthe iboga*	eboga	Flowering bush with yellow or reddish pink petals.	Suppressing of fatigue and appetite in long journeys—initiation.
3. Side posts and subordinate supporting beams.	ovenge	*Distamonanthus benthamianus*	eyen or ele bengang	Very straight tree with reddish trunk and yellow wood.	Reddish powdered wood associated with padouk wood to cure skin infections.
4. Rear central pillar.	etanga	*Pachylobus edulis*	osa or osa biang	Large and beautiful fruit tree. Light red-yellow wood.	Highly edible fruit. Pulverized bark used on suppurating wounds and rashes.
5. Odoriferous resin used in torches and bark candles. Its base a focus of ritual activity.	olumi	*Copaifera religiosa*	andem	One of the largest, straightest, and most impressive trees of the equatorial forest. Reddish bark and trunk	A sacred tree of Tsogo Bwiti—a tree of many religious uses among Fang. Bark used in medicinal washes to bring good luck.

6. Name given to welcoming hut of ancestors constructed out of this wood.	otunga	*Polyalthia suaveolens*	otunga	Short thick-leaved tree, red fruit, whitish yellow wood.	Widespread use in construction and furniture. Leaves and bark used to lift curses and protect against them.
7. Tree representing the road of birth and death.	oil palm	*Elaeis guineensis*	alen	Nut-bearing palm. Very rough trunk, long overarching fronds. Palmnuts red.	Oil used in cooking and toiletry. Heart of palm a delicacy. Used as lactogen.
8. Tree often the locale of ritual activity— otherwise the legendary tree of passage from savanna to forest.	moa bi	*Mimusops djave*	azap	One of the giant trees of the equatorial forest. Reddish bark, very straight trunk.	Seeds of the fruit yield an edible vegetable paste which is much appreciated.

forest to make one last invitation to any still lost ancestors and to illuminate their way back to the chapel. It is a striking moment, for the forest is thick enough at the village margins that all one sees is the glimmer of candle light moving about. And all one hears is the soft strumming of the harp.

In traditional Bwiti as practiced by the Metsogo of southern Gabon one might argue that it is the forest that is being brought into the village. For the members disappear into the forest and suddenly reappear dressed in animal skins and dancing animal dances. The "animals" are "charmed out of the forest," it is said. In Fang Bwiti, though in some respects the forest is brought into the chapel, the much stronger emphasis is to extend the influence of the chapels outward by illuminating the dark forest with the religious events of the evening. By this illumination it is the ancestor spirits, wandering like animals in the deep forest, that are brought back—charmed, though in a different way—to their rightful place in the order of village life.[21]

We have said little about watercourses except to indicate that the far end of the chapel is conceived of as the sea, *mang*, or the "great river," *tame manga* in Popi. We have also said that somewhere in the forest is a pure pool of water sacred to the Sister of God from which a stone is taken which will be emblematic of the fertility to be restored by Bwiti to its participants. The two basins of water in each secret chamber are linked to this pool as they are, in a larger sense, linked to the sea. So it is not only the forest that is represented in the chapel but also the watercourses that have been so important to Fang in orienting themselves in the equatorial forest.

So the chapel stretches out in ritual act and in representation taking in and going out to the forest. This is not surprising. Fang life has long been a cycle of activity which moved from forest to village and back again. The village becomes too hot or too turbulent and men move out deliberately or in exasperation to the forest. In most Fang ceremonials, Bieri, Ngi, Ndong Mba, use was made of forest precincts and special clearings around former village sites (*elik*) for a portion of ceremonies. For the forest has a special power to purify, to simplify too complex thought, and to bring men into contact with the unseen. Of course the forest is no less ambivalently regarded than the village. It can be too cold, too isolated, too lifeless. It is in the movement back and forth between forest and village that vitality lies. And even though in Bwiti it is the movement back and forth between parts of the chapel that is most vitalizing, the religion has not abandoned the revitalizing links with the forest.

In a more limited context, that of the village and the area immediately surrounding the chapel, there is more linearity in the architectonic of activity. There is a directionality reminiscent of Fang migration. In Figure 15.12 we show the main Bwiti arenas outside the chapel itself which are crucial to ritual performance.[22] The most important gathering places here are the njimba and the otunga.

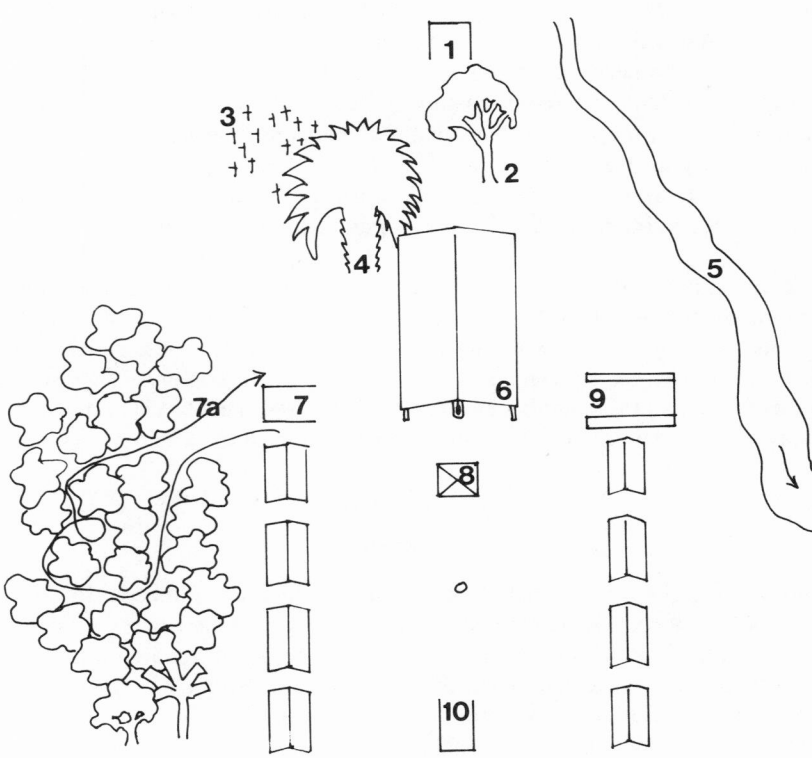

KEY

1. Elik-njimba (mobayi ndongui)—
   secret or final meeting spot (also elem).
2. Eyen tree—zen awu.
3. Song—the graveyard.
4. Alen—the oil palm (also mobayi ndongui).
5. Oswi nlem—the river of
   oneheartedness.

6. Aba eboga—the chapel.
7. Ndabenyaboro—the house
   of the old men.
7a. Path of the lost dead.
8. Otunga—house of the dead.
9. Njimba bidzi—morning and evening
   meeting house.
10. Njimba osu—the origin spot.

15.12 Ritual Arenas Exterior to the Chapel

There is a graveyard close behind the chapel. Here are buried dead Banzie. They are buried close by, where leaders of the chapel can maintain contact with them. At the Kougoulou Chapel of Asumuge Ening there is a grave pit called *tsuga tsenghe* (the last earth) below and behind the altar. The leader of the chapel descends into this pit well before midnight to communicate with the dead. As he lies on a mat in somnolent and expectant state, visions come to him from the dead buried not so far from his head. Other chapels do not dig pits but maintain a secret chamber[23] behind the altar at the place called *mang* where, in the flux of that imaginary element, leaders can be in communication with the dead. At the very rear of the chapel, the leaders, by immersing themselves in the elements of earth or water or air, whether real or imagined, obtain most effective communication with the dead buried nearby.

Before discussing the two most important external structures, the njimba and the otunga, we should note the *nda benyaboro* (house of the old people). In this hut those Banzie who are too old to participate in the rituals—and participation in the dancing is the essence of Bwiti worship—may yet be present at the engosie and benefit from its blessings. This hut is immediately to the left of the death exit of the chapel, for the old people are close to passing on.

THE NJIMBA

In discussing the entrance dances we pointed out that the njimba is conceived of as an origin spot, an Archimedean point from which the Bwiti cosmos can be created and moved into being. The first pinches of eboga are taken in the njimba. It is there that individual prayers are first offered (as opposed to the public prayers that are only permitted in the chapel); and it is there that the members hold council (*esawk*) and plan the particular songs and dances of the evening. The njimba is said, like the forest, to be a cold spot. The word njimba is Tsogo in origin, meaning secret reunion spot. The Fang equivalent would be *elik*, that place in the forest where the ancestors once lived, where certain rituals may be held, and where men can return in brief sojourn and start anew.

In many Bwiti villages there is only one njimba, found at the far end of the village from the chapel where the opposed council house would have been found in traditional villages. The njimba is a place for taking counsel. It is usually a simple structure of three logs open to the courtyard and to the chapel at the far end. But there may be more than one njimba. In the mother chapel of Asumege Ening there are three. There is the customary one in the courtyard facing the chapel. There is one behind the chapel in the forest between the sacred trees. And there is one to the left of the birth entrance. The njimba in the forest, most similar to the Fang elik, is used only on special occasions—

at moments when special dances are being organized such as those dances which syncretize elements out of traditional rituals. The njimba close to the birth entrance is used in this village for the gatherings after the first minkin entrances and before the engosie proper. At that time final preparations are made for the ceremonies and the personal prayers are also made. In the early morning after the engosie this njimba is used for the communal meal of the entire membership (*bídzí bi bandzí*) one of the most euphoric moments in Bwiti. In every case these njimba are either gathering spots for the preparation or launching of that kinesthetic cosmogony which mainly takes place in the chapel or they are spots for the decompression and recovery from that cosmogonic activity.

THE OTUNGA

In the otunga we encounter a space (also a tree) whose meaning is of a special intricacy which reveals something of the thickness in Bwiti representations. The otunga is, on the face of it, the welcoming hut for the returning ancestors. It is a transition spot. Since, in coming in from the forest, they will be accustomed to a cool, wet, and still milieu they must be acclimatized to the vertiginous activity, the heat and fire of the chapel. Candles burn within and a table is set with an offering of food for the ancestors. The care taken to welcome and feed the spirits in this hut is reminiscent of the hospitality offered to the dead in the ancestor cult. Appropriately, therefore, chicken continue to be sacrificed at the otunga.

In the more Christianized chapels the otunga is also held to be the tomb of Eyen Zame. It is said to commemorate his death. The sacrifice of a chicken there is said to commemorate that crucifixion. Instead of killing the chicken in the traditional manner, by cutting the throat, its heart is pierced with a sword in the manner of the Roman soldier who pierced the heart of Eyen Zame on the cross.

But why should this hut be called otunga which is the Fang name of a serviceable tree (*Polyalthia suaveolens*) with a straight trunk and yellowish white wood? It is widely used in house and furniture construction. The trees' leaves were made into concoctions to lift curses or to protect against them, and its leaves were employed in the engan basket.

There appears to be, for the Bwitist, an association between the otunga hut, a place for the lifting of the curses laid down by the ancestors, and the ekat, the circle of grace, the locations where blessings, particularly fertility, are showered down from the ancestors. This association rests on a traditional use of otunga leaves in the engan purification basket. Bwiti is full of this kind of association by reinterpretation—much of it beyond the knowledge or capacity of any stranger to feel or reveal. And yet it is just such present associations resonating with past usages that converge and give a circumstantiality to Banzie experience, a powerful sense of integration which is deeply convincing.[24]

Banzie speak of "paying the otunga"(*atang ôtunga*) or paying the death of the child of man (*atang awu mwan môt*) by which they mean Eyen Zame. Some chapels collect 100 or 200 francs at the otunga hut when the chicken is sacrificed. This is said to "guarantee" one's salvation in Bwiti and appears to have something to do with the lifting of the curse laid upon mankind through the death of Eyen Zame.The Christian notion that Christ died for man's sins is not widely accepted in Bwiti. There *is* the idea that the crucifixion laid a curse upon mankind that ritual acts at the otunga hut, including sacrifice and payment of money, can lift.

The otunga is also called the ladder of heaven since, on the one hand, the spirits of children can come down it to be born, and, on the other hand, Eyen Zame climbed it in his crucifixion on the way to heaven. In several chapels this association has led to the ritual practice of having initiates, when passing from one stage of Bwiti to another, go out in the forest accompanied by their "mothers" and "fathers" of eboga. They actually climb an otunga tree.[25] This action purifies and activates the spirit in its ascent to heaven. The pillar of the chapel remains the main route for this ascent during the engosie as it is the main route of spiritual descent. But the first experience of that ascent can take place in relation to this other tree, the otunga.

In our map of the Kougouleu Bwiti precincts (Fig. 15.12) we indicate two otunga: *otunga meki* (the otunga of blood or birth) and the *otunga bives* (the otunga of the bones or death). The former is in front of the chapel where the ancestors are greeted and the chicken sacrificed. The latter is behind the chapel at that spot where the craniums and other bones of the ancestors were deposited by those who gave up such animistic paraphernalia upon joining Bwiti. Whereas the ancestor spirits appear and are welcomed at otunga meki, at the end of the ceremonies, at dawn, they may depart at otunga bives. The otunga meki is an otunga of the treetops and hence of God Above. The otunga bives is an otunga of the earth and the roots and is the otunga of God Below. Figure 15.13 is a drawing done in this Asumege Ening chapel of the Child of Man, Eyen Zame, crucified upon an otunga tree[26] with the otunga meki stretching above him and the otunga bives stretching out below him. Two African gray parrots are pictured in the tree. The first travelers on the path of birth and death, they pose here, in effect, on another version of this path—the path of the below and the above.

The object of Bwiti is sometimes said to be to give equal attention to the God Above and the God Below. The expectation of equitable attention is expressed in the frequently repeated aphorism, *nge song a ne nti ôtunga me wuang edzô di* (if the grave is as deep as the otunga is high [that is if God Below is as widespread in influence as God Above] I can die peacefully today).

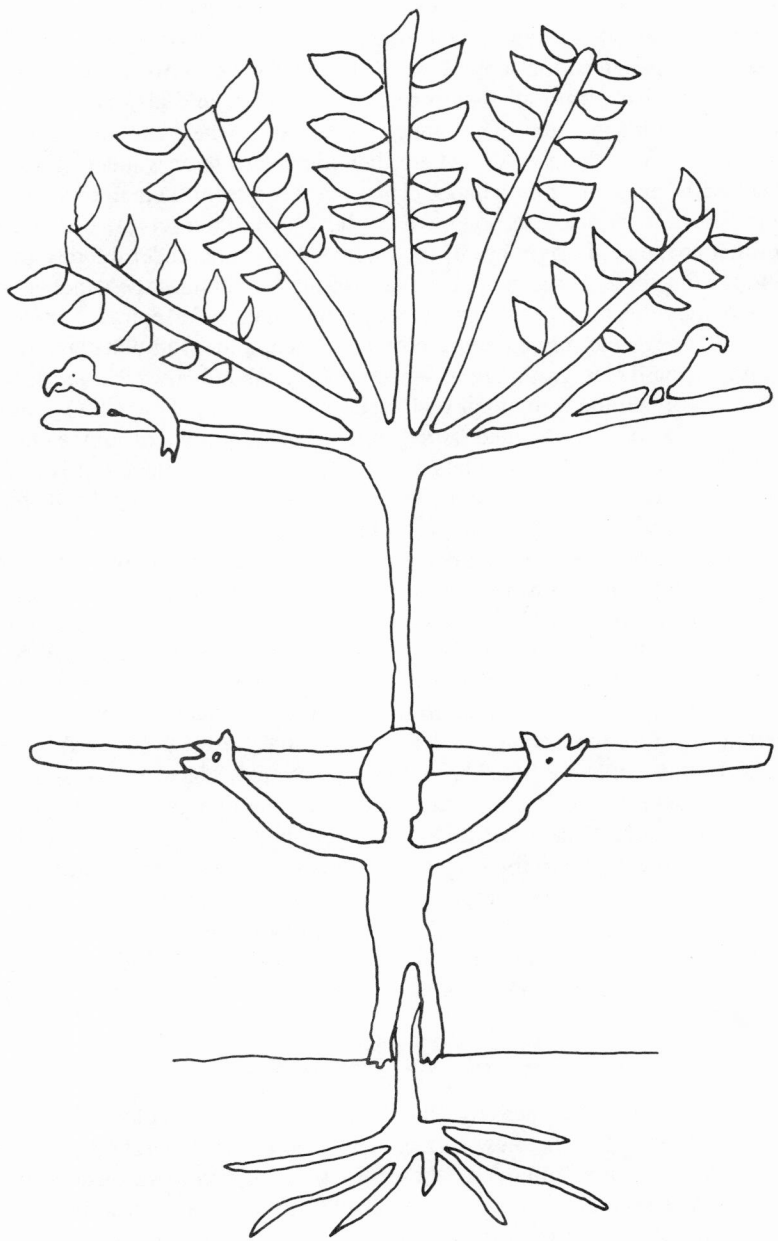

15.13 The Otunga Tree Below and Above

The otunga is also said to be a crossroads and where there is no welcoming hut of the ancestors the otunga will often be represented by a pole with two crossed slats nailed to the top.[27] It is thought of as a crossroads because the spirits gather there from all four corners of the forest and also because it is a transition point in ritual. The otunga is the point where the spirits of the dead can manifest themselves, where they can cease their wandering in the forest and be present in the chapel. They are freed from their imprisonment in the forest. It is also the point where the Banzie themselves, dancing in from that abandoned origin point, the njimba, first come under the discipline of the architectonic of the chapel. Upon passing the otunga, the dance team, *ensama*, must become tightly organized in preparation for entrance into the chapel. Between the njimba and the otunga, otunga meki in our diagram, it is said that the dance group are as wanderers, vagabonds (*eyeye a mot*), and their spirits are confused by their body and vice versa. But beyond the otunga their bodies become disciplined (*tsine*) by the ritual requirements of the chapel and become capable of miraculous activity. At the otunga the spirit is transformed in its relationship to the body. It can now "climb otunga" which is to say free itself from imprisonment in the body.

Considering the entire chapel context, ritual progress proceeds first on the horizontal dimension from njimba, the abandoned origin point, around and past the otunga into the chapel, around and past the central pillar, arriving finally at the altar where the spirits can pass on to the last earth, sugha tsenge,[28] and thence to the sea, mang. This progress is, on one level, a representation of the Fang migration experience from their original abandoned home, elik, uncertainly across the savanna and thence into the forest, finally arriving at the sea. Entrance into the forest brought Fang together. The azap tree entrance brought a convergence.[29] But in the Bwiti view the otunga tree also played a crucial role, for by means of it Fang escaped their ancestral curse. So both the otunga and azap mark the stages of progress in the horizontal dimension. At the same time they are "roads" for progress in the vertical dimension. At the otunga and at the central pillar the spirit of the Banzie can escape its bodybound, earthbound condition and climb to the above. These two trees are crossroads of the vectors of ritual activity.

Heating up the Chapel

By itself, without ritual activity, the Bwiti chapel is a "cold house," an impressive edifice like the new houses with zinc roofs, concrete floors, and plastered walls. But so often, like these structures, it is cold because no fires burn within. Ritual activity warms the chapel up and makes it attractive to the ancestors. Description of the activity that takes place within architectural spaces enables us to understand the architectonic: the feelings and meanings that a given space may evoke. Though most of that ritual is explored in other chapters, where we discuss the song and dance cycle, we should look at the place of fire in heating up the chapel. As in Fang traditional houses, it is important that fires be kept burning in and about the chapel.

The most important fire is at the very center of the chapel where the various sides intersect. This is called *ta mwanga* or *otsa mwanga* (the "fire of the child"). The reference is to the metaphoric "child," that microcosm of activity which Bwiti worship is bringing into existence. It is a "child" that is brought into being by the interpenetration of parts.[30] On some ritual occasions this fire is a large one—a bonfire made of special woods. But since this fire is in the center of the dance arena it is usually a pitch torch (*otsa*) within a bark casing. It is a torch easily moved around to respond to ritual action. Wherever it may be temporarily found this torch is the "fire of the engosie." Its size and the amount of pitch it contains are calculated to burn for the entire evening. The life of the fire is the life of the engosie, it is said, and when the engosie ends so should that fire go out. Banzie also make the point that every man is a torch within which a vital substance burns. When that vital substance burns out, the life of man, like the torch, is extinguished, leaving a withered shell.[31] In a similar way and within the same set of associations it is the Bwiti idea that the engosie itself is a life burning within its casing, the chapel. The vital substance which burns within the chapel is the members' ritual work done for Mebege, Zame, Nyingwan, Eyen Zame, and the ancestors. In the early morning that substance, like the substance within the torch, exhausts itself, leaving but the shell—the empty chapel devoid of that life brought to it by the coordinated activity of the members.

There are other fires or flames. At the origin spot, njimba, at the far end of the courtyard and far away from the heated activity of the chapel, men's and women's souls will be cold with the cold of the deep forest. A fire is thus set there called *mawuba*. Characteristically, two woods are used in this fire. The wood *asas* (*Bridelia grandis*) is a hard wood difficult to break. It represents the strength and perseverance men need to follow the path of birth and death so as to come over successfully to the land of the dead.[32] The other wood burned is *ka* (*Dichostoma glaucescans*), a weak wood, which is the wood of purgatory. It represents that weakness which causes men to fall away from the path of birth and death.[33] This two-wood fire is maintained only as long as the entrance dances continue.

Since the njimba is the beginning of the creation of the life of the ceremonies (*ening engosie*), this two-wood fire will often be laid as the forging fires were laid by Fang ironworkers. That is, it is laid in a square stack alternating the two woods. This stack also represents the forger's house (*nda evolvi*). It is also called the place of innocent beginning (*ebing alona*), where raw materials, the uninitiated, are made into refined materials. This is once again the forging metaphor for the creation of man employed so dramatically in some branches of Bwiti where a fiery forging is enacted within the chapel.

Explanations with theological implications are often given for this fiery forging. Nzameyo Ngema of the Efulan chapel tells us, "To make souls Zame has always used a giant forge, the sun. The fire we build here in Bwiti represents that heavenly fire and forge. During the cold dry season Zame does not work that forge. There is little sun. But the heavenly forge starts up again in the long wet season (*sugu esep*) and Zame once again comes out. Each man within him has something of that fire and when angry that heat starts up within. The heat of Zame is too much with man. That is why we turn to Nyingwan Mebege, his sister, whose cool tranquillity (*evuvwe mvwaa*) offers surcease from the heat of Zame."

There are other fires in the chapel. Candles or a small torch are kept lit in the secret chambers and in the welcoming hut. The most dramatic use of fire, however, occurs after the chapel has been quiescent for a period and particularly after the Banzie have exited in the midnight search of the forest. Before ceremonies begin again the chapel must be purified and heated up lest evil spirits have entered in the absence of ritual activity. A torch of raffia is lit and danced gymnastically around the chapel—tossed from hand to hand, passed through the legs, whirled and suddenly smashed in a burst of sparks. It is a vertiginous pyrotechnic display.[34] The fire whirls through all parts of the chapel, in every corner, and immediately outside the chapel as well.

Though this torch dance seems to be spontaneous, there is a structure to it that suggests the larger architectonic of Bwiti. For the torch is used to open the way again for the coming of the spirits and the great gods. Here is the explanation of the Nganga Metogo Vincent. "I run out into the courtyard thrusting the torch straight up over my head, opening the door for the rising and falling of the child of man, Nganga Eyene Zame.[35] Then I thrust the torch in the four directions of the earth from which the spirits may come. Then I smash the torch upon the ground for God below and all the spirits in the earth. Then I rush whirling back into the chapel to show the disoriented spirits their way."

In the more Christianized chapels the torch is laid down in the form of a cross at the altar and at the two entrances. Or the nganga who dances with the torch will lie down cruciform upon these spots and then smash the torch upon them in a shower of sparks in order to purify the stain brought upon the earth by the crucifixion.

CONCLUSION: THE VALUE AXES OF BWITI QUALITY SPACE

The structure of the aba eboga makes it possible for many things to happen at once and for same things to be replicated in different forms. The sidedness and differently valanced space of the chapel cannot be understood without reference to the traditional Fang village with its sidedness and its male- and female-valanced houses. For the Bwiti chapel does more than simply, though aptly, expand upon the space of the men's council house. It embodies and encompasses within itself the entire Fang village. Even more than that, by having the sea at one end and the legendary azap tree at the other it embodies the Fang legendary-historical experience of migration. In the "forest" of its different pillars and posts it embodies the essentials of the Fang forest experience. In its central pillar it embodies the vertical experience of Fang with God Above and God Below, with sky origins and earthly terminations.

The Bwiti chapel is surpassingly a central place. It restores a centrality to those Fang who are members. By its balanced or integrated oppositions it releases them from the stress of that decentering, that unchecked centrifugality, the passion for journeying, which has become the inclination of Fang as of so many colonial peoples. And by providing for elulua, the pleasure of meaningful group activity, within this central structure it frees its members from the economic individualism and purely material interests of recent years. By ritual activities within the chapel Bwiti reestablishes the content of structure, the interacting and resonating representation of body in building and building in body. For if a sacred space is to have significant quality, an architectonic, it must contain both an extension of personal body images and an intension of mythical and cosmic images.

While we will have a good deal more to say about Bwiti rituals we shall continue to see how these actions within the topography of the chapel restate the progressive movement in space of Fang myth and legend. By interior circulation and by increasingly tighter knitting together of opposites the membership is unified—is brought to "oneheartedness."

In the face of the secularization of modernity, the Bwiti chapel provides a sacred space in which troubled men and women can be reborn. They can dance back and forth over the "crossroads" and up the sacred pillar. They can redistribute in a kinesthetic form modes of being which have gone awry. It is a space away from the glare and oppression of the "sun" of the colonial world. It is a breathing space of the douce lumière of the moon, of the night, of the Sister of God, of the religious imagination in touch with its roots.

There is plenty of syncretism in the chapel. It is not simply a structure returned to the past. For the chapel syncretizes elements traditionally separated as it absorbs elements from the colonial world: evangelical Christianity on the one hand and evangelical mercantilism on the other. Christian elements are recurrent. In respect to consumerism and conspicuous consumption the aba eboga is not simply a house of raffia, bush rope, and forest pillars—a traditional woven house. Often enough it has wattle and daub walls, concrete walkways, a zinc roof. It partakes of the modernity toward which so many Fang desire to move. But even here it is compensating in its modernity. In superficial ways a cold house like so many modern houses, it is recurrently very much heated up with real fires and meaningful activity.

In the richness of replicated associations that reverberate through the chapel during ritual activity we may lose sight of some of the main vectors of movement. But there is a quality space in Fang Bwiti which can be defined in more reduced terms. We are trying to show here by examination of the chapel from a number of perspectives that an architectonic is an organization of space which locates those who live in that space in an optimum position in respect to their own bodies and in respect to their mythological, legendary, historical knowledge and feeling for space—their cosmos. Though we should be cautious in extending a Euclidean three-attribute space to Fang,[36] nevertheless three elemental vectors can be identified and it may be argued that the Bwiti chapel is a quality space because it locates the membership in respect to:

(1) the downriver progression of their legendary-historical migrations (*efa ôswi nkeng*), recently stultified, by restoring progress on the downriver dimension (*ôswi nkeng*);

(2) the convolutions of village life, recently turned centrifugal, by restoring a counter-clockwise centripetal involution toward a central point (*ta mwanga*) in the horizontal cross-village, cross-chapel plane;

(3) the convolutions of the spiritual life, recently become too grounded and bushbound, by restoring a round of descent and ascent in the vertical plane, principally at the central pillar (akon aba).

But though these vectors sum up the essential spatial qualities of worship, there is a paradoxical objective: that of moving the membership beyond life to the other side (*si ayat, mang ayat*). The final qualitative achievement of the Bwiti chapel, perhaps, is to enable the membership to escape its confinements. We may arrive tentatively at the following diagram of the axiology of Bwiti quality space (Figure 15.14).

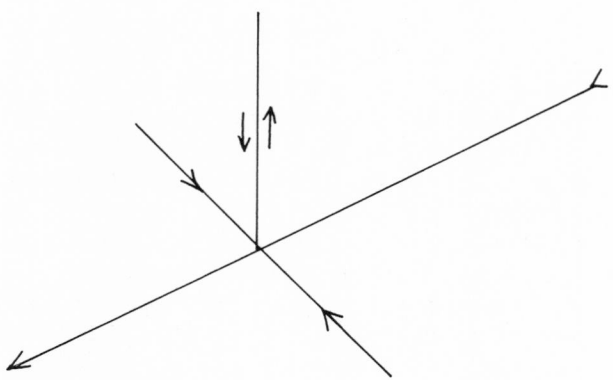

15.14 Axiology of Bwiti Quality Space

❖16❖

The Corporation of Angels

King foré ôsiman abui.
(One voice, many thoughts.)

A Failure of Oneheartedness

THE EVENTS which led to the building of a new chapel at Assok Ening, the chapel whose construction provoked the debate we have examined above, are instructive for the insight they give into the dynamics of the Bwiti worshiping group. Recruitment of members to chapel membership and the perdurability of that membership is a constant preoccupation. We have seen how transitory most chapels are. Leaders feel a constant competition with other chapels for members. They often suspect, and with reason, that another leader is seeking to attract local members. Even the ethnographer may be the object of a mild competition. His presence at a chapel can testify to the value of the Bwiti practiced there.

There are many internal threats to stability. There is the contentiousness, typically Fang though much exacerbated in acculturation, of younger members who question procedures and interpretations of the leaders. They are always a potential challenge to consensus in the chapel—to that "oneheartedness" which the religion seeks to achieve. In such an egalitarian society as Fang variable interpretations of common actions and commonly attended to signals, signs, and symbols are assertive and endemic.[1] The challenge to leadership is to prevent these from rising to "damage oneheartedness" (*endamen nlem mvore*) or "break apart the worshiping group" (*abuk ensama*).

In the fall of 1959 it became impossible to achieve oneheartedness in the old Bwiti chapel of Assok Ening. Events came to a head in a heated debate over several weeks with the old *nima na kômbô*, Zogo Ebu. Though he was gradually changing over to Asumege Ening Bwiti under the influence of his son, the Nganga Metogo Zogo, who had been to the coast at Libreville and been persuaded by the Asumege Ening founder, Ndong Obam Eya, Zogo Ebu still persisted in certain prewar practices. He had never really wanted to build a chapel separate from his house. He refused to change to a red and white uniform. He persisted in a limited song cycle. He did not wish to add the chest drum to the *ôbangô*. These were all minor matters but they were bones of contention. For more than two years the younger members of the chapel had fretted over his outmoded practices. From time to time they suggested modifications to the elderly nima na kombo. And sometimes he was open to them. But he did not keep pace with the possibilities they suggested. Chapel life went on as usual, and the ritual achievement of solidarity—the achievement of consensus at the social level of highly coordinated interaction—continued even while disgruntlement persisted at the cultural level and in connection with the meanings of the coordinated activity.

The occasion of the initiation of a member brought out the disaffection. The younger men questioned the procedures Zogo Ebu proposed to employ, the woods he would use in purification, the amount of eboga he would give and the admonitory preparation he would offer to the initiate. Offended by all this, the old man invited the dissidents to follow Bwiti elsewhere—find another "path" if they could. Thereupon three-quarters of his membership under the leadership of Muye Alogo Michel abandoned his chapel, undertaking an arduous weekly journey of 21 kilometers to another and more progressive chapel, the Kwakum chapel of Mve Asumu André. The old man was left with the immediate members of his family, though not his son the Nganga Metogo Zogo, and a few dependents. Eventually the dissidents returned to the village to build a new chapel. Gradually the old man's family joined the dissidents, for the ceremonies he continued to provide for such a small group seemed a pale reflection of the more satisfying activities at the other end of the village. Finally only the old man and his wife were left in solitary worship.

Contentiousness may be endemic in religious movements actively syncretizing diverse cultural traditions but there were also good family reasons—reasons having to do with male-female relations and with the rivalry between generations over goods—for the breakdown of consensus in the leadership of Zogo Ebu. The family matters asserted themselves in the question of the initiation into Bwiti of Oyana Ndutumu. She was a daughter of the village, just returned from a second divorce, the child of Zogo Ebu's dead brother Ndutumu Ebu. It was Zogo Ebu who administered the marriage monies and it was he who was obliged to return the monies to Oyana's former husband's family. This Zogo Ebu was prepared to do. Since he had long tried to convince his brother's daughter to eat eboga (something his brother, when living, had prohibited), he was also glad of her proposed initiation. Her presence would strengthen the chapel.

His son the Nganga Metogo Zogo, however, was of a different view. He was counting on the marriage monies, that would now have to be returned, for a marriage of his own. And in any case, he had long argued that in order to spread the religion women should join the Bwiti chapel of the village where they were married. He argued that Oyana made little effort to please her husband—this was her second divorce—and that the ndebot should insist that she return to her marriage. Zogo Ebu countered that Bwiti would teach Oyana Ndutumu to live harmoniously with her husband.

Though Metogo Zogo had shared the disgruntlement of Muye Alogo Michel and other young men it had been he more than the others who, out of filial piety, had acted to maintain consensus—a grudging acquiescence in the outmoded practice of the old man. His own disaffection over the initiation of his sister acted to release the contentiousness of the others. In the ensuing argument he took no part. And, in fact, he absented himself from the village before the final rupture. Caught between loyalties he spent a year itinerating to other chapels in other districts. When the rupture was all but healed, he returned to Assok Ening to the new chapel.

The questions which arise here concern the way in which consensus is maintained in Bwiti, the way in which loyalty to the group and a sense of corporateness is assured. These questions—they are very basic ones—are addressed from other perspectives in other chapters. Here we address them from the perspective of the structure and distribution of membership. In particular, we examine the relationship between leaders and followers, males and females, elders and youngers, givers of offerings and receivers of offerings—those who stand to profit from spiritual transactions and those who must pay for the advantages they receive. These are the major lines of cleavage in the corporate group, the major foci of contentiousness that can defeat consensus.

Speaking with One Voice: The Religious Hierarchy

At the conclusion of prayers or at crucial ritual junctures Banzie rapidly recite their benediction upon the membership. *Banzie, Nima na Kombo, Benganga Boga ye!* This benediction is a recitation of the main roles in the Bwiti hierarchy. They are all united, as the benediction concludes, in eboga. The benediction is thus, primarily, a reaffirmation of hierarchical solidarity, frequently enough, let it be said, in need of reaffirmation. The following is a list of the main leadership positions in Fang Bwiti. (It will be noted that most terms derive from the Tsogo although the leadership structure in Fang Bwiti is more intricate than the Metsogo ancestor cult structure.)

BANZIE: The ordinary initiated member or adept. In the folk etymology of Bwiti the Banzie are angels (by derivation from the French *ange*). The word, however, comes from the Tsogo *bandji*, translated as "aspirant to the ancestor cult" or, more exactly, inhabitant of the cult house (*ebandja*).

BETI NGOMBI: The player of the Bwiti harp. From the Tsogo *Beti a ngombi*.

BOMO OBAKA: Beater of the bamboo sounding staves, *ôbaka*.

KOMBO OR KAMBO OR KAMBI: Guardians of the chapel and supervisors of ritual activity. Of uncertain derivation, this term probably derives also from the Tsogo, *Kambi* (an entirely white person or albino). This is apt because the Kambi are the first to daub the white kaolin clay upon their faces. Kambo and Kombo are both words referring to persons possessed by spirits.

NGANGA: Leader of the dances or leader of the songs or both. In either case chief performing member of the congregation. The term is the same in both Fang and Tsogo and means diviner, witch doctor, penetrator of the unseen.

YEMBA: The "knowledgeable one" of the chapel. It is he who presents and explains the rituals, the songs, and the "subtle words" of the evangiles. The term is from the Fang *yem*, to know.

YOMBO: The leader of the women. From the Tsogo *yombo* (adept in the female secret society, *nyembe*).

NIMA OR NYIMA NA KOMBO: The leader of the chapel. From the Tsogo, *nyimah*, master of an art or craft, "he who excels," and kombo, "he who is possessed by spirits: thus, "master of spirit possession." This Tsogo derivation is, however, not as active in Bwiti Fang as the Fang root *kom*, to prepare, make something out of diverse ingredients. The more active meaning, thus, is "master of the preparation of the all-night ceremonies, *engosie*."

Banzie themselves make various observations on requirements of membership. When men or women have eaten eboga and have seen the ancestors and the great gods, they say, they become Banzie for they are pure as "angels." The players of the harp and the obaka are singled out first by their talents, as are the song leaders. But it is important that all of them be pure of heart and body. This is particularly true for the harp player since the harp is the voice of Nyingwan Mebege and is the instrument of communication with the Sister of Zame. Older, unmarried men are often selected for these roles. They are said to be "married" to the harp and to Nyingwan Mebege. The importance of the harp cannot be underestimated, for not only does it tie the membership to Nyingwan Mebege, it is also the chief instrument of intercommunication between the living and the dead. By its rhythms the beauty of the ritual emerges. Lackluster or clumsy ceremonies are often blamed on an apprentice ngombi player.

If the harp and sounding stave are important for setting tone and rhythm for the evening, even more important are the dance leaders, nganga. The centrality of these dance leaders may be less marked in other branches of Bwiti than in Asumege Ening where three nganga—the dance leader and two "serviteurs"—act as principal dancers and leaders of the congregation. Yet in all branches the position of the nganga is regarded seriously because, in the end, it is his responsibility to bring about fruitful activity—activity which is aesthetically pleasing and spiritually efficacious. The nganga may also be the song leader, though just as often this is a different person, the *nyiabia* (director of the songs).

It is an interesting question why the dance leader should have been given the name of the old diviner and witch doctor, he whose task was the penetration of the unseen in favor of the afflicted. The only answer forthcoming is that the Bwiti nganga, by leading the membership fruitfully down the path of birth and death, does, in effect, like the nganga of old, enable them to penetrate into the unseen, to pass over into the land of the dead and, in so doing, to assuage their afflictions.

Dancing successfully down the path of birth and death demands orderliness within the chapel. It demands the exclusion of agents of disorderliness such as witches and other errant supernaturals from the chapel. The men and women who become kambi and whose customary spots are chairs just inside the entrance of the chapel are first of all men and women who have demonstrated orderliness (*okomnge*) in their own married lives. Secondly, they are likely to be large people as Fang go and able to impose themselves by physical presence alone. The kambi of the chapel maintain an orderly context within which the nganga and the musicians can lead the membership through a harmonious ceremonial progress.

Beyond these ritual positions which participate and enact or directly supervise the ceremonial activity are the "knowledgable ones" of the chapel: the yemba, yombo, and the nima na kombo who explain and create the ceremonies. It is they who, out of their knowledge of the land beyond, create (*akom*) the ceremonies of this world. They are usually not directly participant, though the yombo, the women's leader, may dance the role of nganga. They spend their time at the rear of the chapel in aloof supervision of the activities or in communion with the ancestors. At crucial ceremonial moments, for example during rituals for the removal of sin, the nima may take part directly— it is he who takes the sins upon himself. In any event there are really two kinds of Bwiti leaders: leaders directly participant in ritual enactment, and observant leaders, preoccupied with the creation and interpretation of rituals.

The "uncreated creator" of Bwiti chapel is the nima na kombo, though he may be much aided in his understandings by the yemba and the yombo. The yemba, usually a younger man, has the task of explaining and clarifying Bwiti practice to the membership, and also the "subtle words," "évangiles," of the nima. But in his explanations and understandings he may also act indirectly to instruct the nima, particularly if the latter is, like Zogo Ebu, an old man outmoded in his practice. Frequently there is a "tension of understanding" or a "disparity of explanation" between the nima and the yemba. And many a yemba has taken over as leader of a chapel. The yombo is the "knowledgeable one" who clarifies and explains the religion to the women.

Knowledgeability alone is not a sufficient qualification for the assumption of these three leadership roles. For example, Metogo Zogo, besides being an excellent dancer with an impressive voice (and therefore an outstanding nganga) is also a very articulate man, an aggressive and flamboyant speaker. But he is too flamboyant and excitable to be wise and prudent (*akyel*). It is felt that he is more likely to bring disorder by speaking. The "knowledgeable ones" should contribute to the spiritual tranquillity of the chapel. Not only should they have the intelligence and imagination to explain and create liturgy but they should also have those qualities of temperament that are conducive to tranquillity. They should have the patience to make themselves understood (*ewôgan*) and to return the good answer (*mbamba nyalen*) to contentiousness in the membership.

One strategy of leadership widely practiced in Bwiti is to insist upon speaking with one voice (*king fôre*). In inquiry among Banzie, particularly when one is not well known, one will often be told: "Here we speak with one voice." The reference is to the voice of the yembe or the nima. This may be said even though there are many different views present as to religious activities and even though within the chapel there is lively contention. There may be only one voice in the family as Fang say, but there are many thoughts (*ôsiman abui king fore*).

But this rule of speaking with one voice cannot be enforced by itself. Observance rests upon convictions in the membership which are produced by the effectiveness of their ritual experiences: by the fruitfulness of their imaginative journey down the path of birth and death, by the exhilaration or ecstasy they experience in narcotic excursions, by the intriguing experience of hearing the "subtle words" of the évangile. If Bwiti leaders succeed in leading as fundamentally leaderless a people as Fang it is because, to an important degree, they lead with the imagination. They provide in ritual act and evangelical word images and image-related (image-evoking or image-generated) activities that are satisfying and rewarding.

A Convincing Image of Corporateness

As much as anything our object here is to explore these images and their aptness—their powers of conviction. The next chapter explores the path of birth and death itself. Here we may usefully examine an image which is particularly effective in the strategy of incorporation: the image of the *ensama* (the purposeful group). The past is made present in Bwiti in many ways but it is most frequently made present by Bwiti leaders referring to the group of worshipers as an ensama.*[1] The reference mainly in mind here is the nineteenth

---

*[1] The term ensama (nsama) is defined by Galley (*Dictionnaire Fang-Français*, p. 239) as "indian file progressions of a group." He contrasts this with the massing of a group in a phalanx (la marche de front, efakh). The term can also be used more generally to mean "group" or "troupe" or a crowd in motion (foule qui marche). The English notion of "followers" is also

century trading team which collected rubber and ivory upcountry and carried these valuables to the coast for trade. First, the ensama of old knew its way through the forest. Its members were pathfinders and pathfollowers par excellence. Second, as it was an all-male group it was, in principle, celibate as Bwitists try to be. Third, its members had an essentially positive and profitable relationship with the European coastal merchants with whom they traded—something that could not be said of relationships in the subsequent colonial era characterized by the exploitations and dominations of the energetic colonial culture. The ensama trading teams were, in short, apt embodiments of composed intention and successful self-sufficiency—qualities desirable in Bwiti "pathfinding."

That these trading teams turned a profit, in hindsight at least, on their forest ventures is itself not irrelevant to the aptness of the image. It is true that Bwiti leaders regularly inveigh against the appetite for money and goods of the modern world. They see it as a distraction from the path of birth and death. But even though they themselves may practice conspicuous poverty they are expected to make their chapel a success monetarily. They must keep up the chapel and provide for the members' needs.

The ensama image is apt, finally, because it evokes the Fang passion for journeying about. It was the providing of that psychic benefit, added to the prospect of material gain, that as much as anything confirmed the position of the leaders of both the ensama trading teams of the late nineteenth century and the leaders of the dance exchange teams of the twentieth century. In both these cases there was the plentiful satisfaction of journeying about—from deep upland forest to seacoast in the one case, from village to village, district to district in the other. That journeying about, that pathfinding, both demanded leadership and, in the associated satisfactions, confirmed it.

Thus the leader in putting forth the ensama image can also take advantage of the leadership possibilities contained in it. In point of fact, of course, Bwiti ceremonies stay put. They recenter experience. But at the same time they

---

relevant. As much of the dancing and certainly the crucial dance out into the forest at midnight is done indian file, the word addresses itself to the most relevant group configuration in Bwiti. In Asumege Ening Bwiti the term regularly evokes reference to the nineteenth-century trading teams exploiting the forest for purposes of trade. It also evokes group movement through a forest.

There was in these teams a pronounced element of fraternal solidarity if not aggrandizement. This is seen most clearly in the bizima (soldiering) bands of the early twentieth century: marauding teams of young men which both engaged in the rubber and ivory trade and preyed upon other trading teams. (*Archives of Mitzik*: Report of the District Administrator for 1910—Circonscription de l'Okano). This association of ensama with aggressive male solidarity may interfere with the use of this image in Bwiti, since the corporateness sought in the religion is that of men *and* women. On the other hand it may constitute an attraction to women since their own traditional cult, Mevungu, was compensatorily aggressive and aggrandizing.

provide imaginative traveling about—spiritual journeys of the imagination. In that context the ensama image is a central feature in the enactment of these journeys and aptly incorporates the members' diverse intentions.

THE DISTRIBUTION OF MEMBERSHIP

There are three relevant groupings in the distribution of Bwiti membership: distribution by sex, by age, and by clan membership. In respect to the first we should recall the adult male-female ratios in Fang country in the middle decades of this century.[2] Upcountry, because of loss of men to lumber camps and other seaside enterprises, the ratio is on the order of 8 men to 10 women. Around the Estuary and on the coast this figure is by reason of this migratory labor practically reversed: 10 men for every 8.5 women. These ratios are not directly reflected in Bwiti. Indeed, the male-female ratios in fifteen chapels sampled upcountry, in the Woleu-Ntem region, show a slight preponderance of men: 176 men to 170 women. Thirty-two chapels sampled in the Estuary region and around Libreville show virtually an equal number of men and women: 219 men to 215 women.[3] In the Kougouleu Chapel, in which we are mainly interested, there is a preponderance of women: 38 men to 48 women. Only in the southern Woleu-Ntem, on the Mitzik-Medouneu road, are the male-female ratios of the larger society directly reflected in Bwiti. In nine chapels we registered 99 women and 78 men. This is the region of Fang country, outside of the Estuary region itself, which is most accessible to the labor markets of the coast.

In general, Bwiti chapels show a more balanced male-female ratio than the general population in the adult age levels. In one sense this is not surprising since the religion specifically offers an equal and complementary place for women in rituals. Over the longer period this offer, together with the promise to restore fertility, could be expected to lead to a preponderance of women. Indeed, this is what seems to be occurring in the Estuary region where, despite the excess of men in the general population, there is balance in membership and in some important chapels a notable surplus of women.

Upcountry, despite the excess of women, there are more men in practically all chapels. This anomaly may result from the fact that Bwiti has been active in the region only since the Second World War and has been brought in by new male converts returning from labor contracts on the coast. These returning laborers may well account for the male presence in upcountry chapels. There are other reasons for relatively fewer women. Missionary evangelization has been unusually effective in the upcountry region sampled, the Woleu-Ntem, with a higher percentage of women committed to a missionary church than is the case on the coast. Also, for a variety of historical reasons having to do with early German colonization and expansion of cash crops as well as higher per capita income, the upcountry region considers itself more advanced than the coast (an anomaly for Africa) and thus resistant in a general way to taking up what is perceived as a coastal and southern Gabonese "fetish" religion. For such reasons the recruitment of women into Bwiti—although they are preponderant in the population—has been slower.

Bwiti makes a special effort to give equal place to women in ritual, but age pyramids from the Bwiti heartland show an age dominance of men in the upper age levels. Although in Fang culture age alone was never a criterion of leadership and failing powers worked against the capacity to lead, within the ancestor cult age was more closely correlated with leadership. This is also the case in Bwiti where age is accorded more respect than is the case outside the religion. Vigorous and sufficiently imaginative men in their forties and fifties are usually the effective leaders but affective leadership in really stable chapels usually comes from esteemed elders sixty or older. There are few women of this age in Bwiti.

Figure 16.1 is the age pyramid for Kougouleu Chapel of Asumege Ening while Figure 16.2 is the age pyramid for fifteen Estuary and coastal chapels. The figures are those for regular members and not occasional participants or onlookers. The age pyramid for the fifteen chapels sampled on the Libreville-Kango road shows less of a differential between male and female membership than at Kougouleu, but it still shows the paucity of women at the upper age levels.

This falling away of female members as age increases is the consequence of several factors. First, it is an expression of the fact that in many cases a woman's membership in Bwiti is a function of her marriage. Men more often seek to convince their wives to join the religion. Married couples constitute approximately 60 percent of the membership of the chapels sampled. As the differential in age of husband and wife is ten to twelve years on the average there would be, correspondingly, a younger distribution of women. But one must still ask why it is that widows do not seem to participate in Bwiti. This is partly due to the greater satisfaction derived from connubial participation— itself an expression of the ritual unification of male and female periodically emphasized in worship—and is partly an expression of the rigors of all-night ritual observances. It is almost exclusively old men who are granted the status of observer (nima na kombo) and who can effectively retire from the arduous ritual. Finally, widows, unless remarried by levirate or bound to their male children in the village in which they are married, will often return to their own clans and natal villages. They are thus lost to the congregation as the chances are that the village to which they return has no Bwiti chapel.

Bwiti, as these pyramids show, is not an old man's religion. On the other hand, it is not a young man's religion either. The bulk of male membership is in the thirties and forties, the age that coincides with the onset of marriage and family life. It is unfounded to suggest, as outsiders sometimes have, that Bwiti is the religion of footloose young men. It is, however, true that attendance at the engosie gives that impression, for many young men are often present as spectators or casual participants. The pyramids presented here,

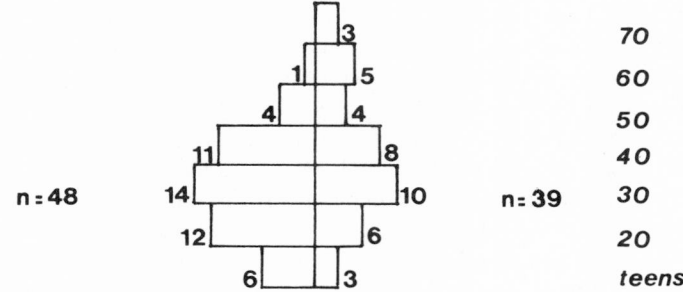

16.1 Age Pyramid: Kougouleu Chapel

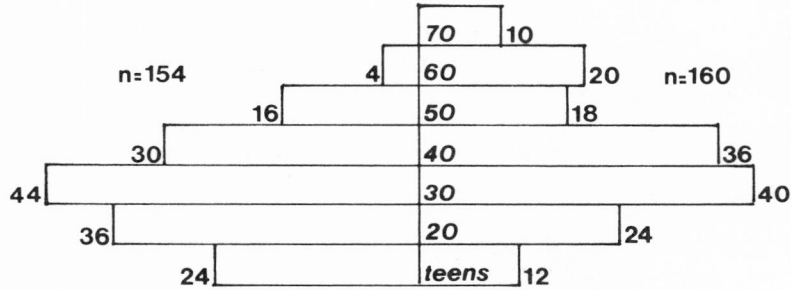

16.2 Age Pyramid: Fifteen Estuary and Coastal Chapels

however, show only those committed and communing, by means of eboga, in regular attendance upon rituals.

The preponderance of men in their vigorous thirties and forties constitutes strong pressure on older leaders that takes the utmost skill to resist. The dispute we detail in opening this chapter is not exceptional, therefore, and others like it are predictable first by demographic distribution and second by reason of Fang preference for leaders at the peak of their physical powers.

Insofar as in former times practically all Fang religious activities were exclusive to the particular clan, a consideration of the clan derivations of members can give us insight into the Bwiti achievement—particularly as Bwiti emphasizes that clan membership is of no relevance to worship. This is argued even though a recitation of clan genealogy is an important form of prayer and even though it is with his or her clan ancestors that every member hopes to make contact. There is, however, except at moments of initiation, a sufficiently generic definition of the dead (this is seen in the term Bwiti itself) as to avoid the problem of particular competing or incompatible clan ancestors. We encountered no Bwiti chapel in which only one clan was represented among males (as a consequence of exogamy women would inevitably be drawn from various clans in any chapel). The following is the clan distribution of the 39 male members of the Kougouleu Chapel.

CLAN	NUMBER OF MEMBERS
Ntoun	9
Oyek	7
Essametak	6
Ngaeng	4
Essoseng	2
Essoké	2
Essakora	2
Yengwi	2
Ngwanmve	1
Bekoue	1
Esseng	1
Essabam	1
Bakoule	1

In this chapel, as in most, the two principal leadership positions are in the hands of that clan, Ntoun, with a preponderance in the membership. Both the nima and the yembe are clan Ntoun. Indeed it is difficult and unusual for leadership in a Bwiti chapel to be maintained by men who are not members of the preponderant clan. In that respect, Bwiti, although it tries to attract multiclan membership, retains a certain clan orientation. Also, the dominant presence of one clan tends to attract women of the same clan, either those from the local village not yet married or those returned from marriage by divorce or widowhood. The distribution of women at Kougouleu shows this in respect to Ntoun women.

CLAN	NUMBER OF MEMBERS
Ngaeng	8
Ntoun	7
Oyek	7
Efak	6
Yengwi	5
Bekoue	4
Essakora	4
Essisis	2
Essimvous	2
Essoseng	1
Yebimve	1
Abeng	1

It is not surprising that one clan should be preponderant in any chapel. Fang for the most part still live in clan villages. Any village that would permit the construction of a Bwiti chapel shows by that fact a significant number of villagers, by necessity of the same clan, committed to and supportive of the religion. Only in those villages close to Libreville where multiclan villages are frequent or in those areas of Gabon, in the Woleu-Ntem mostly, where clans have been regrouped into villages, would large representation of one clan not be inevitable. Two facts are significant. First, it is impressive that Bwiti chapels existing in clan villages manage to cultivate multiclan membership successfully. Secondly, and conversely, it is a testimony to Fang egalitarianism that in no village known to us were all villagers members of the religion. In fact, Bwiti membership rarely exceeds 50 percent of the inhabitants of any village. In both ways Bwiti escapes exclusivity in respect to clan.

Quite frequently, and particularly in the coastal chapels of the Gabon Estuary and heartland, Bwiti members are drawn in from other tribes. But in no chapel surveyed for this study was that membership ever more than a handful. It was never more than 10 percent in any chapel, even in the case of such branches as Yembawe which, recognizing the debt of Fang Bwiti to the Metsogo, makes an active effort to attract Metsogo into membership. There are a variety of reasons for this limited pan-ethnic recruitment despite frequent claims of universalism.[4] Primarily it is a consequence of emphasis upon lineality of worship, that is to say, upon the use of the genealogical principle in making contact with divinity. It is also a consequence of the insistence upon participation in an intricate liturgy accompanied by recondite communications (the "subtle words" of the sermons). These two emphases, combined with drug-induced ecstatic initiation and the tendency of Bwiti to isolate itself in its milieu, create an atmosphere not altogether conducive to participation by other ethnic groups.

THE WOMEN'S PART OF THE WHOLE

In an effort to obtain comparability with an inquiry on divorce made among 85 men in Assok Ening (above, pp. 156-157), a similar inquiry was made among 86 Banzie men in the Bwiti chapels at Kougouleu and Dzoberimintangan (Estuary region) and Ayol (Southern Woleu-Ntem region). Whereas the Fang divorce rate—186 out of 324 marriages—was 57 percent, the divorce rate of the Banzie men was 39 percent—97 of 249 marriages terminated after cohabitation and completion of the first and most substantial stage of the bride-payment. This significantly lower figure is compatible with the Bwiti claim, ritually enforced, that in contrast to the malaise between the sexes in Fang society which has led to high divorce rates, Bwiti men and women are in harmonious relation. This claim is even more dramatically established when we consider the divorce rates of men since they have become fully participating members of Bwiti where their spouses are also members of the religion. Of 87 marriages in this category 16 had ended in divorce—an 18 percent divorce rate.

To assure this harmony, Bwiti urges that its members' wives "eat eboga." This pressure on converted men to convert their wives is itself a cause of divorce because of recalcitrant women. It is interesting that men state a preference for "leading" their wives into eboga rather than marrying women who are already in eboga. The path metaphor is central in the explanation of this preference—not only the path of birth and death of Bwiti itself but the notion that it is the husband's role to be the "pathfinder" for his wife. Banzie men express a desire to show their wives the "true path" and express a mistrust of marrying women who have already eaten eboga. "They will have their own path and will not be good wives." These observations in Bwiti accord with the mistrust among Fang of too much directionality among women—of letting women have too much of a path of their own.[5] (It will be recalled that one metaphor of deprecation among Fang for free-living women is that of the path—"a path upon which many men have trod.")

Although the more traditional paternalistic attitudes toward women are thus still present in Bwiti—despite the dual leadership structure, the overall leadership is male[6]—and although it is preferred that men lead women to eat eboga and to the path of birth and death, at the same time initiation into Bwiti does confirm women in their own genealogical path as the ancestor cult rarely did. At the least it gives them a complementary place in the religion, a complementarity which is recurrently affirmed in ritual. And occasionally ritual dances other than the "oneheartedness" dance go beyond complementarity to suggest interpenetration of the two parts into the whole. (See Figure 13.1a.)

There are a multitude of examples of this ritual affirmation of complementarity, some of which we have already discussed. But there are two examples which are particularly telling. In many Asumege Ening chapels, as part of the euphoria at the completion of the night-long rituals, a morning tug of war (évi nkol) is held between men and women. This is followed by a jocular bout of aggressive backslapping between the sexes. The tug of war in which men pull against women—and which the women often win—is used by the "knowledgeable ones" as an object lesson. "This game," they say, "is only possible because men and women pull against each other." "Were one or another to stop the other would fall down." Men and women in life may appear to pull against each other but actually, they imply, it is that opposition which makes life possible. "It is only by pulling apart that they can really stay together." This lesson is similar to the point so often reiterated: just as a child cannot be brought into being without the complementary effort of male and female so the "life of the engosie and the world of the dead cannot be created without men and women."

A similar complementarity is obtained in those ritual entrances into the chapel (minkin) made by women alone. These entrances are often called *minkin mevungu* (the reference is to the women's secret purification society, Mevungu). In these entrances the women dance into the chapel in a close-knit dance group. The first three rows, of three dancers in each row, are the senior women dressed entirely in white, followed by the younger women dressed in the regular red and white garb. The older women in white are bent over and around the yombo, center front, who carries in her left hand the red pebble of creation sent down by Nyingwan Mebege on a moonbeam and discovered in a pool of pure water in the deep forest.

Various interpretations are given for this formation. Most interesting is the physiological one: that the pebble represents the homunculus in the womb. The women all dressed in white represent the seminal fluid which surrounds it and nurtures it. This pebble—the homunculus—is being brought into the spiritual womb, the chapel itself, for fruition. That the women should dress in white to represent the male seminal fluid is on the figurative level a statement of interpenetration while in terms of dance structure it is in complementary relation to the male entrance dance.

The Bwiti interpretation is that this women's entrance dance represents the "miracle of menstruation." That is, the women in white represent the moon-beams upon which, monthly, Nyingwan Mebege sends the possibilities of creation. As senior women they are all individuals who have presumably given birth abundantly. The younger women behind them are thus being introduced to the monthly miracle, to the "good luck of the womb" (*ma'abum*). But the point is also made, and this is the complementarity, that the women are bringing back to the men what the men gave to them—namely, insemination. Like the mevungu dances of old this is a vigorous entrance. Often the group of women will "catch" an nganga, a male dance leader, and hold him prisoner in the dancing group. As men "attacked" women in the sexual act so they now attack men. The consequence is good luck and fertility for all.

Women may not have the fullness of place in Bwiti that they once held in their own secret society, mevungu. But they enjoy a more integrated and complementary place, vis-à-vis men, than mevungu provided, despite its aggressive engagement with the male community. What these Bwiti rituals do is provide women with a sense of productive place—a sense of incorporation, in the most physiological sense of the word—into the worshiping body of Bwiti. This sense of place in the whole religious experience may be one of the most important explanations for reduced divorce rates among members.

THE MEN'S PART OF THE WHOLE

We offer elsewhere a tabulation of some of the personal reasons for eating eboga, but here we may reexamine the seventy-eight brief histories collected in an effort to discover other satisfactions experienced by these men in their incorporation into the worshiping body of Bwiti. At least six responses were obtained in each five-year age spread, from 20 years to 60, and two responses from Banzie over 70.[7] The responses come disproportionately from the 30-35 age group and the 46-50 age group although this reflects the facts of age distribution accurately enough. Of greatest interest is the number of unmarried men that appeared in the sample, 22 out of 78, which is testimony to the rewards that Bwiti offers to this age group. These satisfactions range, no doubt, from the promise of weekly night-long diversion for lonely men to the possibility of obtaining women from chapel leaders. In some chapels, notably the Kougouleu Chapel, leaders bind the loyalty of younger men to them in the form of clientage known as "marriage of eboga" (*aluk eboga*) with unmarried female members—which many chapel leaders make an effort to attract.

Another important feature of this sample is the high proportion of married men, 30 out of 56, who had no children.[8] This reflects the promise which Bwiti makes to bring children to the infertile, a promise made in the context of very low birth rates. But something more is reflected, and that is the attraction of the surrogate kin-group provided by the religion for those who are unmarried or whose marriages have been barren. In joining a flourishing chapel new members obtain, in the process of initiation, "mothers and fathers of eboga." The leader of the chapel is regularly referred to as the father of the congregation and fellow members as brothers and sisters. But beyond these surrogate relatives of this world is the rediscovery of real relatives in the next world. For eboga can put one back in touch with dead parents or children. In this inquiry with 78 Banzie men they were asked with whom eboga had brought them in contact at the time of initiation. Out of a total of 86 contacts reported—a number reported several contacts—22 were with a dead father, 14 with a dead mother, and 10 with a dead grandparent. Four contacts were made with dead siblings, two with a mother's brother, and two with a deceased child. Thirty-six responses specified no contact with a relative but rather with great gods, an undifferentiated crowd of spirits, or with a supernatural animal—usually the African gray parrot (*kos*). For those who have not prospered in family formation Bwiti offers, then, both a ritual and a spiritual kinship.

Of related interest to the question of surrogate kinship is the family position of the men who convert to Bwiti, for there seems to be a marked presence of either oldest or youngest sons. Twenty-two of the respondents were the youngest sons of either father or mother (6 of the mother, 16 of the father) while 14 were the oldest sons (4 of the mother and 10 of the father). There is nothing statistically significant here, particularly in a situation of high infant mortality rates and reduced family size. Still, informants remarked so frequently on their "oldest" or "youngest" status, one suspects such males are particularly attracted into Bwiti for the possibilities of leadership which can be exercised within—the oldest are normally expected to be family leaders among Fang by virtue of first access to the use of bridemonies—or for the possibility for the youngest of escaping their older brothers' domination in alternative structures. The presence of men so motivated is another challenge to enduring leadership, for they must be incorporated in such a way as to gratify their desires for position.

As in Assok Ening, Bwiti members often come from peripheral ndebot or from impoverished mvogabot who do not "hold the village." One supposes, therefore, that Bwiti membership derives from the peripheries of village kin groupings and that it is an "alternative family structure" and a gratification of the desire for position. In economic and social terms it is the search for a larger part of the whole. But this hypothesis has been harder to maintain in the materials gathered in this study. The facts seem to be that in the relatively prosperous parts of northern Gabon, large villages with numerous mvogabot, as in Assok Ening, show Bwiti membership taken from more peripheral and impoverished families. Bwiti is an "alternate (larger part) structure" there. In central Gabon, in the areas where Bwiti originated and where villages are smaller, often coterminous with the mvogabot, and where there is general impoverishment, one cannot easily make the distinction between central and peripheral family membership in village life. The decision to dance Bwiti is often made by the central and dominant family line, producing more of a Bwiti-village effect. Bwiti is used by such families as a means of restoring the vitality of genealogical descent. At the same time, at another level of comparison, such villages often feel relatively more impoverished than their neighbors. But amidst the general impoverishment of the period and region studied there is no convincing measure of this.

"Paying eboga": The Economics of Incorporation

A striking feature of the inquiry here discussed was the number of men who engaged in no employment other than that of doing the work of the ancestors or the "work of Bwiti" (eseng eboga). Forty-four percent so responded (30 percent described themselves as cash crop farmers and 25 percent as petty merchants, truck drivers, mechanics' aids, and road repair personnel).[9] The question arises: in other than ritual terms what is the "work of eboga" and what is its remuneration?

To begin with it must not be supposed that Bwiti, for all the loftiness of its spiritual purposes—to pass beyond the concerns of the material world and obtain for its members the widest possible communion with the dead and the great gods—yet foregoes the more traditional view of reciprocal obligations in the obtaining of spiritual goods. Knowledge of the unseen was privileged knowledge. Just as diviners obtained recompense for contacting the unseen in favor of clients, or the leaders of the ancestor cult were compensated for initiating new members and bringing them into contact with the dead, so Banzie are obliged to "pay eboga" for spiritual knowledge and spiritual benefits. The phrase applied primarily to initiation and the compensation due for the large amounts of eboga ingested and the spiritual contacts made at that time. But Banzie continue to "pay eboga" throughout their lives. All personal prayers outside the chapel are accompanied by offerings. Offerings are made at all general ceremonies. As members move up the leadership hierarchy and obtain new knowledge and capacities payment is expected to the holder of this knowledge. Much of this payment ends up in the hands of chapel leaders who are, as an earnest of their moral rights to leadership, obliged to redistribute this income in a convincing way. Let us review these economics in a more detailed fashion.

Many chapels maintain "prayer books" which are an account of the specifics of personal prayer—those prayers which are always carefully overseen so that they do not work to the detriment of other members—together with the offerings made. The following are selections from the "prayer books" of the Disumba Bwiti chapel, Tamamanga, at Efulan (Medouneu District).

11 April 1959: The general prayer of this Holy Saturday is accompanied by the following prayers. Monga Nze Ezima prayed in remembrance of the death of her father-in-law Okolongo Edou Eyene: 1 egg, 1 liter of kerosene, 1 demijohn of wine, 190 francs, 1 packet of cigarettes. Ngonde Ndoutoume Nzogo prayed to cure the sickness of his wife, Ada Ndong Edu: 1 chicken, 2 packages of cigarettes, 150 francs. Evissa Etsama Ngema gives 50 francs because eboga came in a dream and told her to do so. Mwanga Avene Egoga came forward seeking grace (abora) from Bwiti: 5 francs. Disumba Mezui Ngema came forward to say farewell and ask for good luck, as he leaves for Spanish Guinea looking for work: 10 francs. Modibo Nze Mebiame comes forward praying that Bwiti will release his brother, a prisoner in Spanish Guinea: 20 francs.

23 May 1959: This prayer of Holy Saturday is accompanied by the following prayers: Micodia asks of eboga that it go and return his absconded wife, Obama Ona, and change her heart: 2 eggs. Ngonde Ntutuma Nzogo asks of eboga that it convince his wife to eat eboga: 2 eggs and 25 francs. Ndzonge Edo Eba says farewell for he leaves for Guinea: 1 egg and 5 francs. Micodia Menge demands again grace for she is still sick: 10 francs.

The average offering which accompanied these prayers was between 10 and 20 francs (with a maximum of several hundred francs) in money together with something in kind, usually candles, a liter of kerosene (for the lamps of the chapel), a chicken, and almost invariably an egg.

The purposes of the prayers are diverse, with the greatest number seeking the alleviation of ill health or bad fortune or the favor of deceased parents, husbands, brothers, or sisters. But prayers are forthcoming to provide safe journey, induce a recalcitrant spouse to enter into Bwiti, or bring children into a marriage. These personal prayers bring in several hundred francs a week together with goods useful in the conduct of the ceremonies and the communal meals.

Midway between these personal prayers held outside the chapel and the communal prayers held within it are prayers and offerings made by families— usually for the family dead. These events generally bring offerings many times greater than personal offerings. But these family prayers are only occasional events and the main source of chapel income is the periodic festival in which offerings by all members are obligatory. (Offerings are made independent of personal prayers at each Saturday night service but this is not required.) The following table lists the offerings made at seven festivals at the Tamamanga Chapel in 1958.

FESTIVAL	EGGS	CHICKEN	WINE	KERO-SENE	CANNED GOODS	MONEY	SHEEP
Awu (Easter)	98	10	5	3	9	4,090	1
Kumba (Ascension)	28	5	4	5	2	2,315	
Madebo Etsengue (Pentecost)	30	2	2	3	5	235	
Tara Zame (Fête Dieu)	7	1	1	1		490	
Nana Nyepe (Assumption)	28	2	5	4	8	1,590	
Olorogebot (St. Michael)	15	1	3		1	1,350	
Bewu (All Saints)	15	1	6	6	12	7,360	
Abiale (Christmas)	24	2	12	3	5	8,265	
Totals	235	25	40	25	41	27,685	

It will be noted that substantially more is given in the three-day Easter ceremonial cycle (Awu Mwan Mot), the All Saints celebration (Bewu), and the Christmas Cycle (Abiale Mwan Mot) than in the others. These are the three big giving periods of the year. It is also the time of the giving of animals. If we calculate both the values of goods together with the actual monetary offerings the total festival giving for the year for a medium-sized chapel amounts to 48,000 francs or $192. This calculation is independent of services offered; all Banzie are obliged to maintain the chapel and outlying ritual arenas in good repair.

The accumulation of offerings at the regular Saturday engosie, independent of the festivals, is not inconsiderable if we combine personal prayer offerings with general offerings. Each Saturday night offering for the 1958-1959 period averages 300 francs, 5 eggs, half a chicken, a third of a liter of petrol, and 1 liter of wine. As there are 8 festival occasions this leaves 44 Saturdays of ordinary services. The yearly average then is:

Monetary	12,600 francs
Eggs (210)	2,100 francs
Chickens (20)	4,000 francs
Liters kerosene (12)	480 francs
Liters wine (40)	4,000 francs
	23,180 francs

The total amount of offering to the chapel then comes to some 70,000 francs or $280. This would be slightly more than the yearly income of a store clerk or a tailor of the period whose incomes averaged 50 to 60 thousand francs yearly. It is a sum substantially less than the amount regularly exchanged in the bridepayment—100 to 120 thousand francs.

It was often argued in Gabon, by missionaries and administrators, that Bwiti functioned primarily to enrich leaders and organizers. These figures give little support to that view. But there are other sources of income available to chapel leaders; in particular the requirement that one pays to obtain a position in the religion. Because it is a matter of ascending the spiritual ladder this is as often called "paying otunga" (atang ôtunga) as "paying eboga." There is certain secret information imparted in the securing of these positions and this is the object of payment. For example, in attaining the yombo position among women there is the secret of the fishing basket (nkun) to be learned, which is to say, the secret of the obtaining of the pebble which is the female principle of creation—the pebble sent by the Sister of God. Yombos pay 15,000 francs over several years to the nima na kombo for the right to dress as yombo and to carry the fishing basket, the sign of their control over fertility. Every initiate must pay eboga between 500 and 1,000 francs at the time of initiation. To become a yembe between 4,000 and 6,000 francs are "paid to the otunga." There are other secrets of the chapel for which compensation must be offered.

It is difficult to estimate what the income to chapel leaders would be from these payments. This is kept secret. Taking the average size of membership in a flourishing chapel to be between 50 and 70 there would normally be about 5 initiations a year, representing an income of 5,000 francs. Advancement in rank might bring in another 20,000 francs and payments for secrets and for consultations with the leader over personal problems—marriage and divorce, difficulties at work—might account for another 10,000 francs. It seems clear that even by the most generous estimate the chapel leader is not likely to receive more from these sources than he, or rather he in the name of the chapel, receives by direct offerings. It is unlikely that a successful nima receives more than twice as much than he could make in menial or mercantile employment outside the religion. It is for that reason, as well as for symbolic reasons, that most leaders continue as hunters or as planters of cash crops.

THE INCORPORATION OF ECONOMIC IMPULSES

Again and again, despite the modesty of chapel economics, the possibilities of profit must suggest themselves to chapel leaders. But there are counter-vailing pressures as well. Since payment must be made for secret knowledge there is a pressure upon leaders to engage in and promote the recondite and arcane. Income can be derived by first suggesting and then untangling dif-ficulties of interpretation. Indeed subtlety—reconditeness—is a recurrent mode of thought in Bwiti, as we see. Though we may concentrate on other explanations for this inclination toward subtlety, reasons that have to do with the protection of leadership status or maintenance of consensus by sugges-tiveness, the economic motive must be included among them. But there is a countervailing pressure: suspicion of that which is too complicated or tricky (*njuk* or *meduk*). The subtle and the recondite may be admitted insofar as they seem to be emanating from the unseen or as they give evidence of a leader's surpassing understanding. But any suspicion that complexity is being created for its own sake is inimical to leadership. Leaders vary to the degree that they can introduce subtlety without being accused of complexity.

More clearly economic is the impulse to advance members in rank because of the payments involved in making this advancement. But this may lead to overcrowding of the higher echelons which often leads to disagreement, fis-sion, and loss of membership. Hence most leaders are hesitant to advance members in rank, surely in respect to the highest ranks such as yembe. Most advancements take place at lower levels. There tends to be a proliferation of yombo and nganga positions.

There is also the pressure to engage in casuistic counsel with individual members or to engage in therapy: the laying on of hands, the prescription of medicines. For these can be profitable activities. On the other hand, such ministrations to individuals is felt to take leaders too easily away from their main task, their main responsibility to the group. This is the task of supervising and enabling the entire membership to make a satisfactory ritual progress along "The Path of Birth and Death." While there is an impulse to par-ticularize the ministerial relation it is also understood to work against incor-poration—against "oneheartedness." This is why the leaders of Bwiti tend to leave healing to the sister cult of MBiri. And that is why that casuistic counsel offered to members as regards their difficulties which takes place in

the euphoric morning hours after the engosie usually tends to group counseling—homilies addressed, usually with some subtlety, to the entire membership. Healing, it is felt, can be found in a fulfilled ritual experience as
much as in individualized ministrations such as the laying on of hands. It is
that healing sense of incorporation that the best leadership provides. The
economic impulse of leaders to individualize their relation to members is
constrained by their received obligation to the whole experience of the entire
membership.

Bwiti leaders do not display wealth. They follow the norm of inconspicu-
ousness that is practiced generally in Fang society by the well-to-do (*nkukuma*). But Bwiti leaders are even more assiduously inconspicuous when
away from ritual activities. For if it is understood that their leadership of the
chapel provides them with income it is also understood that any income
beyond their personal needs should be redistributed to the membership—to
the needy who weekly come forward to make prayers to that effect. Otherwise
any extra funds should be used to support or facilitate ceremonial activity.
The leader who does not redistribute convincingly in communal meals, in
provision of uniforms to the needy, in keeping up the chapel forfeits his claim
to have trod the path of birth and death. He trods only the path of life. He
himself is manifestly not incorporated into the reality of Bwiti and he loses
his power to incorporate others.

Conclusion: Assuagement by Incorporation

Disputes over the meaning and use of ritual forms are implicit in the nature
of a religious movement like Bwiti which is seeking to syncretize diverse
knowledge born of the expanding awareness of members and which is trying
to create a new and more comprehensive world view. Progressive and conservative tendencies will be the more marked—cultural lag and culture innovation the more apparent. In any social situation participants may interact
even though it can be shown that there is a diversity of views on the meaning
of their interactions. This is usually possible because the culture content of
most social situations is implicit and long-lasting and taken for granted. It is
not consciously focused upon nor is it confronted with the realities of other
cultures. The collective representations of group life can signal coordinated
interaction even though there is a diversity of ways those collective representations are understood and will be interpreted under inquiry.

A movement such as Bwiti cannot so take its culture for granted. For one
thing it confronts the new knowledge of several cultures which it must decide
either to incorporate or exclude. Furthermore, in the rivalry between branches
and chapels, leaders will often turn to the intrigue of novelty and innovation
to hold or attract members. In either case both leaders and followers become
much more conscious about the maintenance and the creation of culture than

is the case in more traditional groups that have not expanded their awareness through culture contact. No leader can escape the awareness of his membership that choices are being made and must be justified, and that the religion is moving or not moving in certain directions vis-à-vis a more complex world.

Traditionally for Fang, the most compelling act of incorporation of the individual into the kin-group was the recitation of the lengthy genealogies they remembered. For in that recitation the individual saw himself subsumed in the entire genealogical line. In Bwiti, in personal prayers, that act of incorporation has been preserved. In making these prayers, men and women recite, holding in their left hands the braided red and white "umbilical cord" which links them to their antecedents, the names of their ancestors ending with the great gods, Zame and his sister, who founded all the lineages. In this manner the ancestors and the great gods are alerted to their descendants' needs. The recitation is singularly effective—an "assuagement by incorporation" into the family of Bwiti.

In the end it is just this "assuagement by incorporation" that Bwiti leaders must repeatedly provide if they are to maintain themselves amidst a traditionally contentious and argumentative culture with little inclination to give leadership enduring authority. To this is now added an expanded awareness of other ways of doing things. Bwiti culture does not escape that contentious Fang culture nor that expanded awareness and it is not irrelevant that the chapel is called the aba eboga—recalling in the term aba that central arena of disputatious activity, the Fang council house. Insofar as the Bwiti chapel has taken over the name of that site of dispute and litigation it is not surprising that it is liable to the same contentiousness, despite the imaginative ways that members are incorporated into its birth-and-death-embracing activities.

In an effort to catalyze in a productive and assuaging way the problems of the membership, the chapel is actually turned into a council house for the hearing of complaints and conflicts in the morning hours after the all-night engosie. This is the best possible time to diffuse these antagonisms, for after such long ritual work the membership is in a condition of weary euphoria, satisfied with itself and looking forward to the communal meal. Even the most argumentative spirit will be considerably subdued, assuaged by a night's "incorporation."

That assuagement is not only a product of the euphoria of the situation, it is also a product of the rhetorical skills of the leaders—their capacity to convince by apt images, by "subtle words." This "subtle words," coming from the grave as they are often thought to do, or at least coming from one who has "died many times," give the membership the sense of sharing in secrets that pertain to some larger reality without fully understanding these secrets. The "subtlety" and ambiguity of the midnight sermons (it is also true of the post-ceremony counseling of members) help to protect leaders against contentiousness. For such words either discourage the ordinary member's pretentions to understanding and thus reduce the likelihood of dispute, or they preoccupy the contentious with the plentifully ambiguous possibilities of interpretation.

Contentiousness can be met also by a policy of innovation. The introduction of new meanings and practices—characteristic of any religious movement—is not only a testimony to the leader's imaginative powers, it also serves the useful purpose of keeping the argumentative members off-balance. In sum, though the leadership speaks with one voice the voice provokes many thoughts in the diversity of the membership. One voice can thus in its multivocality speak to many. On the other hand, by the requirement of speaking with one voice—and speaking subtly and with novelty—leaders can manage to subsume such diversities in an apparent unity.

Though one may talk about a Bwiti religious hierarchy, therefore, there is no sacerdotal caste. Leaders are constantly having to confirm themselves by the assuagement of contentiousness. It is hard work to maintain (literally to tie together) the worshiping group (*along ensama*). It demands a kind of concentrated attention that is not easily joined with the requirements of performance. That is why the old distinction, elemental to be sure, between men of thought—in Bwiti the "knowledgeable ones"—and men of action—in Bwiti the Banzie dancing down the path of birth and death—is relevant. At the apex of Bwiti chapels stand those men of thought who must work hard at incorporating the obvious cleavages and the endemic contentiousness by innovation in ritual practices, by subtlety and reconditeness in communications, and by demonstrating, in the end, a greater sense of the coherence, the overarching structure of liturgical activity. They are people able to articulate the cosmos that is suggested by that activity. That power of articulation tranquilly put forth constitutes religious wisdom from the Bwiti point of view. It is in the end the best way to confront contentiousness. But the best way to prevent dissension from arising at all is to place the members fruitfully and surely on the path of birth and death. As the members' inadequacies, their afflictions of partness, are redeemed in that larger momentous whole, so is the leader's right to lead redeemed. We turn now to the path itself.

·17·

The Path of Birth and Death: The Benevolence in the Liturgical Cycle

Eboga zom za kwing minsung.
([My body like] a leaf package of eboga [pounded food]
has come out into the courtyard of understanding.)

THE AMAZEMENTS OF THE METSOGO

THOUGH BANZIE as a rule are ever ready to discuss any aspect of their liturgy and legend there are times, perhaps when a complexity is pointed out to them or a contradictory interpretation arises, when they will speak of an "amazement of our work" (*akyunge eseng*). The word, akyunge, is often translated as "miracle" in the literature. But primarily it means anything done with such surpassing skill and subtlety as to amaze and be beyond ordinary understanding and imitation.[1] Supernaturals amaze by intervening in the natural order of things and contravening the normal. Bwiti amazes its members by intervening in their lives in such a way as to enable them to surpass themselves and come to an understanding of the extraordinary, the unseen, the "death side" of things, and thus be in communication with it. If the members will work hard in the ritual life of Bwiti, they will surpass themselves and be amazed.

It is just here that the Metsogo have gained such a reputation among Fang. For their Bwiti ancestor cult is renowned for surpassing skillfulness, amazing performance. Such amazements caused Fang to take over many things from the Metsogo cult into Fang Bwiti: the name of the members, Banzie (from the Tsogo *banji*, "those of the cult house," *ebandja*) the name of one of the principal dances of Bwiti, the *ôbangô*, the use of the sounding board, *ôbaka*, the use of *eboga*, the forms of initiation, the distinction between the cult of communication with the dead, Bwiti, and the cult of the healing of illnesses caused by the dead, Mweri. All these elements in Bwiti are Metsogo in origin. When we add to this the ritual language, Popi, a pidginized form of Tsogo, we see that the syncretic elements in Fang Bwiti are as strongly Metsogo as Christian. It is no wonder, then, that Banzie everywhere advised us to visit the Metsogo if we wished to understand "miracles." Eventually we were able to spend three days, and a full night of Bwiti in a Macika Metsogo village of the Ngounie region. We could only gather impressions.[2] But it was enough to see what impressed Fang. It impressed us.

As dramatic and constructed as the séance was, the Metsogo leaders and performers were, unlike Fang, resistant to providing extended commentary on their performance. The "miracles" spoke for themselves. As in Fang Bwiti the séance begins in the mid-afternoon with the blowing of the antelope horn to call the men into the Bwiti hut, ebandja, found at the far end of the village. Within it the members cooked and ate a meal of cucumber seeds and game. Women were not present. Eboga was also eaten.

After the meal the curse of the ancestors was lifted in front of the ebandja. As an iron bell was struck, one of the leaders spoke to the spirits and asked their blessing on the evening activities. A circle was then formed around one of the members afflicted by a spirit. Each man in this circle was slapped repeatedly with the tail of a wildcat skin dipped in a pot of water and medicinal leaves. Periodically the skin was sailed out onto the dirt of the courtyard and then returned and washed in the pot. Finally, the afflicted man's shoulders and head were stroked with the skin which was thrown out into the courtyard a final time and left there. Now the men in groups of three reached into the pot and retrieved the leaves with which they swatted and scrubbed the afflicted. Finally all three ritual objects, bell, wildcat skin, and bundle of leaves were pressed in the air together above the afflicted. A purifying chant was intoned and the objects allowed to fall to the ground.

This lifting of a spirit curse was an impressively elaborate ritual compared with similar rites in Fang tradition; indeed the actions were reminiscent of the "oneheartedness rite" in Fang Bwiti. The Metsogo were careful to describe this as a Mweri healing ceremony, to be distinguished from the Bwiti which would come in the evening. The latter started about nine o'clock, after dark, with a long and slow shuffling entrance dance (eya) from far out in the road. There were repeated entrances each of two songs' duration. The songs were intended to attract the spirits in from the edge of the forest. As the dance group arrived at the entrance of the ebandja they staggered back and forth before finally surging into the hut. The succeeding dances were of superb quality and highly coordinated. This was particularly true of the obango dance in which the three dancers—also as in Fang Bwiti called nganga—exited through the secret chamber in the rear of the ebandja to appear suddenly in mid-village dancing vertiginously with torches. These dancers appeared in various raffia costumes simulating animals which had been charmed out of the forest. There were also individual dances of such intensity that the dancer finally fell exhausted to the floor. Immediately the membership sprang up from the benches along the wall to cluster around him, concentrating their forces upon him to bring him "back to life."

The highlight of the evening consisted of the "amazements" themselves: torches that glided eerily across the courtyard, the apparent growth over several hours of a small tree from a banana shoot, the sudden production of a cock from an egg, and the falling of a dancer into the fire without being burned. Some of these miracles were simply sleight of hand but others were the result of surpassing skill and planning. Wires had to be carefully guyed to "float" the torches across the courtyard. Or take a strange sound heard in a nearby tree top. Is it a spirit? A dancer volunteers to climb the tree and find out. And he does so with a torch tied to his arm. But just as he reaches the top he is cast down, the torch and what appears as his body falling with a terrible scream through the trees. In the next instant the same man jumps out from the secret chamber.

For us the most intriguing moment was the "appearance" of the local French District Administrator. A table is set up far out in the courtyard with a pile of books and papers. Suddenly out of the darkness of the road a "white man" appears in full administrative dress. Waited upon obsequiously by a staff of Africans he approaches the table, sits down, and shuffles the papers in authoritative and bureaucratic fashion and, as quickly, rises and disappears. Truly a "miraculous" series of apparitions—even the District Administrator can be produced—and calculated to impress anyone in search of arresting ritual.

The surpassing skill and careful attention which Metsogo devote to their Bwiti ceremonies is a value very much adhered to in Fang Bwiti. Because of their demonstrated competence authority is granted to Bwiti leaders to ensure precision in ritual performance. For example, the chapel leaders paint the feet of the members with red padouk paste at the *njimba* before final entrance. This is done so that they will dance flawlessly down the path of birth and death. And chapel leaders watch the ingestion of eboga lest inebriation confound the ritual progress and vitiate the "amazements." The Banzie of Fang Bwiti do not trace this concern with precision to a Metsogo precedent, however, but rather to the dances of the land of the dead of which their visions have made them aware and which they seek to imitate.[3] By such skillful performances they can obtain the blessing, surely the benevolence, of the above. They can make the amazing passage of the path of birth and death in a single night.

GENERALITIES OF THE ENGOSIE

There are some generalities useful to an understanding of the Bwiti all-night ceremony (*engosie*). The timing of the ritual, for example, is of pronounced importance in Bwiti, for it is said that rites in the land of the dead are all exactly timed. Frequently, in the back of the chapel where the leaders sit and observe the dances, an alarm clock guarantees precision of performance. The entrance phase should be over by 9 p.m., the path of birth should be concluded by midnight and the path of death before sunrise at 6 a.m. These three time points are observed at a minimum, and many chapels are more exacting than this. Time is of such importance in some chapels that dance leaders (nganga) and "knowledgeable ones" (yemba and nima na kombo) will journey from chapel to chapel carrying alarm clocks. These are set to ring every three hours and remind them of prayer periods.

Banzie say that the clock and the harp walk together for the clock gives time to the harp.[4] As the harp is the voice of the Sister of God, the clock is the heart of Zame himself. In part this emphasis upon timing is an acculturative response to the emphasis on timing in colonial administration as well as to the frequent deprecation in the colonial world of the African time sense.[5] It also responds to the value placed on surpassing performance. The following are the time phases of the engosie.

6:00 to 7:00 p.m.	Soft playing of the harp to clean out the chapel
7:00 to 7:30 p.m.	First njimba
7:30 p.m.	First entrance (minkin)
8:00 to 8:30 p.m.	Second njimba
8:30 to 9:00 p.m.	Second entrance (minkin)
9:00 to 12:00 p.m.	Path of the harp: Path of birth and beginning
Midnight	Prayer cycle, Yombo Songs
12:15 to 12:45 a.m.	Nlem mvore—Oneheartedness
12:45 a.m.	The Word—"Évangiles"
1:00 to 5:00 a.m.	Path of the harp: Path of death and destruction
5:00 to 6:00 a.m.	Exit (minkin)
7:00 to 8:00 a.m.	Morning (final) njimba

There is some variation in these times in different chapels and branches of Bwiti. In most general terms the engosie begins after sunset and concludes before sunrise. Bwiti belongs to Nyingwan Mebege who is of the night and the moon. It is not of the day or the sun.

Ritual clothing is important in Bwiti and only the newest chapels have not developed a special garb. There is much diversity. One branch, Mekombo Kombe of the Muni Estuary, dresses in extravagant yellow, white, and blue. But generally red and white are the central colors in clothing as would be expected from the fact that the two sides of the chapel are as often associated with red and white as with female and male whose respective colors these are. The physiological association is ever-present. Red is the color of the female blood of fertility and white is the color of semen. Of course fertility lies in the coming together of blood and semen so conceived and it is a main object of Bwiti to produce that fertility by, among the various synesthesias of the ritual, bringing together red and white. Black is not nearly as frequent a color in the Bwiti scheme though it appears occasionally.*¹ Red, white, and black streamers are often hung from the circles of grace. Banzie sometimes conceive of the overall progress of the engosie as being a movement from the blackness of the forest through the redness of the village, to the brilliant white of the land of the dead beyond the sea. The engosie itself concentrates on the red path of birth and death.

The ritual garments of Bwiti play variations with red and white. In Asumege Ening Bwiti the garments of ordinary Banzie are red from the waist down and white from the waist up. This color scheme is first explained by reference to sin and goodness. The source of goodness is from the waist up and of sin from the waist below. All men and women are made up of good and evil— we remember the Fang phrase "good and bad walk together"—and the engosie enables those parts to be brought into harmonious relation. And there is a purpose beyond this synesthesia of colors. The garments Banzie wear should be light and flowing. They should billow in the dances and enable the wearer to fly. For the object of Bwiti is to escape corporeality as a man would take off his clothes. The synesthesia of colors, the bringing together of corporeal good and corporeal evil, as it were, enables the transcendence of the corporeal.

With any such central representations as these a plurality of meanings is inescapable. Red is not only the color of sin but it is also, as manifested in the red path of birth and death, the color of pain and suffering. It may be the color associated with the pain of birth but there is also a dimension of joyfulness to it as well—a "réjouissance" as the Banzie say. A replication of

---

*¹ The ritual colors red, white, and black have widespread use in African ritual symbolism, as Victor Turner has pointed out (*The Forest of Symbols*). Turner gives physiological explanations for the primacy of these colors which are similar to the physiological explanations given by Banzie for their widespread use of white and red. Of course white, black, and red are the basic color terms found in every language previous to any of the other primary colors. These are the colors of State I and II in B. Berlin and P. Kay's *Basic Color Terms*. It is an interesting question why black is a subordinate color in Bwiti even though the three colors (red, white, and black) seem to have equal place in Metsogo Bwiti. For one thing it is precisely their blackness of condition which is interpreted as sinfulness and which Bwiti seeks to escape by knowing death and thereby surmounting blackness and obscurity. For another thing black is taken for granted while the other two colors cannot be. But in any event the interesting thing about red, in addition to its association with physiological process, is its capacity, perceptually, to mediate between black and white—that is, to play a dark color in relation to white and a light color in relation to black. It can maintain saturation over a wide range of brightness values. In my view, red does both these things in Bwiti. Most obviously it plays a dark color in relation to white. But it also plays, in a less direct and obvious sense, a light color in relation to black. It is very much a color of mediation and that is why, among other reasons, the path of birth and death is conceived of as a red path—the red not the golden mean as it were.

the synesthesia of colors is seen in the *ngômbí* harp. The right side of the sounding board is covered with white kaolin and the left side with red padouk powder. The music of the harp brings together redness and whiteness, female and male. That synthesis is the benevolence in the voice of Nyingwan Mebege.

Bwiti ceremonies employ four kinds of instruments: the eight-string *ngômbí* harp, the bamboo sounding stave (*ôbaka*), the skin head drums (*nsom*), and on occasion the one-string musical bow (*mbe*). The path of the harp, both the birth path and the death path, occupies most of the night and its songs and dances are accompanied by the harp and by light rhythms on the bamboo sounding staves. These are played by two men seated on either side of the harpist. Periodically during the path of the harp, however, and particularly during climatic moments, the *ôbangô* chants and dances are interjected. These are accompanied by intense drumming and by beating upon the sounding stave. The softness of the harp music and the harshness of the obango drums go together, Banzie say.

The one-string harp represents in Banzie thought that figurative umbilical cord that attaches each person through all his ancestors to sky spider. The one-string harp is played only at the njimba where Banzie are figuratively in the pristine condition and are trying to come into being and to become attached.

Other instruments that make an occasional appearance are the antelope horn bugle (*nlak mvu*) which is blown before njimba to alert the ancestors in the forest, and the iron bells (*alenga*) which are played by women during the yombo songs in the women's chamber. All songs are of three varieties: nganga songs sung only by the dance and song leaders, responsorials sung between leaders and congregation, and songs sung in unison by the entire congregation. The engosie not only has an extensive "book" of songs, well over two hundred, from which to choose (less than half the total repertoire is sung at any one engosie) but it also can select among a variety of instruments and song modes.

THE PATH OF THE HARP

THE PATH OF BIRTH

In Chapter 14 we followed the origin legend of Bwiti as recited by Muye Michel and we related it to the Bwiti song cycle. Indeed, Muye Michel himself in recounting the legend often broke into song as an accompaniment to his recital. For Bwiti song and dance do correlate, although imperfectly, with the origin legends.

In the earlier chapter we were mainly interested in the origin and beginning of things, cosmogonic events which are featured largely in the minkin songs although they are also present in the path of the harp songs (the path we will study in this chapter). In fact, the path of the harp, which comprises 115 songs (of which 24 are obango songs), begins with creation ex nihilo and follows the sky spider as she drops the egg of creation upon the ocean. Still, this path, divided into two parts, the path of birth (*zen abiale*) with 49 songs) and the path of death (*zen awu* with 66 songs), mainly features events out of a more biblical scenario. Early on we encounter Adam and Eve, the archetypal pair, whose coming to terms with their sexuality is what is largely featured in Muye Michel's legend. Just as this pair recurs archetypically in Bwiti legend, so a song referring to them—we will not refer to all songs in our discussion—recurs thematically in the path of the harp. It is first sung in relation to the experience of Adam and Eve in Paradise and to their expulsion from Paradise. The song traces (and recurrently reminds Banzie of) the origin of mankind in the archetypical pair.

Abora Tara Zame, bemvama bebaé be fwéng ening engura ye bôt abwi.
Ebwan e Zame ye Mebege be fwé ening engura ye bôt abwi.
Blessings Father Zame, two ancestors announce the coming of life itself and many people. The children of Zame ye Mebege announce life itself and many people.

But to correlate the songs, and most songs appear only once, we pick up the Bwiti legend we were following in the last chapter as it concerns itself with Noah and the flood.

Muye tells us that after Eve gave birth to the ball of gristle and bone (*kigile*), which Adam placed in a bark reliquary and decided to worship equally with Zame as the first ancestor, she gave birth to many children. The last child was Noah who, born with the harp in his hand, grew to be the master of the ngombi harp. The harp brought the news to him that the world was come to an end. His brothers refused to listen. The flood came and they were drowned. But Noah had made a large canoe in which he saved his twelve children. This canoe floated on the waters and passed the only remaining thing above the water, the azap tree, upon whose topmost branches clung Adam and Eve. Noah watched these ancestors piteously as the waters rose. They too were drowned. To commemorate their death he turned and taught his children the following song. (This song is also thematically repeated in Bwiti.)

Meyong me nga zibang. Taroo. Me nga zibang. Meyong me nga zibang.
Tarooo. Meziban, Meziba mekodia, Mekodia etsenge, Etsenge Dibobia,
Zambe A Pongo, Mongabenda. Meyong meziban.
The clans have sunk and drowned Father. They have sunk and drowned. The clans have sunk and drowned, Father, in the swampy earth. The rainbow (cord of earth) marks the spot of their sinking, the last rainbow of the earth, that leads to the sky spider, to God the creator, the padouk tree that foretells the future, the clans sunk in the swamp.

This song telling of the drowning of the clans, it should be noted, also contains a kind of genealogy of salvation. It is a litany of ascent to the above from the foot of the rainbow at the end of the earth to sky spider and finally to the creator God (Zambe a Pongo) who holds the future in his hands (*monga benda*).

We return to Muye Michel's account.

The waters rose higher until the canoe came close to a brilliant white cloud from which Zame's face shone. And Zame reached out of heaven and gave the fire to Noah for the use of man. And the waters began to descend and the canoe became lodged in the azap tree from which Adam and Eve had perished. Noah made a prayer at the foot of this tree. He was in obscurity for the torch had gone out. The voice of Zame came to him to cease his prayers and to dig in the earth beneath the tree for there he would find the skulls of Adam and Eve. And those two skulls struck together would produce fire.

Noah began wandering on the earth. He heard the voices of many spirits locked in a rock cavern (*nda akawk*). He realized that these were the spirits of the dead of all the clans that had perished because of the sin of Adam and Eve. And Noah was perplexed about how to avoid that sin because among his children he had to give brothers to sisters to populate the earth. And thus Noah continued the great sin. But, at least, he made his children leave the canoe and propagate in the forest secretly and separately. Whereas the animals propagated in the canoe, and indiscriminately, brothers and sisters, sons with mothers, fathers with daughters.

These six boys and six girls of Noah went off into various parts of the earth and formed the various races from which we are all descended. After many generations the earth was populated again and men were falling again into their old evil ways because the sin of incest was still with them. And Zame went to Nyingwan Mebege his sister who was Eve and said to her, "You must go below again and save these people."

The songs which express this part of the origin legend are, including the oft-repeated "*meyong me nga ziba*," six in number. Noah is given the Banzie name "kombo" because he was possessed of a subtle and clairvoyant spirit which enabled him to anticipate the flood (from the Tsogo *kômbô*, "one possessed of a powerful clairvoyant spirit"). These songs of the Noah sequence are called prayers by Banzie because they are sung quietly without dance or movement of any kind. They are also mainly supplicative rather than descriptive of legendary events. This distinction is often difficult to maintain, however, as so many songs, whether called prayers or not, are supplicative in nature. We pick up the Noah story in Song No. 28 of the path of birth in the Kougouleu-Kwakum song cycle.[6]

28. *Kombo kobege akal da. Wa o betang oyo. Kombo oh! Kombo a kang edjop! Kombo wa o betan betara.*
Kombo speak in our behalf. You who have gone above on the flood. Kombo has gone to the sky. Kombo you who have gone above to the fathers.

30. *A kombo bi zaghé avwale. Vwalege bot. Avwale te da so ebe Zame. Minsutimibot mi wuang, a Tara Zame. Engongol, engongol. Kombo bi sili abora. Vwalegebot.*
Ah Kombo we beseech your aid. Help maintain the help that comes from God. Black men are dying in great misery. Kombo we ask grace of you. Help mankind!

Two of the other songs, Nos. 29 and 31 in the sequence, are the prayers of Noah to Zame from the canoe (*byal*) upon the waters.

29. *Kombo mwan Zame a nga kobo byal été.* Response: *Kombo na disoso a nga wa zu yen. Wa mien o vele bot a Tara Zame. Kombo na disoso a nga wa zu yen.*
Kombo son of Zame spoke out in the canoe. Response: Kombo na Disoso has come to see you. You yourself have prepared mankind Tara Zame. Kombo Disoso has come to see you.

The last song of the Noah sequence, No. 31, is Noah's prayer to Zame to open the door of the cave in which all the spirits of the drowned are locked after the flood. Their release will enable their descendants to flourish again.

31. *A Tara Zame za' kule mbi. Oh! Oh! A Tara Zame za' kule mbi. Bot abui be nto mimbok—ka yen vyé. Engongol, Engongol! A mwan nima za' yen bwan bia.*
Oh Father Zame come open the door. Oh Father Zame come open the door. Many people have been held prisoner and do not see the light. Sadness, sadness. Oh son of the first one come see your children.

There are several important elements in this Noah sequence. First of all, what seems to attract Banzie to the Noah story is the drowning of the clans in the water. This resonates with the Fang migration legends of the crossing of the great rivers and the drowning of whole clans in the waters. It also resonates with a favorite Banzie image—we see it in the midnight sermon given in Chapter 12—of Banzie suffocated in dank thickets and swamps cut off from the light and heat of the above. The songs feature the rising of Noah above the watery suffocation and stifling swamps. Otherwise the customary theme of Banzie despair occurs throughout the songs.

We note also that Noah's main source of preternatural intelligence is the harp. This accords with the Banzie view of the harp as mainly an instrument of communication with Nyingwan Mebege and the above. It is also of interest that the tree to which the old order (Adam and Eve) clings and at the base of which the new order is begun is the azap tree. This is the tree which marks, in traditional migration legends, the transformation from the old savanna life to the new life in the equatorial forest. The legend also accounts for the origin of the custom of keeping the craniums of the dead in reliquaries. It begins in that miscarriage of gristle and bone (kigile), a consequence of the incestuous sin between brother and sister. The ancestor cult among Fang is not derived from a miscarriage but it is an apt derivation for Banzie to whom reliquary worship is a miscarriage of religious devotion. This is true even though Banzie still believe that the path to the great gods lies through devotion to the ancestors. The fact that Noah saved six sons and six daughters is closer to older notions of the six tribes of the Pahouin (Ntumu, Fang, Mvae, Okak, Ewondo, Bulu) than to the Bwiti notion of the four races—black, white, yellow and red.

Noah's prayer to the gods to release the imprisoned spirits and have them come to the light of the above is granted immediately in the song cycle with the next song. This release is obtained by Nyingwan Mebege. It should be noted that the same kind of release of imprisoned spirits is obtained in the path of death under the aegis of Eyen Zame Onyibot (He Who Sees God the Ransomer of Men), the Banzie Christ figure.

32. *Mora ensama (nking) ô sô adzal. Oh! A Nyingwan Mebege. Oh!*
ensama ô ne mbembe! Mora ensama o so mang ayat ye endendang.
Oh! Oh!
A great band of beings comes toward the village (of the dead). Oh, Nyingwan Mebege. Oh! The great band is forever. The great group comes beyond the sea and into the light. Oh! Oh!

But though the release of the spirits guarantees the new creation and the recommencement of life, the second half of the path of birth largely concerns the coming of Eyen Zame (He Who Sees God). This coming is a "miracle," the Banzie carefully explain, because the sister Nyingwan Mebege, who is Eve, becomes the mother Marie. And the brother, Zame ye Mebege, who is Adam, becomes the son, Eyen Zame Nganga, the Christ figure. In this amazement the original sin is finally lifted. It is the miracle that the Christians refer to as the Virgin Birth. For the narrative of this amazement we return again to the legend recounted by Muye Michel.

After long generations Zame responded to Noah's prayer. He said to Eve, "You must return to earth and become the mother of Adam who will be Emwan Mot the Nganga. And he will die a terrible death and become Eyen Zame Onyibot (the ransomer of people). And in that death all the evil of the Garden of Eden and of Noah's children will finally be forgiven. And Zame sent a guardian angel who was to become Joseph. And Joseph never saw Marie naked. And she took pillows and feigned pregnancy. And at the last moment God sent Adam below and he appeared from beneath Marie's skirt. And a star appeared at this moment and three rich men (*minkukuma mile*) came and bathed the infant and prepared him (*akômnge*). The first placed an ivory bracelet in the basin saying that his life should be as perfect and valuable as the circle of ivory. The second placed a piece of resin incense (*ôlak ôban*) to protect Emwan Mot against all sorcery. And the third placed six pieces of money. Because of these six pieces Emwan Mot would lose his life.

Now the first "miracle" that Nganga performed was to throw a piece of earth upon the ground and it turned into *mvekum* (the gray African house sparrow—*Passer griseus diffusus*). After this "miracle" Emwan Mot discovered he was not living in his proper lineage (ndebot) so he crossed over the courtyard to the ndebot of David. And there he made many miracles and became known over the countryside. Finally he decided to go to Jean Baptiste and demand the eboga. And Jean Baptiste demanded why Zame (for he recognized Zame in Emwan Mot Nganga) should ask baptism of a poor man. Nganga said that all of that was decided in heaven. Then Jean Baptiste asked if Nganga had any sins and Emwan Mot said, "Only one. The sin of being born which he would repay when he died." Then Jean Baptiste gave him the eboga.

Emwan Mot Nganga remained in the village of his father and made more and more miracles. Finally the Jews heard of this. They worried when they heard that Nganga was intending to go to Africa[7] and make his miracles there. They summoned him and questioned him. He showed them the eboga and he affirmed that he was going to Africa with his miracles and to show the true path of eboga. And the Jews determined to kill him so that others should not know of his miracles. And that is why the Europeans have remained with all the amazements of Nganga. And that is why the blacks have remained in despair (*engôngôl*) and obscurity (*zibe*) and in limbo (*tôtôlan*).[8]

The last songs in the path of birth are those which celebrate the coming of Emwan Mot. They are eighteen in number of which seven are obango chants. The first of these songs celebrates the birth itself. Eve who has become Marie is referred to by her Tsogo name, Nana Nyepe.

34. *Abiale e ne mbembe, Nana Nyepe. Ônyíbot a bialiang. Ah, Nana Nyepe, Nana Nyepooo! A bialiang Nana Nyepe.*
    Birth is for ever, Nana Nyepe. The savior (He who offers ransom) is born. Nana Nyepoo.

Three obango chants and the vertiginous dances which accompany them follow this song. They represent the turmoil of birth. Song No. 38 introduces a subtle and very Fang image. The umbilical cord with the placenta attached is compared to the forest swing (*ndem-kawle*). In Bwiti and frequently among Fang the afterbirth (*ku*), which is to say, the umbilical cord with placenta, is considered as a second person. It is the twin of the newborn who must die and be carefully buried lest animals or witches discover and devour it and bring harm to the newborn. In Bwiti the afterbirth is considered as a guardian spirit, the twin of the newborn, who accompanies the newborn to the moment of birth and then dies, returning to the forest and the land of the dead.[9]

The association of the afterbirth with the forest swing, the swinging vine into which a stick is tied and upon which the swinger sits, has an obvious structural basis. They are both two "persons" at the end of a cord. But the association also works because of the forest locale appropriate to both ku and ndem-kawle. And the association may also work by opposites, for in the song the ku cries out in pain at the wrenching it has undergone whereas the ndem-kawle causes swingers to cry out in pleasure. At any event the ku is taken as a surrogate for the newborn in order to give dramatic voice to the pain of birth.

38. *Engôngôl a ndem-kawle mot. Tarooo! Be nga biale bebae. Taroo!*
    Mwan ye ku Taroo! Me kanayang ye abum nyia. Nima Tarooo! Tara
    Zame me wuang. Oh Nima. Tara nget e ne ening. Me kanayang
    abum nyia.
    The despair of the person who is the forest swing. Father. They have
    been born as two. Father. Child and afterbirth. Tara. The separation
    from the stomach of the mother. Father. O first one. Life is hard.
    Already the separation from the stomach of the mother, swinging
    at the end of the vine.

The next song celebrates the bathing of the child and his being fortified in the basin of leaves (*esawk*), the same basin in which the three rich men make their gifts. It is the voice of the newborn, the old Adam and the new *emwan mot* that is here raised in song. He is already fully adult and speaks for himself.

39. *Eyong me nga wôban Tara, me wôban.*
    Eyong me nga woban, Tara, me woban.
    Me woba minkodia, minkodia etsenge, etsenge dibobia, dibobia.
    Nzambe, Nzambe a pongo, Mongabenda. Me nga soba.
    Now I have bathed father, I bathe. Now I have bathed Father I
    bathe. I bathe at the rainbow which is at the end of the earth, at the
    place of the spider, the spider of Nzambe. He who foretells. I have
    bathed.

It is a frequent device in Bwiti songs for the singers to take the voice of the divinity, especially so when the subject is Eyen Zame, Nganga, the Christ figure. The identification with man found in Eyen Zame's popular name, Emwan Mot (child of man) is strengthened in this practice. We note again in this song the hierophantic sequence of rainbow, end of earth, sky spider, and Zambe. In this case the newly bathed and fortified spirit returns to the above.

This song is followed by a number of obango chants, very rapid in rhythm, in which various actions appropriate to the legendary events are carried out: the washing of the child, the coming of the three rich men, etc. The obango chants are mostly sung in Popi Fang.

Song No. 45 is simple in content but the accompanying dance is interesting. The song occurs in the concluding phase of the path of birth. Men and women sing it in unison. And we see, again, the shift of voice and person.

> 45. *Tara Zame, mwan a bialiang. A tara Zame mwan a bialiang. Me*
> *ke yen emwan Zame a bialiang. Abora betara o ne abialing.*
> Oh Father Zame the child is born. O Father Zame the child is born.
> I am going to see the child of Zame already born. Thanks to all the
> fathers you are born!

During this song men and women on their respective sides of the chapel gather and exit into the courtyard. Women leave by the birth exit and men by the death exit, for both the life of the newborn and the death of the afterbirth are being celebrated. The leader of the woman's group, yombo, carries a candle which represents the brief life of the afterbirth as well as the guardian star it will become. The men and women sing and dance an interweaving pattern out in the courtyard. Finally all return single file through the birth entrance. In the end it is the birth of Emwan Mot that is being celebrated.

The next two songs celebrate the birth and its revitalizing consequences for sky, earth, and all mankind.

> 46. *A Nana Marie, Maria a bieng Zame Onyi Bot Oh. Maria a bieng*
> *Zame Onyi Bot. Oh! Oh! A nana Maria, Oh! Marie a bieng Zame*
> *Onyi Oh. Marie enye a bieng Zame.*
> Oh mother Marie. Maria gives birth to Zame Oh. He who ransoms
> men. Marie gives birth to Zame (repeat).

Typically the songs refer variously to the principal divinities as Marie, Maria, Nana Nyepe, Emwan Mot, Eyen Zame, Onyi Bot, and Jesus. This shifting back and forth between vernacular and biblical names is indicative of the alternation in Bwiti itself between Christian and more traditional beliefs. Full syncretization has not been obtained, and in any given situation a more traditional or a more acculturated view of a particular divinity may emerge.

Song No. 47 celebrates the resurrection or revival in earth, sky, and men accomplished by the coming of Eyen Zame Onyi Bot. There are two important verbs in this song: *vele* and *koré*. The first has the meaning of resuscitating or returning to life and more particularly it refers to bringing the initiate who has fainted from the drug of initiation back to the land of the living. It also refers to the keeping of the names of the dead alive through the worship of their skulls in the reliquary. In this context Eyen Zame revives earth, sky, and men by putting the dead and the living back into contact. The verb kore refers to the act of ransoming a prisoner taken by another clan. The Bwiti sense is that Nganga, by paying the price of his life, brought men, imprisoned from each other, back into communion.

> 47. *A vele si, a vele djop a vele môt ase. Tare Zame. Zame a vele ening oh! A zame Oh! Nkorébot a koré môt ase. Onyibot a bialiang. O nyi bot bese.*
> He revives the earth, he revives the sky, he revives everyman. Father Zame, Zame revives life. O Zame Oh. The ransomer of men is born. You ransom every man.

The last song of the path of birth already forebodes the coming of the path of death, for it refers to the palaver and discord which reign on earth and prevent people from hearing Zame and which will eventually lead to Nganga Emwan Mot's death.

> 49. *Nte me nga sô, ka wôk na, Zame a kôbeyang. Oh Zame a kôbeyang Oh Zame. Engongol Zame a kôbeyang.*
> The discord for which I have come, [They do] not listen. Zame has spoken. Zame has spoken. Despair. Zame has spoken. Oh Zame.

THE OBANGO CHANTS AND DANCES

Interspersed among the songs of the path of the harp are the obango chants and dances. The word is Tsogo in origin and in that language refers to any action which is intense and laborious in execution. In Metsogo Bwiti the name applies to any vertiginous dances. Much of what attracted Fang to Metsogo Bwiti was the intense quality of the dancing. In Fang Bwiti these pounding chants and dances are contrasted with the songs and dances of the harp. Although the harp can be played with a driving rhythm it is basically an instrument of soft tones and gentle rhythms. It is an instrument suitable to its patron, Nyingwan Mebege, who speaks through it to the membership. While there is tranquillity in the harp, there is powerful activity in the obango which is always accompanied by intense drumming. The obango drum is described as *king fam* (the male voice) of the engosie. It is the voice of hunger, cruelty, and pain. The harp is the *king mininga* (the female voice) of pity and consolation. It sees and understands the despair of the Banzie (*a yene engôngôl*). The path of the harp, in any case, is a synesthetic alternation of tranquil harp music and intense drumming.

The obango dance, although it has different meanings at various parts of the evening, is generally taken to represent the turmoil of the soul as it either enters the body, at birth, or departs it, at death. This cleavage of spirit from flesh is an intense experience best represented by the drums and whirling of the body typical of obango. This is why obango is most continuously celebrated those several hours after midnight when the death of Eyen Zame and the separation of his soul from his body are being celebrated. Similarly, at the death of a Banzie, obango figures prominently at the funeral in his honor. The funeral dance comes at 5 p.m., the time, in Banzie thinking, when the soul separates from the body.[10] Banzie go on to say that the drums of the obango also represent the pounding torment of the life of the soul in the body and the whirling around and uncertainty of the recently released spirit in taking direction toward the village of the dead. For this reason, though the obango dancers generally whirl around Ta Mwanga,[11] the central spot of the chapel, (where the main fire burns) at one point or another they touch the central pillar. (See Figure 13.1c.) This puts the confused spirit correctly on the path of birth and death. Touching the central pillar also puts the spirit of the dancer in contact with the other spirits clustering at the top of the chapel. Another device to assure the soul's orientation upon leaving the body is to draw a straight line of redwood powder down the middle of the forehead. As the spirit, however spun in the dance, exits from the head it will find itself straightaway on the path of birth and death.

There are, thus, different explanations for what the obango represents and what it accomplishes. For example, obango dances by the women's nganga team take place when the women take charge of the dancing after midnight. Suddenly the raffia mat of the women's chamber is thrown aside and the three women dancers rush out in obango. They shake their buttocks, laden with sleigh bells, before the three male ngangas who are about to retire. They whirl around Ta Mwanga and then shake themselves again before the birth entrance and death exit and the central pillar. They are calling the souls out of the men's bodies. But there is a sexual element. For the buttocks of the women are bedecked with sleigh bells which represent the child in the womb, while their shaking of their buttocks is directly enticing. We see again that sexuality is both represented dramatically and prohibited in actuality. Obango has the meaning, if not of sexual passion, at least of ecstatic activity with fertile consequences. The promotion of that condition is always a purpose of Bwiti if only by indirection.

Of the 115 songs of the path of the harp some 35 are classed as obango chants. We list these songs below (by number in the Kougouleu-Kwakum cycle) and give the legendary activity they give expression to in Asumege Ening Bwiti. The obango really begins in earnest at songs 35-37 in which the birth of Christ is sung.

Two obangos, however, precede the birth obango. Song No. 5 is an obango which celebrates the descent to the ocean and the bursting open of the spider's egg of heaven. Song No. 21 celebrates the pregnancy of Eve. In both cases the noise and turmoil of obango accompany an important transformation of matter: from the potential of the egg to the actuality of the three precursors and from virginity to pregnancy.

This is a fuller list of obango chants than is actually used in Asumege Ening which has translated some of these into Fang and assigned them to the ngombi harp. Branches of Bwiti and chapels differ as to whether they prefer to sing in Fang or Popi and, thus, what are obango chants in some chapels are harp songs in others.

SONG NUMBER	LEGENDARY ACTION CELEBRATED
2-9	Creation in the wind, the egg drops to the ocean, the three precursors appear, land is created, Adam and Eve are created.
21	Eve becomes pregnant.
35-37	Noah surmounts the flood. The birth of Emwan Mot.
41-44	The death of Nganga adumbrated.
54-55 & 57-59	Death of Nganga planned.
64-65, 67, 71	Eyen Zame anguishes on the cross and is killed by the Roman soldier.
78 & 86	Eyen Zame is put in the grave.
93-94	Eyen Zame Onyi Bot climbs above on the wind. No. 94 is an ngombi song in the Noah sequence (Noah's going above in the flood) here made into an obango.
98-102	Eyen Zame escapes the rock cavern, dies a final time, and joins his father above.
106	Eyen Zame established as mankind's savior (Onyi Bot) and the ruler of the dead.

The obango chants taken all together are a survey of practically all phases of the Bwiti legend. The more use made of the obango the older the branch of Bwiti and the closer to the original Metsogo influences. Still, in every branch of Bwiti there is a contrast between the obango drumming and the ngombi harp strumming. That is to say that there are two qualitative sides to the legends: a harshly turbulent side and a tranquil, resigned side. By distributing activity in the obango and tranquillity in the ngombi Bwiti celebrates both these sides.

We cannot examine all obango of the night any more than we can examine all the ngombi songs. But we may single out two sequences for comment. The word "chants" is used here rather than "songs" because of the brevity of the lyrics and because, usually, there is a chanting call and response relationship between the leader (*nyiabia*) and the congregation which does not occur in the ngombi songs. These latter are much longer and often sung in unison. We will provide such translation of the Popi lyrics as was available. But Banzie themselves, though they may give translations and explanations, are usually unsure of the exact meaning. Here are the three obango chants that occur when the birth of Emwan Mot Nganga is being celebrated.

35. *Disumba me konga, a ngona, motsaenya. Motsaenya monganga madouma môpende kô.* Response. *Motsaenya, motsaenya monganga madouma mobendiko.*
This chant is said to tell of the turning of the child in the womb.[12] The child turns in the womb and faces the earth below. It is during this song that one of the nganga dancers climbs the central pillar, reverses himself and descends headfirst through the legs of the principal dancer.

36. *Aduma na disumba to ngadi na duma.* Response. *Engadi na duma mwan abialiang.*
This obango is translated as the celebration of the beginning brought about by lightning and the groaning of thunder—by sexual activity. The nganga who has descended through the legs of his co-dancer first whirls to the male side, the lightning side, and then to the female side, the thunder or groaning side, of the chapel.

37. *Disumba ma kondja womeniga disumba. Disumba ma buran zae.* Response. *Disumba disumba bi buran zae.*
The translation of this obango is a bit surer in part because as in No. 36 it employs some Fang, in this case the word *bura* (to replace, substitute for). It refers to the substitution of Emwan Mot for Adam. The specific Banzie translation is: "The beginning, I fabricate the newborn. The beginning. The beginning I substitute him." The dance action is the customary whirling back and forth between the altar and the central pillar.

Obango chants Nos. 64, 65, 67, and 71 celebrate the suffering and death of Eyen Zame on the cross. We give the first two of these.

64. *Ma duma nawoseli obango na pinji.* Response. *Ma duma nawoseli Obango na pinji aiii!*
"Eyen Zame cries out in pain as his soul prepares to leave him whirling out into the forest." [The dance action is that normal to the obango except the Nganga fling themselves arms outstretched against the central pillar.]

65. *Minkendi ye, minkendi ye. Obango minkendi ye.* Response. Repeats.
"The soul of Eyen Zame reaches the crossroads between life and death in great turmoil." [The dance action is this obango may be frequently that of whirling out into the courtyard.]

The remaining obango of this sequence, Nos. 67-71, celebrate successively the final sword thrust (*ezomo*) of the Roman soldier, the removal from the cross, the placing of the cadaver upon the ground, and the placing of the cadaver over the thighs of Eyen Zame's mother, Marie, the old Eve. All of these are painful and turbulent events suitable for obango performance.

THE PRAYERS

At the conclusion of the path of birth just before midnight a long prayer made up of a number of songs takes place before the altar. The Banzie kneel upon the ground with hands clasped and with eyes toward the ceiling where the ancestor spirits are gathering. They may intone up to thirteen prayer songs. All the prayers express the state of despair (engongol) in which Banzie are living. Prayer songs can also occur at any time in the process of the path of the harp. The main difference between these and the other songs and chants is that the membership is quiescent and the three nganga, the three dance leaders, are quiet as well. We have already given Noah's prayer, No. 30, which occurs midway through the path of birth. Its declaration of despair and its appeal for help is typical of all thirteen prayers of Banzie. As a further example here is Prayer No. 2 in the prayer sequence.

2. *Tara Zame bia zôba minsem. Tare, Tare! Nyonge bia. Bia wuang engôngôl, engôngôl. Tare Zame nyonge bia, engôngôl engôngôl.*
   Father Zame we regret our sins. Father, Father. Gather us in, we are dying of despair. Father Zame take us. Despair, Despair.

The last or thirteenth prayer echoes a frequent theme in the songs which we have examined above in Song No. 31 of the Noah sequence.

31. *Ah Tara Zame za' kule mbi (bis). Abwi bôt be ne mimbôk. Ka yen vyé.*
   Oh Father Zame come open the door (*bis*). Multitudes are prisoner and do not see the light.

This final prayer is repeated over and over again each time a different deity or version of deity is appealed to. In place of Tara Zame the object of appeal may be Nzambi Avanga (Zame who has arranged everything) or Enyepe Nzambi (the sister of Zame) or Minsengi Nzambi (Zame father of the earth). The prayer cycle alternates between prayers in unison accompanied by the ngombi and prayers led in call and response by the nganga.

ONEHEARTEDNESS

We have now arrived at midnight in our all-night scenario. Amidst and beyond the vectors of movement—and the paths of the harp have definite vectors—is the quiescence of the prayer and the integrity of "oneheartedness." There is in Bwiti—it is constrained by the architectonic—what we call a saving circularity, which holds the vectors around a vital center. In the ritual of oneheartedness (*nlem mvôre*) these vectors and that circularity develop into a final flowing together—an ultimate recentering of Banzie experience. Until the decentering of the colonial situation, Fang migration is well represented as a series of centripetal poses of village life strung along (subsumed in) an overall vector of migration northeast to southwest. It is an achievement of the Bwiti architectonic to have brought both vectors of progressive spiritual movement and centripetal circularities into harmonious relation in the same ritual arena.

The key ritual event in which this occurs is held at midnight and first light. After the prayers for the membership have been made at midnight, all the Banzie follow the cult harp out into the forest upon narrow precut paths. They have candles in their hands, for they are searching for those lost ancestor spirits which have not yet returned to the chapel. Returning from this forest procession, the membership, following the nima na kombo, enters the chapel and, just before the central pillar, begins to weave a tighter and tighter circle until they are compressed, virtually, into one being around the nima na kombo. Raising their candles above their heads (ideally they should be able to make one flame out of all candles) they intone *bi antô nlem mvôre* (now we become one heart).

The ritual also occurs at first light after the dances of farewell to the ancestors. But at this time it does not occur within the chapel but rather before the ancestors' welcoming hut (*ôtunga*). And the members, instead of raising the candles in their right hands raise and bring together the yarn umbilical cords in their left hands. For they are not celebrating the lighting of the chapel by the ancestral presence and by communication with the great gods. They are reaffirming the "umbilical linkage" that binds them to the departing ancestors. "Oneheartedness" may otherwise be celebrated by men and women in separate groups in the midst of nearby streams. But midnight and first light are the two occasions for this celebration in the process of the engosie. It is a climactic celebration in the engosie. It is usually said that the engosie leads beyond death to mang ayat. As often it is said that the path of engosie leads to "oneheartedness."

As we have learned to expect of Banzie, there is imaginative and replicative virtuosity in the interpretation of the clustering into one heart. "As we speak with one voice," it is said, "so we act as one heart." But also remarked is the appearance of the nima na kombo, dressed all in red, at the heart of the mass of the membership all in white (as far as their upper garments are concerned). The nima na kombo represents the heart itself surrounded by the white flesh. In replication of another body image, that of procreation, he is also said to represent the drop of blood, the homunculus, surrounded by the protective and nurturant seminal fluid which will enable the homunculus to come into fruition. So there is a fertile and procreative meaning to this ritual as well as its essential meaning of solidarity and centering of membership.

1. Ekang Engono, The Parrot's Egg, the Uncreated Creator (nima na kombo) of the mother chapel of the Commencement of Life Religion (Asumege Ening). Kougouleu, Kango District.

2. The Parrot's Egg at rest in the gravepit under the altar with two assistants just before the beginning of the engosie. Kougouleu Chapel, Kango District.

3. Men's prayers at the hole before the altar that communicates with the gravepit and thence with the land of the dead. Kougouleu Chapel, Kango District.

4. Gathering the roots of the eboga plant preparatory to the all-night services (engosie). Efulan Chapel, Medouneu District.

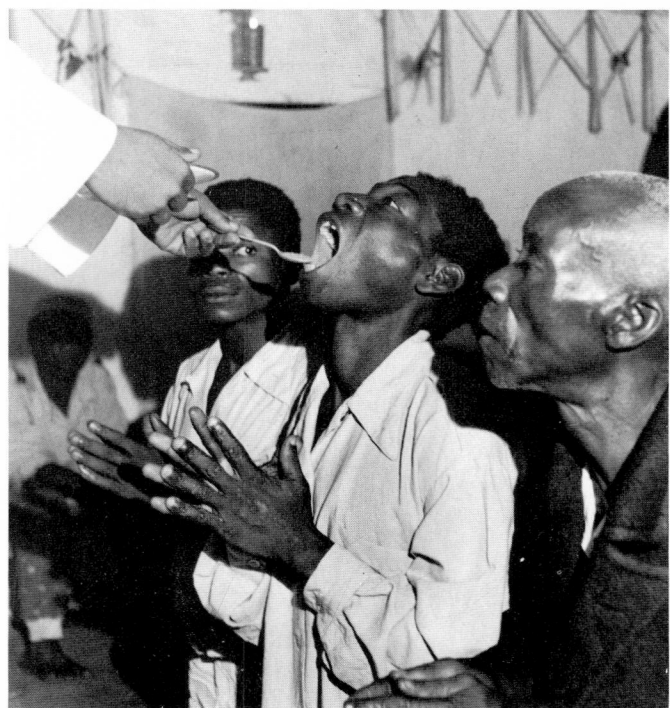

5. Taking communion with eboga. Kwakum Chapel, Oyem District.

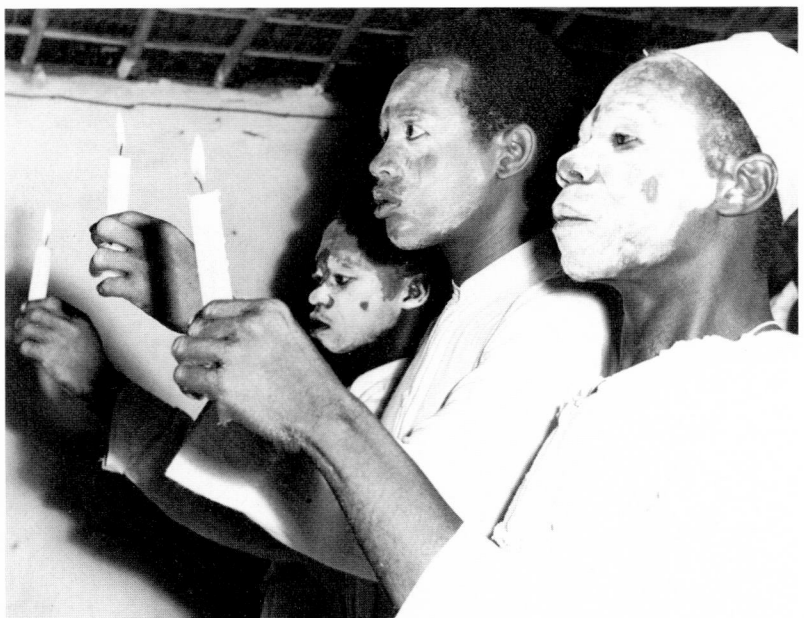

6. Checking for the effects of eboga by looking for rainbows (color spectra) around the edges of candle flames. Kwakum Chapel, Oyem District.

7. The drug-steady gaze of the harp player whose ingestion of eboga must be most carefully controlled. Efulan Chapel, Medou-neu District.

8. Descent of the sacred harp from its secret chamber above the altar. To the right the circle of grace. Efulan Chapel, Medouneu District.

9. The Bwiti harpist accompanied by the two beaters of the sounding stave (obaka). Kwakum Chapel, Oyem District.

10. Women in the women's quarters waiting their turn to dance. Ayol Chapel, Mitzik District.

11. Men in the men's chambers applying kaolin chalk to their faces. Ayok Chapel, Mitzik District.

12. Women in the women's quarters grinding red padouk powder (fim) and depositing it in the sacred pool. Kougouleu Chapel, Kango District.

13. Women exiting from women's quarters shortly after midnight and replacing the male dancers. Kougouleu Chapel, Kango District.

14. The women dance forward to replace the men. Ayol Chapel, Mitzik District.

15. To the accompaniment of the harp the back pillar of the chapel is placed in the ground. Assok Ening Chapel, Oyem District.

16. Burying the collection of protective substances at the base of the central pillar of the chapel. Assok Ening Chapel, Oyem District.

17. The raising of the central pillar of the chapel. Assok Ening Chapel, Oyem District.

18. Final dedication of the central pillar to both men and women. Assok Ening Chapel, Oyem District.

19. The pillar as the central point of orientation in the most rapid dances. Efulan Chapel, Medouneu District.

20. Gathering strength by periodic touching of the central pillar during the dances. Ayol Chapel, Mitzik District.

21. The central pillar as path of the descent of the spirit of newborns. New birth enacted at Antom Chapel, Minvoul District.

22. Women's Belebele dances. Efulan Chapel, Medouneu District.

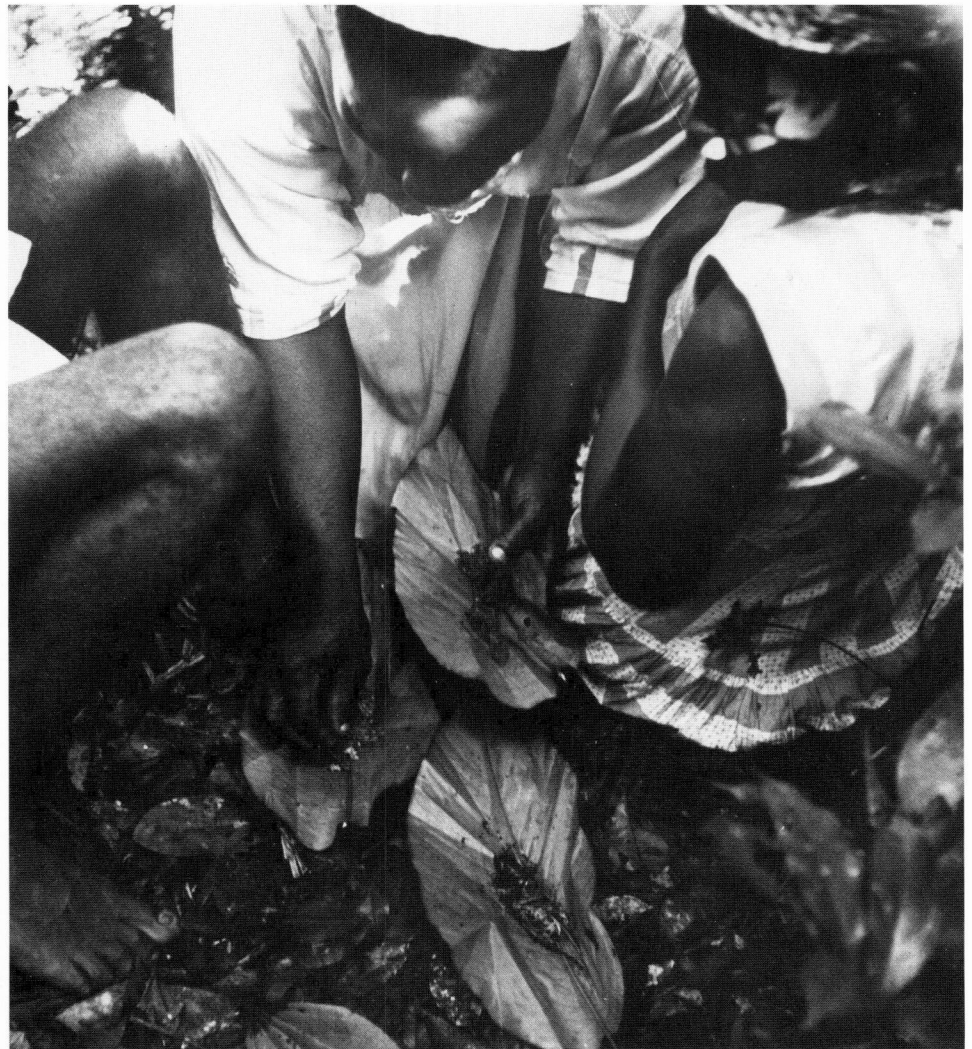

23. The various sacred substances to be eaten by the initiate are laid out upon their separate leaves. Assok Ening Chapel, Oyem District.

24. The soul boat with a cube of burning pitch passes between the legs of the initiate and her "parents in eboga" on the way to the sea and the ancestors. Assok Ening Chapel, Oyem District.

25. Final view of the soul boat as it disappears around a bend in the stream.

YOMBO SONGS OF THE WOMEN'S CHAMBER

Around the midnight hour between the path of birth and the path of death and usually after the evangile and the celebration of oneheartedness, the women retire to their secret chamber to sing the yombo songs. Yombo songs may be sung at three in the morning and at six in the morning but midnight is their main hour. Accompanied by only an iron clacker—or sometimes by iron struck upon a bottle—the head of the woman's group (*yômbo ensama*) calls out the songs, which are all responsorial. The women sing of both birth and death. There are nineteen birth songs and twelve death songs. The main emphasis is on conception, gestation, and parturition. We shall give representative songs of both birth and death. As these are all in Popi we shall give Banzie explanations without translations.

There is no singing in the men's quarters in response or in company with the women's singing, although a man, during the yombo songs, will be grinding kaolin clay over his sacred pool just as next to the singers a woman is grinding the red padouk in the women's quarters. Banzie say that it is the men who lead the minkin entrance songs and the njimba songs.[13] It is they who initiate Bwiti, so to speak, while it is the women who sing the songs that balance the ceremonies between birth and death and between night and morning. The yombo songs also anticipate the appearance of the women's dance team which comes out and takes the lead in dancing the early phases of the path of death.

The yombo songs, then, replicate the entire evening's events, both birth and death, except that they concentrate upon the female experience of giving birth and seeing die one to whom one has given birth. The songs are brief, detailing moments in the conception, growth, birth, and maturity of the infant, Emwan Mot. Examples of the brevity of subject matter are the following: "spirit and a fistful of earth makes the man"; "the spirit is in the stomach"; "the woman agonizes in labor"; "the newborn is bathed," etc. Yombo songs also introduce apt images as in Song No. 4 of the yombo cycle.

4. *Ye mewuma ya yôbe tsenge bôtô a ntô biamo yengae.*
   The new plantations brought into being by Nyingwan Mebege they
   give the fruit of the rubber vine.

This image of Nyingwan Mebege as bringing a flourishing plantation into existence is satisfying. But that this should be a plantation giving the fruit of the rubber vine (*avôm nzik endama*) is resonant. For it conjures up both the difficulties and satisfactions involved in the collection of rubber by the nineteenth-century trading teams (*ensame endama*). The fruit of the rubber vine is those balls of latex that were painstakingly amassed and then taken to the coast for trade. The ball of latex is an apt image here, as the growth of the child in the womb is being referred to and implicitly compared to the growth of the rubber ball by the accumulation of latex around the core. This is an image which also accords with Fang notions of the fertilization and strengthening of the homunculus in the womb.

Another highly resonant image for men and women of Fang culture is introduced in Song No. 6.

> 6. *Menzongo abige Tame Manga. Yee ee Tame Manga. Mendzongo abige. Yee Eee Tame Manga.*
> The spirit has descended into the water, into the sacred pool. Oh Oh into the sacred pool.

In the explanation given for this song Banzie make a connection between the sacred pool in the forest, the two pools of the secret chambers of the sexes, the area named sea or "great river" at the back of the chapel, *and* the bag of waters in the woman's womb. The sacred pool referenced here has, thus, corporeal, architectonic, ecologic, and cosmic associations.

Song No. 7 of the yombo songs introduces another comparison with considerable resonance—that between the woman's womb and a bird nest.

> 7. *Midwandzi monga môma kanga. Yeee môma kanga. Yeee eee moma kanga. Atin Yeee wooo.*
> The womb of the woman is the child's nest. Yee the nest of a bird. Yee the nest of a bird.

This association is serviceable to the recurrent attempt in Bwiti to integrate village and forest or, at the least, bring about fruitful communication. It also resonates with other images of birds we have encountered and particularly the African gray parrot who first traced the red path of birth and death and whose eggs condense the potential knowledge of that path. The association between the path of birth and path of death and the birth canal is contained in Song No. 15.

> 15. *Ma zaba zaba ekôpe, Ekope! Ma zaba zaba ekôpe.*
> This is translated as "the vulva of the woman is the path of the spirit."

The path of birth and death begins in the birth canal where the child of man's first sinful abuse of another being takes place. This beginning in the blood of birth is also for many Banzie the main reason for the redness of the path.

The yombo songs concerned with the death of Emwan Mot also contain their resonant images. Like the birth songs these death songs are generally brief descriptions of various stages in "the betrayal," "the trial," "the beating," and "the crucifixion" of Eyen Zame. Song No. 7, however, gives us particular insight, as translated, into Bwiti attitudes toward their Christ figure, Eyen Zame.

7. *Diveyô diveya ya monga sumena divaya. Divayô divaya monga su-*
   mena divaya.
   This is translated as "Eyen Zame he is the father of all the spirits,
   he is the elder of the dead, the first of the dead (*kon osua*). He
   commands the dead as Nana Nyepe commands the living."

The concluding six songs of the yombo songs of the dead celebrate the
ways in which Eyen Zame's spirit left its body. For not only is Eyen Zame
the Elder, the first, of the dead, he is also the one who showed men and
women how the spirit could leave the physical body (*ekokom*) and still return
to it. That is, he showed men that they could know death and still be living.
The final yombo song pronounces the curse of Nyingwan Mebege upon the
earth for having killed her son and brother. It is a curse that Bwiti in its
ceremonial devotions to the female principle seeks to lift.

THE PATH OF DEATH

The path of death, also called *Kombi*, comprises in most chapels between
sixty and seventy songs including obango chants. There are more songs than
in the path of birth because the path of death lasts two hours longer, from 1
to 6 a.m. The path of death shows more Christian influence in the events
described than the path of birth, although the great majority of the songs are
Banzie in origin and style. But the more pronouncedly Christian scenario may
account for the paucity of legendary materials lying behind the songs and
actions of this part of the path of the harp. The events of the betrayal and
crucifixion of Eyen Zame are left to the liturgy and not expanded upon.

The path begins (we shall ignore the obangos here) with a series of laments
on the part of Eyen Zame as to his fate. Song No. 50 establishes identification
between Eyen Zame and all the Banzie in their common fate of having
committed the sin of being born.

50. *Engongol Tara Zame me ne Banzie. Tara Zame me ne Banzie. Me*
    bele nsem abiale me ne Banzie.
    Despair Father Zame I am a Banzie. Father Zame I am a Banzie.
    I carry the sin of birth I am a Banzie.

The identification has an ambiguity since Eyen Zame, the old Adam, really
escaped that sin through the ruse of the Virgin Birth. In the next song Eyen
Zame complains of how many men first tempt him before his fate and then
pretend not to know him.

51. *Bôt be kông me, bôt be wing me Oh! A Bendembe Disumba, a*
    bendembe Monga Bendembe.
    People tempt me, people kill me and people deny knowing me. The
    beginning one is the denied one. The child is the denied one.

Song No. 52 calls out for guidance from Zame and from Olorogebot ("He who shows the way," St. Michael). This song anticipates the identification between the soul of Eyen Zame and the souls of all Banzie.

> 52. *Tara Zame O lerege bôt. O lerege bôt Tare Zame. Minsisim mi bwan be bôt mi ye ke djôp. St. Michael O lerege bôt engôngôl e dang Tarooo!*
> Father Zame show men the way. Olerogebot Father Zame. The spirits of the children of men are going above. St. Michael show the way to the despairing people.

The final song of this series, before a series of obango chants expressing the pain of the crucifixion, declares Eyen Zame's frustration at speaking and not being heard, at showing miracles and not being appreciated. *Me buran mwan* (I die for the child of man), he goes on to say. But he also lays a curse upon those who do not appreciate him.

The curse laid upon mankind by the death of Eyen Zame is more clearly expressed in Song No. 66 which refers to the spearing by the Roman soldier—the instrumentality of his death.

> 66. *Ngum môt wa ye bô ke wu mekong, Zame ye Mebege! Tarooo! Nde me wuang mekong, ooh! Alumayang.*
> Hardly a person but will not die by the spear, Zame ye Mebege.
> Father. Because I die by the spear oh! general destruction!

In these early songs of the path of death Eyen Zame is notably referred to by two names: *mongabenda* (the child crucified or possibly, in a play upon words, the clairvoyant child) and *nguba* (the shield or protector). Though several of these songs suggest the curse rather than the salvation laid upon mankind by Eyen Zame's crucifixion, there is evidence in the death songs that Eyen Zame also seeks to shield the descendants of man against the consequences of their blindness. The typically Fang notion of the blood debt incurred in the crucifixion thus contests in these songs with more redemptive notions.

Periodically in the path of death the women take over as leaders in dance and song although not usually when Eyen Zame himself is lamenting his betrayal, crucifixion, and death. An appropriate moment for the women to take over is after the obango sequence, 67-73. Here begins a series of songs in which a third party (it could be Nyingwan Mebege) is lamenting the death and arrival in the land of the dead of Eyen Zame. For example, Song No. 75:

> 75. *Mwan Zame a kang mora nkin bekongô a ntô mwan nima. A ntô mwan Zambi Avanga. Onyi Bot Mwan Zambe.*
> The child of Zame arrives amidst the great crowd of the dead. He

becomes the young first one among them. He becomes the child of
Zame the creator. He who ransoms men, Child of Zame.

Focus, however, can change quickly in these songs. Thus the next song, No.
76, laments the departure of the corpse from its house into the courtyard—
always a poignant moment in Fang funerary rites for it is the definitive
testimony to the final incapacity which has descended upon the dead.

76. *Olang o koroyang nda, o kang nsung. Olang o kang ekéké. O Tara
Zame. Engôngôl, engongol enen. Nzambi a wuang. Ya ya Yi Yi Ya.*
The pall abandons the house. It comes away into the courtyard. It
comes away forever. Father Zame! Oh great despair. Nzambi has
died (lament).

From time to time in the path of death the same songs that have appeared
in the path of birth are sung with a different sense. This gives, at once, a
thematic recurrence as well as a sense of transformation or plurality of meanings of basic elements. At the moment in which Eyen Zame has been lowered
into the grave the Banzie sing again, Song No. 77, *Nkôl o bele ening* (the
cord holds life). In the two previous instances in which this song was sung
it referred first to the cord upon which sky spider lowered the egg of creation
to the sea and, second, to the umbilical cord which attached all newborns
through their mothers to the first people and the creator gods. In this instance
the cord which held life now holds death, for the reference is to the cords
used to lower the body into the grave.

One also notes a similar kind of persistence *and* transformation in respect
to the Christ figure, Eyen Zame (He Who Sees God). In the process of the
song cycle the names for him change. Early on he is referred to mainly as
Emwan Mot (the Child of Man) or Nganga (the Chief Priest and Guide to the
unseen). But gradually he comes to be referred to more and more as Eyen
Zame or Mwan Nima (Child of the First One) or Onyi Bot (He who ransoms
men). It is evident that this Christlike figure enjoys, no less than Fang themselves, different names of encouragement (*eyôle mebara*), each suitable to
different situations and life circumstances. It is only natural that that pleni-
potentiality of being which Banzie themselves seek should be granted to their
Christ figure.

In subsequent songs, 78-92, besides a number of obango chants we note
a thematic crying out to Zame and his Sister and to Onyi Bot to take pity on
the imprisoned souls of black people. Eyen Zame's imprisonment in a rock
tomb is compared to the plight of the souls of all blacks. Song No. 92 is a
song of triumph by Eyen Zame as he obtains release from the tomb.

92. *Ebôt be nga bôme bisô na me se ki Zame: Be dege, be dege ane me
ke. Zame ye Mebege a bele ening engura. Me ke ezen jôp. Me ke
ezen Zame* (repeat).

The people who were skeptical that I was Zame: Let them look as
I go. Zame ye Mebege has all of life. I go on the path to the sky.
I go on the path of Zame.

This song of triumphant ascent is accompanied by the rising of the ngombi
harp from the seated position in which it is normally played. The harpist
shakes slightly as he gets up. The membership rises with him and, following
the harp, faces around in the four directions.

Though Eyen Zame may have arisen, the souls of black people are still
trapped, and subsequent songs, until No. 103, continue to plead for their
release from the rocky cavern. Song No. 103 is a triumphant song of celebration, for the black souls are now released and pass to heaven.

103. *Minsutimibot mi kang ejop kômbô oh! Benyaboro be kang edzal
     bô. Minsutimibot mi ye yene Zame. Oh!*
     Black people have departed for the sky. Oh creator Black people
     have departed for the sky. Oh. The elders have departed for their
     village. Black people will see Zame. Oh!

The songs following, Nos. 104-106, continue to celebrate the release by Eyen
Zame of the souls of black people.

By this point in the path of death dawn will be perceptible over the eastern
forest. It is time to conclude the engosie, for the rising sun who is Zame
should not shine upon the engosie which belongs to Nyingwan Mebege. Song
No. 107 is one of the most beautiful in the repertoire and also one of the best
known. It marks the beginning of the concluding phases of the engosie.

107. *Onyibot a bô okan. Tara Zame a bô ôkan. Oh Zame Oh. A bô
     ôkan. Mbamba môt a bô ôkan. Oh Zame Oh.*
     He who has ransomed people has remained undefiled by sex. Father
     Zame. He is undefiled. The good man is undefiled. Oh Zame Oh.

While the song sings ostensibly of the celibate existence of Onyi Bot, at the
same time it testifies to the undefiled condition of Banzie themselves who
have passed the entire night in sacrifice of sexual congress. *Ôkan* was traditionally the condition of sexual purity maintained by hunters and warriors
and cultivators before arduous or uncertain action in order to bring good luck
and success. In the wider sense, then, *a bô ôkan* means to have obtained good
luck, success, and blessing by self-discipline and self-denial.

This song really marks the end of the engosie within the chapel. And though
the concluding nine songs are classed as path of death songs by Banzie they
are all sung in various stages of exit from the chapel. Song Nos. 108-112
take the membership out into the courtyard and village and even into the
forest to announce "the good news." Song No. 108 is very similar to Song
No. 32 in the path of birth and is an example of transformation of a thematic

element. Looking back at No. 32 we find it celebrating the coming into the chapel of the spirits of the dead and the promise of fertility, specifically the birth of Emwan Mot, that they bring with them. While singing this song in the path of birth all the women exit to dance around the otunga welcoming hut. Then they dance back into the chapel. Here is that song.

32. *Oh. Oh. Mora nking (ensama nen) wa sô adzal. Oh Nyingwan Mebege. Nking a ne mbembe. Mora nking wa sô mang ayat ndendang.*
Oh a great crowd of spirits come from the village of the dead. Oh Nyingwan Mebege. The crowd is everlasting. The great crowd comes from beyond the sea of light.

In Song No. 108, on the other hand, the same great crowd of spirits appears again but returns now beyond the sea to the great light.

108. *Mora nking wa bulan mang ayat ye Endendang oh. Mora nking a kang ye muya. Mora nking a kang.*
The great crowd of spirits returns beyond the sea to the great light oh! The great crowd has departed amidst lamentations. The great crowd has departed.

The actions are very similar to those of Song No. 32. The women exit with candles, whirling out into the courtyard to carry the news throughout the forest of the release of black peoples' spirits. Also, as in No. 32, the ngombi harp ceases to play and the women sing unaccompanied. Often the men, carrying torches, circulate around the women in a much larger circle to drive away any evil.

As the song concludes, the dance continues, the membership humming and all joined together to circle around the otunga hut. They finally kneel before it to say farewell to the ancestors. There are three songs that may be sung at this time. All celebrate the arrival of Mwan Nima and the crowd of ancestral dead either above or beyond the sea. As we have seen, both above and beyond are interchangeable vectors of Bwiti worship.

Just as *a bo okan* expresses the metaphysical achievement of sexual purity, Song No. 111 expresses the acquisition of another kind of metaphysical or superordinate view of life. It expresses the achievement of a markedly above and beyond perspective.

111. *Ma ke yen ane besaint be vwing endama. Ma ke yen. Ma ke wé. Ma ke yen.*
I will see how the saints play ball (with the earth). I am going there. I am going to see!

The explanation given is that the earth, with all its passionate struggles which people take so seriously, is just a ball which the saints playfully contest.[14] This is the kind of Archimedean perspective, beyond and above, which is one of the main promises which Bwiti makes to its members who feel themselves wandering, here and below, lost in the earthly thicket.

After the crowd of ancestral spirits has been dispatched along with Eyen Zame to the land of the dead, the ngombi harp, the voice of Nyingwan Mebege and the sacred instrument of the night must be put away into its special light-tight chamber at the end of the village. In order to achieve okan, male and female must not have sexual congress during the all-night ceremonies. In the same way the male orb, the sun, should not be allowed to shine upon the female principle, the harp which belongs to the moon. There are four songs which are sung for the putting away of the harp. They begin with No. 112.

> 112. *Ngombi e ntô mbamba étô. A taraoo! A sumena. A bobedzang e*
> *ntô mbamba etô. Mbamba etô mbembe.*
> The harp has come to a good place. It begins, it starts up (in its
> true place). Brothers and sisters, it has come to a good place, a
> good place forever.

But, of course, it is not only the ngombi that has come to its good place forever. This is also the achievement of each Banzie whose body is represented in the harp.

The final song of the dawn, No. 116 in the Kougouleu-Kwakum song sequence, may be sung once again back in the chapel as the Banzie return to gather up their belongings. Or it may be sung in final njimba where men and women come together for the morning meal. It is a rapid and very beautiful responsorial of very brief verses. As they sing this the men and women, in two lines on either side of the chapel, dance with rattle and brush. First they shake the rattle and brush to one side and then to the other. Then jumping one foot forward they shake to the below and one foot back they shake to the above. Then joining in a long line they shake to the central fire.

116.

Eboga zôm za kwing minsung.	(My body like) a leaf package of eboga (pounded food) has come out into the courtyard of understanding.
Eboga mwan zame a kwing minsung. Eboga!	The eboga of the child of Zame has reached the courtyard of understanding. Eboga!
A tara Zame me kwing adzal!	Father Zame I arrive at the village.
Tara Zame ye Mebege (Response) *Eboga zôm*	Father Zame ye Mebege. The package of eboga.
Me sane me nlem (mesane me nen) Eboga zôm	I jump with joy in my heart (a great satisfaction). The package of eboga.

Me vak me nlem (mevak me nen) *Eboga zôm*	I rejoice in my heart (a great rejoicing). The package of eboga.
Me bune me nlem (mebune me nen) *Eboga zôm*	I have conviction in my heart (a great conviction). The package of eboga.
Me kuliya zôm Eboga zôm	I have opened the package. The package of eboga.
Dzé e na zôm Eboga zôm	What is in that package? The package of eboga.
Me yeneya eya Eboga zôm	I see nothing! (for the soul has departed) The package of eboga.
Ndo zôm e ne mvé Eboga zôm	For the package is good. The package of eboga.
Me kang edjop Eboga zôm	I am going to the sky. The package of eboga.

This joyous song and dance is figuratively a complete catechism of what has been accomplished in the engosie—a catechism expressed in three central images of Bwiti: the leaf package of pounded food,*² the heart, and the path. The leaf package has been opened up, untied, so that it can be consumed by Zame, the heart has been made to rejoice and have confidence in its several ways, and the path around obstacles has been discovered which avoids ambushes and imprisonment and leads to the above and the beyond. Altogether for Fang Bwiti an apt set of images upon which to end the engosie.

STAGES OF THE LITURGY

The song and dance cycle as discussed above enables us to outline the liturgical scenario of Bwiti.

I. *Preparatory*

1. *Minkin* entrance songs and dances. These come in three phases, usually at 3 p.m., 6 p.m., and the final minkin after the njimba at 8:30

---

*² The leaf package metaphor (zom) emerges frequently in Bwiti sermons. The leaf package referred to here, we should further add, is the leaf package of pounded food such as manioc (mbo) or plantain or yams. In this case it is powdered eboga. This package contrasts with the packages of solid foods (game or fish) called mvua. The aptness of this image lies in its reference to the pounding of the body in the all-night ceremonies which reduces it to its spiritual fundaments. There is occasional reference in Bwiti to Nyingwan Mebege wielding the pestle of Bwiti upon the membership in the mortar which is the chapel (mbekh aba). The image is also apt because it makes reference to Bwiti worries that black people are held prisoner, tied in leaf packages as it were, and unable to commune with Zame. But in the case here, instead of consuming deity in communion, Bwiti opens the package and enables deity to consume the Banzie. Finally, this song is apt as the concluding song because shortly, in the morning njimba, the Banzie are going to be having a communal meal of pounded foods.

p.m. The minkin songs refer, generally, to cosmogonic events. Overall they are understood as invitations to the ancestral host to enter the chapel.

2. *Njimba* gathering of the entire membership generally occurring between 7 p.m. and 8:30 p.m. and from 7 a.m. to 8:30 a.m. These are ceremonies of foregathering and preparation and aftergathering and fellowship. In the evening personal prayers are heard in the njimba and ritual garments and ritual body decoration are arranged. In the morning a communal meal of pounded tubers is shared.

II. *The Path of the Harp (Zen Ngômbí)*

3. The path of birth and beginning (*Zen Abiale Disumba*). These are the songs and dances celebrating the origins of men and women and the birth of the spirit in the person of Emwan Mot (the Child of Man who is the Bwiti Christ figure) into this world. These songs and dances are interspersed with obango chants.

III. *The Midnight Interlude*

4. Prayer Songs and nlem mvore (oneheartedness). Prayer songs to the gathered ancestors take place at midnight, followed by a procession out into the forest to invite any lingering spirits. Unification of membership follows within the chapel.

5. *Nkobo akyenge* (miraculous words). The brief, highly figurative sermons given by the head of the chapel.

6. *Yombo* songs. The special women's birth and creation songs are sung in the women's chamber.

IV. *The Path of the Harp*

7. *The path of death* (Destruction and New Creation [*Zen Awu-Kombi*]). Songs and dances interspersed with obango from 1 to 6 a.m. Celebrates the death of Eyen Zame and his rising above as Onyi Bot, releasing with him the imprisoned ancestors.

V. *Conclusion*

8. *Minkin* exit songs. These exit songs, farewell to the ancestors and farewell to the harp (the voice of the Sister of God) are often included in the path of death. The ngombi harp is danced out to its special chamber. Women and men may perform "oneheartedness" in nearby streams.

9. *Njimba* reunion of the entire membership in a "réjouissance." Banzie men and women partake of a communal meal of manioc and plantain foods.

This is the obvious way to organize the particulars of the liturgical cycle but it is not usually the organization of the engosie given by Banzie when put to the question. They prefer to speak of the engosie as properly a three-day celebration: *Efun* engosie, *Nkong* engosie, and *Mesoso* or *Meyaya* engosie. And usually an elaborate description is given of these three engosie.

Efun engosie. The name refers to the uninhabited or abandoned spot in the forest where those lost or hunting or returning to old plantations spend the night. This is an engosie of purification, for the forest is pure. On this night Banzie wash themselves with the bark of the pure and powerful trees of the forest. But it is a night when Banzie are also regretful (*zôba*). It is a disagreeable engosie, for Banzie are not sure they can find the path. They may be lost. They are in a black and obscure state (*envin*). The forest is pure but men's sins confuse them. This is also the engosie for the preparation of creation. Rituals create the earth at otunga and the first man is created at the large fire in the center of the chapel so that things begin to emerge out of confusion and isolation.[15] These two rituals are the only ones that should be performed this evening. Afterwards the members remain to sleep in the chapel.

Nkong engosie. This is the midpath engosie (from nkong, the distance on a path between two rivers).[16] It is also called *ezizang zen* (the middle of the path). The universe is in turmoil on the way to a new order. The sky has separated from the earth, the sun from the moon, and the stars from each other. God above has separated from God below. That is why the chapel is full of fires, torches, and candles. The separation is seen in the singing of the harp and the chanting of the obango. The oil palm (*alen*) is the tree of this engosie, for the path, like its bark, is rough and spiny yet there is a delectable core and the joyful promise of palm nuts high in the tree. In this engosie the Banzie feel themselves to be on the path, and making their way through the thicket. But it is a painful path yet. Whereas in Efun, one's clothes are black and dirty, here Banzie don red clothes. They say: "We have split open our obscure and sinful body and discovered the red heart beneath."

Meyaya engosie. The last evening of the three-night cycle is meyaya (or mesoso) and everything is now fresh and clean. The path in between the two rivers has been trod. The ancestor spirits are fully descended, prepared to carry the Banzie over to *mang ayat*. This is an engosie of full light (*endendang*). Banzie say, "Whereas we were as a cup turned over upon the earth [*elas osi*] we are now turned up to be filled with the above [*abôra ôyô*]." Everything that was complicated and difficult in Nkong engosie becomes very simple. Instead of struggling over the ground "Banzie can now lie flat upon it and rise to the above."[17] Banzie say: "This is the engosie of tranquillity (*mvwaa*). We have triumphed over the cold loneliness and isolation (*engoégoé*) of Efun and the turbulent confusion (*ngamla*) of Nkong.

Though Banzie prefer to talk about the sequence of events by reference to three engosies moving from the qualities of cold and inert isolation through turbulent confusion to final spiritual tranquillity, it will be seen that every engosie undergoes much the same progression as it moves in from the njimba of the first minkin, the njimba of the forest, along the path of birth and death to the final state of okan and the tranquil goodheartedness of the final morning njimba.

THE RITUAL CALENDAR

In some branches of Bwiti there is no ritual calendar beyond the weekly engosies. These may be in abatement during the summer cool dry season (ôyôn) because of much journeying around typical of Fang. Of course there will be the occasional three-day engosies held around the initiation and death of a member. But most branches, and most committedly Asumege Ening, have a yearly calendar. Here again there are differences among the various chapels in what they recognize as that calendar. In some it is nothing more than the Fête Abiale (ceremonies of birth taking place around Christmas time) and the Fete Awu (ceremonies of death taking place around Easter).

The following calendar is one in general use in Asumege Ening. Here there are six main festivals with a seventh optional festival in the midsummer dry season. These festivals correlate with the Christian calendar except that the Bwiti year, as the old Fang year, begins in late September with the cool rainy season (*sugu esep*). Many chapels are content to follow the Christian calendar feast days but for Asumege Ening an appropriate relationship to the four Fang seasons is overridingly important, as the table on the next page shows.

CONCLUSION: CATEGORIES COLLAPSED AND BENEVOLENTLY REALIGNED

The leaders of Bwiti, the nima na kombo, the yemba, yombo, the guardians of the chapel, the nganga and the beti ngombi are all granted in the context of the ceremonies as much if not more authority as any possessed by traditional Fang ritual figures. It is a less transitory, less context-bound authority than that of traditional figures. Of course the leaders of Fang Bwiti are still Fang and they must still struggle, as we have seen, to attract and hold together a membership. Disgruntled younger members, if they do not directly contest the leaders' position in Bwiti society, frequently enough question their religious imagination and their understanding of the meaning of Bwiti. In a religion as richly cosmologic, as fertile in syncretisms and the production of apt and resonant images, and as readily exegetical as Bwiti, such questions easily arise. And such questions can be used as an attack upon the leader's authority. Still, by the "miracle," the amazements of surpassing skillfulness in ritual organization and explanation most leaders can acquire and justify unusual amounts of authority for Fang. It may be one of the most interesting consequences of contact with Metsogo.

But perhaps the more important consequence of contact with Metsogo "amazements" is the stirring up of the Fang religious imagination. To a high degree these dramatic ceremonies confound the ordinary categories of experience. We find in them a liminal atmosphere in which the dead are suddenly again the living, animals are yet men, seedlings are suddenly mature trees,

FESTIVAL	TIME	PURPOSE
Olorogebot (St. Michael)	End of Sept. at beginning of cool rainy season (*sugu oyon*) late Sept. to Dec.	Celebrates the discovery of the path through the thicket to the beyond and the above. 3 days.
Bewu (also called All Saints)	In mid-*sugu oyon* early in November.	Celebrates the ingathering of all the souls of the dead. 3 days.
Abiale Emwan Mot (Christmas)	At the end of *sugu oyon* and the beginning of *esep* (hot dry season, end December).	Celebrates the birth of Emwan Mot (the Child of Man). 3 days.
Awu Emwan Mot (Easter)	At the end of *esep* (mid to late March) and the beginning of *sugu esep* (the hot rainy season).	Celebrates the death of the Child of Man. 6 days.
Kumba (Ascension)	At the beginning of the hot rainy season (April).	Celebrates the passing of Eyen Zame (He Who Sees God) over the sea, taking with him the imprisoned souls of black people. The festival often called "The Founder of the Fang Race." 3 days.
Madebo Etsenge	At the end of sugu esep (early June) and beginning of oyon (the cool dry season).	The purpose is to bring eboga to earth—to make it tranquil until September.
Nana Nyepe or Nyingwan Mebege (Assumption)	In mid-*oyon* in August.	Occasionally when Banzie feel the need for a festival in the long, cool dry season they celebrate Nana Nyepe in honor of the sister of Zame. An optional festival dedicated to She who is the object of attention of every engosie. 3 days.

and whitemen are really blackmen or vice versa. Things are confused, lose their categories—Metsogo "miracles" make things "amazingly ambiguous." As Metsogo Bwiti procedes, these ambiguities, as a matter of course, are resolved and reclassified by the potent manifestations of the ancestors, the living dead. In a manner of speaking, after the stimulating ambiguities of the "miracles," men and women are lined up again in genealogical allegiance. They are placed upon the path of birth and death.

There is plenty of evidence that these "amazing ambiguities" excited the imagination of Fang and Fang Bwiti spectators. Time and again Metogo and Muye would recall their own visits to Metsogo Bwiti. But the point is that the excitement of collapsing categories also opened up the possibility of religious creativity, of recategorization and reconstruction. These Metsogo rituals were not mere trickery. They were edifying. This edification is present in pronounced degree in Fang Bwiti which attempts, like Metsogo, miraculously to collapse categories while at the same time it steps back from the abyss of misunderstanding implicit in such collapse by lining up "miraculous things" along the path of birth and death. Indeed it was a "miracle" of leadership in "knowledgeable ones" when they could both excite by collapsing categories while they lined up participants in an orderly progression with benevolent consequences.

Traditional authority that was enduring among Fang rested, for the most part, on how well it assured those who agreed to be followers that it was working benevolently and protectively in the interests of the kin group. And this is so for the authority of Bwiti leaders. It is assured to the degree that Banzie feel satisfaction in their ritual experience. That satisfaction can have several sources. If Banzie are asked why they have joined Bwiti and work so hard through the night worshiping in it they will generally respond that Bwiti enables them to see the ancestors, to communicate with them and receive blessings from them. In the more Christian chapels they will speak of seeing Eyen Zame, the ancestor of us all, and receiving blessings from him. There are other reasons frequently given: "to enable our spirits to escape our bodies which have held them prisoner"; to make "one person" or "one heart" out of the many persons and the many clans that come to join into Bwiti. The engosie should make the body "feel like a silk shirt through which the spirit can easily pass."

So the expectations Banzie have of the pounding excitements of the engosie are various. Is it leading them to tread the path of birth and death so as to pass over above and beyond and come to know the ancestral dead? Is it opening them up to greater forces of the universe? Is it taking the many and making them into the one? Leaders of Bwiti have elaborated a complex body of experience by which to satisfy these expectations. In this chapter we have been looking at the backbone of the body of Bwiti, namely the night-long song and dance cycle and more centrally,[18] the path of the harp. It is a path that moves by various forms of synesthesia from birth to death, from black through red to white, from the imprisonment of ancestral spirits to their release, from despair and isolation to community and tranquillity. It is a path that reveals many apt images from Fang tradition and many subtle syncretisms with the legends and history of Christianity as conveyed by missionaries. Bwiti leaders with such ritual tools at their command may easily use them to become convincingly benevolent, clearly qualified to lead their despairing fellows down the path of birth and death.

⁓18⁓

Equatorial Excursions:
The Quest for Revitalizing Dreams
and Visions

Za' kulu mbí awu.
(Come open the door of death.)

THE NEW LIFE OF OYANA NDUTUMU

WHEN OYANA NDUTUMU made up her mind that she wished to become a member of Bwiti the leaders of the chapel at Assok Ening asked why. She was a daughter of the village, the sister of a man who had long been a Banzie. She had just been sent back from her second marriage and her family was in turmoil trying to gather the bridepayment they were obliged to return. She replied that she hoped that Bwiti would enable her to make a successful marriage and to have children. In part her two divorces came, she said, because she was a nervous woman and infertile.

That evening the membership held a ceremony to "put the question," to find out from Bwiti whether the woman was a sorcerer and thus inadmissible or whether she had strength enough to eat eboga and to see Bwiti. Banzie only very occasionally died in initiation from an overdose of eboga but it was just such deaths that brought missionary reaction and administrative repression. So at midnight the membership filed out with candles in their hands to the forest to the spot where an *ôtunga* sapling had been located. It was pulled out of the ground without difficulty, a good sign that Bwiti was in favor of the initiation. Also that night the *nima na kômbô* ate large amounts of eboga in order to "talk" with the ancestors. He received no objections from them. So at the first hour, at dawn, after the engosie, the woman was brought to the chapel and admitted to initiation.

The first spoonful of eboga is given at 9 a.m. The initiate was seated in the front of the chapel close to the central pillar looking inward toward the altar. Before her on a *môsingi* skin (the skin of the wildcat *esinga*) was placed a basket full of eboga. Two members of the chapel, male and female, were assigned to be her father and mother of eboga (*essa ebôga, nyia ebôga*). Before midday they had urged upon her sixteen teaspoons of eboga. At midday the antelope horn is blown as a first alert to the ancestors that a descendant is coming among them. By 3 p.m. the initiate had consumed sixteen more teaspoons of eboga and was taken to the stream for initiation.

As Oyana was a slight woman I expressed concern to the kambo, the supervisor of ritual activity who was directing the initiation, about the possibility of an overdose. But Ona Pastor replied that no man or woman would *ku ebôga* (fall under the spell of eboga) in less than thirty teaspoons and it often took sixty teaspoons to swell the soul on the tendons and veins of the body so that it could break free and journey off to Bwiti. When the soul begins to expand, he said, the skin begins to feel like a silk shirt which will easily burst and allow the soul to escape. The father and mother of eboga were, in any case, keeping careful track of the initiate's condition in this respect.

Preceded by the *ngômbí*, the initiation procession made its way down to the stream. The initiate (*etema*, Popi, or *ebín*, Fang) was followed by her mother and father of eboga and by the director of initiation and his assistant. In final place came an old woman proffering a plate full of eboga. The procession made its way into the deep forest to a glade where the stream widened. The walking made the initiate sick from the eboga she had consumed and she had to be allowed to vomit before purification could proceed. This worried the Banzie present, for if she could not stomach eboga she would not "see" Bwiti. In any case it would simply lengthen the time before she would see it. The director of initiation ran his finger through the ejecta to see if there was any blood or evil substance, but none was found.

When she had recovered herself she was led into the stream and up beyond a bend by her mother and father of eboga to confess her sins. She was there stripped to the waist. Periodically the voice of the father of eboga would be raised beyond the intervening trees, remarking on a particular sin. Meanwhile the various leaves and powders of initiation were laid out on a leaf upon the bank. After the confession was over the father and mother of eboga waded back to get the plants of purification. The father took back a mixture of flowers and leaves of the plant called by Fang *myan* (*Costus lucanusianus*). In Bwiti it is called by the Pongwe term *ôkosakosa*. The mother took the leaves of the *abômenzan* plant (*Piper umbellatum*). Both of these plants give off a strong perfume. The father of eboga first chewed the myan and spat it out upon the initiate. He then washed her down with stream water. This was to purify her and open her eyes so that she would see Bwiti. Then the mother rubbed her down with abomenzan. The odor of this plant was attractive to the spirit of the dead and to Bwiti and would excite them to have pity and take interest in the plight of the initiate.

The father of eboga now returned downstream to obtain the final packet of powdered bark which he handed to the mother of eboga. The initiate, stripped entirely naked, was rubbed down with this bark powder. This powder was a mixture from the bark of twelve trees (one was actually a forest bush). They were named to the initiate one by one. They were described as good and pure trees, well regarded by the ancestors and all of important medicinal use. "Learn these trees!" the initiate was admonished, for they are the "forest of Bwiti" (*afan Bwiti*). Because of her infertility Oyana had once attempted to be cured in an MBiri ceremony, the curing cult collateral to Bwiti. The director of initiation therefore took the occasion to tell her, "Remember that Bwiti is a religion of trees (*nyiba bile*) while MBiri is a religion of herbs and plants (*nyiba bilawk*)." The twelve trees from which the barks were taken were: *asam* (*Kapaca guineensis*), the "palétuvier," *eyen* (*Distmananthus benthamianus*), *azap* (*Mimusops djave*), *ôvung* (*Guibourtia Tessmannii*), *azem* (*Psilanthemus manii*), *mfôl* (*Enantia chlorantha*), *eteng* (*Pycnanthus angolensis*), *aseng* (*Musanga acropioides*), the *ôtunga* umbrella tree (*Polyalthia suaveolens*), *mbel* (*Pterocarpus soyauxii*), *asas* (*Bridelia grandis*), and *adzam ntoma* called *elegalenga* (*Ocimum americanum*), the plant added to the mix to give it a perfume.

Though eight of these trees were those customarily sacred to Bwiti, four were unusual. But no special explanation was given. No one, said the kambo, knew the exact number of trees in the forest of Bwiti. In fact the membership had debated as to whether there were to be twelve or thirteen trees. They had settled on twelve barks as being the midnight number, the hour in which Bwiti would come to the initiate.

After being rubbed down with these barks the initiate donned her white dress of initiation and returned to the glade. Her father and mother of eboga stood spreadlegged in the stream. Oyana Ndutumu got down in the water and crawled through their legs. This represented her birth in Bwiti. The director of initiation then stepped into the stream and struck the initiate over the head with the large phallic-shaped flower of the parasol tree (*zôseng aseng*). There had been some joking about the phallic shape of this flower while descending to the stream. But the purpose of the action was to open the woman's head again, as it was when she was an infant, so that her soul might escape. Her mother and father of eboga followed suit in striking her head.

Finally, with only the initiate left in the water the director of initiation went 15 or 20 feet upstream and lit a cube of pitch on a manioc leaf. Gently placing the leaf in the water he floated it down through the woman's legs. All watched as, still alight, the "soul boat" (*byal nsisim*) disappeared around a bend on its way to the ancestors in the sea (*mang*). In a like manner, later in the initiation, the woman's soul would drift off to the ancestors, but in an opposite direction.

The initiate was brought to the bank and given eleven more teaspoonfuls of eboga. The procession back to the chapel reformed. The initiate, now quite rubber-legged, had to be helped up the hill. The procession circled the chapel once, the central pillar once, and then stopped just before the chapel. The otunga sapling that had been pulled up in the forest was now planted just in front of the chapel. All Banzie present aided in tamping down the earth around the plant. The otunga was to be the ladder by which the spirit of the initiate would mount to heaven. A chicken was then sacrificed at the otunga. The chicken would go to heaven and announce the coming of the spirit.

As it was still a long time until the commencement of the engosie, at 9 p.m., the initiate was taken off to a special chamber where she continued to eat eboga. At 10 p.m., now virtually comatose, she was brought out before the altar to face the harp. Propping her up, her father and mother of eboga listened carefully to her mumblings. It was apparent that she was having a visionary experience—that she was "seeing Bwiti." But the specifics of her vision could not be communicated or elaborated until the next morning when she had recovered from her narcotic inebriation to begin her "new life." At that time she claimed to have traveled up the path of birth and death and seen her dead grandmother who took her over a crossroads in which a red road intersected with a black one. Not far beyond she found herself in a great crowd of voices. One in particular repeated insistently what she took to be her new Banzie name, Nanga Misenge. She heard or saw nothing more.

THE EATING OF EBOGA

In important part the initiation experiences of Oyana Ndutumu (and of all Banzie) are stimulated by the large amounts of eboga ingested. "Eboga" or "eboka" is the Fang name for *Tabernanthe iboga*. The species name as well as the Fang name is taken from the Galwa-Mpongwe or Miene language term, *iboga*. The bush, which occurs in at least two varieties (*T. iboga* and *T. manii*—not always distinguished botanically and apparently of similar psychotropic qualities), is common in the equatorial underforest. Its psychotropic properties have long been known,[1] particularly its capacity, in small quantities, to maintain wakefulness and confer resistance to fatigue. This may have induced German colonial authorities to allow the use of the drug by Africans building colonial roads and railroads in the Cameroons at the turn of the century.[2] Indeed the capacity of the plant to suppress fatigue—quite

[1] In his "Sketch of Gabon and Its Interior," Edward Bowditch mentions the "eroga" under fetish plants. It is a "favorite but violent medicine" which he took to be a charred fungus since he probably saw it in its powdered state (*Mission to Cape Coast Castle and Ashantee*, p. 445). French explorers knew it in mid-century and Griffon du Bellay brought specimens back from Cape Lopez ("Le Gabon"). The plant was investigated intensively after the turn of the century by the French. Raponda-Walker and Sillans give a bibliography of this French work (*Rites et croyances des peuples du Gabon*, pp. 89-91).

[2] The Germans became interested in the drug in the 1880's when references to it appear in the reports of District Officers from Kamerun in *Mitteilungen aus den Deutschen Schutzgebieten* (in particular, Vol. I, 1888, p. 49). In Volume XI of this colonial journal (1898, p. 29) the instrumental value of the root is recognized: "Its exciting effect on the nervous system makes

apart from its capacity to produce visions—has been a principal attraction to Banzie. They must dance all night and hence they value the euphoric insomnia produced by the drug. So important is eboga that in some chapels the members are not called banzie but *nziebôga* (eaters of eboga). And the usual form of asking why a Banzie joined Bwiti is to ask him why he ate eboga. Indeed in some chapels there is a pervasive synecdoche in which eboga is taken for the whole—it is eboga that is prayed to and sung to and not Bwiti or any of the gods or ancestors.

The eboga bush, an apocynaceous shrub, grows to about four feet in height. It is cultivated in the open courtyards of Bwiti villages, usually at the sides of the chapel and the ancestral welcoming hut. It produces yellowish or pinkish-white flowers and a small orange fruit whose sweet pulp is edible though not narcotic. In Bwiti the fruit is sometimes used as a medicine for barrenness in women. The main alkaloid[1]—ibogaine—is contained in the roots and particularly in the root bark. The mode of consumption in Bwiti maximizes access to the alkaloid. The root bark is rasped and eaten directly as raspings or ground as a powder or left to soak in water to be drunk as an infusion.

Eboga was the psychotropic drug of choice in Metsogo Bwiti whereas in the Fang ancestral cult, Bieri, two *different* narcotics were employed: *malan* (*Alchornea floribunda*) and *ayang beyem* (*Elaeophorbia drupifera*).[2] We have seen how Bwiti origin legends credit the discovery of eboga either to the Pygmies (they may actually be the source of the drug for all equatorial peoples), or to the intervention of the ancestors, or the great gods. In point of fact the extensive use of eboga in Fang Bwiti diffused to them from the Metsogo.

The Metsogo claim to be surprised by the casual use of eboga by Fang and are not surprised to hear that death results. Before giving large amounts of eboga to initiates Metsogo test them out with small amounts first "to see if they can support the drug or if they have evil spirits which will use the drug as an excuse to kill their host." Metsogo also claim to watch over the initiate much more closely in the process of initiation. But in Fang Bwiti, the mother and father of eboga (roles, it appears, taken over from Metsogo) provide very close supervision.[3]

Eboga is taken in two ways. (1) At each engosie it is swallowed in small doses of two to three teaspoonfuls for women and three to five teaspoonfuls for men before and in the early hours of the ceremony. There may be an additional several grams eaten at mid-course, after midnight. This represents

its use highly valued on long tiring marches, on lengthy canoe trips, and on difficult nightwatches." Old informants in northern Gabon, formerly German Kamerun, say that the use of eboga was permitted, if not encouraged, by the Germans in their work gangs and colonial projects such as the Douala-Yaounde railroad. See J. W. Fernandez, "Symbolic Consensus in a Fang Reformative Cult."

ingestion of between four and twenty grams of powdered eboga. (2) Once or twice in the career of a Banzie a massive dose of eboga is taken for purposes of initiation and to "break open the head" in order to effect contact with the ancestors through collapse and hallucination. One to three small basketfuls may be consumed at this time over an eight to twenty-four hour period. This represents an ingestion of between two hundred and one thousand grams, up to sixty times the threshold dose and, in the upper reaches, close to a fatal dose. Though the range between threshold and fatal toxicity in the alkaloids is great, it is not surprising that the death of initiates is commented upon in all chapels. In the past forty years a dozen charges of murder or manslaughter have been brought against Bwiti leaders who have lost initiates. The effect of such high dosages can last up to a week and for that reason Banzie say they can only tolerate this dosage once or twice in a lifetime.

The lighter regular dosage of two to five teaspoons does not produce hallucinations, though adepts of Bwiti claim that once a man has "met eboga" and been taken by "him" to the "other side," any subsequent amount will raise in his mind many of his former experiences. The regular dosage, therefore, may have that associative power, but it is taken primarily to enable the adepts to engage in the arduous all-night ceremonies without fatigue. Members often say that the eboga taken in this way also lightens their bodies so that they can float through their ritual dances. It enables them to mingle more effectively with the ancestors at the roof of the chapel. They do not report visions under the influence of such amounts, only modest change in body perception and some dissociation.

The massive doses taken at initiation produce both physical and perceptual changes—such things as a gross reduction in the initiate's ability to moderate or program motor activity, the appearance of chromatic spectrum on the margin of objects in the perceptual field, and a sense of "objectivity" or distancing from one's own body. This latter is a crucial sensation as far as Banzie are concerned. It is evidence of the beginning of the visionary excursion as well as of the rising to the ancestors at the roof of the chapel. But practically all physiological and perceptual consequences of eboga are given meaning in Bwiti.

Early in the day of initiation the initiates are allowed to rise and evacuate when they wish. Several hours into the initiation, as we have seen, they are taken down to a stream to be purified in preparation for their meeting with the ancestors. As ingestion of the drug proceeds the initiates rise no more. They sit upon their white cloth gazing expectantly toward the rear of the chapel and continuing to eat eboga heaped upon the civet-cat skin between their legs. They may gaze with fascination upon a mirror propped before them in those chapels which employ this device. In it their ancestors may seem to appear to them, though they are actually seeing their own faces perceived under the influence of eboga. Behind them sit their mothers or fathers of eboga, calming their anxieties and listening carefully to their excited mumblings as the eboga works upon them. They may already be experiencing a sense of departure from self and of visionary encounter. Their mumblings may convey important information to the entire membership.

Eventually the initiate will fall over and have to be supported and carried from the chapel to a special chamber within it or to a special hut or arena behind it. Being initiated and eating eboga is often called "sitting down" or "getting down" to the earth. All members of Bwiti have to "get down." The final stage of that process is collapse. The collapse is an indication that the initiate's soul has left him and in the company of the ancestors is wending its way through the forest to a final and confirming vision in the land beyond— the land of the dead.

The phrase "wending through the forest" describes the visionary experience of practically all initiates. For the forest is experienced first, whatever subsequent elements may appear. The visions thus confirm the fact frequently emphasized by Bwiti leaders that Bwiti is a religion of the forest (*nyiba ye afan*). It also explains why eboga, a plant of the forest, represents something beyond itself—it represents the forest and power over the forest. Banzie take the forest unto themselves in many ways, but most fundamentally and powerfully in the eating of eboga; it gives them both an identification with and mastery over the forest. Amidst the pressures upon Fang in the colonial world to leave the forest, to abandon their villages and launch themselves upon the arteries of commerce and wage labor, this powerful powder of the forest returns Banzie to that milieu in a meaningful way.[4]

EBOGA VISIONS

Dreams did not play a meaningful role in Fang life.[5] In initiation into the ancestral cult, however, visions were cultivated, and the dreams which took place after initiation as men slept close to the reliquary were studied carefully. In Bwiti the visions which accompany initiation and the eating of massive amounts of eboga are always elicited by leaders and interpreted for the adequacy of the experience, the acceptability of the initiate to the spirits and great gods, and the future role of the initiate in the religion. An eboga name is usually given in the vision as well as, very often, a religious specialty such as the playing of the harp or the guarding of the chapel. The eboga visions are an important part of the "breaking open of heads" (*abwing nlo*) and the opening up of the Banzie to the fuller possibilities of self and of universe which Bwiti promises.

More than sixty open-ended discussions were held with individual members of the religion concerning both their reasons for joining and the nature of their initiation. Fifty of these discussions contain reliable information on the initiation experience. Thirty-eight vision experiences or lack of experiences were reported. Twelve members of a particularly secretive chapel were reluctant to discuss the visions in any way.[6] Twenty-one vision experiences were noted in their entirety. Failure to see visions and refusal to tell them are frequent enough to be honestly reported. Before summarizing the reasons given for eating eboga and the contents of the visions it is instructive to give seven representative visions.

We begin with two visions which were refused. The particular chapel in which the following vision was refused had years before undergone severe repression by colonial authorities and by missionaries. This chapel tended to be wary of imparting any information to anyone. As far as the failure is concerned, our figures show it to be frequent enough in encounters with eboga. Not all initiates are as equable as this particular informant, however, and most would try the initiation again at a later time. Many who found nothing in the plant would leave Bwiti, since so much of its promise hinges upon "going down with eboga."

1. The vision (refused) of Engomo Obama (Zambi Evanga). Age 28, Clan Essabam. A younger brother, with one wife, no children. Has a small cocoa plantation but gets nothing from it. District of Medouneu, Bwiti Chapel at Efulan. Ate eboga two years before.

   REASONS GIVEN: I danced and ate a bit of eboga when I was in Libreville years ago. But I saw very little. But now, recently, my brother became sick in the head. He began telling me to eat the eboga. I ate eboga because the *beyim* (witches) had put thunder (*zalan*) in the head of my brother, and he became a fool. He had already seen the road and was going to become a Banzie. But when the thunder came into his head he said he could no longer see in the eboga. He told me to take it because I should see what he had been looking for. The nima na kombo of our chapel said not to tell what we saw in our vision, because it belongs to us here. But I saw those whom my brother was seeking to see.

2. The failed vision of Nyimeh Ondo (Mendombo). Age 42, Clan Yebingwan. Five wives and four children. District of Mitzik, Bwiti Chapel at Ondondo. Ate eboga eight years ago.

   REASONS GIVEN: I ate eboga at Ondondo. My father of eboga was Mba Ngwe, my mother's younger brother. He kept after me to eat eboga, but I could see no reason to eat it. But finally he convinced me to eat it because I would see something in it and perhaps my mother. I ate only because I wanted to see what was in it. He told me I would have to go to the ground to see. But then I ate the eboga several times and saw nothing. But I have continued to be a Banzie because my heart tells me it has been the right thing even though my head has not been opened. The heart of the Fang is more at home in the music and dance of Bwiti.

The following two visions have the incomplete quality of many that are collected in category 2 below (hearing voices) and particularly category 3 (seeing ancestors). The incompleteness may be a consequence of many factors—quality of the eboga taken, attitude set of the individual and the nature of the guidance he has received from the leaders of the chapel, and so on. But often it is a consequence of the initiate becoming so violently ill that he cannot complete the initiation, although he may still have visions. That is the case in these two accounts. The first account shows, incidentally, how similar delirium in sickness is to eboga hallucinations in the eyes of the Banzie. Their visionary component is essentially the same except that eboga has a therapeutic result.

3. The vision of Mebang Mbe (Ngondo Ekumu). Age 33. Last wife of a Banzie. No children. District of Oyem, Bwiti Chapel at Kwakum.

    REASONS GIVEN AND VISION: For a long time I resisted eating eboga although my husband encouraged me. But when I became very sick and nearly died, my husband decided to transport me to the Chapel at Kwakum. I was in agony and saw a road going through a house. I followed this road a long way to a crossroads, where a man with a great lance stopped me and said, "Where are you going? You are not dead." And he pointed back. I found myself in bed in Kwakum. I remained sick for some weeks and my experience decided me to find the solution to this illness in eboga. But when I took it a year ago I saw only my father and a woman carrying a basin with various herbs. The woman was washed by my father, and my father turned to me and said, "You must return all the things that are in your stomach." I got up and with the help of my mother of eboga went to the river and threw up. I have not been sick since.

4. The vision of Abeso Mungeh (Nzambi Evanga). Age 54, Clan Nkojeng. Has a small coffee plantation. Has three wives and one child. District of Oyem, Bwiti Chapel at Kwakum.

    REASONS GIVEN: I ate eboga here five years ago. I had seen Bwiti in Libreville but I had not danced it. I am a *mimia* (a person without a witch) and I have nothing to protect me, so I decided to eat eboga to see if that way our old people and God would listen to our prayers and grant them. Nothing was coming to me as a Christian.

    VISION: I didn't see much. I traveled a red path and came to a village of one house with one door and one window. Two white men were sitting at either end of a table. They were writing. That was all. I returned then. But I was dissatisfied, so I took a big dose of eboga again and this time I saw my mother and she was surrounded by many people. She died when I was young and I didn't recognize her. But men surrounding her said it was my mother. She came and stood at my right. Another woman came with a child and stood at my left. I reached for the child but she held it away from me. Then I became sick and had to pass out to the edge of the forest to throw up. As I came back I saw a host of small babies laughing and playing together in the air. That was all I saw.

The following five visions, arranged by increasing length and showing some diversity within type, all have those stereotyped features characteristic of category 4 (walk down the long path) which comprises one-fifth of the visions collected. These visions are treated in more detail in our analysis below.

5. The vision of Biyogo Ondo (Zambi Evanga). Age 45, Clan Evon or Nkojeng. Two wives. A planter of four hectares of cocoa and coffee. District of Mimvoul, Bwiti Chapel at Engoen.

   REASONS GIVEN: I worked at Libreville in a shop many years ago and I saw much Bwiti but I never ate eboga. When I returned to Mimvoul seven years ago I ate eboga. I was a man who ought to have been rich in the preparations my father gave to me (akômnge ening). But I have not become rich. Witches closed the path to me. The Banzie, whom I came to consult, told me to eat eboga. For if I ate eboga I would see my father again and he would give me counsel.

   VISION: When I ate eboga I saw my elder brother. He didn't see me or speak to me. Then I next saw another brother, who was not dead, but I saw him there in the eboga. I saw his body on the ground beside the road I traveled. (Two weeks later, that brother died!) This road led to a great desert that had no limit. There my father descended before me in the form of a bird. He would accompany me back. On returning, I saw Christians dressed in animal skins—belts of antelope. They carried heavy crosses around their necks. They were to the left on a path that led off the path we followed. As we returned, my father gave me a ngombi, the harp, and he told me that would guarantee me in my life.

6. The vision of Mve Ndong (Mvanga Abena Mokuku Kanja). Age 36, Clan Efak. Two wives, no children. Coffee planter with four and a half hectares. District of Mitzik. Chapel at Amvan.

   REASONS GIVEN: I have married many women, of whom I have only two now, but I got no children from them. One day after work I was asleep resting, and suddenly in my sleep my mother came from the left of the room and my father from the right. This was when I was working in Libreville some years ago. They asked me why I didn't eat eboga. I responded that it was mad medicine. My mother said no, and she showed me a small leaf package from which she ate eboga. She bid me go to a

certain friend of mine who was a Banzie and have him give me eboga.
Then I ate eboga these three days and three nights. [Interviewed just after
initiation.]

VISION: I started up a red road and passed through a village full of people
whom I heard in their huts crying and wailing. On each side was a hill
with a fine house on each. Beyond the village I came to a river, and three
women were there fishing bones out of that river and placing them on the
bank. I floated across the river, at the other side of which was a crossroads
with three roads: silver, gold, and red. Standing in the center there was
my father. He said, "See where you have arrived with the power of
eboga." I passed through his legs and started up the gold route, which
became brighter and brighter. I came to another crossroads, where I found
the otunga planted. There, under the otunga, the chicken that had been
killed for me when I started eating eboga was alive and scratching. Beyond
the otunga a man was shining on a cross. I knew him from his pictures.
It was Eyen Zame. I passed beneath the cross to a house of glass on a
hill. It was the house of Nyingwan Mebege. Within was my brother. He
was secretary and writing for two men all in white, who sat at either end
of a long table. He was writing my history and my name as a Banzie.
Then my father of eboga called me back, for I should go no farther.

7. The vision of Mendame Nkogo (Ngadi). Age 32. Cocoa planter. One wife,
two children. District of Oyem, Bwiti Chapel at Sougoudzap.

REASONS GIVEN: I was skeptical. The Banzie challenged me, so I decided
to eat eboga. They actually convinced me by giving me three teaspoonfuls.
I felt something. That was several years ago.

VISION: I saw in the mirror that they had set in front of me a great crowd
of black men approach. They were then changed to a great crowd of white
men. I found myself in a garden surrounded by a crowd of people whose
color I do not know. I was surrounded by eboga bushes, and by two
chapels of Bwiti. Then I saw my grandfather at the other end of the garden
in a hollow in the rocks. And I saw myself as a child sitting between his
legs. Then that child which was me changed into a ngombi (the cult harp),
which my grandfather was playing. And now, whenever I play the ngombi
I know it is my grandfather playing through me. My grandfather arose
and took me in something like a plane to the land beyond. He took me
to Nyingwan Mebege. She was a beautiful woman—just a glimpse I had.
She was too beautiful to look at. Then my grandfather showed me again
the ngombi and said that I must play. It would always lead me to another
land and be the route of the Banzie. My grandfather then explained to me
all the parts of the ngombi. At midnight the ngombi is no longer of wood.
Nyingwan Mebege comes into it and it becomes her. Grandfather told me

to look at the sun. It blinded me. I saw a path to Eyen Zame. I knocked against the door but Eyen Zame said I could not enter. This was because I still had black skin. All the dead are white. When I die I will become white like the *ntangan*. My father of eboga saw that I was already gone too long with eboga. He brought me back. He gave me sugar cane to eat. Now whenever I eat eboga, I see or hear my grandfather.

8. The vision of Ndong Asseko (Onwan Misengue). Age 22, Clan Essabam. Not married, he is an "aide-chauffeur" but also plants coffee in his father's village. District of Oyem, Bwiti Chapel at Kwakum. Taken several weeks after initiation.

REASONS GIVEN: Nzambi Evanga Beyogo Ondo mwan Evon gave me the eboga. I was a Christian but I found no truth in it. Christianity is the religion of the whites. It is the whites who have brought us the Cross and the Book. All the things in their religion one hears by the ears. But we Fang do not learn that way. We learn by the eyes, and eboga is the religion that enables us to actually see!

VISION: When I ate eboga I found myself taken by it up a long road in a deep forest until I came to a barrier of black iron. At that barrier, unable to pass, I saw a crowd of black persons also unable to pass. In the distance beyond the barrier it was very bright. I could see many colors in the air but the crowd of black people could not pass. Suddenly my father descended from above in the form of a bird. He gave to me then my eboga name, Onwan Misengue, and enabled me to fly up after him over the barrier of iron. As we proceeded, the bird who was my father changed from black to white—first his tail feathers, then all his plumage. We came then to a river the color of blood, in the midst of which was a great snake of three colors—blue, black, and red. It closed its gaping mouth so that we were able to pass over it. On the other side there was a crowd of people all in white. We passed through them and they shouted at us words of recognition until we arrived at another river, all white. This we crossed by means of a giant chain of gold. On the other side there were no trees but only a grassy upland. On the top of the hill was a round house made entirely of glass and built upon one post only. Within I saw a man. The hair on his head piled up in the form of a bishop's hat! He had a star on his breast, but on coming closer I saw that it was his heart in his chest beating. We moved around him, and on the back of his neck there was a red cross tattooed. He had a long beard. Just then I looked up and saw a woman in the moon—a bayonet was piercing her heart, from which a bright white fire was pouring forth. Then I felt a pain in my shoulder.[7] My father told me to return to earth. I had gone far enough. If I went farther I would not return.

9. The vision of Eman Ela (Misango ki Nanga). Age 30, Clan Essamenyang. One wife, who is a Banzie, and no children. He is the oldest of his brothers and a planter. District of Mitzik, Bwiti Chapel at Akuruzok.

REASONS GIVEN: A man of the Mvang Clan gave me the eboga. I ate the eboga for other black men. I am sorry for the other black men and their suffering. I also ate the eboga to be able to play the ngombi well. I also searched in it to have many children. Years ago my father, who was a Banzie for a time, gave me some eboga. But I saw nothing in it.

VISION: When I ate eboga, very quickly my father came to me. First he had black skin. Then he returned and he had white skin. My grandfather then appeared in the same way [i.e., in a white skin]. It was he that gave me my eboga name. Because my grandfather was dead before I was born, he asked me if I knew how I recognized him. It was through eboga. He then seized me by the hand and we found ourselves embarked on a grand route. I didn't have the sense of walking but just of floating along. We came to a table in that path. There we sat and my grandfather asked me all the reasons I had eaten eboga. A man there wrote all these down. He gave me others. Then my grandfather disappeared, and suddenly a white spirit appeared before me. He grasped me by the arm and we floated along. Then we came to a crossroads. The path on which we were traveling was red. The other two routes were black and white. We passed over. Finally we arrived at a large house on a hill. It was built on one post. Within, I found the wife of my mother's father. She gave me my eboga name a second time and also gave me the talent to play the ngombi harp. She told me to work it until eternity. We passed on and finally arrived, after passing over more crossroads, at a great desert. Nothing was there! There I saw descend from the sky—from the moon—a giant circle, which came down and encircled the earth, as a rainbow of three colors—blue, red, and white. There were two women in white at each side of that circle. I began playing the ngombi under the rainbow and I heard the applause of men. I returned. All the Banzie thought I had gone too far and was dead. Since then I have seen nothing in eboga. But each time I take it I hear the spirits who give the power to play the ngombi. I play what I hear from them. Only if I come into the chapel in a bad heart does eboga fail me.

In all the visions collected, not only the ones given here, we noted five different reasons given for eating eboga. In order of frequency the reasons given were: (1) because of the urging of a dead relative in a dream; (2) because of attacks by witches, causing impotence, sterility, pain, and sleeplessness; (3) because of discontent with the missionary religions; (4) because of a desire to know Zame; (5) because of a general malaise and sickliness. Inquiry was also made as to the content of what was seen. But this is a tricky question and subject to secondary elaboration. The visionary is likely to become a folk narrator, and standardized elements from Bwiti culture appear that were not part of the original vision. Also, the vision is more elaborated the further one is from the experience itself. Many Banzie solidify and embellish their visions the more they recount them. We shall not attempt the difficult task of sorting out secondary elaboration. Both primary and secondary vision experiences are an integral part of Bwiti culture.

CONTENT	N = 38	PERCENT
1. Saw nothing and heard nothing.	9	24
2. Heard many voices, a great tumult, and recognized the voices of ancestors. Saw nothing.	8	21
3. Heard and saw various of my ancestors. They walked with me and instructed me on my life in Bwiti and elsewhere.	13	34
4. I walked or flew over a long multicolored road or over many rivers, which led me to my ancestors, who then took me to the great gods.	8	21

It was not clear from these discussions whether the high percentage who claimed to have no significant experience (24 percent) were those who, infrequently, became so nauseated as to vomit repeatedly and finally withdraw from the initiation. The last two categories of vision experience and particularly the fourth, the most detailed, show an instructive stereotyping. In general, women's accounts of their visions are much shorter than men's accounts though there is no belief in Bwiti that women have shorter excursions than men. It appears that women's primary objective is to make contact with a dead relative, very often a dead child, and when this is accomplished the vision experience is fulfilled. Men are more elaborative. They also confess to being, initially, more skeptical, and their visions tend as a consequence to be more exploratory, as if the very richness of what they discover overcomes their skepticism.

Looking directly at the twenty-one most fully reported visions we note four categories of experience, including the physical reactions to initiation. These reactions were seldom reported by the members except under prodding.

1. CONTACT WITH THE DEAD. All the visions involved visual contact with some dead relative or with a whole group of relatives. These could be children (7) or babies waiting to be born (2). In one vision a black baby Jesus (Emwan Mot) provided passage to the great gods. Other cases involved a paternal grandmother (5), a paternal grandfather (2), a mother (4), a father (7), an elder brother (2), unspecified brothers (3), or unspecified relatives (3). Sometimes these relatives appeared in exceptional manifes-

tations. Father or grandfather descended in the form of a bird and took the initiate flying with him (3). In one case the grandfather took the initiate in a small airplane. On occasion the relatives changed from black to white (4). Or they might be all dressed in white. In one case the relatives wore brilliant uniforms. They might be sitting at a table, occasionally in a large house, doing paper work (3). The dead engaged in various actions besides escorting the visionary. They gave eboga names to initiates (8), gave ngombi (harp), or the power to play ngombi (5), taught initiates how to cure themselves (4), passed the initiate through their legs (1), or made the initiate eat eboga (1). Once, the father washed a woman.

2. EXPERIENCES OF THE VISIONARY EXCURSION. Fifteen of the visions involved a prolonged excursion up a long path usually in the company of a relative or with relatives along the way. Often the road was specified as red (8). In all cases, the mode of progress was unusual, sometimes being suggested as similar to floating or flying (6). The end of the road might offer a remarkably different landscape from that of the road itself, such as a large, grassy clearing, a grassy upland, or a grassy hill (6), or a desert (4). A house built on one post was sometimes found on this landscape (5), with entry either permitted (3) or denied (2). Descriptions of this house stated that it was built entirely out of glass (2), had one supporting pillar, one door, one window (2), or was simply a great house. In two cases eboga plants were seen on the grassy clearing. In one case a many-colored circle (full rainbow) descended from heaven on this clearing; in another case the otunga (sacred tree or post of origin) was reached. Rivers of various colors, but never more than three, were encountered as obstacles along the route (7). Twice a monster was discovered in a river—a giant snake or a giant crocodile who, however, enabled passage across. Once a giant gold chain spanned the river, and once women were seen fishing bones in the river. Crossroads were also encountered (11), but never more than three times. The intersecting roads were varicolored. Sometimes white men or white Africans sat at a table in the crossroads checking identity, shuffling papers, and allowing passage (4). Once a man with a spear, and another time a white man, barred passage. Visionaries commented on various features experienced on the route: passing large crowds of black people (5), or white people (2), the whites once being a crowd of Christians in animal skins; passing a village taken to be the village of the dead (5), once having only one house, the chapel of Bwiti; and once seeing a Catholic and a Protestant church on hills on either side of the village.

3. EXPERIENCES WITH THE GREATER POWERS. In twelve instances the visionary encountered one of the greater supernatural powers, in particular Nyingwan Mebege, the Sister of Zame and the female principle of the universe. She was seen in various manifestations (9), as a beautiful woman (4), as

the moon, which is her orb (2), once with a bayonet piercing her heart, as a ngombi (cult harp) that changed into herself and back again into the harp. Once she appeared inside the house of one post, and once she was doubly manifested, descending on either side of the many-colored circle.

The initiates viewed the personage of Eyen Zame Onyi Bot (5). He was seen three times as a person inside the one-pillared house, once as a bishop with a cap of hair and a star heart visible in his chest, and once as a black babe that retreated into the one-story house and locked the door against the visionary (his Mwan Mot aspect).

4. PHYSICAL REACTION TO THE EXPERIENCE. Visionaries infrequently volunteered any information about their physical reaction to the vision. They often described nausea, but not as a part of the visions. Three times they mentioned a floating, flying feeling, once a feeling that their body color was changing, and once a sensation of the heart burning and becoming pure as flame.

The Banzie consider the many diverse elements present in these visions as contained in the power of the root itself to reveal realities of the land beyond. But, of course, these visions have their source in previous experiences, the first of which is the experience of other Banzie who have taken the drug in initiation doses. Though there is no formal instruction preparing the initiate for his visions, the experiences of others are recounted to him. Since an occasional overdose, moreover, may lead to the death of an initiate, there is an air of expectancy to the whole experience, which is heightened by the hope of seeing a dead relative. These experiences together lead to an anxious search for preinformation on the part of many initiates. But afterwards there is remarkably little detailed recounting or anything approaching excited recall. The initiate soberly recounts his experience to the chapel leaders to confirm the power of eboga and to see whether an inspection of the vision will reveal any secret knowledge of value to the members. Otherwise a decorum of disinterest is shown toward the initiate. It is recognized that the eboga vision is an intimate affair which must be free from public prying.

EBOGA AND THE CONTINUITIES BETWEEN LIFE AND DEATH

It is clear that a fulfilled and satisfying eboga vision is an extension into the unseen, the death realm, of the path of birth and death which the all-night ceremonies evoke and follow. Most visions are a following of that path. What the liturgy can only suggest, the taking of eboga actualizes. The visionary experience of probing or passing out into unseen realms has long been a source of what Bot ba Njock calls "intellectual preeminence"[8] among Fang. Banzie do pride themselves on their "intellectual preeminence," at least in the cosmologic sense—and the visual intelligences brought to them by Bwiti confirms it. They repeatedly say of communion in the missionary churches, "There you take communion and only taste. In Bwiti you take communion with eboga and you see!"

It is eboga that fulfills the eschatological promise of Bwiti, the promise to pass members over to the realm of the dead. This coming to terms with death and the reestablishing of contact with the dead was fundamental in the ancestor cult as well. Indeed, mortality seems to have been of particular vexation to Fang. Early missionaries frequently found Fang asking them to explain death to them.[9] They were especially interested in Christian notions of resurrection. Correspondingly, commentators on Fang culture, beginning with Largeau, noted with surprise that Fang seemed to feel that a person who had fainted was dead. Alexandre, as well,[10] commented on differing Fang views of the definitiveness of the process and hence their different views of the possibilities and miraculousness of resurrection. Such diffused views of death were supported by Fang ideas of multiple souls. For while one soul was tied to the body as its animus, another could come and go until the disappearance of the body, and still another soul had permanent existence independent of the state of the body.[11] From such various views of death and such beliefs in multiple souls Bwiti could easily derive the belief that those inebriated, alienated, or comatose under the influence of eboga had passed over and explored the death side of things. They were as "dead men."

Beyond a notion of death which contained the possibility of experiencing death while still not dying definitively there was also an old notion of the struggle with death, the struggle to prevent its taking hold of mankind. Nassau says that among the Miene people of the coast there was an old salutation, "What evil law hath god made," which referred to death.[12] He interprets the Miene greeting "mbolo," widely adopted by Fang, as expressing the wish that the stranger should be free of the threat of death. The claim to have died, to have known and to have mastered death, and to have the power to resuscitate the dead, is a very old one among would-be religious leaders in western Equatorial Africa.[13]

Among the branches of Bwiti, Asumege Ening takes a particularly strong interest in the problem of death and frequently refers to the engosie as *akômnge awu*—the preparation for death. Accordingly, the chapels of Asumege Ening are often called Metsugu Etsenge (the last of the earth). The leaders of the chapel carry prestige in virtue of the number of times they have "died." Of any Banzie it is true to say, as they say themselves, that "he is accustomed to death," "he knows death because eboga has showed him death."

There are a variety of metaphors which Banzie, as Fang before them, escaped the discontinuity between life and death. These images suggest in fact that continuity is the more natural condition. There is the crossroads metaphor, which is an intermediate image between continuity and discontinuity, being both at the same time—a road that continues and yet a road that must be crossed over. The image even more suggestive of continuity is the umbilical cord, the cord that holds together life and death. The umbilical cord is ever-present in Bwiti and is represented in the braided red and white yarn. It is worn around the waist and held in the left hand as, during prayers, the genealogy is recited. For the genealogy is, figuratively, a long line of umbilical cords that attach a person directly to all those beings, ancestors and great gods, in the land of the dead. When a Banzie dies his genealogy is recited in order to alert all these ancestors whose names appear there of his coming. This "clears the path" in his genealogy. This recitation, said to "open the door of death" (*kulu mbí awu*), presents a motif which is recurrent in the song cycle. For Banzie feel that the door of death has been closed upon the African and that he or she has come to live in a state of pronounced discontinuity between life and death. A final image is the mirror employed in initiation (much more widely in MBiri than in Bwiti) in which the ancestor, actually the reflection of the initiate, appears during the final stages of the ingestion of eboga. This image implies not only a continuity but a unity of the living with the dead.[14]

Though the conditions of the colonial world have acted to exacerbate discontinuities between the living and the dead in the eyes of Banzie, such discontinuities were always a possibility for Fang. This is seen in the old custom of the lifting of the curse (*ava meteng*) on the deathbed. This was done in case any hostilities between generations had acted inadvertently to create discontinuity in the genealogical line and had thus blocked up the benevolence that should naturally flow down it. We recall as well that the elder generation might in the custom of showing naked (*alere shéshé*) abruptly cut off the younger generation from genealogical continuities.

THE DEAD AND THE DYING REDEEMED

The old Fang "lifting of the curse" was generally understood to proceed from elder generations to younger generations, and that is seen in its primary locale—the deathbed. It was initiated by the dying. But the lifting of the curse could also be initiated on the part of the younger generation about to embark upon some dangerous enterprise, hunting, or warfare. In Bwiti the lifting of the curse has entirely that emphasis. It is a redemptive act undertaken by a younger generation, the living, to restore the line of communication and the flow of benevolence from those older than they and particularly the dead.

There are two acts of ava meteng in Bwiti: the *apongina* and the ava meteng proper. The apongina is an act of respect and the Fang word for respect (*eseme*) is often used. It is an action performed by one younger to one elder. It removes bad feeling and assures blessing and benevolence from that person. The engosie itself is often called an act of respect to the dead. The younger person kneels in front of the older person, who takes the younger's two hands in his own, slides them against the sides of his chest under his arms, brings them forth, cups them, and blows into them. (In the old "lifting of the curse" the older blew on the head of the younger.) Then the younger person takes his hands, rubs them down his chest, and throws them wide in thanksgiving. Older Fang notions of the power and potential for enmity that resides in the chest (*nkuk*) appear to be involved here. That power is sought by rubbing from without and by blowing from within. The blessing is a passing down rather than a storing up of power.

An elder of the chapel does not need to be present as the agent for the passing of power. During prayer periods apongina may be made directly to the ancestors and the great gods. The kneeling membership taps three times upon the ground and then raises its cupped hands to the "above." Receiving the power they "pour" it over themselves. They rub the flats of their hands over their chests. Apongina is rarely given or taken unless under some influence of eboga. Eboga is felt by Banzie to be efficacious in all that concerns spiritual flow and in the passing of power.

Sometimes accompanying the apongina but usually independently of it and at appropriate moments in the path of birth and death, particularly in the path of the harp, a "lifting of the curse" will be recited in Popi Fang. This recitation is given together with the translation prevalent in the Kougouleu-Kwakum Chapel of Asumege Ening.[15]

> *Ye ye kebwe Oh miwandzi etsenge. Oh miwandzi a kombi oh, nanga mi suo. Oh tita Zambi a Pongo oh! Me mana memboka o. Me mokaenya pasa bilondo ngadi ye duma ye nkumbe ye ngondo ye. Me pasama. Bebaé. Lube ye. Tsenge ye. Mepasama bebaé. Bazingo ye bama ye. Me pasama begaé. Naki, naki Ekoso. Kombi na mombango me. Yoki yoki, zaa ka, zua ka. Esumba na motina. Ngak, ngak, Angumba kambondo. Maga buti ye. Mikando miasiga. Vengo vengo. Mabondo musigo. Vengo vengo. Oh vengo vengo. Tsetsae tsae. Kubengi ngi, nzok ngi ngi. Adendang dang. Me yena nati, etuga medenga.*
>
> *Banzie, nima na kombo, banganga bokaye!*

Ye the beginning. Spirits of the earth. Spirits of the heaven. The place where we pass through. Father Zame who is the Gate Keeper. I come to a new country which is the cemetery. I strike out with the raffia streamers. Lightning and thunder. Sun and Moon, Sky and Earth. They are twins together. They are life and death. They are twins together. The yawning hole of the grave and the new life, they are twins together. Stamp stamp and no answer. The spirit is in the turbulent wind of the village of the dead. Joy, joy the ancestors give joyful welcome and hear the news. The troubled life of the born ones is finished, finished, finished. And now the disciplines of the dead. I go to the dead. All the misfortunes are shorn away! They leave, they leave. They leave. They leave. Every-

thing clean, clean. All is new, new. All is bright, bright. I have seen the
dead and I do not fear.

Banzie, leaders, priests, people of eboga!

The "lifting of the curse" in Bwiti, we see, makes a significant change
from the traditional Fang recitation which was much shorter and more concentrated. The two forms are similar only at the end, in the cleaving away
of the dirt of misfortune and unsuspected malevolence. The Bwiti lifting of
the curse is otherwise a much more dramatic series of images portraying the
voyage of the soul into the land of the dead. It is a lifting of the curse designed
to facilitate that voyage and restore continuities between the living and the
dead. But it is also integral to the whole dramatic celebration of the path of
birth and death. The living who are to die are redeemed in relation to the
dead who once lived. They are but "twins together."

There is a recondite and eliptical quality to this chant—a need for ampli-
fication that is also found in the midnight sermons. The effect produced is
one of a succession of images which are not readily grasped without cultural
context. For example, the phrase "stamp stamp and no answer": this refers
to the Fang custom of the elders solemnly stamping down, in a kind of last
farewell, the newly reshoveled dirt of the grave. In this stamping one is
imagined to be knocking on this last earthly house of the departed. Because
the chant is in Popi it is recondite and often inaccessible to Banzie.[16]

STAGES AND STEREOTYPES IN INITIATION

Initiation is expected to go through several stages and have a certain content.
Both the mother and father of eboga watch the initiate and listen with this
in mind. There are stages in both the mechanics of initiation and in the
visionary experience itself. Though there is some variability in the Banzie
sense of the divisions of initiation, six stages can be distinguished. First,
Stage I, there is a period of probing the night before the day of initiation to
see if the candidate is acceptable to Bwiti and to eboga. To test this a small
amount of eboga may be given. The next day, Stage II, there is a long period
from morning into the afternoon of quiet ingestion of substantial amounts of
eboga (up to a hundred grams). With the initiate well under the influence of
the narcotic he or she is taken, in Stage III, into the forest to be confessed,
bathed, and purified as we have described. In Stage IV the candidate is
returned to the chapel and continues to eat eboga amidst the activity of the
engosie. Finally around midnight he or she will collapse—fall over in a
stupified or comatose state. This is "eboga death" and it signifies arrival in
the land of the dead. At this stage, V, the initiate is removed to a special
chamber in the chapel or behind it in order to conclude in peace the visionary
experience and to recover. No more eboga is given. The final stage, VI, is

that of the morning return to the membership and the recounting of the experience. In a word, six stages: testing, ingesting, purifying, stupifaction, "dying" or excursion, and reintegration. This division accords well with the Banzie tendency to speak of stages or "sojourns" (*azak*) during the initiation: (1) "the stage of preparation" (*azak akômnge*); the stage of journeying (*azak awulu*); the stage of collapse and death (*azak awu*); the stage of wondrous reverence in the presence of the spirit (*azak awume*); and the stage of going to the above—to the ancestors and Zame (*azak abet*). Banzie do not consider the "return to the living" to be a stage in initiation, although it must be performed carefully as the reported experience of the returning initiate makes an important contribution to his own sense of membership as well as to the entire membership's sense of the surpassing reality with which they are dealing.

These stages of initiation constitute a set of expectations which are communicated to the initiate before he begins his narcotic journey.[17] His journey is adumbrated for him. It is not enough that he should merely pass out. In mild doses inebriation and uncoordinated physical behavior are condemned because they interfere with or confuse the proper treading of the path of birth and death. In the initiation, where stupefaction must inevitably take place there is, nevertheless, a certain orderliness that is expected. Thus the setting in which eboga is taken is controlled by chapel leaders; a set of attitudes and expectations about the experience is also conveyed. It is not surprising, therefore, that there is considerable stereotyping in the content of the visions.

The stereotyping is, in part, a consequence of the sequence of experiences the initiate undergoes. The experience of being moved out into the forest to a stream for purification and then being brought back into the tumult of the ongoing engosie in the chapel undoubtedly accounts for the frequency with which the crossing of streams and tumultuous encounters with a host of spirits are reported. There are other recurrent elements. It is very common in these visions to be met by a relative who guides one over the obstacles in the visionary landscape. Often these relatives are white of skin, clothed in white, or change to white, for white is the color of the dead and those entirely purified of the sin of birth. Crowds of black people may be seen at first. But they have not eaten eboga and are, therefore, not able to pass completely to the beyond.

In addition to the reasons already given, the frequent reference in visions to river crossings and a great snake in the waters is a motif taken directly from Fang migration legends, which involved difficulties in crossing various watercourses until aided by any of various giant chthonic animals: crocodiles, snakes, hippopotami, lizards. It is of interest that in crossing these rivers the visionary (as in number 8) comes finally to a grassy upland. This reverses the migration experience of the Fang, which began in a grassy upland (the savanna) and descended into the rainforest. We frequently note a correlation, in reverse then, between the eboga-induced visions and the events of Fang migration legends as shown in various collections and particularly in the literary version of Engutu, *Dulu Bon be Afri Kara* (1951). The visionary experience is very often represented as a journey down a long road that eventually leads to great powers. As the initiate pursues this route, other, older ancestors are presented to him. Various obstacles are encountered, including rivers of various colors. Finally the initiate passes out of the forest onto a bare hill, where he makes his confirming encounter with the great gods. Since Bwiti itself is, in important part, a ritual celebration of primordial Fang experiences, and since a key technique of worship is the recitation of long genealogies in which men ascend, ancestor by ancestor, to their clan origins and to the antecedent gods, it is not surprising that the eboga visions themselves follow a legendary genealogical framework, albeit in reverse. Eboga initiation is "miraculous," for it both takes the initiate forward to the other side of the sea and it takes him or her back to savanna origins.

This "going back" in the vision is true in another sense. Banzie also say that eboga enables a man or woman to return to infancy and to birth—to the life in the womb. All the sins of life cause people to forget their origins and particularly their ultimate origins in mang ayat, the land of the dead beyond the sea. This is the land from which all spirits come to be incarnated and to which they return. The two sins of early life which cause forgetfulness of this ancestral land are sins of violating one's mother's private parts. One sins in being born and one sins in eating at one's mother's breast. If this propensity to violate another's being is allowed to continue into adulthood it eventuates in witchcraft, the consuming of another's substance. But eboga, by returning initiates to the uterine condition, a condition in any case very close to life in the land of the dead, restores them to their own integrity—their pristine conditions. By carrying initiates forward to the land of the dead and backward both to savanna origins and the original uterine condition, eboga miraculously returns them to the same original and final place. It is another form of the "saving circularity."

Bwiti seeks in a variety of ways to attain to this "original and final" place—a spiritual Archimedean point, as it were, from which birth and death in all their contrarieties and complexities can be uniquely contemplated. This point is represented in several ways. The frequent reference in these visions to a one-stanchioned house—a glass or metal house built on a post—is an example. This visionary configuration seems to derive from Fang experience with a world globe seen in schools or colonial dwellings. Such a complete representation of the earth is more metaphysically impressive, Archimedean, than we might suspect. A similar ultimate place is obtained in the visions when the initiate arrives at the center of the rainbow. It is the spot from which he can see the entire circle of the rainbow as well as the entire circle of the earth. Even though the visionary may not have seen any spirits or gods in his journey this is a sign of the success of his vision.

The stereotyping of the visions reminds us of the fact, well recognized in the study of hallucinogens, that the content of the experience is more a function of the attitude set of the individual himself, of the social situation in which he takes the drug, and of the cultural setting of beliefs and values than of anything in the drug itself. The various chapels of Bwiti and the various branches of the cult differ, of course, in the sets they provoke in their initiates, the situation of initiation, and the Fang and Christian cultural setting they invoke.

When heavy doses of eboga are being taken, some chapels modify the ritual. Sometimes the initiate is surrounded by a vertiginous circle of members dancing, singing, and shouting. Drums may be beaten incessantly even in the initiate's ear, in representation of the sufferings of life pounding upon the spirit within the body until it is finally enabled to break through and fly. So fierce and insistent is the ritual turmoil that hardly any drug would be needed for the initiate to be astounded, mesmerized, and carried away in enthusiasm or ecstasis. Most chapels provide very careful supervision of the initiate. The eboga parentage, the mother of eboga and the father of eboga, watch over him solicitously and encourage him against anxiety while protecting him against overdosage. Initiates often begin to mumble or even shout incoherently under high dosage; the eboga mother and father listen intently to see if they can make out any message from eboga. It is their own soft voices whispering in the initiate's ear that he may take as the voices of the dead, while the turmoil of dancing and drumming is easily interpreted as the turbulent crowds of the dead. Some chapels provide none of this careful construction of set and situation, and these tend to be the houses afflicted with bad visions (*ndem abé*).

CONCLUSION: LIGHTENING THE BODY, RELEASING THE SPIRIT

Eboga is often described by Banzie as a "miraculous" plant. It amazes by opening up both the initiate (once in a lifetime by massive doses) and all the Banzie (regularly by smaller doses) to greater possibilities of the self. In the one case this is the possibility of knowing the land of the dead and the dead themselves, of reestablishing forgotten or obscured continuities between the living and the dead. In the other case it is the possibility of performing an arduous all-night ritual without faltering. In both cases the once clotted body is transformed (*afwalen*) into something it always had the potential to be, and the once benighted and bush bound mind is given privileged—preeminent— intelligence.

Eboga makes the body lighter so that it can dance beautifully and so that the spirit within can be released. Eboga also acts to purify the body—this is its capacity as a forest bush—so that the "sins" accumulated by the body, first and most notably the "sins" of birth and lactation but subsequently the sins that arise out of the angers and desires of village life, can be removed. For these "sins" sully and clot the body and make it "obscure" and unable either to recollect or hope for the continuity of the living and the dead. Eboga, in short, acts to make the part which is the individual body and the individual animus of everyday life aware of the whole, the surpassing genealogical body and encompassing spirit. It enables Banzie to act upon that awareness—to become the whole—in all-night dance and song and in those initiatory excursions energized by eboga among the dead.

ⵈ19ⵈ

The Word in Bwiti

Mbôfak mwan nsôsôm.
(The thinker is the child of the hunter.)

THE PARROT'S EGG: THE MAN WHO RETURNS TO SEE

VISITORS to Fang Bwiti seeking details of religious practice that escape local explanation will often be referred to the "mother chapel" of the particular branch. In a peripheral chapel like Assok Ening, affairs in the "mother chapel" are closely followed. Members visit this chapel to see for themselves the "miracles" that take place there. We were repeatedly advised to go to the "mother chapel" of Asumege Ening, Metsugu Etsengue on the Libreville-Kango road, and to Ekang Engono, its leader.

This necessary visit turned into a sojourn of several months in the chapel at Kougouleu. Ekang carries the Banzie name of Aki Kos Zamba Avanga a Bera Yene (The Parrot's Egg, God Who Creates, He Who Returns to See). He was from the first a hospitable man, making sure we were well accommodated and always accompanied by someone to explain the religion, usually the "knowledgeable one" of the chapel, the Yemba Michel Bie. But he himself was elusive. A tall, sinewy man of imposing dignity, Ekang was of such austerity of life-style as to be very difficult to approach. He was proud to be a hunter. When he was not leading Bwiti, he was hunting. In the village he was only in his element at night. The forest was his arena during the day.

Though the yemba was well equipped to spell out the intricacies of the liturgy and particularly the leader's subtle midnight messages (évangiles), at the same time one naturally desired to go straight to the "parrot's egg." Only after several months, and with reluctance, did he agree to an extended discussion. Though he might be persuaded to speak of the details of liturgy or of his sermons he would not speak of his own life. The most he would say was that "his father was a great hunter." He had been married four times and divorced once. Even his former wife could not provide much information about her former husband; in any case, she wished to rejoin him. Indeed, for both intimates and strangers, Ekang Engono was as hard to discover as the Parrot's Egg.

It is of interest to remark on Ekang's relations with his wives—what we know of them—in view of the Bwiti emphasis on marital stability. After many years of her infertility, Ekang reluctantly divorced his first wife because of a witchcraft accusation brought against her by his second wife at the time of the death of an infant of a third wife. Ekang's wives had difficulty conceiving. Only his fourth and last wife produced two surviving daughters. In such infertile households there is an intense focus on every conception and the likelihood of witchcraft accusation of one wife against the other in the event of miscarriage or the infant's early death—events with high probability given infant mortality rates. Ekang tried patiently to mediate these accusations but, in the end, decided that for the sake of the tranquillity of the house and the chapel, he had to send his first wife away. He did this reluctantly, he said, because he had introduced her to eboga and she had been a devoted Banzie. A preoccupation with the malaise between the sexes and with conception is a notable theme in Ekang's sermons as it is in Bwiti generally.

Ekang's two daughters followed him into eboga and stayed with the chapel. He had also readily accepted other young women into the chapel, forming a father-daughter bond with them. As with his own daughters, he encouraged these young women to marry and bring their husbands into the local Bwiti chapel. Since the father-daughter bond is much the most positive and un-ambiguous among Fang, the number of women—as many as ten—who feel that tie at Kougouleu Chapel creates and helps preserve the stability of the chapel. The uxoricality of a number of marriages also is a stabilizing factor as the young men who might otherwise challenge Ekang's leadership owe him, for the wives he provides, a kind of in-law respect. These young men also lack a local lineage base upon which to stand and from which to make a claim. Indeed, there is an incipient matrilineality in the Kougouleu Chapel, compatible, to be sure, with the lineal relationship sought by Bwiti with the Sister of God as well as with the matrilineality of the southern Gabonese people from which Bwiti is derived.

Ekang Engono's personality, his practice of priestly removal, and his appearance only at climactic ritual moments, add to the power of his sermons. His personality is a factor in the influence he is able to wield in holding the various factions of the chapel together. It is said with awe that he is a man who has "died" many times and who knows the other world better than this one. He is a man who not only sees hidden things, he "returns to see them." The young people of the chapel hold Ekang in awe as one who belongs to the land of the dead more than to the land of the living. This familiarity with the land of the dead influences the leader's character. Ekang himself says that his many trips to the land of the dead teach him the cardinal virtue: patience (*zongbe*). "My ability," he says, "to tolerate all the petty irritations of this world comes from knowing death. . . . Before Banzie have traveled fully the path of birth and death, they are constantly irritated and in a state of anger at the things of this world. But knowing death gives tranquillity." Above all, Ekang presents himself as a tranquil man. It is helpful to this presentation of self that he avoids social contact, escaping as much as possible to the forest.

Ekang's familiarity with the unseen gives him particular power to take away the sins of the membership. This was represented by his wearing a red robe during the hours of worship. The red represents the sins of the membership shed upon him to be carried away in the ritual of cleansing. This assimilation of sins and the periodic taking of the posture of crucifixion suggests the black Christ, though Asumege Ening Bwiti does not generally subscribe to the notion that Christ died for men's sins. On the contrary, while Christ's birth removed the primordial sin of incest, his crucifixion cursed the earth again. Ekang Engono does not hesitate to take the role of the crucified Eyen Zame, and at climactic moments of the obango on the path of death he appears posing as a man crucified against the central pillar with a candle in each outstretched hand.

But above all, his leadership lies in his "miraculous and amazing" words. His Bwiti name conveys his verbal powers. For in Fang folklore it was the parrot who first brought the word, the capacity of speech, to man. To be the Parrot's Egg is to be the very essence of that capacity—the sheer potentiality of that power.

The name is meaningful for other reasons. It was the parrot, and his red tail feathers signify this, who first flew along the path of birth and death from the red pool of birth (the pool of the sister of Zame) to the final reaches of the azap tree. The man who is the very potential of the parrot should be particularly skillful in guiding his membership along the red path of birth and death. And the Parrot's Egg is well hidden in the heights of such great trees, as well hidden as Ekang Engono himself from daily scrutiny. As well hidden as, very often, are the meanings of his messages.

In the little he will say about these sermons, Ekang Engono describes himself as interested in showing the membership that the world is one thing (*dzam da*), or a great whole (*engura dzam*), by showing the connections between things. He offers to tie things together (*atsing mam*) or coagulate things too much in flux (*a lighe mam*). He says that Mebege made the world as one thing, "the great egg of the sky spider shows us that, the one hole in the adzap tree shows us that, but people and the world have split into many parts. People have lost their way." That is to the liking of the witches, for their object is to "isolate men the easier to eat them. When men and the world are all together the witches cannot work."

In explaining his sermons Ekang used two important words: *efônan* (a likeness, a resemblance, and a word used nowadays for a portrait or an image) and *ndem* (a sign, a mark, an indication of something). He made the following statement. The eliptical and pontifical style has something of the ring of his sermons.

Ndong Obam Eya (the founder of Asumege Ening) is gone but yet he remains for I am his likeness on earth and I will carry on his work. So Everyman's ancestor is gone but still here for we are their likeness. So the things of the world which really seem separated can be shown to be likenesses of each other. Our sermons speak in likenesses. It is the good wind that comes from Nyingwan Mebege that sends these likenesses. The signs come to me in my dreams[1] and clarify our path for us. All the bad spirits act to confuse and confound our life. But they are kept in their place by this good wind. And all the good things otherwise separated by the bad are brought together and shown their resemblance to each other. Signs come to me in *tsuga tsenge* (the last earth) which is the grave under the altar. And these signs are the miracles that lead us down the path of birth and death.

"Amazing Words" from Above and Below

The "last earth" in which the "amazing words" come to Ekang is a special arena. He descends during the ceremonies into a grave pit excavated just behind the altar. The cult harps and the bamboo sounding staves are played upon the planks that cover the front half of the pit so that the sound below is mindfilling. The pit also provides a resonance for that music, projecting it throughout the chapel. Ekang descends into this pit after nine in the evening when he is sure that the rituals are in orderly progress. He has ingested a double portion of the powdered roots of the eboga plant and as he settles himself into the canvas of an old beach chair, his mind floats away in an easy reverie. The insistent rhythms just above his head put a steady if not stultifying pressure upon his mental excursion. He is communing with the dead—with the powers of the below and of the earth (*Zame asi*—God Below). Around midnight these powers bring amazing words (*nkôbô akyunge*) to him in the form of a sermon or "évangile." Ekang Engono will either rise from his pallet or call the knowledgeable one (yemba) and dictate to him these "amazing words" as they have formed in his mind. These "sermons," highly condensed, image-laden and with an elliptical and illusive quality, as we shall see, have the hypnagogic quality of the mind passing into or out of a somnolent state of inattention and flooded with images. The sermons are mysterious in the sense that they convey more than the membership can easily paraphrase in any explicit way. There is much more to them than at first meets the ear. They provide rich insight into the meanings of the religion. Here is the sermon put forth by Ekang at midnight on the second celebration of Kumba (*Fête bebe Kumba*) on March 9, 1960. I have placed in parentheses paraphrases and expansions of the vernacular text (which is found in Appendix II A).

Sermon Fête Kumba

"Eboga tells us that the purity of the spirit is in the blood. Women must close the back door of the cookhouse before seven in the evening. The

member of Bwiti is buried in a white robe (with ashes on his face) and
that is the destiny of Fang. The spirit flees the dead (inert) body because
it is (causes) agitation. It is asleep. (It has gone above.) (The spirit wanders
fitfully.) In this way the child honors the father and the mother. The
father is the agitated spirit, the mother is the inert body. The congregation
must ponder these things. Zame ye Mebege and Nyingwan Mebege
created all life, those two did. They said, 'three rich men attended the
birth of He Who Sees God (Jesus).' . . . They gave him three gifts: the
malan leaf, the eboga plant and a leaf of paper. The malan leaf goes
with the old harp, the eboga goes with the Fang harp (we now play) and
the slip of paper goes with our downriver brothers (the European). The
Fang have come to announce their presence sounding the vibrating string
(the one-string bow) on which music is made between heaven and earth—
between God Above and God Below. That string vibrates eternally. God
below is the recipient of the soul, the dwelling place of the soul. God
above is the wind. Those are the strings with which Nyingwan Mebege
binds up mankind as women wrap up the umbilical cord. (Man can be
tied as a package with the string—as his afterbirth is tied and buried in
the earth—as leftover food is tied in a leaf package to be eaten later.)
We are all of us leaf packages of food—the food reserves of God above.
These are the reserves that provoke strife. Brothers eat of these packages.
. . . You should not eat of these packages . . . the food packages of
God—we should untie that vibrating string of the food package of God.
Nyingwan Mebege has sent us the grave. Metsugu Etsengi below is the
grave . . . it is God Below. Our fathers played the old raffia harp. The
clan of Nyingwan Mebege (womankind) are the seat of the soul and (we
remember) that our fathers sat upon leather stools (when they were
debating the brideprice) in the council house. For that then Fang perhaps
began to construct the (Bwiti) "chapel" (a better sitting place). This is
what Fang call the "foundation stone"—founding place—the "fortified
place" of the house. (And within it the people—the members—are as
the staff of the crossbow ready to speed their soul like a bolt on its way.)
The ngombi is the crossbow. The folk are journeymen and work by day.
(We work by night.) The clock stands at twelve. He Who Sees God has
taken the souls from the rocky house, from the grave, from the rocky
sepulcher. The place the Fang call "the rock house" the European calls
"limbo." Moreover, He Who Sees God was accompanied by twelve
followers. And there are twelve races in the earth. Fang will return again
(to the path that leads) to God. And that is the Otunga. And he will
glorify God and Nyingwan Mebege. The moon (the young woman) is
in the water. Do not eat the food of God. Do not eat of men. Do not
keep bones of the dead. Do not make sorcery. Do not take the belongings
of others. Aki Kos (the egg [the power] of the parrot) Zambi Avanga
it is he that has spoken. I have finished speaking."

We shall examine something of the fabric of associations brought into play by these sermons in another analysis below. But here we can point out several movements and tensions which offer insight into Bwiti images of moral order. As usual this order is implicit. To be sure, Fang, so as to see Zame and to know him, must obey some rules. They must not eat the food of God, that is, they must not eat men. They must not keep the bones of the dead nor make sorcery nor steal. But the moral order of Bwiti, we have learned, is a more complex state than can be summarized by reference to such moral rules. They are usually added as an afterthought at the conclusion of the sermons.

It is in the interplay of images in the metaphors and metonyms which are put forth by the evangelist that the Bwiti moral order, in all its tensions and transformations, lies. In this sermon there is both a continuum of transformation and an enduring tension. Two Gods are central: the God of the Below and the God of the Above. These two gods suggest the persistent tension in Fang theology as they also suggest a continuum of transformation from the below to the above, that general vector of change in Bwiti. We see that in the name for the Bwiti member, Banzie (angels, or those who fly above). And there *is* a predominance of metaphors of height, of loftiness, of vectors of aboveness. We see this aspiration to aboveness in the focus on the African Gray Parrot as the Bwiti "totem animal." For "kos" nests in the tallest trees of the equatorial forest and frequently in the azap, one of the tallest trees and a sacred tree to Banzie. He is predominantly a bird of the above.

At the same time his red tail feathers showed that he followed the earthly path of life and death. And while what is most emphasized, besides his power of the word, is his occupancy of the high realms of the forest and his purposeful, rapid, and unambiguous flight, yet upon the ground he has a curiously human manner of walking, grasping, and climbing. Though it might be argued that the parrot is a liminal creature, difficult to categorize and mediating between the below and the above, it would be closer to Fang thought to say that predominantly a creature of the above, he is yet of the below. And being of both realms, he knows where he is going for he has lived and died on the path of birth *and* death.

Metaphors with vectors of aboveness and associations with belowness are evocative for Fang in Bwiti. The metaphors make a proper movement in respect to their condition. In recent years, Fang have found themselves badly situated. As they would put it, they are too much of the ground, of earth and thickets. Figuratively they feel themselves wandering through dense undergrowth. Images of the earth and undergrowth abound in Bwiti "évangiles." Clay and swamps and fens appear, and men are lost in the leaves of the underbrush and wander unable to see each other, let alone their tutelary supernaturals. In such a context, it is apt that the speaker compares the Bwiti chapel to the hunter's bower of leaves in the deep forest. For within this spiritual "bower" men can become, as he suggests, like crossbows, tensed to "shoot" their souls to the above.

The image is apt, for while vectored to the above, it also evokes the powers and gratifications of the below. The obscure and tangled forest does continue to hold for Fang the gratification of hunting and fishing. And there continue to be, as there always were, powers of the below: the powers cultivated by the old religion of the ancestors and the antiwitchcraft societies; the powers of the dead, of forest spirits and nature sprites, secret powers of the living. For these powers and their ritual evocations and endorsements are invested in, Zame asi, God of the Below. In Bwiti, Fang recognize the inescapable attraction of the evangelical God of the Above, but Bwiti seeks to establish by syncretism a communication between these two gods—a communication that is represented in this évangile by the vibrating cord of the one-string harp, *ben*, seen as truly binding "God Below" and "God Above" together.

The metaphors of Bwiti évangiles—this can hardly surprise—move the membership predominantly toward higher things, toward realms of the above. They do this by treating the members as Banzie—"spirits of the wind." They do this by giving the leader his name—"the egg of the parrot"—which connotes the essence of superior knowledge. For the leader, like the parrot, with his superior and arresting cry and unambiguous flight, calls out to men below, struggling and wandering in the suffocating thickets of the forest, and gives them direction upward. He transforms them into crossbows so that they can shoot their souls to the above. This évangile with its gods below and above joined by a vibrating cord shows a general movement upon a continuum from belowness to aboveness which is a main parameter of Bwiti quality space.

Still and again, rare is the évangile that moves only in one direction on this one continuum. In the sermon given, something, surely, is said for belowness. Men are born to it. It is gratifying. It gives stability. It is the seat of the soul. Banzie can stand on it though it soils their feet and obscures their vision. In the end they stand on belowness the better to launch themselves to aboveness. The Bwitist does not abandon Zame asi in moving upward. It is a rich source of creative tension in this religion and the very nature of its edifying moral order to try and keep Zame above *and* Zame below, to try and move between the forest canopy where the parrot nests and the leafy underbrush where the hunter waits. It is the tension of this double commitment that keeps the communion cord of Bwiti vibrating.

To reduce any of these évangiles or Bwiti itself to movement on a continuum or set of continua violates, then, a deeper richness—a tension embodied in their most apt metaphors. Consider finally the metaphor in this sermon of man as a leaf package of leftover food tied by a string that should be connecting the below and the above. How well that image captures the notion of forest-bound men closed in by leaves. How aptly it captures the feeling of bodily decay, so widespread a feeling in the colonial period. How concisely it summarizes the anxiety Fang have felt about the increase of witchcraft and

the consumption of brother by brother. "Men are as food to each other." At
the same time there is a positive element in the image, for these leaf packages
of leftover food are a delight and solace to hunters and gatherers in the cool
forest glades at noontime.

With all this there is a predominant movement implied. Despite all the
things that can be said about the package metaphor, its object in the end is
to convince the Banzie to disentangle themselves and become properly attached to the above.

THE RHETORICAL RESOURCES OF THE FOREST

A mark of maturity among Fang and a chief requisite of leadership was
speaking ability. Activity in the council house was salient in the lives of men.
Interaction there was almost constant—daily discussions, debates and moots
involving marriage, divorce, brideprice, fraternal rights and debts, land claims
and inheritance. Reputation (*ewôga*) was gained by expressing oneself well
on these issues. The term was derived from *wok* (to listen, understand) because
such men were listened to and could make themselves understood. As virtuoso
language use occurred regularly in the old council house (*aba*) so it occurs
in the aba eboga, the Bwiti chapel, and is important to the reputation of Bwiti
leaders. Though sermons of the kind we consider here do not occur in all
chapels, the leadership of any chapel must address itself convincingly to its
membership. It must be listened to and understood.

Eloquence, in the Bwiti context as in the more traditional setting, rests
upon a resourceful culling of the crucial domains of experience in search of
apt images. Insight into what Fang, and Fang Bwitists, consider eloquence
or persuasiveness in speakers is obtained by noting those images with which
they assess a speaker's performance. Take the Fang distinction between one
who breaks disputes (*abuk adzô*) and one that slices them (*akik adzô*). If one
is so clumsy, however powerful, as to break apart a palaver one leaves jagged
ends which are hard to fit back together again. Things are not reconciled.
They are simply put off to another day to surge forth again in a more festering
condition. But if one cuts or slices, the parts may be easily put back together
again. One chooses language to "cut and slice" and not to "break."

This image of techniques of judgment—he is a slicer or a breaker of
palaver—refers the listener to the domain of forest work. Over and over again
we find that forest activity, activity between men and women and things of
the forest, is a source for the understanding of social interaction. The Fang
proverb, the thinker is the child of the hunter (*mbôfak mwan nsôsôm*), fits
the situation well, for Fang repeatedly cull their forest experience to gain
understanding of their social and ideological affairs. In Fang culture the
distinction between breaking and cutting is naturally loaded, for the forest
must be worked skillfully. All of the various woods must be carefully cut.

Out of these materials Fang make their shelters, their essential tools, their comforts, their arts. For a people heavily involved in forest exploitation and forest crafts the linking of this realm to techniques of argument and judgment is persuasive. Men cannot be esteemed in either arena if they break rather than cut.

The council house dispute, the palaver, is also a forest through which one must knowledgeably wend one's way. It is said at the end of a successful judgment, *nkikmesang a kui elik* (the slicer of the affair has arrived at the site of the former village deep in the forest). He has found that former clearing where the resentments which have given rise to the conflict lie. By casting light on these resentments he has clarified them if not cleared them up. He has also (this is implied in returning to the elik) encouraged in the parties sentiments of their common origin, sentiments of value in settling the strife of a segmentary family structure.

The litigant also should wend his way carefully through the forest. In his argument a litigant (*nteamadzô*) may be complimented or may compliment himself on being a *nyamoro nsôm adzô*, a mature man and a hunter in the affair. He is proceeding skillfully through the "forest." By verbal powers he reaches the "game" and makes it his own. Should he wish to disparage his opponent he may refer to him as *nyamoro ôzem*—a man mature as the bearded monkey (*Cercopithecus talapoin*). With his beard he may appear as a full man but he is a chatterer not a debater. He does not dominate the "forest" but simply plays around within it, failing, as we would say, to know the forest for the trees. Rather than the hunter he is the hunted—the dominated one in the palaver situation.

This opportune use of forest images to make the palaver situation graspable is part of a profound tendency in Fang to see thinking itself as a kind of forest craft and to envision, in more than the proverbial sense, "the thinker as child of the hunter." We discover this in the Fang vocabulary of ratiocination. An examination of this vocabulary shows that thinking and knowing have very much to do with seeing one's way, one's path, clearly in obscure circumstances. It is a capacity of vision.[2] It has to do with paying close attention to signs. And it has to do with pausing on one's way to reflect and think back on the way that one has come in order to know how one has to proceed. We know how important and central the path metaphor is in Bwiti. We can show in terms of the lexicon of ratiocination that that choice of metaphor is embedded in the figurative resources of the Fang language.

SEEING HIDDEN THINGS

In the Fang lexicon of ratiocination the verb *yem*, usually translated as "to know," is more adequately translated as "to be right about something in perplexing circumstances" and "to have the capacity to do difficult things well.'' This capacity is to be distinguished from that knowledge based on a trained and habitual skill (*kale*). Yem implies the hunter's talent of being able to read signs. Indeed the two Fang words for signs or marks which give directions in the forest are *ndem* (low tone) or synonymously *ayema* (low mid-tone),[3] which are both derived from *yem*. Thus, more fully, ''to know'' is to have the capacity to read signs or marks which appear spontaneously or in uncertain circumstances. Knowing is being able to find a path by reading available signs where no path exists.

The spontaneous element in knowing emerges in the cluster of terms derived from or cognate with the verb *yem*. For example, there is the noun *ayem* (mid-tone) ''the state of being in astonishment or surprise at something.'' There is also the verb *tem*, ''to be astonished or surprised at being shown something.'' The Fang word for dream is *ndem* (low tone) which is generally derived from *tem* and is thus, derivatively, an occurrence full of amazing manifestations. Lexicons may properly stress the distinction between ndem, ''sign'' and ndem, ''dream,'' but Banzie play on the homophony of these terms.[4] In any case the distinction is not absolute for a dream, particularly to the Banzie, is an occurrence full of surprising signs from which important knowledge can be derived. Whatever distinction must be made between the terms, they make up a verbal constellation which shapes the imaginative formulation of experience in Bwiti.[5]

We have pointed out that the verb to think, *siman* (*osiman*, thought) implies a reflective action, a thinking back, an imagining once again, as it were. It is the using of previous experience as a guide by analogy to present experience. The words are probably derived from the root verb *sim*, ''to arrest oneself,'' ''to hold oneself in suspension a moment before going forward.'' Similarly the word yem appears to be derived from the stative verb *ye*, ''to be in suspension,'' without movement of one's own. Thinking and knowing, from the perspective of these terms, are passive states of reflecting upon past experience and searching for likenesses (efonan) to present circumstances which will act as a guide, a set of signs, to further movement along a right path.

There is a pronounced emphasis upon the visual mode in thinking and knowing. Another derivative of the stative verb, *ye*, is the verb to see, *yen*. It has the meaning of pausing to look around and gather in visually before moving on. This emphasis upon pausing to study the situation prudently, sagaciously, is contained in other Fang terms for knowledge. The term *nkyel*, frequently translated as science or intelligence, is better translated as prudence or sagaciousness. It is derived from the verb *kyelbe* whose meaning is ''to be attentive, cautious, forewarned'' as a consequence of looking carefully about. In Bwiti we see a repeated emphasis upon the visual mode, from the name of the Bwiti Savior figure, Eyen Zame (He Who Sees God) to one of the names of Ekang Engono, A Bere Yene (He Sees Over and Over Again).

Dying again and again, he is informed by hidden things seen in the land of the dead.

Seeing these hidden things is facilitated by the taking of eboga and by the visions it produces. In these visions are the signs from which "the miraculous words" of the sermonizer arise. He returns with these words to the congregation like a hunter who has made wise use of all the signs granted to him in following the trail to his quarry.

The figurative resources discoverable in the Fang language are rich and diverse and derive from a variety of domains of experience. But fundamentally they derive from a notion, figurative in itself, that knowing and thinking are pathfinding processes. Knowing and thinking come from a reflective and prudent reading of visible signs, or signs by drugs made visible, in a thick forest of experience. It is that fundamental notion that makes "the thinker the child of the hunter."[6]

THE VOICE FROM THE GRAVE

The word for thinker in our epigraph proverb, *mbôfak*, is itself figurative and derives from the verb *fak*, to dig out, excavate, disinter. The mbofak is he who is active in digging things out (*fak sông*, to dig a grave; *mfak sông*, gravedigger). The term is also used figuratively for one who seeks to get at the roots of an affair (*fak adzô*, to dig down and clarify a palaver). Any judge must be a thinker in this sense. He must not only return to the site (*elik*) where present resentments and quarrels had their origin, but he must also dig below appearances.

This metaphor for thought is not unusual. But what is interesting here is that the sermonizer, Ekang Engono, digs a large gravepit behind the altar to which he descends in a somnolent and drug-influenced state to obtain those sign-laden visions and those surpassingly meaningful words which he conveys to the membership. It is an interesting congruence in this man of amazing words that he is both a gravedigger *and* a hunter.

He is also a playful man, for it is said of him by the membership that he gives pleasure by "playing with words" (*a vwing bifia*). Any one word of his may have many meanings (*eyola evore ve a kane meyili*). Such playfulness is a widespread characteristic of Bwiti itself. And the potentialities of this kind of play are great in Fang, a highly tonal language. Utterances are short and contrast is frequently provided by tone alone. Bates, the first linguist to study the Pahouin languages, described them as being "averse to long words." The number of possible words is much restricted, he found, and there is great employment of homonyms, two or more words pronounced alike but different in meaning.[*1]

[*1] G. Bates (*Handbook of Bulu*, p. 5). Of course there are many other grammatical and phonological resources in Fang, besides high dependence on tone and extensive homophony,

Homonyms carry with them the potential for association of their multiple meanings. In principle at least, they offer to the Fang speaker rich opportunities for punning. Nevertheless, outside of Bwiti, punning is not a frequent speech device among Fang. In fact, speakers of such a language may not be as free to pun as might be supposed. For if homophony makes the possibility of punning omnipresent, capitalizing upon it risks a plethora of "double entendre"—clarity constantly betrayed in bemusement. This possibility may have made Fang speakers hold more securely to the cognitive principle of all or nothing selection of alternative interpretations in decoding messages,[7] and thus reticent to play with words in the punning way.

But punning of a concentrated kind occurs in Bwiti and particularly in its subtle sermonizers. There are several causes for this pronounced word play. In the first place, such word play—where one sound or set of sounds is associated with several meanings—accords with a main point the sermonizer seeks to make: that the diversity of things is really one thing. If a unity of sound can be played upon for a multiplicity of meaning so a multiplicity of meaning can be shown to derive from a unity. Second, and perhaps more obvious, fertility in punning can be taken as indicative of "miraculous" powers of speech. Indeed local commentators do take this word play as evidence of "surpassing skill." There may also be the influence of bad language habits of European speakers who rarely mastered tone. The resulting tonal confusions were a kind of inadvertent word play.

Finally word play of this kind can be shown to be an integrating element in the sermons. There are many examples. A recurrent double entendre, for example, concerns the name for the Bwiti Christ figure, Eyen Zame. A short sermon concerning him (given on page 516) plays upon the verb yen, "to see." The play basically is between yena, "mirror," and Eyene, "he who sees." Both nouns are derived from the verb. But the word pool (enyenge, or alternatively, enyenyen) derived from the same verb appears also. Thus three central words in this brief sermon play with the verbal root yen. Sermonizers frequently "play on roots" to achieve an integrity in what otherwise appears to be a rambling and elliptical presentation. An expectation is created in the audience that a root embedded in one way at one point may later on and at another point be embedded differently. Subsequent confirmation of that expectation gives a sense of integrity that does not emerge when one approaches the sermon with a more explicit logical progression in mind.

that make it an instrument for such rhetorical messages as Ekang Engono seeks to deliver. There is, for example, the rich lexicon of ideophones—exclamatives—and there is the form class system which, however vague the principles by which nominatives are classified, does give a sense of major noun classes which can be played off against each other. Most of these grammatical and phonological matters are implicit. They are not consciously manipulated by speakers even though they are an indubitable resource for them. We are choosing to analyze here figurative resources, the characteristic choice of tropes, which are more explicit, more consciously selected. Surely in Bwiti they are often quite explicitly manipulated.

Not only is there an expectancy that roots will be played with, but often it is felt that such playfulness can adumbrate the whole argument of the sermon. We can see this with the play upon the root "to see" (of particular interest in view of the importance of the visual mode of "making things intelligible"). Essentially, this sermon, and other sermons as well, for it is a recurrent theme, are concerned to make the point that heaven and earth, the above and the below, are reflections of each other. In a play on words Eyen Zame, "He Who Sees Zame," is also interpreted as the "mirror [eyena] of Zame"—His reflection. At the same time Eyen Zame, in other contexts known as Emwan Mot—the "Child of Man"—is the reflection, the mirror, in which mankind can see themselves. He is thus both a mirror of the above, that is, of Zame, and the below, of mankind. The same paradoxical theme is contained in the reference to the deep reflecting pool in the forest (enyenge or enyenyen ["that in which one sees oneself," or "that in which something is seen"]). It is standard Bwiti belief that not only do men and women see their own faces in these forest reflecting pools but that the sky and Nyingwan Mebege are also reflected in these pools. Here again the above and the below are united by the mirroring effect of the forest pool which has the particular power of integration of realms. (This notion of reflecting surfaces is central to Bwiti and we shall return to it below). But the reference to the pool itself emerged in the sermon by this process of "playing on roots," in this case the root *yen*.

Another instance of the adumbration of the whole argument by playing on roots can be seen in the long sermon, Sermon Fête Efun, we examine below (and in Appendix II B). It is seen in the play on the words *nlong* (savanna) and *nkôk* (sugar cane). The punning is not perfect, in the sense that these utterances are repeated exactly with other meanings further on in the sermon. Rather the speaker plays on the root *long*, "to construct," "to make something" and *kôk*, "to be sufficient," "to go," "to arrive well," "to be able to carry through." Thus the notion of an abandoned savanna homeland mentioned in the second sentence leads to the notion of the construction of a new life, a new home out of the forest. (*Edô a nga sum nzu long Afan* [line 2] and at the very end of the sermon [line 106], *ane a nga long nda.*) The speaker takes advantage of a contrary possibility of meaning, that of construction, long, contained in the word for the former savanna homeland, nlong, which had been destroyed. It is "surpassingly skillful" to have plucked from a destroyed homeland a newly constructed home in the forest. One of the major objects of Bwiti is to offer a new spiritual home to the membership.

The second play on the roots of words is begun in the mention of sugar cane (nkôk) and is seen in most condensed and alliterative form in the phrase *nkôk wa kôk mwan mot* (line 56). This translates as "the sugar cane pushes the child of man through to his goal"; that is, by taking life section by section, as the sugar cane is divided, man arrives well to his death. The root verb, kôk, brings to mind a capacity which Bwiti takes pride in offering to its members—the capacity "to push through and arrive well" at the end of the path of birth and death. It is just this capacity "to carry through and arrive well" that is felt to be lacking in contemporary Fang life. Arriving well, then, is the result of taking life stage by stage. The image in mind is that of eating the sugar cane section by section. It is also implied that following the path of birth and death in this manner is a "sweet process." Since the sermon seeks to establish the stages of the religious life in the passage from birth to death, the sugar cane as path image is apt. It is even more apt when the word itself is broken down so as to extract from its roots the very verb for that process of determined pathfinding, that is, pushing through and arriving well.[8]

As a final example of this word play we take a sermon text examined in another place.[9] Early on in this sermon the images of the Fang smelting furnace and the iron that comes out of it are introduced. The speaker complains that all the good things which Fang ironworking brought with it—strength in battle, cooperation among men in production, order in the exchange of women, etc.—have been abandoned as that iron has been abandoned. The furnace and the production of iron represent what Fang have lost and need to regain in Bwiti. But a pun is involved. For while the furnace and iron images are being used to deplore the disappearance of brotherly and cooperative feelings among clansmen, we come to realize that the word for furnace (akua), when pronounced in low mid-tone, means mutual aid among men. A homonymic association foreshadows the thrust of subsequent statement, adding weight and integrity to the sermon. It is the sermonizer's talent to perceive the multiple possibilities of his words so as to give the impression of a tying together what might otherwise seem a kaleidoscope of images.

While admiring the verbal powers of Bwiti sermonizers one must recognize the dilemma they face. They seek to testify by subtlety and richness of imagery and by double entendre to surpassing powers to see signs of the unseen, but they also feel the obligation to "clarify the path." There is always the risk of too great a subtlety, of arousing typically Fang suspicions of craftiness and complicatedness (meduk). In Fang culture generally there is a practicality of style that is impatient with those who seek to "dig too deep" or pause too long in reflection (bôt be edô fek). Bwiti sermonizers as "knowledgeable ones" are given more leeway to give evidence of surpassing mastery and subtle skill. Still, the dilemma is there and various sermonizers seize the horns of this dilemma in different ways.

Sermonizers range in type from the highly Christianized, who simply repeat Christian homilies or give traditional missionary-type sermons with little Fang content, to those, like Ekang Engono, who offer up subtle and culture-embedded words. That Ekang Engono can do this without developing a reputation for "complicatedness" is in part due to the suggestiveness of the images he offers, their local coloration and their aptness to circumstances. In part it is due to the context of his message. For not only does he project an impressive austerity and simplicity of life style—the very opposite of complicatedness—but his creative use of liturgy has convinced his auditors that he has descended into the tomb and that his is truly "a voice from the grave."

But there is another element: an excathedra or ecclesiastical style of presentation. With all the verbal playfulness, there is something terse, solemn, and simple about these sermons. Predication runs straightforwardly from subject to object with a tendency to employ the simple form of the verb. The mood is indicative, for these are matters of unquestionable veracity. It is not in morphology and syntax that the subtle nature of the message is enfolded. Syntactical simplicities contrast with semantic subtleties.

This style has two important associations: (1) with missionary sermons and (2) with the traditional night speech (nkôbô alu) of elders. Oftentimes the sermons are declaimed so slowly as to remind one of the painfully composed sermons delivered in the vernacular by missionaries.[10] This deliberate style of delivery, linking the sermons to the solemnities of Europeans preaching Christianity, attains or seeks to attain to the authority and knowledge of the unseen credited to the missionary. But these deliberate solemnities are also reminiscent of the "night speeches" delivered by village elders in the quiet of the late evenings when the village was on the verge of sleep. The elders in former times took these moments to counsel the village on current difficulties. These speeches were, like Bwiti sermons, full of proverbs and proverbial references. The Bwiti sermons themselves coming in late evening, though perhaps more subtle than solemn, yet recall those night speeches and the spirit of community espoused by them—that community lost under the disintegrative impact of colonization and restored in some measure in the sociable extended family of Bwiti.

ONE WORD, MANY MEANINGS:
ONE VOICE, MANY UNDERSTANDINGS

We should emphasize in going on, now, to interpret specific sermons that there is a range of interpretations. In an egalitarian society such as Fang, variation in interpretation is frequent. It is true that chapel hierarchies, the "knowledgeable ones," try to enforce "speaking with one voice," and some chapels do manage to limit interpretation to the nima and his assistants, the yemba and the yombo. Still, disputes over interpretation arise frequently. In any case, with such subtle and condensed words as are characteristic of Bwiti sermons there are bound to be various resolutions of the ambiguities involved, not to mention different foci of interpretation as to the signal importance, the significance, or the symbolic referents of the sermon.*[2] In such heavily laden,

---

*[2] In mind here are the distinctions among signals, signs, and symbols, distinctions as regards the way in which the elements of communication are responded to, which first arose in the study

thickly interwoven vehicles of figurative speech, then, a full range of meanings is not available to everyone, and elaborate interpretations are in fact rare— limited to the chapel hierarchy, the "knowledgable ones" who feel it incumbent upon their status to offer elaborate exegesis.

The interpretations offered here are based on those given by chapel leaders, in particular the yemba of various chapels. Our primary interlocutor was the yemba of the Kougoulou Chapel of Asumege Ening, Michel Bie. But we also spent many hours with the yemba at the Kwakum Chapel, Andre Mvomo Asumu, with the yemba at Assok Ening, Muye Alogo, and with the nganga at Assok Ening, Metogo Zogo. As for the posture with which to approach these sermons, the observation of Michel Bie is appropriate. These sermons, he said, are not for simple-minded people, *mimia*,[11] such as those who will understand the proverb, "the goat eats where he is tied," to mean that if you tie up a goat you can count upon him to eat where he is tied. These sermons are not intended for goats.

ELEMENTS OF FOLKLORE IN SERMONS:
EDIFICATION BY PUZZLEMENT

The words that arise from the grave are words that have come to Ekang from the land of the dead and from the ancestors. They are also described as being "old words" or "words of the past" (*nkobo ye okua*). Accordingly, elements of folklore, proverbs, riddles, and segments of tales often appear. The following two sermons show the use of such materials. If anything, the ambiguities inherent in this lore are used to increase the puzzlement the sermonizer seeks to induce, by which he edifies his audience.

This first sermon[12] was given on the first day of the Easter cycle, *efun*. Mostly these are the words of the yemba of the Kougouleu Chapel of Asumege Ening. When he descended into the grave pit on that night Ekang Engono had only a few words for him. He told the yemba otherwise: "Recall to them the story of Osuga Kwe, the red-tailed monkey." The yemba preached:

Sermon of the Yemba Fête Efun-Nana Nyepe

"Eboga! Leaders of the religion of eboga." Let us go to the ceremonies. The last of the earth. Many souls are present. Here is an old story of the red-tailed monkey. He entered a thicket of branches high in a tree. Four fruits of the *abam* [*Chrysophyllum lacourtianum*] hung in there. Monkey entered but he was clumsy and the fruit fell far to the ground below.

---

of Bwiti. For it was apparent that elements which some members regarded as deeply meaningful and about which they could speak at length were regarded by others as signs or simply as signals that were clues to the proper sequencing of behavior. There are many members of Bwiti, perfect performers of its rituals and rapt auditors of its sermons who, at least as far as the ethnographer is concerned, seem to derive very little that they can articulate as to the meaning of the sermon.

Monkey cocked his head down but he was clumsy and the fruit fell far to the ground below. He would not eat abam fruit today. The body of monkey climbed down to look at the fallen fruits. He found they were not ripe (not red). The child of man is the abam. And witches will not know the simple and virtuous man unless Zame himself detaches him. Our flesh is the abam fruit. Monkey could not triumphantly eat the fruit because the abam is a good man. It is eboga that cocks our head downward. The eater of eboga, he who speaks under the influence of eboga, has a body very awkward in hunting and fishing. We should not shake the tree of the child of man to get the fruits out. Only Zame himself knows what to suspect of good and evil in us. The spirit has one important sin (lack of hospitality). Do not refuse to help others because it is difficult. Take care of strangers who have come among the people of Zame. The tribe of Nyingwan Mebege must listen to the tribe of Zame ye Mebege. The tribe of Zame must listen also to the tribe of Nyingwan Mebege. For the tribe of Nyingwan Mebege can create destructive situations. Because they are in the process of mixing with people who can be discovered with bad acts. If one understands eboga one ought to prohibit such things. This is after all a festival for Nana Nyepe too. All of us are blood after all. People should take their own portion for they do not know how to tie up another's portion in a leaf package. The Parrot's Egg God Who Creates has spoken. This is the festival of Nana Nyepe. The Harp Emerging, Yembe Eboga, the Bad Burden That Zame Carries, he has given these words because he is constantly astonished at the words that Aki Kos speaks to the group. The Last of the Earth, the Repose of the Ancestor Spirits.

In elaborating on the folktale suggested by the nima, the yemba is seeking to follow images and phrasings characteristic of Ekang Engono more than the tale itself. The moral of the original Fang tale concerns the fruits, or lack of fruits, of clumsy overeagerness in hunting. In the sermon the identification, however, is not primarily between the monkey and the clumsy hunter but between the tree and man. For the monkey is identified both with clumsy people who violate others' integrity and also with witches and other evil forces that would seek to despoil others. We have seen this identification between the forest and people and between specific trees and the spiritual life of Banzie arise in numerous ways. The tree metaphor was also a favorite one of missionaries.[13]

The sermon, then, is not, or is only secondarily a cautionary tale about hunting. It deals primarily with the respect for the integrity of persons which Bwiti preaches. We remember that for Banzie the two primal sins in the life of the person (as opposed to the primal sin in the life of the group which is incest) are the sins of being born and nursing. Both of these are violations of the integrity of the mother's body. Rather than shaking the tree of another to see what fruit may fall, therefore, one should respect others and leave it to Zame to determine their value. Let the fruits of another fall of their own accord. But the sermon also suggests in its indirect way that Zame will protect the integrity of a person (the tree) against witches. The eater of eboga and one who speaks under the influence of eboga, himself clumsy by intoxication, should know the clumsiness of people to each other. They should teach respect for each other. For eboga, by its own disequilibrium, informs those who take it how far they can cause others to fall.

This theme of respect leads, as is often the case, to a more direct and moralistic conclusion, a moralism more typical of missionary-influenced African churches and politicians than of Bwiti.[14] This is the observation on the respect due strangers (in this case the ethnographer and his wife) and on the mutual respect due between men and women (the tribes of Zame ye Mebege and Nyingwan Mebege).

Two other recurrent images appear. The sermon ends on the image of the person as "leaf package of food." The image has multiple functions in Bwiti texts. Here it serves to evoke the theme of respect. Each person should be left, it is argued, to tie up his own portion of life, make his own package. Others cannot do it for him. Another recurrent image appears early in the sermon, that of the thicket in which men and women must find their way. In this phrasing the fruits of life are found in a thicket protected by Zame, a thicket that the clumsy or evil-intentioned hunter cannot penetrate and the respectful eater of eboga will not seek to penetrate.

It is of interest that it is the tale of the red-tailed monkey that was chosen by Ekang, a choice that arose by association with the red-tailed Gray parrot and the red path of birth and death, both images occurring with great frequency. It was a choice, however, that was otherwise apt in relation to other forest imagery in the religion. The abam tree, which is not the tree of the original Fang folktale upon which the sermon is based, and whose acidic fruit is bright red, may well have been chosen out of the same associational complex of colors, color vectors, and animal and body elements (blood). Finally there is a play on words for which Ekang is well known. *Abong* (clumsiness) is also the word for nest in the crotch of a tree. As there is recurrently a subordinate focus on sexual activity and menstrual blood in this sermon and as there is regularly an association between nest and womb in Bwiti the word play is apt and suggestive. It is strengthened by the person-tree association. The discussion of the monkey's clumsiness early in the sermon, then, anticipates, as is typical of Bwiti word play, later discussion of women's infidelity and the consequent sickness in the womb—the nest of Fang blood.

From time to time a short sermon is put forth in the form of a riddle. One night after several hours spent in questioning Ekang Engono, the "words from the grave" came up from below in the form of questions put by the

European visitor and answers given by Ekang. This created smiles in the congregation. But typically both the answers given to us and the ones reproduced in the sermon were elliptical and ambiguous, showing the principle, dear to Ekang Engono, that edification follows after puzzlement. Here is the first portion of that sermon given at Nkung Fête Minkol.

Sermon Nkung Fête Minkol

A stranger has come among us at the Repose of the Spirits during this festival of Minkol. Many questions that stranger has asked. The first question: What is the water that comes to the secret chamber of the men on the left? Akikos has responded saying, "Yes! the water arrives there." Second question, etc.

The sermon went on to give ten short questions and to provide ten brief answers, all of them puzzling in their brevity, but all, at the same time, dealing with fundamental questions of chapel or liturgical organization and thus edifying if puzzled out by the membership.

Traditionally it was the riddle that Fang employed in order to provoke "edification by puzzlement." Not surprisingly, then, some of "the midnight words" are put before the membership in the form of riddles. The following sermon was given on a regular Saturday night engosie.

Sermon Samedi Engosie

Aki Kos Zame Avanga, our elder, has gone on his journey to the dead alone. He has returned with a host of people and he has thrown out this riddle:[15] Our mothers cooked food, some of them placed their pots in the lower end of the hut, some at the upper end and some in the middle. So our elder asks the people: "the far corner, the near corner, which is the elder (nyamoro)." Those of you who come to the "Last Earth Chapel" here have good heads. Hold Aki Kos in awe for he is the man from whom the clans flee.[16]

The point of the riddle, the yemba said, was that there was no better, no "older," place to prepare the food. Rather it was the woman's role to prepare the food in whatever place. By this interpretation the riddle addresses a recurrent theme in these sermons. In response to the malaise between men and women and the high divorce rate Bwiti attempts to find the complementarity of the sexes irrespective of the preeminence, the seniority, of one over the other. It is of interest that in making this point the term *nyamoro* (elder or mature man) is employed, for this is a term typical of the old Fang society of male dominance. The usage thus stands in contrast to the point being made, though, it is true, being made in a peremptory authoritarian manner. In fact there is a presumption in many of these sermons as to the right of the sermonizer informed by spirits to baffle and "hold in awe" the membership,

and often enough it is the less informed members—women and children—
who are "held in awe."

Proverbs, although they do not directly challenge the auditor like riddles,
are also by nature puzzling. They are frequently employed, sometimes simply
dropped into the sermon for the audience to puzzle out contextually. But they
are often explained, as in the following example from Words of the Festival
of Olorogebot (St. Michael).

Sermon Fête Olorogebot

"*Ele e ne nkang. Eboga a bele nkung* etc.*"* "The tree is contained in
its smallest roots. Eboga has the capacity to procreate." "Zame has
come out of hiding for us but he still hides himself. In the eboga left by
Ndong Mba there is the proverb." The little red-tailed monkey [*Cercopithecus cephus*] is not yet able to eat or yet move with the big black
monkey [*Colobus satannus*]." The little monkey is the pure and innocent
one. The big black monkey is the sorcerer. That proverb is a proverb
of sorcery. The Fang child is a bone. The bad has gained over the good
in this world but Zame still knows the Fang child. Brothers, let's start
up the forge. The bellows are still in place within. It is the pool of eboga
that has the capacity to procreate. The tree is uprooted by the wind,
because it is rooted in the ground. Mankind is not uprooted by wind
because they are rooted in the pool of eboga. Death will come to an end.
The Parrot's Egg, Zame Avanga, I speak. I have finished speaking.[17]

The proverb is explained by reference to sorcery although it might be
explained by Fang in a variety of ways. The comparison of the red-tailed
monkey with the man and woman innocent of sorcery, and the comparison
of the big black monkey with the sorcerer is very much a Bwiti comparison.
The red-tailed monkey occurs repeatedly in these sermons as a surrogate for
the red-tailed parrot. Both animals are physically marked to follow the red
path of birth and death. Sorcery destroys that path.

A PLENIPOTENTIARY PLAY OF IMAGES

There are many other referents in this dense, short sermon, Fête Olorogebot.
These link to experiences in Fang culture and so extend the listener's imagination. Take the phrase, "the tree is contained in its smallest roots." This
is apt first of all because the power of eboga is, indeed, contained in its roots.
But the speaker goes on to say that eboga, the "tree" implied, has the power
to procreate—that power recurrently sought in Bwiti. It seems apparent that
the root referred to has been extended to mean, by virtue of the man-tree
association, "male procreative organ." This interpretation is supported by
the reference to Zame coming out from hiding. The association here is to the

ritual act of "showing oneself naked" to one's descendents (*alere shéshé*) in order to remind disobedient offspring of the genealogical line from which they were descended and to cut them off from it. But here the meaning is different. For Zame, showing himself in Bwiti, "shows" the line or path by which men and women are descended, enabling them to recapture their patrimony. Outside Bwiti, however, as the sermonizer goes on to say, Zame still "hides himself."

Subsequently we are told that the bad has gained over the good in this world, the world of flesh. In the world of bone of which Fang are made (bones were the principal sacra of the ancestor cult) the relationship to Zame is still secure. For it is the bone that Zame knows and not the flesh. It was the bones that were made in the forge of life by Zame at the moment of creation. The sermonizer is saying that if Fang in Bwiti will remember that they are made of bone and not of flesh—that is, if they will remember that they were created by Zame and perpetuated by all the ancestors (whose bones are kept in the reliquary)—then they will be saved and properly placed on the path of birth and death which is the genealogical line.

These sermons require interpolation by reference to experiences otherwise acquired in Fang and Bwiti culture. If a ready explanation of the sermons is not forthcoming from the "knowledgeable ones"—it is almost exclusively they who will offer explanations—then we must search out those domains of Fang culture where the referents have their resonance. For example, the brothers are asked to "start up the forge, for the bellows are still in place within." Knowledge of Fang forging is required to identify this as a sexual image. It calls to mind the Fang two-bag bellows with its long clay nozzle. This remains in the forging pit. If this is heated up again—by activity in the chapel, for the chapel is often metaphorically equated with a forging pit where souls are created—it can give life anew. Life and potency can be restored to Banzie by heating up the "chapel-forge" of Bwiti identity.

On the other hand, the chapel-forge, the ritual arena of heated-up activity, is not the only arena of creation. There is another primary arena with an opposite quality. This is the cool, still pool of Nyingwan Mebege in which procreation is ritually enacted, particularly at midnight. The souls of mankind have their origin in this pool, and procreative power is found in it. It is congruent with Bwiti belief to point out that the first creation of the soul takes place in the cool, still pool while the second creation of the Bwiti soul—its rebirth—takes place in the hot arena of the chapel in mid-performance. There is a progress implied from cool to hot creation just as in Fang legends there is a progress (ignoring the savanna experience) from the cool, still primeval forest existence to the hot society of village life.

Further, the sermonizer argues that procreative power can be obtained if Fang will remember that they are rooted in that pool rather than in the earth as are trees. In that remembrance they will find the possibility of enduring and prospering under the wind of the above. That wind will not blow them down. They will, in that remembrance, surpass death, and that which terminates mankind will itself terminate.

If one looks in these sermons for an explicit argument, one that proceeds by clear progression and which seeks to avoid contradiction, included middles, and other ambiguities, one will not find it. What the play of images characteristic of these sermons is concerned to bring out, by reference to the multitudinous arenas of Fang life, are the many-faceted aspects of Fang Bwiti identity: cool in some respects, hot in others, treelike in some ways yet rooted in water in other ways. These sermons are prime instruments for the suggestion, if not the actual recapturing, of that plenipotential self which Bwiti seeks to release. Their interpretation provokes an awareness of many possible different arenas of activity, and hence of identity, in interaction.

Most sermons call for culture-informed powers of interpretation. But one does not always have to interpolate recondite references. For however plenipotentiary and difficult these sermons may often be, they frequently contain striking images that stand by themselves. The following is a passage from a long and otherwise obscure sermon on the differences between Bwiti and Bieri and between these two and Christianity.

> The clay of our flesh collapses and the spirit comes forth arriving in rapid waves of wind. And the wind of bright light is brighter than the light of the mirror. And it passes away forever. The hot tobacco we smoke brings reflections (thoughts) upon that light . . . it becomes hot and takes fire and it endures forever. These reflections (thoughts) come that the spirit should become hot and take fire and endure forever. These reflections (thoughts) arise, climb up as the smoke. They become hot. They take fire. They endure forever.[18]

The poetic quality of this passage—the movement of the spirit out from the body to the heat and light and divine wind of the above is self-evident. Still, two elements must be further explained: the reference to tobacco and to the light of the mirror. The smoking of tobacco (sometimes hemp) is employed in chapels of Bwiti to represent the distillation of the spirit out of its corporeal substance and its rising to "the above." Often the reference to tobacco occurs, though not in this sermon, in relation to the forging of the body in the ritual activity of the chapel—its reinvestiture with spirit upon its rebirth in Bwiti. But smoking is an image with opposite implications here, for it implies the destruction or burning down of the body and the divestiture of spirit.

We have discussed the place of the mirror in Bwiti and its aptness as an icon for the reflective nature of thought (*siman*). We have also discussed the notion that the past and the beings of the past (the ancestors) and the present and the beings of the present (the living) are reflections of each other. In this passage the mirror and thought are brought into more direct association. For the mention of thought directly follows the mention of the reflected light of the mirror. There is also a considerable metaphysical achievement here. The speaker discovers a light (the light of the wind of the soul) brighter than the light of the mirror—brighter thus than the light of the past reflecting upon the present and vice versa. We also note in this short passage a synesthesia of elements—heat, light, and motion. But synthesia is not the only kind of condensation which occurs in these sermons.

THE POWERS OF A CONDENSED COMMENTARY

The "miraculous" words may sometimes be straightforward and brief,[19] but characteristically they condense meanings in a rambling, recondite way. The following short sermon shows condensation. It was given on the second night, nkong, of a three-day engosie. In order to give some sense of the use of alliteration the Fang is given here in the text.

> *Eyen Zame a dzi ki yene enyeng. Nge a nga yene a berege lir akyenge awu. Engong a nga bulan adzal edo a nga yen enyeng. Ekôkôm da yian yege mezo me ye mefonge. Ensama wa kam. Aki Kos Zame Avanga enye a nga kobo. Me mana dzo.*
> He who sees Zame did not see the still pool. If he had seen the still pool he would not have had to return to be shown the miracle of death. When he returned to the village that day he saw the still pool. The cadaver must listen to the words of the wind. The group protects. Aki Kos Zame Avanga has spoken. I have finished speaking!

These brief "midnight words" were, perhaps for their brevity, received with awestruck silence. In part this was because of the masterful alliterative effect of a rapid sequence of nasal and glottal consonants. But there was also a creative power in these words arising from condensation of meanings.[20] The yemba, Michel Bie, felt that this sermon was a fine example of Ekang Engono's surpassing powers, particularly his power to give many meanings in one word (*eyola evôre ve a kane miyili*).

Take the ironic observation that "he who sees Zame" (Eyen Zame) nevertheless did not see death because he was not shown the still pool known to every Banzie. He had to return to the living to show, in that resurrection, the possibility of death in life and life in death. We know that the still pool refers to (1) the primordial ocean (mang) into which the creator Mebege sent the spider with his egg in order to raise the land; (2) the ocean from which Fang migrated and to which they are migrating; (3) the small, cool, clear "rain pools" in the forest into which the moon, the manifestation of Nyingwan

Mebege, shines and sends the spirits of new infants in the form of the sacred pebble of fertility; (4) the pool of decaying fluids into which the dead body collapses; and (5) the actual pools of water in the male and female chambers of the chapel representative of all these pools but most particularly the bag of waters in the pregnant woman. Rituals of "fertilization," as we know, are performed around these pools at the midnight ritual pause between the path of birth and the path of death.

In the "still pool" are condensed origins and conclusions, birth and death. This condensation of ultimate experiences is something that every Banzie learns in treading the path of birth and death—for every Banzie dies as he lives and lives as he dies. But Eyen Zame, the sermon tells us, did not have that knowledge. He had, therefore, to die painfully, be crucified, and go to the village of the dead before he understood what every Banzie learns in initiation and in each engosie. He had to learn that before he could return. That is the lesson of his resurrection. Banzie die and return at every Bwiti celebration. This knowledge of life in death and death in life is contained in the wind in Bwiti thought. It is "the wind of life," the wind that animates what would otherwise be a lifeless cadaver. Banzie should learn to listen to that wind, to know its secret (it is, for example, present in the harp music) before it abandons their body and leaves a cadaver without hope of resurrection. The sermon thus speaks to the potential of death in the living and, as well, to the verbal powers of condensation by which that fate can be escaped, or at least by which life and death can be condensed into each other and thus surpassed. Those who have not heard the "miraculous words" will not benefit from such powers of condensation of the separated domains of experience.

Following the Hunter
through the Midnight Forest

With the various qualities of these sermons in mind—their plenipotentiary play, their condensations—let us turn to a complete sermon, given at an efun festival for St. Michael, to gain a fuller sense of the leaps of imagination and labile associations characteristic of the sermons at their most "miraculous." It is not possible to account for every leap and every linkage. But in many cases knowledge of Fang culture enables us, even without the aid of the yemba, to find the underlying connection which makes them plausible and intriguing to Banzie. We will try, thinking like the sermonizer, to hunt through the forest of these images and give a more explicit account of the path he is following—the venery he is offering up to his auditors. We will not be able to dog his every move for he periodically disappears from view, baffling the interpretive task. To make the sermon more comprehensible to Western ears (a literal line for line translation is given in Appendix II B) a relatively free translation is given here.

Words from the Fête Efun of
"He Who Shows the Way" (St. Michael)

1. This thing which I recount is no longer. Zame made us first out upon the savanna. And it was he that pierced and prepared our way through the giant azap tree. And it was he that began to make it possible to make things in (and out of) the forest. For Fang are of the forest.

2. Humankind shows four miracles. First he leaves the earth and comes to his feet. And he leaves there and comes to the calf. Then he leaves there and comes to the knee. Then he leaves there and is perched upon the shoulders of his father. On the shoulders he is put into the balance for the first time.

3. One fans (in vain) the cadaver in this earth of our birth. The first bird began (to fly) in the savanna. The night Cain slew Abel the people built the village of Melen. And after that they never turned back. What we Banzie call Elodi Tsenge Fang call rainbow and Europeans call arc-en-ciel. It was raised over the people. Then they passed through the azap tree. Then they used the forest to construct things. That was the auspicious invasion from the north, the invasion of Olu Menyege.

4. The land of humankind was formed as a drop of blood. And that drop whirled round and grew big like a white rock or as two hailstones, the white hailstone and the black hailstone. That is the ball of birth and of the earth.

5. Now Fang say that "the star is suspended there high up above." The fruit of the azap tree is suspended up there high in the azap. What is found suspended there just below that fruit? Why it is the (pure) raindrop. And that raindrop is the congregation—the group—of Banzie.

6. The first food of mankind was the sugar cane; therefore the child takes and presses in his mouth the sweet fruit of the breast. It was Ndong Zame of legend who began to whine and wheedle for children. We are children of the rainbow because we are made of clay.

7. The first people had furry (feathery) skins. These people were the angels. The "Rays of the Sun—The Master of the Bellows," he is St. Michael. The heavens are never dark. The Rays of the Sun—the Master of the Bellows struggled up out of the dark forest and obliged the bright rays to strike into the courtyard. And disorder and strife became apparent with the arrival of that day. It came from night-time escapades now become clear by day.

8. Adam and Eve they began kneeling in supplication. They are the first priests—knowers of the unseen. Then Eyen Zame died by a spearing. The sharpening stone executed by the knife! The great machete has killed the sharpening stone. The spear it has killed Eyen Zame.

9. Eboga says: "Môpasema beba, môpasema beba ndembe." That means twins. "Môpasema beba, mopasema beba ndembe"—twins over

and over again without change. And that is sister and brother. And that is wife and husband, and that is child and mother. But still one dies alone and one is sick alone.

10. Eyen Zame has no wings. Angels have wings because they are born from eggs. Also they have furry (feathery) bodies. The father of us all made life counting six nights. Then Zame shaped the egg that descended upon the ocean. And therefore we were all born in an egg. Life has many divisions like a piece of sugar cane. By taking his life section by section mankind is driven on to the end.

11. Nyingwan Mebege she is the oil palm. Zame ye Mebege he is the otunga tree. And the death that came to them and which has come to us all is that of the lazy and wandering one, the slovenly one of legend, Ndapiat. And she was caught by surprise in the forest. And Ndapiat gave birth between the spreading roots of the azap tree. These roots were the first stool. And the azap we know protects the newborn, distracting sorcerers and causing them to climb into its branches. And we Fang began at the azap but thus protected we set out quickly from under azap tree. Then Zame sat upon the stool and gave it to his child Eyen Zame. That stool is the otunga and it is also a cross. Azap-mboga is the road of death. And the first stool, the azap, was the door to death.

12. The spirits descend into the pool of Nyingwan Mebege which Banzie call Tame Manga. In that water we bathe ourselves. That is the pool of Maria. And it has the name of Miwandzi Amwanga Tame Manga. The black is the elder but white is the refuge—the refuge of the spirit. We see it in the white powder of our ceremonies. We see it in the color of the ancestor spirits.

13. The black child is five times older. And the moon (the maiden) began to tie together the congregation in the pool. Eboga has two sections to it—birth and death.

14. Eyen Zame has gone to the rocky sepulcher with the twelve spirits. Twelve apostles accompanied him. And he left them behind to wander in this world for twenty years.

15. The living body is the second-born of twins. The caps of Zame— the halos men wear—are black, red, and white. The cap of Zame is called blessing. And we refer to it as of the water clan. There is the blessing. Mankind does not know he has been born unless others tell him of it as I tell you here. It is not for the man to wash his wife in water. The tadpole—the first transformation of the child—in the womb is for both of us, male and female, a blessing. Thus woman should carefully guard and protect the water.

16. The convulsions of the soul, that considerate death agony, is what we give to women when we marry them. And that death is a payment of the earth. And it is the seed of humankind.

17. The ligaments of the small green bird who cries like boiling water they tie together the earth. Woman has the pierced azap tree below. Man holds the azap tree up above. And thus is life tied together. Zame makes life with two materials: the twin drumming sticks is the male. The drum is the female.

18. Nyingwan Mebege cooked twelve leaf packages of manioc. She carefully laid eboga leaves in the bottom of the cooking pot and in the cooking basket. She twisted off the sinewy veins from the green leaves in order to tie up the packages of food. Then she put into the leaf package the tadpole, the fruit of the nsom, and the flintstone. Then she saw small lizards. One of those she placed down within also. Then she placed a little water in the package. Then she went to the river to scoop up water in order to boil the packages over the fire. The black water bugs were left behind scurrying about and causing disorder.

19. Now Zame ye Mebege cut apart the leaf package and with these sinews he tied together the Fang house. The human child begins as a tadpole, he is a flintstone, he is a lizard, and he dies. The little waterbug it is the spirit and it performs miracles as it goes above.

20. These words are the words of the wind. The earth is of one speaking. Having the word is listening to the words of the wind. The earth still contains bones but now (in Bwiti) it listens to the words that come from the village (of the dead). I have finished speaking.

IMMEDIATE CONTEXT AND THEMATIC INTENTIONS

The sermon is influenced by its immediate context. Since this sermon was given in September at the start of the cool rainy season—the prime season for Fang, as it is the main season for the planting and weeding and growing and harvesting of crops—its preoccupation with water and seed and rain and generally with the origin and growth of things is appropriate to its season. The reference to the preparation of food, although it is figurative, referring to the cooking of mankind, is also apt, for this season is a time of hunger—the food reserve of the previous year are low or all but exhausted. Since the sermon was given on the first (efun) day of the three-day festival for Olorogebot (St. Michael, who herein is given a praise name—Rays of the Sun), it is appropriate that it be concerned with matters of origin. For efun is the originating night of the three-day engosie—the night in which Banzie gather themselves in the dark forest before coming into the light of the village. The recurrent references to experiences of the forest are thus particularly apt here, although it is true that the forest occurs in all the sermons as a domain full of resources for the imagination.

As this sermon was written down in the sermon book of Ekang Engono,[21] and as it was read again by the yemba and tape recorded, there was no segmentation. The division into twenty paragraphs corresponds to our own sense of the sequence of topics. That sequence may appear to be random but it coheres in various ways. It is the sermonizer's main intention to speak of things that "are no longer." The sermon holds to that intention. It maintains its theme of being about origins. But the theme is tricky. For example, in paragraph five, Ekang puts forth a riddle whose purpose is to teach the congregation its exalted and exposed nature. It is the kind of calculated puzzlement that frequently occurs in these sermons and has nothing obvious to do with matters of origin, although in a vague way the clinging raindrop is resonant with the water motif which is recurrent as origin imagery. Very likely the idea of origin in a drop of blood which occurs in the previous paragraph brought the riddle of the raindrop to mind.

In order that this puzzlement not turn into "complexity" and confound its listeners, the sermons can as often take a didactic approach and seek direct explanation. Paragraphs nine, twelve, and sixteen have that explanatory quality: nine explains a Popi phrase and the emphasis on duality in Bwiti; twelve explains an architectonic feature of the rituals; and sixteen explains the sacrificial nature of male-female relations as conceived in Bwiti. None of these topics is made to conform directly to the overall interest in origins. And yet we perceive how each of these paragraphs is linked to previous elements in the sermon and how, by bringing a larger cultural perspective of interpretation to bear, an interest in origins may be seen to be contained in each reference. The sermonizer, however he may explain particular passages, rarely refers to overall principles which are guiding his thought. One must seek these by referring out to the larger cultural context. Interpretation, therefore, is a moving back and forth—as is so often the case—between text and surrounding context. The elliptical quality of the text obliges us to proceed by indirection in our interpretation, to seek in the "unseen" culture which surrounds this text its "raison d'être."

In paragraph nine, for example, our knowledge of Bwiti views on typological transformation of Zame and his Sister into Adam and Eve into Eyen Zame and his mother, Marie, allows us to grasp the transformation which the speaker has in mind in his various versions of twinness. This transformation is linked to the transformation of the child in paragraph two and there is reason to interpret it as addressed to the matter of origins.

The same interpretation by indirection may be made in paragraph twelve. Ostensibly it is an explanation to the membership, recondite to be sure, of the sacred pools and the use of colors in the chapel. But the paragraph is appropriately linked to the previous discussion of the descent of the "spider's egg" into the inchoate ocean. And in the larger context we recognize that the speaker is correlating the origin of the earth by the descent of the spider's egg to the ocean with the origin of the individual human being by the descent of the spirit to the sacred pool through the agency of Nyingwan Mebege. We have also seen that there is a ritual progression of colors in Bwiti from black to red to white, so that the discussion of colors, the reference to the eldership of black and the refuge of white, also has to do with origins and evolution.

Paragraph sixteen correlates the death agony with male sexual climax—a "gentle death" or "sacrifice" that men offer to women in marrying them. This "sacrifice" not only offers the seed and fructifies mankind but it also "pays the earth." From the larger context we know the Banzie belief that mankind has fouled the earth by the sin of incest, the violation of the integrity of another by being born, by the cannibalism of nursing, and by self-indulgent, nonsacrificial sexuality. The European has paid that earth and become white. But Banzie are in the process of paying it. Reading this paragraph in this way we find implicit in it matters of origin and evolution. Otherwise the paragraph accords well with other paragraphs which are devoted directly or figuratively to physiological creation. Applying the larger cultural context enables us to see how, in recondite and elliptical fashion, certain themes are being threaded through the text.

THINKING IN COMPLEXES

With a view to understanding the kind of thinking characteristic of the sermon let us turn to a progressive explanation of the parts. One must recognize that for such recondite and indirect speech—such miraculous words—a full exegesis could be lengthy indeed, a contextualization which would lead out to the entire culture of Bwiti, if not all of Fang culture.

Paragraph one explores briefly the major events of Fang origin and migration from savanna through azap tree into a fully forest existence. The leitmotif phrase, "for Fang are of the forest," is asserted as a principle around which the sermon can be constructed. This assertion can also act as a recurrent controlling emotion, for Bwiti takes pride in being a forest religion. The forest imagery which recurs in this sermon is a main source of its emotional integrity.

The four miracles recounted in the second paragraph concern the successive transformations of the child as he passes to adulthood: from lying to crawling to standing at the knee to being put upon the balance of the father's shoulder and gaining thereby the perspective of adulthood. For adulthood in the sense of elementary body-wisdom is a sure sense of up and down and of balance in all things. The balance image here is also meant to refer to the balance in which St. Michael, the saint to whom the sermon is devoted, places the souls of men upon judgment.

In the third paragraph we encounter another recurrent image, the wind. The sermons of many Banzie leaders are considered to be "words of the wind." Like the path metaphor the wind is felt to bind together life and death. But men are not birds to take that wind for granted. Just as Banzie must assiduously follow the path so they must cultivate the wind, for once the wind is lost one cannot fan it back into a cadaver.

The third paragraph contains several references to Fang legend and history—the rainbow and the nineteenth-century invasion of Fang territory. In some versions of Fang legend the rainbow, which is a cosmic path image, guided Fang in their flight and migration through the savanna and across the great rivers into the forest. In Bwiti it is taken as a sign of the blessing of the above upon that migration. The Oban, an actual invasion of Fang country in the late nineteenth century by the Bane, a more northern people cognate to Fang, is here equated with both Cain's assault upon Abel—a conflation of Fang history and Christian myth-legend—and the Fang invasion of the equatorial forest.

Paragraph four evokes Fang notions of gestation. One begins with the drop of blood, the homunculus in the female, which is then quickened and protected by male seminal fluid until the egg-sac of birth is formed. This physiological process is associated by the microcosm-macrocosm extension so typical of Bwiti both to the cosmic egg of sky spider which created the earth and to the formation of hailstones in the air. And finally, since one of the preoccupying themes in Bwiti is the relation between black and white, the two parts of the egg, physiologically red and white, are transformed into black and white[22]— a white hailstone and a black hailstone. Thus is the egg of creation linked to the black earth surrounded by the white sky.

The notion of the suspension of drops of blood and of cosmic eggs and of hailstones leads to the sequential association of suspended things in paragraph five: the stars, fruit in tall trees, and finally raindrops. The raindrop is taken as an analogy for the worshiping group of Bwiti because they, like the raindrop, are suspended between heaven and earth, the below and the above, yet possess a clear, forewarned awareness of both their heavenly origin and their final destination, their earthly dissolution.

In paragraph six we move from one fruit which is virtually unattainable and quite bitter—the fruit of the azap tree—to another fruit, quite sweet and obtainable. This is the fruit which is the breast, a familiar association to Fang. But since Fang are tough people of the forest rather than softer people of the village the speaker argues that they come to the breast first by sucking the sweet milky liquid from the sugar cane. Coming to the breast has, however, the speaker goes on to warn, produced a wheedling character in Fang that they did not previously possess. Since the theme of "crying out in despair" and of "asking pity," both a kind of wheedling, is a constant one in Bwiti this seems to be Ekang's way of accounting, ruefully perhaps, for its origin— in the easy access to the sweet fruit of the breast. We remember, in regard to this warning, that eating at the breast is considered an original, if inescapable sin in Bwiti. Thoughts of their dependence upon the breast should lead Banzie to recognize that they are made of clay and dependent upon the rainbow to lead them forth to salvation.

We have enough of this sermon before us now to pause and consider what kind of thinking is going on. It is elliptical thought which puts a burden upon the listener for interpolation, extension, and contextualization. It is thought that forces the listener out to a larger context. Insofar as the listener has that larger context as a frame of reference this kind of sermonizing returns him or her to the whole. It is another form of "edification by puzzlement" and it acts to revitalize the larger religious culture.

The thought in these sermons rarely coheres by reference to explicit organizing principles and declared objectives. There is rarely a purpose stated to the membership in the manner of "tonight I wish to speak about our origins," or "about perdition" or "about the threat in village life to our integrity." Such explicitness would violate the principle of "edification by puzzlement."

Where an explicitly conceived purpose is lacking the selection of subject matter seems volatile. By indirection we can usually discover implicit subjects which are recurrently addressed. In the case of this sermon the subject is origins and it is addressed in several ways through a variety of images: forest imagery, atmospheric imagery, cooking imagery, birth imagery. But since all these images condense many meanings and as they are put forth virtually unconstrained by a conceived purpose they easily conduce to the evolution of other themes and to the bringing of these other themes into focus, if only momentarily.

It is fruitful to recognize in these Bwiti sermons what Vygotsky has called "thinking in complex."[23] As the sequence of associations which are put forth is not dominated by any overall conceived purpose, often the materials cluster around recurrent nuclear, organizing images. New materials from various domains of Fang experience are introduced on the basis of association by similarity or contiguity, contrast or complementarity with these nuclear images. But then again, abruptly and apparently spontaneously new elements with their attributes are allowed to enter the thought process, introducing new topics and even new nuclei. The sermons in this way become diffuse and challenging to interpretation. For example, in these sequences from this long sermon which we are examining we find drops of blood, hailstones, and cosmic eggs exemplifying the theme of origin. They are associated with physiological and cosmological origins. But since they have the attribute of suspendedness they immediately bring into association a collection of suspended items: stars, fruit, and raindrops. Then abruptly one of the elements of this collection, the fruit, is allowed to assert itself by association with the breast. This then brings to mind other themes than that of origin: the violation of another's integrity by the sin of lactation and self-indulgent wheedling and search for pity in response to existential despair. Both of these are edifying themes in Bwiti but vis-à-vis the main theme are produced spontaneously here out of puzzlement. After reviewing briefly these edifying themes the speaker returns abruptly to another element in the collection of suspended objects: the raindrop. This leads to a focus upon an image associated with the path of birth and death: the rainbow. The rainbow, itself a cosmic path, is a guide, a salvation, for humans who, made of clay, cannot without this guide save themselves by following the right path. Thus a third theme is produced—that of "salvation by following the path."

THE WORKING OUT OF PROBLEMS AND PARADOXES

These sermons seem fanciful in the Coleridgian sense—an unchecked subliminal flow of images in association—were it not for the recurrence of a main theme which restrains pure spontaneity, determines to some extent the choice of edifying images, and constructively returns to the whole. The sermons are too edifying to the membership to be simply fanciful. They also work out, albeit subtly, some of the problems in Bwiti theology and cosmology. A major theological problem for Banzie, for example, has been the status of the angels vis-à-vis the ancestors. Paragraph seven of the sermon attempts to solve that problem by assigning the angels to a different order of being: furry or feathery creatures who were born from eggs and are hence different from mankind and from Eyen Zame. Of course it is true, as the sermon goes on to say, that all beings were originally born from the egg of creation so that, whatever the subsequent differences in the order of being, they still have a common origin.

It is unclear why St. Michael, the patron saint of the sermon, should be referred to in paragraph seven as the "Rays of the Sun"—Mebege is usually thought of as the sun and Zame ye Mebege as the rays of the sun.[24] The reference may be intended to link St. Michael or Olorogebot, "He Who Shows the Way or Opens the Way" more directly with Zame and with Mebege. The relation of the saints to the great gods is a problem in Bwiti.

In any event it is edifying to realize that things of the forest and of the thicket below are never obscure to those great powers who periodically emerge, as the sun emerges out of the dark forest of the east, to cast light into the thickety disorder of village life—a disorder due to clandestine night-time activity, escapades. Paragraph seven lauds, in effect, that capacity in the great powers—a capacity which Bwiti itself claims—to cast light upon and thus bring order into night-time activity. Whereas the great powers, Zame and Olorogebot, accomplish this by day, Bwiti, with the aid of the Sister of God, accomplishes this by ordering the disorderly night itself.

In paragraph eight the reference to the kneeling of Adam and Eve is a reference to their sin of incest and to the despairing search for pity it brought upon them and upon mankind. Their incest is a problem, for while this sin brought spiritual awareness of hidden things it eventually led to the death of Eyen Zame. The death of the savior figure is the problem that next presents itself to the sermonizer. It was a death by spearing and thus an ironic death. For he who sharpened men's senses of the unseen—the "sharpening stone of mankind" as the sermonizer calls him—and he who put mankind on the path of birth and death is cast aside and killed by those he might have sharpened and guided. The problem of the death of a culture hero is "solved" by ironic detachment from the event—by pointing up the paradoxes involved.

In paragraph eleven we have a particularly recondite use of forest imagery and of folktale. It is apt that Nyingwan Mebege be taken as the oil palm because of the tree's association with a beneficial red fruit (her color is red) and its succulent heart (heart of palm) which is a Fang lactogen. The otunga, on the other hand, as a tree of the "last earth" is more appropriate to Zame and is more generally associated with death than with birth. The death that is referred to is of Eyen Zame again. In this context the sermonizer mentions a Fang folktale of a woman, Ndapiat, so sloppy and careless as to have been caught by surprise having to give birth in the forest.[25] In Bwiti sermons there is often an admonitory undertone directed toward women and their habits, and this is an example of it. But other associations are at work. A forest birth and, additionally, a birth in the buttressed roots of the azap tree, is appropriate to the forest imagery of the sermon and, of course, brings in the thematic tree of Bwiti. But the major point of this part of the sermon is to contrast the natural condition of unplanned birth and death with the careful organization of life in Bwiti as it follows the path of birth and death.

Abruptly we are returned to forest imagery and to two of the central trees in the Bwiti image inventory: the azap and the otunga. The azap tree, whose roots act to couch the giving of birth, and whose branches protect against sorcerers (by attracting them), is associated with the four-legged stool upon which the leaders of the Bwiti chapel sit. This stool in turn is associated by its four legs to the cross of crucifixion, four-legged in its way. The stool of birth which is the azap tree becomes in an abrupt association the stool of death which is the otunga tree. The azap as the tree of life, then (the main azap tree in Bwiti thought is the pierced azap tree, *azapmboga*, through which the Fang were born into the equatorial forest), is quickly linked to the otunga as the tree of death. Similarly, we remember, the central pillar of the chapel— a generalized tree—has both a birth and a death hole in close association. While this paragraph seems extreme in spontaneity of associations, in fact the associations relate to the problem of closely relating life *and* death already resolved in the Fang architectonic. Also they are associations which solve the problem of life and death by bringing these contrary conditions into conjunction in a forest of two trees—a birth tree and a death tree. In like manner the path metaphor integrates life and death.

The sermon now embarks upon a series of paragraphs concerned with the problem of birth order and the coming into maturity. Water imagery becomes predominant, particularly the origin pool of mankind, the sacred forest pool of Nyingwan Mebege. Basic colors appear. It is frequently stated in Bwiti, as in paragraph twelve, that black is the elder while white is the younger. White is also said to be the refuge in the sense that for those growing old the youngest and favorite child will become the refuge of his aging parents. This precedence of black applies to the dark primordial condition of the cosmos to which both Mebege and Zame ye Mebege brought the whiteness of light. We know, as well, that the three-day ritual progress is from black to white— from the blackness of the origin spot to the whiteness of the above and beyond which is the final refuge which Banzie seek. Blackness to whiteness is the progression in color terms from origin to spiritual maturity. Otherwise birth and water imagery is predominant here.

A PLAY OF ELEMENTARY IMAGES

The sermonizer not only plays on roots, producing the effect of greater integrity of the sermon, he plays on elemental images. One recalls here Tessmann's argument that each of the Fang cults he discussed was devoted to one or another of the elements: sun, moon, water, and fire. He identified these elements in the process of his search for the "elementary ideas" which lay embedded in the religion of the "*Naturvölker*." Indeed, the sun and the moon are organizing images in the Bwiti architectonic, but elementary ideas in the sense that Tessmannn sought them out do not emerge in any explicit way. *Prima materia* come up in Bwiti discussions of their religion. For example, in the constellation Orion, the four outer stars of the quadrangle are said to be the stars of water, of fire, of earth, and of air or of the wind. But elementary ideas, as Tessmann despaired, live on in Bwiti, as in Fang, unrealized.

Yet one notes in these sermons a playing with elements or with elementary images such as water or fire so as to have them emerge in different embodiments and different contexts throughout the sermon. This, like the playing on roots, gives a sense of integrity to the "miraculous words"—a sense of their being founded on something elemental and recurrent. In paragraph fifteen, for example, we have a dense flow of associations, although the theme is still that of birth. The nuclear organizing image, however, becomes that of water, and the birth theme is here embodied in spirit pools, amniotic liquids, and seminal fluids. The element emerges in recondite references to caps of Zame and to twins, for the first-born of twins is the fetal membrane which is often, as a portion of the caul, carried on the infant's head. The reference to the cap of Zame is a reference to this membrane. We are not so far away from the bag of waters, the human "spirit pool," whose remnant it is. But also the Banzie cap is rainbowlike.[26] It displays the three basic colors of the religion. The rainbow-like nature of this fetal "halo" is in general constellation with the elemental underlying concern with water.

This concern emerges more directly as the sermonizer next associates Banzie with the water clan, Yemenzim.[27] Though there is a Fang clan by this name, the reference is rather to the Banzie themselves whose origins lie in waters of various kinds. Indeed, as the sermonizer has pointed out in paragraph thirteen, the moon has tied together the congregation in the pool. The water image continues to maintain its associative power and in further sentences brings to mind the fetus in the form of a tadpole growing, without distinction of sex, within the amniotic fluid, the bag of waters. It is to the woman particularly that the guardianship of this water of birth belongs. For it is not the man who washes his wife in the end, although in the climactic convulsions—the little deaths—of the sexual act, he provides a nurturant and protective seminal fluid for her. It is rather the woman who washes all mankind in the amniotic sac of creation.

Though this, like all sermons, rests upon close observation and knowledge not only of physiological process but also of equatorial forest and fauna, one or another of these images will generally be taken as underlying and organizing. Here water is a commanding sign and exerts a principle of selection amidst the plethora of natural objects available for purposes of representation. Take, for example, the small green bird, ôtok, whose song is reminiscent of boiling water (from tok, to boil) and who seems to have been brought to mind by that association with the water image. Of course this bird has other attributes. Since the tendons of its legs are sometimes used as ligatures in leather and woodwork, it has an attribute of "tying together" that Ekang goes on to exploit. Then abruptly we return again to the azap tree of Fang origin. Here with the ligature in mind the tree is employed to tie together male and female. For as the hole in it is female, in its erectness it is male. Thus is life tied together, the sermonizer says, and, indeed, thus does the sermon tie life together by a fertile exploitation of the attributes of its organizing elemental images and of those images that arise in association with them.

The final paragraphs contain a series of cooking images which resonate with the boiling water and the "tendon as ligature" images previously. They are also very much origin images and conform to that thematic preoccupation. The specific reference is to the preparation by Nyingwan Mebege of the "human package." The "human being as package" metaphor we know is recurrent in Bwiti and in Bwiti sermons. Mankind, the sermon has it, is enclosed in leaves and cooked up. The notion of thickety enclosure in leaves and the feeling of suffocation recurs in these sermons, although here that enclosure is given more positive valence, for Fang and Bwiti notions of ontogeny, phylogeny and transformation of being are afoot. As the sermon implies, men and women in gestation begin in the form of tadpoles and pass through various transformations such as flintstones and lizards.[28] Water imagery comes back into this paragraph in a major way and the bag of waters is transformed into a leaf package of boiling food. Various kinds of waterbugs enter here as well, representing those spiritual forces that know how to live above the water of life. Black waterbugs represent the evil spirits and little waterbugs the good spirits.

If we follow the sequence of images, we find a climactic complexity in paragraph nineteen. Here, Zame opens the food package in order to make a Fang house. And, indeed, the walls of Fang dwellings were lined with leaves and tied with fibers similar to those used in cooking packages. But in doing this, Zame also releases the spirit from its various leafy enclosures, enabling it, like the little water bug, to go above and find a larger heavenly house. The general vector in most of these sermons may be toward "the above," but we see how that tendency is constantly grounded in the immediate and often microscopic resources of Fang experience. The sermonizer "thinks through" the sign-images of this experience, organizing them in relation to a succession of recurrent and more elemental images.

CONCLUSION: IMAGES OF EDIFICATION
OFFERED TO THE EYES

Ekang Engono, the "Parrot's Egg," the "first among the creators," the "inveterate hunter," offers by his miraculous words to "tie the world together," to show—for Fang emphasize the visual mode—by a sequence of "likenesses" that the world, fallen into a devilish particularity, is yet really one thing. That is truly edifying, but it is not didactic. For these sermons are most markedly a flow, often thick and multilayered, of images whose relationship to each other is rarely expository. The linkage between images is indirect and recondite. The visions that the hunter's mind's eye is following in the gravepit, in his semisomnolent state under the influence of eboga, lead here and there, disappear from view in the thicket amidst the trees, and suddenly again emerge in another place or direction. And yet for the membership these sermons are not especially disjointed. They do not seem to be the product of a mad or drugged mind. Approaching them with their cultural knowledge—the sort we seek to approximate in interpretation—they find an integrity in them. Amidst the trees of this forest of images these sermons remind the members of the forest itself. Amidst the thickety convolutions of these sermons the membership is repeatedly reminded of the above and beyond to which they are being carried despite the difficulties they, as we, may have in explaining individual passages or sequences of passages. For ambiguities both playful and somber abound in these sermons. They are full of words with divided meanings. Their very ambiguity, indeed, is a measure of their "miraculousness," a testimony to their august provenance. They are words that arise out of the gravepit and come from the land of the dead. The Banzie by and large seem ready to accept in a voice from the grave such "edification by puzzlement" and they demand little direct explanation. How could such words be of easy access?

If these sermons are difficult to understand in any lineal sense they are always full of images which steadily fill the mind's eye in a satisfying way, however these striking images are to be linked together by reference to larger contexts. And it is not only in striking images but in intriguing reference to old folklore, in playing on roots, in unifying condensations, in double entendre and in the ironies of double perspectives that these sermons are edifying and lead out to a larger whole.

In many of these sermons (we see this in the long sermon examined here) there is an impressive interlinkage of various domains and various levels of interest into something that suggests cosmological integrity if it does not actually explicate it. Thus physiological, domestic, architectonic, ecological, and legendary-cosmic experiences are made to reflect each other. The bag of waters at birth is the forest pool is the great river of migration is the cosmic sea of origin. Or the azap tree of legendary entrance into the great forest is the pillar of heaven and earth while it is also the male organ and the female organ. One obtains in these sermons as, indeed, one obtains in the architectonic of Bwiti life and in the ritual drama of their celebrations, a sense of reverberation, resonance between levels and domains of interest. In talking about one thing and circling around one image there is always the suggestion of other things, other attributes of that image, implied at other levels and in other domains. We are forced to extend ourselves to larger integrities in wider contexts.

In mentioning reverberation and resonance we must also keep in mind that there is a tradition to this sermonizing such that any one sermon is, in part, to be heard in the context of previous sermons. This is true to some degree of any communication in any culture, for tradition plays its inescapably important part. But to a greater degree in Fang sermons the nima na kombo has the argument and images of other sermons in mind. Things said in any one sermon may be referring not to other portions of that sermon or to the immediate context of presentation but to other sermons at other times and even to the largest context—the culture itself. This makes for real difficulty of interpretation unless one has as good a memory as the sermonizer of his previous somnolent sermonizing states or has been a steady attendant of the engosie. Indeed it is difficult unless one is fully participant in Fang culture. At the same time the need provoked in the hearer for the larger "unseen" context in ordering the sermon is itself suggestive. It is an important part of the message. It suggests that larger whole to which Bwiti constantly refers, and which the religion seeks to bring into existence by a variety of methods, recondite reference among them.

The mental state of Bwiti sermonizers such as Ekang Engono is just that which would generate the "likenesses" by which he can "tie together" the world and approximate that larger whole. The close atmosphere of the gravepit together with the late hour and the influence of the drug, eboga, promote that optimum mental state for the production of ideas by analogy: that state characterized by neither extreme nor overly relaxed motivation. The relaxed mental state of the nima na kombo relates in fact to that type of mentation often discussed by students of the mind as basic to the creative process, that state by which domination of the object-world-oriented mind is escaped so as to exploit preconscious processes. Such exploitation is claimed to lead to highly fertile use of symbolic forms in the allegorical and figurative mode. Experience is reshuffled and, by processes of analogy, dissimilar ingredients are recombined, often with a high degree of condensation, into new perceptual and conceptual patterns. The vehicle of this new message is the nima na kombo, Ekang Engono, the drugged hunter who upon descent into the gravepit becomes as one "dead to the world and to the flesh." But at the same time he becomes in his somnolent state very much alive to the resources of his people's imagination and language—alive to the resources to be found in the most resonant domains of their experience: the forest, the cook house, the womb, the watery surround of the humid equatorial world. Amidst a plethora of such images and in the fashion of a good hunter he finds visual signs (ndem) that lead him surely along the path of birth and death and likenesses (efonan) that enable him to tie together the larger whole of the Bwiti cosmos.*3

*3 We have emphasized, in this chapter, the images which are in argument in these sermon texts. After all, they arise in visions in the gravepit and produce visions in many auditors, or so they testify. At the same time these sermons are full of signs (ndem)—better called signals, perhaps—which have no pictorial content but which simply provide directionality to thought. They move the mind along to new considerations, imageless ideas—opening it up, routing it, and rerouting it and closing it up again. The hunter in his task has to be sensitive to signals and signs of this kind. It may be well to recall that our epigraph maxim tells us that the thinker is the child of the hunter and not the hunter himself.

Also, we are emphasizing here an analysis of Ekang Engono's imaginative virtuosity. But we should not overemphasize its idiosyncrasy. The "argument of images" we analyze here (that is, the condensation of references to various domains at once) as well as the punning or playing upon homophonous terms (another form of linkage or condensation of references) was common practice in ritual recitations. The "pleasure" Ekang gives to the membership by his verbal ingenuity—the spiritual powers over the "hidden" manifest in it—was a "pleasure" frequently provided by occult discourse.

⚜ 20 ⚜

The Pleasure Dome Emergent

Edô e ne atsinglan ening.
(That is the tying together of life.)

A MORNING MEAL OF MANIOC

AFTER THE NGOMBI HARP has been put away in its light, tight chamber, for the sun is brightening in the East; after the ancestors have been bid farewell in a brighter dawnlight by dances which circle around the welcoming hut which belongs to them; and after the compressed circles of "oneheartedness" have been danced in front of the hut, on the edge of the forest, and, by the women, down in the center of the nearby stream, the membership can feel the all-night ceremonies at an end. The rising sun is slanting through the trees and there are just two remaining events.[1] Neither are obligatory, although both are usually fully attended. These are the communal meal (*bídzí bi banzie*) and the hearing and untying of the embittered complaints of the membership against each other (*atia mezô me banzie*). The communal meal takes place in an open-sided hut to the left (the birth side) of the chapel. The hearing of the palavers takes place in the chapel itself. This hut of the morning meal is placed close by the birth entrance because after the ritual is over, men are as reborn into village life.

Most of the membership, understandably, is in a state of deep fatigue, for they have danced most of the night and have tried to remain alert and sacrifice their sleep. Yet there is voluble talk as the men settle into their side of the hut and the women move about preparing the morning meal. Men and women joke with each other about some misstep during the dance or for having dozed off during the wee hours. There is also a deep sense of satisfaction for they have done their ritual work well. And it has been hard work. The members are also satisfied because they are in a state of purity (*ôkan*). They have avoided the contamination of sexual congress. In the vertiginous activity of the night, by copious perspiration they have purified the impurities in their bodies.

The main food presented to the membership out of one large basin is a mix of small chunks of peeled white manioc tubers. They have been long boiled and previously long soaked to remove the prussic acid characteristic of the bitter manioc (*ôsa mboe*) which is the favorite of Bwiti. The chunks of this manioc are chosen with a purpose. For just as the manioc has been purified of its poisons by long soaking and boiling, so the members of Bwiti, now long-bathed in the humidity of the night and in their own perspiration and aroused to heated activity, have become purified of their poisons. The ethnographer and his wife sit down in their respective spheres of the hut. They are offered pieces of manioc. For though they danced few dances and did not perspire at all, it is joked, yet they remained awake the whole night and were probably pure enough, that is to say free of connubial contamination, to partake of the meal. Sometimes roasted peanuts are passed around for they, too, like the Banzie, have had their heads broken open and have come free of their skins, their external appearances, having been purified by fire.

If there is no immediate business and no palavers the membership will linger long in this hut in diverse conversations and with strong euphoric sentiments of solidarity and collective effort. If there are any palavers the *nima na kombo* will call the membership into the chapel to hear them out. As he has taken the sins of the membership upon himself during the night and transferred them to the forest, so he is ready to take their quarrels upon himself in the morning. But in this euphoric atmosphere, animosities have been mostly satiated in activity. Steeped in the flow of ritual, most of the bitterness has gone out of them. It is a rare member who can vigorously recall and espouse the insults or injuries he felt before the night began. If there is deep bitterness, a man or a woman is not likely to bring it to these early morning moots. Thus, the moots are conducted, most often, in an atmosphere of only mild recrimination. The nima na kombo does not have to say much. He mildly reproves and suggests. Often the mere relating of an offense satisfies the injured party, while the offending party is usually ready to make amends, already persuaded by the general atmosphere.

The engosie does not always end on such a tonic note, but it usually does. The rituals work effectively to the pleasure of these morning hours. In this final chapter, although we have addressed ourselves to such issues in our previous chapters, we will explore in a final way the sources of the satisfactions bound up in the activities of this equatorial pleasure dome. These sources are various. Also, the experiences of the membership are diverse; what is meaningful to one member, say a nima na kombo, may be simply routine to another member. What gives one member pleasure, say a particular symbolic conceit or a particular ritual routine, may be quite opaque or without interest to another member. If, as Ekang Engono boasts, Bwiti "ties the world together" it does not do so by achieving uniform experience in the members. It does so only by insisting on common activity, by coordinating core and peripheral ritual action despite the diversity of referents that action may have for the members.

First of all, if Bwiti does "return to the whole"—put the world together again—it does so by requiring common, highly coordinated activity, but not common meanings or common feelings. Perhaps the basic satisfaction in Bwiti for the members is that which suffuses this morning meal of manioc. It is the satisfaction of having danced together in unison, of having "worked" for the dead and the great gods in well-coordinated fashion with others and for an entire night. But there are also many subordinate satisfactions, pleasures, fulfillments, and reconciliations.

The Handing About of Symbols

For many members there is a pleasure in the invention and handing about of symbols[2]—various substances or objects that have a place in the religious interaction and, while fulfilling a function, bring into association other domains and levels of experience. The use of manioc at the morning meal is an example of this. In addition to the satisfaction of the meal, it is pleasurable to realize that the manioc chunks, pieces of the now white and purified tuber, stand for the members' own bodies purified by the water and heat of worship of the dirt of the earth, of the bitterness of life. The same kind of compounded pleasure, physical and symbolic, is present in the eating of peanuts. For this food also stands for the broken heads and the discarding of the external body which Bwiti seeks to achieve. The surpassing skillfulness (*akyenge*) involved in "saying something" about the purified bodies and released spirits of Bwiti adepts in the offering of food is pleasurable. For these symbols offer an elemental kind of "knitting together" and reconciliation of the parts of experience—in this case at least the body part and the food part, if not the material part and the spiritual part.

The Banzie are inventive and there are many such pleasurable symbols. Sometimes very novel objects are introduced. For example, Banzie have replaced the traditional raffia bustle of Fang women dancers with sleigh bells. Not only do these add an attractive sound to the dance; there is a symbolic conceit. For the ball in the bells represents the baby in the womb and the bells' action, sexual activity.[3] These are both apt associations, given Bwiti emphasis upon restoring fertility to women.

Another novel item is rubber balls. In the Kombé branch of Bwiti, rubber balls are introduced into the ceremonies and passed around from member to member and hand to hand—particularly after the exhausting obango dances. There are also dances in which rubber balls are bounced. These rubber balls (*endama*) have a variety of meanings[*1] but fundamentally they refer to the

---

[*1] They are also said to represent the sky spider's egg (aki abop) which contained the primordial threesome—Zame, his sister Nyingwan, and Nlona Mebege, "the evil one." Mention is also made of the modern game of football in which the players run around after the ball. Despite chaotic appearances the ball actually holds all the players under its discipline, the rules of "its" game. The rubber ball then stands for that which organizes and orders the "running around." It is a dynamic "point de repère."

resistance that the good wind (*mba-mba mfônga*) of Zame provides to the Banzie. For the rubber shell of the ball is the skin of the Banzie, and the air within is the "good wind." It is the good wind of Zame that enables the Banzie to rise again after falling to the ground in a state of despair or exhausted from the all-night dancing. In the same way, although in being born the infant falls to the earth, the "wind of Zame" causes him again to spring aloft. Equally, at the end of life, although the body falls to earth, the soul yet goes up. The rubber ball, in short, represents the resilience Banzie obtain by incorporation of the good wind of Zame.

The thinking up of these symbols is said to be an example of akyenge, surpassing skillfulness. It testifies to that religious and intellectual preeminence to which the "knowledgeable ones" of the religion lay claim. It is mostly they who introduce these symbols and, in introducing them, they show their capacity to make one thing or set of things out of something else, and by this reconciliation, this collapsing of two things into one thing, their capacity to return to the whole.

The general atmosphere of Bwiti is conducive to the use of conceits in this way. The equatorial world, village and forest, is full of things apt for use as symbols. There is, for example, the *evegé-e-ngogé* plant (*Cassia alata*) the so-called "indicator of the evening" which closes its leaves at about four in the afternoon. In some branches of Bwiti this plant is used in initiation when the initiate, already eating eboga, is brought down to the stream for the purification ritual we have described in Chapter 18.[4] The plant was rubbed over the body and its sense ran by contraries to its natural meaning. While the evegé closed in the late afternoon, the initiate was expected to be opened up to the unseen at the same time. It is also said, on the other hand, that as the plant indicated to women in traditional life the approach of the evening meal so its use in initiation signaled the spiritual repast of the evening rituals of Bwiti.

The flora and fauna of the equatorial regions were widely culled for apt symbols. We have seen the frequency with which the African Gray Parrot appears—an animal apt because of his red tail feathers (the first to follow the red path of life and death), his capacity of speech (miraculous words), his direct and unambiguous flight (he is not lost in the thicket), and his recondite nesting places. Another symbolic animal is the civit cat (*esinga: Genetta cervalina*) whose skin was placed between the legs of the seated initiate. The basket of eboga was placed upon it from which the initiate steadily dipped. Banzie say that the spotted fur of this wildcat, reddish-brown spots upon white, reiterates the two basic colors of Bwiti. It is thus a good representation of the bringing together of redness and whiteness which Banzie seek to achieve in their rituals. They also say that as the wildcat is a deft and agile forest animal, so Banzie can learn from it to be deft and agile in the forest of the dead.

These explanations must be complemented, however, by reference to an older tradition of observations on the sexual meaning of the esinga skin, probably derived from the notable screeches and yowls that accompany wildcat copulation. Dating back to Largeau,[5] it has been noticed among Fang that love-fetishes have been made out of wildcat skin and that this usage relates to its use as a genital covering (*cache-sexe*) or otherwise as a hanging decoration from the breech strap. Binet, Gollenhoffer, and Sillans, in fact, consider the wildcat skin as a symbolic penis.[6] Other observers, while not giving a direct sexual interpretation, point up the degree to which, among Fang and elsewhere in Gabon, the wildcat skin is potent in magic and sorcery and can bring bravery in combat or protection (*akamayong*) to the clan.[7] These sexual meanings may be present in the Bwiti symbol—its placing between the legs in initiation suggests this—so that it not only reconciles red and white and village with forest, but also the enforced celibacy of the night rituals with sexuality. We have seen sexual representations at one level and the exclusion of sexuality on another level before. After all, while the Banzie must enforce the ''sacrifice'' of night-long celibacy, they must also seek fertility and potency for their membership. The wildcat skin would, therefore, be an apt symbol of sacrificed, yet resurgent, potency coupled with confident and protective power.

The central hands-on symbols of Bwiti, however, are the ritual garments and the various musical instruments, the rattle and brush, the drums of the obango, the bamboo pounding staves, the one-stringed harp, and the ngombi harp itself. During the all-night ceremonies, the membership, appropriately garbed, is in constant interaction both with these instruments and with their own clothes. All chapels explain both the instruments and the clothing although meanings differ from chapel to chapel as the uniforms themselves differ.[*2]

In the Asumege Ening branch of Bwiti, the two-colored (red and white) uniforms[8] are washed in the river the morning before the all-night celebrations. It is the first act of purification. For the clothes will be full of the impurities sweated away in the last engosie. They are hung out to dry under a thatch porch. Though the sun may strike the white cloth, the red cloth ''fears the sun.'' The red cloth is the giver of life while the sun is the ''life-taker'' or death-giver, the heavenly body which belongs on the death side of the chapel. The red cloth ''fears'' the sun also for a quite practical reason: it easily fades.

The explanation of the red and the white is typically multivocal. Most simply it is said that red is the color of sin and it is therefore appropriate that the lower half of the uniform is red, for men and women sin in the lower halves of their bodies. The white of the upper half of the uniform is purity,

---

[*2] The diversity of views and the problem of consensus in views as regards the meaning of the harp is discussed in J. W. Fernández, ''Symbolic Consensus.''

the purity of the upper body. But it is also clear that the red and white are the blood and the semen out of which living beings are made. The uniforms make a statement about the contrasting and interacting elements of life. In the end, Banzie say, the purpose of the engosie is to enable the soul to escape the body as easily as the body can shed its clothes. The clothes are to the body as the body is to the soul. Hence, the uniform symbolizes the body: the redness its bloody tissues, the whiteness its sinews and bones.

But the color scheme of the uniform replicates the ritual process as well. That process is launched on the path of life which is the red path of the lower body. After midnight, the ritual proceeds to the path of death which is the white path of the upper body until, finally, the soul escapes the body entirely to merge above with the dead. As the ritual progresses in a passage from the below to the above, so it is replicated in the uniforms—red below and white above.

An apt comment on this passage through the colors of the clothing is made in the Ayol Chapel where the uniforms of dead Banzie are piled in a corner of the altar during Easter ceremonies. This is a reinterpretation of Fang mortuary ceremonies where the clothes of the dead are displayed upon the roofs of their huts. The explanation is that the dead soul, though it is disembodied and about to embark definitively for the land of the dead, may still be affirmed, one final time, in its loyalty to its descendants, by being shown the familiarities of its former abode. The Banzie add that in every engosie the soul, through the power of eboga, becomes disembodied, flying up beyond its uniform and its body to mingle with the dead. The body in its uniform dances on, but the soul regards its abode ecstatically from a distance. So, in the Ayol Chapel the returning dead are shown their former abodes, their clothing, from which they are now permanently distanced.

The Bwiti uniform as symbol is tied, then, in manifold ways to the body, to the ritual process, and to the overall architectonic of the religion. The ritual progression from life to death to a mingling with the ancestors is the progression understood in the soul's rising out of the body and the body's clothing, red to white to the above. In the vertical division between lower red and upper white there is a reiteration of the horizontal division of the chapel, the red side and the white side. The uniform represents those complex emotional states: vitality and sinfulness, suffering and mortality, which inhere in red; calm and perduring transcendence of impulse, and control and mastery, which inhere in white. This simple garb of red and white cotton cloth thus extends out to many facets and levels of Bwiti experience.

The same "extension out" to the religious universe can be shown for the main musical instruments. Practically all of them have at least physiological reference. The one-string harp stands for the reverberating umbilical cord which attaches mankind to all the ancestors ascendent and to the great gods.[9] The drums, and particularly the skin-headed standing drum (*nku*), stand for the human body loud in its complaint and suffering from the assaults and insults, the abuses of this earth. A similar extension is made for the bamboo sounding stave (*ôbaka*), the backbone of mankind beaten upon constantly by life. The obaka is also the path of birth and death, for its support piece on the left end is made of redwood (*mbel*) and is said to be the birth or moon side of the stave, while its support on the right side made of the very white wood (*osa*) is the sun or death side. So men and women's backbones are stretched between birth and death.

But it is the ngombi harp which, above all, symbolizes the microcosm and macrocosm of Bwiti life. It represents the body directly. The hole below is the birth hole; the two holes above are the breast holes from whence comes the nurturance of Nyingwan Mebege. Very often the entire harp, particularly if it carries a sculpted head post (Figure 20.1) represents Nyingwan Mebege

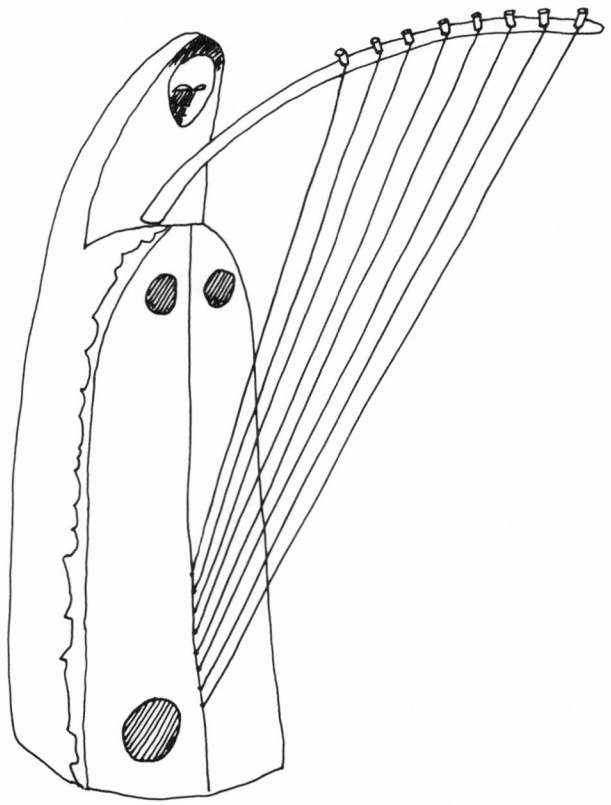

20.1 The Ngombi Harp

herself. The support post is her backbone, the keys her ribs, the strings her sinews, the sounding box her stomach. During the engosie her voice comes into the harp and speaks, in musical mode, to the membership.

But the ngombi is also associated with the chapel for it has a white half and a red half and its four lower strings are male and its four upper strings female. Played together, they represent the harmony of the engosie and men and women dancing together. The ngombi is also carved out of the wood of the two sacred trees of the chapel: its body out of osa and the support post and the keys out of the redwood, mbel. This ngombi-chapel association is carried further by the belief that the spirits of the dead, particularly the spirits of former ngombi players, can come into the ngombi as it is played just as the dead spirits come into the chapel.

There is an extension here which goes beyond Bwiti to the ancestral cult, Bieri. For as the bark reliquary contained the dead, so does the hollow ngombi. Upon both "containers" heads are posed and both at certain points in the ceremonies were and are cradled in the arms and danced out into the forest and back. When this association is pointed up, it is also quickly added that while the reliquary contained only the bones of the dead, the ngombi, like the chapel, contains the spirits of the dead.

The ngombi has, therefore, both a spiritual and a corporeal meaning; extending to the body of the worshiper it also extends to the body of Nyingwan Mebege. At the same time it welcomes the spirits of the dead. This double identity gives it a special "miraculous" quality, for while all members of Bwiti are born into the chapel through the birth entrance and pass out of the chapel through the death exit, the ngombi enters the chapel through the death exit and leaves by the birth entrance. It affirms its spiritual quality by undergoing its corporeal transformations by contraries. Dying out of the spirit world and passing through the death door, it is made alive in the chapel. And passing out of the chapel, through the birth door, it is reborn into the spirit world.

These objects of ritual interaction, the symbols of Bwiti, are pleasures to behold and to hold, to interact with or hand about. Not only are they satisfying as "things in themselves" (as food, as playthings, as music-makers), but also they extend out and link to themselves and reconcile other domains and levels of experience. They give these other domains and levels, usually very uncertainly conceived, an intriguing concrete representation. The Banzie can "see" their sad and despairing bodies in whole or in part made more graspable and manageable in manioc chunks, in peanuts, in rubber balls, in sleigh bells, in red and white uniforms, in drums and pounding staves, and in a harp. But in seeing their bodies reflected in these things, they also see their bodies associated with other referents with which these things are connected. The harp which is the Banzie's body is also the body of Nyingwan Mebege with whom Banzie most devoutly wish to be reconciled. The harp, *their* harp, is also the reliquary and the chapel. In the red and white uniform which represents the two elements of corporeal existence are also the stages of the ritual progress of the soul as it moves from fleshly creation of the lively world to the more enduring armature of sinew and bone of the upper body, finally passing out beyond and above. It is in these symbols which pass through the hands of the Banzie at every engosie that the most elemental kind of "tying together" is achieved.

The Ordering of Images

As evocative as these inventive symbols are, they are not, as we saw in the last chapter, the only vehicle of meaning. They may, it is true, have a particular force, for they condense and store into a unitary and palpable configuration a variety of apt associations which suggest a totality—and in that sense they are the elementary forms of Bwiti cosmogony. And they can be handed around. But Bwiti is rich in the experience of recurrent images—mental pictures which may be but are not usually stimulated by the entities and icons actually manipulated in the ritual process. We have discussed not only the stereotyped hallucinatory images of initiation by deep dosage of eboga— images of the multicolored road, of the crossroads, of the rivers, of the crowd of the dead, of the upland savanna and the one-legged house—but also the recurrent images of the sermons: the descent of the egg from heaven and the oceanic creation ex nihilo, the forging imagery of the creation of man and woman, and forest and hunting imagery of all kinds. The most crucial images of all are the images of their own dead which Bwiti can produce for its members. For though members regularly attest to how much they "see" in Bwiti as opposed to other religions, it is the "seeing" of the dead that conclusively convinces them of the worth of their religion.

The emphasis upon the visual metaphor for thought in Bwiti, upon "seeing," covers a variety of ways that the images of the religion are experienced. Some of the images, those of the dead, for example, may have the vivid reality of drug-induced hallucinations. Many of the images are, undoubtedly, much less clear—"thought images" as they are called, which give the impression of seeing something without vivid outline. Some of the images, surely those in initiation, are principally auditory, a hearing of voices without any distinct picture of those who embody the voices or of the setting in which the voices are heard.

One cannot underestimate the problems involved in speaking about images either in respect to their vivid picture quality or as regards their generality among the membership. It has long been recognized that images are difficult to dictate or direct in subjects. They are not easily constrained by circumstances. Images tend to occur relatively independently of overt circumstances and requirements and have a spontaneous quality. Indeed, the greater the requirement for motor activity of any kind including speech, the fewer the images produced.[10] But it is just here that Bwiti is conducive to image formation. For amidst its vertiginous activity, it still provides many periods of quiescence, drowsiness, and fatigue and other periods of drug-induced lassitude propitious for image formation. We have already studied the rich imagery of the sermons produced in just such circumstances.

But more important is the fact that certain images have come to be perceived as particularly significant—as "sign images" pregnant with potential meanings.[11] These have been made into organizing images of ritual activity. One need not assume that all Banzie experience the same images in the ritual process, or even that the images are especially vivid, to recognize that there are certain recurrent, stereotyped images which all Banzie recognize and about which they have been instructed by the "knowledgeable ones," and that these images act to organize activity. It is to the formation and ordering of these recurrent images that we now turn, in the sermons first and in the rituals second.

THEMATIC TROUBLES

The play of images in Bwiti sermons, since it is not constrained by an explicit argument, seems to move unpredictably. The "thinker as hunter" analogy seems very apt, for the sermonizer's game seems shifty and elusive. It is indeed, as Banzie say, a "midnight forest" of images and the words often seem, indeed, "the words of the wind." And yet the listener is edified while he may be also puzzled. How is this so?

It may be true, if we had large numbers of these sermons, that one could discover a tendency toward an instructive progression of images in them— say from savanna imagery to forest imagery to ocean imagery. Indeed, water imagery often occurs at the ends of these sermons, as in the long sermon given above. Other progressions which are suggestive would be those from earth to water to wind imagery, or ground to forest to sky imagery, or forest to village of the living to village of the dead imagery, or animal to human to spirit imagery. But none of these progressions can, without forcing, be discovered in the corpus of thirty-five texts collected. Even if we were to discover such ordering progressions, the discovery would be made at a lofty and unsatisfying level of abstraction.

From what we have before us, we can say, however, that Banzie are edified first because these sermons adhere to one or several recurrent themes*[3] in Bwiti. These themes, of course, are rarely explicitly stated. We discover them by indirection or in other spheres of Bwiti life. By themes is meant those recurrent preoccupations of Fang life as Banzie see it, which are problematic

---

*[3] It has been the tendency in the literature to discuss themes as "dynamic affirmation" about the givens, the common-sense facts of existence, which are recurrently expressed in various modes (M. E. Opler, "Themes as Dynamic Forces"). Themes as we understand them here are more aptly called "dynamic dilemmas" which are motivating to image formation.

and which require some kind of resolution. Bwiti as a religion, and particularly the sermons, seeks to make edifying comments on these problems. The most salient thematic preoccupations in Bwiti which motivate the sermons are the following. We have sought to give in previous chapters the historical, the social, the economic, and the political contexts which account for these preoccupations.

1. The problem of the relationship between men and women, that is, the malaise between the sexes.
2. The problem of the relationship to the abandoned ancestors.
3. The problem of the violation of another's bodily integrity.
4. The problem of ignorance and dwelling in obscurity.
5. The problem of origin ex nihilo, of procreation and the continuing capacity to procreate.
6. The problem of the European and of colonial domination.
7. The problem of poverty and suffering and the piteous and despairing condition.
8. The problem of isolation from others in the breakdown of family life and filial and fraternal piety.
9. The problem of the relationship to the great gods—the problem of theology.
10. The problem of the relation of the corporeal to the spiritual.
11. The problem of death.

When Fang speak of these preoccupying problems, they generally use two related general terms for states of mind and body: *nzuk* (a fatiguing sense of uncertainty and worry) and *nzukla* (a sense of physical or moral trouble or confusion; the term is used also as a verb for the troubling or stirring up of water). These "troubling" states burden human relationships with bad feeling and prevent the reaching of goals.

We have given the eleven "troubles" that most often emerge in discussion with Banzie and which underlie and motivate the sermons. But there are more abbreviated forms of stating these troubles. There are, for example, three very frequent exclamations in Bwiti which are a capsule summary of these thematic preoccupations: "the land of life is good no more" (*si e se fe mvé*); "how fallen apart is the relationship of brothers" (*bôbenyang be daman nlam*); "how piteous and full of despair is the life we lead" (*O tara bi ne engôngôl!*). These exclamations might otherwise be labeled as the "times out of joint" theme. In even more capsule form, Banzie speak, as we have seen above (Chapter 12), of the undesirable qualities of a former way of life: bad body (*nyôl abé*), turbulence (*ebiran*), vengefulness (*akun*), and so on. They also speak of the good qualities that they hope will emerge through the practice of the Bwiti religion: clean body (*nyôl nfuban*), tranquillity (*mvwaa*), forgiveness (*azame*), and the like. The sermons, then, are motivated by a set of continuing problems—in briefest form this is a preoccupation with the qualities of personal or social life—and every sermon gains some coherence from the fact that it treats, in its fashion, one, or perhaps several, of these problems or unacceptable quality states.

But can we say more about how the problems are treated and how the images of this figurative hunter's argument are formed? In briefest terms the view taken here is that the sermonizer's semi-somnolent mind, motivated by the recurrent preoccupations of Bwiti and seeking to move the membership to a more satisfactory condition or quality state, forms images which aptly speak to the unsatisfactory condition and accomplish that movement. We will have more to say about the specifics of movement below, as that is, in part, the consequence of ritual activities performed in respect to certain central and more stereotyped images. For movement from undesirable to desirable quality states, we have pointed out, is obtained by ritual activity in conjunction with the visual and verbal metaphors of the liturgy.

Let us seek a further understanding of the way that the more original and transitory images of the sermons are formed and of the "arguments" of the sermon made by reference to what we can call "elemental images of association" on the one hand and "syllogisms of association" on the other.

ELEMENTAL IMAGES

"Elemental images" are those simple images of experience, such as those of water, dirt, or fire, which have the capacity to expand[12]—or better to say perhaps, suggest expansion—into more complex images in the process of the sermon. The sermonizer, in a manner similar to the "playing on roots" we have discussed, plays with these experiences, forming complex images with them by inserting them in various contexts. This elemental "play" organizes his imagination in certain directions. It directs the formation of certain more complex images built upon these "root" images. It gives a sense of coherence to the presentation. We have seen the way that water imagery is an elemental image running through the long sermon we have considered in Chapter 19. It is the basis of a sequence of complex images which cohere by common inclusion of that elemental attribute: the image of the rainbow and the raindrops, the images of the spirit pools of the forest, the image of the amniotic bag of waters, the images of seminal fluid, of waterbugs, of boiling water, and of leaf packages, of boiled food, and of various other cooking images. And there are certain "plays" upon the word associated with the image as well, as in the mention of the water clan, Yemenzim, or of the bird, *ntok*, whose song is like boiling water. Water is a nuclear element in the sermon out of which more complex images are formed and around which they cluster. It should also be clear that for both sermonizer and audience there is a satisfaction in seeing these elementary images emerge in different ways into complex patterns. It is another variety of the experience of emergence*⁴ which is so basic an attraction of Bwiti.

SYLLOGISMS OF ASSOCIATION

In addition to recurrently emergent elemental images Ekang's sermons employ what we may call "syllogisms of association": analogic arguments which employ the various images and bring them before the mind in such a way as to argue for a larger unity. By the use of analogy various more concrete objects in Fang experience are predicated upon the problematic subjects of the Bwiti religion. What are these subjects? The individual Banzie, man and woman, the worshiping group, the Fang people, the ancestors, the various significant deities. All of these subjects of the Bwiti religion are, we would argue, inchoate. That is, their identities are problematic and not precisely defined. It is the role of Bwiti as a religion to predicate some more concrete and manageable identity upon them. This is done by the use of various analogies—the predication of metaphoric or metonymic identities upon these objects. In the very first paragraph of the long sermon treated it is said: Fang are Forest (or of the Forest). That identification of one of the central social subjects of Bwiti with trees or a forest of trees is recurrent and basic. Another subject of continuing concern, perhaps more so in the Commencement of Life branch of the religion, is life itself. The sermon offers the metaphor, "Life is sugar cane." This is meant to instruct the Banzie in the fact that life comes in sections and that, if approached slowly, section by section, life can be, like the sugar cane, consumed with sweet satisfaction. And there are other analogies, quite frequent in Bwiti, which compare life to a thicket or, most commonly as we know, to a path.

More interesting, however, are the syllogism-like predications in which two subjects are related to a middle or common image which disappears in the process of the argument, leaving the two subjects in a situation of identity,

---

*⁴ We argue below that the Bwiti ritual experience, satisfactorily conducted, is the kinesthetic achievement by synesthesia of a state of emergent qualities in the membership. This emergence is a main pleasure provided in the religion. The analysis rests, in part, upon the distinction between primary and secondary qualities—a troubled distinction in philosophy, to be sure, and one that is not likely to receive definitive clarification here. But it is useful to relate this notion of elementary images to the notion of qualities. These images would seem to be particularly striking and anomalous constellations of qualities that arrest the attention as one passes from primary perception of them to a more direct secondary interaction. Thus water is a substance that appears to have mass but turns out to have neither taste, color nor resistance. Or fire is a substance that has color, sound, and configuration without, as it turns out, weight or mass. Elemental images, then, are composed of surprisingly anomalous qualities that emerge as one passes from primary perception to secondary interaction. There is an emergent shock of recognition in them.

of equation, or some other satisfying form of reconciliation.[13] Thus, in paragraph seventeen of the long sermon, Fête Efun-St. Michael, of Chapter 19, women are first equated with the azap tree below and men with the azap tree above. By eliminating the common term, men and women, if not equated, are at least reconciled. This, of course, is one of the main objects of Bwiti and it is achieved in other ways by an equal and complementary place in the ritual procedures as well as by insistence on the suppression, through special clothing, of differentiating sexual characteristics. We cannot overlook a continuing thread of domination-subordination, incidentally, in this reconciliation through the azap tree.

The same kind of identification or reconciliation of the focal subjects of the Bwiti religion is accomplished in paragraph nine of the long sermon where twins are used as the common term. We are told that brothers and sisters are twins, and wives and husbands are twins and mother and children are twins. By dropping the mediating image, all three of these pairs are equated as, indeed, they are equated in the archetypal interpretation of the stages of creation which we have reviewed above (Chapter 13). In the face of the generational divisiveness and the divisiveness along the various axes of relationship in the Fang family, this syllogism neatly knits together the contentious elements. In a subsequent analogy, interestingly, man as living body is equated with the second-born of twins. This introduces a new divisiveness between the spirit twin and the corporeal twin. But it is precisely this tension that Bwiti finds of most dramatic value in the liturgy and which it seeks constantly to reconcile.

There is another variety of syllogism that involves complementarity of relationship. We have already noted, for example, that in the equation of man and woman with the azap tree, there is a complementarity—men above and women below—suggested in the assertion of the identity. This achievement of complementarity by association is seen more directly in the equation of men to the drumstick and women to the drum in paragraph seventeen of the sermon. Such analogies of complementarity are generally handled in the literature by the Aristotelian formula $a:b :: c:d$ or drum:drumstick :: woman:man. The overall associative effect is one of complementarity in the relation between men and women; that is, they make music together. Indeed, it is precisely this happy condition that is a hoped-for consequence of male-female participation in Bwiti. The syllogism should really read therefore, drum:drumstick :: woman:man $\therefore$ they make music together. Finally, we see sequences of associations in the sermon in which the social subjects of Bwiti undergo transformations of identity, gaining polyvalence in the process and, at the same time, equation with other social subjects. For example, in paragraph eleven, we begin with an association of Zame with the otunga tree. He is subsequently connected sequentially to the stool of birth, the cross, and finally the azap tree. Later, as we have seen, man and woman are linked to the azap tree and thus to Zame. The sequence of associations is the following:

$$Zame = otunga = stool\ of\ birth = cross = azap$$
$$men\ and\ women = azap\ below\ and\ above$$
$$\therefore Zame = man = woman\ etc.$$

By this sequence God (Zame) is found in every man and woman, another intended purpose of Bwiti. But rather than being achieved by direct statement, this reconciliation is obtained by a gradual transformation of Zame's inchoate nature through a sequence of predications upon him which transform him from an otunga tree into an azap tree. In the end, all these mediating images of the transformation, the stool of birth and the cross, drop away, leaving the equation of Zame to man and woman.

One should be cautious here, for, as always where analogies are being manipulated, one is obliged to tease out probable associations. There is such a range of interpretations possible that one cannot be absolutely sure one has discovered just those or all of those associations actually at work.[14] But while interpretations may be tentative, the principles by which the sermons proceed to have their effect upon the world view are clear. There is an ordering obtained by the skillful use of analogy and persuasive power. To turn inchoate subjects of religious attention into something graspable and then to turn them into each other, to reconcile them, is a pleasure. The outsider who approaches these sermons with a preference for a more rational and explicit argument may tend to discount this figurative thought—it may be interesting but not convincing or fundamental. But for the Banzie it is both. It suggests an overarching integrity of things, a cosmology, by a convincing form of argument: the argument of images.

THE WELL-FORMED SERMON

Banzie regularly comment on the sermons and generally find something in them (*a ne été*) of great authority and significance (*ebam nen*). Indeed the listeners are pointed toward that significance, for as the sermonizer is apt to say at the end of the sermon: "Listen to these words of the wind for they are of great authority to you" (*me ne mina ebam nen*). The image of something being inside (été) and brought to the surface is another kind of emergence that not only is part of the Bwiti religious experience, but was also part of the former experience of divination. The chief criterion of a diviner was that he could "see" what was hidden and make it emerge (*ku*). The appraisal of a sermon thus has some similarity to the appraisal of a diviner's performance. Does it bring the hidden to view?

While it was difficult to obtain commentary from Banzie themselves by which an authoritative sermon could be distinguished from one that failed, our own discussion here has advanced a series of criteria for a "well-formed" sermon. Sermons that work pleasures for Banzie in the sense that they offer fulfillment and suggest a larger integrity to things whether that be in the relation of object or subjects do so because:

1. They address themselves to thematic preoccupations.
2. They play with elementary images, as they play with verbal roots, giving the sense of the emergence of these images into various, more complex images.
3. They reconcile as they identify by syllogisms of association, the inchoate religious subjects of Bwiti: The great gods, the ancestors, men and women, the European, the individual Banzie. This is done first by predicating concrete and more easily grasped objects upon these subjects, thus identifying them. Then, by dropping the middle terms or images, they reconcile the various subjects upon which they have been predicated.
4. They offer to the congregation images which are apt to their situation and move them in appropriate ways. These images, like the symbols we have discussed, are polyvalent and knit together the parts of experience. Thus, the prevalent image of the spirit pool of the deep forest knits together associations with itself. Not only is this the deeply meaningful forest experience, that old Fang feeling for hunting and gathering, but also it resonates at the cosmic level with the primordial ocean of creation and at the physiological level with the bag of waters out of which the person is born. The deep forest pool is a polyvalent image of creation.

Another of those polyvalent images which resonates at various levels is that of the leaf package of food boiling in the pot. Not only does that image resonate with the "pools of creation" images above, but it resonates with the other "containers for nurturance and strengthening of potential" images: the female body and specifically the womb; the forging pit for the formation and strengthening of man and woman; the nest of the sacred birds of Bwiti (particularly the parrot) who are harbingers of greater realities; the ngombi harp which is the container of that sacred music which nurtures the congregation; and the Bwiti chapel itself which is associated in this long sermon with the womb, the forging pit, the nest, the body of the harp. It is the chapel which contains all these other nurturant images. The acting-out of these images strengthens the membership for their lives beyond these containers. The authoritative and significant sermon, then, works by various processes of knitting together, by processes of emergence, and by resonance between levels of experience. We may wish to represent this achievement by reference to a cube of several levels. There is the surface level of experiences directly treated in the sermon. And underlying this level are various other levels[15] of experience, with which it resonates: the physiological level of birth, procreation, gestation, and death; the ritual-cosmological level of the creation myths; the socio-political level of colonial and family life; the subsistence level of the modes of existence. The art of the sermon is to hunt through and master the various domains at the surface level while resonating with other levels of experience not directly present. The hunter's eye may seem to be following, virtually randomly, a willful game and thus may appear susceptible to spontaneous associations and unbidden images. But, in the end, however circuitous, backtracking, or crosstracking this pursuit by the imagination may seem to be, it is just such a moving about that fleshes out and suggests the totality the sermonizer is trying to tie together.

Not only do these sermons suggest an overall integrity to things by moving by analogical argument from domain to domain, they are themselves shaped by the need to produce that integrity. They are shaped by (1) the thematic preoccupations of Bwiti; (2) the challenge of bringing elementary images into recurrent emergence; (3) the challenge of identifying the essential subjects of Bwiti and reconciling them; (4) the requirement of creating apt images that resonate at various levels of experience.

THE SACRED FOREST AS QUALITY SPACE

Throughout our discussion, we have treated the Bwiti chapel as a space in which the membership undergoes significant changes in their quality states. We may think of this in terms of the list of desired and undesired qualities and the promise in the religion to move from the former to the latter. We have also made clear that the chapel has a complex architectonic. It is an edifice made up of a variety of spaces of different qualities between and through which Banzie move back and forth. They obtain in that movement the quality of each of those spaces and in the overall movement of the liturgy are edified by a complex overarching configuration of qualities.

But it is more than the chapel—although this is the main arena of this qualitative movement and overarching edification. It is the religion itself which is a quality space in which the membership can, with satisfaction, learn to dwell and in which they can undergo significant transformations of quality. We have yet to demonstrate this for the ritual sequences although we have demonstrated the pleasures of emergence, of condensation, and of resonance between levels of experience that are obtained in the handing about of symbols and in the argumentative sequencing of images in the sermons.

As a transition, now, to the discussion of the ritual itself, we consider how Bwiti, this self-proclaimed "religion of the forest," returns Banzie to the forest as a quality space. We consider what kind of a quality space it is. This discussion applies also to the discussion of symbols, for barks and roots and

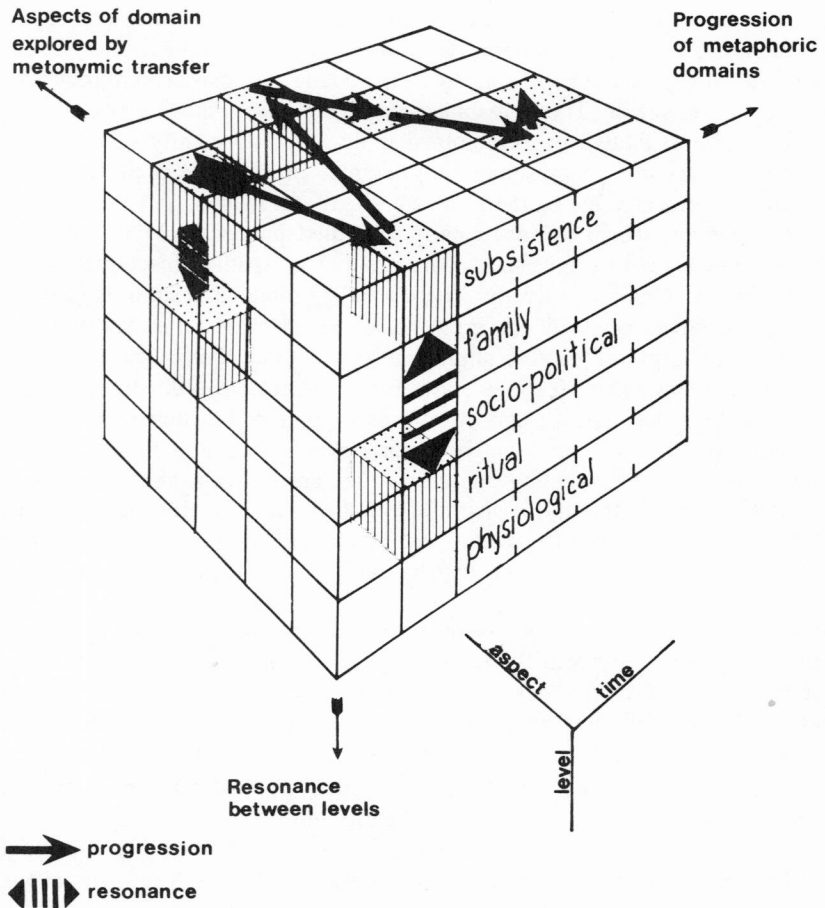

Aspects of domain
explored by
metonymic transfer

Progression
of metaphoric
domains

subsistence

family

socio-political

ritual

physiological

aspect   time

level

Resonance
between levels

➡ progression

◀||||▶ resonance

20.2 Emergence and Resonance in the Well-Formed Sermon

leaves are regularly handed around in Bwiti. It applies also to the sermons which place many forest images in sequence. In the case of the sacred forest, however, we have a limited number of trees.

Each of these sacred trees possesses a distinct set of qualities, and their successive consultation, while suggesting the totality of the forest, also suggests a quality space. One must argue that the sacred trees of Bwiti are no more chosen randomly than are the images of the sermon. Their choice is constrained because taken together these trees suggest, blockout as it were, a quality space of Banzie experience.

Several axiomatic assumptions are necessary to the support of this argument. First of all, we presume qualitative continuum as a principle of discrimination; that is, our judgments of the qualities of things, their feeling tone, fall along a set of continua, say from good to bad, masterful to impotent, active to inactive, etc. There are innumerable continua for qualitative judgment in any culture, though every culture has its characteristically salient set of continua. Second, we presume the principles of affective predication and parallel alignment. That is, there are subjects of our interest, or of the interest of the Banzie, which are not clearly identified in our thinking. They are inchoate and need to have more concrete and graspable objects predicated upon them to obtain an identity. These are the problematic subjects of Bwiti which we have discussed: the great gods, the ancestors, man and woman, etc. The principle of parallel alignment argues[16] that though these subjects are inchoate, we have feelings about them and that in order to concretize these feelings we tend to choose objects of predication that more or less embody the same feelings, that is, occupy parallel positions on the relevant qualitative continua. Feeling aggressive, we are tigerish; abashed, we are sheepish. But the principle of parallel alignment also implies the possibility of qualitative change or strategic movement along a continuum. Feeling abashed I can predicate a tiger upon myself.

The point is that the various sacred trees are concrete objects, relatively clear images, which the members of Bwiti interact with and in effect predicate upon themselves, confirming (paralleling) or changing (moving) their identities. More importantly, these trees constitute a system or quality space within which Banzie may affectively locate themselves and within which they may affectively move or be moved. Let us see how this works.[17]

Since we are dealing with trees with which the reader has had little experience, let us take, as an example, the difference between a willow and an oak as they operate on the continuum, let us say, of flexibility and tough resistance. A system is created when a third tree is introduced, say a pine tree, which creates two new dimensions in respect to the oak and the willow: the deciduous (oak and willow)--coniferous (pine) dimension, and the canopied (oak and willow)--receding (pine) dimension. As we add trees our quality space becomes multidimensional and the possibilities for multiple qualitative predication and movement are enriched.

If we will recall the sacred forest of Bwiti (discussed in Chapter 15), we can see how, in the ritual process, it is constituted as a quality space within which, through interaction with the various trees, Banzie may obtain both an identity for themselves and sense of a microcosm in which to dwell. The key to this forest quality space, the entrance by which Banzie emerge into it, is the azap tree through which the ancestors tunneled. This is the master tree of Bwiti around which all the other trees and, in a sense, the entire religion are arranged. For it is the tree which mythologically brought about the transformation of Fang into a forest people. The qualitative transformation of Fang is represented in the passage through the azap tree. They pass from being savanna wanderers, dominated and fleeing from others, to equatorial forest dwellers, dominating others. This is the lesson of Fang legend and history.

Bwiti has chosen a set of sacred trees to represent that forest existence. These trees, since they have distinct and contrasting qualities, when taken together give dimensions to a quality space. Since there are upwards of twelve sacred trees in most branches of Bwiti, this will be an "n"-dimensional space. But for purposes of illustration, we may take eight of the sacred trees of Bwiti and show a three-dimensional space. First we should list the eight sacred trees with their qualities.

MBEL: tall, imposing redwood which secretes a red, "bloody" resin. Used medicinally to solidify the bowels after dysentery or fluxes of blood.

ETANGA: large and beautiful tree whose pulverized bark (*osa biang*) is used on suppurating wounds and rashes.

Both of these are large and imposing, dominant, trees of the equatorial forest. But one has largely internal medicinal uses and the other external uses. Next, we list the two most sacred trees of Bwiti which are associated with the spirit world or direct access to that world. The two previous trees serve functions of corporeal healing. These next trees serve purposes of spiritual access.

OLUMI: one of the largest, straightest, and most impressive trees of the equatorial forest, with reddish bark and trunk. "Tree of the spirits," its bark is used for medicinal washes to bring good luck. Most typically, it is the tree of the male members of Bwiti.

OTUNGA: short, thick-leaved tree of the underforest—the tree of death. Its leaves and bark are also used as a medicinal wash on the surface of the body.

While one of these trees is a dominant tree of the forest, the other is subordinate. Both function to give access to the spirit and both are used in medicinal washes and in healing of the external body. The two following trees are both more squat and less imposing trees in the forest configuration.

OVENGE: very straight tree with reddish trunk and yellow wood. Its reddish powdered wood is associated with padouk wood in the curing of skin infections. Thus it has external use.

ALEN: the oil palm whose rough and forbidding exterior is contrasted with the succulent interior—the heart of palm, which is eaten as a lactogen by women. It is the women's tree and the tree of Nyingwan Mebege especially.

In final contrast, we have the two other main "trees" (beside the azap) of Bwiti: the eboga bush (spoken of very often as a "tree" in Bwiti) and the

asam, the false paletuvier. The latter is a very large tree of the forest whose
bark is taken as a purgative and whose ground roots have the effect of a
stimulant for those who wish to stay awake to see their ancestors. A tree that
has virtually the same qualities as asam would be the ovenge, one of the
largest trees of the equatorial forest. Portions of its bark are taken against the
affliction of evil spirits, hence its name *ele beyem* (the tree of the witches).
Like the azap, it serves in Bwiti thought as a tree of access to the land of the
dead.

These eight trees may now be contrasted with each other on three dimensions so as to form the most elementary kind of quality space (Figure
20.3). These three dimensions are: dominance-subordinance in the forest canopy; external or internal medicinal use; corporeal or spiritual valency in respect
to afflictions. We should not congratulate ourselves that this elementary kind
of quality space exhausts all the qualities present in these trees. Nor does it
adequately register some ambiguities in qualities. Decoctions of some of these
woods or barks are taken, for example, both internally and externally. The
chart does nothing more than suggest what, in the end, is a space of many
more dimensions. But this "suggestion" I believe yet indicates what is so
suggestive about Bwiti itself: its capacities for cosmogony, an achievement
that we argue here to be an important part—a dimensioning and redimen-
sioning of qualitative experience. We may not have got the dimensions just
right—analytic knowledge of these dimensions is very difficult to achieve in

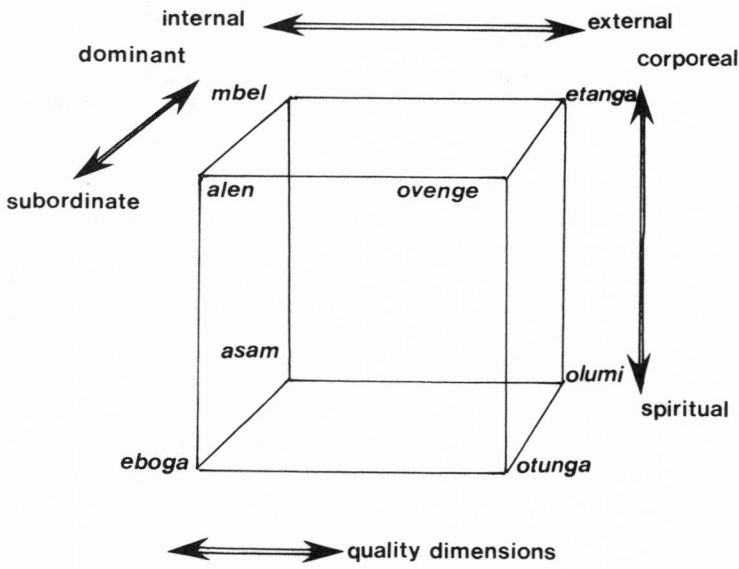

20.3 The Sacred Forest as Quality Space

anthropological fieldwork—but there can be no question that these trees are presented to the membership in such a way as to suggest a forest space and to bring movement in that space so that the member is himself moved—presumably through moods of dominance, subordinance, external or internal preoccupation, and corporeal or spiritual orientation.

Since their several-century-old emergence into the forest Fang have become adapted to it. The aimless wandering of the modern condition, upon the highways and satellite urban slums of the colonial and postcolonial world, is something that Bwiti seeks to counter. We see how effectively this is achieved in this forest quality space. It is the restoration of an old adaptation within which the membership can yet undergo the fulfillment of qualitative excursions from mood to mood.

THE PERFORMANCE OF RITUAL METAPHORS

In the handling of symbols, in the pursuit of elemental images, and in the laying out of a sacred forest, there is usually such an appearance of spontaneity that we cannot be sure that such ordering principles as we have constructed are those intended by Banzie themselves. In respect to the all-night liturgy, we have greater assurance of the intentionality. For that ritual process is specifically, and over and over again, conceived as the following of the path of birth and death. It is almost as if Banzie are seeking to tie down the volatility of their hunter's thought, a kind of pathfinding in any case, to a straight and narrow path. That would certainly not be an unexpected consequence of missionary evangelization.

But while we may have a good idea of where the path of birth and death may be headed—from life to death to life again—we are much less clear about the kinds of experiences encountered along the way and the specific kinds of movement that occur during this all-night excursion out to and back from the land of the dead. We can, however, come much closer to these experiences if we examine the key images that are being brought into play in the ritual progress. For behind the ritual, it is to be argued, is a set of images which the ritual performance seeks to put into effect. These images are a kind of template for ritual performance. The point has been frequently enough argued in the anthropological literature.[18]

Ritual organization is in part, to be sure, patterned according to received images or by schemes of orderliness that do not have any very clear-cut or informative images behind them. The nesting of the ''évangile'' or ''word'' within the two paths of the ngombi and these paths in turn within the two *njimba* (origin spots) and the *minkin* (entrance dances; see Chapter 13) would be an example. We could elicit no clear-cut image of this ''neatness'' although it is tempting to speculate that there is an image of the ''layers of the onion'' type in the all-night rites, with the ''word'' as the pith or core experience.

On the other hand, there are some images which accompany performance and which account for what is being performed that are vivid in members' minds.

More important than identifying these images is the recognition that they are predicated upon what we are calling the "inchoate" central subjects of Bwiti. They are metaphors or metonyms that provide an identity for these subjects—an identity most satisfactorily achieved through the possibility of performance. We will define metaphor here as a strategic predication upon an inchoate subject. The first-order, essential subjects are the personal pronouns, I, you, we, he, and they. But also to be included are the second-order abstract religious subjects of Bwiti which we have identified: the great gods, the ancestors, man, woman. The predication of these images upon these subjects not only gives them a concrete identity but, inasmuch as the images lead to performance, makes possible apt movement in them.[19]

Metaphors, it must be said, can serve a variety of functions. They can be informative, acting to bring additional information to bear on a subject where logical processes of superordination and subordination in semantic hierarchies seem inadequate. They can serve merely to express the speaker's feelings about the subject—including himself—or to declare his intentions or, in an indirect way, to argue or to give directions to the subject—to persuade him in certain ways. The ritual metaphors discussed here have, in varying degrees, all these uses, but their particular use approximates the last in that they give direction and are persuasive to the moods of ritual participants. They may appropriately be called performative metaphors because, as we shall see, they bring about actions appropriate to their realization. They imply performance.

There are four metaphors which arise as Banzie comment on various constellations of the ongoing ceremonies in this fashion: here we are such and such; there he is such and such; *eyong dzi bi ne*; *eyong te e ne*. These summary declarations look very much like metaphoric predications. Four of the recurrent predicates are:

bi ne ensama da	we are a trading team (in file through the forest)
bi ne ayong da	we are of "one clan."
bi ne emwan mot	we are the child of man (manchild).
bi ne nlem mvore	we are "one heart."

This liturgical commentary was easy to obtain and was not just a product of the situation of focused inquiry. These metaphors, as we know, run throughout Bwiti as leitmotifs. We have already obtained a feeling for their aptness and the ways in which they accomplish through performance those transformations of experience which are a prime objective of Bwiti.

Indeed, it can be argued that the fitness of ritual lies in the aptness of its metaphors (and metonyms), for it is through these tropes that inchoate religious subjects are better able to grasp their circumstances and experience satisfying affective movement.*⁵ In the absence of declared purposes it is still possible for the ritual to succeed by an argument of images; this kind of argument, we seek to show, can be quite purposive. For explicit purposes are difficult to obtain in movements of this kind and when obtained, often have the status of pseudo-concepts—that is to say, ad hoc explanations that have little to do with the actual ritual. The best place to look for purpose is in the metaphors themselves.

Taking first the metaphor of ensama (trading team), we know it as the metaphor that belongs typically to the minkin (the entrance dances). The metaphor connects members with the cohesive nineteenth-century bands of young men who marched with determination through the forest collecting rubber and ivory and trading these with the Europeans on the coast. These groups had high solidarity, the euphoria of hunting and gathering, and a rewarding trading relationship with Europeans—in brief, a sense of fulfilled purpose. Acting out this metaphor makes for satisfying movement if one reflects upon the lack of solidarity in kin-group and village, the aimlessness of the colonial world, and the ambivalence and unrequitement of relations with the European. Such conditions provide experience to which the metaphor was and is a compensatory representation.

The second metaphor to emerge into ritual activity is that of *ayong da* (one clan). It is the metaphor of the njimba, the gathering together for prayers and songs between the entrance dances and the path of birth and death. Since the membership of a Bwiti chapel is derived from many clans, this is a metaphoric and not a literal statement. A key movement in the "sitting together" of the njimba is the prayerful recitation of genealogy, the "pièce maîtresse" of clan identification. These are always the genealogies of particular lineages but the periodic affirmation by the membership, "we are one clan," during the njimba has the effect of knitting together these disparate lineage genealogies. The metaphor is also apt in view of the decline of clan allegiance and allegiance to the ancestors who are the guarantors of the clan. The metaphor is apt because it is a compensatory reaction to the kinds of individualism and opportunism which have undermined these allegiances.

The third metaphor here singled out, *emwan môt*, "child of man" or "manchild," is typical of the path of birth portion of the path of the harp and the concluding midnight search for the ancestors in the forest. This metaphor (we should note that it is predicated upon the individual and not the entire group of Banzie) yields a complex of associations, including a Christian one—

---

*⁵ It is axiomatic to our discussion here that people undertake experience in religious movements (perhaps in all religions) because they desire to change the way they feel about themselves and the world in which they live. They want to change the way they think about these things as well. They desire to achieve a greater grasp of their inchoate selves and significant others. A metaphor is an image, then, which, predicated upon a central subject of concern and acted out, gives both greater comprehension and satisfying affective movement.

the regular reference in Bwiti to Eyen Zame (the savior figure), not only as the son of Zame, but as the son of man. This metaphor is apt, first of all, because the full spiritual experience can only be achieved by escaping from the contaminated condition (bad body, *nyôl abe*) of adulthood where sexuality and fraternal strife burden the spirit. There is, in asexual childhood, despite its impotence and dependence, an innocence propitious to passing over to the other side. Other associations make this an apt metaphor—for example, the notion that the younger the child, the closer he is to the ancestors. The metaphor also aptly expresses that state of dependence, that piteous condition (*engôngôl*) which Bwiti desires to impress upon the ancestors. Finally, this metaphor emphasizes the corporeality, the primordial facts of birth, death, and the intervening dependent condition of the life of the organism which is celebrated at this point and which Bwiti seeks to pass beyond.

This last implication of the child-of-man metaphor is even more aptly conveyed in the metonym[20] of "oneheartedness" (*nlem mvôre*) affirmed periodically in Bwiti, but particularly at midnight after the single-file progression out into the forest in last appeal to the lingering ancestors. The returned members spiral more and more tightly together in the chapel until they form a compact mass with candles raised so as to form one flame. They intone "we are one heart"—a figurative condition which the ritual performance is designed to achieve.

Corporeal metaphors, that is, the predication of parts of the body or the entire body on secondary structures, are, we know, frequent in Bwiti. We have seen the body in the chapel, the assimilation of the body to the pitch torches; both are shells in which a vital substance burns its allotted time. Paradoxically, the linking of corporeality to these "objective correlatives" is part of the process of escaping the burden of that corporeality. At the same time, this association is efficacious in respect to the body's problems. For moving about within spaces associated with the body, whether in the chapel or the sacred forest, is a therapeutic moving about within the body itself. The paradox of this association is a paradox of Bwiti which seeks both to vitalize corporeal existence and escape the burden of it.

The aptness of this particular metonym, the heart, derives from several context. It is first of all the most alive of the bloody organs and, therefore, an apt representation of that vitality (*ening*) which Bwiti seeks to achieve for its members in this world. At the same time, it is the organ of thought, as opposed to the brain which is the organ of will and initiative. It thus connects to another objective of Bwiti which is to bind men together thoughtfully so as to escape the afflictions of vitality: concupiscence and corporeal self-interest. To affirm "we are one heart" is to affirm Banzie solidarity beyond corporeal individuality. Finally, the heart as the bloody organ par excellence is linked to Nyingwan Mebege, the female principle to whom Bwiti is mainly dedicated, as far as the great gods are concerned (blood and the bloody organs are the female portion of the corporeal; semen, bone, and sinew the male portion) and to the red path of birth and death which is, in the end, the bloody path of salvation. Thus, this metaphor acted out in the midnight procession moves Banzie closer to vitality in their corporeal being, closer to their fellow worshipers on an enduring spiritual basis, closer to the female principle, and closer to the path of birth and death along which salvation lies.

TRANSFORMATION BY METAPHOR

As the metaphors emerge into performance by those upon whom they are predicated, they produce desirable quality states in the membership. We may speak of emergent qualities. Looking at the four metaphors we have before us we may summarize the contribution of each metaphor: confident invigoration and intentionality in the case of the performing of the ensama metaphor, solidarity in the case of the ayong da metaphor, dependence and the restoration of a pristine potentiality in the case of the emwan mot metaphor and, finally, proclamation of the paradoxical but essential "spiritual corporeality" in the case of the nlem mvore metaphor. Each of these predications makes its particular contribution to the overall master metaphor of Bwiti, *bi ne banzie*, "we are angels." This metaphor argues for lofty spiritual mastery of the realm of the living and the dead, combining aboveness and beyondness. Thus Fang who entered into the Bwiti religion as wandering, "thicketbound" colonial subjects of low confidence; who enter as individualistic and self-isolated men and women; who enter caught up in the prurience, concupiscence, and covetousness of adulthood; who enter enmeshed in sluggish corporeality—are by this sequence of performances transformed in their condition so that they may become angels.

We may be skeptical in various ways about this formulation. Do all participants experience the same movement, the same assuagement of a troubled subjectivity? Of course they do not. But at some point in the history of the religion the metaphors were produced by the visionaries as a means of grasping inchoate troubles. The "knowledgeable ones" gave and continue to give prophetic impulse to the religion.

Metaphoric innovation, like innovation of any kind, rests with the few and not with the many. The many who are attracted to the performances need only entertain what may be called "social consensus":[21] an agreement about the appropriateness of the ritual actions required. They need have little concern for "cultural consensus," that is, insight into the meaning of that action, or the associations being brought into play. In the end, through long participation in the rituals, such participants may inductively come to an understanding of the attendant associations.

Yet there are those, the originators and maintainers of revitalization movements such as Bwiti, who have the insight, force of character, and talent for organization to envision and "create" a new religious culture. It is the images of these visions predicated metaphorically (or metonymically) upon focal religious subjects which give rise to the persuasive rituals. As the leaders of the various chapels constantly have new visions, new metaphors appear frequently to bring about revitalization. The dynamics and fissionary ferment in Bwiti are often, in the end, a dispute over metaphor.

In respect to this distinction between social and cultural consensus, it must also be recognized that participants may be paying variable attention to the particulars of the ritual activity while yet going through it in an acceptable way. There are always differences regarding the level of activity upon which participants are focused. Attention at certain junctures may be so removed from the level of activity which is just then "qualifying" a particular metaphor as to make for bodily presence only. This hyperstatization or removal of attention is never so complete as to prevent the participant from recognizing those signals by which scenes are changed and new metaphors put into operation. It is for this reason that chapel leaders, outside of initiation, guard against the overuse of eboga lest it degrade the precision of the ritual progress.

A closer look at the associations evoked by the metaphors will give us a better understanding of the affective transactions brought about by them. Here we must introduce the two laws of association: (1) the law of contiguity, or cause and effect, and (2) the law of assimilation by similarity. These two laws differentiate metonym and metaphor: the former are figures of speech resting on relationships of contiguity; the latter rest on perceived or felt similarities in the quality of experiences which are not contiguous but lie in separate domains.[22]

It is generally recognized in associationist theory that the contiguity principle fails to explain many phenomena.[23] Things are associated which have never appeared together before. Structures of association seem to be formed as the result of schema or hypotheses which associate elements from diverse experiences or from different domains.[24] In our view metaphors are hypotheses of a kind—insofar as a predication is a hypothesis—which are brought to bear upon inchoate subjects out of the need in those subjects for more concrete identity and apt movement. But they are also hypotheses about a certain kind of connectedness of the parts of experience, and they imply a transcendental sense of order—a cosmology.

But in what manner are diverse experiences brought together under the aegis of metaphor and metonym? The answer is almost redundant: by interplay of similarities and contiguities of experience. The consequence of this interplay is microcosmic fulfillment, the sense of exploring the parts of single domains and of interconnecting different domains of Fang life. Microcosmogony in this perspective, then, is the laying out and fulfilling of the quality space of religious subjects by metaphor and metonym—that is to say, by predications upon these subjects based on similarity or contiguity principles.

We may, therefore, add this kind of microcosmogony to the varieties already discussed: by condensation of associations in symbols, by recurrent insertion of elemental images, by pursuit of thematic preoccupations through different domains of representation, by syllogistic processes of argument, and by architectonic construction of a quality space.

We may illustrate the particulars of this final kind of microcosmogony—the sequential laying out upon the path of birth and death of a series of metaphoric and metonymic predications upon inchoate subjects—by considering the chain of associations which are activated by each of the four metaphors in successive performance. This is a complex matter in such a thickly layered performance. We may concentrate here on the chain of associations which was brought into existence by each metaphoric rephrasing, each metaphoric "acting out" of the progress being made upon the path of birth and death. Banzie, as all men and women, live in bodies to which they must give an interpretation, an identity. The overall identity which brings them into the religion and launches them upon the path is that of despairing, devitalized, impoverished, and wandering Fang. They wish to master these afflictions and achieve a spiritual rather than a corporeal identity. To achieve this transformation, the members perform the four subordinate metaphors. Each of these performances brings into association a chain of primary experiences typical of the corporeal life of a social animal seeking spiritual fulfillment—experiences having to do with relatedness to significant others first, and to the self second.

Each metaphor or metonym performed has its particular set of primary associations. In Figure 20.4, under a statement of the overall transformation from a state of despair to the state of banzie (angel), we indicate the sequence of subordinate performances and the set of associations and transformations in attention they provoke. These subordinate metaphoric performances successively bring into focus and scan, as it were, different aspects of that primary corporeal sociality. Thus the members find at various successive moments in their ritual celebrations different dimensions of primary experience in play. Compounded, these experiences suggest a totality, a total body, a total society, a total range of human effects and qualities. Taken together the succession of these metaphors offers a fulfillment, a return to the whole of experience.

Two of these metaphors refer primarily to social groups: the trading team and the clan. Two refer primarily to corporeal existence: the child of man and "oneheartedness." But all metaphors suggest a linkage of the social facts of relatedness to more primary corporeal matters.

The sequencing of metaphors is not only, then, a sequencing of attention upon aspects of primary experience, it is a sequencing of attention upon social experience—from euphoric group adventure (ensama) to somber and enduring allegiance to ancestor cult (ayong da) to a dependent filial piety (emwan mot) to final individual and group transcendence in thoughtful reflection (nlem mvore). In the metaphors there is a linking of these two attentions. Thus, while the succession of metaphors moves the attentive participants along the path to spiritual fulfillment, each metaphor is itself fulfilling to that linkage between the primary, that is, the corporeal, and the social. Such linkage must be the characteristic of an apt metaphor, for there is necessarily a corporeal

Figure 20.4 The Sequence of Associations in Transformation

OVERALL BASIC TRANSFORMATION				
suffering devitalized individual	is incorporated into	worshiping body of Bwiti	which is incorporated into	spiritual body of Bwiti as Banzie (angel)

SUBORDINATE TRANSFORMATIONS				
	Ensama	*Ayong da*	*Emwan mot*	*Nlem Mvore*
primary corporeal experience of	chain of associations	chain of associations	chain of associations	chain of associations
relatedness to others	celebration of the achievement of solidarity through the cooperation of corporeal parts	celebration of lineal relatedness	sorrowful and beseeching celebration of helplessness and dependence, desire for relatedness	celebration of the achievement of unity by liquefaction
color spectrum	white	white	black	red
body effluent	sweat	semen	cloacal exuviae	blood
sexuality	young manhood	mature manhood	childhood and latency	incorporation with the mother
body constituents	sinews tendons & muscles	skeleton & brain	flesh and body surfaces	veins, arteries, and bloody organs
attitude or posture	energetic adventuresomeness, self-confidence, euphoria	pensive and serene reflection	inferiority and self-abnegation	self-transcendence

component in the memorable experiences of social life, whether birth, puberty, or marriage. Apt ritual metaphors must return to the "wholesomeness" of that linkage[25]—wholesome in the sense of the assurance that that which is done with one's body is good for society and that which is done in society is good for one's body.

The primary associations implicated in the metaphors are those appropriate to the activity performed. Thus the intense movement of the trading teams in the entrance dances implicates primarily the sinews, the tendons, and the muscles, while the quiescent prayerful observances of the njimba, with its celebration of one clanhood, implicates the main objects of worship and sources of strength of the ancestor cult: the bones of the dead and the brain as the organ of ancestral and clan willful determination. So the child-of-man phase—the phase of infantile dependence—implicates both the gastrointestinal tract and the body surface, the body parts most in need of control in the advance toward maturity. They are also the body parts most susceptible to suffering (beating and flagellation) and deprivation (hunger and starvation). And finally "oneheartedness" quite obviously implicates the bloody organs.

The various body effluents and the sexual or sensual aspects of these metaphoric performances seem plain enough, although the implicated color spectrum seems less obvious. It is the purpose of the entrance dances to move out of the blackness of the origin spot to the white light of the chapel. The celebrations of clanship take place in that light in the presence of the ancestors (white) and Nyingwan Mebege (red). The child-of-man performance moves the membership out from the chapel into the black forest, while "oneheartedness" gathers the membership all together again under the flame of the combined candles. It resolves the previous ambivalence of colors in an unambiguous and saving red.

The chains of associations offered here are interpolated from knowledge of the referents of these metaphors in Fang culture and from watching the ritual performance of the metaphors. These interpretations were not given by the "knowledgeable ones" nor were they confirmed subsequently among them. One cannot pretend that these are *just* the associations evoked by the various metaphors. There are undoubted ambiguities, and not only in respect to the color associations. The body effluents evoked under the child-of-man (or mankind) metaphor may be either cloacal exuviae or breastmilk, the essential effluents of infancy and dependency. Oneheartedness both nourishes and vitalizes corporeality as it makes possible escape from it. The manchild metaphor figures both dependency and pristine possibility. The associative possibilities of any of these central images are quite complex. Watching them in performance in the context of Fang culture and Bwiti revitalization encourages but does not confirm the view that they are rich in associations and that the movement from one set to another gives each metaphor and the sequence of metaphors their power.

The same problems of interpretation arise when we seek to state the affective movement achieved by these metaphors—their aptness. We have argued that in the first half of the night, along the path of birth, the metaphors move the members from the needful condition of isolation and subjugation through celebrations of (1) a confident and coordinated intentionality, (2) enduring lineal solidarity, (3) the pristine individual condition of dependence and possibility, and (4) the final liquefaction and spiritual unification of "oneheartedness." Each metaphor or metonym picks out a part of the inchoateness of experience and explores a set of associations with implications for affective movement. But each metaphor only succeeds in exploring the part and not the whole, so another metaphor is generated seeking to "return to the whole" by evoking another part of it.

Here we note another source of the impulse to progressive transformation of metaphor: the constant search to "return to the whole"[26] out of dissatisfaction with the "partness" of any of the devices of representation. Wholeness, the suggestion of cosmology, is only achieved by a sequence of metaphoric explorations performing the parts of experience. Only when various parts have been explored is the moment ripe for a convincing assertion of wholeness by "oneheartedness," even though that assertion is metonymic, the celebration of a part. For only in exploring the many parts of experience can the ritual progression come to the "salvation" of finding "wholeness in a part."

From the point of view of the predications involved, we should also note an important shift in the pronoun subjects of these metaphors. We move from the collective "we" as the subject to the individual "I" or "he" back finally to the collective "we." Part of the motivation in the change of metaphor and consequent change of scene is this desire to explore the variable pronominal relationship between the individual and the collective.

CONCLUSION: THE RECONCILIATION OF VOICES, THE ARGUMENT OF IMAGES

In this chapter we have explored the ways in which the "knowledgeable ones" of Bwiti bring into being and reveal to their membership a "pleasure dome" where they can be reconciled with the world and themselves and feel at home. It is a process of "tying together" (*atsinge*) that which witches and sorcerers and the agents of the colonial world and simply modern times have rent asunder into that anxious, isolated condition where men and women, bereft of the solidarity of the group, the strength of the whole, are, like the doomed Mba Muzwi, preyed upon. This chapter is really about the capacity of the masters of the Bwiti word and rite "to return to the whole," tying together by an argument of images that overarching integrity and bringing about that final euphoric gathering around the morning meal of manioc.

This "tying together" is accomplished in diverse ways: by the handing about of symbols that condense in themselves a diversity of associations; by what appear to be the random walks of Bwiti sermonizers through a thicket of images but which, in reality, comprise a determined hunting about with a quiver full of elemental images seeking to expand them into a series of more complex images; by syllogistic argument; by the choice of a set of sacred trees that, in effect, give dimension to a quality space for experience; and, finally, by embarking by metaphoric enactments along a path of performances that sequentially and aptly transforms the participants' focus of attention and their sense of quality in self, in others, and in situation. This moves them finally to an overarching sense of solidarity in the sacred society of Bwiti in which they act and of integrity in the cosmos in which they dwell. This tying together into a whole, then, is accomplished by condensation, by extension and expansion, by qualitative dimensioning, and by the performance of metaphoric predications. Though we may give this analytic account of the way that fulfillment is obtained in Bwiti, we cannot pretend that our interpretation of the materials is unexceptionable and in any sense easily verifiable or replicable by anyone employing the same concepts. The Banzie themselves recognize that, though they may speak with one voice, there are many meanings. And there also are many voices. The materials in association with each other with which we are here dealing are thickly layered and not fully congruent or even compatible one with another. We made the same point about the myths and legends of Bwiti, on the one hand, and the rituals on the other. They give us rather different accounts of the past and the present and are not simply saying the same thing in different ways along different channels by different modes of presentation. In the same way we learn different things from the song cycle than from the myths and legends or the rituals. In part, this multiplexity and discordance is a consequence of the syncretism in Bwiti of various religious traditions. For syncretism rarely renders the religious sources by which it is stimulated fully compatible. In part, this multiplexity arises from the fact that the traditional culture did not come all together into a whole. Fang were taught different and not fully compatible things by different aspects of their traditional culture, whatever impression they now have (an impression urged upon Banzie by their religion) that they once had a fuller existence which was more of a piece.

The point is that the student of Bwiti learns rather different things about this religion not only according to the informant with which he works but depending on where he begins his analysis: with the songs, with the sermons, or with the rituals. For that aspect of the religion with which he begins will tend to frame and shape his subsequent questions and frame his progressive understanding as he or she seeks, like the Bwiti sermonizer himself, some integrity in his materials. Indeed, the strong impulse toward cosmology in Bwiti may arise out of a sense of the discordances, the discrepant syncretisms stacked upon the diverse perspectives of the older Fang culture. But while Bwiti sermonizers may be permitted their search to "return to the whole," the student cannot indulge himself with the expectation of finding complete integrity in the materials. He can only hope that he has stayed close enough to the argument of images to make for future replication by another student.

That this multiplexity of materials can work at cross-purposes is shown in the relation between the symbols of Bwiti and the metaphoric transformations. The condensation of meanings characteristic of symbols gives them a multivocality which is highly volatile in the metaphor scenario. By virtue of their many meanings, symbols are always likely to shift the member's attention to a meaning, say filial dependence rather than lineal solidarity, not appropriately voiced by the metaphor being acted out. For though the metaphoric context in which a symbol appears tends to focus attention on a particular meaning of the symbol, the latter is volatile in that it is always likely to shift attention away from a current focus or at the least to add another level of awareness.[6] Symbols thus add the possibility of the experience of other levels of meaning during the basic transformations of the ritual progress as discussed at the end of this chapter. They fill out the Bwiti universe of religious experience and give it a resonance and complexity, a plenipotentiary quality, which the discussion of the sequence of metaphors, or any mode of knitting together of the whole, does not fully capture.

It is precisely this plenipotentiary quality that engages the member's attention, that satisfies his need to escape the one-dimensional condition of colonial domination and administration, and that pleases by appearing to reconcile those many aspects of his life which have fallen apart: the dead reconciled with the living, man reconciled with woman, children with parents, the old ways of life with new ways of life, the past with the present, the corporeal self with the social self, the villagers with the forest, the infant with the adult.

---

[6] In a different context, I have tried to assess this quality of the symbol (J. W. Fernández, "Symbolic Consensus," p. 922). "It appears, thus, that the tension between society and culture, between causal-functional systems and logico-meaningful systems, is not only a consequence of their inevitable incongruities, but can be summed up in the tension between the symbol and the signal—the one immediate, dependent, embedded in the existential situation of coexistence and coordinated interaction, the other autonomous with super-added meanings forever pulling the culture carrier's attention beyond his immediate situation to the larger implications of his actions—creating in him, in other words, self-awareness." I would simply add here that this impulse toward "transcendence of the existential situation of coordinated interaction" is even more the character of the metaphor than of the symbol as here defined.

Afterword: The Suggestion of Coherence, The Impression of Momentum

AFTER THE MORNING MEAL of manioc and the chapel moot the membership disperses for another week. In all likelihood the nima na kombo, Ekang Engono, will already have disappeared into the forest. But the achievements of the Bwiti "pleasure dome"—its return to the whole—will linger on throughout the day and with any luck will provide an overarching shelter for human relations well on into the coming week. Of course, there are many anxious circumstances of modern equatorial life and the pluralistic post-colonial society that can easily trouble and dissipate the "even-handed tranquillity," the "oneheartedness," and the "transcendence" achieved in Bwiti.

The achievements of this new religion are various: reconciliation of the subjects of worship, the tying together by architectonic linkage of different levels and domains of experience, the satisfaction of emergent qualities. But they may be more easily stated. Where there was a failing sense of the past, cosmic and human origins have been vividly revitalized. Where there was a decentering in Fang village experience, a sense of peripherality, there has emerged a vital center of activity, the Bwiti chapel, in which the principal powers of the unseen congregate or come into communion. Where there was a loss of genealogical identity, there is a new sense of umbilical connection not only to the ancestors ascendent but to the cosmos. The lines to the ancestors have been cleared and the membership restored to the reciprocal flow of protective benevolence. Where there was a sense of perdition, of wandering in thickets, the membership has been set on the path of birth and death. Where village structures had collapsed into the confrontation of "cold houses" with warm houses—the council house falling out of its central role to become the limbo of disgruntled men—there is a new architectonic linking the levels and domains of Fang experience into an overarching structure—the new council house of eboga. Where men and women had fallen out in their relations with ever greater recourse to recrimination and divorce, there is a new sense of their complementary contribution to cosmology. Where the authority of leaders had become increasingly transitory and suspect, "knowledgeable ones" have appeared and have achieved a more enduring respect by their inventiveness in liturgical elaboration, by their eloquence in figurative argument, and by their wisdom in easing the resentments of their members toward the world, toward each other, toward themselves. Where Fang were increasingly cast out into "night foolishness" and the perilous, self-aggrandizing search for individual capacity with witches or with strange imported powers, these powers have been constrained or made familiar and benevolent, and the individual members accommodated to the night, have been incorporated into the purposeful team of Banzie and into the cosmos itself. The old, declining, self-restrained image of full manhood, of even-handed tranquillity and confident but unaggressive knowledge of the unseen—the image of the *engôlengôla*—has been brought back to counter the various egocentric images which have flourished in the modern period—images of the *nem*. Where there was a sense of bodily isolation and decay and vulnerability to circumambient evil, a burdensome sense of accumulating impurities, there is vigorous purifying engagement in ritual enactments followed by ecstatic transcendence of the corporeal.

All these achievements have been personified in these pages. The presence of these achievements or their absence has been exemplified in the persons of the argument, the individual subjects of religious predication and reconciliation. In them the conditions of Fang life have become the motives for despair or revitalization. For what has been achieved in Bwiti by the subtle words of Ekang Engono or the dynamic persuasions of Metogo Zogo, by the practical mindedness of Muye Michel or the sense of pattern of Michel Bie, would have spoken very much to the condition, would they have listened, of Ze Azi, who felt the declining power of his people; of Ndutumu Zogo, who was unsure of his place in genealogy; of Bibong Leon, who suffered the collapse of his prestige; of Antoine the nightfool, who had lost his patrimony; of Mba Muzwi, who sought to make a private pact of power and encountered death in a female guise; of the entire family of Mba M'Oye which was losing its sense of solidarity. Even that pragmatic man of affairs, Ngema Mve, who has been the skeptical antagonist of all the cosmological matters recounted here, might have found in Bwiti a more satisfying relation with his infertile wives and a more appreciative arena for the display of his oratorical powers than anything offered to him in the feckless and fretful villages of his retirement years.

These undoubted affective achievements in microcosmogony of the Bwiti religion, we need only reiterate, are accomplished at the expense of an effective contribution to the building of the new Gabon Republic as undertaken by those in the modernizing elite who seek to integrate this equatorial country into the modern world. The achievements of Bwiti are not without their cost measurable in the currency by which the world measures such things. But to reduce—to monetize—all that Bwiti accomplishes to the all-purpose measure of modern man is to dismiss it in a simple-minded prejudicial manner.

As we reflect back on the long road we have traveled, we will remember the narratives, more or less coherent, with which we started: European narratives about their African experiences and about Africans on the one hand, and Fang narratives making plausible to themselves the European presence in the equatorial forest and their relations to the Europeans on the other. Of course, there were also detached and ironic observers among the authors of these accounts. Mary Kingsley and Trader Horn and Commissioner General Dolisie were hardly handmaidens to every imperial attitude. And there was variation and discrepancy in Fang versions of azapmboga or the Whiteman-Blackman episodes. Nevertheless, these narratives made plausible to most Europeans their role in the "civilizing mission" as they made plausible to Fang the dynamic of their equatorial existence—their drive toward the coast at first and subsequently their subordinate place in the colonial situation.

These narratives worked more or less convincingly until after the Second World War. Then they lapsed into incoherence—epistemological crises[1]—buffeted by new images and alternative scenarios to European hegemony and African subservience. Of course, the beginnings of this collapse were older and may be traceable, as Albert Schweitzer argued, to the First World War which took from Europeans their moral authority, their capacity for convincing mission and captivating self-narrative. This was the time, to be sure, when Bwiti itself arose as a reconstituted scenario and a reenergized narrative apt for Fang fulfillments in an increasingly unintelligible culture. Of course, there were other scenarios and vigorous narratives. The missionaries had their periodical revivals, the colonial administration their galvanic changes of regime and ideology, and Fang their recurring antiwitchcraft movements, their constantly renovated dance-dramas, and more recently a total historical-legendary narrative: *The Journey of the Children of Afri-Kara*. The troubadours also became increasingly popular, singing of the monstrous heroes of *mvet*, the race of *engong*. These were robust but cold-spirited narratives celebrating strategic enmities and a world of blood feuding and internecine conflict—a part of the truth, to be sure, of Fang migration and Fang relations among themselves and with others.

But it was not the whole truth by any means, for just as the increasing assertion of witchcraft spirit, the nem character type, represented a perversion of what had long been the most esteemed kind of "full man"—that is to say, the well-balanced engolengola—so the increasing emphasis on strategic enmity was a perverse account of what it was to be fully human. It ignored the protective benevolence, the even-handed tranquillity, the satisfying solidarities in the Fang imaginative repertoire. Such virtues are very much at the center of the Bwiti scenario.

Without doubt the "agape" in the missionary message has been influential in the particular constellation of virtues emphasized in Bwiti. But it is important to recognize the continuities with the Fang past in the Bwiti narrative, for the scenario of conversion (to which we have long been accustomed in the West as the accomplishments of the "civilizing mission" have been extolled to us by furloughed missionary and administrator) ignores the persistence of autochthonous elements. Bwiti, we have argued, in confronting the crisis of doubt about what Fang know about the world and themselves, is as much a way of understanding and revitalizing old commitments[2] as it is a way of converting to new ones. For that reason we have devoted many chapters to examining these old commitments and their increasingly troubled and conflictive condition: commitments to a fertile harmony between the sexes, to protective benevolence between the generations and between the living and the dead, to the balancing of emotions in social life, to mutuality and saving circularities in relations involving authority, to a patient, slow, and humble accession to supernatural powers on the part of the young rather than the dangerous "quick fix" of occult literature.

While one cannot argue that something entirely new has been created, it is not just something old either. For if essentially old, dead and dying tropes such as the forest metaphor or the body social metaphor or the genealogical metaphor are reanimated in the Bwiti scenario, at the same time essentially new organizing images appear in Bwiti narrative as central to its vitality: the red and white uniforms, the red path of birth and death, the world as globe or ball, to mention just a few. For what emerges in Bwiti—and the Banzie do experience a feeling of emergence through ritual activity of new qualities in their lives—is something achieved by the interdigitation of old and new. Revitalization, as it must always be, is a syncretism, a tying together, a time-binding of old and new.

As more traditional Fang sought the emergence in village life of the complementary states of "even-handed tranquillity" and "pleasurable activity" so Banzie seek "oneheartedness" and beyond that a spiritual buoyancy, a distancing from their earthbound bodies, that will carry them beyond and above. As fatigued as they may finally feel in the early morning hours after the all-night ceremonies, they will yet, if these have worked well, have the satisfying sensation of emergent selves in an emergent congregation. They will have the impression of a momentum in the night's experience whatever the actual inertia of their village lives. That momentum is inescapably temporal, a consequence of the binding together of old and new.

These most general emerging qualities of Bwiti and the impression of momentum which Bwiti is so skillful in conveying are compounded out of activity in many domains and along many dimensions. There is moral movement from feared to desired feeling states which is didactic. There is architectonic movement in actual structures which is kinesthetic and synesthetic. There is figurative movement in the ritual progress which is performative. Bwiti attacks the inertia and the troubled and confused condition of its members on many fronts. The consequence is the emergence of Banzie into more momentous circumstances of greater spiritual potentiality than anything the

administered existence of the colonial world could offer. It was the sense of
these emergent achievements that turned so many members of the religion
to dynamic or subtle persuasion of others—that gave them a sense of mission
that was irritatingly countervailing to the missionary presence.

Amidst all these achievements, what of the intellectual one? If the crisis
Bwiti faces is essentially an epistemological one and its challenge that of
making things once more intelligible when Fang had lost confidence in what
they knew and their ways of knowing—what of that intelligibility? Mentality
is a thematic question in anthropology, perhaps because it is felt that the field,
by exploring so far beyond the bounds of the literate, offers more perspective
on mind than any other discipline. Perhaps. In any event, as John Peel in one
of the best studies of African religious movements has made very clear,[3] it
is a mistake to ignore attempts by leaders of these movements to grapple
thoughtfully with their circumstances as they seek to provide for themselves
a better set of explanations for their transitional condition than any which lie
at hand. In fact Bwiti, like Peel's Aladura Church, has been if not self-
consciously rationalizing at least volubly exegetical about the constructions
it is putting on the world by word, by ritual deed, and by artifact. But this
very Weberian word, "rationalize," a favorite one of Peel's, can too easily
lead us to a schoolmasterish analysis which misses the imaginative lucubration
by which Bwiti moves and convinces its membership. For what we have had
before us, mainly, is iconic thought rather than thought which is conceptual
or expository in a discursive and abstract, logically consistent sense. We have
been treated over and over again to the argument of images, whether this was
the flow of images in the sermons or the performance of the sequence of sign-
images in the ritual progress or, what is most convincing of all, the insertion
of images of the ancestral dead that come to the members in narcotic trance.
Literacy is not extensive in Bwiti, and education, for the most part, is of a
primary kind, and this may account for this orientation to images. Bwiti is
also a movement with a strong nativist impulse—a strong desire to recapture
a traditional world—and is thus resistant to the modern rational-purposive
style of thought which is incompatible with that world.

The generation and patterning of these images has undoubted adjustive
consequences[4] for individual Banzie in respect to the conflicts of their colonial
condition. But these "iconic adjustments," we need only reiterate, are
achieved at the expense of effective adaptation to modern circumstances.[5] For
while the argument of images enables the Banzie to construct a world to live
in, which if not self-explanatory at least gives the impression of self-con-
sistency, it is a world that has closed itself off from the modern challenge.
It is not a modern world, and with some reason, given the way the pluralism
of that world has been employed as a double standard against the African.
The kind of thought going on here, with its emphasis on images, is a deval-

uation or a rejection of language-based thought and the discursive reason that lies in it and that has been the intellectual power tool of modern technical-rational man.

The kind of thought we have had before us resembles the "imagist" thought of the symbolist movement in literature or the more contemporary Theater of the Absurd.[6] It is a thought which, when it appears in modern guise, is labeled "decadent," "mystical," "primitive." The argument for Bwiti thought, of course, would be similar to that for imagist thought: it is the kind of thought which points to the whole, that does not desiccate and contort or impoverish the fullness of experience, that intuits the integrity of being. In short, it is the kind of thought most suggestive of the coherence of experience. It is the kind of thought most useful to microcosmogony.

Like the products of imagist literature, however, Bwiti thought leaves a great deal to the interpretation of the audience. The ethnographer, like that audience, is often forced to make his own creative effort at interpretation and integration. Of course, the Banzie, as we have seen over and over, are volubly forthcoming with their own interpretations. There is a yeast of conceits. This exegesis gives invaluable insight, but so much is unexplained. And so much is inconsistent; these interpretations are rarely discursive or explanatory in any overall, orderly way.

All this raises the question of the coherence of the Bwiti cosmos. It seems incontrovertible that for most members their religion skillfully suggests, if it does not actually achieve, a coherent worldview. But given all the argumentation about various interpretations to which one is submitted by disputatious Banzie, and given the fact that rather different worldviews are contained in the different modes—the songs, the myths and legends, the ritual progress, and the sermons—it is much easier to demonstrate incoherence than coherence. This would certainly be true in the logical sense, although a refutation of this kind that ignores their edifying kinesthetic accomplishments would be of little interest to Banzie.

In any case, we have been cautious not to play here the virtuoso ethnographer constructing out of the elements of Bwiti thought—but beyond them—a logically coherent cosmology. That would be to falsify the real nature of their "intellectual achievement." Nor did we meet any Banzie who in the manner of Marcel Griaule's Dogon interlocutor, Ogotomelli,[7] were in special possession of a thickly consistent cosmology. The "knowledgeable ones" of Bwiti could explain many things, but their explanations were not overarchingly coherent in that way. This may be symptomatic of the difference between a settled Sudanic culture which for hundreds of years has been close to Islamic centers of learning and an equatorial forest culture agitated by constant migration and internecine strife and isolated from any great tradition except for the recent colonial period.

Yet there is this sense of an emergent coherence—a sense of the whole.

And though such accomplishments, such "surpassing skillfulness," defy verbal description, we have attempted to give some account of them. For example, a certain coherence is obtained by the marked dualism in the Bwiti architectonic. Binary thinking of this kind may provide for the most elementary kind of coherence in human thought.[8] At the same time we have noted how recurrently that dualistic sidedness is transcended—by the "saving circularities" and by the rituals of "oneheartedness." Another kind of coherence occurs in the linking of levels of experience—the physiological with the natural, with the social, with the cosmic. Polyvalent images often reasserted provide for a kind of coherence by reverberating at these various levels. A third kind of coherence is that of time-binding by archetypal thought; archetypal events or personages of the past manifest themselves over and over again in that past, in the present, and expectantly in the future. A fourth kind of coherence is by insistent complementarity. This is seen most clearly in the relation of men and women, a relationship in marked confusion and incoherence outside the religion. The sexes within Bwiti are given dramatic complementarity of function. As with dualistic ordering of thought, which they resemble, these complementarities are collapsed in "oneheartedness" to begin with and by the achievement of spiritual status to end with. For the dead are without sexual distinction.

There have been three particularly challenging sources of incoherence in colonial life. First, there has been the increased scale of relationships in which the reality of the far away has come to challenge what was previously the overriding reality of the near and the parochial. Secondly, the old protectively benevolent powers of the below have been challenged by the missionary message of divinity in the above. And thirdly, there has been the pluralism of colonial life—the double standard, applied differently to colonizer and colonized.[9] In the first case, we have seen how the excursions taken under the influence of the drug eboga go out to the far and convert it into the near and also how the ritual progress on the path of birth and death encompasses the far—both the origin spot and the "sea beyond"—uniting microcosms within the macrocosm of the chapel and its surrounding ritual arena. In the second case, a complementarity and a creative tension are created between the gods of the above and the gods below. In the third case, plurality is collapsed into "oneheartedness."

As must be so often the case in cosmology, the trick seems to lie in taking what is apparently incoherent or plainly contradictory and then discovering some higher principle of complementarity, of archetypal identity, of time-binding, of linkage which demonstrates that the opposition is only apparent and is subsumed in that higher principle. In the suggestion of these higher principles, Bwiti operates not so differently from any science whose discovery procedure is to take things apparently incoherent and inconsistent and show them to be instances of a more general principle. The important difference is that Bwiti only suggests and does not aim to discover and state those principles in so many verifiable and refutable words. Rather than struggling relentlessly to deprive puzzles of their mystery, Bwiti works with puzzles.

Here I think "edification by puzzlement" is a useful phrase for what is occurring in Bwiti microcosmogony. For though the religion is undoubtedly edifying—that is, it combines world construction with spiritual improvements—it does so by indirection and suggestion and other kinds of puzzlements. It leaves many loose ends and inconsistencies. Instead of working through these in a consistent manner, it counts on what B. N. Colby has called "unconscious collusion" and "symbolic accommodation"[10] in a well-disposed membership to catch the hint of a pattern of overarching relationships where such may not be specifically stated. Given the many possible associations that inhere in the images of the Bwiti argument, a well-disposed membership can intuit, as the "knowledgeable one" says, that "many things are in fact one thing." And this can be intuited in many ways. This may be why Bwiti, by the use of drugs and esthetic elaboration of ritual, pays special attention to assuring the disposition of the members.

The multiple ways in which the membership can collude with the leadership in cosmogony and can accommodate themselves to the "discovery" of a coherent worldview must caution the ethnographer in his own pretentions to have discovered *the* overarching order. He may be in collusion, too, and unconsciously accommodating. Certainly Tessmann's confidence,[11] as the first Fang ethnographer, that he had discovered the "Grundstufe" of the Fang worldview seems unwarranted, particularly since his informants were not accommodating enough to confirm his interpretations. The interpretations lay, as he deplored, "unrealized in them."

Still, Tessmann paid close attention to Fang images. He was working with the same materials, and his constructions—hardly sui generis—are quite useful. In one important way, though he understood it backwards, Tessmann offers us insight into this edification. While Tessmann maintained that Fang escaped their human problems of good and evil by transferring them over to nature, it was rather that they were using the orderliness present in natural images to argue by analogy for orderliness in human affairs which are more inchoate. In the relationship between trees in the forest, between birds in the sky, between waterbugs on the waters, between the wind and the land, Banzie find arguments for orderliness in human life. This is traditional proverbial wisdom and Bwiti continues to make major use of it. Most often that wisdom is stated in puzzling fashion. The connection between a "rolling stone" or a "bird in the hand" or a suspended raindrop and the social situation to which the image is to be applied lacks clarity. The auditor must puzzle out the meaning. This is even more the case with the riddle, a truncated proverb, in which puzzlement is directly provoked. Just as Bwiti sermons make use of riddles, so much of the communication in Bwiti has that calculatedly puzzling character, seeking to edify by puzzlement.

The edification in that puzzlement is cosmogonic. For if one domain of experience is used to comment upon another, say nature upon human affairs, one creates a transcendent sense of their relatedness. What was only a similarity in domains of experience is transformed into a contiguity. One achieves a higher sense of coherence.[12] This transcendent sense of the relatedness of things is an inevitable consequence of analogic thought and the argument of images. It is implicit in such thought. The "knowledgeable ones" of Bwiti, those masters of imagery, recognized this in their way when they argued that "likenesses" showed that "all things were merely one thing." No more edifying statement could be made in the context of a microcosmogonizing religion.

In the end, any attempt to demonstrate the coherence of the Bwiti cosmos founders upon the paradoxes with which it plays. The chief of these is the emergence by ritual activity of life in death and death in life, or what comes to the same thing, the transformation back and forth of the linear path of birth and death into a "saving circularity." Perhaps the use of the mirror in initiation and the reflectivity in Bwiti thought implied by it shows this best. For as the living Banzie travel down the path toward death, so their ancestral dead travel up the path to rebirth. In the truly satisfying night-long ritual the living become the dead and the dead become the living, confounding in that paradox the somber inexplicability of death which no amount of coherence in cosmology could explain away. This paradoxical transformation of, to use the phenomenologist's terms, the subjectivity of the living into the objectivity of the dead, and vice versa, is an "intellectual achievement" that surpasses simply logical account.

We hardly need to reiterate that these achievements are all microcosmic in scope. The path of birth and death, in the end, does not lead out, significantly, to any current macrocosm. It reflects back upon itself. There are other religious movements in Africa that lead out efficiently to the macrocosm of the modern world. But the Bwiti tendency is introversion, the closing and maintaining of imaginative boundaries, however political in some respects and otherwise evangelistic Banzie can be. Theirs is a preoccupation with the parochial. Their achievement is to make it seem the cosmos itself. Such microcosmic tendencies are not unique to Africa or to religious movements. They may be a recurrent phase in the life of cultures. If we began with Coleridge as a romantic guide to the nature-oriented "pleasures" in our subject, we may end with John Donne as a guide to its metaphysics.[13] For we recognize in the Bwiti sensibility a kinship with the early seventeenth-century preoccupation with the small, and a capacity similar to Donne's to "make one little room, an every where."

Appendix I:
Glossary of Key Terms

Terms or phrases within parentheses are variant spellings found in the literature from other dialect areas or orthographies, occasionally quoted in the text.

abing ôjeng (abí ôje)
> The presentation by the mother of the newborn male child to the patri-lineage in the men's council house in order to obtain a name. Meaning literally, the "capture of the antelope," the presentation was accom-panied by a meal prepared by the mother—usually of fish.

abô
> Generic name for all spiders. In Bwiti, *dibobia*, the sky spider, the agency of creation, working at the instance of the creator gods.

abôbôn (abôbông)
> The fontanelle of a baby, where the life of the spirit, *nsisim*, can be seen beating.

abôra
> "Thanks," thanksgiving, words of blessing given by elders in favor of the enterprises of youngers; in Bwiti, the blessing (or grace) obtained from ancestors by night-long ritual worship.

abukh bifia
> "Breaking apart words" in order to develop folk etymologies; a Fang tendency much more pronounced in Bwiti.

abum (abmum)
> Stomach, stomach of a pregnant woman, a locality particularly suscep-tible to the attack of the demon.

abum (abmum) da
> "One stomach," referring primarily to the pregnant stomach, the syn-ecdoche or quality which bound together clansmen at whatever level of the kinship structure.

abwia
> Misfortune, usually caused by unfavorable disposition of the ancestors.

afa abong
> Payment of funeral money by sons and brothers-in-law at the death of a brother or father-in-law. Literal meaning, "to dig out honey from the hive in the tree."

afan
> "The forest." The milieu of Fang, who in folk ethnology derive their name from it, hence "people of the forest." In origin Fang are a savanna people who have adapted to the forest only in the last 200 years.

afôn (afônbe)
> Action of looking very carefully at something; by extension, "the dance of mockery" on the part of in-laws as their new relatives examine the gifts they have brought, sometimes involving the display of the private parts. Sometimes confused with *afoge*, activity which agitates and disturbs others.

akam (nkam)
> Protection; the closing of boundaries to evil influences often obtained by interdictions and taboos usually acting within the patrilineage from elders to youngers.

akiage (aki yagha)
> The promise to observe interdictions and taboos accepted in order to strengthen oneself. The preparation with the demon in infancy. *Yaghe*, to promise.

akôm (akomé)
> The protective arrangement of things on the part of elders for the benefit of youngers.

akômnge (nkomnge)
> The "plans" in a man's head, the anticipatory arrangement of things; as *akomnge nda*, the plan to build a house. From *nkom*, the fact of doing something well and the radical, *kom*, arrange, form, prepare, make, dispose. Also *akomnge awu*, the "preparation for death," a central object of Bwiti characteristic of its eschatological orientation. To be contrasted with the traditional *akomnge*, which was a preparation for the challenges of life. Akomnge mwan refers to the "preparation" of the child for the challenge of life and particularly the preparation with the *evus*; opening up one's nature for the fulfillment of its potentialities.

akôn aba
> The "pillar of the council house," in Bwiti, the central pillar, highly charged with meaning.

akwia (akulé) nlô
> "To break open the head" so that it can understand things of the dead and of death, things of the "outside." Important in both Bieri and Bwiti.

akyenge (akeng)
> Surpassingly skillful activity, often translated by Banzie as "miraculous activity."

Alar Ayong
> The "knitting together" or the "reunion of the clan." A clan regroup-

ment movement begun by the northern Ntumu in the late 1940's and continuing until the late 1950's.

alere shéshé (svísvíe)

"To show naked," a form of parental discipline of recalcitrant sons, a showing of the private parts.

asiman (osiman, asimda)

Thought, point of view, that which gives direction to determination.

atan esi (si)

"The paying of the earth" by which the Banzie of Bwiti mean the paying for sins of this earth in preparation for the next.

atu minsem

Confession, the spitting out of the sin, also known as *atu menden*, the spitting forth of the (bad) saliva.

ava meté (meteng)

To lift or remove the insults and curses either purposefully or inadvertently passed from father to son. To remove the saliva.

avwie bifia (víe)

Plan, amuse oneself by manipulating words or arguments, playing with words. A pronounced interest in Bwiti. Contains the root *vi*, to transform, convert one thing into something else.

awume

Respectful action; act of adoration; religious observance.

ayegle

Instruction in the doctrine or principles of a group or society.

azapmbôga (adzapmboga)

The pierced azap tree of Fang legend. The event which represents the entry into the Equatorial Forest from the savanna, the event and place (thought to be in Cameroon) from which Fang trace their identity.

axôba

Repentence, regret; the main emotion in the state of despair (*engongol*) felt by Fang and particularly felt in respect to the ancestors for having been abandoned by them as regards preparation for the modern world.

baa

The red powder of the wood of the padouk tree (*mbel*); mixed with oil, it is spread on the newborn, on the craniums of the ancestors, and also on the feet of the Banzie. It signifies joy, fertility, but also suffering. It is also the female blood of creation.

Banzie

The members of Bwiti, properly "those of the chapel" from the Metsogo *ebanja*, cult house, but also translated as "angels" from the French *ange*.

bemle

To push, excite, "push beyond" appropriate activity or tranquillity.

bewu

The three incisions cut in the back of the neck of the initiate at the Soo-Ndong Mba puberty ceremonies, in order to protect the initiate and to enable him to eat certain meats.

beyeme mam

Knowledgeable ones, particularly knowledgeable in the unseen, and hence, likely to be dangerous. Plural of *nem*, those possessing the witchcraft spirit, *evus*.

biang (byañ)

Medicine, remedies, charms, remedies for lack of capacity or excess capacity. Substances having to do with the gaining of power over unseen forces.

bidimi mam

Ignorant ones; those who dwell in obscurity (*zibe* or *dibe*) and are not enlightened by the witchcraft spirit.

bídzí bi nengôn (nyéngon)

The "meal of the mother-in-law" prepared for the men of the patrilineage into which her daughter has married in order to honor them and to guarantee their good treatment of her daughter.

Bieri (byeri)

The Fang ancestral cult. The cranium or piece of cranium which is the sacrum of the cult.

bilaba (bilap)

Competitive gift exchange, ceremonies of mocking exchange; from *bilap*, words of deprecation and denigration.

bílôbôlôbô

Non-Fang, gibberish, strangers, those who speak gibberish.

biôm (byom)

Goods, tradegoods, merchandise, riches, particularly goods obtained by trade or by marriage.

biôm be nkia

The father-in-law's gifts (*nkia*, he who is possessed of dangerous power) to the son-in-law and son-in-law's family as a response to their own gifts and as a guarantee of their good treatment of his daughter.

bipwé (bapwé)

To be carried in a balanced fashion; from *bap*, to be carried on the back in a balanced fashion. In Bwiti, the balance with which one should walk the path of birth and death. Also, *vyemle (vomle)*.

djop (yô, jô)

Heaven, the abode of Zame oyo, the god of the above.

dibôbia

The sky spider (*abop*) in Bwiti, who as the chief agent of the creator

god, Mebege, structured the world and brought the first beings to the
sea.

duma

Glory, renown, reputation, particularly sought by young men, *nduman*.

ebame

Authoritative and significant statements in respect to the management
of human activity; the kernel of Bwiti wisdom.

ebíbí

The "monster of the forest or rivers" who demands tribute and sacrifice
but who can be helpful.

ebin

The "state of ignorance" in which the initiate begins his initiation.

ebiran (ebira)

"Bad action," "injustice," social disorder, a constant threat to village
life and lineage relations.

ebôga (iboga, eboka, ebogha)

The psychoreactive alkaloid drug employed in Bwiti to obtain visions
of the ancestors (*Tabernanthe iboga*).

ebwan (menzvia)

"Adultery," a main preoccupation of midcentury males.

efa meyal

The left or female side, "side of the woman" (*ngal*).

efa meyom

The "male or sperm side of things"; the right side (*meyom*).

efôna (efonan)

Portrait, resemblance, likeness, image; the element of thought with which
the Bwiti sermonizer works.

efongla

Mutual respect.

efufum

The state of excessive whiteness, of having dirty white spots on the
body.

ekí, bekí

"Something powerful," sacred, to be approached carefully; taboos, prohibitions.

ekí akyage

Complex of prohibitions laid on a person and the promises (*yage*) made
in fulfillment of these prohibitions.

elibege

Counsel, instruction, advice, provided by elders to youngers.

elik

Former village sites in the deep forest; secret place for cult activities or
where initiates are isolated.

elulua (elukeluk)

Joyful activity; pleasurable, animated, not excessive village activity (*luk*, to be very animated).

engang (engañ, angan)

The art of knowing hidden things; *asok engang*, to search for hidden things and make them known.

engan

The unseen, the realm of magical power.

engang a mot

Courageous leader, leader worthy of respect.

engôlengôla (ngôlengôla)

One who possesses the demon (*evus*) but who controls it and prevents its secret aggressive activity.

engôngôl

The state of deep sadness, despair, in which, according to Bwiti, Fang are living and which it counteracts by ritual activity.

engôsi (engosie)

The night-long Bwiti celebration along the path of birth and death.

engungul

A shade, *kon*, doomed to wander interminably in the forest.

ening (enyiñ)

Life, duration of life, capacity, determination to survive.

ensama (nsama)

A corporate group formed to fulfill a specific purpose or task. A trading team, a master metaphor of Bwiti.

envalen

Old men who magically exploit children in order to strengthen the power of their demon.

epogain

Possession, loss of bodily control, usually through a heavy dose of eboga or through turbulent presence of an offending spirit. Viewed as undesirable in Bwiti except during initiation.

essaebôga

The ''father'' or ''mother'' (*nyiaeboga*) assigned to keep watch over the initiate while he or she is consuming eboga, the alkaloid drug, during initiation into Bwiti.

essamalan

The ''father'' assigned to keep watch over one's well-being during the ingestion of the alkaloid *malan* (*Alchornea floribunda*) while being initiated into Bieri, the ancestor cult.

eseng (ésé)

Work, physical labor that has confirming power in Fang thought, an antecedent condition to marrying a woman or to a true religious experience.

esinga (mosingi)

The wildcat or civit cat whose white and reddish skin is a central ritual object.

evus (evur)

The "spirit" that dwells primarily in the trunk and the chest; the "demon," the essential animating principle of forceful personalities, usually aggressive and difficult to control.

ewuma

Respect, honor, particularly shown to the patrilineage.

eyôle mebara

"Name of encouragement," nickname, often kept secret and recited at difficult or stressful moments to bring the power of the family into play.

ezing

Friendship, mutual aid between people of the same sex, sometimes extended to spouses.

fem (fim)

White kaolin clay applied to cadavers and also to the face in the Bwiti religion.

fiang

Ironic commentary on human affairs, practical joking.

kí

To respect something, abstain from something for the force or power contained in it.

kígíle (kíkile)

The stomach of the woman in the first three months of pregnancy; by extension, the undifferentiated ball of gristle and bone thought to be the content of the womb. *Kigile ki*: a being of gristle and bone, energetic and active, but without human capacities. A miscarriage produced by sin.

kôm

To give elemental form or shape to something.

kôn

The spirit, essential nature, of the dead, which perdures beyond the shadow of spirit; the ancestral dead, *bekon*.

kos

The African gray Parrot who brought the "word" to man.

maa (maghe)

Good luck, particularly the good luck experienced within the kin-group.

mbamba éyala

The "good answer" which mature men should offer in the face of provocation in order to assure social order.

mbek

A game, the widespread African Warri or Kala, played on a pitted board with pebbles.

mbim

The cadaver.

mbôbian

The "maker of medicine," usually herbal remedies against afflictions from the unseen.

mbôfak

The thinker, the delver into things.

mbôm

The new bride just brought into the village by "capture" or negotiation.

mbune

Believer, one who has faith.

mbwôl (ngwel)

Night flights of the demon *evus*, use of the demon *evus* for personal aggrandizement. The "eating" of others.

mefule (biyem)

"Habits of action," propensities.

mekí

Blood.

Mevungu

The women's purification and initiation society.

meyôm

The right side; sperm; the male principle.

mienlam

The "incumbent" of the town, the man who holds the town together by reason of wealth.

mimia (nkebe)

Innocent one, simple man or woman without demons.

minkí

Fathers- or mothers-in-law. One who has to be respected.

minkin

The entrance dances of Bwiti in which the cosmos is begun to be created.

mvam

Sentiment of protective benevolence, succor, affectionate fidelity; promotion of the interests of youngers.

mvama

Grandfather or grandmother; those who act benevolently or protectively.

mvamayong

The protective benevolence of the clan.

mvele me bot
> The red people who first dislodged Fang from the eastern waters and started them on their migration.

mvet
> The Fang chest harp around which an extensive genre of troubadour legends is built; the legends themselves.

mvôgabot (mvokbot, mvôgebot)
> "Village of people." For most purposes the maximally effective lineage segment among Fang. Also village family.

mvole mvole
> Mutual aid, emphasized as a value in Bwiti.

mvon
> Initiated person, disciple; the state of secret knowledge acquired after initiation.

mvuk
> "Dumbness," particularly the dumb, unresponsive state brought about by the transgression of a taboo.

mvwaa (évuvwé)
> Wise, tranquil, soft, calm, pacific, evuvwe is the conjunction of *evo*, silent, and *avwe*, cool; in Bwiti, even-handed tranquillity.

mwan biang
> "Child of medicine," the Fang reliquary figure, containing qualities of infancy and old age. Latter-day name of *eyima bieri*.

mwan mot (emwan mot)
> The generic person, literally the child of man in the genealogical sense. Used with this literal meaning in Bwiti.

mwanenyang (mônenyang)
> Brother or sister (same sex speaking), siblings. Literally, child of the mother.

ndan ayong (éndan)
> The genealogy of the patriclan, the masterpiece of Fang social education.

ndébot
> "House of people," "house family," the minimal lineage segment of Fang.

ndem
> Signs, particularly those received from supernaturals in Bwiti.

nduman
> Young persons full of themselves and interested in renown.

nem
> One who possesses the demon but fails to control it and/or uses it in secret aggression against others. Plural, *beyem*.

ngang (angang)
> A basket formed of a circle of lianes and leaves, used, when filled with a therapeutic mixture, in a curing rite.

nganga (ngungan)
> "Doctor," person powerful in the knowledge of hidden things, also a courageous one in dealing with the demon.

Ngí
> The antiwitchcraft cult still practiced in some villages in the mid-twentieth century.

ngômalan
> Initiated member of Bieri, the ancestor cult; he who has eaten *malan* the psychoreactive alkaloid.

ngômbí
> The eight-string Egyptian harp employed in Bwiti.

ngomge
> Orderliness in social life and in village affairs.

ngul
> Force, capacity, power to do, determination.

ngwel
> Malicious use of the demon (*evus*); *sortilège*; the action of the sorcerer, *nem*.

nima na kombo
> The leader of the Bwiti chapel. From the Metsogo language.

njia (njiabot, nzvia)
> Commander, war leader, a temporary position of authority.

njimba
> The "origin spot" out of which Bwiti ceremonies proceed.

nkana nlang
> "Just-so" stories.

nkande
> An accounting of events of genealogical history.

nkôabot (ngôma)
> "Informal friendship," solidarity groups of age mates.

nkôbô akyenge
> "Miraculous words," the surpassingly skillful words of Bwiti leaders explaining recondite doctrine, particularly during the midnight sermons.

nkuk
> The chest cavity or trunk of the body and its organs; the seat of most demonic activity and most sickness.

nkukuma (kuma)
> Rich man (in wives) of the village.

nkukwan (nkôkôn)
> The sick person, sick in the chest or body cavity; *nkukwan nlem*, psychically sick person, deranged in thought.

nkus (nkur)

   Widow or widower, also the particularly burdensome mourning rite imposed upon widows.

nkyel

   Sagaciousness, prudence, cunning, latterly translated as science.

nlang

   Narrative history, fabulations.

nlem

   Heart, seat of thoughtfulness.

nlem abé

   "Badheartedness," bad disposition, resentment.

nlem mvôre

   "Oneheartedness," the main emergent sentiment aimed at in Bwiti.

nlôabé

   "Badheadedness," recalcitrance, lack of goodwill.

nlugha

   "Affectionate care" between spouses, the favored spouse in a situation of plural marriage.

nôm (nhom)

   Old person, elder, greatly experienced one.

nôm Ngi

   The "old of Ngi," the leader of the Ngi antiwitchcraft rite.

nôm ngwan

   Son-in-law, the most susceptible to requests for further bridepayments.

nsem

   Sin, ritual sin in the sense of transgression of a taboo; act against cosmic nature such as incest within the clan.

nsing (esinga)

   Wild cat, tiger cat, genet or civet whose skin is an important symbol in Bwiti (see *esinga*). The word is homophonic with *nsin* ("an enemy in the family") and that association may add to the symbolic importance of the cat skin.

nsis (nsir)

   Sinews, integuments, veins, and arteries. The essential structure of the body, and seat of the demon. The structure of the "body soul" (*nsisim*) in Bwiti doctrine.

nsisim

   The "essential nature" of the visible body which disappears at death. Taken by the missionaries as the soul.

nsôkngang (nsôkangang)

   "He who searches out hidden things," "doctor" of powerful revelation.

nsua

   Bridemonies.

nsuk bieri

The reliquary, the bark box containing the craniums.

nsusok eki

Person out of his mind, inebriated, hallucinating through transgression of a taboo.

nsut mot (nsurmot)

"Blackman," the African.

ntangen (ntana)

White man, European; also *bivele-bi-bot* (red man), he who has paid (*atan*) the sins of the earth, or, alternatively, he who counts everything.

ntebezang

Intermediary, the person who negotiates between two social groups.

ntôawu

A "sitting" of relatives in the village of a dead man on the day of his death.

ntôbot (ntôbe)

People cast off from their own families or, having lost them, who come to live in and be adopted by other families in other villages. If these people are from other clans, some degree of servitude is required until the second generation.

ntôlomot

Elder; oldest man of the lineage still actively participating in its affairs.

nyamoro

Full man, complete man, an early middle-aged man.

nyangndum

The mother's brother, a particularly strong relationship for a sister's son.

nyebe

Acceptance, agreement, responsiveness to a certain point of view, particularly in evangelization.

nyôl abé

The condition of "bad body," or dark body (*nvin*), of being in a state of sin.

nzang (onzan)

Hunger for meat.

nzeng (nze)

General hunger.

nzieboga

The "eater of eboga," another name for the members of Bwiti.

nzong (anzong)

Patience, tolerance, perseverance, the chief mark of a full man.

nzuk

The fatiguing sense of affliction, worry, uncertainty, moral trouble, or confusion to which Bwiti seeks to give a revitalizing answer.

ôbaka

    The bamboo sounding stave in Bwiti, a main instrument of Bwiti music, usually played upon by two players.

ôban

    A late nineteenth-century invasion of Fang country by the more northern Pahouin, the Bane in particular.

ôbangô

    The vertiginous, ecstatic dance of Bwiti.

ôkan

    Abstaining from sexual intercourse, or the state of purity which results.

ôsa biang

    A tree (*Pachylobus edulis*) whose fruit, leaves, and bark are felt to make highly effective medicine. Of central symbolic importance in Bwiti.

ôsiman (osimda)

    "Thought" in the sense of reflection on the past in search of useful analogies; also communion with the past.

ôson

    Shame, timidity, particularly the shame of having transgressed a taboo.

ôtunga

    Gathering place of the shades, transition spot between life and death, arena of reflection, crossroads; sacred tree (*Polyalthia suaveolens*) connecting the realms of being.

sok

    To seek out hidden truth.

sông

    The grave.

tsuge tsengé

    The grave; in Bwiti, the place of transformation.

ta mwanga

    The very center spot of the Bwiti chapel, the umbilicum, the navel, where the main fire of the chapel is lit.

yemba

    The "knowledgeable one" in Bwiti.

yena (eyena)

    The mirror, a key Bwiti symbol because of the reflective nature of thought and the reflective relation between the living and the dead.

yíle

    "To mean" in the sense of the import something has as a consequence of experience with it; meaning based on what one concludes from experience.

yômbô

    The head of the woman's group in Bwiti.

Zame asi, Zame ôyô
> God of the Below and God of the Above. The god of two parts which "is" the ancestors and also the old series of creator gods syncretized with the missionary divinity. This is a theological tension omnipresent in Fang culture of the twentieth century but pronouncedly emphasized in Bwiti.

zen
> "The road," the master metaphor of Bwiti; *zen abiale ye awu*, the path of birth and death, the main figurative dimension along which Bwiti songs and dances proceed.

zok
> Ceremony of protective cleansing.

zôm
> Leaf package of (usually pounded) food. A key metaphor in Bwiti.

Appendix II:
Sermon Texts

A. Evangile Fête Kumba

Ebôka a zô na: ku nsisim a ne mekí. Nyi na, nkawla mewala mesamen ye etun ongoase mininga ye ayong Nyingwan Mebege a yian dzip nda mbi atarege. Mwan amot a dzebe ye mfum etô, ening mon Fang e dzo alé. Nsisim wa mara ekôkôm akale e ne engongom. Edô a ne ôyô. Edô mon a adjughle essa ye nyia. Essa a ne nsisim. Nyia a ne ekôkôm. Nsama wa yian siman dzam ete. Zame ye Mebege be Nyingwan Mebege ebô be nga kôm ening ese bebe. Edô ba zô na: bekuma belal be nga sô abiale Eyene Zame—be nga ve nye biveve bilal: alan, ebôka, afep ezangô. Alan a nga wulu ye Ngombi-long. Ebôka a wulu ye Ngombi Fang, edô afep ezangô da wulu ye bobedzang nké. Mwan Fang a nga sô a dzô a sok béng. Nyi na: Zame asi, Zame ôyô. Nyi na a ne fe etuge nzum, nyi na Zame esi enye a ne etok nsisim, Zame ôyô a ne mfônga. Minkôl mite emyô. Nyingwan Mebege a nga kak mwan—bininga bi kak nkôp. Bia bise bi ne nyim Zame. Edo nyim a nga sô asô etôm. Bobedzang be dzi nyim—ô ta dzi nyim—nyim Zame. Bi nga van esi mben nyim Zame. Edo Nyingwan Mebege a nga lôm song. Metsugu Etsenge asi a ne song, Zame asi. Betara be nga bôm ngômbi long. Ayong Nyingwan Mebege edô é ne etô nsisim—dzam ete edô ebô be nga môbôba betara bekwa. Mwan Fang enye a ne tara long "la chapelle." Dzom eté edzô mwan Fang a lé na, ebem. Ngombi enye e ne nzele. Bot bevok be ne minkwas, nkawle o ne awom mewala ye mewale mebe. Eyene Zame a nga nyong minsisim, kôkô nangunda, Mezaman Obai, Obai Ndongi. Edzo Mwan Fang a lé na "nda akok," ntangan, enye, a lé na "limbo." Edô fe Eyene Zame a nga wulu ye beyegele awom ye bebe. Edô ening e ne meyong awôm ye bebe. Edo mwan Fang a bere ye ke kwing ebe Zame. Edô e ne Ôtunga. Edo e ne atsing Zame ye Nyingwan Mebege. Ngwan e ne mendzim. Mina ta dzi môt. Mina ta bele eves emôt. Mina ta kwing ngwel. Mina ta zu biôm bôt bevôk. Aki Kos Zambi Avanga enye a nga kôbô. Me mana zô.

B. Medzo me ye Fet Efun Olorogebot

(1) *Dzam te e se fe! Enye Zame a nga kom bia nlong.*
This thing is no more!/He, Zame, made us out upon the savanna.

(2) *Edô enye a nga tugan Azamboga. Edo a nga sum nzu long Afan.*
And he pierced the Azap mboga,/And he came and began to construct in the forest (and with the materials of the forest).

(3) *Edô mwan Fang a ne Afan. Mwanmot a ne mekyenge meni.*
For that Fang is (a person of) the forest./Humankind is (made of) four miracles.

(4) *Ane a koro así a kwing akyenge abô. Ane a koro vale a ntô mbien.*
Thus he leaves the earth and miraculously stands up (comes to his feet)./And he leaves that (posture) and rises to the calf.

(5) *Ane a koro va a ntô abon. Ane a koro va a ntô betate.*
And he leaves there and comes to the knee./Then he leaves there and perches on the shoulders (comes to his father).

(6) *Eyong te a nga fep así. Betate a bet adol osua.*
Then he spied down from the shoulders of his father./On these shoulders he was first put into the balance.

(7) *Ba fep ekôkom esí abiale.*
One fans the cadaver in (this) earth of (our) birth.

(8) *Onwan osua a nga sum nlong.*
The first bird began in the savanna.

(9) *Alu Caen a nga wing Abel edô be nga long Melen.*
The night that Cain slew Abel that was when they constructed the village of Melen.

(10) *Edô ka bulan omvus!*
And they never turned back!

(11) *Edô Elodi Atsengue Fang a lé na ndutum.*
And Elodi Atsengue Fang call rainbow.

(12) *Ntangan a lé na Arc-en-ciel.*
Europeans call it Arc-en-ciel.

(13) *A nga dage ebe bô.*
It was raised over the people.

(14) *Edô be nga tuga Azamboga.*
Then they passed through the Azap tree.

(15) *Edô be nga long afan.*
Then they constructed within (and out of) the forest.

(16) *Oban ewole. . . .*
That was the great (and auspicious) invasion.

(17) *Oban Olu Menyege.*
The invasion of Olu Menyege.

(18) *Esi mwanmot e nga kombe ye e ne atui mekí.*
The land of humankind was formed as a drop of blood.

(19) *Edô da vigele ye ke kwing mfum a kok meteng mebe.*
Then it whirled around and grew big like a white rock or as two hailstones.

(20) *Aten mfum ye aten nsut.*
The white hailstone and the black hailstone.

(21) *Ebuma ezoale.*
That is the great ball (the globe or earth).

(22) *Edô Fang a dzô na:*
For that reason Fang say that:

(23) *Oteteng ô kele ôyô na ka ndung.*
The star is suspended (high) above without falling.

(24) *Ebona e kele Azap.*
The fruit of the Azap is suspended in the Azap.

(25) *Dze e mbe e kele así ele? Atui mveng!*
What is suspended there below that fruit? The raindrop!

(26) *Edô e ne ensama.*
That is the group (of Banzie).

(27) *Adzô osua e ne nkok.*
The first food was the sugarcane.

(28) *Edo mon a nyong ebuma.*
Therefore the child takes the fruit (of the breast).

(29) *Ndong Zame enye a nga tare nzang ebwan.*
Ndong Zame he began to whine and wheedle for children.

(30) *Bi ne bwan ndutum akal bi ne metek.*
We are children of the rainbow because we are of clay.

(31) *Ebot ôsua be mbe mimvur.*
The first people had furry skins.

(32) *Ebô be mbe ''les anges.''*
These people were the angels.

(33) *Minkukwe mi zop Mfolo enye a ne St. Michel.*
The rays of the sun, the chief, he is Saint Michael.

(34) *Zop e ne ka dzibi.*
The heavens are not obscure (dark).

(35) *Minkukwe mi zo mfole a nga tele farga minkukwe na mi keng a nsung.*
The Chief of the rays of the sun obliged them to go into the courtyard.

(36) *Ene ebiran za nga sum mos te.*
So that disorder and strife began with that day.

(37) *Za so, za nga so, mbi.*
(That disorder) comes, it has always come, from (night-time) escapades (escapes into darkness).

(38) *Adang ye Eve abô be nga tara kut mebong.*
Adam and Eve they began to kneel.

(39) *Be ne benganga osua.*
They are the first masters of the unseen.

(40) *Edo Eyen Zame a nga wu mekong.*
Then Eyen Zame died by a spear.

(41) *Bizoghe e nga wu ekige!*
The sharpening stone killed by the knife.

(42) *Nsomo fa edô e nga wing Bizoghe.*
The great war knife killed the sharpening stone!

(43) *Akong edô e nga wing Eyen Zame.*
The spear it has killed Eyen Zame.

(44) *Edô Eboga a dzô na:*
And Eboga says:

(45) *Mopasema beba, mopasema beba, mopasema beba—mbembe!*
Mopasema beba, mopasema beba, mopasema beba, forever!

(46) *Da yili na, mbías: mopasema beba, mopasema beba—mbembe!*
It means twins: mopasema beba, mopasema beba—forever!

(47) *Edo be ne kal ye ndum, edo na ngal ye nôm.*
And that is sister and brother, and wife and husband.

(48) *Edo fe be ne mwan ye nyia.*
And that is mother and child.

(49) *Be wu etam, be kwan etam.*
One dies alone, one is sick alone.

(50) *Eyen Zame a se mefap.*
Eyen Zame has no wings.

(51) *Beange be ne mefap akal be nga biale aki.*
Angels have wings because they are born from eggs.

(52) *Edo fe be ne ye mimvur.*
And for that they have furry (feathery) bodies.

(53) *Tara a nga kômô ening tang melu mesamen.*
Father made life counting six nights.

(54) *Edô Zame a nga vigile aki.*
Then Zame stirred up the egg.

(55) *Edô bia biale aki.*
And we were born in an egg.

(56) *Ening mebong mebong ane nkok, nkok wa kok mwan mot.*
Life has many divisions like a piece of sugar cane, and man is driven on section by section.

(57) *Nyingwan Mebege a ne alen.*
Nyingwan Mebege is the oil palm.

(58) *Zame ye Mebege a ne otunga.*
Zame ye Mebege is the otunga.

(59) *Awu a nga wu edô a ne Ndapiat.*
The death that came to them was that of the lazy and wandering one, Ndapiat.

(60) *Akal enye, Ndapiat, a nga kwing abum mizi mezap.*
Because she, Ndapiat, gave birth in the spreading roots of the Azap tree.

(61) *Emô mi ne ekwa ôsua.*
These were the first chair (place where Fang were first thrown down in fighting).

(62) *Edô azap da kom wa na beyim be bet mintem.*
And the azap protects the newborn by causing the witches to be distracted and climb into its branches.

(63) *Edô bi nga koro azap asi.*
And thus we set out from underneath the azap.

(64) *Edo Zame a nga tôbô ekwa a ké mwan, Eyen Zame.*
Then Zame sat upon the stool and gave it to his child, Eyen Zame.

(65) *Edô e ne ôtunga, e ne croix.*
That is the otunga, it is the cross.

(66) *Azapmboga ô ne zen awu.*
Azapmboga is the path of death.

(67) *Ekwa ôsua a ne mbí awu.*
The first seat is the door of death.

(68) *Minsisim mi asighle etam Nyingwan Mebege, edô e ne Tame Manga.*
The spirits descend into the pool of Nyingwan Mebege, and that is Tame Manga.

(69) *Menzim mite emô bi awôban.*
In that water we bathe ourselves.

(70) *Edô e ne etam Maria.*
That is the pool of Maria.

(71) *Edô e ne eyola na Miwandzi Amwanga Tame Manga.*
Thus it has the name of Miwandzi Amwanga Tame Manga.

(72) *Nsut ô ne nyamoro.*
The black is the elder.

(73) *Mfum ô ne asueng—asueng nsisim.*
White is the refuge—the refuge of the spirit.

(74) *Edô ô ne fim. Edô ô ne kôn.*
And it is the white powder. And it is the ancestor spirit.

(75) *Mwan enye a ne ntô nyamoro betan.*
This child is the elder—five times elder.

(76) *Edô ngwan e nga tara lar esame.*
And the moon (the maiden) began to reunite the congregation.

(77) *Eboga e ne mebong mebe, abiale ye awu.*
Eboga comes in two sections, birth and death.

(78) *Eyen Zame e nga ke "kôkô nangunda" ye minsisim awom ye mebe.*
Eyen Zame has gone to the rocky sepulcher with the twelve spirits.

(79) *A nga wulu fe ye "bepotre" awom ye mebe.*
Twelve apostles accompanied him.

(80) *Edô a lige bô mimbu mewom mebe ye ndender ening.*
And he left them twenty years of wandering life in this world.

(81) *Nyol ening e ne "mwanga."*
The living body is the second-born of twins.

(82) *Mefak me ne misut, bevele, mefum. Afak Zame ba lé na abora.*
The caps (halos) are black, red, and white. The cap of God is called blessing.

(83) *Edô bi alé na Yemenzim. Abora edô ale.*
And we call it of the waterclan. That is the blessing.

(84) *Mwan mot a se yim na abialiang ka na ebôt bevô ba dzo nye dô.*
Mankind do not know they have been born unless others tell them of it.

(85) *Fam za wa nga menzim.*
The man (husband) does not bathe his wife in water.

(86) *Akoroge mon e ne bia bise avora: fam ye mininga.*
The first transformation of the child in the womb (as tadpole) is for us both, man and woman, a blessing.

(87) *Edô mininga enye a yian ba'ale menzim.*
For that reason woman must be the guardian of the water.

(88) *Asingele nsisim—ankongle—enye e ne edzom befam bi ave mininga engung bi abô aluk.*
The death agony of the soul—that gentle consideration—is what we men give to women when we marry them.

(89) *Edô e ne mintang asi. Edô e ne mvong bwan be bot.*
And that is the payment of the earth. And it is the seed of humankind.

(90) *Nsis otokh ewô ô ne si.*
The ligaments of the green bird who cries like water boiling it is (ties together) the earth.

(91) *Mininga enye a bele azapmboga asi.*
Woman she has azapmboga below.

(92) *Fam e bele azapmboga ôyô.*
Man he has azapmboga above.

(93) *Edô e ne atsinglan ening.*
That is the tying together of life.

(94) *Zame a bô eseng mam mebe.*
God makes life with two materials.

(95) *Mbias ngom ewô ô ne fam. Ngom e ne mininga.*
The drumming sticks (the twins) that is the male. The drum is the female.

(96) *Nyingwan Mebege a nga yam awom mbom ye mebom mebe.*
Nyingwan Mebege cooked twelve leaf packages of manioc.

(97) *A nga tara ake azar eboka mvi.*
She carefully laid leaves of eboga in the cooking pot.

(98) *A nga tughle minkol akal a woghle mom.*
She twisted off the sinews from the green leaves to tie together the leaf package of food.

(99) *Edô a nga ve akorge, ye nzong, ye akok eseng.*
Then she placed in the leaf package the tadpole, the fruit of the nsom tree, and the flint stone.

(100) *Edo a nga yen bensue.*
Then she saw small lizards.

(101) *Vale a nga sile bo été.*
Then she placed them down within.

(102) *Edo a nga ve menzim avitzang azom été.*
Then she placed a little water in the package.

(103) *Edo a nga ke osvi a ke lal menzim na a tele mom nduan.*
Then she went to the river to scoop up water in order to place the packages over the fire.

(104) *Ye bibebam be nga ligan ba bô ebiran omvus.*
The black waterbug was left behind making destructiveness.

(105) *Edo Zame ye Mebege a nga kik aket.*
Then Zame ye Mebege cut open the package.

(106) *Ane a nga long nda.*
And he tied together the house.

(107) *Mwan a sum akorge, a ntô séng, a ntô nsue, edô a wu.*
The child begins as a tadpole, it becomes a flintstone, it becomes a lizard, then it dies.

(108) *Mengabe-me-nzoge a ne nsisim wa bo akyenge eyong a ke ôyô.*
The little waterbug, it is the spirit, it performs miracles when it goes above to heaven.

(109) *Mezô mete me ne mezô ye mfonge.*
These words are the words of the wind.

(110) *Esi e ne ye nkôbô mbore.*
The earth is of one speech.

(111) *Ezô e ne wôk mezô me ye mfonge.*
This is what one can understand from the words of the wind.

(112) *Esi e ngenen e bele bives e ne wok mezo me ye adzal.*
The earth still possesses bones but it listens to the words of the village (of the dead).

(113) *Me mana dzô.*
I have finished speaking.

Appendix III:
The MBiri Curing Societies

WE HAVE LABELED the subject of this book an equatorial microcosm so as to contrast the small-scale, self-sufficient cosmologizing going on here with the macrocosm of the world system, which in the form of the colonial and post-colonial world has been gradually encroaching on Fang as upon all third-world peoples. In another sense, however, we know that Bwiti itself is a macrocosm in relationship with the corporeal microcosm of the individual participant whose ritual activity within the quality space of the chapel has revitalizing consequences—at least, it puts him or her in contact with the whole. Bwiti healing is thus healing in the etymological sense of that term: "to make whole." It makes whole by cosmogony, by placing the body-microcosm directly in relation to the macrocosm of Fang experience—in relation to mythological, legendary, migratory, and ecological experiences as well as in relation to experiences of kinship and clanship. Bwiti ministers to the affliction of partness.

The Bwiti sense of healing, then, is largely symbolic. It heals indirectly, for the most part, by representations—by definitions of ritual situations and by consequent performances which involve the individual participants in qualitative transformations. Rarely in Bwiti is there a direct laying on of hands, a providing of specific remedies or a focusing upon possible causes of individual cases of disease. Indeed Bwiti tends to look upon such therapeutic preoccupations as detrimental to cosmogonic activity. It is the same way Bwiti looks upon such excessively individuated behavior as is found in possession (*epogain*).

MBiri chapels take a more direct and curative approach to disease and affliction. Banzie of Bwiti (both MBiri and Bwiti members call themselves Banzie) sometimes refer to MBiri as a "sister religion" or as "our hospital." In view of this perceived complementarity it is revealing to distinguish Bwiti from MBiri, for although Bwiti seeks to build a self-sufficient healing world of its own, the fact that Banzie often look to MBiri for a more direct curing of a specific disease or spiritual malaise makes, for such Banzie at least, MBiri an essential part of the Bwiti whole. This is true even when, as often enough, MBiri functions as an alternative religious institution with mutually exclusive membership. Individuals inclined towards religious revitalization must, then, choose which path to follow. In this context as well, some knowledge of MBiri is relevant to an understanding of Bwiti and the kind of commitment it represents.

Foster's distinction between personalistic and naturalistic orientations in disease etiology is relevant here,[1] although the coexistence of these sister systems points up the dialectic in disease strategies in Fang culture and the impossibility of classifying the entire culture in Foster's terms. The point is that Bwiti understands the afflictions of its members in systemic terms, seeking to bring the isolated individual back into orderly and balanced relations with the cosmic system—the "complex whole." We see in the ritual relating of parts in the Bwiti chapel something very like an equilibrium model of well being. Of course the attributes of the ancestors and the great gods are taken into account and their benevolence solicited in the rituals, but little attempt is made personalistically to diagnose specific diseases. The major effort in cosmogonizing is to persuade (or conjure) the great gods and errant or abandoned ancestors to assume their appropriate and benevolent place in the cosmic system. When they are in that place all will be right with the individual Fang world. The Bwiti response to malaise is kinesthetic restoration of system. That is what cosmogony is all about. That restoration is therapeutic in a general way to all diseases but specifically therapeutic to none. Thus Bwiti is better described as redemptive—seeking to redeem a world in which participants can live fruitfully and hopefully.[2]

MBiri chapels and leaders, on the other hand, are mainly concerned with the diagnosis of specific illnesses and with the identification of the specific agents responsible for them. Initiates to MBiri are most often brought to seek its ritual offices by a sense of a specific troubling spirit, the MBiri, who must be encountered through initiation and eboga-induced visions. The focal event in MBiri is these initiations—not very different in their stages from Bwiti initiations—and it gives central place in its ritual procedures to the encounter with the troubling spirit. These initiation curings or reinitiations (often one large dose of eboga is insufficient and another "eating" is required) provide the "raison d'être" for MBiri. This is not the case in Bwiti where initiation, though important, is peripheral to the night-long cosmogony. The events surrounding MBiri initiation, the orientation of the ongoing dances around the initiate, pressuring him or her toward the spiritual revelation, are all more intense and dramatic than in Bwiti. The mirror, for example, into which the drugged initiate peers fixedly in order to see the troubling spirit come forward out of the ground is much more purposefully, instrumentally employed in MBiri. The initiate's attention is forced upon it. It is a crucial technique and part of the cure. When the vision is received the initiate is rushed out of the chapel to the *epiko* (the three-log arena directly to the side of the birth entrance), in which the vision is recounted, the afflicting spirit identified, and specific herbs and medicines prescribed. The presence of a formulary in MBiri causes Fang to describe it as a religion of herbs and plants (*nyiba bilok*) and to distinguish it from Bwiti as a religion of trees (*nyiba bilé*). Accordingly, eboga is never taken alone in MBiri but always mixed with various efficacious plant powders.

Because of the complementarity of Bwiti and MBiri, either by overlapping membership or by mutually exclusive membership, the relations between the two sects pose a problem for Banzie—and for Fang generally—and they are usually ready to provide a set of differentiations. Here are some of the differences which arose in inquiry.

BWITI	MBIRI
A religion of one path.	A religion of two paths.
A religion of trees.	A religion of plants.
A religion of voluntary membership.	A religion in which membership is compulsory.
A religion.	A hospital.
A religion of the ancestors.	A religion of afflicting spirits.
A religion of the other world.	A religion of this world.
A religion of men.	A religion of women.
A religion that breaks open the head.	A religion that cleans the body.
A religion of light, of seeing and following the path.	A religion of the wind (mfonge) and of possession (epogain).
A religion of Nyingwan Mebege and the great gods.	A religion of the family.

We have already spoken to some of these distinctions, but others bear commenting upon. MBiri is said to be a religion of the family because many chapels are family enterprises, because its influence spreads along family lines, and because in its ministrations it is mainly thought to promote family (not world) well-being. The spirits discovered to be troubling family well-being will be, quite often, nonancestral. There are no great gods such as Nyingwan Mebege to which the entire membership is devoted. Each MBiri initiate has his or her own troubling spirit, deity as it were, to which he or she must be devoted. The object of MBiri is visionary fulfillment through possession and the purifying action of the good wind—*mbamba mfonge*—whereas in Bwiti the object is visionary intelligence, enlightenment, and a more precise following of *the* path of birth and death. MBiri, thus, is perceived by Fang as having many paths—each initiate has a path appropriate to himself and his afflicting spirit. In MBiri it is not only the "good wind" that purifies; the rituals themselves emphasize cleansing and purification through the administration of purgatives and through the forcing of vomiting in initiation. In Bwiti purification is only incidental to initiation and vomiting is accidental. There is thus a much greater emphasis upon cleanliness in the MBiri chapel, including the lavish use of freshly laundered sheets wrapped around the central pillar and draped elsewhere.

The sex distinction in informants' observations derives from the fact that most leaders of MBiri chapels are women, whereas in Bwiti, despite the ritual place women have obtained, there are no overall female leaders. The this-world/other-world distinction derives from the fact that MBiri emphasizes the bringing of the troubling spirits from the other world, Ekongi, to this world, while Bwiti emphasizes the penetration into the other world of the dead, although it may seek to make the ancestors present as an aid to that penetration during the night-long worship. MBiri, besides being sensitive to troubling ancestors, recognizes a group of troubling spirits, *okinda*, which are causative of specific diseases and whose recognized presence can lead to the curing of specific afflictions. Some of these spirits, identified with their afflictions are:

ODUMBO: spiritual affliction of the head, which gives signs of increasing pressure and feels as if it might explode. Untreated, this affliction leads to madness.

MDUMBULA: afflictions of the chest which are cured by purgation and cleansing of the interior body with the cooperation of the spirit cause.

NJEMBE: afflictions of the bones and joints cured by action of the "good wind" in dancing.

MBUMBA: afflictions of the stomach and bowels caused by a water spirit of the same name who exists in the form of a serpent. With the cooperation of this spirit and by action of eboga mixed with various plants (a mixture called *ekaso*), the watery bowels, chief symptom of the disease, are solidified. This spirit is sometimes called *mamywateh*.

There is a tendency in MBiri for various chapels to specialize in one or another of these spirit-afflictions, all of which derive, although there has been syncretic reinterpretation, from spirits well known among coastal peoples. Though one can be called by disease or malaise into Bwiti, as we have seen in discussing reasons for membership above, Bwiti membership is still felt to be a voluntary search for a path. In MBiri one is compelled by affliction to seek membership. The spirit forces one's hand.

DYNAMICS IN THE DEVELOPING RELATION
BETWEEN BWITI AND MBIRI

Fang also say that MBiri is a religion of the coast and Bwiti a religion of the interior forest. By this is meant that MBiri derives from coastal peoples and particularly from the Miene-speaking peoples living along the coastal estuaries from Libreville to Fernan Vaz and also along the lower reaches of the Ogowe river and in its delta. Among the Miene, the Mpongwe and the Galwa particularly, the Ombwiri were nature spirits associated with trees, caverns, rocky promontories, rivers, pools, lakes, and waterfalls.[3] These spirits had to be pacified in order that men and women could carry out their activities in these places. But these spirits could also interfere with human well-being, good fortune, and health, and various Ombwiri societies had long existed on the coast to prevent or beneficially manage that intrusiveness. These Ombwiri societies were organized and led by women, though unlike the Fang Mevungu women's rites (the equivalent among the Miene was Nyembe), men also participated.

In the first decades of the century Fang women who had visited or lived on the coast and who had consulted Ombwiri returned up-country and created Fang MBiri chapels. This seems to have occurred after the First World War. Between the wars MBiri among Fang was largely a female curing society fully complementary to Fang Bwiti, which at that period was predominantly a male religion, much more faithful to its heritage from the male ancestor cults of interior peoples, Metsogo and Massango principally. The aftermath of the Second World War included a substantial shift in male and female participation in Bwiti. Women became much more important than previously in most branches. Fang say that in part this was the result of the pressure of MBiri upon Bwiti. At the same time men became more influential in MBiri. This latter influence was so noticeable that some MBiri curing centers became substantially more than "hospitals." They became religious centers with a redemptive claim upon a participant's lifeways. Some MBiri chapels became difficult to distinguish in their cosmogonic claims from Bwiti chapels. Swiderski gives us a 1974 report on an MBiri tradition, *Erendzi Sainte*, that in most respects is difficult to distinguish from a Bwiti tradition (in its systematic claim on the patient's worldview) even though it preserves much more of a personalistic orientation than most Bwiti chapels.[4] What has, in effect, occurred since the Second World War under the mutual effect of Bwiti and MBiri on each other is the institutionalization of the latter and its entrance, perhaps by aspiration to a calling higher than transitory therapeutics, into the sectarian dynamics of Bwiti as we have discussed above.

Notes

Preface And Linguistic Note

1. B. Weinstein, *Gabon: Nation Building on the Ogooué*.
2. H. Arendt, *Between Past and Future*, p. 275.
3. S. Galley, *Dictionnaire Fang-Français et Français-Fang*, p. 262.
4. P. Alexandre and J. Binet, *Le Groupe Dit "Pahouin."*

Entering Into An Equatorial Microcosm

1. John Livingston Lowes, *The Road to Xanadu*.
2. Ibid., p. 366.
3. The understanding of Africa which we obtain by considering these images has been fully demonstrated by Philip Curtin, *Image of Africa*. We have sought, taking advantage of the anthropologist's participation, to register Fang images which are a reaction to European images.
4. This awareness of the "circumstantiality" of ethnography and the understanding of the description of culture as dialogue is represented most insightfully in the work of Clifford Geertz, *The Interpretation of Cultures*. But the argument that meaning in human experience arises in social interaction, if not a Wittgensteinian point, is central to the argument of the symbolic interactionists (H. Blumer, *Symbolic Interactionism: Perspective and Method*).
5. D. Sperber, *Rethinking Symbolism*, and F. Barth, *Ritual and Knowledge among the Baktamen*.
6. J.D.Y. Peel's study of the Yoruba prayer churches, *Aladura*, is a very good example of a study which gives full credence to the conscious thought of church leaders—of which there is an abundance. He offers a detailed "sociology of knowledge" for that thought, treating it as a dependent variable to be explained by other antecedent changes in the social system. At the same time he treats the thought itself as logically prior to the emotional and behavioral consequences of it (p. 156). While giving full credence to Bwiti thought, we do not necessarily give it priority. Images and concepts emanate from action as often as they give rise to behavior and emotional states.
7. O. Lewis, *The Children of Sanchez* and V. W. Turner, *Schism and Continuity in an African Society*.
8. The basic ethnographic monographs on Fang are those of G. Tessmann, *Die Pangwe* and H. Trilles, *Totemism chez le Fang*. Alexandre and Binet's *Le Groupe dit "Pahouin"* monograph in the International African Institute

Series, though primarily on Bulu, applies in good part to Fang. The Fang are also one of the African peoples abstracted and categorized for ready consultation in the Human Relations Area Files.

9. I hope the reader will not think it egocentric to have included ourselves in these events. The presence of the ethnographer is, after all, the reality of the field situation. It is the reality of the interactive process in which meaning emerges. Soon enough, in any case, the ethnographer's self-conscious presence is replaced, as it should be, by participation in the observed reality of Fang culture and the Bwiti microcosm.

10. Max Gluckman, "Ethnographic Data in British Social Anthropology," and J. Van Velsen, "The Extended Case Method and Situational Analysis."

11. R. Brown, *Explanation in the Social Sciences*, p. 41.

12. Some of the most illuminating work on African religious movements is being done by historians or historians of religion (M. L. Daneel, *Old and New in Southern Shona Independent Churches*; H. W. Turner, *African Independent Church*). An anthropologist has to recognize the powerful understanding obtained through what Vansina, the master in this, calls the "study of cultures through time." J. Vansina, "Cultures Through Time," pp. 165-179. For a historian's study of a dance movement, not so different from a religious movement, which brings successive historical contexts illuminatingly to bear, see T. O. Ranger, *Dance and Society in Eastern Africa*.

13. C. Lévi-Strauss, *The Savage Mind*, p. 21.

14. Samuel Coleridge, *The Ancient Mariner*, pp. 366-436.

15. Jack Goody and Ian Watts, "The Consequences of Literacy."

16. V. Lanternari, *Religions of the Oppressed*.

17. A.F.C. Wallace, *Culture and Personality*, 2nd ed., Introduction.

18. The resistance to reasoning by self—or problem—contained rules has been a discovery of the Rockefeller ethnographic psychology team working among the nonliterate rural peoples of Liberia. When presented with syllogisms the tendency was to respond by searching contexts or direct personal experience for an answer, although all the rules necessary were contained in the syllogism itself. Sylvia Scribner calls this mode of thought "empiric" rather than "theoretic" ("Modes of Thinking and Ways of Speaking: Culture and Logic Reconsidered"). It ought to be said that riddles, widespread in Africa and particularly cherished by Fang, force contextualization because they rarely or never provide in themselves sufficient rules or information for their own solution.

19. V. Largeau, *Encyclopédie pahouine*, pp. 14-15. Largeau is not the only early observer to comment upon the thoughtful questions put to Europeans by Fang, and in counterpart, the thoughtful answers provided. The exegetical nature of Fang may not then simply be a product of acculturation but a characteristic of Fang having to do with the institutions of the council (or debating or palaver) house as well as their penchant for riddling.

20. P. Bohannan and L. Bohannan, *The Tiv of Central Nigeria*, p. 18.

21. L. Doob, "Presuppositions and Perplexities Confronting Social Psychological Research in Developing Countries."

22. J. W. Fernandez, "Symbolic Consensus."

23. I have argued this point in greater detail in a critical appreciation of the work of Victor Turner: "On Reading the Sacred into the Profane."

24. J. W. Fernandez, "African Religious Movements—Types and Dynamics"; *Microcosmogony and Modernization in African Religious Movements*; "The Ethnic Communion: Interethnic Recruitment in African Religious Movements."

25. J. W. Fernandez, "Rededication and Prophetism in Ghana."

26. A point convincingly made in T. O. Ranger and I. Kimambo, eds., *The Historical Study of African Religion*.

27. See particularly John M. Janzen and Wyatt MacGaffey, comps., *An Anthology of Kongo Religion: Primary Texts*. For a virtuoso cosmologizer who, however, goes well beyond any of the Bwiti "thoughtful ones," see A. Fu-Kiau Kia Bunseki, *Le Mukongo et le monde qui l'entourait*, with an introduction by John Janzen. The BaKongo, of course, have had a much longer contact with the West and structurally are a different society from Fang.

28. J. Mbiti, *New Testament Eschatology in an African Background*, and N. S. Booth, "Time and Change in African Traditional Thought."

29. J. W. Fernandez, "Unbelievably Subtle Words."

30. N. S. Booth, "Time and Change in African Traditional Thought," p. 87.

31. Alexandre, "Proto-histoire de groupe beti-bulu-fang," p. 109.

32. This "nowness" is very much at the heart of the microcosmogony we seek to explain. In doing that, we may contribute to a better understanding of an important recent debate in the literature which conceives of conversion as the shift from a microcosmic to a macrocosmic perspective (R. Horton, "African Conversion," and "On the Rationality of Conversion." It is a debate which is weakened, however, by a neglect of our understanding of how a microcosm can be imaginatively constructed and how it can be so constructed in the face of modernizing pressures (J. W. Fernandez, "Microcosmogony and Modernization").

CHAPTER 1

1. This estimate of travel time to the Woleu is much exaggerated, as Tessmann walked from the Woleu south to the point in the Gabon Estuary of which Bowditch speaks in fifteen days. G. Tessmann, "Verlauf und Ergebnisse der Lubecker Pangwe Expedition," p. 28. For commentary relevant to our considerations see Bowditch, *Mission to Cape Coast Castle and Ashantee*, see pages 422-452.

2. The drive of the missionaries toward the interior is seen in such letters to the Home Board from 1840 on. Two books summarize the history of the mission in Africa and treat this "drang nach Osten": Arthur J. Brown, *One Hundred Years*, and W. R. Wheeler, *The Words of God in an African Forest*. In later chapters, 2 and 6 particularly, this drive is examined carefully.

3. The American presence has been examined in l'Abbé André Raponda-Walker and Robert Reynaud, "Anglais, Espagnoles et Nord Americains au Gabon au XIXe siècle."

4. Benjamin Griswold, "Reasons for Selecting the Gaboon," letter to the Home Board. *The Missionary Herald*, 38 (December 1842):499.

5. John L. Wilson, "Visit to the Upper Waters of the Gaboon," *The Missionary Herald*, 39 (June 1843):238.

6. Ibid., p. 239.

7. His death and reference to this journey are reported in *The Missionary Herald*, 41 (January 1845). He made extensive notes of his trip, but unfortunately for science left them at his death in "so incomplete a state that they will be of little value to us and none to the world," p. 27.

8. Letter of William Walker, *The Missionary Herald*, 45 (April 1849):121.

9. Ibid., p. 122.

10. Ibid., p. 123.

11. His two expeditions are noted in the *Annual Reports of the Board of Foreign Missions* of the Presbyterian Church in the United States of America: 17th Annual Report (1854), p. 22; 20th Annual Report (1857), p. 34. The 20th report contains an accurate map of his journey. A more extensive report is given in *The Home and Foreign Record* of the Presbyterian Church, 9 (1858):110-115.

12. *The Home and Foreign Record*, 9 (1858):102.

13. Discussed fully in Guy Laserre, *Libreville: la ville et sa région*, pp. 87-96.

14. Pigeard's exploration is reported in Laserre and in Charles Pigeard, "Exploration du Gabon effectuée en août et septembre 1845."

15. A. Mequet, "Nouvelle excursion dans la haut de la rivière du Gabon effectuée en novembre et decembre 1846."

16. Ibid., p. 71.

17. Ibid., p. 75.

18. "Voyage au Como." A map of this river and an account of the riverine inhabitants are given in this 1861 article. As far as I know, we have no record of his explorations to the Cristal Mountains, though he mentions his voyages far up the Como in the above article. He seems dependent on the experiences of the American missionaries, Bert and Hendrick, for his knowledge of the plateau.

19. The author notes (ibid., p. 359) that the Fang of the region of the

Gabon Estuary are of two groups: the Meké and the Fang proper or Fang-Fang. The former are those Fang clans which have migrated directly into the estuary from the east-southeast, primarily down the Ogowe. The Fang or Fang-Fang are those clans which migrated primarily from the north and north-east directly from the plateau down the Como and the Abanga.

20. Mequet, "Nouvelle excursion," p. 77.

21. These are reported in the following books: *Explorations and Adventures in Equatorial Africa* (1861); *Stories of the Gorilla Country* (1867); *Wild Life under the Equator* (1869); *Lost in the Jungle* (1869); *My Apingi Kingdom* (1870); *A Journey in Ashango Land* (1871); *In the Country of the Dwarfs* (1872). A biography of DuChaillu was written by Paul Vaucaire in 1930, *Paul DuChaillu, Gorilla Hunter*. But it incorporates many materials from DuChaillu's own writings and is hardly adequate to cover his career.

22. This defense is in *Globus*, Band I, p. 167 (1863) under the title, "Paul DuChaillu—Forschungsreisen und Abendteurer in West Afrika." DuChaillu had been roundly attacked by H. Barth in *Peterman's Mitteilungen*, Band VII, p. 367 (1961), "Analyse der Reiseschreibung DuChaillu." Barth sought to show that DuChaillu falsified his data and dates, and even plagiarized materials from other explorers and gave his own name to specimens found previously.

23. DuChaillu gives a very good account of the middle-man trading system in *Explorations and Adventures in Equatorial Africa*, Chapters I-IV, particularly pp. 17-19.

24. Ibid., pp. 46-47.

25. Ibid., p. 80.

26. Ibid., p. 78.

27. G. Tessmann, *Die Pangwe*, Vol. I, pp. xi-xii. "Seine Berichte Vielfach in der Verallgemeinung Unrichtig und Masslos Übertrieben Sind."

28. DuChaillu, *Explorations and Adventures*, p. 39.

29. Ibid., p. 14.

30. Ibid., p. 59.

31. One has only to compare the maps of the Rev. J. L. Mackey's journey as reported in *The Home and Foreign Record*, 4(1858):110-115, with that of DuChaillu (*Adventures*, opposite p. 1). DuChaillu's contemporary, Dr. Griffon du Bellay, made the most balanced critique, perhaps, while stationed in Libreville: "Le Gabon." Du Bellay maintains that DuChaillu made the explorations claimed but greatly exaggerated cannibalism and confused material culture from the coast with that of the interior. Du Bellay implies that these faults of character and intellect may arise from the fact that DuChaillu, by birth a French Creole, became "depuis et du même coup un citoyen américain plein d'ardeur pour sa nouvelle patrie et un anglican plein de ferveur pour la bible" (p. 278).

32. R. Burton, "A Day Amongst the Fang," reprinted in *Selected Papers on Anthropology, Travel and Exploration by Sir Richard Burton*, ed. N. W. Penzer (New York: Philpot, 1924).

33. Ibid., p. 93.

34. Ibid., p. 99.

35. Ibid., p. 100.

36. DuChaillu, *Explorations and Adventures*, p. 78, had appealed to Reverend Walker to support his testimony as to cannibalism.

37. Ibid., p. 108.

38. In *Death Rides a Camel: A Biography of Richard Burton* (1963), Allen Edwards describes the contradictions in Burton's character which drove him on: his "two personalities each of which hated the other . . . the sensualist versus the ascetic . . . the idealist versus the realist . . . ," p. 11.

39. G. Roullet, *Annales des Voyages* (December 1866), Tome IV, pp. 273-282.

40. Ibid., p. 282.

41. A major exploration of the area between French and German territories was that of the Spaniard, Manuel Iradier y Bulfy, in the years 1875 and 1877-1884. His report is in two volumes, *Africa: Viajes y Trabajos de la Asociación Euskara—La Exploradora*. His observations are mainly pertinent to the coastal peoples living about the Muni Estuary—the Benga and the Bapuku. He did penetrate to the plateau and made brief contact with Fang. But he is often inexact and confirms the old stereotype. For example, he finds the Fang a race "fuerte, valiente y anthropófaga . . . saguinaria y cruel. They order for the slightest reason the death and consumption of a slave . . . the head and testicles reserved for the chief." (Vol. I, p. 313). The report contains valuable data on material culture, and dance patterns.

42. See Griffon du Bellay, "Le Gabon." R.B.N. Walker's explorations are reported in the *Annales des Voyages* (February 1870), I, pp. 9-80, 120-144, in "Über Ogoue und Ngunie," and in "Letter of a Journey up the Ogowe." R. H. Nassau's work on the Ogowe and his friendship with de Brazza are reported in *My Ogowe*.

43. Marquis de Compiegne, *L'Afrique équatoriale: Gabonais, Pahouins, Gallois*. The Marquis reviewed the debate over DuChaillu and hunted up the old trackers of the famous hunter. They, unfortunately, claimed that their "massah" had killed no more than one gorilla and that already wounded. Compiegne, however, pays DuChaillu the respect of repeating his stereotypes.

44. Ibid., Vol. 1, p. 155.

45. Ibid., p. 159.

46. Du Bellay, "Le Gabon," p. 310.

47. De Compiegne, *L'Afrique équatoriale*, Vol. 1, p. 207.

48. Savorgnan de Brazza, "Voyages dans l'ouest Africain," pp. 289-336, pp. 1-25. De Brazza divides the Fang into two branches: the Fang Osyeba

or Ogowe Fang and the Fang Batchies or Fang of the Como, Woleu, and coastal escarpment. The Fang split into these two groups at an unknown time and at an unknown place, probably in the Sudanic Plateau (Vol. XLV, 1888, p. 2).

49. Ibid., Vol. XLV, p. 11.

50. Ethelreda Lewis, ed., *Trader Horn or the Ivory Coast in the Earlies: Being the Life and Works of Alfred Aloysius Horn*, with illustrations from the Metro-Goldwyn-Mayer Production, pp. 19-27.

51. Horn discusses three branches of the MPangwis: the Binvoul on the north bank between Lambarene and Ndjole, the Fang inland to the north and penetrating to the river around the mouth of the Okano, and the Osheba on the south and north bank of the Ogowe upriver from Ndjole. His report would accord with the view of the Osheba as Ogowe river Pahouin coming originally from the Ivindo.

52. Ibid., pp. 4 and 179.

53. M. Kingsley, *Travels in West Africa*, particularly Chapter XIV.

54. Her ethnological intuition in Ashanti was praised by Rattray as "inspired" (R. Rattray, *Ashanti*, p. 81).

55. Kingsley, *Travels*, pp. 429-430.

56. Besides *Travels in West Africa* her other important book is *West African Studies*.

57. J. E. Flint, in "Mary Kingsley—A Reassessment," has argued that Mary Kingsley was mainly committed to commercialism in West Africa and to the defense of the traders. But he does not explain why she took this position. Self-interest was surely not involved (p. 97). Nor was personal liking, for she liked the missionaries just as well. The reason seems to be that in the exchange relationship practiced by the traders, the justice of the marketplace prevailed and there was no direct or unfairly coercive attempt to impose one way of life on another—as was the case with missionaries and administrators. She ignored the creation of new needs through trade, perhaps more insidious and damaging to native cultures. Also, the primary rationale of Mary Kingsley's expedition was the collection and preservation of new species of fish. She often extended the taxonomy metaphor to the African and African life; he and it were of a different species and entitled to description and preservation.

58. In respect to her Gabon materials, she consulted extensively with Dr. Nassau, much profiting from his long experience (cf. *Travels*, pp. 443ff.). Nassau's own materials are found in *Fetishism in West Africa*.

59. Kingsley, *Travels*, pp. 504-508.

60. Ibid., p. 307.

61. Ibid., p. 117.

62. Ibid., p. 130.

63. Ibid., pp. 729, 282, 400, 409.

64. Ibid., p. 264.

65. Ibid., p. 285.

66. Kingsley, *West African Studies*, p. 119.

67. Kingsley, *Travels*, pp. 440-441.

68. Kingsley, *West African Studies*, p. 386.

69. Flint, "Mary Kingsley—A Reassessment," p. 100.

70. Kingsley, *Travels*, p. 104.

71. Ibid., p. 501.

72. Ibid., p. 485.

73. Louis Franc, *De l'origine des Pahouins: essai de resolution de ce problème ethnologique*. Mentioned in Brian Weinstein, *Gabon: Nation Building on the Ogoowe*, p. 37.

74. Paris, Ministre de Marine et Colonies, *Archives de la France d'Outre Mer (Paris): Gabon-Congo IV*, Dossier 10, Document no. 47. Lettre de 1 juillet 1876, lettre de 27 octobre 1883.

75. Ibid., lettre de 18 octobre 1888.

76. Ibid., lettre de Ndjole 3 août 1894, lettre de Ndjole 9 août 1894, telegram 21 décembre 1894.

77. Ibid., Rapport politique du 20 septembre 1897 and lettre du 20 septembre, Rapport du Capitaine Vernoeldi sur le 5ᵉ de *l'Avant Garde* Cap Lopez.

78. Ibid., lettre du 18 octobre 1897.

79. The extensive exchange on this issue, "Affaire echouage de l'eclaireur," comprises a separate bundle of papers within the mentioned dossier—*Gabon-Congo IV*, Dossier 10. Dolisie's letter in response to previous pressures is dated 9 octobre 1897.

80. M. J. Ellenberger, Letter to the Paris Board, *Journal des Missions Evangéliques*, 3ⁱᵉᵐᵉ Serie, 26 (1901):513. There are numerous letters on this subject in the journal from 1885 on. The Protestants were more critical than the Catholics in these matters, in keeping with the fact that the latter had something of the status of a state church. In fact, the archives of FOM give evidence of administrative attempts to restrain the too-forceful evangelization of the interior by Catholic missionaries. *France d'Outre Mer, Gabon-Congo IV*, 10, Procès Verbal 22 avril, 18 août 1888. The American missionaries had early remarked a tension between French administration and missionaries reminiscent of the church-state dichotomy in Spanish colonization. *The Missionary Herald*, 47 (April 1851):32, letter of August 24, 1850: "The civil authorities continue to be friendly to us but inimical to them (the Catholic mission), I hardly know how to account for this unless it is because of that hostility which all Frenchmen feel towards Jesuitism on being extricated from its trammels." These administration-mission relations undoubtedly followed the fluctuation of "secularism" in France itself.

81. Letter of A. Fondere, Commandant de la Région de l'Ogooué, 24 juillet 1899, *Archives France d'Outre Mer*.

82. Afilan azok; Nzok! Bot bese be baa nye? Ntangen!

83. *Archives France d'Outre Mer, Gabon-Congo IV*, 10, lettre de 11 janvier 1884.

84. The American missionaries left Gabon and their stations on the Gabon Estuary and the Ogowe for the German Kamerun. Dr. A. I. Good, first missionary among the Cameroon Bulu, preached to them in the Fang he had learned in Gabon. From 1842 on, *The Missionary Herald* testified to the anxiety of the Americans concerning what they called "French aggression" and exertion of hegemony despite the primacy of the American presence. But there was a tendency to blur this anxiety with a preoccupation with the coming of "Romanism." See especially Vol. 40 (August 1844):349-352.

85. This "tertium quid" positioning between Germans and French is particularly apparent in the report of the Cottes expedition to establish the boundaries in northern Gabon between French and German claims. A. Cottes, *La Mission Cottes au Sud-Cameroun (1905-1908)*. From the German side, the view of the Fang as a pawn in French-German relations is seen in a report on the Batanga-Expedition by Lieutenant Kund. *Mitteilungen aus den Deutschen Schutzgebieten*, Band II (1889), pp. 105-110.

86. *France d'Outre Mer, Gabon-Congo III*, Dossier 10. Rapport politique no. 364. Ndjole, le 29 juillet 1896.

87. *France d'Outre Mer, Gabon-Congo IV*, Dossier 19, 1902-1903, Rapport politique no. 656, 19 septembre 1902, p. 94.

88. J. B. Roche, *Au Pays des Pahouins*, passim, but especially pp. 38, 53, 79, 91, 113, 118.

89. Ibid., p. 140.

90. French administrators, following the warning of Roche, perhaps, tended to overestimate the political threat represented by Bwiti. Cf. J. W. Fernandez, "The Affirmation of Things Past: Alar Ayong and Bwiti as Movements of Protest in Central and Northern Gabon."

91. Hoxie Neale Fairchild, *The Noble Savage: A Study in Romantic Naturalism*.

92. Philip Curtin, *The Image of Africa*, p. vi and passim.

93. Bernard Schnapper, *La Politique et le commerce français dans le Golfe de Guinée de 1838-1871*, Part I, La Politique des points d'appui.

94. Ibid., p. 101.

95. Cf. George W. Stocking, "French Anthropology in 1800." Stocking points out that the romantic view of the primitive was dispelled in the decade after 1800 by actual field work. A benevolent primitivism was thus purged in favor of the developing doctrine of social evolutionism and its uncharitable view of savage life. As our data makes clear, these intellectual developments seem to have been confined to professional circles. None of our French observers was influenced by them.

96. Georges Hardy, *Histoire sociale de la colonisation française*, speaks

of the double problem: the imperial problem of the relation of the metropole to the territories; and the colonial problem of the relation of the transplanted Europeans to the natives. He suggests that French colonization can be studied as a series of poses or swings back and forth between grasping one horn of the dilemma or the other.

97. Albert Schweitzer, *On the Edge of the Primeval Forest*, pp. 96-97.

98. This characteristic of African religious movements has been widely remarked. Among others, Dorothea Lehmann has noted this for the Lenshina movement in Zambia (Alice Lenshina Mulenga and the Lumpa Church), in *Christians of the Copperbelt* by John V. Taylor and D. Lehmann, pp. 248-268. Raymond Leslie Buell remarked the preoccupation of the followers of Simon Kimbangu with sin in the early twenties. R. L. Buell, *The Native Problem in Africa*, Vol. II, pp. 601-609.

99. *Archives of the District of Mitzik*. Note Circulaire Colonie du Gabon, Bureau des Affaires Politiques, No. 10bis., Libreville, le 9 février 1912. Le Lieutenant Gouverneur du Gabon aux Commandants des circonscriptions militaires. Pour copie conforme transmis à M. le Lieutenant comt. la subdivision de'Essone. Objet: Rappel des dispositions de principe qui définissant les rapports de l'autorité locale avec les indigènes.

CHAPTER 2

1. All the Pahouin speak dialects of mutual comprehension. In Guthrie's general classification of Bantu languages (M. Guthrie, *The Classification of Bantu Languages*), the Fang are found with six other peoples as Group 6, Zone A. In Guthrie's later study of Western Equatorial Africa the Fang give their name to the Yaounde Fang group (A70) (Guthrie, *The Bantu Languages of West Equatorial Africa*, pp. 40-44). In both cases Guthrie uses Fang or its closely related dialect, Ewondo, as the type language for the group and for the Zone.

2. The most recent and comprehensive is that of Alexandre "Proto-histoire." He locates the origin zone, in the middle eighteenth century, between the upper Sanaga and the Adamawa region of the Benue, although the possibility of an earlier origin in the northern Congo is accepted. Alexandre admits that considerable speculation attends any such enterprise of historic reconstruction. Other attempts at the reconstruction of migration routes are seen in Gonzalez Echegaray, "Rutas y Etapas de los Pueblos," and R. Avelot, "Recherches sur l'histoire des migrations dans le bassin de l'Ogooue et la région littorale adjacente."

3. Alexandre calculates the Pahouin migration at about 10 km a year ("Proto-histoire," pp. 504 and 532). If we find the first Fang in the Cristal Mountains above the Gabon Estuary in 1840, this places them in the western Sudan, between the headwaters of the Benue and the middle Chari, in the early eighteenth century, fully half a century before Fulani hegemony in that

area. Though the later Fulani expansion undoubtedly exerted pressure on Fang migration, it must have been indirect. Direct pressure was probably exerted by the earlier Islamic states south of Lake Chad: Bornu and Baguirmi. Later, pressure was probably exerted further south by the Cameroons highland kingdoms: Tchamba and Bamun. There has been an interest, in the French literature, in the resemblance between the Fang and the Fulbe. Both were admired for their Caucasoid appearance. The speculations advanced for the origins of the Fulbe—very similar to speculations over Fang origins—are summarized in R. Cornevin, *Histoire des peuples de l'Afrique noire*, pp. 346-355.

4. G. Balandier, *Sociologie actuelle de l'Afrique noire*, p. 159.

5. Independence and nationalism in the new states in Africa have tended to change this picture. The new Gabon government in Libreville regards the attachment and esteem manifested by the Fang for the Cameroons Pahouin as a threat to their allegiance to a wider Gabon, and have made every effort to discourage it.

6. H. Deschamps (*Traditions orales et archives au Gabon*, p. 85) collected an account of the Oban from the Fang (Zaman or Meké) of Makokou far removed from the area of invasion. Ramon Alvarez (*Enseñanza en la Guinea Española*, p. 33), at an equal remove in Kogo (southwestern Spanish Guinea), elicited reference to the Oban in a clan history (Clan Ogumo Esakoran). In Makokou the Oban warriors are identified as Dzem of the Middle Congo while in Kogo they are identified as Pahouin of northern Spanish Guinea.

7. V. Largeau. *Encyclopédie Pahouin*, pp. 210-213.

8. Ibid., pp. 394-406.

9. P. Alexandre, "Proto-histoire," p. 548.

10. G. Tessmann, *Die Pangwe*, Vol. II, Chapter 2.

11. Ibid., II, 30. Alexandre finds a play on words in respect to another saurian, the crab, kara. It comes in the title of the pseudo-legend we consider below, *Dulu Bon be Afri Kara*. He says, "le nom d'Afri Kara est en lui intéressant: c'est un calembour phonetique . . . prononcé avec l'accent *ntumu*, le sens litteral étant 'l'espoir du crabe' ou 'l'avenir du crabe,' ce crabe étant celui qui a donné son nom au Cameroon. Le jeu de mots est à double entendre les Bulu Fang sont l'avenir du Cameroon et de l'Afrique." (*Système verbal et predicatif du Bulu*, p. 551).

12. Tessmann, *Die Pangwe*, Vol. II, p. 62.

13. H. Trilles, *Totemism chez les Fang*.

14. Ibid., p. 193.

15. The mvet is a cordophone made from the branch of the raffia palm. Four sinews from this branch are stretched out to make the cords, which are taut in relationship to the bridge in such a way as to give an imperfect pentatonic scale rich in minor thirds. Cf. Eno-Belinga (*Découverte des chantes fables Africaines des beti-bulu-fang*, pp. 120-124) and Tessmann (*Die Pangwe*, Vol. II, pp. 327-328).

16. The 1964 festival of the mvet in Yaoundé, Cameroons, is reviewed by G. Towo-Atangana: "Le Mvet—genre majeur de la litterature orale des populations Pahouins."

17. Ekot Nsila is sometimes said to have been a woman (Towo-Atangana, p. 169) though I know of no woman bomo mvet. There is, however, as discussed below, a tendency to trace significant cultural innovations to women.

18. Eno-Belinga, *Découverte des chantes fables*, Chapters III and IV.

19. Ndong Philippe wrote a series of articles on the mvet which appeared in successive issues of the journal of the Gabonese Ministry of Education, *Réalités Gabonaises*, 1959 through 1961.

20. This is Ndong Philippe's argument in introducing his series on the mvet. *Réalités Gabonaises*, no. 1, pp. 7-8.

21. Eno-Belinga, *Littérature et musique populaire en Afrique Noire*, p. 141.

22. Ndong Philippe, "Le Mvet," no. 1, p. 7.

23. Ibid.

24. Eno-Belinga calls it "the contradiction between man and woman," *Littérature et musique populaire en Afrique Noire*, p. 149.

25. The character of the chimpanzee, waa, particularly as it contrasts with that of the gorilla, ngi, is well remarked by Fang, Animal symbolism arises in traditional Fang religion. The chimpanzees generally represent the evil of uncontrollable impulse (Tessmann, *Die Pangwe*, Vol. II, p. 69).

26. If there is a paternal role it is most likely to be taken by the grandfather, as in the case of the mvet legend given by Ndong Philippe where Oveng Ndoumou Obame, the chief of the Tribe of Flames, is prepared supernaturally by his grandfather when an infant. This is done by having all his organs replaced by iron parts ("Le Mvet," no. 10, p. 6). In payment for this, the grandfather himself must shortly die and be consumed by the elders of the tribe.

27. Towo-Atangana, "Le Mvet," p. 171.

28. Ndong Philippe, "Le Mvet," *Réalités Gabonaises*, no. 3, p. 19.

29. Ndong Philippe, "Le Mvet," *Réalités Gabonaises*, no. 3, pp. 3-7.

30. Defeated enemies are also turned into women, thus binding them in perpetual service to the men of Engong. Mvet heroes may also take the shape of a woman beguiling opponents into marriage, learning the secret of their magic powers and killing them. These motifs may reflect the ambiguous status of women in any strongly patrilineal society—at once intimate and alien (since by exogamy they are members of other clans).

31. Towo-Atangana, "Le Mvet," p. 172.

32. In respect to the ruthlessness valued traditionally as the most convincing manifestation of "courage" (ayok), Bates, in his Bulu dictionary (*Handbook of Bulu*, p. 72), remarks, regretfully it would appear, that "no distinction is made between aggressive and proper courage."

33. By Ondoua Engutu, *Dulu Bon be Afri Kara*. One takes some liberty in translating the work *Dulu* as pilgrimage. Properly it means a walking, a journey, a more casual and less goal-oriented progression. But in the context of the entire narrative, pilgrimage is an appropriate gloss.

34. Discussed in J. W. Fernandez, "The Affirmation of Things Past: Alar Ayong and Bwiti as Movements of Protest in Central and Northern Gabon."

35. O. Engutu, *Dulu Bon*, p. 7.

36. V. Largeau in his version has the Fang migrating "in search of their father, he who possesses all the riches." (*Be nga nzou ba bi esa woa é mor a nga so y'a kouma besese, Encyclopédie pahouine*, p. 105). In the missionary journals of the late nineteenth century, conversations were reported with Fang in which the European is identified with the departed deity who now lives behind the sun in the West. The missionaries must therefore know him personally. *Journal des Missions Evangéliques*, 2ième Série, 20 (1895):261.

37. O. Engutu, *Dulu Bon*, p. 27.

38. Ibid., p. 55.

39. "One could not see one's brothers and without permission one was helpless to aid one's brothers. Just see what kind of a sad situation was that." Ibid., p. 61.

40. Among the Bukwe of Gabon, access to *Dulu Bon* affected their sense of identity. After reading it they began to refer to themselves more and more as Ndong.

41. Engutu, *Dulu Bon*, p. 36.

42. Ibid., p. 49.

43. Ibid., p. 50.

44. Ibid., p. 52.

45. The reference to the white man in the early part of the narrative is literal—mfummot, mimfum mi bot (white man, white people). Ntangan, the common term whose etymology is examined below, is not employed.

46. H. Trilles, "Proverbes, légendes, et contes fang," pp. 93-109.

47. V. Görög-Karady, "L'Origine de l'inégalité des races."

48. S. Galley believes the term comes from the Galwa, otañgani, but he attempts no etymological derivation (*Dictionnaire*, p. 245.)

49. J. W. Fernandez and P. Bekale, "Christian Acculturation and Fang Witchcraft," p. 257.

50. H. Deschamps, *Traditions orales*, p. 82.

51. F. Muye, "L'Oban," *Réalités Gabonaises*, no. 17, pp. 11-14.

CHAPTER 3

1. There may be some recent degeneration and collapsing of genealogies. Galley, working between the Meke and the Okak in the twenties and thirties, gives 30 as a normal list of names in the ndan (*Dictionnaire*, p. 109). However,

Tessmann gives 15 as the longest number of names (*Die Pangwe*, Vol. II, p. 125), and Trilles, though he collected up to 33 names, gives 20 as the average number of names (*Totemism*, p. 114).

2. J. Middleton and D. Tait, eds., *Tribes Without Rulers*, p. 10.

3. The Spanish naturalist and ethnologist Jordi Sabater believes Mobum to be a defunct subgroup out of which the Ntumu formed by copenetration with other subgroups (A. Panyella and J. Sabater, *Esquema de la anthroponímia Fang de la Guinea española desde el punto de vista etnológico*, p. 77 and unpublished manuscripts). In respect to Ndong and Bukwe, Alexandre ("Un conte Bulu," p. 250) considers them to be, among the Bulu, special endogamous clans derived from the gradual absorption of pygmoid elements. There was no trace of either pygmy or pygmoid origin, other than that mixture all Fang recognize, in Fang Bukwe. Nor was there any trace of clan endogamy.

4. G. Balandier, *Sociologie actuelle de l'Afrique noire*, p. 110.

5. Largeau, *Encyclopédie pahouine*, p. 37.

6. Ibid., p. 557.

7. Galley, *Dictionnaire*, p. 190.

8. This ethnocentrism might seem to suggest a preference for tribal endogamy. But such a preference is hard to identify. For any clan where such marriage arrangement is territorially feasible, tribal exogamy ranged between 10 and 25 percent in northern Gabon (my figures). Alcobe and Panyella in Rio Muni (*Estudio cuantitativo de la exogamia de los Pamues (fang) de la Guinea continental española*, p. 71) give figures between 2 and 42 percent.

9. R. Naroll, "A Preliminary Index of Social Development," p. 284.

10. Various folk etymologies are often given for the names of the tribes. The name Bulu, for example, is said to mean those who have returned north (from bulan, to return).

11. Largeau, *Encyclopédie pahouine*, p. 4.

12. This emergence is also a decentering as seen in the next chapter. In both cases, disincorporation is a basic process.

13. C. D. Forde and A. R. Radcliffe-Browne, *African Systems of Kinship and Marriage*, p. 15.

14. Panyella and Sabater, *Esquema*.

15. The mvogabot was a grouping concept of primary use among the Ntumu Fang and northern Fang of Mitzik and Medounou districts. It had been moving south and replacing a term of more natural use among southern Fang, essabot.

16. In respect to the anthropologists' own analytic use of the term family, I would agree with Bender that it is fruitless to try and define it by reference to a specific set of persons or functions ("A Refinement of the Concept of the Household: Families, Coresidence, and Domestic Functions"). For there are families in which there is no male genitor present, as in the case of a girl being kept to have village children, or in which the head of the family is not the male genitor but a rich sister who has brought in a male ntôbot to continue

the family line in consort with her sisters, her brother's daughters, or herself.

17. A. L. Kroeber, "Basic and Secondary Patterns of Social Structure," pp. 210-218.

CHAPTER 4

1. Or as it was sometimes said: "We flee from the forest for the obscurity it casts upon us" (*bi amara jíbí akal ndendam, afan da bô bia jíbí*). Fang did not hesitate to acquaint casual visitors with this attitude to the forest. The first American ambassador to Gabon was told by the president, Leon Mba, when the former regretted the cutting down of some magnificent trees on the Palace grounds, "You do not understand. We have always fought to keep the forest from engulfing us. We have to cut trees down." (Charles F. and A. B. Darlington, *African Betrayal*, p. 23). This war with the forest carried out by "slash and burn" agriculture has been very destructive, and French agronomists referred to Fang as "butineurs des champs" (buccaneers of the fields), not only to indicate how their method of agriculture exhausted the fertility of the soil but also to indicate how destructive they were of the forest.

2. As often Fang credited their moving to an accumulation of effluents: *Nge ô tôbô nlam, eduk e dze . . . ô ntô va akoro* (If you live in a village [where] the latrines are full . . . you have but to depart).

3. Various etymological soundings have been made for the name Fang. Alexandre and Binet (*Le Groupe*, pp. 4-5) find its signification obscure. But they give some credence to Trilles's attempt to attach it to the root, *fa*, connoting the idea of virility and violence.

4. When the French missionary Maurice Hermann was on a deep forest trek at the turn of the century, he noticed a strong perfume in the air. He asked his guides what it could be. They responded innocently: "Cela doit être le parfum des feux du village." *Journal des Missions Evangéliques*, 2ième Série, 35 (1910):225.

5. Burton speaks of villages more than a mile long (in N. W. Penzer, *Selected Papers*, p. 94), as does DuChaillu. G. du Bellay in 1862 noted villages of 200 to 300 houses ("Le Gabon," p. 305). Largeau (*Encyclopédie pahouine*, p. 677) speaks of some exceptional villages as over a kilometer long with a dozen council houses strung out along the central court.

6. The rectangularity or "carpentered" nature of the world in which Fang live is exceptional. Tests carried out with them in respect to visual illusions (M. H. Segall, D. T. Campbell, and M. Herskovits, *The Influence of Culture on Visual Perception*, Chapter 6) show them to be more susceptible to these than most non-Western people. The theory is that this is a consequence of the rectangularity of their experience.

7. As in the Fang riddle: "*zom da sô meyop ka akule*" (What is the package that comes from above and cannot be opened?) The answer is: the child in the womb.

8. Thus any strange or foreign part of the earth was referred to as afan. For example, *me so afan America*, I came from America.

9. The concept is that of E. Z. Vogt, "Structural and Conceptual Replication in Zinacantan Culture."

10. Galley, *Dictionnaire*, p. 181.

11. J. M. Roberts, M. J. Arth and R. R. Bush, "Games in Culture."

12. These houses were, as quickly as possible, roofed with zinc sheets. Solar radiation during the day made them much hotter than those buildings with thatch roofing, despite their nicknames.

13. Tessmann, *Die Pangwe*, Vol. II, p. 110.

14. Though easy births were given upon the bamboo beds, particularly difficult births were carried out upon the earth of the hut. The woman's head was placed toward the front door and she gave birth toward the rear door.

15. L. Martrou, "Les 'Eki' des Fang"; J. W. Fernandez and P. Bekale, "Christian Acculturation and Fang Witchcraft."

16. Tessmann, *Die Pangwe*, Vol. I, pp. 68-69.

17. The data here are not personal observations but arise from detailed discussion with villagers of Sougoudzap, Kolabona, and Antom, Oyem District, Woleu-Ntem.

18. The bark of this tree was used, according to my experience, in purifying lotions and baths, hence its particular use in this ceremony. But its aptness may be greater than that, for Raponda-Walker and Sillans (*Les Plantes utiles du Gabon*, p. 179) say that the fruit was used as an aphrodisiac. A picture of this scaffolding is found in Tessmann, *Die Pangwe*, Vol. II, p. 58.

19. In addition to the plan of a journey and the plan of a house informants frequently gave the "plan of the palaver" (akômnge ntia or etôm); the "plan to go hunting" (akômnge nsôm); and the "plan to establish a liason with a woman or to get married" (akômnge ngwan or ebwan). Since in any village there was always a mare's nest of disputes not fully resolved, the "plan of the palaver" reflected every man's determination to right long-suffered wrongs. Young men often gave akômnge akuma (the plan to obtain riches) as paramount.

20. We have been mainly concerned here with the images Fang possess of the space they occupy. The images we present are, in part, the result of empirical observation (Figure 4.3 and Figure 4.4), or a combination of empirical observation of space and Fang activities in space (Figure 4.1 and the discussion of the associations of the various dwellings), or the result of direct elicitation of mental pictures (Figure 4.2). The relation between these images variously produced in our inquiry and Fang behavior is problematic. At the least we should recognize, after C. Geertz ("Religion as a Cultural System," in *The Interpretation of Cultures*, that some of these are images "of" behavior and some are images "for" behavior. One key term of our discussion, *ar-*

chitectonic (discussed mainly in Part III) is taken to mean "a spatial structure subdivided into many qualitative parts—hence a quality space—which is at once a set of images (a complex image) *of* Fang experience as well as a set of images *for* Fang experience."

21. Tessmann, *Die Pangwe*, Vol. I, p. 58.

22. Tessmann, *Die Pangwe*, Vol. II, p. 72.

23. The differences in logico-aesthetic integration are discussed in Fernandez, "Principles of Opposition and Vitality in Fang Aesthetics."

24. Zinc roofing was very much desired, and Fang and other African groups with which I am familiar rated themselves and others by the percentage of zinc roofs in a village. Fang who journeyed to the Cameroons were impressed by the Bulu in this respect. Zinc roofs, though hotter, had the distinct advantage of durability; they lasted at least 20 years. Raffia roofs had to be replaced every 5 years or so. A zinc roof added 50 thousand francs to the value of a "cold" house.

25. G. Dieterlen and M. Griaule, *Le Renard pâle*. Also, J. P. Lebeuf, *Les Habitations des Fali*.

CHAPTER 5

1. Tessmann gives pictures of the varieties (*Die Pangwe*, Vol. II, pp. 217-218). Though no longer in use at the time of the fieldwork I was able to make a complete collection from the Ntumu for the Lowie Museum, University of California, Berkeley. Fang did not take to European currency very quickly, probably because of their nonmarket economy. The Germans were forced to manufacture their own bikuela for trading purposes. These, an example of which is in the Lowie collection, were very much larger than the ordinary and made of a much higher grade of iron. They were, in short, inflationary.

2. Ibid., pp. 214-217.

3. This figure appears in *Selected Economic Data for the Less Developed Countries*, Statistics and Reports Division, Agency for International Development, June 1967. This is one of the lowest figures for Africa. Only Botswana and Mauritania give a lower figure. For Fang, the estimates have varied over time and from district to district—between $10/km^2$ and $2/km^2$. In the earlier part of the century, higher estimates were common. Higher population densities are characteristic of the northern districts (G. Balandier, *Sociologie actuelle*, pp. 84 and 94). In every case the density is low for Africa.

4. Binet's account of the economic life of the Pahouin (Alexandre and Binet, *Le Groupe*, pp. 27-29) does not fit the facts for the Gabon Ntumu and Fang. There was still a rich supply of game for them. Binet described Pahouin fishing as being ineffective without dams or nets. But as Tessmann shows

(*Die Pangwe*, Vol. I, p. 119) and as we witnessed many times over, very large nets were used. Massive earth dams were built to block streams and an intoxicant, môkwa, was employed, both to considerable effect. There were often very large catches which were dried and smoked.

5. In Assok Ening, of the 51 nyamoro among the 85 married men only 12 did not maintain traps. Three of these 12 possessed permits for shotguns and felt it unnecessary to trap. The average number of traps was 12. The range, among those who possessed them, was between 3 and 100. The mode (7 men) had 30 traps. Each trap was checked at least once every 3 days. For every 3 traps a man could count on one animal per month. Men with more than 30 traps caught enough to sell game to others.

6. Wild meat was also supplemented by village sheep or goats and by ducks and chickens. Villagers kept very few pigs but each man had 4 or 5 chickens and ducks. half the nyamoro had sheep or goats averaging 3 per adult male.

7. The age pyramids of these villages are telling in this respect. They show lacunae in the younger age groups from 15-29. In 10 villages surrounding Assok Ening, this 15-year span, in gross figures 174 men among the 595 counted, constituted 29% of the male population while the 15-year age span, 30-44, constituted 34% of the population—204 of 595 counted. Actuarially one would expect a decrease in percentage of the older age group. The Gabon Census of 1960-1961 shows the same though a less marked distinction for the Woleu Ntem. The 15-29 age group is 23% of the population and the 30-44 is 23.3% (Gabon, *Recensement*, p. 32).

8. During the late 1950's most villagers kept coffee trees behind their houses. But the beans, often picked too early, were not of good quality. The average return was 15 kilos, which was sold in Spanish Guinea, because of the supported prices prevailing there, at between 450 and 600 pesetas (6 and 10 dollars). This money was changed into cheap Spanish wines and cognac which, provided the customs patrols were avoided, could be sold in the village at a 50% markup. Coffee crops were worth between 3 and 4 thousand francs CFA.

9. A downpayment on the brideprice (one-quarter to one-half the amount) was paid on the majority of girls well before puberty. The ideal was that the young girls, around the time of puberty, should go and live with their husband's mother so that they might learn the ways of the family and go finally to sleep with their husband, usually a man much older, after pubescence. But there was many an impediment between payment and bed. The girl as she grew older might get other ideas. She might enter into sexual relations elsewhere, violating the terms of the agreement. Even if she went to her husband's village, her much younger age made her an object of adultery to her husband's sons or younger brothers. This custom of early brideprice payment, useful from the point of view of the bride's father or brothers who could use the

funds for their own wives, was yet a source of constant debate and reclamation
as the hopes of the future husband were frustrated or violated.

10. There were nine devaluations of French currency from 1913 to 1960.
M. Palyi, *A Lesson in French Inflation*.

11. Tessmann, *Die Pangwe*, Vol. II, p. 260.

12. Real value adjustments made by reference to *Economic Almanac 1967-
1968* (ed. Paul Biederman, New York: Macmillan, 1967) and A. D. Webb,
The New Dictionary of Statistics. It should not be forgotten in this calculation
that Tessmann was estimating the value of Fang iron money. Fang of his time
had not, by and large, committed themselves to colonial currency. There is
an anomaly in Tessmann's report. He says higher brideprices were paid in
the hinterland than in the areas close to trading centers. This situation had
just reversed itself by the end of the colonial period.

13. Taking 20 francs as the average value of the 1936-1939 dollar and 500
francs as the value of the 1959 dollar together with the fact that the purchasing
power of a 1936-1939 dollar was approximately twice that of a 1959 dollar.
(The colonial franc is valued at approximately half of the metropolitan franc.)
Cf. *Economic Almanac*, p. 98 and the U.S. Census Bureau, *Statistical Abstract*, Washington, D.C.: Government Printing Office, 1936, 1939, 1959.

14. The suspicion, however, that sexual relations might be included in the
Commmandant's powers caused many husbands to refuse their wives' requests
to dance. Since some of the songs could be quite suggestive, this added to
suspicions. Husbands could follow the team on its tour. From some teams,
for this reason, it was expensive to buy a dance. They were accompanied by
too many jealous husbands.

15. G. Balandier, "Phénomènes sociaux totaux et dynamique sociale," pp.
23-24.

16. The archaic form of bilaba has been analyzed by Balandier in
"Phénomènes sociaux."

17. In P. Alexandre and J. Binet, *Le Groupe*, pp. 46-48.

18. Cf. P. J. Bohannan, "The Impact of Money on an African Subsistence
Economy," p. 500. Bohannan suggests the different spheres of exchange in
traditional African life and the special-purpose currency appropriate to each
sphere. He points out the difficulty involved in converting the values in one
sphere—say the values of women in the sphere of kinship relations—to the
value of another—foodstuffs in the subsistence sphere—by means of general
purpose money.

19. Ezing could refer to the friendship between spouses but refers here to
the friendship between people of the same sex—namely, women. The women
were referring—this was rather a late song in the mangan dance—to the strong
bonds between the women as opposed to the men. There was a play on words
with eziézié—the shameless act of having eaten or enjoyed something without

giving recompense. The women may also be understood as accusing the men of inadequate compensation of that which they were enjoying.

CHAPTER 6

1. Balandier, *Afrique ambiguë*, p. 24.

2. *Môt a luk mininga nsua na; a yam nye bidzi, a ba'ale nye beyun ye fe na e môn a ne biale a bô evia.*

3. *Nge bôt be bô ka ve nsua nge môt e bele ki mininga . . . mininga a se tôbô ebe môt ka nsua.*

4. Relative sex is reflected in the kinterms for brother and sister (ndun zam and ka zam), for they are only employed across sex lines. Siblings of the same sex call each other mwan nvan or mwadzan, "child of the mother."

5. Fang kinterms for wife, nga, and husband, nôm, are the generic terms for male and female. Since there is no grammatical gender in Fang, these two terms are often used to distinguish between the male and female of animals—nôm ku, male chicken or cock. The translation of the terms of address, nga wum or nôm wum, as "my male" or "my female," though harsher and more unadorned in our ears than to Fang, does point up their perception of the relationship in its predominantly sexual dimension.

6. The slaying of the adulterer seems to have taken place only when he was discovered in flagrante delicto. Ngema's account here is much dramatized. By and large, adultery was more matter of factly regarded, principally setting in motion a series of negotiations to recover payment.

7. Tessmann, *Die Pangwe*, Vol. II, p. 262.

8. Tessmann puts the figure at the turn of the century at 300 pieces of iron money or 21 marks (*Die Pangwe*, Vol. II, p. 263).

9. J. Binet, *Le Mariage en Afrique noire*, p. 150.

10. I am indebted to my wife for many of these observations. She established family cooking quarters in the kisin of Ngema's first wife and thus was as privy as Fang women to the ongoing round of events. This chapter, however, is being written from my point of view. In respect to bridemoney, incidentally, she found the village women to take, despite missionary and administration views, a remarkably positive view. They regarded it as the most effective demonstration of the husband's affection. It was the bridemoney that made clear that the woman was not being taken for granted. The question was several times asked, in view of the fact that I had given no bridemoney, how it was that she had any evidence of my real consideration.

11. Tessmann (*Die Pangwe*, Vol. II, pp. 256 and 263) only gives the reasons which might lead the man to ask for divorce: (1) meanness or rebelliousness toward the husband; (2) unsurmountable aversion toward him; (3) repeated stealing; (4) witchcraft against others' children; (5) too slow a maturation; (6) certain chronic diseases such as leprosy or elephantiasis and

barrenness. In mid-century women much more readily gave the reasons why they would divorce a man: his failure to give material signs of his affection, his conversion of her to the single role of a mother in the household (avungan nyia or avengsan nyia) and hence the denial of her connubial rights, his failure to eat her food, his not giving a just portion of the family fields. The readiness of women to total up their resentments caused men to say of them that they were like a book in carefully preserving all the bad acts of their husbands until they came to the end of the page and fled home.

12. There is some variability here. In the marriages I observed, these two kinds of foodstuffs were so distributed between the two parties. But other informants insisted that the wild meats and fish must come with the in-laws. What seemed to be constant was the sense of complementarity in the provision of the foodstuffs. There was a tradition I did not observe that the mother-in-law prepared two meals: one of plantation food and one of food from the river.

13. The table is taken from *Evaluation of Basic Demographic Data in Some French-Speaking African Countries*, United Nations, January 1968, pp. 22-24. Total Fertility Rate is the average number of children brought into the world per woman and Gross Reproductive Rate is the average number of girls.

	GABON	CONGO	CHAD	CAR	UPPER VOLTA	IVORY COAST	TOGO	NIGER	GUINEA
Birth Rate	30	42	47	44	49	52	50	53	49
Death Rate	27	25	32	29	35	33	32	29	38
Growth Rate	.3	1.7	1.5	1.4	1.4	1.9	1.8	2.4	1.1
Total Fertility	3.5	5.5	5.5	5.0	6.0	6.5	6.5	7.0	6.0
Gross Reproductive Rate	1.7	2.7	2.7	2.4	3.0	3.2	3.2	3.4	3.0
Life Expectancy at Birth	35	37	31	34	31	32	34	36	29

14. Gabon, *Recensement*, p. 87.

15. Ibid., pp. 89-90.

16. Estimates of venereal infection are not readily available. I was told by a WHO team doing an etiological survey of northern Gabon in 1959 that between 30 and 40% of the population gave evidence of venereal infection. That is, if true, a figure of such magnitude as to itself explain a good many of the difficulties between male and female.

17. As seen in the event which opens this chapter, there was a tendency that should not be ignored for these sisters who had stayed on in the village to bear children to become the focus of hostilities of the women who had married in. For in the end, the daughter of the village did not really belong there in the view of other women. They tended to resent her staying on and her special advantages.

18. There is some wordplay in this aphorism with eyeya, vagabond woman, or (as a verb) to get angry without reason.

19. At.the same time, Fang said, "The man is the route that the woman must follow." Ntumu play on words here, for they used the word nomô for forest path. From this, they said, comes the word for husband, nnôm.

20. M. Douglas, *Purity and Danger,* p. 159.

CHAPTER 7

1. Hierarchical organization was not demanded among the Fang. Since they rarely come together in gatherings of more than several hundred, they may be classed as one of those societies that can dispense with almost all officials. Raoul Naroll, "A Preliminary Index of Social Development," p. 609.

2. J. W. Fernandez and P. Bekale, "Christian Acculturation and Fang Witchcraft," p. 260.

3. G. Tessmann, *Die Pangwe,* Vol. II, p. 208.

4. The names of these two cults are homophonic with the names for gorilla (ngí) and elephant (nzôk), and they were sometimes referred to by Fang as the Cult of the Gorilla and the Cult of the Elephant. However, Ngí, the cult, is pronounced in low tone and ngí, the gorilla, in high tone. The cult of Nzok or Dzok is probably to be traced to the root, *sok,* "to search out evil and reveal truth by supernatural means." The association of these cults with the gorilla and elephant is seen, however, in the fact that an essential part of the ritual was the construction of massive earthen figures sculpted in relief in the cult precincts. They wee often gorilla-like or elephant-like (cf. Tessmann, *Die Pangwe,* Vol. II, pp. 74-90). Among the northern Pahouin (Bulu and Ewondo) Ngí was organized into a permanent semisecret society with considerable enduring authority, according to Alexandre and Binet (*Le Groupe,* p. 45). But among Fang Ngí was sporadic with temporary authority.

5. Under the pressures of contact with Europeans and in an attempt to preserve discipline and cultural orthodoxy which was challenged by that contact, it was often these secret antiwitchcraft societies that installed themselves on a permanent basis in the villages. Thus the missionary Robert Nassau, *Fetishism,* pp. 140-149, comments upon the power of the secret societies (Nkuku with the Benga, Yasi with the Galwa, and Ngi with the Fang) in resisting mission influence and even in restricting trade. Nassau found

himself threatened on the Ogoowe by Yasi which accused him of "teaching our children to disobey us."

6. Literally "to remove the saliva."

7. Père Trilles in his unrelenting pursuit of Fang totemism took the concept of mvam as a keyword in Fang culture. In fact, the viability of the lineage did rest upon the exercise of such benevolence. But Trilles attempted to trace its source to animal totems. Fang clearly perceived it as the cement of lineage affairs sanctioned by both the ancestors and by older men who had the interests of their lineage and not exclusively their own interests at heart. The lineage was extraordinary, in that sense, because it produced mvam in human relationships. But mvam was not a totem.

8. Envalen were acccused of persuading children and young people to steal vulnerable personal objects from their elders with which the envalen could work his secret powers. The envalen promised to make the child powerful as well. Often this was done, it was said, by giving him powdered pieces of human flesh. It was a "pact with the devil" that foredoomed the child to evil activity throughout his life. One sees, in this notion of a pact between old and young as a threat to the most active members of the society, a generational dynamic close to the European explanation as to why grandfather and grandson are so close: "They have an enemy in common."

9. The plight of the old and their "lassitude de vivre" is well described in P. Alexandre and J. Binet, *Le Groupe*, p. 101.

CHAPTER 8

1. Cemeteries are an innovation with Fang. Traditionally they had no common cemeteries. Their cemetery was the reliquary. This distinguished them from the Gabonese people south of the Ogoowe who oriented themselves toward common cemeteries. Cf. Raponda-Walker, "Les Cimetières Gabonaises," p. 7.

2. Fully accurate statistics on disease rates have not been compiled for Gabon despite the excellence of the Census of 1960. Fang faced the oppressive spectrum of diseases common to tropical countries with, however, a particularly high incidence of syphilis and gonorrhea. I was told by a medical team doing a survey of disease in the Woleu-Ntem region of the 40% figure for venereal disease affliction mentioned above. But a 7% venereal rate is reported as a maximum figure for the Woleu-Ntem region in the *Plan quindécennal de développement des services de santé—1966-1980*, Libreville, 1965, Chapter VIII. The pressure of disease generally is reflected in the life expectancy figure, at birth, of 32 years (ibid., p. 58).

3. There are numerous reports on mad people in the villages in missionary archives. See *Journal des Missions Evangéliques*, passim, 1890-1920. The

missionaries seem often to have been confronted with mad people and were usually beseeched for a cure. Albert Schweitzer reports the numbers that showed up at his hospital when he opened it in 1913, with which he was not prepared to deal. He rapidly constructed stockades, however, for it was his understanding that the Africans trussed up the troublesome fool and threw him into the river (*Journal des Missions Evangéliques*, 2ième Série, 39[1914]:322). He blamed brain-degenerative parasites—spirochetes, trypanosomes—that were a particular affliction of tropical countries. We are interested here in the alienation, usually temporary, that afflicted young men on the frontiers of full manhood and that illuminates problems of Fang maturation.

4. This was much reduced since 1950. In 1960 it stood at 8.4% among the Fang. Gabon, *Recensement*, p. 101. But formerly this figure was 30 to 40%, and parental attitudes survive from that period.

5. Why this ceremonial presentation of fish was called "the capture of the antelope" was not clarified for me. The antelope referred to is the small antelope—*Neotragus batesii*—whose meat was much appreciated. I was told that this was a custom learned from the Pygmies but that Fang had substituted fish for antelope since antelope was hardly a food women could provide.

6 The nkôabôt was also called the nkwinabot (people who arrive together) or mien abôt (people who were born together). Age grading was not institutionalized among Fang in any formal rites of passage nor did age mates have a series of progressive responsibilities as they grew older. Age mates, however, continued throughout their lives to maintain sentimental ties. Nkôabot meant those who shared or were generous with each other. It was the group in which one showed intimacies, passed on sexual information, and planned small adventures into the forest.

7. Tessmann, *Die Pangwe*, Vol. II, pp. 293-330.

8. This notion is discussed in Fernandez and Bekale, "Christian Acculturation." But for a more extended discussion of a similar notion or image, see George Foster, "Peasant Society and the Image of the Limited Good."

9. The following is Tessmann's diagram, *Die Pangwe*, Vol. II, pp. 8-10:

	Diesseits	Zwischenreich	Jenseits
Vergänglicher aichtbarer Teil	Körper Körperwesen		
Fortlebender, unsichtbarer Teil	Seele Seelenwesen	Seele Seelenwesen	Seele

10. I had long discussions with Gabonese from other ethnic groups about the evus among Fang. They almost all remarked how suggestible, from their view, Fang seemed when they believed their evus was attacking them. They themselves claimed to take witchcraft more matter-of-factly and were openly

astounded at Fang behavior in this instance. They were also amazed at the particularly exacting nature of Fang taboos and promises. See the discussion in Fernandez and Bekale, "Christian Acculturation," pp. 247-248.

11. These three character types are discussed more fully in Fernandez and Bekale, "Christian Acculturation," p. 246. The ordinary meaning of the term engolengola was a large and powerful animal that lacked its aggressive instruments, e.g., an elephant without tusks, a leopard without teeth, a buffalo without horns.

CHAPTER 9

1. Fang spoke of several stages of sleep during the night. A first stage (ôyô adzal), the sleep of the village, was often interrupted by village sounds, night talks, etc. A second stage after midnight (ôyô beyem) and in the deep of night was dangerous for it was ominous with the threat of witchcraft, hence its name, the sleep of the witches. The final stage before sunrise (ôyô kiri) was supposed to be deep and untroubled.

2. The dearth of young men in the age brackets 15-24 was a remarkable feature of age pyramids drawn up in Gabon, both in the official census and the age pyramids we personally collected. This has never been satisfactorily explained, and appears in both gross and adjusted pyramids (Gabon, *Recensement*, pp. 25-29). Fang, as we see here, sensed this lack and blamed it on witchcraft.

3. There was a panoply of procedures in Fang medicine. Two principal methods may be distinguished: the voiding, actually or sympathetically, of the interior of the body; and the washing down of the exterior. There was also a distinction to be made between two kinds of medicine: bile (tree barks and woods) and bilawk (various grasses and leaves). The former was used primarily to strengthen the interior of the body and the latter to cleanse the exterior.

4. C. Gaulen, "L'étiologie des malades et l'influence des sorciers chez les pahouines."

5. Tessmann, *Die Pangwe*, Vol. II, pp. 5-6.

6. Largeau, *Encyclopédie pahouine*, p. 547.

7. Bates, *Handbook*, p. 141.

8. Alexandre and Binet, *Le Groupe*, p. 104.

9. I have attempted elsewhere to point out how the prestige of various kinds of artists in Fang society arises out of the order they were able to suggest or achieve in that society as the result of their work. "The Imposition and Exposition of Order—Artistic Expression in Fang Society" in Warren d'Azevedo, ed., *The Traditional Artist in African Society*.

10. We concentrate here on the spirits that preoccupied Fang. There were other sprites and monsters of forest (ebíbí) and stream (menzim sôsô). Some

evus did not entirely disappear at death but became monsters of the deep forest (esenege). But these transformations were less intrusive.

11. Tessmann, *Die Pangwe*, Vol. II, pp. 64-94.

12. Tessmann says that Ngí, besides eradicating witchcraft, could be used to protect sins of any kind: adultery, thieving, etc. Men could call up Ngí against any evildoers and make them, as Tessmann called them, ngíkrank (*Die Pangwe*, Vol. II, p. 79). In visiting the remnants of one of these mounds—they are found everywhere in Fang country near abandoned village sites—I made the mistake of spitting in its vicinity. In getting back into the truck, I hit my head sharply against the door frame which caused significant comment among my companions. Two days later, I came down with a light case of malaria—a head and neckache. Knowledge of this was greeted with further nods.

13. Tessmann, *Die Pangwe*, Vol. II, p. 80. "Das Holzstück ist eine Medizin gegen Zauberwesen und soll andeuten das die Zauberwesen ebenso 'zugrunde' gehen sollen wie das wasserschwangere Holzstück."

14. J. Maignan, "Une Ngi-fête chez le nkoje," p. 3.

15. Ibid., p. 5.

16. Tessmann, *Die Pangwe*, Vol. II, p. 78.

17. Maignan, "Une Ngi-fête," p. 8.

18. The fact that these succeeding versions of Ngi were taught from village to village and clan to clan gave it wide scope and made it of some importance in the social cohesion of the Fang, as Alexandre remarks (Alexandre and Binet, *Le Groupe*, p. 62). But there is no evidence that Ngi had any tribal-wide political importance or that it gathered together initiates from many clans to resolve interclan litigation, serving on a broad scale as police and judicial system, as he also suggests. There was a general tendency in Gabon and Cameroon for administration archives to overinterpret the political implications of any Fang cult or movement (cf. Fernandez, "Affirmation of Things Past").

19. The particulars of one cult leader who had sold the cult in five villages and who was brought to justice by the Spanish colonial government are given in Moreno, *Reseña histórica de la preséncia de España en el Golfo de Guinea*.

20. Assok Ening bought Ndong Andrike for 9 chickens, 9 pieces of cloth, and 900 francs. The number 9 was sacred to Ndong Andrike.

21. This evolution was also noted by the Protestant missionary André Junod ("Possédé par un evur," p. 79) who speaks about the degeneration of the belief in the evus. "Il tend à devenir une puissance impersonnelle, une espèce d'esprit malfaisant, de demon au sens neo-testamentaire du term qui n'est plus liée necessairement à un être humain."

22. Fernandez and Bekale, "Christian Acculturation," pp. 262-263.

23. The Ndende movement was only one of a great rash of antiwitchcraft movements of the period. Every district saw men and women arise proclaiming

power over evil, but few gained any adherents. Bekale has that interest in folk etymologies—in breaking apart words (abukh bifia)—which is frequent among Fang of two cultures. Of Emane's name he says, quite justly, "This name means 'he who finishes.' It is also the root of Emmanuel, Envoy of God and he who finishes sorcerers." This commentary is taken from Fernandez and Bekale, "Christian Acculturation," pp. 268-269.

24. Though the shrine was usually called ambam or abam, Alogo Zogo insisted on calling it amvam probably by association with mvam, protective benevolence. To protect a new village Fang often dug a hole and filled it with powerful medicines—ebem.

25. A great catalogue of different kinds of medicine was brought before Ndende. I counted 30 different kinds of biang. Students of Fang art, aware of the rareness of the reliquary figures, will regret that Ndende removed and burned a large number of these.

26. For 150 francs Ndende would make individual shrines of Ambam. He made six additional ones in the village. He was paid 10 francs for every person he consulted. His perfume sold at 50 francs the flask. He also had individual consultations about illness and misfortune for which he charged 100-200 francs. In a little less than two weeks' time, he probably made 6 to 8 thousand francs in the village (a good return in a time when the average monthly salary was 4 thousand francs).

27. In Assok Ening the two establishments from which this literature was ordered—both offering a wide selection of books on the occult—were: "Establissements R. Micheleau," 4 bis Rue de la Turbie, Monaco; and "La Diffusion Scientifique," 3 rue de Londres, Paris 9.

28. No date. "La Diffusion Scientifique," Paris, pp. 24 and 36.

29. Perhaps the same thing, for as Fang often said, "Paris, Paradis!"

30. Gabon, *Recensement*. In the Fang regions the figure varies between 23 (Woleu-Ntem) and 37 (Estuaire) per thousand. The figure for men (39) is almost twice that of women (22).

31. R. P. Briault, *Dans la forêt du Gabon*, pp. 62-63.

CHAPTER 10

1. Allegret, *Les idées religieuses*, p. 1.

2. Compare E. E. Evans-Pritchard on the Azande (*Witchcraft, Oracles, and Magic Among the Azande*, xvii), "The Azande actualizes . . . his beliefs rather than intellectualizing them, and their tenets are expressed in socially controlled behaviour rather than in doctrines. Hence, the difficulty in discussing the subject of witchcraft in Azande, for their ideas are imprisoned in action and cannot be cited to explain and justify action."

3. Galley, *Dictionnaire*, p. 378.

4. Tessmann, *Die Pangwe*, Vol. II, pp. 32-34, 40-51.

5. Ibid., p. 56.

6. Ibid., p. 14.

7. Largeau, *Encyclopédie pahouine*, pp. 384-388.

8. Like "Thimble-Thimble" in Shalé (or Tsaghle or Salé), children sit around spread-legged. A bystander—usually a man—then comes forward with a piece of wood or a stone in his fist. He thrusts his fist up between the legs of each child in turn, leaving it under one. There is much giggling. He sings: "Trapdoor Spider, Trapdoor Spider" [salé] you are very foolish! Hide this for me." Now another player comes out from a hut and attempts to guess where the object is hidden. As he reaches up between the legs, the seated player attempts to trap him.

9. Tessmann, *Die Pangwe*, Vol. II, p. 299.

10. It is true, as Tessmann points out (ibid., p. 42), that the southern Pahouin, Fang, Meke, Betsi, show a greater diversity of cults than the northern Bulu, Ewondo, Ntumu. Tessmann worked primarily in the north. It appears that the southern Pahouin—the spearheads of Fang migration—were also much more open to diffusion from autochthonous peoples. Thus, in recent years, the southern Pahouin have been much more hospitable to syncretist religions such as Bwiti or MBiri.

11. Ibid., p. 96.

12. It is of interest that Tessmann makes this distinction between shame and guilt. The distinction between shame and guilt cultures was to become important in anthropology—between cultures, that is, which demand that their members internalize personally a heavy responsibility for the evil in the universe, and those who would accept that evil as a natural condition and ask only that man be ashamed for exacerbating that condition. The slippery quality of this distinction has been well pointed up in the work of G. Piers and M. Singer, *Shame and Guilt: A Psychoanalytic and Cultural Study*.

13. Tessmann, *Die Pangwe*, Vol. II, p. 13.

14. He argues that the name for the initiate to these cults (mvôn) also derives from this radical and means "He who dies." But this etymology is mistaken. The etymology is much more likely to be vô (to stand great trials) or vôr (to be astonished or stupified) or vôe (to pass on habits, to instruct). The exercise of tracing radicals in the Bantu languages, always difficult, is simply gratuitous unless tied down to local perceptions of the matter. Tessmann is sometimes spurious in his etymology.

15. Tessmann, *Die Pangwe*, Vol. II, p. 42.

16. Here again, Tessmann puts forward a mistaken etymological derivation between soo and nsem (sin), which he spells nsom (ibid., p. 213), so that by implication, a sin is something of the night. This association is purely an artifact of his argument.

17. Ibid., p. 52. Compare the insults of a similar kind offered to the male genitals in the women's purification cult Mevungu (above, Chapter 6).

18. The "soo" masks are a little known aspect of Fang art. We were able

to collect an impressive one, in which the branches of the tree were used for the horns, thus making it a single piece. It is now in the Lowie Museum, University of California, Berkeley.

19. Tessmann traces the name of the cult to a word for dizziness, ndong, which we could not confirm. The meaning of the cult, following this definition, would be "the dizziness which is good."

20. Tessmann, *Die Pangwe*, Vol. II, p. 57.

21. Ibid., p. 59.

22. C. Lévi-Strauss, *Totemism*.

23. Tessmann, *Die Pangwe*, Vol. II, p. 56.

24. The ancestors are sometimes and more familiarly referred to as grandfathers (bimvama) or the fathers (betara), placing them inextricably, despite the fact of their intervening death, upon the continuum of age and seniority. No Fang with whom I spoke regarded them simply as older persons, however. They have a special stature or power which derives from the fact that, as the dead, they have penetrated and are aware of the "unseen." This quality is contained in the term "kon." It is probably derived from the verb, kôn, to grow tough or hard as a consequence of growing big. It is appropriate that the hard cranium should be taken to represent them in the reliquary.

25. Missionaries, and the lexicographer Galley among them (*Dictionnaire*, p. 41), have usually translated engang as the realm of sorcery or the malevolent manipulation of the supernatural, which it often is. But only in part. In more general terms, it is the realm of hidden things which can be either benevolently or malevolently approached and manipulated.

26. Tessmann, *Die Pangwe*, Vol. II, p. 116.

27. Fernandez, "Principles of Opposition."

28. The nsuk bieri always carries a name (a sign of the personalization we are discussing). This name is often of the "strongest skull" in the collection. Often it is an ancestral name which otherwise functions as a name of encouragement—eyôle mebara. The name need not appear in the genealogy.

29. "A ba" or "A baa" is a very familiar, almost diminutive way of speaking of father in both reference and address. It is an early term of employ among very young children. In this context it is highly appropriate, for it combines both respect and familiarity.

30. Skulls were exhumed after a year or so in the grave but never by the initiate himself who was to enter into the cult with this ancestor. It would be too dangerous for him to do so. It takes special spiritual fortification to remove the cranium.

31. Fernandez, "Principles of Opposition."

32. Fang knowledge of any part of anatomy should not be surprising. It should be remembered that they regularly performed autopsies. In respect to knowledge of the skull: as it was the chief sacred relic, it was very well known.

33. Tessmann, *Die Pangwe*, Vol. II, p. 118.

34. Largeau (*Encyclopédie pahouine*, p. 391) says of the malan, "It is eaten from the morning until two or three in the afternoon. It progressively produces a kind of ecstatic state accompanied by a sort of intense cerebral excitation that lasts two or three days. In this state the initiates believe the souls of their ancestors, parents and defunct friends come to converse with them, tell them the past and announce the future."

35. Tessmann (*Die Pangwe*, Vol. II, p. 121) gives us a sketch of two *Bieri* precincts. In the 1940's and 1950's the Bulu-Ntumu revitalization movement of Alar Ayong tended to reproduce this configuration in their forest precincts. We give a sketch of such a precinct in Fernandez, "Affirmation of Things Past," p. 434.

36. Trilles, *Totemism*, pp. 234-236.

37. Ayang is said to have been used on slaves in the old days to baffle their sight and prevent them from fleeing.

38. If after this treatment the initiate still did not "fall dead," the director of initiation (nyile bemvon) would hurry up to the cult precincts to consult the craniums. He would take up the bark barrel and, cradling it in his arms, rock it before the craniums reminding them thus that a new child was coming to them and they should take care of him. He would then whirl around with the barrel in his arms to produce vertigo in the initiate. One remarks here the assimilation of the bark barrel to the body of the initiate. This is another indication of the fact that the bark barrel was taken as the body or the stomach to the ancestor figure—which was classically simply a head (nlô biang— medicine head) and not an entire figure.

39. Trilles, *Totemism*, pp. 333-335.

40. This is pictured in Tessmann, *Die Pangwe*, Vol. II, p. 125.

41. If the initiate was long in reviving, this subsequent part of the ceremony might take place the following day. It would become part of the akulu malan.

42. Trilles, *Totemism*, p. 372.

43. Ibid., p. 94.

44. This is Ayang Ndong's re-creation of the council given.

45. Tessmann, *Die Pangwe*, Vol. II, p. 122.

46. Trilles, *Totemism*, p. 372.

47. Tessmann, *Die Pangwe*, Vol. II, p. 116.

48. There is a play on words here, for contemporary Fang are probably conditioned by the Bwiti tendency to engage in word play. "So" (high tone) is the nocturnal antelope while "So" (low tone) is the verb for washing and rinsing the body—thus purification.

49. Bieri was also known by the name of Okôma Zame Asi, a reference perhaps to increasing control exerted over the ancestors. Okôma derives from kôm (preparation of something living) as in akôm nkuk, preparation of an animal or person as a Zombie. Bieri was also sometimes called Okuma Zame Asi, derived from kuma (riches); the translation would be, "The God below who brings riches."

The tendency to distinguish between gods of the below and gods of the above has been recurrent in Africa as an intellectual response to Christian evangelization. It is discussed as the distinction between little and big gods among the Lo Dagaa by Jack Goody (*The Myth of the Bagre*, p. 32). Robin Horton argues that these two-tiered theologies appear when the old microcosm is shattered by acculturation, as a kind of intellectual compromise between allegience to the old microcosm and recognition of the reality of the new world view—the European-imported macrocosm ("On the Rationality of Conversion," pp. 220, 234).

CHAPTER 11

1. *Journal des Missions Evangéliques*, 2ième Série, 34 (1909):399. Hereafter cited as *Journal*.

2. *Journal*, 46 (1921):444. This is in a letter from F. Grébert, a missionary who maintained good relations throughout his more than three decades.

3. *Journal*, 18 (1893):90-96.

4. Ibid., pp. 90-96.

5. *Journal*, 24 (1899):99.

6. *Journal*, 18 (1893):435.

7. This new perception was true of the missionaries, as we see below. But Balandier also finds the principal cause of Fang migration to be the desire for trade goods. *Sociologie actuelle de l'Afrique noire*, p. 159.

8. Felix Fauré, *Le Diable dans la brousse*.

9. By Charles Cadier, 1928, Paris.

10. By Charles Cadier, 1933, Paris.

11. F. Grébert, *Au Gabon*. See particularly pages 113-118 and 150-152.

12. The Fang lexicographer, Samuel Galley, was another missionary who accurately assessed the cultural inertia with which village Christians had to contend. His *Eben 'Avo—L'Apôtre Fang* is an account of an enterprising village evangelist whose difficulties finally bring him to his grave.

13. *Journal*, 46 (1921):298.

14. *Journal*, 42 (1917):238. Letter of C. Cadier.

15. *Journal*, 49 (1924):179. Letter of C. Cadier.

16. R. P. Briault, *Dans la forêt du Gabon*. Especially Chapter X, "La Notion du temps chez les noirs," pp. 107-120.

17. By the 1860's, both the American Protestants and the Catholics had printing presses in Libreville turning out prayers, language manuals, Gospels, and Gospel stories. Most of these earlier publications were in French or English or MPongwe, the main coastal language. Catechisms and biblical lessons in Fang were in circulation by the 1890's. The earliest Fang catechism in my collection was published by the American Presbyterian Mission in 1889, *Nteni ôsu, Nteni Fanwe* (First Book of Fang Readings [Talaguga,

1889]). It contains six pages of lessons (lesenyi): word recognition, phrase recognition, paragraph reading. This is followed by four biblical stories: Adam ye Ivi, Abí ôsua (the first sin), Jenesis 3:14-24, Luki 1:6-55. The Bible was entirely translated into Fang by the end of the Second World War. The Catholics published earliest in MPongwe; the first Fang catechism appeared in 1891. After 1900, half the Catholic vernacular publications were in Fang. *Bibliographie Secrétariat General*, Congregation du Saint Esprit de Marie (Paris, 1930), pp. 17-21.

18. F. Grébert, *Au Gabon*, p. 120. Fang are sometimes referred to, because of their migratory ways, as "juifs errantes" in the literature.

19. The missionary Lavignotte complains of Fang who "prendre la puissance de l'Evangile à contrasens." *Journal*, 50 (1925):286.

20. Both systems, Horton points out, seek to explain and predict and control, and both work toward increasing levels of abstraction in explaining problems of existence. African thought, however, is not guided by any "body of explicit acceptance-rejection criteria" and it tends to employ, as we say, different models. But in both systems the investigator is impressed by an analogy between the puzzling observations he wants to explain and the structure of certain phenomena whose behavior has already been well explored. Because of this analogy, he postulates a scheme of events with structure akin to that of the prototype phenomena, and equates that scheme with the reality behind the observations that "puzzle" him ("Ritual Man in Africa," p. 98).

21. As argued above in Chapter 10.

22. *Journal*, 35 (1910):125.

23. *Journal*, 32 (1907):448.

24. *Journal*, 49 (1924):216.

25. *Journal*, 55 (1930):41.

26. Another form that the evus takes is that of the palm squirrel (*rat palmiste*). The goat has about the same connotation to Fang as to the European, a lecherous creature not in control of its appetites.

27. C. Cadier, *Sauvons les paiens du Gabon*, p. 66.

28. *Journal*, 44 (1919):135.

29. *Journal*, 50 (1925):169. Letter of C. Cadier.

30. This is Grébert's complaint, but it is also echoed in the frequent criticism of African literalmindedness (*Au Gabon*, p. 204).

31. Cf. *Biblical Revelation and African Beliefs*, ed. Kwesi A. Dickson and P. Ellingworth, p. 43.

32. S. G. Williamson, *Akan Religion and the Christian Faith*. Accra: Mission Press, 1965, p. 144.

33. Grébert shows a tolerant amusement in this regard (*Au Gabon*, p. 204).

34. D. Barrett has pointed to this deprecation of African culture in missions as one of the chief causes for the appearance of African independent churches (*Schism and Renewal in Africa*).

CHAPTER 12

1. W. de Craemer, J. Vansina, and R. Fox have argued that religious movements, at least movements seeking fecundity, riches, and protection against witchcraft, are an "integral part of the pre-colonial African tradition" and not simply a response to colonization ("Religious Movements in Central Africa: A Theoretical Study."

2. *Presbyterian Mission Archives*, Philadelphia. Microfilm Missionary Correspondence, Reel 71-no. 382.

3. Ibid. Reel 67-nos. 104, 105, 107.

4. Ibid. Reel 71-nos. 335-337. Ikengue, incidentally, seems never to have joined that movement and retired in good standing. He is mentioned as a remarkable man by A. Judson Brown in *One Hundred Years*, p. 136. This is a history of the American mission in West Africa.

5. C. Cadier, *Ces Hommes ont peur*, pp. 35-38.

6. F. Grébert, Letter in the *Journal des Missions Evangéliques*, 2ième Série, 46 (1921):38-40.

7. *Relations sur le Congo du Père Laurent de Lucques 1700-1717*, ed. M. Cuvelier.

8. R. P. Hee, "Les Adouma du Gabon."

9. Brian Weinstein presents a succinct account of the Vernoud revival based partially on interviews with Pastor Vernoud in Paris (*Gabon: Nation Building on the Ogooue*, pp. 64-67). I also visited and interviewed Gilles Vernoud, but at his small mission station close to Medouneu in 1959.

10. *Journal des Missions Evangéliques*, 2ième Série, 61 (1936):116.

11. G. Balandier, *Sociologie actuelle de l'Afrique noire*, p. 515. Balandier was involved in fieldwork at the height of Ngol.

12. Pierre Alexandre, "Proto-histoire," p. 515.

13. Letter of M. P. Ochswald, "La Danse 'de Gaulle' à Lambaréné," p. 7.

14. Ochswald ("La Danse 'de Gaulle' à Lambaréné," p. 12) says that the dance came from Spanish Guinea where a dream vision of it was brought to a Fang man by his dead wife. From Spanish Guinea, Ochswald argues, it passed to Libreville and then to the Gabon interior. But as this was the origin described to me for the Flanco dance, also widespread in the fifties, Ochswald may be confusing the two. It is possible that the Flanco dance changed its name to Digol in some parts of Gabon and that the later Digol is to be distinguished from the earlier Ngol of the upper Ogooue. For the Spanish Guinea version see J. Moreno Moreno, "Los Digols," p. 88.

15. J. W. Fernandez, "Affirmation of Things Past."

16. A Flanco head collected in Oyem district in 1958 is in the collection of the Lowie Museum, University of California, Berkeley. It is pictured in Fernandez, "The Exposition and Imposition of Order," p. 211.

17. An nlô bekege mask is also in the Lowie Museum (ibid.). The Fang

in my experience give no explanation of the Janus face, though we may see it as a manifestation of the doubling of personality which cult and ceremony are meant to achieve and which is possessed by the ancestors as a matter of course—they are valent in this world and the next, as are initiates (ngômalan) to the cult.

18. An nlô nge mask is pictured in Fernandez, "The Exposition and Imposition of Order," p. 211. There is also a picture of one in the process of manufacture (ibid.).

19. "The Daughter of the White Man" was a mask and associated dance which appeared after the Second World War. In the dance, a "beautiful white woman in a mask" made a sudden appearance.

20. Birinda de Boudieguy, *La Bible secrète*.

21. The feedback from this book has influenced Bwiti thought in Gabon, posing problems of interpretation for students of Bwiti doctrine in the 1960's.

22. Birinda de Boudieguy, *La Bible secrète*, p. 41. Also see his footnote 9 (p. 129). As Daughter of the Night, Dintsouna is black but she appears white, luminous, because light is born with her.

23. Birinda de Boudieguy, *La Bible secrète*, p. 129. And not only in the occult literature. It seems likely that Birinda also read and had been influenced by M. Griaule's masterwork, *Dieu d'eau*. This ethnographic revelation of the Dogon cosmology through the words of the sage Ogotemelli contains elements very similar to Birinda's Bwiti cosmology—the stages of creation, the necessity of redemption from earlier stages, etc.

24. These progressive ritual predications and their performance are discussed in J. W. Fernandez, "The Mission of Metaphor."

25. Birinda de Boudieguy, *La Bible secrète*, p. 31.

26. The cosmic tree image in Birinda—the universal tree in everyman—frequently arises in recitation of Bwiti traditions. An element of cosmic order, it is also a principle of intercommunication between spheres of existence.

27. Birinda de Boudieguy, *La Bible secrète*, p. 32.

28. Ibid., p. 47.

29. "La composition de l'homme est analogue à celle de l'univers; en lui se trouve une hiérarchie de trois par le moyen de trois, divisée en trois régions." (Ibid., p. 112.)

30. Ibid., pp. 111-112.

31. André Evan, "Le Voyage de Jacques Ngoya au pays des morts."

32. Cf. J. W. Fernandez, "Equatorial Excursions—The Folklore of Narcotic Inspired Visions."

33. See J. W. Fernandez, "The Exposition and Imposition of Order: Artistic Expression in Fang Culture."

34. Charles Cadier in a letter to the home board, *Journal des Missions Evangéliques*, 2ième Série, 49 (1924):179.

35. The frequency of cleansing, atunba, was observed by Tessmann, though

he did not follow it through, to be one of the main themes of Fang religion. (Tessmann, *Die Pangwe*, Vol. II, pp. 24-34.)

36. The missionaries sometimes observed that if the black was destined to remain black, at least he could become white of soul. A missionary reports a convert as saying, "In a few days I shall bring here two children and a woman child, our whites will wash them with water from a little glass . . . they will keep their skin like ebony, but their hearts will be white as milk." Eugène le Garrac, *Au Fernan-Vaz: La Rencontre de deux civilisations*, quoted in B. Weinstein, *Gabon: Nation Building on the Ogooue*, p. 58.

37. This quote is taken from a circular of 1911 to all district officers in Gabon reminding them of their obligations to the "civilizing mission." *Archives of the District of Mitzik: Affaires Politiques*, no. 106, 6 bis, 9 February 1912.

38. The two books put out by the French Evangelical Mission for children's reading in France, *Ekomi* (1951) and *Avema* (1946), both emphasize how the young hero and young heroine learn to do the "work of God" although they live in the village atmosphere of "dolce far niente."

39. Such comments as the following can be culled from the *Journal des Missions Evangéliques*. Grebért, in a letter in this journal for 1921 (p. 299), quotes a "typical" Fang response, "*Hoi, nza ke yem bô abim eseng te*" (Who can do such an amount of work). He goes on to say (p. 300), "Immediately they lay hands on an instrument of work the idea of repose comes into their heads."

40. This redistribution of activities and work values creating cultural dilemmas for men is discussed in J. W. Fernandez, "Redistributive Acculturation and Ritual Reintegration in Fang Culture."

41. See J. W. Fernandez, "Principles of Opposition and Vitality."

42. These cultural dilemmas in Fang life in transition are discussed in Fernandez, "Redistributive Acculturation."

43. In fact the principal ritual sins, nsem (incest) and mbwôl (the appropriation of another's corporeal substance), have very much to do with relationships to others as well as to the cosmos.

44. The relationship between ethics and aesthetics is a snarled one, with some arguing that right action is essentially good form and nothing more. I have explored the notion off the universe as a moral order and men's aesthetic responsibilities to it in "The Exposition and Imposition of Order."

45. E. Allegret, *Les Idées religieuses des Fang*, p. 14.

CHAPTER 13

1. This comes from the Tsogo word "ndjimbé," "place of secret reunion for the members of Bwiti" (Raponda-Walker, *Dictionnaire Metsogo*). The creation spot also bears other names—for example epíkô. Also it is not the

only gathering spot outside the chapel. Some leaders prefer to reserve the name njimba for the "secret gathering spot" in the forest beside the chapel, and call this origin spot by another name.

2. The derivation of the word minkín is uncertain. The folk etymology in Bwiti derives it from the Fang miñking—paths or trails, for each minkín is a series of paths followed into or danced into the chapel. A series of paths from obscurity to light, from coldness to heat, from disorderliness to orderliness.

3. This association of wind and Holy Spirit is very widespread. For example, in the Zulu "umoya oyincwele" (Holy Wind). Fernandez, "Bantu Brotherhood."

4. The Miene languages are Guthrie's B:10 and the Tsogo B:30 in M. Guthrie, *The Bantu Languages*.

5. Raponda-Walker in his *Dictionnaire Metsogo* translates apongo as "voûte etherée."

6. This theme is also explored in Henri Marcel Bot ba Njock, "Prééminences sociales et systèmes politico-religieux dans la société traditionnelle Bulu et Fang," p. 162.

7. We discuss the "sacrificial element" in Bwiti below but it might be mentioned here that in practically all administrative accounts of Bwiti between the wars it was presumed that Bwiti sanctified human sacrifice and that human sacrifice was necessary for the religion to accomplish its ends.

8. Veciana, *La Secta del Bwiti*, pp. 13-16.

9. I have published another version of this legend collected in the Asumege Ening chapel at Ayol, southern Woleu Ntem (J. W. Fernandez, "Equatorial Excursions," pp. 352-354.

10. In Veciana's version (*La Secta del Bwiti*, p. 14) the woman called Banjuku killed the cat and wrapped the bones in its skin. While she was carrying them home they spoke to her and directed her to build a hut to house them. In the Ayol version she is guided to the cave by a porcupine, a dog, and a man—a revealing configuration for these are the three stars in Orion's belt, a constellation otherwise associated with ancestral blessing of the crops in the long cold rainy season.

11. We will discuss the meanings of the wildcat or civit cat skin below.

12. This reference to a possible psychoreactive mushroom is unique. We have no direct evidence that mushrooms were ever consumed in Bwiti, though informants had heard of a mushroom being eaten in powdered form. No special psychoreactive quality is mentioned for this mushroom by Raponda-Walker and Sillans in *Les Plantes utiles au Gabon*, p. 457.

13. When this small sweat fly enters the eye it is said to warn that a wrong path has been taken. The interjection of Olarazen at this moment recalls the brushing of the eyelid with the latex of ayang beyem to baffle the vision at

a crucial moment of initiation in the Fang ancestral cult. The purpose of this "eyedrop" was to place the initiate on the proper path to the dead.

14. Given recent sensitivities about keeping bones in Bwiti (see the previous chapter), the beginning of the cult in the guarding of bones is also an embarrassment.

15. The necessity that a parental figure, in particular a mother figure, be sacrificed for effective transformation as a theme in African folklore is explored in J. W. Fernandez, "Filial Piety and Power."

16. Though Veciana's version of this legend from the coast does not speak directly of the Pygmy, the principles are said to be of the Bakui tribe—probably from the Fang Beku or bekui for Pygmy.

17. The distribution of this psychoreactive plant is confined to the equatorial deep forest zone, the habitat of Pygmies.

18. C. Turnbull, *The Forest People*.

19. Banzie say that one of the best lessons Pygmy could teach Fang was how to live as a conquered people in a state of despair (engôngôl).

20. Wyattt MacGaffey has written an important, yet unpublished, article on this topic, "The Dwarf Soldiers of Simon Kimbangu: Explorations in Congo Cosmology." For a discussion of the place of dwarfs or "little people" in Kimbanguisme see P. Raymaekers, "L'Eglise de Jesus-Christ sur la terre par le prophète Simon Kimbangu: contribution à l'étude des mouvements messianiques dans le Bas-Kongo," p. 711.

21. J. W. Fernandez, "Principles of Opposition and Vitality."

22. John Janzen and Wyatt MacGaffey, *An Anthology of Kongo Religion: Primary Texts from Lower Zaire*. For the new world Gossen has demonstrated how clearly the Chamula of Southern Mexico hold in mind the three successive creations. Gary H. Gossen, *The Chamulas in the World of the Sun*.

23. Customarily it is said that Mebege carried life to the earth—from bege, to carry. Muye ignores this.

24. The descent of a container of creation, an egg, shield, box, or musical instrument is a widespread creation motif in West Africa from the Niger to the Congo.

25. God's name may be taken from zame (high tone), to leave, pardon, or abandon; Nlona derives from lôa (high tone), to bite with the teeth, hence he who bites. Nyingwan means literally "mother of the girl" and usually refers to the mother of the girl espoused into one's family. She must be especially cultivated in order to assure her blessing of the marriage—see "bídzí bi nengon."

26. Veciana, *La Secta del Bwiti*, pp. 17-19. These trees are not identified by Veciana but would appear to be: the yellow wood (eyen), the copal (ndem), the ebony (evila), and the padouk or redwood (mbel). See below (Chapters 8 and 9) for a discussion of the meaning of these trees in Bwiti.

27. As quoted in J. Binet, J. Gollenhoffer, and R. Sillans, "Textes religieux du *Bwiti-fan* et de ses confréries prophétiques dan leurs cadres rituels," p. 221.

28. The derivation of Nlona's name from "he who bites with teeth" makes for a ready association with the serpent.

29. Literally this means sperm, the white liquid of the body. In some of these legends Nlôna ejaculates semen which he places in the ball of earth and which is the origin of the white parts of the body—the bones and the brain principally. Men have three parts which they owe to the three gods of origin.

30. Discussed and pictured in Tessmann, *Die Pangwe*, Vol. I, p. 234.

31. This is the translation of the song given by Banzie. There is a general fit with Tsogo words: ngadi (lightning); duma (growling of thunder); tômbô (young woman); kômbô (to be possessed).

32. This is the Bwiti play on words: "Paris—Paradis."

33. Textes religieux du *Bwiti-fan*, pp. 223-225.

34. E. Allegret. Note found in the *Journal des Missions Evangéliques*, 2ième Série, 18 (1893):435. On the Fang side they came to the conclusion that missionaries weren't really helping them to know their God—were standing between. Various Bwiti leaders promised contact with the Great Gods without interpreter.

35. Such a formulation of the Trinity to suit Bwiti understanding is not idiosyncratic. Balandier presents a similar myth from the Ndong clan and not from Bwiti, in which the Trinity is composed of Zame (Adam), Eve-Mvôm (Eve or Nyingwan) and their first son, Mvôm-Adam (Balandier, *Afrique ambiguë*, p. 178). Inventiveness and syncretism in the handling of the Trinity is also remarked by Soeur Marie Germaine (*Le Christ au Gabon*, p. 68).

36. Fang have always been inventive in explaining the divine genealogy. Allegret in his study of Fang religious ideas (*Les Idées religieuses des Fang*, p. 9) is rapidly frustrated by the diversity of explanations offered him for the phrase, *Zame enye a ne Mebege, Mebege Menkwa, Menkwa Sokuma, Sokuma Mbongwe*. For some Fang take Zame as the son of Mebege who was son of Menkwa. And others take Sokuma as the wife of Menkwa, etc. Allegret seeks clarification in the roots of the proper names: Menkwa from the radical kwa (to judge) is the supreme arbiter of the world; Sokuma from kum (to arrange) is the arranger of all things. He offers no radical to explain Mbongwe.

But the hazards of interpretation by reference to radicals is seen in the fact that Largeau (*Encyclopédie pahouine*, p. 261) derives quite different meanings. He traces Mebege to beghe, to share out, and Nzame to sameghe, to pardon. Largeau's version of the creation is of interest. Mebege, the sun and principle of light and heat, combines with the universal matrix, Anghe Ndongwa, to engender Nzame, the pardoner, who combines with Oyem Mam, his sister, to create humanity. The name of Nzame's sister Oyem Mam (the knower of things) is of interest. Largeau says the name is synonymous with "science universelle." This name for either Eve or Nyingwan Mebege never appeared during our fieldwork but the fact is Bwiti often claims that it is Nyingwan Mebege's all-knowingness that makes of Bwiti a "science universelle."

37. Cain and Abel are not mentioned in Muye Michel's myth. But they are frequently presented as a new husband and wife type in Bwiti. They figure frequently in songs. The etymology of their names is obscure. Folk etymology derives Obolo from bôlô, to break apart, and biôm, the name for trade goods, merchandise. This etymology is in accord with the splitting apart of man and woman in the struggle over possessions.

38. There is virtually a circularity in this view: the sense that I am my ancestor and my ancestor is me. Banzie often enough argue that men and women die and are reborn as the dead and the dead die and are reborn as the living, although such a view is in contradiction with the view of "a genealogical line." The view that one is a "reflection" of one's ancestors is actually acted out in MBiri and Bwiti initiation (see below).

39. See the discussion of appropriate progressions in family relationships in J. W. Fernandez, "Bantu Brotherhood," pp. 363-366.

40. We discuss below the views of the nima ka kombo, Ekang Engono, and his use of likenesses in his sermons (efônan-bifônan) in knitting together the world.

41. See Galley's discussion of these two gods, Dictionnaire Fang-Français, pp. 263 and 453. The God Above-God Below distinction was firmly established in the missionary literature. See the Journal des Missions Evangéliques, 2ième Série, 62 (1937):729.

42. For a collateral branch of Bwiti, Disumba, I have discussed the idea and symbol of the Savior (J. W. Fernandez, "The Idea and Symbol of the Saviour in a Gabon Syncretist Cult").

43. Banzie, playing on words, say that Jesus (Jesu in French) is also a judge (juge) who has taught men to work their religion in this life and who judges finally how well they work it.

44. This is the assumption made by Barrett in his comparative study of the new African religious movements (D. Barrett, Schism and Renewal in Africa).

45. This is the case even though there is frequent speculation by individual Banzie as to the historical personage of Jesus, his wealth, wives, color, etc.

46. Les Idées religieuses des Fang, p. 9.

47. Ibid., p. 12.

48. "Prééminences sociales," p. 162.

49. Tessmann presumes that dualism throughout is study of Fang religion in Part II of Die Pangwe, but he succinctly identifies it in an article written for the colonial journal, Globus, "Verlauf und Ergebnisse."

CHAPTER 14

1. Abbé A. R. Raponda-Walker in his *Dictionnaire Metsogo* gives the spelling as Bwete. He gives three definitions of the term: (1) fetish statue, (2) dance held in the Bwete cult, and (3) secret society of those initiated into the secrets of Bwete. In his *Dictionnaire MPongwe-Français*, he gives the same approximate definition for the MPongwe term Bwiti.

2. P. DuChaillu, *In The Country of the Dwarfs*, pp. 238-245. The Apinji are a dialectical subgroup of the Metsogo.

3. M. D. Le Testu, "Réflexion sur l'homme tigre."

4. Ibid., p. 155.

5. The administrator Maclatchy in his report on the Massango uprising of 1917 emphasizes (referring also to their neighbors the Metsogo who had revolted in 1904) their strong attachment to their customs and the occult authority of their leaders. Report of M. Maclatchy for 1936 on the subdivision of Mimongo. Referenced in Brian Weinstein, *Gabon: Nation Building on the Ogooue*, p. 162.

6. T. E. Bowditch, *Mission to Cape Coast Castle and Ashantee*, pp. 449-452.

7. The missionary M. E. Haug writes in the *Journal des Missions Evangéliques*, 2ième Série, 29 (1904):435 that a "buiti" fetish from Lake Alombie had arrived in his district. "The 'Buiti' properly speaking is the only idol of the country. It is adored by a congregation composed in the most part of slaves which reunite in a house where the idol is installed and eat an exciting and hallucinatory root called Iboga . . . since 1897 I noticed that buiti house on Lake Alombie (with central post adroitly sculpted)."

8. *Journal des Missions Evangéliques*, 2ième Série, 39 (1914):65.

9. Ibid., pp. 234-235.

10. Reference to Bwiti is found in *L'Echo Gabonaise*, Libreville, for March 7, 1923, no. 6, p. 108, for example, and periodically in the Spanish missionary journal, *La Guinea Española*, Santa Isabel, Spanish Guinea. It is not until 1931 (no. 2, p. 277) that extensive coverage is given to it.

11. G. Vuillaume's thirty-page study, "La coutume pahouine dans l'estuaire du Como," has never been published but was available for study in the archives of the Presidency of the Government in Libreville. Though Vuillaume's attitude was very negative, his account of Bwiti was accurate as far as it went.

12. The three cases known to us of Europeans initiated into Bwiti in the forties and fifties, Messrs. Benoist, Gamm, and Massey, were all bachelors who were living with Fang women.

13. Until after the war the "indigenat" system prevailed which allowed local administrators much latitude in their treatment of the African.

14. I am grateful to Maître Julien for showing me the Benoist letter and commenting upon it.

15. In Muye's view, Catholicism and Protestantism were appropriate religions for the European because they had found God. But the African had not found God. Therefore he should practice Bwiti—a kind of ritual politics which led to god.

16. All these phrases appear in Governor Vuillaume's manuscript, "La coutume pahouine," p. 21: "Les pratiques du bwiti sont nuisibles aux races qui l'adoptent," "dangereux et les manifestations qu'il exerce ont une répercussion telle que le pahouins sont absolument terrorisés," "des troubles mentales annilent toute volonté . . . la race s'abrutit."

17. These events are discussed in John Ballard, "The Development of Political Parties in French Equatorial Africa."

18. Freemasonry, in my view, has had very little effect in Bwiti. It was present very early in Libreville, as Nassau mentions it (*Fetishism*, p. 306). French commentators on Bwiti, probably because of the conspiratorial reputations of freemasons prevalent in France, overemphasize its importance (Raponda-Walker and Sillans, *Rites et croyances*, p. 287).

19. The abolition of the "indigenat" and the series of reforms (1944-1947) initiated by Felix Eboué, the wartime Governor of AEF, resulted in the "Loi Cadre"—virtually the application of the legal rights of Frenchmen to Africans.

20. See above (Chapter 9) for the discussion of an antiwitchcraft session in Northern Gabon in which the BDG was associated with witchcraft. The Woleu-Ntem was long a progressive region and a stronghold of the UDSG, the opposition party.

21. The Congress is given extended analysis in Balandier, *Sociologie actuelle*, pp. 198-218.

22. Cour d'Appel de l'AEF. Chambre des Mises en Accusation. Année 1952. Juillet.

23. Tribunal Territoriale de Libreville: Audience criminelle du 2 décembre, 10 décembre 1952 et 28 janvier 1954.

24. In my interviews with Père Sillard he showed an extraordinary comprehension of and affection for Fang. He spoke the language well. In the case of Bwiti, however, his views seemed much influenced by the evangelical struggle and lingering stereotypes of cannibal savagery.

25. For example, in the Territorial Archives of Libreville there is a letter of September 14, 1956 from Matthew Engouane, a Chef de Terre of Cocobeach, to the Governor of Gabon, complaining of Bwiti activity and the touring of Bwiti leaders in his zone. He particularly complains of the large amount of money "they have collected from their members, 39,000 francs ($156.00) in one night." He refers to the religion in terms more customary in the thirties as "une odieuse et tragique religion anti-nationale, cause de

la denatalité de la depopulation, et de la misère.'' The Bwitists are "fetisheurs vivent dans l'analphabetisme absolue.''

26. Leon Mba carried an "eboga" name: Mabengo. This was known only to Banzie. Several different chapels, including the mother chapel of the Commencement of Life Branch of Bwiti at Kougouleu (Kango), claimed to have secretly initiated him. On the other hand, intellectuals of Leon Mba's own party, the BDG, often said that Leon Mba joined Bwiti only out of intellectual interest. It was argued that his interest was equivalent to ours as an anthropologist. Indeed, Leon Mba qualifies as a scholarly observer of his people (see his "Essai de droit coutumier pahouin").

27. Report of 1ʳᵉ Trimestre, 1934, Archive of the District of Medouneu. Also official letter no. 177 of May 22, 1934 to the Chef de Division from Chef de Subdivision.

28. Brian Weinstein refers to a church "Livre des Tournées" written in 1945 for the Woleu-Ntem in which the missionary writes: "I have had their hut at Aderayo destroyed, also that of Nkein, but once I leave they build it again and even more beautifully than before" (*Gabon*, p. 64).

29. Notably M. Lecuyer, District Administrator at Mitzik, and M. Carly, adjunct at Libreville. But there was always some sympathy. Father E. Philippot, in a discussion of Bwiti's criminal nature and its promotion of wealth and plural marriage, mentions with exasperation a young colonial administrator who asked him incredulously: "Do you really believe sincerely, Father, that this dance is a criminal ceremony?" P. E. Philippot in "Etudes Missionaires," *Revue Bi-Annuelle*, Paris, IV (1936), p. 251. Father Philippot's study, which also mentions the loss of catechists to Bwiti, expresses all the missionary suspicions of Bwiti in the 1930's: human sacrifice, polygamy, sorcery, materialism, etc.

30. M. Lecuyer, Report of 2ᵐᵉ Trimestre, 1951, Archive of the District of Medouneu.

31. Gilles Sautter, "Les Paysans noirs du Gabon septentrional," pp. 133-134.

32. Mission correspondence indicated clearly that both the war and the influenza epidemic were blamed on the European (*Journal des Missions Evangéliques*, 2ième Série, 44 [1919]:155). The English authority on religious movements, H. W. Turner, argues that it was the influenza epidemic of the late teens that accounted for the growth of independency in Nigeria (*African Independent Church*).

33. These conditions are testified to in Grébert, *Au Gabon*, p. 39. This unsettlement was a consequence of the battle between German and French expeditionary forces in the Woleu-Ntem in 1914, the uncertainty of administration because of the recruitment of administrators to war, and the uncertainty of wage labor.

34. These periodic food shortages as well as the famine of 1924 are amply

depicted in the reports of the *Journal des Missions Evangéliques*, 2ième Série, 49 (1924). The famine produced a fatalistic despair and sense of "laisser aller" in most of the population, according to the missionaries.

35. Figures on venereal disease have always been difficult to come by. We reported above the observation of a WHO health team in the Woleu-Ntem in 1959 that they were encountering a 35 to 40% venereal disease rate. In the BSRC for 1930, no. 12, Dr. C. Caperan working in Woleu-Ntem remarks on the peril of syphillis—"a deplorably high figure of infection." He remarks on the recency of the disease among Fang and on its tragic impact on their lives. He also gives infantile mortality rates, 54 to 64% of live births, but does not give fertility rates ("Notes sur l'état sanitaire des populations mfangs du Woleu-Ntem 1924-1925").

36. Medecin General LeDentu. Démographie de l'A.E.F. 1937; archives au Service de Santé. Brazzaville. Quoted in Balandier, *Sociologie actuelle*, p. 93.

37. The same situation prevails in other vital centers of worship. The Efulan Chapel of Disumba in Medouneu District registers a membership of 80. But we have counted over 125 at certain periods. In Oyem the active Kwakum Chapel registers a membership of 21, but services usually find 50 or 60 people present.

38. The dispersal and hiding-out of Banzie in the thirties and forties could mean that the density of Bwiti was greater in the forest than along the roadside. Still, in the decade of the fifties there was a remarkable forest exodus and resettlement along the roadsides.

39. Similar zones, though not perfectly congruent, are mentioned by Brian Weinstein (*Gabon*) referring to political development. Tessmann, in his final trip through Gabon in 1909, after his last field trip, mentions, interestingly enough, the much greater development of cult life among southern Fang ("Verlauf und Ergebnisse").

40. This is calculated by our figure of percentage of density for the region applied against the number of Fang inhabitants over 15 in that region. The regions of Fang inhabitation are: Estuaire, Woleu-Ntem, Ogooué-Maritime, Moyen Ogooué, Ogooué Ivindo. In regions such as the Woleu-Ntem which fall into two density zones of population the mean percentage was used. Cf. Gabon, *Recensement*, p. 42.

41. The average number of years of membership of this sample was 16 and the average length of time spent in one branch of Bwiti worship was 12.

42. The tendency was to treat Bwiti as an undifferentiated movement.

43. From the Western Bantu root verb, sum (in Fang), to commence or begin. The same root was involved in the name of the branch upon which we focus here: Asumege Ening (the beginning or Commencement of Life).

44. Vuillaume, "La coutume pahouine," p. 19.

45. This development of a "Christianism Africaine" is discussed in an

interesting account of some recent founders of Bwiti by Stanislaw Swiderski, "Notes bibliographiques sur les fondateurs et les guides spirituels des sectes syncrétiques au Gabon."

46. Yembawe is discussed in Swiderski (ibid., pp. 40-47).

47. André was present at the chapel construction discussed at the beginning of this chapter.

CHAPTER 15

1. While our concern here is to give the reasons that make the name aba ebôga and the positioning of the chapel apt for Fang Bwitists, the influence of Metsogo Bwiti should not be overlooked. For the Metsogo Bwiti hut, the obandja, stands at one end of the courtyard facing out upon the village precisely in the manner of most Bwiti chapels. Like so many elements in Fang Bwiti, chapel location may originally have been adapted from the Metsogo.

2. Our observations are based mainly on the chapels in Kwakum village (Oyem District), Ayol and Abangayo villages (Medouneu District) and the Mother Chapel of Asumege Ening Bwiti at Kougouleu (Kango District).

3. This moon is always pictured as quarter rather than full because the quarter moon (efas ngwan) commands the full moon (ndugu ngwan). Children created at quarter moon will be wily and tough, while those created at full moon will be big in size but will die quickly.

4. The notion of structural replication has been developed by Vogt, "Structural and Conceptual Replication."

5. In the Kougouleu Chapel of Asumege Ening, the ngombi harp is played upon a spot where a network of raffia cords are focused. These take the blessings of the instruments out to the secret chambers, to the roof, and to the grave pit below.

6. Though this is typical Banzie word play, nsisím, the Fang word for shadow, reflection (water shadow), and by extension soul, spirit, or that which has existence beyond one's corporeal being may actually be related to nsís, the word for sinew, integument, vein, and arteries, since these are considered to be the essential parts, the structure of the body. This is opposed to the flesh which is, as it were, mere content.

7. It is a particular sign of blessing in chapels which have adopted this ekat when a circle is seen around the moon—a powerful conjunction of meaningful representations.

8. C. K. Ogden, *Opposition: A Linguistic and Psychological Analysis.* See also R. Needham's collection of articles on the widespread use of dualistic thinking in cultures. *Right and Left: Dualistic Symbolic Classification in Culture.*

9. The dualism in Fang aesthetics is pointed up in J. W. Fernandez, "Principles of Opposition and Vitality."

10. Cf. Otto von Mering, *A Grammar of Values*, p. 71.

11. Confusions in value distribution as a consequence of acculturation, and ritual attempts at redistribution were a focus of a first analysis of the Fang data. J. W. Fernandez, "Redistributive Acculturation."

12. This discussion applies particularly to the Asumege Ening chapel at Kougouleu, Kango District.

13. Some informants identify this pool in the forest and its imitation in the chambers with the sea (mang) from which all souls come and to which they return.

14. S. Swiderski, "Le Symbolisme du poteau central au Gabon."

15. Tessmann, *Die Pangwe*, Vol. II, p. 59.

16. Indeed the relationship between the birth and the death hole may have a primarily female association with Banzie. Given the frequency of perineal rupture among Fang at time of delivery there may be a preoccupation with maintaining the separateness of the two orifices, anus and vagina, which expresses itself in the akôn aba design. We have some evidence from discussions with Fang women about giving birth, which indicate that it is a preoccupation. The frequency of perineal rupture in this part of Africa is discussed in *Bulletin de la Société de Recherches Congolaises*, no. 6 for 1925, pp. 6-10.

17. There is replication here, as well, for coating the akôn aba white is felt to have a fertile and quickening effect in the same way that the male coat of semen over the female drop of blood—the homunculus—is felt to have a fertilizing and quickening effect.

18. On those pillars where Nana Nyepe is sculpted, the space between her legs is the birth hole and the space between her arms held above her head is the death hole.

Bot ba Njock ("Prééminences sociales et systèmes politico-religieux dans la société traditionnelle Bulu et Fang," p. 155), recognizing how much importance Fang assigned traditionally to the main post of their houses, feels that it relates to Fang cosmogony and a belief that Mebege is the principal pillar who supports the weight of heaven. He has in mind the interpretation of Mebege's name that traces it to the verb bege—to support or carry.

19. In the minkín entrance dances there are a number of sequences of genuflections which begin the dance. With rattles and raffia brush in hand the membership first bends to touch the earth then rises on its toes, arms outstretched to the skies. This movement is said to attract the spirits in the deep forest, for it imitates their fundamental movement. Spirits come down to earth and rise up again.

20. We list eight trees so as to accord with the Bwiti view that there are eight sacred trees. These, in my view, are the trees most often singled out. There will always be variability, however, as to which trees are sacred. So many trees have medicinal properties. About the padouk, eboga, the ôtunga, and the azap there is rarely dispute.

Many commentators (Trilles, Raponda-Walker, Nassau) have commented on Fang orientation toward various sacred trees. The early explorer, Braouzec, was shown the azap tree and told that it was there that God had created mankind and distributed to each man a ration of honey for his sustenance ("Voyage au Como," p. 354).

21. In some chapels of Bwiti the two principal dancers of the night, the yômbô, and the nganga, are "searched for" in the forest, discovered, and brought back into the chapel under a raffia arch to begin the dances. The custom is reminiscent of the Metsogo "discovery" of dancing animals in the forest.

22. This drawing is particularly true for Asumege Ening Bwiti and more particularly for the Kougouleu Chapel, Kango District.

23. The idea of special chambers in the Bwiti chapel could come from either Fang tradition or from Metsogo Bwiti. For in the forest clearing in Fang Bieri there was an inner sanctum where the skulls and reliquaries were kept and where the leaders of the cult kept council. At the back of the cult house, ebandja, in Metsogo Bwiti there was a secret chamber, mandaka, known only to initiates.

24. The terms "convergence" and "circumstantiality" are key terms in the methodological vocabulary of Clifford Geertz (*The Interpretation of Cultures*). Anthropological method must aim at understanding how the data of experience converge in the minds of participants and how the events of their lives convince them by their circumstantiality.

25. The ôtunga tree is not always involved in this climbing. It may as often be the eyen tree, the tree of the shaman (élé bengang), whose medicinal properties were traditionally thought to enable one to see the unseen and become invulnerable.

26. There is some variability in respect to the tree of crucifixion. It is sometimes said to be the élé bengang.

27. Behind the Kougouleu Chapel where there is an ôtunga bives, a concrete cross is half buried in the ground. This is where the spirits all come to be judged. They arrive from the "four corners" of the earth to the ebôm (the judgment spot or place of sorrow) where they are to be judged. The ebôm is the square at the center of the cross.

28. We have been translating tsenge as "earth." The chamber at the rear of the chapel behind the altar where elders sit watching over the action in communication with the dead (also the chamber associated with the sea) is called sugha tsenge. Banzie translate this "the last of the earth." But tsenge is Tsogo for the ôtunga tree. Thus when Fang call the central pillar elôdi or mikodi tsenge and translate it "rainbow of the earth," it might better be translated, referring to the Tsogo, as "rainbow of the ôtunga tree." This would make of the ôtunga an even more central image of transition and transformation. I am unable to comment on the Metsogo use of the ôtunga.

But there must be some correspondence to have caused Fang Bwiti to pick up the word at the same time that it was misinterpreted by them.

The reference to the rainbow is not only to the Mboumba cult of riches and well-being but also to the southern Gabonese belief that the ancestors came into the forest walking on a rainbow. This contrasts with the Fang image of the pierced azap tree. In Metsogo Bwiti, apparently, the "rainbow tree of ôtunga" (mikodi tsenge) is the equivalent to the pierced azap tree (azapmboga) in Fang Bwiti.

29. Compare Pierre Alexandre in his "Proto-histoire" (p. 524) where he discusses the symbolism of the azapmboga as a "convergence et intégration culturelle—suivie historiquement et géographiquement pour un phénomène de divergence et de desintégration." This is certainly true of Fang understanding of their past, as we show in Chapter 2 above. The intent in Bwiti, however, is to counter the historical dispersion after azapmboga with increased discipline and integration after the ritual passage of the ôtunga and the azap (central pillar).

30. This follows the Bwiti aphorism: "As only men and women together can bring a child into existence so only men and women together can bring Bwiti into existence."

31. This "man as pitch torch" association is also seen in the more Christianized chapels where during the Easter season a much smaller torch is fixed upon a spear. This torch is lit and carried about. It represents the crucifixion of Eyen Zame. For Eyen Zame, like all men, was a container within which a vital substance burned its allotted time and then gave out. The spear is the spear of the Roman soldier thrust into the side of Eyen Zame. The flickering flame is the changing vitality the spirit gives to man each day of his life, while the smoke represents the desire of the spirit to return to heaven.

32. The wood may be significant for other reasons. Raponda-Walker and Sillans (*Rites et croyances des peuples du Gabon*, p. 162) record that the bark and leaves of this tree are used to purify the milk of new mothers and also that boiled bark of this tree is used in fumigations to remove bad luck. The dance group at the njimba does stand in the smoke of this fire and is thus, if these old uses are still present in mind (I have no direct evidence that they are), purified and made strong for the journey over the path of birth and death they are about to embark upon.

33. "Ka" may have additional significance. Complementarily to asas bark, the powdered bark of this tree is given to nursing children to enable them to take more advantage of their mother's milk. It is also used as a purgative (Raponda-Walker and Sillans, *Rites et croyances*, p. 165).

34. This fire dancing may have been picked up from the Metsogo who also use fire dancing and "miraculous" pyrotechnics in their Bwiti.

35. In this chapel, as in many, straight up is the most important direction. It is the direction from which the great spirits come and to which every spirit

departs. One sees that in every infant for on the top of his head is a hole, the fontenelle (abôbôn) within which we can see the newly lodged spirit trembling.

36. This caution is discussed in Chapter 4. While we should be cautious about three dimensions we do not have to suspect the linear conceptualizations themselves as being a bias of Western translation, as, for example, in Dorothy Lee's re-examination of the Trobriand materials in which she shows Trobriand adherence to pattern and systematic avoidance of linear conceptions. Dorothy Lee, "Linear and Non-Linear Codifications of Reality."

CHAPTER 16

1. Cf. J. W. Fernandez, "Symbolic Consensus."

2. Cf. Footnote 18, Chapter 4.

3. The Estuary chapels are, on the average, smaller than the chapels in the Woleu Ntem. This is the result of a much longer presence of Bwiti there, and a fissionary process that has left behind many chapels with only a vestigial membership.

4. In fact there is continuing ethnic dominance of one group in African religious movements despite efforts to universalize membership. The factors that account for this throughout Black Africa are discussed in J. W. Fernandez, "The Ethnic Communion: Interethnic Recruitment in African Religious Movements."

5. Missionaries in my experience regularly accounted for the high divorce rate among Fang by reference to the inability of Fang men to live with intelligent women. It was believed that the Fang male's love of domination of women was such that no marriage to an intelligent, self-willed woman could last long. Fang men prefer "simple country girls." There is some truth to this rather stereotypic view although it expresses the missionary tendency to deprecate males and to espouse the women's part in evangelization.

6. This contrasts with the sister curing cult, MBiri, where most often leadership is in the hands of women. See Appendix III.

7. The distribution of responses was: 20-25, 6; 26-30, 8; 31-35, 18, 41-45, 8; 46-50, 14; 51-55, 6; 56-60, 8; over 60, 2.

8. There are slightly fewer plural marriages in Bwiti than outside the religion. Of the 78 men, 36 had one wife, 12 had 2 wives, 4 had 3 wives, and one man had 7 wives. Comparing these figures in respect to the incidence and intensity of polygyny in Fang society generally, we find only suggestive and not significant differences. Taking as a measure of incidence the percent of all married men who are polygynous, the figure for Fang in the 1950's was 39 percent and for Bwiti 32 percent. The figure for sub-Saharan Africa of the period was 38 percent (V. Dorjahn, "The Factor of Polygyny in African Demography," pp. 102-104). Taking as a measure of intensity the number of wives to 100 polygynously married men the figure for Bwiti is 249, for

Africa 246. These figures, of course, are a projection of our inquiry with 78 men.

9. It should be kept in mind that this inquiry was made predominantly in rural chapels at a considerable remove from urban opportunities of employment. Peri-urban chapels show a greater number of the gainfully employed, about 60 percent, although there is still much "parasitisme," as it is labeled.

CHAPTER 17

1. This understanding is an interesting one for it is compatible with a widespread Fang view of the European and of the indignities of colonization. The former is surpassingly skillful and hard-working and the latter is subject to indignities because "our ancestors didn't even teach us how to make a match." This view, of course, was not just developed by Africans themselves. It was frequently contained in the administrative and missionary message. Bwiti, in any case, offers, according to its lights, hard all-night work (eseng eboga) and surpassing skillfulness.

2. We use the word advisedly as three days among Metsogo hardly entitles one to speak with any authority about Bwiti among them. But it can be helpful in explaining what impressed Fang about Metsogo. Many in Fang Bwiti have spent very little more than that among Metsogo. At the same time I should emphasize that this whole study of Fang Bwiti, since it arises out of my study of Fang culture, emphasizes those cultural continuities. A student of Metsogo culture and Metsogo Bwiti coming to Fang Bwiti would undoubtedly find more there than is pointed out here. In the same way one approaching Fang Bwiti from a Christian perspective would encounter much stronger Christian influence.

3. It is generally said that all the rites, songs, and dances have come to Bwiti in visions received from the land of the dead. This view is maintained even though it is evident that some songs stem from Christian songbooks and many others were invented by leaders without benefit of vision.

4. In fact the clock is often called nlôdjop (head of heaven or sun) which is the chief manifestation of Zame.

5. I have discussed the deprecation of the African time sense and Fang responses to it in J. W. Fernandez, "Fang Representations."

6. We collected song cycles at two chapels of Asumege Ening: at the mother chapel at Kougouleu, Kango District, and at one of the most active of outlying chapels, at Kwakum, Oyem District. There was a high degree of agreement between the two cycles. Where differences arose we have taken the cycle of the mother chapel as more authoritative. This is also the case in respect to the language. I have generally used the Meke Fang versions of Kougouleu instead of the Ntumu Fang versions of Kwakum. But at the time of collection the Kwakum chapel often sung the Meke versions.

One cannot argue that these are fixed cycles. We should not take the numbering system as being immutable. The Kwakum cycle compiled by Henry Schmald and Mvomo Asumu André five years after our collection shows considerable change and creativity. (Asumu and Schmald, *Medzo.*)

7. There are various versions of the legend. Other versions have Nganga making a short trip to Africa where he imparts knowledge of eboga to the Pygmies. Another form has Nganga being tricked by the Hausa and in retaliation turning their children into cattle and donkeys. "And that is why the Hausa, who are Muslim, hate Nganga, and that is why there are so many of them."

8. There is no pronounced anti-Semitism in Bwiti. The Jews appear in this devilish role, to my knowledge, only in the legends and not in the liturgy. Nevertheless, it is interesting that Fang have not missed this disagreeable aspect of the "bonnes nouvelles."

9. Banzie say the ku is both male and female. It partakes of both the mother and the father. It represents, however, the paternal line (nkô'bôt) which traces back as a succession of umbilical cords to Zame himself. It is a line to heaven and paternal benevolence. In some chapels the ku is important enough that a special festival, tchoi, is devoted to it.

10. This belief is reminiscent of the intense, often obscene, dances in Fang funerary ceremonies which also relate to the turbulence experienced by the spirit in first separating from the body. Generally Fang conceived of the spirit as exiting from the body in the early morning hours. The pounding of the drums image, incidentally, relates to the pounded food image we have used for an epigraph in this chapter.

11. The Ta Mwanga is generally conceived of as the spot of spirit interchange between this world and the next, while the central pillar is the path between this world and the next.

12. In the legend, Adam and Eve, alias Marie and Emwan Mot, fake the virgin birth. In the songs this is treated ambiguously, sometimes as a real birth and sometimes as a substitution.

13. On occasion one or another of the yombo songs may be sung by the entire congregation in the njimba.

14. The reference to the rubber ball here is resonant with the "placenta as rubber ball" image examined above.

15. In some chapels the festivals are four days in length and the efun phase is two days: The Efun mbeng and the Efun ngômbi. On the first night only the one-string musical bow (mbeng) is played. Its pure and uncomplicated sound is said to be the music of the forest. On the second night the ngômbi harp is played. Some of the Path of the Harp songs can be sung and danced. Still, on both these nights rituals end early and the membership remains to sleep in the chapel.

16. The two rivers in mind here are the river of birth, represented by the

sacred pool, and the great river of death (mang) beyond which the spirits must pass.

17. This statement enables us to understand the meaning of the third stage of the engosie. It is difficult to derive it from Banzie. Apparently it is derived from the verb "ya" (to lie flat upon the ground while looking up). It should not be forgotten that this is the position taken by initiates as well as by the "figure of the chapel" (Chapter 15 above)—the body that is said to lie along the outline of the Bwiti chapel.

18. This follows the metaphoric sense of Fang expressed in the riddle, *Ze e ne nkal ye si?* (What is the vertebral column of nature?) The answer is *zen!* (the path).

CHAPTER 18

1. Isolation of the crystalline ibogaine from the dried roots shows a chemical structure typical of many alkaloids. Ibogaine, although the major one, is not the only alkaloid in *T. iboga*, and it may be the work of several alkaloids in combination rather than ibogaine alone that gives the effect. See H. Pope, "Tabernanthe iboga: An African Narcotic Plant of Social Importance," for the most recent compilation on iboga.

2. See also J. W. Fernandez, "Tabernanthe iboga: Narcotic Ecstasis and the Work of the Ancestors." There is some indication of earlier use of eboga by Fang, particularly in the ngi cult.

3. Indeed Banzie are quite cautious about giving eboga to people who otherwise seem susceptible to psychic disturbance such as Antoine the night-fool discussed in Chapter 8. It is said that eboga will carry such a person too far—to his death. It is also said that such a person will bring back a vision that is "difficult" (njuk). That is, it will be too idiosyncratic and a threat to the expected experience and its ready interpretation.

4. Indeed Banzie say of Bwiti that it is a "path of trees" (zen bile). They contrast it with their sister, curing-cult, MBiri, which is described as a path of plants, zen bilok. The reference is to the much greater therapeutic orientation in MBiri and hence the greater use of medicinal plants. For example, plants are used to provoke vomiting in MBiri while this is regarded as undesirable in Bwiti.

5. This fact about Fang was noted by Mary Kingsley (*Travels in West Africa*, p. 518) in arguing against the English anthropologist Tylor's notion of the origin of religion in dreams. Fang influenced by the coastal peoples, however, seem to have given more credence to the dreams, as the early American missionaries noted (R. H. Nassau, *Fetishism in West Africa*, p. 161). Later on missionaries throughout Gabon made use of troubling dreams as signs interpretable as the will of God. They could be used to effect conversion. This is recurrently discussed in the journal of the Paris Mission Society (*Journal des Missions Évangéliques*), for example, 33 (1908):376.

6. It is sometimes the case that the visions will contain some information that can be used against a person or a chapel. It may be for this reason that in most chapels the leaders wish to be the first to whom the vision is recounted so as to detect and suppress such information.

7. Several elements may be clarified. The bishop with the piled hair in the first vision may be Eyen Zame (Jesus), while the woman in the moon is Nyingwan Mebege. Their pierced and streaming hearts can probably be traced to Christian iconography which features the sacred heart of Mary in intra-thoracic display.

8. Henri M. Bot ba Njock ("Prééminences sociales," pp. 155-156), points out the frequency with which intellectual preeminence had a visionary source.

9. Letters commenting on this persistent Fang question are frequent in the *JME*. See particularly the volume for 1893, p. 96.

10. Alexandre and Binet, *Le Groupe*, pp. 104-106. Observations on Fang views of death are also found in Largeau, *Encyclopédie pahouine*, pp. 460-468. In *Fetishism*, Nassau comments on this problem among Gabonese coastal people (pp. 10, 53-54).

11. The existence and perdurance of multiple souls, the belief that souls could die and yet live, led to the curse of two deaths—wishing two deaths upon a person—a definitive death, as it were.

12. Nassau, *Fetishism*, p. 209.

13. This was essentially the promise made by the Antonian movement in the Kongo in the sixteenth century. Of course the suggestion that they can control death is frequently part of the attraction of religious movements.

14. Kopytoff has demonstrated linguistically that Western notions of the discontinuity between life and death falsify the understanding in a good many African societies of the continuities between the living and the dead and the perception of the dead as, essentially, more distant elders. (I. Kopytoff, "Ancestors as Elders in Africa.")

15. Once again the caution: since the words are in Popi the translation is not literal but a creative interpolation on the part of Bwiti informants. There is, however, a certain basic lexical knowledge of Tsogo on the part of most Banzie. Mabasema does mean twins in Tsogo, duma does mean thunder, etc.

16. The leader of the Asumege Ening chapel at Kougouleu who translated this chant says that Popi is the Tsogo name for the narrator of eboga visions. "He is the one," he said, "who relates to the ancestral cult house, ebanja, the miraculous experiences of those who have eaten eboga."

17. There are other ways of conceptualizing the stages of initiation. In chapels where other drugs are taken the stages are sometimes named after the drink or drug: the stage of eboga, the stage of "malamba," the stage of hemp, etc. Since Banzie believe that people occupy various earths (esí) on their voyage from the below to the above, another way of conceiving of the stages is by reference to the four earths through which the spirits of men pass on

their way to the land of the dead beyond the sea: the earth of birth (esí abiale), the earth of death (esí awu), the earth of the spirits (esí minsisim), and the earth of Zame (esí Zame).

CHAPTER 19

1. Ekang was playing on words here for the word for sign or guidemark (ndem [low tone]) is the same as the word for dream (mid-tone).

2. It is also in this way that eboga with its capacity to produce visions is understood as a source of intelligence—a source, furthermore, that will compensate for missionary denials of vision and insight. The complaints are frequent that the missionaries with all their good will have "kept things hidden." "They have kept us from really seeing."

3. Galley, *Dictionnaire Fang-Français*, p. 223. Ndem is more frequently used than ayema.

4. Indeed there is a third homophone which is playfully associated by Banzie, given the frequent reference to seminal fluid in ritual and sermon, and that is ndem (mid-tone), sperm. Thus we have a constellation of associated terms—dream, sign, sperm—all vital signs of something, which is useful in the kind of word play we discuss below.

5. The same interassociation of separate though phonetically very similar terms is seen between the nouns nyem and beyem, those who know, and nem and beyem, those who have the evus and are thus sorcerers. Though quite different terms in the singular, in the plural they are often identified with each other; Fang speak of sorcerers as those who know because their evus enables them to see the unseen.

6. It has been pointed out by Paul Shepard that one aspect of the "man the hunter" hypothesis argues that human thinking is a topological adaptation to the Pleistocene need to master landscape for hunting purposes (*The Tender Carnivore and the Sacred Game*). The Fang data would seem to accord with that view. Of course, as we see below, there are other root metaphors for thought in Fang. The degree to which the hunter metaphor is basic to natural languages elsewhere awaits further comparative philological research.

7. This cognitive principle of the avoidance of ambiguity is discussed in C. E. Osgood, "Behavioristic Analysis of Perception and Language as Cognitive Phenomena."

8. There is a third association to the nkok-akok complex and that is nda akok, house of stone or sepulcher, the proper culmination or point of arrival of the child of man on the path of life and death. The Tsogo term, kôkô nagunda, is employed preferentially in this sermon.

9. J. W. Fernandez, "Unbelievably Subtle Words: Representation and Integration in the Sermons of an African Reformative Cult."

10. It has been a rueful observation of missionaries that their bad Fang has gained currency among Fang themselves. Bates points out that new speech forms were developed because of European awkwardness with the copula. (George Bates, *Handbook of Bulu*, p. 141).

11. It is of interest that Michel Bie uses the term mimia, "he or she who does not possess the witchcraft spirit and thus is defenseless before the complexity of the unseen"—unable to confront complicated and difficult challenges such as these sermons pose. The more usual word for simpleton or simple-minded is nzime.

12. Tapes of these sermons (and others) together with translations are available for consultation in the Archives of Folkmusic and Folklore at the University of Indiana. This is sermon no. 1. These sermons are catalogued under accession number 71-255-F.

13. See the discussion of characteristic missionary images of evangelization in J. W. Fernandez, "Fang Representations under Acculturation," pp. 20-23.

14. Balandier has commented upon the moralistic solemnities, often banal, of Africans making speeches in French as opposed to the much more inventive rhetoric in the vernacular. *Afrique ambiguë*, pp. 208-209.

15. The phrase employed here was "wa nkanen," "throw out a tale before one." The more usual word for riddle is afilan. But since riddles in this sense are presented highly formalistically the word was inappropriate for this more rambling presentation. Tales or proverbs (nkanen) that contain a puzzlement may also be spoken of as riddles.

16. The Fang of this sermon is the following: AkiKos Zambi Avanga, Nyamoro! a nga ke ekena dze etam. Nyamoro a nga sô ye abwi bot, ane a nga wa nkana na: benana be nga yam bidzi, bevôk be telege atum, eba bevôk esu, eba bevôk anding. Edô nyamoro a nga sili bôt na: ye mina wôk? Edô a nga bera sili bôt na: ye atum, ye esu ye anding! ze e ne nyamoro? Ebôt be tôbô Mesugu Tsenge be ne bôt be ne minlô: kôan Akikos wong ane a mot meyong me mara.

17. The Fang of this sermon is given in J. W. Fernandez, "Unbelievably Subtle Words," p. 52.

18. This passage is taken from sermon no. 25 in the Kougouleu collection. The Fang is as follows. Metek me ku, nsisim wa kwing ngongngong. Mfonge, mfonge, mfonge endendang ye ô dang endendang yena. Wa lot mbembe. Ta a siman mesiman me endendang . . . a yoé nya na a kôba ye langan mbembe. Mesiman me so nyi na wa yoé ye kôba . . . ye langan mbembe. Mesiman me betan nyi na me yoé ye koba ye langan mbembe.

19. Some sermons can be brief indeed. Here in entirety are the words to the congregation given on the occasion of the death of the Yembe eboga, Ngema Ndong Mbema. "You must not eat people. You must not preserve bones of people. You must not make sorcery. The spirit reflects upon Zame. Our brothers mock us in the land of birth. We must pardon them. A person

should not speak much when a man has died.'' This brief funerary homily is also straightforward. It confines itself to admonishing the membership against just those practices that would traditionally have come to mind at the time of a funeral. The reference to the mockery of Bwiti by other Fang was apt in the context because the dead man was the only one in his family and village to join Bwiti and had been mocked by his clansmen.

20. The verbal creativity that arises in states of reverie such as Ekang Engono obtains in the grave pit characteristically shows a high degree of condensation of meaning. Kubie, *Neurotic Distortion of the Creative Process*, p. 34.

21. Half of the thirty-five sermons which I transcribed in the vernacular were taken from the sermon book and read into the tape recorder by the Yembe Michel Bie. There is very little difference in the phrasing and rhythm between these sermons and the sermons directly recorded at midnight. This is because practically all sermons are transcribed slowly first in the grave pit. This is often the version in the sermon book.

22. See above, Chapter 17, ''Generalities of the Engosie,'' for discussion of the easy transformability of red—its ability to play ''black'' to white and ''white'' to black.

23. L. Vygotsky, *Thought and Language*.

24. In some chapels Zame ye Mebege is conceived of as the rays of the sun and Nyingwan Mebege as the rays of the moon. Mebege may himself be conceived of as the totality of the original orbs, sun and moon, and his offspring as the rays.

25. Neither I nor any of the Fang who aided me as assistants are personally acquainted with the specifics of this tale. It is unfortunate that I was not able to pursue it at the time that the sermon was recorded.

26. This halo cap may also have a perceptual basis—the spectrum around the margin of objects produced by hallucinogenic substances such as eboga.

27. There are a large number of Fang clans which are associated by use of the prefix, *Ye*, with various natural objects, Yengwi (clan of the bush pig) Yebimvé (clan of the beautiful people), etc. Here the association is with water, menzim. There is an enduring dispute among students of the Pahouin as to the priority of this clan prefix over the other predominant prefix, essa, father of, as well as the origin of the prefix. It would seem to mean clan (Galley, *Dictionnaire Fang-Français*, p. 373), but it is also a conjunction that means a reunion of things by addition.

28. The lizard and the tadpole are standard transformations of primordial beings, but there is no explanation of why the flintstone is included in the birth package. Men are sometimes referred to as ''sharpening stones'' and here in this sermon we see reference to Eyen Zame as a sharpening stone. Elsewhere Banzie speak frequently of men and women as being rocks upon which other persons can strike the spark of life.

CHAPTER 20

1. On certain festival days, of course, there are other events such as the tug-of-war between males and females which we have discussed above or the playfully aggressive backslapping between men and women. For another example of a ritual tug-of-war, see Charles F. Keyes, "Tug-of-War-for-Merit: Cremation of a Senior Monk."

2. Given the diverse ways that symbol has been defined—a diversity that undermines its utility for clear analysis (J. W. Fernandez, "The Mission of Metaphor in Expressive Culture")—we will define it here, simply, as any concrete, palpable device of representation which condenses several meanings.

3. Banzie make reference to the French euphemism for coitus: "taper la cloison."

4. Traditionally a mess of this plant was used as a curative wash for skin ailments (Largeau, *Encyclopédie pahouine*, p. 690).

5. Ibid., p. 97.

6. Binet, Gollenhoffer, and Sillans, "Textes religieux," p. 237. Paul DuChaillu in *Explorations and Adventures in the Great Forest of Equatorial Africa* makes repeated reference to the wildcat skin—tiger skin he calls it— as pudenda covering. He offers a suggestive picture of its arrangement (p. 61).

7. For further references on the wildcat skin see Cadier, *Sauvons les paiens du Gabon*, p. 16 and Trilles, *Totemism*, pp. 325-327.

8. Other branches have other uniform designs. The flowing golden satin robes, the ballooning white pants and white capes of Mekambo Bwiti are said, for example, to be a direct imitation of the garb of the angels in heaven. Whereas Asumege Ening Bwiti seeks to escape the symbolics of its clothing in going to the land of the dead, Mekambo clothes itself in heaven.

9. It can have an even more direct body referent. Since the string is held in the teeth as it is played, Banzie call it the "tongue of Bwiti." Bwiti "speaks to mankind" by means of it.

10. The tendency toward image formation in periods of overt inactivity has been shown by R. Fischer, "The Perception-Hallucination Continuum, and also by R. D. Bugelski, "The Definition of the Image."

11. The idea of the "sign image" is discussed in Fernandez, "African Religious Movements," and above in the Introduction.

12. These elemental images are discussed by Banzie as "those things out of which the Universe is created." See Metogo Zogo's discussion of the meaning of the four framing stars of the constellation Orion. The first ethnographer of the Fang, Günter Tessmann, was in constant search of "elementary ideas" which, when he discovered them, looked like "elementary images."

13. A syllogism is defined here in the usual way as "an argument of two propositions (premises) containing a common or mid term (our common image) with a third proposition, the conclusion, which follows necessarily." This kind of argument of images is similar to enthymemic argument. In Aristotelian logic this is syllogistic argument of a "probable or a persuasive sort" in which one of the propositions or premises is implicit, "kept in mind" but unstated. Robert Paine has brought to my attention the importance of this kind of argument in modern political rhetoric. ("Rhetorical Creativity and Political Power," unpublished manuscript.)

14. On the very large number of properties which adhere in any image or in any natural category of thought and which are thus available for gratuitous interpretation, see B. N. Colby, "Plot Component and Symbolic Component in Extended Discourse."

15. Brenda Beck, expanding on the work of J. M. Lotman (*Die Struktur literarischer Texte*, Munich: Wilhelm Fink, 1972) has argued that the essential role of metaphor is to provide "creative linkages" or mediations between planes or levels of experience. ("The Metaphor as Mediator between Semantic and Analogic Modes of Thought.")

16. The principle of "parallel alignment" is discussed in J. W. Fernandez, "Persuasions and Performances," but that discussion is an expansion of Osgood, Tannenbaum, and Suci, *The Measurement of Meaning*.

17. The analysis we make here takes up from the analysis made by David Sapir of the variety of animals (chickens, hawks, vultures, doves) brought into play to concretize the various positions taken by patriots, professors, good soldiers, and exiled sons during the Vietnam War ("The Anatomy of Metaphor," p. 29).

18. As for example, Charles Frake: "In acting as well as speaking persons have an image of the pattern to be completed and make plans accordingly ("A Structural Description of Subanum Religious Behavior," p. 125). Also Clifford Geertz in his article, "The Impact of the Concept of Culture on the Concept of Mind," p. 57: "Culture is best seen not as complexes of concrete behavior patterns—customs, usages, traditions, habit clusters—but as a set of control mechanisms—plans, recipes, rules, instructions for the governing of behavior."

19. The theory of metaphoric predication and movement is discussed in J. W. Fernandez, "Persuasions and Performances," "The Mission of Metaphor," and "The Performance of Ritual Metaphors."

20. One-heartedness is a metonymic rather than a metaphoric predication because rather than predicating an object in one domain upon a subject in another—predicating a trading team upon a worshiping group—a part (the heart) is predicated upon and made to stand for the whole, the entire corporeality of the worshiper.

21. See J. W. Fernandez, "Symbolic Consensus."

22. These are very basic notions in anthropology, linguistics, and psychology: Jakobson and Halle, *Fundamentals of Language*, and F. Lounsbury, "Similarity and Contiguity Relations in Language and Culture," pp. 123-128. They were recognized very early in anthropology by Tylor (metaphor and syntax) and by Frazer (sympathetic or similarity magic and contiguous or contiguity magic). They are otherwise discussed by Plato, Locke, Hobbes, Hume, and others.

23. J. Deese argues, "We must be willing to admit the possibility that obtained associations may never have occured together in the experience of the person who yields them—they may instead by the result of schemata which serve the function of bringing together structurally related elements from diverse experience" (*The Structure of Associations in Language and Thought*, p. 20).

24. As Deese elsewhere says (ibid., p. 159), "our cognitive structures are the outcome of the operation of hypothesis upon our experience."

25. This capacity of the apt metaphor has been argued by Victor Turner to be the fundamental capacity of dominant religious symbols. He points out that the multivocality of religious symbols tends to polarize between physiological referrents on the one hand and references to the normative values of social life on the other. Ritual dramas in which these symbols are manipulated create an exchange between physiological and social experiences ennobling the former and investing the latter with emotional significance. Thus are social relationships revitalized. (Turner, *The Forest of Symbols*, Chapter 1.) The socially necessary is made desirable by having it shown that the requirements of social structure are as necessary as the primary processes themselves. No doubt if what we are physiologically can be shown by religion to have a socially relevant manifestation, and vice versa, then religion accomplishes a fundamental transformation. Two of our metaphors aim at this goal. But religion often aims at more than that. It aims at showing that what we are physiologically and socially can be transcended. This is particularly a Christian intention and is present as well in Bwiti. Two of our metaphors aim at that. And they challenge us to find that "totalistic" level of analysis where "body, soul and society—everything merges" (Mauss quoted by Lévi-Strauss, "The Scope of Anthropology," p. 113).

26. Lévi-Strauss makes such an observation about the function of metaphor in returning to the whole. "Various forms of metonymy," he points out, "and in particular synecdoche celebrate the parts of experience while the more eloquent metaphors of myth refer back to the whole for significance" (*The Raw and the Cooked*, p. 342).

AFTERWORD

1. Alisdair Macintyre, "Epistemological Crises, Dramatic Narrative and The Philosophy of Science," pp. 454-472. This article, highly pertinent to

the perspective offered here, was brought to my attention by Jeffrey Stout after completion of the manuscript. Macintyre suggests, although he does not tell us in any detail, that coherence can only be recaptured by a different kind of "reason" than is characteristic of strict scientific method. Quoting T. S. Kuhn, the historian of science, he suggests that "our notion of rationality needs adjustment here and there if we are to understand the development of science." This book, in its way, aims at that readjustment. It is about a different kind of coherent "reasoning" in situations of what Kuhn would call paradigm change.

2. A point made effectively by Macintyre in "Epistemological Crises," p. 461.

3. J.D.Y. Peel, *Aladura*.

4. The distinction between adjustment and adaptation is that made by Clyde Kluckhohn in "Myths and Rituals: A General Theory." Practices which are adjustive enable individuals to cope—manage—the contradictions (culturally derived) of their existence. Practices which are adaptive enable a society to master the objective challenges to its existence. The distinction cannot be perfectly maintained, for the adjusted individual is better able to contribute to his society's adaptive efforts.

5. The difference may be said to lie, in such religions as Bwiti, between esoteric or embedded knowledge which, though edifying, is difficult to act upon and exoteric knowledge, which is easy to formulate in ideas and ideologies and has dynamic implications for social and political structure. Bellah, in his examination of religious evolution, discusses the first, primitive stage, of religion in such terms. The symbolization characteristic of that stage is so "fluid and flexible," such an "all encompassing plethora of images of the general order of existence as to give little leverage with which to change the world . . . it is a barrier to radical innovation." R. N. Bellah, "Religious Evolution."

6. For the influence of imagist thought in the symbolist movement on the understanding of primitive thought in contemporary structuralism see James Boon, *From Symbolism to Structuralism*. On the Theater of the Absurd see Martin Esselin, *The Theater of the Absurd*.

7. Marcel Griaule, *Conversations with Ogotemelli*.

8. As argued in C. K. Ogden, *Opposition: A Linguistic and Psychological Analysis*.

9. The theory of plural societies, mainly those created by colonization, offers insight into identity dynamics produced by multiple and often invidious cultural frames of reference. See the work influenced by M. G. Smith and his students. For the classic statement see *Pluralism in Africa*, ed. by Leo Kuper and M. G. Smith.

10. B. N. Colby, "Plot Component and Symbolic Component." Due to the multivocality of symbolic configurations a resourceful auditor of communications laden with such elements has a wide range of ways to make

sense out of what he hears but does not "really" understand. He can "collude" to produce an acceptable meaning.

11. Günter Tessmann, "Verlauf und Ergebnisse der Lubecker Pangwe Expedition," p. 8.

12. For the "transcendent" consequences of analogic argument and particularly of the use of metaphor see K. Basso, "Wise Words of the Western Apache," and also Ellie Kongas Maranda, " 'A Tree Grows'—Transformations of a Riddle Metaphor."

13. See the discussion by Toshikiko Kawasaki in "Donne's Microcosm."

APPENDIX III

1. As discussed in "Disease Etiologies in Non-Western Cultures." Foster summarizes the two etiologies as follows:

System:	Personalistic	Naturalistic
Causation:	Active agent	Equilibrium loss
Illness:	Special case of misfortune	Unrelated to other misfortune
Religion, Magic:	Intimately tied to illness	Largely unrelated to illness
Causality:	Multiple levels	Single level
Prevention:	Positive action	Avoidance
Responsibility:	Beyond patient control	Resides with patient

2. The distinction between redemptive and therapeutic orientations in African religious movements is discussed in J. W. Fernandez, "African Religious Movements—Confluents of Inquiry," in *Expanding Horizons in African Studies*, ed. Gwendolyn Carter (Evanston: Northwestern University Press, 1969), pp. 27-45.

3. These Ombwiri spirits are discussed in Raponda-Walker and Sillans, *Rites et croyances*, pp. 22-28. The authors remark that Fang were one of the few Gabonese peoples not to have beliefs in Ombwiri spirits and this may be why they were attracted to these cults in transitional circumstances. Such spirits could minister to transitional afflictions. Nassau, who had as much contact with nineteenth-century Ombwiri practices as anyone, makes two points about these spirits. Though they are troubling spirits the object is to convert them into "guardian spirits." Second, their similarity to ancestor spirits comes from the fact that they are often the abandoned ancestor spirits of peoples who once occupied the land another people now occupies. Hence their association with places. *Fetishism in West Africa*, pp. 67-68.

4. S. Swiderski, L'Ombwiri: Société d'initiation et de guérison au Gabon.

Bibliography

Agency for International Development. *Selected Economic Data for the Less Developed Countries*. Washington, D.C.: A.I.D. Statistics and Reports Division, 1967.

Alcobe, S. *Los pamues en el complejo racial del Africa negra*. Madrid: Archivos del Instituto de Estudios Africanos, no. 13, 1950.

———— and Panyella, A. *Estudio cuantitativo de la exogamia de los Pamues (fang) de la Guinea continental española*. Madrid: Archivos del Instituto de Estudios Africanos, no. 18, 1951.

Alexandre, P. *Manuel élémentaire de la langue Bulu (Sud Cameroun)*. Paris: Centre des Hautes Etudes D'Administration Musulmane, 1955.

————. "Un conte Bulu de Sangmelima—La Jeune Albinos et le pygmée," *Bulletin de la Société des Africanistes*, 33(1963):243-254.

————. "Proto-histoire du groupe beti-bulu-fang," *Cahiers d'études africaines*, 20(1966):503-560.

————. *Système verbal et predicatif du Bulu*. Paris: Librarie C. Klinksieck, 1966.

———— and Binet, J. *Le Groupe dit "Pahouin."* Paris: Presses Universitaires de France, 1958.

Allegret, E. *Les Idées religieuses des Fang*. Paris: Ernest Lerous, 1904.

Alvarez, R. H. *Enseñanza en la Guinea Española*. Madrid: Archivos del Instituto de Estudios Africanos, no. 22, 1951.

American Presbyterian Mission. *Ntensi osu, Nteni Fanwe*. Talaguga: Foreign Mission Board Press, 1889.

Andersson, E. *Messianic Popular Movements in the Lower Congo*. Uppsala: Studia Ethnographica Upsaliensia XIV, 1958.

Anon. "Paul DuChaillu—Forschungreisen und Abendeteuer im West Afrika." *Globus*, Band I(1863):167.

Arendt, H. *Between Past and Future*. New York: Viking, 1961.

Asumu, A. Mvomo and Schmald, H. *Medzo meye Nfefe Enig Biere Gningon Mebeghe Angome Ebogha Fang*. Oyem: privately published, 1964.

Avelot, R. "Recherches sur l'histoire des migrations dans le bassin de l'Ogooue et la région littorale adjacente." *Bulletin de géographie historique et descriptive*, 20(1905):357-412.

Balandier, G. *Sociologie actuelle de l'Afrique noire*. 2d ed. Paris: Presses Universitaires de France, 1963.

————. *Afrique ambiguë*. Paris: Plon, 1957.

Balandier, G. "Phénomènes sociaux totaux et dynamique sociale." *Cahiers Internationaux de Sociologie*, 30(1961):23-34.

Ballard, J. A. "The Development of Political Parties in French Equatorial Africa." Ph.D. dissertation, Fletcher School of Law and Diplomacy, 1963.

Barnes, J. A. "Measures of Divorce Frequency in Simple Societies." *Journal of the Royal Anthropological Institute*, 79(1949):37-60.

Barrett, D. *Schism and Renewal in Africa*. Nairobi: Oxford University Press, 1968.

Barth, F. *Ritual and Knowledge among the Baktamen*. New Haven: Yale University Press, 1975.

Basso, K. "Wise Words of the Western Apache." In *Meaning in Anthropology*, edited by K. Basso and H. Selby. Albuquerque: University of New Mexico Press, 1976, pp. 93-122.

Bates, G. L. *Handbook of Bulu*. Elat: Hasley Memorial Press, 1926.

Beck, B. "The Metaphor as Mediator between Semantic and Analogic Modes of Thought." *Current Anthropology*, 19(1978):83-97.

Bellah, R. N. "Religious Evolution." *American Sociological Review*, 29(1964):358-374.

Bender, D. R. "A Refinement of the Concept of the Household: Families, Coresidence, and Domestic Functions." *American Anthropologist*, 69(1967):493-510.

Berlin, B. and Kay, P. *Basic Color Terms*. Berkeley: University of California Press, 1969.

Biffot, L. *Facteurs d'intégration et desintégration du travailleur Gabonais à son entreprise*. Paris: Office de la recherche scientifique et technique outre-mer, 1960-1961.

Binet, J. *Le Mariage en Afrique noire*. Paris: Editions de Cerf, 1959.

————. *Sociétés de danse chez les Fang au Gabon*. Paris: Orstom, 1972.

————, Gollenhoffer, J. O., and Sillans, R. "Textes religieux du *Bwiti-fan* et de ses confréries prophétiques dans leurs cadres rituels." Cahiers d'Etudes Africaines, 46(1972):197-253.

Blumer, H. *Symbolic Interactionism: Perspective and Method*. Englewood Cliffs, N.J.: Prentice-Hall, 1969.

Bohannan, P. "The Impact of Money on an African Subsistence Economy." *Journal of Economic History*, 19(1959):491-503.

———— and Bohannan, L. *The Tiv of Central Nigeria*. International African Institute Ethnographic Survey of Africa. Western Africa. Part 8. Oxford and London: International African Institute, 1953.

Boon, J. *From Symbolism to Structuralism*. Oxford: Blackwell, 1972.

Booth, N. S. "Time and Change in African Traditional Thought." *Journal of Religion in Africa*, 7(1975):81-91.

Bot ba Njock, H. M. "Prééminences sociales et systèmes politico-religieux dans la société traditionnelle Bulu et Fang." *Journal de la Société des Africanistes*, 30(1960):150-171.

Boudieguy, Prince Birinda de. *La Bible secrète des noirs*. Paris: Omnium Litteraire, 1952.

Bowditch, T. E. *Mission to Cape Coast Castle and Ashantee*. London: John Murray, 1819.

Braouzec, M. "Voyage au Como." *Revue Coloniale*, Oct.-Dec. 1861, pp. 349-360.

Briault, R. P. *Dans la forêt du Gabon*. Paris: B. Grasset, 1930.

Brown, A. J. *One Hundred Years*. New York: Revell, 1936.

Brown, R. *Explanation in the Social Sciences*. London: Routledge and Kegan Paul, 1963.

Bruner, J. "The Course of Cognitive Growth." *American Psychologist*, 19(1964):1-15.

Buell, R. L. *The Native Problem in Africa*. 2 vols. New York: Macmillan, 1928.

Bugelski, R. D. "The Definition of the Image." In *Imagery: Current Cognitive Approaches*, edited by S. J. Segal. New York: Academic Press, 1971.

Burton, Sir R. "A Day Amongst the Fang." *The Anthropological Review*, 1(1864):43-54.

Cadier, M. C. *Sauvons les paiens du Gabon*. Paris: Société des Missions Evangéliques, 1924.

———. *Ces Hommes ont peur*. Paris: Société des Missions Evangéliques, 1947.

Caperan, Dr. C. "Notes sur l'état sanitaire des populations mfangs du Woleu-Ntem 1924-1925." *Bulletin de la Société des Recherches Congolaises*, No. 12(1930).

Colby, B. N. "Plot Component and Symbolic Component in Extended Discourse." In *Discourse and Inference in Cognitive Anthropology: An Approach to Psychic Unity*, edited by M. D. Laflin and J. D. Silverberg. The Hague: Mouton, 1978, pp. 104-108.

Compiegne, le Marquis de. *L'Afrique equatoriale: Gabonais, Pahouins, Gallois*. 2 vols. 3rd ed. Paris: Plon, 1878.

Cornevin, R. *Histoire des peuples de l'Afrique noire*. 3rd ed. Paris: Editions Berger-Levrault, 1963.

Cottes, A. *La Mission Cottes au Sud-Cameroun (1905-1908)*. Paris: Leroux, 1911.

Curtin, P. *Image of Africa*. Madison: University of Wisconsin Press, 1964.

Cuvelier, M., ed. *Relations sur le Congo du Père Laurent de Lucques 1700-1717*. Brussels: Institut Royal Colonial Belge, 1953.

Daneel, M. L. *Old and New in Southern Shona Independent Churches*. Vol. 1, *History and Traditional Influences*. The Hague: Mouton, 1971.

Darlington, C. F. and A. B. *African Betrayal*. New York: D. McKay, 1968.

d'Azevedo, W. L., ed. *The Traditional Artist in African Society*. Bloomington: Indiana University Press, 1973.

de Craemer, W., Vansina, J., and Fox, R. "Religious Movements in Central Africa: A Theoretical Study." *Comparative Studies in Society and History*, 18(1976):458-475.

Deese, J. *The Structure of Associations in Language and Thought*. Baltimore: Johns Hopkins Press, 1965.

Deschamps, H. *Traditions orales et archives au Gabon*. Paris: Berger-Levrault, 1962.

Dickson, K. A. and Ellingworth, P., eds. *Biblical Revelation and African Beliefs*. London: Butterworth Press, 1969.

Dieterlen, G. and Griaule, M., *Le Renard pâle*. Paris: *Memoires de l'Institut d'Ethnologie*, no. 72(1965).

Doob, L. "Presuppositions and Perplexities Confronting Social Psychological Research in Developing Countries." *Journal of Social Issues*, 24(1969):71-84.

Dorjahn V. "The Factor of Polygyny in African Demography." In *Continuities and Change in African Cultures*, edited by M. J. Herskovits and W. H. Bascom. Chicago: University of Chicago Press, 1959.

Douglas, M. *Purity and Danger*. London: Routledge and Kegan Paul, 1967.

Du Bellay, G. "Le Gabon." *Le Tour du Monde*, 12(1864):278-279, 304-307.

DuChaillu, P. B. *Explorations and Adventures in Equatorial Africa*. New York: Harper and Brothers, 1861.

―――. *Stories of the Gorilla Country*. New York: Harper and Brothers, 1867.

―――. *Lost in the Jungle*. New York: Harper and Brothers, 1869.

―――. *Wild Life under the Equator*. London: Low, 1869.

―――. *My Apingi Kingdom*. New York: Harper and Brothers, 1870.

―――. *A Journey in Ashango Land*. New York: Harper and Brothers, 1871.

―――. *In the Country of the Dwarfs*. New York: Harper and Brothers, 1872.

―――. *Explorations and Adventures in the Great Forest of Equatorial Africa*, abridged and popular edition. New York: Harper and Brothers, 1890.

Echegaray, C. G. *See* Gonzalez.

Edwards, A. *Death Rides a Camel: A Biography of Sir Richard Burton*. New York: Julian Press, 1963.

Engutu, O. *Dulu Bon be Afri Kara*. Ebolowa, Cameroon: American Presbyterian Press, 1952.

Eno-Belinga, M. S. *Découverte des chantes fables Africaines beti-bulu-fang*. Paris: Klincksieck, 1965.

―――. *Littérature et musique populaire en Afrique Noire*. Toulouse: Editions Cujas, 1965.

Esselin, M. *The Theater of the Absurd*. New York: Doubleday, 1961.

Evan, A. "Le Voyage de Jacques Ngoya au pays des morts." *Bulletin de la Société des Recherches Congolaises*, 25(1938):109-121.

Evans-Pritchard, E. E. *Witchcraft, Oracles, and Magic among the Azande*. London: Oxford University Press, 1937.

Fairchild, H. N. *The Noble Savage: A Study in Romantic Naturalism*. New York: Columbia University Press, 1928.

Fauré, Felix. *Le Diable dans la brousse*. Paris: Société des Missions Evangéliques, 1938.

Fernandez, J. W. "Folklore as an Agent of Nationalism." *Bulletin of the African Studies Association,* 5(1962):3-7.

————. "Redistributive Acculturation and Ritual Reintegration in Fang Culture." Ph.D. dissertation, Northwestern University, 1963.

————. "The Idea and Symbol of the Saviour in a Gabon Syncretist Cult." *International Review of Missions*, 53(1963):281-289.

————. "African Religious Movements—Types and Dynamics." *Journal of Modern African Studies*, 3(1964):428-446.

————. "Symbolic Consensus in a Fang Reformative Cult." *American Anthropologist*, 67(1965):902-927.

————. "Unbelievably Subtle Words: Representation and Integration in the Sermons on an African Reformative Cult." *Journal of the History of Religions*, 6(1966):53-64.

————. "Principles of Opposition and Vitality in Fang Aesthetics." *The Journal of Aesthetics and Art Criticism*, 25(1966):53-64.

————. "The Shaka Complex." *Transition* (Kampala), 29:10-14.

————. "Filial Piety and Power: Psychosocial Dynamics in the Legends of Shaka and Sundiata." *Science and Psychoanalysis*, 14(1969):47-60.

————. *Microcosmogony and Modernization in African Religious Movements*. Occasional Papers of the Center for Developing Area Studies. Montreal: McGill University Press, 1969.

————. "Rededication and Prophetism in Ghana." *Cahiers d'Etudes Africaines*, 10(1970):228-305.

————. "The Affirmation of Things Past: Alar Ayong and Bwiti as Movements of Protest in Central and Northern Gabon." In *Protest and Power in Black Africa*, edited by R. Rotberg and A. Mazrui. New York: Oxford University Press, 1970, pp. 427-457.

————. "Bantu Brotherhood: Symmetry, Socialization and Ultimate Choice in Two Bantu Cultures." In *Kinship and Culture*, edited by F. K. Hsu. Chicago: Aldine, 1971, pp. 339-366.

————. "Persuasions and Performances: Of the Beast in Every Body—And the Metaphors of Everyman." *Daedalus*, 101(1972):39-60.

————. "Fang Representations under Acculturation." In *Africa and the West: Intellectual Responses to European Culture*, edited by Philip Curtin. Madison: University of Wisconsin Press, 1972, pp. 3-48.

Fernandez, J. W. "Tabernanthe iboga: Narcotic Ecstasis and the Work of the Ancestors." In *Flesh of the Gods: The Ritual Use of Hallucinogens*, edited by P. T. Furst. New York: Praeger, 1972, pp. 237-260.

———. "Equatorial Excursions—The Folklore of Narcotic Inspired Visions in an African Religious Movement." In *African Folklore*, edited by R. Dorson. New York: Doubleday, 1972, pp. 241-261 and 511-521.

———. "The Exposition and Imposition of Order: Artistic Expression in Fang Culture." In *The Traditional Artist in African Societies*, edited by W. L. d'Azevedo. Bloomington: Indiana University Press, 1973, pp. 194-220.

———. "The Mission of Metaphor in Expressive Culture." *Current Anthropology*, 15(1974):119-145.

———. "The Ethnic Communion: Interethnic Recruitment in African Religious Movements." *Journal of African Studies*, 2(1975):131-147.

———. "On Reading the Sacred into the Profane: The Dramatic Fallacy in the Work of Victor Turner." *Journal for the Scientific Study of Religion*, 14(1975):191-197.

———. "Dance Exchange in Western Equatorial Africa." *CORD Dance Research Journal*, 7(1975-76):1-7.

———. "The Performance of Ritual Metaphors." In *The Social Use of Metaphors*, edited by J. D. Sapir and J. C. Crocker. Philadelphia: University of Pennsylvania Press, 1977, pp. 100-130.

——— and Bekale, P. "Christian Acculturation and Fang Witchcraft." *Cahiers d'Etudes Africanes*, 2(1961):244-270.

Fischer, R. "The Perception-Hallucination Continuum (A Re-examination)." *Diseases of the Nervous System*, 30(1969):161-171.

Flint, J. E. "Mary Kingsley—A Reassessment." *Journal of African History*, 4(1963):95-104.

Forde, C. D. and A. R. Radcliffe-Browne. *African Systems of Kinship and Marriage*. London: International African Institute, 1950.

Foster, George. "Peasant Society and the Image of the Limited Good." *American Anthropologist*, 67(1965):293-315.

———. "Disease Etiologies in Non-Western Cultures." *American Anthropologist*, 78(1976):773-782.

Frake, C. O. "A Structural Description of Subanum Religious Behavior." In *Explorations in Cultural Anthropology: Essays in Honor of G. P. Murdock*, edited by W. H. Goodenough. New York: McGraw Hill, 1964, pp. 111-129.

Franc, L. *De l'origine des Pahouins: essai de resolution de ce probleme ethnologique*. Paris: Maloine, 1905.

Fu-Kiau Kia Bunseki, A. *Le Mukongo et le monde que l'entourait: N'Kongo Ye Nza Yakun' Zungidila*. Kinshasa: Office National de la Recherche et de Développement, 1969.

Gabon. *Recensement et Enquête Démographique: Ensemble du Gabon 1960-1961.* Libreville: Ministère de la Coopération, 1965.

Galley, S. *Eben 'Avo—L'Apôtre Fang.* 3d ed. Paris: Société des Missions Evangeliques, 1926.

————. *Dictionnaire Fang-Français et Français-Fang suivi d'une grammaire fang.* Neuchâtel: Henri Messeitler, 1964.

Gaulen, C. "L'étiologie des malades et l'influence des sorciers chez les pahouines." *Annales Medicales et Pharm. Coloniales,* 3(1934):364-370.

Geertz, C. "The Impact of the Concept of Culture on the Concept of Mind." In *Theories of Mind,* edited by J. Scher. Glencoe: The Free Press, 1965, pp. 713-740.

————. *The Interpretation of Cultures.* New York: Basic Books, 1973.

Germaine, Soeur Marie. *Le Christ au Gabon.* Brussels: Louvain University, Museum Lessianum, 1931.

Gluckman, Max. "Ethnographic Data in British Social Anthropology." *Sociological Review,* 9(1961):5-17.

Gonzalez Echegaray, Carlos. "Rutas y Etapas de los Pueblos Playeros de la Guinea Continental Española." In *Conferencia Internacional de Africanistas Occidentales,* Vol. II, pp. 327-351. Trabajos Presentados a la 3ª Sección (Medio Humano). Madrid: Dirección General de Marruecos y Colonias, 1954.

Goody, Jack. *The Myth of the Bagre.* Oxford: Clarendon Press, 1972.

———— and Watts, Ian. "The consequences of literacy." In *Literacy in Traditional Society,* edited by J. Goody. Cambridge: Cambridge University Press, 1968, pp. 27-68.

Görög-Karady, Veronica. "L'Origine de l'inégalité des races: Etude de trente-sept contes africains." *Cahiers d'Etudes Africaines,* 30(1968):290-309.

Gossen, G. *The Chamulas in the World of the Sun.* Cambridge, Mass.: Harvard University Press, 1974.

Grébert, F. *Avema.* Paris: Société des Missions Evangéliques, 1946.

————. *Au Gabon.* Paris: Société des Missions Evangéliques, 1948.

————. *Ekomi.* Paris: Société des Missions Evangéliques, 1951.

Griaule, M. *Conversations with Ogotemelli.* London: Oxford University Press for the International African Institute, 1965. English translation of *Dieu d'eau—entretiens avec Ogototemmeli,* published in 1948.

Griswold, B. "Reasons for Selecting the Gabon." *The Missionary Herald,* 37(1842):499.

Guthrie, M. *The Classification of Bantu Languages.* London: Oxford University Press for the International African Institute, 1948.

————. *The Bantu Languages of West Equatorial Africa.* London: Oxford University Press for the International African Institute, 1953.

Hardy, G. *Histoire sociale de la colonisation française.* Paris: Larose, 1953.

Hee, R. P. "Les Adouma du Gabon." *Les Missions Catholiques,* Vol. 3, no. 299 and Vol. 3, no. 330.

Horton, R. "Ritual Man in Africa." *Africa*, 34(1964):85-104.

———. "African Conversion." *Africa*, 41(1971):85-108.

———. "On the Rationality of Conversion." *Africa*, 45(1975):219-235, 373-399.

——— and Peel, J.D.Y. "Conversion and Confusion: A Rejoinder on Christianity in Western Nigeria." *Canadian Journal of African Studies*, 10(1976): 481-488.

Ifeka-Moller, C. "White Power: Social Structural Features in Conversion to Christianity." *Canadian Journal of African Studies*, 8(1974):55-72.

Iradier y Bulfy, M. *Africa: Viajes y Trabajos de la Asociación Euskara—La Exploradora*. Santander: Sociedad Euskara de Exploración, 1888.

Jakobson, R. and Halle, M. *Fundamentals of Language*. The Hague: Mouton, 1956.

Janzen, J. and MacGaffey, W. *An Anthology of Kongo Religion: Primary Texts from Lower Zaire*. Lawrence: University of Kansas Press, 1974.

Junod, A. "Possédé par un evur." *Journal des Missions Evangéliques*, 83(1960):78-80.

Kawasaki, T. "Donne's Microcosm." In *Seventeenth-Century Imagery*, edited by Earl Miner. Berkeley and Los Angeles: University of California Press, 1971, pp. 25-43.

Keyes, C. "Tug-of-War-for-Merit: Cremation of a Senior Monk," *The Journal of the Siam Society*, 63(1975):43-62.

Kingsley, M. *Travels in West Africa—Congo Français, Corisco, and Cameroons*. London: Macmillan, 1897.

———. *West African Studies*. London: Macmillan, 1899.

Kluckhohn, C. "Myths and Rituals: A General Theory." *Harvard Theological Review*, 35:45-79.

Kongas Maranda, E. "The Logic of Riddles." In *The Structural Analysis of Oral Tradition*, edited by P. Maranda and E. Kongas Maranda. Philadelphia: University of Pennsylvania Press, 1970, pp. 189-234.

———. " 'A Tree Grows'—Transformations of a Riddle Metaphor." In *Structural Models in Folklore and Transformational Essays* by E. Kongas Maranda and P. Maranda. The Hague: Mouton, 1971, pp. 16-39.

Kopytoff, I. "Ancestors as Elders in Africa." *Africa*, 41(1971):129-142.

Kroeber, A. L. *The Nature of Culture*. Chicago: University of Chicago Press, 1952.

——— and Kluckhohn, C. *Culture: A Review of Concepts and Definitions*. Cambridge, Mass.: Papers of the Peabody Museum of American Archaeology and Ethnology of Harvard University, no. 47, 1958.

Kubie, L. S. *Neurotic Distortion of the Creative Process*. Lawrence: University of Kansas Press, 1958.

Kuper, L. and Smith, M. G. *Pluralism in Africa*. Berkeley: University of California Press, 1969.

Lanternari, V. *Religions of the Oppressed*. New York: Knopf, 1963.

Largeau, V. *Encyclopédie pahouine*. Paris: Leroux, 1901.

Laserre, G. *Libreville: la ville et sa région*. Paris: Colin, 1958.

Lavignotte, H. *L'Evur—croyance des Pahouins du Gabon*. Paris: Société des Missions Evangéliques, 1936.

Lebeuf, J. P. *Les Habitations des Fali*. Paris: Hachette, 1961.

Lecomte, A. "Notes sur quelque poisons de la côte occidentale d'Afrique." *Archives Medicaux Navales*, 7(1864):260-264.

Lee, D. "Linear and Non-Linear Codifications of Reality." In *Freedom and Culture*. Englewood Cliffs, N.J.: Prentice Hall, 1959, pp. 105-120.

Le Garrac, E., ed. *Au Fernan-Vaz: La Rencontre de deux civilisations*. Abbeville: C. Paillot, 1896.

Leighton, A. H., Lambo, A. T. et al. *Psychiatric Disorders among the Yoruba*. Ithaca: Cornell University Press, 1963.

Le Testu, M. D. "Réflexion sur l'homme tigre." *Bulletin de la Société de Recherches Congolaises*, 25(1938):147-167.

Lévi-Strauss, C. "The Structural Study of Myth." *Journal of American Folklore*, 68(1955):428-444.

―――. *Totemism*. English translation by Rodney Needham of *Le Totemisme aujourd'hui*, 1962. Boston: Beacon Press, 1963.

―――. *The Savage Mind*. English translation of *La Pensée sauvage*, 1962. Chicago: University of Chicago Press, 1966.

―――. "The Scope of Anthropology." *Current Anthropology*, 7(1966):112-123. English translation by Sherry Ortner Paul and Robert Paul of *Leçon inaugurale*, 1960.

―――. *The Raw and the Cooked*. New York: Harper and Row, 1964. English translation by John and Doreen Weightman of *Le Cru et le cuit*, 1964.

Lewis, E., ed. *Trader Horn or the Ivory Coast in the Earlies—Being the Life and Works of Alfred Aloysius Horn*. London: Jonathan Cape, 1927.

Lewis, O. *The Children of Sanchez*. New York: Random House, 1961.

Lord, A. B. *The Singer of Tales*. Cambridge, Mass.: Harvard University Press, 1963.

Lounsbury, F. "Similarity and Contiguity Relations in Language and Culture." In *Report of the Tenth Annual Round Table Meeting on Linguistics and Anthropology*, edited by R. S. Harrell. Georgetown: Georgetown University Press, 1959, pp. 132-138.

Lowes, J. L. *The Road to Xanadu—a Study in the Ways of the Imagination*. Boston: Houghton, 1927.

McClelland, D. *The Achieving Society*. Princeton, N.J.: Van Nostrand, 1961.

Macintyre, Alisdair. "Epistemological Crises, Dramatic Narrative and The Philosophy of Science." *The Monist*, 60(1977):454-472.

MacGaffey, W. "The Dwarf Soldiers of Simon Kimbangu: Explorations in Congo Cosmology." Unpublished manuscript.

Maignan, Captain J. "Une Ngi-fête chez le Nkoje." *Bulletin de la Société Recherches Congolaises*, 8(1925):1-15.

Mallart, Louis. *La Médecine traditionnelle chez les Evuzok au Cameroun.* Paris: Ecole Pratique des Hautes Etudes: VIe Section, 1970.

Martrou, L. "Les 'Eki' des Fang." *Anthropos*, 1(1906):745-761.

Mba, L. "Essai de droit coutumier pahouin." *Bulletin de la Société Recherches Congolaises*, 25(1938):5-51.

Mbiti, J. *New Testament Eschatology in an African Background.* London: Oxford, 1971.

Mequet, A. "Nouvelle excursion dans le haut de la rivière du Gabon effectuée en novembre et décembre 1846." *Revue Coloniale*, 12(1847):45-77.

Mering, Otto von. *A Grammar of Values.* Pittsburgh: University of Pittsburgh Press, 1961.

Middleton, J. and Tait, D., eds. *Tribes Without Rulers.* London: Routledge and Kegan Paul, 1958.

Moreno Moreno, J. *Reseña histórica de la preséncia de España en el Golfo de Guinea.* Madrid: Instituto de Estudios Africanos, 1952.

———. "Los Digols." *Cuadernos de Estudios Africanos*, 7(1949):88.

Muye, F. "L'Oban." *Réalités Gabonaises*, 17(1962):11-14.

Naroll, R. "A Preliminary Index of Social Development." *American Anthropologist*, 58(1956):609-628.

———. "A Fifth Solution to Galton's Problem." *American Anthropologist*, 66(1964):863-887.

Nassau, R. H. *Fetishism in West Africa.* New York: Young Peoples' Missionary Movement, 1904.

———. *My Ogowe.* New York: Neale, 1914.

Ndong Philippe, M. "Le Mvet." *Réalités Gabonaises*, 1-12(1959-1961).

Needham, R., ed. *Right and Left: Dualistic Symbolic Classification in Culture.* Chicago: University of Chicago Press, 1973.

Ochswald, M. P. "La Danse 'de Gaulle' à Lambaréné." *Journal des Missions Evangéliques*, 7(1950):7-13.

Ogden, C. K. *Opposition: A Linguistic and Psychological Analysis.* Bloomington: Indiana University Press, 1967. Originally published in 1932.

Opler, M. E. "Themes as Dynamic Forces." *American Journal of Sociology*, 51(1945):198-206.

Osgood, C. E. "Behavioristic Analysis of Perception and Language as Cognitive Phenomena." In *Contemporary Approaches to Cognition* by J. Bruner et al. Cambridge: Harvard University Press, 1957, pp. 75-118.

———, Tannenbaum, P., and Suci, G. *The Measurement of Meaning.* Urbana: University of Illinois Press, 1957.

Palyi, M. *A Lesson in French Inflation.* New York: Economists National Committee on Monetary Policy, 1959.

Panyella, A. *Esquema de Etnologia de los Fang Ntumu de la Guinea Española*. Madrid: Instituto de Estúdios Africanos, 1959.

———— and Sabater, J. *Esquema de la anthroponímia Fang de la Guinea española desde el punto de vista etnológico*. Madrid: Archivos del Instituto de Estudios Africanos, no. 34, 1955.

Peel, J.D.Y. *Aladura: A Religious Movement among the Yoruba*. London: Oxford University Press for the International African Institute, 1968.

Penzer, N. W., ed. *Selected Papers on Anthropology, Travel, and Exploration by Sir Richard Burton*. London: A. M. Philpot, 1924.

Piers, G. and Singer, M. *Shame and Guilt: A Psychoanalytic and Cultural Study*. Springfield, Illinois: Thomas, 1953.

Pigeard, C. "Exploration du Gabon effectuée en août et septembre 1845." *Revue Coloniale*, 11(1847):263-295.

Pope, H. "Tabernanthe iboga: An African Narcotic Plant of Social Importance." *Economic Botany*, 23(1969):174-184.

Radcliffe-Brown, A. R. "Introduction" to *African Systems of Kinship and Marriage*, edited by A. R. Radcliffe-Brown and D. Forde. London: Oxford University Press for the International African Institute, 1950, pp. 1-85.

Ranger, T. O. *Dance and Society in Eastern Africa*. London: Heinemann, 1975.

———— and Kimambo, I., eds. *The Historical Study of African Religion*. Berkeley and Los Angeles: University of California Press, 1972.

Raponda-Walker, Abbé A. *Dictionnaire Metsogo*. Libreville: manuscript, n.d.

————. *Dictionnaire MPongwe-Francais*. Metz: La Libre Lorraine, 1934.

————. "Les Cimetières Gabonaises." *Réalités Gabonaises*, 4(1959):5-9: 5(1960):7-10.

————. "Anglais, Espagnoles et Nord Americains au Gabon au XIXᵉ siècle." *Bulletin de l'Institute d'Etudes Centre-Africaine*, IIᵉ serie, 12(1948):254-279.

———— and Sillans, R. *Les Plantes utiles au Gabon*. Paris: P. Lechevalier, 1961.

———— and Sillans, R. *Rites et croyances des peuples du Gabon*. Paris: Presence Africaine, 1962.

Rattray, Captain R. *Ashanti*. Oxford: Clarendon Press, 1923.

Raymaekers, P. "L'Eglise de Jesus-Christ sur la terre par le prophète Simon Kimbangu: contribution à l'étude des mouvements messianiques dans le Bas-Kongo." *Zaire*, 13(1959):675-756.

Roberts, J. M., Arth, M. J., and Bush, R. R. "Games in Culture." *American Anthropologist*, 61(1959):597-605.

Roberts, J. and Ridgeway, C. "Musical Involvement in Talking." *Anthropological Linguistics*, 11(1969):223-246.

Roche, J. B. *Au Pays des Pahouins du Rio Mouny du Cameroun*. Paris: Lavauzelle, 1904.

Sapir, J. D. "The Anatomy of Metaphor." In *The Social Use of Metaphor*, edited by J. D. Sapir and J. C. Crocker. Philadelphia: University of Pennsylvania Press, 1977, pp. 3-32.

Sautter, G. "Les Paysans noirs du Gabon septentrional: Essai sur le peuplement et l'habitat du Woleu-N'Tem." *Les Cahiers d'Outre-Mer*, 14(1951):119-159.

Savorgnan de Brazza, P. "Voyages dans l'ouest Africain." *Le Tour du Monde*, XLIV and XLV (1877-1888):289-336, 1-25.

Schnapper, B. *La Politique et le commerce français dans le Golfe de Guinée de 1838-1871*. Paris: Mouton, 1961.

Scheub, H. "The Techniques of the Expansible Image in Xhosa Ntsomi Performances." *Research on African Literatures*, 1(1970):119-146.

Schweitzer, A. *On the Edge of the Primeval Forest*. London: Black, 1955.

Scribner, S. "Modes of Thinking and Ways of Speaking: Culture and Logic Reconsidered." In *Discourse Production and Comprehension*, edited by R. O. Freedle. Hillsdale, N.J.: Ablex Publishing Corporation, 1977, pp. 121-148.

Segall, M. H., Campbell, D. T., and Herskovits, M. *The Influence of Culture on Visual Perception*. New York: Bobbs-Merrill, 1966.

Shepard, P. *The Tender Carnivore and the Sacred Game*. New York: Charles Scribner's Sons, 1974.

Sperber, D. *Rethinking Symbolism*. New York: Cambridge University Press, 1975.

Stocking, G. "French Anthropology in 1800," *ISIS*, 55(1964):134-150.

Stoll, R.P.A. *La tonetique des langues Bantu et Semi-Bantu du Cameroun*. Paris: Institute Français D'Afrique Noire, Memorandum no. 4, 1955.

Swiderski, S. "Le Symbolisme du poteau central au Gabon." *Mitteilungen der Anthropologischen Gesellschaft*, Band C(1970):299-315.

———. "Notes bibliographiques sur les fondateurs et les guides spirituels des sectes syncrétiques au Gabon." *Anthropologica*, 14 (1973):37-88.

———. L'Ombwiri: Société d'initiation et de guérison au Gabon. Extract from *Religione e Civiltà*, Vol. 1. Rome: Dedalo Libri, 1974.

Taylor, J. and Lehmann, D. *Christians of the Copperbelt*. London: S.C.M. Press, 1961.

Tessmann, G. "Verlauf und Ergebnisse der Lubecker Pangwe Expedition." *Globus*, 97(1910):no. 1, pp. 1-10 and no. 2, pp. 25-29.

———. *Die Pangwe—Völkerskundliche Monographie eines Westafrikanischen Negerstammes*. 2 vols. Berlin: Ernst Wasmuth, 1913.

Towo-Atangana, G. "Le Mvet—genre majeur de la litterature orale des populations Pahouins." *Abbia*, 9 and 10(1965):163-179.

Trilles, H. "Proverbes, légendes, et contes fang." *Bulletin de la société neufchâtelloise de géographie*, 16(1905):49-295.

————. *Totemism chez le Fang*. Munster: Bibliothèque-Anthropos, 1912.

————. *Les Pygmées de la forêt equatoriale*. Paris: Bloud, 1932.

————. *L'Ame du pygmée du Afrique*. Paris: Seures, 1945.

Turnbull, C. *The Forest People*. New York: Simon and Schuster, 1961.

Turner, H. W. *African Independent Church*. 2 vols. Oxford: The Clarendon Press, 1966.

Turner, V. W. *Schism and Continuity in An African Society*. Manchester: Manchester University Press, 1957.

————. *The Forest of Symbols*. Ithaca: Cornell University Press, 1967.

United Nations. *Evaluation of Basic Demographic Data in Some French-Speaking Countries*. New York and Geneva: UNESCO, 1968.

United States Bureau of the Census. *Statistical Abstract*. Washington, D.C.: U.S. Government Printing Office. For 1936, 1939, 1959.

Van den Berghe, P. "Some Comments on Norbeck's African Rituals of Conflict." *American Anthropologist*, 67(1965):485.

Vansina, J. "Cultures Through Time." In *A Handbook of Method in Cultural Anthropology*, edited by R. Naroll and R. Cohen. Garden City, N.Y.: Natural History Press, 1970, pp. 165-179.

Van Velsen, J. "The Extended Case Method and Situational Analysis." In *The Craft of Social Anthropology*, edited by A. L. Epstein. London: Tavistock, 1967, pp. 129-152.

Vaucaire, M. *Paul DuChaillu, Gorilla Hunter*. New York: Harper and Brothers, 1930.

Veciana, Vilaldach, A. de. *La Secta del Bwiti en la Guinea Española*. Madrid: Instituto de Estudios Africanes, 1958.

Vogt, E. Z. "Structural and Conceptual Replication in Zinacantan Culture." *American Anthropologist*, 67(1965):342-353.

Vuillaume, G. "La coutume pahouine dans l'estuaire du Como." Unpublished manuscript available for study in the archives of the Presidency of the Government of Libreville, 1930.

Vygotsky, L. *Thought and Language*. Translated and edited by E. Hahnfmann and G. Vakar. Cambridge, Mass.: M.I.T. Press, 1962.

Walker, R.B.N. "Letter of a Journey up the Ogowe." *Proceedings of the Royal Geographical Society*, 17(1875):354-355.

————. "Über Ogoue und Ngunie." *Mitteilungen aus den Deutschen Schutzgebeiten*, 8(1875):51-57.

Wallace, A.F.C. "Dreams and Wishes of the Soul: A Type of Psychoanalytic Theory among the Seventeenth Century Iroquois." *American Anthropologist*, 60(1958): 234-248.

————. "On Being Just Complicated Enough." *Proceedings of the National Academy of Sciences*, 47(1961):458-464.

————. *Culture and Personality*. 2d ed. New York: Random House, 1970.

Webb, A. D. *The New Dictionary of Statistics*. London: G. Routledge and Sons, 1911.

Weinstein, B. *Gabon: Nation Building on the Ogooue*. Cambridge, Mass.:
    M.I.T. Press, 1966.
Wheeler, W. R. *The Words of God in an African Forest*. New York: Revell,
    1931.
Wilson, G. and Wilson, M. *The Analysis of Social Change*. Cambridge:
    Cambridge University Press, 1945.
Wilson, J. L. "Visit to the Upper Waters of the Gaboon." *The Missionary
    Herald*, 39(1843):236-239.

Index

Library of Congress Cataloging in Publication Data

Fernandez, James W.
  Bwiti: an ethnography of the religious imagination
in Africa.

  Bibliography: p.
  Includes index.
  1. Fang (West African people)—Religion.   2. Fang
(West African people).   I. Title.
BL2480.F3F47   299'.67   81-47125
ISBN 0-691-09390-3   AACR2
ISBN 0-691-10122-1 (lim. print. ed.)